Thirteenth Edition

Teaching Science Through Inquiry-Based Instruction

Terry L. Contant
LEARN Regional Educational Service Center

Anne L. Tweed
McREL International

Joel E. Bass
late, of Sam Houston State University

Arthur A. Carin
late, of Queens College

Pearson

330 Hudson Street, NY NY 10013

Editorial Director: Kevin M. Davis
Portfolio Manager: Drew Bennett
Content Producer: Yagnesh Jani
Portfolio Management Assistant: Maria Feliberty
Executive Product Marketing Manager: Christopher Barry
Executive Field Marketing Manager: Krista Clark
Development Editor: Martha Trydahl
Procurement Specialist: Deidra Smith

Cover Designer: Taylor Reed, Cenveo Publisher Services
Cover Art: Chris Johnson/Fotolia
Media Producer: Allison Longley
Editorial Production and Composition Services: SPi Global
Full-Service Project Manager: Benjamin Gilbert and Michelle Gardner
Text Font: Garamond MT Pro 10/12

Credits and acknowledgments for materials borrowed from other sources and reproduced, with permission, in this textbook appear on the appropriate page within the text.

Every effort has been made to provide accurate and current Internet information in this book. However, the Internet and information posted on it are constantly changing, so it is inevitable that some of the Internet addresses listed in this textbook will change.

Library of Congress Cataloging-in-Publication Data:

Names: Contant, Terry L., author. | Bass, Joel E. | Carin, Arthur A.
Title: Teaching science through inquiry and investigation / Terry L. Contant,
    LEARN Regional Educational Service Center, Joel E. Bass, late, of Sam
    Houston State University, Arthur A. Carin, late, of Sam Houston State
    University.
Description: Upper Saddle River, NJ : Pearson Education, [2018] | Rev. ed.
    of: Teaching science as inquiry / Arthur A. Carin. 11th ed. 2009.
Identifiers: LCCN 2016058655| ISBN 9780134515472 | ISBN 0134515471
Subjects: LCSH: Science--Study and teaching (Elementary)
Classification: LCC LB1585 .C6646 2018 | DDC 372.35/044--dc23
LC record available at https://lccn.loc.gov/2016058655

6 2021

ISBN 10:   0-13-451679-6
ISBN 13: 978-0-13-451679-0

Contents

KD 03.08.2021 0840

ACTIVITIES FOR TEACHING SCIENCE THROUGH INQUIRY-BASED INSTRUCTION   245

III   Life Sciences   A-101

IV   Earth and Space Sciences   A-145

V Engineering, Technology, and Applications of Science   A-204

Teaching Science Through Inquiry-Based Instruction provides theoretical and practical advice to elementary and middle school teachers who are expected to help their students learn science. Written during a time of substantive change in science education, this book strives to help readers connect their own prior science education experiences, and their understanding of what school administrators have traditionally expected of teachers who teach science in elementary and middle school classrooms, to the new vision of three-dimensional, student-centered, inquiry-based teaching and learning. For this reason, the book references, the *National Science Education Standards* (NRC, 1996), which still provides the basis for many states' current science standards; *A Framework for K-12 Science Education: Practices, Crosscutting Concepts, and Core Ideas* (NRC, 2012), which builds on previous science education reform documents, including the NSES and contemporary learning theory; and the *Next Generation Science Standards* (NGSS Lead States, 2013), which were released in April 2013.

Many years of work and research in the science education community have provided a coherent, research-based vision for a new era of science education. This vision is encompassed in the *Next Generation Science Standards*, adopted by many states as we go to press. Reference to the *Framework*, and to the NGSS throughout this book, makes this edition applicable to educators in states that have adopted the NGSS and those that are still making decisions about revising state standards.

Text Organization

Important concepts and skills for new educators and guidance for those who are working to improve and accommodate the new demands of science teaching are addressed in the first ten chapters of this text. These chapters scaffold an understanding of current practices, concepts, and ideas necessary for effective science teaching in elementary and middle schools. They relate traditional methods of science instruction to the emerging strategies suggested by the NRC *Framework* and the *Next Generation Science Standards*.

Chapter 1: *Science and Science Education*, explores the nature of science, its importance in today's world, trends in science education, and national science standards. It discusses "What science is" and "What it means to do science" because it is difficult to effectively teach a subject unless you understand what that subject is and how it is applied.

Chapter 2: *Getting Ready for Inquiry Instruction* and Chapter 3: *Creating a Positive Classroom Environment* discuss initial concerns that both new and veteran teachers may have about science teaching. They include information about how to determine the important science concepts to teach, and discuss strategies that help create positive classroom environments where students are intellectually engaged with science ideas.

Chapter 4: *Learning Science with Understanding* presents contemporary learning theory that relates to science teaching and learning. The focus is on inquiry-based instruction, which is discussed along with its application in science classrooms.

Chapter 5: *Engaging in Inquiry-Based Instruction and Using the 5E Model* clarifies the nature of inquiry-based instruction and the importance of using an instructional model that supports constructivist learning through inquiry-based approaches. This chapter provides foundational information about the 5E instructional model, which is referred to and applied throughout the text. It identifies the essential features of classroom inquiry and elaborates on the 5E instructional model, its phases—Engage, Explore, Explain, Elaborate, and Evaluate—and the functions of each phase. Guidelines express what teachers say and do and what students say and do during each phase of this model.

Chapter 6: *Effective Questioning* explains how teachers first teach students how to ask scientific questions that are testable, and then discusses how questioning changes throughout inquiry from questions that are investigated during the inquiry to those that guide discussions leading to explanations and student learning. Using a variety of questions and approaches, a shift from closed questions to open questions promotes student reasoning that leads to conceptual understanding.

Chapter 7: *Assessing Science Learning* covers appropriate shifts in assessment of inquiry from only assessing student factual knowledge to assessing students' scientific reasoning and what students know, understand, and are able to do to provide evidence of mastery. Both formative and summative assessment strategies are discussed.

Chapter 8: *Using Technology Tools and Resources for Science Learning* provides a review of appropriate technology that teachers can use to support data collection during inquiries, along with an explanation about the relationship between science and technology and their link to STEM (Science, Technology, Engineering, and Mathematics) instruction.

Chapter 9: *Connecting Science with Other Subjects* provides an overview of the important links between mathematics and English language arts standards to science education standards. Additionally, connections are made to issue-based learning in social studies and science as a component of STEM teaching and learning.

Chapter 10: *Making Science Accessible for All Learners* focuses on making meaningful science education available for all students, including those with special needs and disabilities, those who need assistance with language acquisition, and those who are identified as needing individual education plans.

The initial ten chapters incorporate valuable pedagogical elements that support readers. They include:

- Clear learning goals provided at the beginning of each chapter that link to each chapter section.

- An introduction to invite the reader to access their prior knowledge.

- Narrative text that develops each learning goal along with self-assessments and embedded links to engage the readers with actual teacher examples.

- Exploration activities interwoven through the text narrative and designed to encourage readers to grapple with science concepts and classroom decision-making.

- Reflective questions, at the end of each Exploration, challenge readers to determine how to help students make connections among the investigations or inquiry activities they do, and also push readers to practice making instructional decisions.

- Links to point-of-use videos (in the Pearson eText) to see science classrooms in action. Marginal notes link e-readers to video segments that illustrate STEM (Science, Technology, Engineering, and Math) teaching, inquiry-based teaching, questioning strategies, cooperative grouping, and the use of technologies.

- Vignettes also present various examples of classroom teachers and the execution of science activities. Online quizzes at the end of each section of the chapter enable readers to self-evaluate their understanding while progressing through the text.

- At the end of each chapter, there is a summary of key ideas organized by Learning Goals and related discussion questions, as well as questions designed for the reader to use during field experiences.

An appendix presents details about the science process skills that have long been an important element of science education. Appendix A is designed to familiarize the reader with science process skills including: observing, measuring inferring, classifying, communicating, predicting, hypothesizing, and experimenting, It includes definitions, descriptions and explanations, and examples of science process skills used in elementary and middle school science classes.

Unique Science Activities Sections

At the end of this text, the reader will find suggested activities for teaching science through inquiry-based instruction, using a three-dimensional approach that reflects the influence of NGSS in organizing inquiry-based activities and incorporating engineering and design skills.

Five additional sections of this enhanced Pearson eText relate to activities designed to support science learning for elementary and middle school students. Section I provides an introduction to the scope and structure of the activities included in the other sections that are organized by the domains of the NGSS Disciplinary Core Ideas: physical sciences, Earth and space sciences, life sciences, and engineering design.

Each of the activities includes and models a complete 5E lesson, including all of the phases of the inquiry-based learning cycle. Each activity begins with a *Framework* context box that specifies Scientific and Engineering Practices, Crosscutting Concepts, and Disciplinary Core Ideas emphasized within that lesson. The specific, lesson-based, learning targets and success criteria are identified along with the related performance expectations found in the NGSS documents. The activities themselves are not meant to be a complete lesson but should be a starting point for teachers as they plan for inquiry-based instruction. The activities can be used to:

- Illustrate and expand on learner understanding of scientific and engineering practices, crosscutting concepts, and disciplinary core ideas since they provide examples of the three dimensions of the new science framework that can be intertwined in a lesson.

- Model the 5E lesson procedures, engaging students in constructivist inquiry. The 5E instructional model, clarified in Chapter 5 of the text, serves as a framework for ALL of the activities. By keying each activity to the three dimensions of the framework, the text further provides new and experienced teachers with a solid foundation for science teaching.

- Provide a comprehensive view of how *A Framework for K-12 Science Education: Practices, Crosscutting Concepts, and Core Ideas* can be used to organize curriculum and inform instruction in elementary and middle school science.

- Demonstrate for readers how to set up activities that weave science and engineering design into their science teaching.

- Prepare for teacher preparation exams and state licensure.

- Draw on a bank of inquiry-based activities that provide significant and critical models for lesson planning.

Enhanced Pearson eText[1]

Teaching Science Through Inquiry-Based Instruction is available as an enhanced eText exclusively from Pearson. The Enhanced Pearson eText provides a rich, interactive learning environment designed to improve student mastery of content with the following multimedia features:

- **New Classroom Videos** illustrate STEM (Science, Technology, Engineering, and Math) teaching, inquiry-based teaching, questioning strategies, cooperative grouping, and the use of technologies.

- **Check Your Understanding** quizzes are included in each chapter and allow students to gauge their understanding of key learning outcomes.

- An **Activities Library** allows students to search suggested activities using specific criteria (more details below).

Activities Library

In the Pearson eText it is even easier to search for a specific activity. Click on "Activities Library" in the left navigational bar in your eText to explore activities sorted by disciplinary core ideas, scientific and engineering practices, and crosscutting concepts. Clicking on the "Browse Full Library" option will sort all of the activities by appropriate grade level.

You can also do a keyword search using the search box available at the top of the Activities Library page. Each activity is coded by useful criteria, for example, by title, grade level, component idea, or scientific and engineering practice, making it extremely easy to find exactly what you need.

All of the activities are downloadable and printable, so you can save what you'll need for use in your classroom.

---

[1] Please note that eText enhancements and Activities Library are only available through the Pearson eText and not through eTexts provided by third-parties. The Pearson eText App is available for free on Google Play and in the App Store. Requires Android OS 3.1 – 4, a 7" or 10" tablet, or iPad iOS 5.0 or newer.

Support Materials for Instructors

The following resources are available for instructors to download on www.pearsonhighered.com/Educators. Instructors enter the author, title of the text (13e), or the ISBN of this book and click on the "Resources" tab to log in and download textbook supplements. New users will need to request access to the Instructors' Resource Center in order to download these useful supplements.

Online Instructor's Resource Manual and Test Bank

Free to adopters is an Instructors Manual that provides chapter-by-chapter ideas and resources for enriching each class meeting. Within the Instructors' Manual, there is a test bank, as well as suggested activities, objectives and overviews, suggested readings, and other tools for teaching.

PowerPoint Slides

New to this edition are chapter-by-chapter PowerPoint slides that present key concepts and big ideas. These PowerPoints are also available via the Instructors' Resource Center.

Acknowledgments

The revisions and modifications incorporated in the thirteenth edition would not have been possible without the insightful reviews of the twelfth edition and suggestions for improvement from colleagues. We acknowledge and express our gratitude to the following reviewers: Teresa Higgins, University of Northern Colorado; Julie K. Jackson, Texas State University-San Marcos; Suzanne Nesmith, Baylor University; and Margarita Wulftange, Western New Mexico University.

We want to thank the many managers who helped make this edition possible, especially: Beth Kaufman, Editorial Project Manager; Drew Bennett, Portfolio Manager; Megan Moffo, Managing Producer for Teacher Education; Miryam Chandler, Content Producer; Karen Sanatar and Lokesh Bisht, Permissions Managers at APTARA, and Linda Bishop.

We also want to thank Meredith Fossel whose oversight and amiable advice has enriched the efficacy of this text. and Martha Trydahl, who patiently guided the revision work and skillfully nudged us when deadlines became critical.

We are grateful as well for the coordination skills of Hope Madden, for making the inclusion of new video of classrooms where teachers were working toward three-dimensional teaching and learning possible. We also want to thank Jon Theiss and his team from Many Hats Media—who captured authentic classroom video and the ideas of exemplary teachers on video.

The production of these new videos would not have been possible without cooperation and expertise of Dr. Harry Rosvally, STEM Curriculum Administrator, and teachers from Danbury Public Schools: Nancy Michael at Pembrook Elementary, Bernado DeCastro at Rogers Park Middle School; and to Dr. Heather Harkins, STEM Coordinator, and teachers: Sheri Geitner, Ashley Welch, Nicole Bay at Charles H. Barrows STEM Academy.

We appreciate everyone's attention to bringing this long-awaited new edition to completion. On a more personal note, I especially want to acknowledge the support and hard work of my friend and coauthor, Anne Tweed. The day she agreed to collaborate with me on this project was one of the happiest in my professional life. I also want to thank my patient, loving husband, Charlie. His encouragement and belief in me, and the importance of furthering science education, made it possible for me to remain committed to this extended project. Both Charlie and my daughter, Heather, helped me immensely with the writing process by reading drafts and providing a platform for reflection about the clarity of the work. It is wonderful to have a family of scholars who are also interested in my area of scholarship! I'd also like to thank my feline family members, Si'i and Fiefia, who kept me company through many long nights of writing.

Terry L. Contant

I would like to thank Terry Contant for inviting me to work with her on this revision. It has been a labor of love and an experience that I will cherish. I value her as a professional colleague, thought partner, and friend! Teaching inquiry-based science has been a passion of mine for more than forty years. I would like to thank many of my professional colleagues that were significant contributors to this journey including: Jack Carter, professor emeritus from Colorado College who taught me about the ESS (Elementary Science Study) and SCIS (Science Curriculum Improvement Study) programs; Nancy Kellogg my mentor and former science coordinator from Adams Five Star School District in Thornton, Colorado; Mary Gromko, long-time friend and current NSTA President; and Laura Arndt who I have worked with for more than 25 years and shares my passion for developing curriculum and learning experiences for students that invites creativity and inspires them to inquire and make sense of science phenomena.

I am also grateful for the support and patience of my best friend Michael King who understood the importance of meeting deadlines for this project even when they happened during our vacations. My family has also been there to support me as the work continued into long evenings, holidays, and weekends. I want to thank my sons Matt and Josh, my daughter-in-law Tia, my precious grandson Gavin.

Anne L. Tweed

THIS BOOK IS DEDICATED to the memory of Dr. Joel E. Bass, who passed away after completing the eleventh edition. Dr. Bass inspired many science educators during his 35 years at Sam Houston State University, and he touched thousands more through his work on the ninth, tenth, and eleventh editions of *Teaching Science as Inquiry*. Joel, your passion for teaching science lives on in our memories, and in this book.

THIS BOOK IS ALSO DEDICATED to the memory of Dr. Arthur A. Carin, author of the first eight editions of the book (then called *Teaching Science as Discovery*). Through five decades of exemplary writing, teaching, research, and service, Dr. Carin had a significant, positive impact on science education. Art, you are remembered and honored.

Chapter and Learning Outcome Alignment to NSTA Standards for Science Teacher Preparation

Chapter	Learning Outcome	NSTA Standard
1	1.1 Science is observing, analyzing, and investigating to learn how the natural and physical world works.	1a, 1b, 1c, 5b
	1.2 Educational initiatives related to science education increasingly emphasize student conceptual understanding and student-centered, inquiry-based learning.	1a, 1b, 1c, 2a, 5b, 5c
	1.3 The Next Generation Science Standards provide guidance on what to teach and how to teach to provide students with high-quality science education.	1b, 1c, 2b, 2c, 3a, 3b
	1.4 It is important for teachers to develop lessons that are inquiry-based and initiate conceptual change.	2a, 2b, 2c, 3b
2	2.1 Learning goals aligned to standards identify what students should know, understand, and be able to do at their grade level.	1a, 1b, 1c, 3b, 5c
	2.2 When getting ready for instruction, teachers must first select the science concepts, procedures and skills they will use during inquiry learning.	1a, 1b, 1c, 2a, 2b,
	2.3 Units of instruction, curriculum maps, or guides along with a variety of resources assist with pre-planning for instruction and creating content storylines.	1a, 1b, 1c, 2a, 2b, 2c, 3a, 3b, 6a, 6b
	2.4 Familiarity with aspects of "doing science" (process skills and Practices) is needed prior to planning inquiry-based instruction.	1b, 1c, 2a, 2b, 3a, 3b, 5c
	2.5 Determination of the appropriate type of investigation in which to engage students is dependent on the question that is asked.	2a, 2b, 2c, 3a, 3b, 5c
3	3.1 Positive classroom environments exist when teachers plan for the physical and social/emotional environment of students, where students find the learning rigorous and engaging, trust is evident and everyone (teachers and students) believe that they can learn.	2a, 2b, 2c, 3a, 3b
	3.2 Designing a positive classroom environment is essential to promote active inquiry learning.	2a, 2b, 2c, 3a, 3b, 3c
	3.3 Procedures for maintaining student safety must be planned prior to doing science with students.	3d, 4a, 4b, 4c
	3.4 Teaching procedures will help you manage student behavior.	3a, 3d
4	4.1 Knowing science facts involves memorizing information that can be recalled, while understanding science ideas means being able to explain, to interpret, to apply and adapt knowledge.	1a, 1b, 2b, 3b, 5a, 5c
	4.2 A child's ability to construct learning depends on age and experiences.	5a, 5c
	4.3 Students can be led to deeper understandings of science concepts using a variety of approaches.	2a, 2b, 3a, 3b
	4.4 Students' alternative conceptions of science concepts can be changed using a conceptual change model.	2c, 3c
5	5.1 Inquiry-based instruction features Practices needed to ask and try to answer a scientific question.	2a, 2b, 3b
	5.2 Research says that inquiry-based instruction refers to the diverse ways in which students study the natural world and propose explanations based on the evidence derived from their work.	2a, 2b
	5.3 The essential features of classroom inquiry include engagement with scientific questions, collect evidence, formulate explanations, evaluate explanations, and communicate and justify explanations. The levels of inquiry vary depending upon the degree to which students make the decisions or teachers scaffold and guide the inquiry.	2a, 2b, 3b
	5.4 Instructional models that support inquiry-based instruction in science differ from the models used to design lessons in other content areas.	2a, 2b, 3b, 5c
	5.5 The 5E model of science instruction includes five phases where students are intellectually engaged in learning about science phenomena that leads to explanations based on evidence.	2a, 2b, 2c, 3a, 3b, 3c, 5c
	5.6 Each phase of the 5E model (engage, explore, explain, elaborate, and evaluate) of science instruction supports science learning.	2a, 2b, 2c, 3a, 3b, 3c, 5c

Chapter and Learning Outcome Alignment to NSTA Standards for Science Teacher Preparation (*continued*)

Chapter	Learning Outcome	NSTA Standard
6	6.1 Asking the right question is at the heart of teaching and learning.	2a, 2c, 3a, 3c, 5a, 5c
	6.2 Different kinds of questions when used at the right time are important to move learning forward.	2a, 2c, 3a, 3c, 5a, 5c
	6.3 Different kinds of questions are needed to align with the different phases of the 5E model of inquiry-based instruction.	2a, 2c, 3a, 3c, 5a, 5c
	6.4 Teachers responses to questions will guide learning and classroom discourse.	2a, 2c, 3a, 3c, 5a, 5c
	6.5 Implementing science talk in the classroom will support conceptual change that results in student understanding.	2a, 2c, 3a, 3c, 5a, 5c
7	7.1 Assessment processes provide opportunities to gather evidence of student learning (summative) or for student learning (formative) which can be evaluated to determine level of mastery of the identified learning goals.	2c, 3c, 5a, 5c
	7.2 Formative assessment processes when implemented as a part of effective teaching practices use feedback loops that helps move student learning forward.	2c, 3c, 5a, 5c
	7.3 Summative assessments provide evidence of student knowledge and understanding at the conclusion of a learning cycle.	2c, 3c, 5a, 5c
	7.4 Performance assessments can measure student understanding of several learning targets.	2c, 3c, 5a, 5c
	7.5 Large scale (state and national tests) assessments indicate the effectiveness of science programs at schools and are used to inform changes needed at the school and district level.	5a
8	8.1 General educational technology to support science instruction in K-8 classrooms should minimally include a computer with internet access that is connected to a classroom projector.	1b, 2b, 3a
	8.2 Digital technologies for gathering scientific information, data collection and analysis by students, creating and using models of scientific phenomena, and communication support student engagement in specific Science and Engineering Practices.	1b, 2b, 3a
	8.3 Social media can be a useful resource to support science teaching and learning.	1b, 2b, 3a
9	9.1 Science doesn't happen in isolation but is connected to mathematics when the learning goals from each discipline and the student practice skills from both disciplines are linked.	1b, 1c, 2a, 2b
	9.2 STEM (science, math, engineering and technology) teaching and learning links the knowledge and skills from each area to answer questions and solve problems.	1b, 1c, 2a, 2b
	9.3 Events and issues studied in social studies link to inquiry and problem-based learning in science.	1b, 2a, 2b
	9.4 Science and English Language Arts are linked with reading and writing goals and student practices.	1b, 1c, 2a, 2b
10	10.1 Equity, diversity, and achievement gaps must be considered when guiding all children to learn science.	2a, 3a, 3b
	10.2 Teachers of science must utilize the instructional strategies that enable students from linguistically and culturally diverse backgrounds to learn science.	2a, 3a, 3b
	10.3 The same research-based instructional approaches that are recognized as best practices in any science classroom are effective in an inclusive classroom when appropriate differentiation is used to meet student's individual needs.	2a, 3a, 3b
	10.4 Providing the least restrictive environment can support the learning of students identified with various disabilities.	2a, 3a, 3b
	10.5 Students identified as gifted and talented require the use of alternative instructional strategies to maximize their science learning.	2a, 3a, 3b

Immediately following Chapter 10 you will find suggested activities for teaching science through inquiry-based instruction. This section is organized into four major areas: Physical Sciences, Life Sciences, Earth and Space Sciences, and Engineering, Technology, and Applications of Science. Each activity contains a suggested grade level and is mapped to the NGSS framework with respect to Scientific and Engineering Practices, Crosscutting Concepts, and Disciplinary Core Ideas. Additionally, each activity was designed using the 5E model

Teaching Science Through Inquiry-Based Instruction

Curiosity and Learning Science

AN INTRODUCTION

"Every year, 5 million children enter kindergarten armed with one word: 'Why?' They continuously ask questions in what seems like an unending loop. On the other side, parents, caretakers, and teachers do their best to come up with answers to manage this kiddie-inquisition. Yet there's no allaying it. Behind that question hides another. And another. And another. And another. As painful as this activity may be for adults, the process is important for children. Their brains are busily creating pathways. They are trying to understand how things work. They are learning—and learning how to learn.

Early-childhood research says that we have a curious scientific nature from the beginning of life. A recent study says that toddlers and preschool children behave like scientists. They are observant and curious as they soak in information about the world. Like little experimenters, they light up when unpredictable events happen, and they can decipher causal relationships.

But something happens as children get older. That curious nature fades, and those 'why' questions grow silent. Students no longer feel that it's OK to ask questions. Somehow, they fail to remember that they started off curious. They fail to remember their inner scientists" (www.edutopia.org/blog/a-case-for-curiosity-ainissa-ramirez).

Why does this happen? Numerous research studies and articles point to the connection between curiosity and student motivation to learn. From the quotation you just read, which appeared in a blog written by Ainissa Ramirez in February 2016, inviting students to ask questions and to be curious should be an essential goal for both science and science teaching. As you learn about inquiry-based instruction in this course, we encourage you to think about how you can support curiosity in your classroom. Remember that students will stay curious when we show them how important it is to wonder about science phenomena and to ask questions. Embrace the process of asking questions and inviting students to generate questions as part of everyday learning. Staying curious leads to both creative and critical thinking abilities, which are foundational student skills leading to a love of science. All kids are naturally curious! If science literacy is our goal, then inviting students to ask questions is a science practice that matters!

Science and Science Education

Hero Images/Getty Images

LEARNING GOALS

After reading this chapter, you should understand that . . .

1. Science is observing, analyzing, and investigating to learn how the natural and physical world works.

2. Educational initiatives related to science education increasingly emphasize student conceptual understanding and student-centered, inquiry-based learning.

3. The *Next Generation Science Standards* provide guidance on what to teach and how to teach to provide students with high-quality science education.

4. It is important for teachers to develop lessons that are inquiry-based and initiate conceptual change.

What do you think about when you hear the terms **Science** and **Science Education**? Try this free-association exercise. When you think about the term *science*, what are the first three ideas that come to your mind? Record your thoughts using words or drawings. Repeat this activity when thinking about *science education*. Reflecting on your current thinking about these terms will provide a context for the ideas developed in this chapter.

It is important that you are clear about the differences between science and science education and what it means both to you and to your students. This is a good place for us to start since the two ideas are closely linked. Look at Table 1.1 and compare your ideas to the ones expressed in the table. What do you notice? What additional questions arise when looking at the table?

Now that you have more knowledge about these terms, let's get started. In the twenty-first century, it is important for teachers responsible for helping students learn science to understand the nature of science and the educational standards designed to guide science learning. This chapter presents information and ideas to help you develop these important understandings so that you will be prepared to teach science well.

What Is Science?

Many times on the first day of school, I've asked students the question, "What is science?" I've heard some interesting responses over the years, depending on the age and experiences of the students or adult learners, including: "Science is what scientists do"; "Science is biology, chemistry, and physics"; "Science is hard"; "Science is easy"; "Science is fun", "Science is about doing investigations"; and as a sad commentary on the elementary school schedule, "Science is taught opposite of social studies."

When the word *science* entered the English language from French during the fourteenth century, it referred to "the knowledge (of something) acquired by study," and to "a particular branch of knowledge." It is thought to have been derived from the Latin words *scientia* "knowledge" and *sciens* "to know," or "to separate one thing from another, to distinguish" (*Online Etymology Dictionary*). Table 1.1 lists common attributes of both science and science education. In Exploration 1.1 you have an opportunity to further investigate current definitions for the term science.

TABLE 1.1   **Attributes of Science and Science Teaching**

Common Attributes of Science	Common Attributes of Science Teaching
Science is more than a collection of facts.	Science teaching is more than lecturing or doing hands-on activites.
Science knowledge is made up of current understandings of our natural systems and is subject to change.	Knowledge of science teaching is based on current understanding of effective teaching and learning and is subject to change as new research becomes available.
The body of scientific knowledge is constantly being revised, extended, and refined.	The body of knowledge about science teaching and learning is constantly being considered, expanded, and refined.

Today, there is no single accepted definition of *science*. Use your favorite web browser to find at least four statements that answer the question: *What is science?* Record the statements you select, and cite your sources.

Working alone or with several of your peers, compare, contrast, and synthesize the statements to develop your own definition for *science*.

Reflection Questions:

1. What similarities do you find in all of the statements you selected?
2. How do these statements differ?
3. Based on what you have discovered, which statement do you consider to be the "best" definition of science? Why?
4. What is your current definition of science, in your own words?

Since you may soon be teaching science to children and/or adolescents, really understanding what science is would be beneficial. You probably realize by now that developing a precise definition of *science* is not that simple. So, rather than just defining it, consider the key characteristics of science listed in Table 1.2.

Notice that the left column in Table 1.2 lists typical characteristics of inquiry-based activities that are science. If an inquiry-based activity exhibits all or most of these features, it is reasonable to call it science. Things that don't exhibit most of these characteristics should not be considered to be science.

Other ideas that are often included in a discussion of the "**nature of science**" are

- Science is based on the premise that the things—**phenomena** in nature—and events that happen occur in consistent patterns that are comprehensible through careful, systematic study.

- Science is a process for generating knowledge. Scientific knowledge is simultaneously reliable and tentative. Having confidence in scientific knowledge is reasonable while realizing that such knowledge may be updated or modified in light of new evidence or reconceptualization of prior evidence and knowledge. For example, the idea that atoms are the smallest particles was changed when subatomic particles were discovered. Or, for another example, the theory of continental drift was replaced with the plate tectonics theory once we had evidence of what occurs along plate boundaries.

> Listen to Nancy Michael's goals for science learning in her 2nd grade class. Consider how they relate to your ideas about what science is.

TABLE 1.2 **Some Characteristics of Science with Examples and Non-Examples**

Characteristics of Science	Example	Non-Example
It focuses on explaining the physical and natural (not the supernatural) world.	Investigating why tides vary in height at different locations along the shore.	Investigating the effect of prayer on the growth of crops during droughts.
It involves testable ideas using investigation and inquiry approaches.	Investigating the relationship between the number of coils of wire in an electromagnet and its strength.	Investigating what the world would be like without sunlight.
It relies on evidence determined by observation and analysis.	The investigators based their conclusions on statistically significant evidence.	The investigators based their conclusions on their beliefs.
It involves the scientific community in communication and argumentation processes.	The investigators presented their research to their peers at an international conference and appreciated the feedback they received.	The researcher refused to publish or share his results.
It utilizes scientific behaviors to intellectually engage in the systematic study of a question or problem.	The investigators reported their results, even though their evidence was insufficient to support their hypothesis.	The investigators deleted data from their data set in order to get the results that they had predicted.

Source for left column: "What is science?", 2012.

Appendix H, "Understanding the Scientific Enterprise: The Nature of Science," in the *Next Generation Science Standards*, presents grade-level understandings about the nature of science for each of these themes. It is available online at www .nextgenscience.org /next-generation-science -standards.

- There is an expectation that scientific results can be replicated by other investigators when they follow similar procedures. When this does not happen, the validity of the initial results and inferences is questioned. In 2011, physicists were astonished when they found evidence of neutrinos (one kind of subatomic particle) traveling at speeds greater than the speed of light. Before immediately reconsidering Einstein's theory—that matter cannot travel faster than light—to be invalid, other researchers repeated the experiment. The initial results were not confirmed by other research teams, and it was discovered that an equipment malfunction (a loose connection) explained the original, unexpected findings.

- "Science is characterized by the systematic gathering of information through various forms of direct and indirect observations and the testing of this information by methods including, but not limited to, experimentation. The principal product of science is knowledge in the form of naturalistic concepts and the laws and theories related to those concepts" (National Science Teachers Association [NSTA], 2000).

- While science and technology do impact each other, basic scientific research is not directly concerned with practical outcomes, but rather with gaining an understanding of the physical and natural world for its own sake.

- The scientific questions asked, the observations made, the evidence gathered, and the conclusions in science are to some extent influenced by the existing state of scientific knowledge, the social and cultural context of the researcher, and the observer's experiences and expectations. After all, scientists are human.

Scientists display certain attitudes and **habits of mind** when doing science. During science class, you should model these and explicitly teach them, since children should also acquire and display scientific attitudes and habits of mind as they do science. Some of these attitudes are

- *Curiosity*—an enduring interest and fascination about the physical, natural, and human-constructed worlds is a vital, yet personal, ingredient in the production of scientific knowledge.
- *Desire for Knowledge*—an urge, even "rage" (Judson, 1980), to know and understand the world (intrinsic motivation to learn).
- *Placing a Priority on Evidence*—using data as the basis for testing ideas, engaging in analysis to determine evidence, and respecting scientific facts as they accrue.
- *Willingness to Modify Explanations*—changing initial conceptions and explanations when the evidence suggests different ones.
- *Cooperation in Investigating Questions and Solving Problems*—working in collaboration and more importantly, cooperatively—with a shared goal—with others, is fundamental to the scientific enterprise.
- *Honesty*—presenting data as they are observed, not as the investigator expects or wishes them to be (National Center for Improving Science Education, 1989).

Can you think of other characteristics or terms you would need to teach and model? It is important to clarify for students the language of science in particular for terms that have a scientific explanation and another definition when used in everyday language like the terms *communication* or *argumentation*. You will learn more about this later in the chapter and throughout the course.

When used in the context of science, certain common words have specialized meanings. You should be aware of these nuanced meanings so that you consistently use appropriate terminology and encourage your students to do the same. Certainly there are many technical terms specific to the various science disciplines, but that is academic vocabulary you learn in science courses. Some of the words that describe the main product of science, knowledge in its various forms, are clarified in Table 1.3.

When teaching science, keep in mind that "Science is both a body of knowledge that represents current understanding of physical and natural systems and the process whereby that body of knowledge has been established and is being continually extended, refined and revised" (National Research Council [NRC], 2007, p. 26). Remember that science has certain characteristics, often referred to as the nature of science, that distinguish it from other ways of knowing and that scientists are expected to apply certain habits of mind as they work. Exploration 1.2 challenges you to consider examples of the major themes related to understanding the nature of science. Also, recall that in science some words have specific meanings that may be different than their common meanings. As you provide your class with numerous opportunities to develop science concepts, skills, and practices by letting your students "be" scientists, explicitly model and point out examples of scientific attitudes, actions, and terminology. Over time, your students will better understand what science is, the nature of science, how scientists reason, and how to properly use of the language of science.

Teachers can **engage children in investigations and inquiry-based learning** that provide opportunities to develop the same habits of mind scientists exhibit. As you watch this video clip, identify the scientific attitudes that teachers encourage children to use while doing inquiry-based activities and investigations.

Nature of Science Themes   **EXPLORATION**

1.2

During the development of the *Next Generation Science Standards* (**NGSS**), which you will learn more about later in this chapter, the writers described eight major themes or categories related to understanding the nature of science. On the following chart, those listed in the left column are associated with Scientific and Engineering Practices, while those in the right column are associated with Crosscutting Concepts:

Nature of science themes related to Scientific and Engineering Practices	Nature of science themes related to Crosscutting Concepts
Scientific investigations use a variety of methods.	Science is a way of knowing.
Scientific knowledge is based on empirical evidence.	Scientific knowledge assumes an order and consistency in natural systems.
Scientific knowledge is open to revision in light of new evidence.	Science is a human endeavor.
Science models, laws, mechanisms, and theories explain natural phenomena.	Science addresses questions about the natural and material world.

Source: Achieve, 2013a.

Look back at the information presented earlier in the chapter for examples that relate to each theme. Discuss your ideas with a partner or a small group of your peers.

Reflection Questions:

1. What examples did you find related to the various themes?
2. In what ways do the themes help you understand the enterprise of science as a whole?
3. Why do you think that K–8 students should develop an understanding of the nature of science? What are the implications for teachers?

TABLE 1.3   **Some Words That Have Special Meanings in Science**

Word	Meaning in Science	Everyday Meaning
Theory	A complex explanation about how nature works that has been well tested and is supported by a wide body of evidence. A theory is so well established that it is unlikely that new evidence will totally discredit it.	An untested idea or conjecture. A guess, speculation, opinion, or belief.
Law	A description of what happens naturally under very specific conditions. It will predict what will happen as long as those conditions are met. A scientific law only describes; it doesn't explain.	An enforceable rule. Something that must be followed and may have legal consequences.
Hypothesis	A testable prediction (idea) that may contribute to the development of a scientific theory.	(Not generally used outside of science.)
Data	Observations, measurements, or inferences recorded for later analysis.	Information in the form of numbers.
Evidence	The cumulative body of data or observations of a phenomenon that have been analyzed.	What detectives look for and use to solve a crime.
Claim	Always based on evidence. May or may not stand the test of time; some will eventually be shown to be false.	Anything people say is true and it may represent their beliefs.

(Table 1.3 continued)

(Table 1.3 continued)

Word	Meaning in Science	Everyday Meaning
Fact	An understanding based on confirmable observations and is subject to test and rejection (Bybee, 1997). An example of a scientific fact is: *The speed of light is 186,000 miles per second.* Evidence and claims related to phenomena can contribute to the generation of scientific facts.	Anything that is considered true and may be based on the trust given to an individual who said it was a fact. (Unfortunately, some information is considered factual because it appeared in the newspaper, it was on the Internet, or an authority says so!)
Communication	Scientists share their explanations in such a way that their experiments can be reproduced. This sharing helps to resolve contradictions and solidifies arguments.	Anything that is shared with others either verbally, in writing or nonverbally.
Argumentation	Logical descriptions of a scientific idea and the evidence for or against it. The process can precede any evidence relevant to it, and other times the evidence helps inspire the idea.	The process of reasoning systematically to present ideas logically. This occurs in education and everyday lives and often is about contrary points of view.

 CHECK YOUR UNDERSTANDING 1.1
Click here to gauge your understanding of the concepts in this section.

Science Education in Elementary and Middle Schools

Science surrounds us, all day, every day. True, you don't have to understand science ideas and concepts for them to affect you, but understanding science and the processes used to inquire can be very useful. For example, here on Earth, gravity will pull you down whether you know the related equations or not. And when a cold front comes through, carrying your umbrella is a good idea. Meteorologists analyze weather data so their predictions can advise you to act on them. Science knowledge can affect the quality of your life. Consider the following additional examples.

- In a collision, the heavily loaded moving van nearly always "wins" against an economy car. Knowing a little bit of physics and practicing defensive driving based on an understanding the laws of motion and about unbalanced forces might save your life if you are the car's driver.

- Realizing that germs that cause the common cold can survive on surfaces provides the rationale for frequent hand washing when those around you are sneezing.

In the modern world, some knowledge of science is essential for everyone (NRC, 2007). Young students should begin to learn science in kindergarten or even pre-K.

Science Education

Science education is about teaching and learning that involves students in inquiry-based investigations in which they interact with their teachers and peers; establish connections between their current knowledge of science and scientific understandings; apply science concepts to new questions; engage in problem solving, planning, reasoning from evidence, and group discussions; and experience an active approach to learning science.

The National Science Teachers Association (NSTA) has advocated for years that inquiry-based science instruction must be a basic part of the daily curriculum of every elementary school student at every grade level because of the importance of early experiences in science in developing problem-solving skills needed to be productive citizens in the twenty-first century (NSTA, 2002).

NSTA also considers middle school to be a critical time in students' science learning journey. Studies indicate that if students aren't interested in and excited by science by seventh grade, they may never be. It is important that middle school teachers present science concepts in ways that are both age appropriate and engaging so that students continue to build on their prior knowledge and attain the necessary background to participate successfully and responsibly in our highly scientific and technological society (NSTA, 2003).

Scientific Literacy

Another reason to start teaching science in elementary school is to begin early to build **scientific literacy**. Learning to think scientifically and to understand the scientific view of the physical and natural world takes time. Science experiences from the earliest grades are essential for helping students to learn to think and understand. Many learning progressions begin with foundational concepts that are best understood in the early primary grades.

Some of your students will likely choose careers in a scientific, technical, or health-care profession, but *all* of them will need to be scientifically literate to take an active role in recognizing problems, contributing to solutions, and making informed decisions about local, state, national, and global issues.

The *National Science Education Standards* **(NSES)** define scientific literacy as "the knowledge and understanding of scientific concepts and processes required for personal decision-making, participation in civic and cultural affairs, and economic productivity" (NRC, 1996, p. 22).

According to the NSES, "Lifelong scientific literacy begins with understandings, attitudes, and values established in the earliest years" (NRC, 1996, p. 114). More recently, the National Research Council's *A Framework for K–12 Science Education* defined science literacy by all K–12 students by identifying the Science and Engineering Practices, Crosscutting Concepts, and Disciplinary Core Ideas that will enable all students to make scientifically sound decisions about the world in which they live (NRC, 2012, p. 3). Whether from the NSES or the ***Framework*** and NGSS documents, all definitions of scientific literacy indicate that it is important for literate citizens to have both knowledge of science facts and concepts and the skills to "do" science and then use the information for personal decision making about societal issues.

National Concerns

Many people believe that what happens in elementary science today can have potentially dramatic effects, not only on the lives of children, but also on the economic future of our nation. A prestigious panel sponsored by the National Academies of Science produced a report, *Rising Above the Gathering Storm* (National Academies of Science, 2006), that details some of the global issues our nation faces.

The report noted that the "high quality of life" in the United States, "our national security, and our hope that our children and grandchildren will inherit ever-greater opportunities" is derived, in large part, from "the steady stream of scientific and technological innovations" produced in this country since World War II. But there are indications that our global leadership position in science and technology is changing. Among the findings of the committee and recent followup reports are these:

- Since the early 1990s, the United States has been a net importer of high-technology products.

- Other nations are graduating considerably more engineers, computer scientists, and information technologists than the United States.

- Lower labor costs and the availability of highly trained scientists and engineers have led to the location of factories by U.S. companies in foreign countries and the outsourcing of many jobs.

- International assessments in math and science indicate that U.S. K–12 students lag behind students from other industrialized countries and we now rank 22nd in graduation rates and 14th in numbers of students 25 through 34 years of age with 2- or 4-year college degrees (OECD, 2012, p. 26).

- The National Science Foundation recently reported that there are between 2 and 3 million STEM (Science, Technology, Engineering, and Mathematics) positions that are unfilled.

- The Department of Commerce studies show for more than a decade, STEM jobs grew at three times the rate of non-STEM jobs, which is a trend likely to continue and accelerate (Langdon et al., 2011).

In response to such findings, recommendations from the reports and from White House initiatives suggested, among other things, that the United States vastly improve science and math education to increase the pool of students prepared to choose science and STEM fields as a career. Improving science and math education must begin in the early grades.

Language Literacy and Mathematics Competency

In the *Common Core State Standards for English Language Arts*, expectations for reading and writing in science are identified, and guidance is provided for the skills students will need. In the *Next Generation Science Standards* (NGSS), connections to the *Common Core State Standards* (CCSS) in English Language Arts and Mathematics are included in the Foundation Boxes and in Appendixes L and M (Achieve, 2013). The NGSS development team recognized that the literacy standards and student practices work closely with the content demands and performance expectations outlined in the NGSS documents. Additionally, science is a quantitative discipline, so linking to the CCSSM standards and student practices is reflected in the NGSS document, and specific suggestions about the relationship between mathematics and science are provided for grades K–8. More information about the connections is included in Chapter 9.

Science provides a rich context for children to apply and further develop their language and mathematics skills. In the process of acquiring scientific information, students have opportunities to improve their reading skills. For example, children learn to apply skills of reading informational texts as they seek to comprehend the science in trade books, articles, and children's literature. Skills of reading in the content area are not only necessary in acquiring new information, but they are also essential in preparing for and taking standardized tests in reading, science, and other content areas.

Writing observations in science journals, editing collaboratively, refining procedures, and rewriting at each stage of the inquiry process can be effective ways to enhance inquiry and science learning and to improve writing skills (Champagne & Kouba, 2000).

Science also provides a context in which children can apply and practice their math skills, such as counting, estimating, measuring, putting data into tables, and constructing and interpreting graphs.

Legislation

Responding to growing concerns about the quality of education for all students in our nation, Congress passed the No Child Left Behind (NCLB) Act in 2001. Science education was an important part of this legislation. According to the NCLB Act, by the 2007–2008 school year, every state had to administer annual assessments of reading, math, and science at elementary, middle school, and high school levels. Results of these assessments provided information that determined whether schools were demonstrating adequate yearly progress (AYP) toward the goal of 100 percent proficiency for all students. Schools that did not maintain adequate yearly progress were subject to severe sanctions.

In response to the NCLB Act, all 50 states adopted science standards for their states to guide the development of their state assessments. A review of state science standards in 2012 by the Fordham Foundation did not give the state standards very high marks. The report found that the standards were often too general or too specific in nature and required further unpacking or interpretation by teachers (Fordham Institute, 2012). The Institute continues to review state standards including the many states that have adopted the *Next Generation Science Standards*. You may want to check and see what "grade" has been given to the state standards where you live. What is important about this task is the conversation that can occur with other teachers when you look at their findings.

Many believe that the best way to prepare elementary and middle school students for the science portion of these statewide examinations is a coordinated K–8 effort built around inquiry approaches to science.

The most recent legislation, signed in December 2015, is the Every Student Succeeds Act, which is a reauthorization of the Elementary and Secondary Education Act. In summary, this new legislation terminates aspects of the No Child Left Behind legislation in 2016 and transitions to a system of state plans in 2016–2017. As part of the legislation, states are required to provide challenging, academic content standards in science with at least three levels of achievement. Science must be assessed once in grades 3–5 and once in grades 6–9. State assessments must provide multiple measures of student achievement and must include higher-order thinking skills and understanding. More about assessments is included in Chapter 7.

Table 1.4 briefly describes several reform programs and documents that can impact the "whats and hows" of your science education program and includes websites for additional information.

TABLE 1.4   National Science Education Reform Documents

National Science Education Reform Document	Summary
Science for All Americans AAAS Project 2061 (1989) www.project2061.org/publications/sfaa/default.htm	• describes the nature of science and technology, including historical perspectives and their impact on society. • describes understandings and ways of thinking that are essential for all citizens.
Benchmarks for Science Literacy AAAS Project 2061 (1993) www.project2061.org/publications/bsl/default.htm	• states what all students should know and be able to do in science by the end of grades 2, 5, 8, and 12. • presents specific, grade-span learning goals (benchmarks) that can help educators develop a core curriculum that leads students toward adult science literacy goals presented in *Science for All Americans*.
Atlas of Science Literacy, Volumes 1 and 2 AAA Project 2061 (2001 and 2007) www.project2061.org/publications/atlas/default.htm	• presents conceptual strand maps that show how K–12 students' understanding and the ideas and skills that lead to scientific literacy interconnect. • based on the specific learning goals presented in *Benchmarks for Science Literacy*.
National Science Education Standards National Research Council (1996) www.nap.edu/catalog.php?record_id=4962	• defines science education standards for science content, teaching, professional development, assessment, programs, and systems. • emphasizes scientific literacy. • focuses on inquiry approaches to teaching.
Inquiry and the National Science Education Standards National Research Council (2000) www.nap.edu/catalog.php?record_id=9596	• provides a learning research foundation for the science standards. • serves as a companion volume to the science standards.
Rising Above the Gathering Storm National Academies of Science (2006) www.nap.edu/catalog/11463.html	• provides a view of science in the national economy and describes the growing precariousness of our nation's leadership in the global economy. • recommends that U.S. K–12 science and math education be vastly improved.
Taking Science to School: Learning and Teaching Science in Grades K–8 National Research Council (2007) www.nap.edu/catalog/11625.html	• provides a critique and evaluation of the science standards movement. • presents new research on how children learn science. • suggests that science content should be further reduced to concentrate only on core conceptualizations in science.
A *Framework* for *K–12 Science Education: Practices, Crosscutting Concepts, and Core Ideas* National Research Council (2012) www.nap.edu/catalog.php?record_id=13165	• proposes a new approach to K–12 science education in order to address U.S. global competitiveness and develop our workforce. • informs the development of new K–12 science standards. • identifies three dimensions to be reflected in new standards: scientific and engineering Practices, Crosscutting Concepts, and Disciplinary Core Ideas.
Next Generation Science Standards NGSS Lead States (2013) www.nextgenscience.org/	• developed through a collaborative, state-led process. • based on the *Framework for K–12 Science Education*.

Source: Compiled by authors.

The American Association for the Advancement of Science (AAAS) established Project 2061 to begin to explore what all U.S. students should know and be able to do in science in the twenty-first century. The year 2061 marks the next return of Halley's Comet to our region of the solar system. By including this distant date in the project title, AAAS implied that it intended to take a very long view indeed in determining what students will need to know, understand, and be able to do to be scientifically literate throughout a new century.

Project 2061 published a number of pivotal documents, including *Science for All Americans* (AAAS, 1990), *Benchmarks for Science Literacy* (AAAS, 1993), and the *Atlas of Science Literacy*, Volume 1 (AAAS, 2001) and Volume 2 (2007). These documents have effectively expressed and clarified ideas about the nature and importance of science and science teaching. They have also laid the foundation for the development of national standards for science education that still inform standards in many states even today.

Building on the work of Project 2061 and other groups, a distinguished panel coordinated by the National Research Council (NRC) worked on standards for science education throughout the early 1990s. In 1996, the *National Science Education Standards* (NSES) were published. The NSES offer the U.S. public a coherent vision of what it means to be scientifically literate.

There are six categories of standards in the NSES (NRC, 1996), including Science Content Standards, Assessment Standards, Teaching Standards, Professional Development Standards, Science Education Program Standards, and Science Education System Standards. For teachers, the heart of the standards is the Science Content Standards, which include (1) standards related to conceptual knowledge and understanding in physical science, life science, and earth and space science; (2) specific abilities of scientific inquiry; and (3) understandings about the nature of scientific inquiry.

The NSES did not prescribe curriculum; that is a state and local responsibility. Rather, they described what all students must understand and be able to do in science as a result of their cumulative learning experiences.

The central message that the NSES content standards convey, and that the other types of standards support, is that students should be engaged in an *inquiry* approach to learning science that basically parallels the procedures scientists use and the attitudes they display in doing science. The standards emphasize that inquiry can involve many different approaches to science instruction, including hands-on–minds-on investigations, reading books, using internet resources, talking and listening to scientists and teachers, and direct teacher instruction on the concepts, principles, and procedures of science. A common feature of all inquiry methods of instruction is a shift from a teacher-centered to a student-centered classroom. Through engaging in the many forms of inquiry, students learn how to investigate on their own and to work cooperatively with others. They learn important science knowledge and the process of generating science knowledge. And they learn to use science knowledge in understanding the objects, organisms, and events in their environments. It is clear why the NSES have declared that "inquiry into authentic questions generated from student experience is the central strategy for teaching science" (NRC, 1996, p. 31).

In response to the NSES and advances in science, brain research, learning theory, and assessment approaches, in 1994 the Governing Board of the National Assessment of Educational Progress (NAEP) decided that a new Framework for the NAEP Science Assessment was needed. NAEP, the nation's only ongoing survey of students' educational progress, is an important tool for measuring and monitoring student science achievement in the United States. The *Science Framework for the 2009 National Assessment of Educational Progress* (NAEP, 2008) specifies content to be assessed by describing key facts, concepts, principles, laws, and theories in three broad scientific disciplines: physical, life, and earth/space science. The other dimension of the NAEP *Framework* is composed of four science practices: identifying science principles, using science principles, using scientific inquiry, and using technological design. NAEP assessment items address performance expectations that combine both content and practices. A more recent version, the *Science Framework for the 2011 National Assessment of Educational Progress* (NAEP, 2010) includes hands-on performance tasks and interactive computer tasks in addition to maintaining a focus on student conceptual understanding.

In the mid-1990s, the National Research Council commissioned a panel to examine the state of science education in elementary and middle schools in our nation. In the report, *Taking Science to School: Learning and Teaching Science in Grades K–8* (NRC, 2007), the panel critiqued and evaluated the standards movement and made recommendations about science education for the future. The panel also reviewed contemporary studies from psychologists and educators about how children develop understanding in science. Among the recommendations of the committee was the call to reduce the K–12 science content taught and to emphasize fewer well-chosen core concepts to focus more on understanding rather than just accumulating knowledge.

This report also addressed a new view of what it means for students to be proficient in science. It stated, "Students who are proficient in science:

1. know, use, and interpret scientific explanations of the natural world;
2. generate and evaluate scientific evidence and explanations;
3. understand the nature and development of scientific knowledge; and
4. participate productively in scientific Practices and discourse." (NRC, 2007 p. 36)

FIGURE 1.1
Four Strands of Proficiency

Understanding Scientific Explanations

Generating Scientific Evidence

Reflecting on Scientific Knowledge

Participating Productively in Science

4 intertwined learning strands

That lead to

Science Proficiency

FIGURE 1.1
Four Strands of Proficiency

As illustrated in Figure 1.1, the four strands of proficiency were presented as broad learning goals that could best be achieved when addressed simultaneously, rather than in isolation, since advances in one strand support advances in the others.

☑ **CHECK YOUR UNDERSTANDING 1.2**
Click here to gauge your understanding of the concepts in this section.

K–8 Science Education in the Present and Future

In response to new findings about how students learn science, *A Framework for K–12 Science Standards: Practices, Crosscutting Concepts, and Core Ideas* (NRC, 2012) was developed to guide the current effort to ensure that all U.S. students understand science well enough to be effective and productive twenty-first-century citizens. By high school graduation, the expectation is that all students:

- appreciate the wonder, elegance, and beauty of science,
- are curious, lifelong science learners,
- understand enough about science and engineering to publicly discuss **STEM** (Science, Technology, Engineering, Mathematics) issues,
- critically evaluate STEM information and apply it to their everyday decision making, and
- have the skills to follow their chosen career path, whether it leads to work in STEM or other fields (NRC, 2012).

The *Framework* presents an innovative, coherent structure for K–12 science education and provides the basis for the *Next Generation Science Standards*, Figure 1.2 graphically represents the principles on which the *Framework* is based and its organization around **three dimensions**: Scientific and Engineering Practices, Crosscutting Concepts, and Disciplinary Core Ideas.

Notice that six guiding principles appear as inputs to the *Framework* circle in Figure 1.2. These are based on the research-based findings about science learning that support the *Framework*, that is, the assumptions on which it is built.

Children are natural investigators Through direct experience, media, friends and family, children develop their own ideas about the world around them long before entering school. Though some of children's ideas may be misconceptions—often listed as preconceptions since they are the naïve conceptions prior to learning—many of those early ideas provide a base on which to build instruction. Reasoning skills of young children are much more sophisticated than had been thought. Young children can do more than describe; they can also begin to build explanations. Your role as a teacher of science is to help learners develop progressively more sophisticated explanations of natural phenomena over time. Even in the early grades, students can also engage in meaningful ways

FIGURE 1.2 A *Framework* for
K–12 Science Education Overview

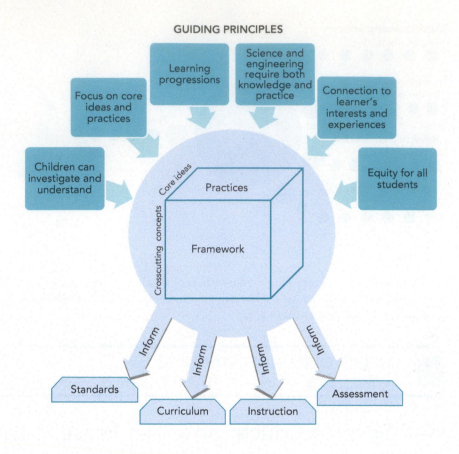

GUIDING PRINCIPLES

Focus on core ideas and practices

Learning progressions

Science and engineering require both knowledge and practice

Connection to learner's interests and experiences

Children can investigate and understand

Equity for all students

Core ideas
Crosscutting concepts
Practices
Framework

Inform — Standards

Inform — Curriculum

Inform — Instruction

Inform — Assessment

with each of the Scientific and Engineering Practices described in the *Framework* and in the *Next Generation Science Standards*.

Focus on Core Ideas and Practices   The number of Disciplinary Core Ideas in the *Framework* is limited in order to avoid superficial coverage of too many disconnected topics and in favor of deep investigation of important concepts. Studies have shown that by developing understandings of Disciplinary Core Ideas and engaging in Scientific and Engineering Practices, learners move from being novices, who may know many facts but can't effectively use their disconnected knowledge, to being experts, who understand core principles and theories well enough to use them to make sense of new learning and grapple with novel problems (Mestre & Cocking, 2002).

Learning progressions   It takes time to develop deep understanding of core disciplinary ideas. Students need to engage with core ideas multiple times at more sophisticated levels as they progress through school. Many scientists have worked toward mastery of a Disciplinary Core Idea all of their lives, so it should be no surprise that many learning progressions found in the *Framework* extend from kindergarten to grade 12. Ideally, learning progressions are based on research about how students' understanding of an idea develops over time and the impact of instruction on learning. Analysis of

What ideas might this child develop about the world and how things work by investigating with these materials?

learning progressions is a relatively new area of education research, so some of the pathways described in the *Framework* are more accepted than others. When the *Next Generation Science Standards* (NGSS Lead States, 2013) were developed, they were sequenced based on the learning progressions presented in the *Framework*.

Science and engineering require both knowledge and Practice The goal of science is to better understand the physical and natural world. The goal of engineering is to solve problems to address a need or desired product improvement. In each of these fields, professionals need an understanding of a certain body of knowledge, and they must apply certain Practices in order to discover, expand, and enhance that knowledge. The eight major Scientific and Engineering Practices identified by the *Framework* are described in more detail later in this chapter. These Practices were incorporated into the *Next Generation Science Standards* (NGSS). The summaries of what students should know and be able to do related to Science and Engineering Practices at the end of 12th grade from the *Framework* were further elaborated into learning progressions with grade band endpoints in the NGSS. Further information is provided in Appendix F (Achieve, 2013) of the NGSS.

As they work, both scientists and engineers integrate their knowledge base with accepted ways of finding out, effectively merging the elements of knowledge and Practice. Likewise, when learning science and/or engineering, rather than studying facts and concepts in isolation from the ways they were established, learners should be involved in active experiences that integrate content knowledge and Practices. "When children use their ideas about the natural world to design investigations or argue about evidence, it strengthens their understanding of both phenomena and the means used to investigate those phenomena" (Michaels, Shouse, Schweingurber, 2008, p. 17).

Connection to learners' interests and experiences During your educational career, you may have noticed that it's often easier to learn when you have an interest in, some familiarity with, and/or excitement about the topic or skill you are learning. Among the many variables that affect learning, students' personal interest, experience, and enthusiasm have been shown to impact academic achievement as well as future educational and career choices. Students are more likely to be intellectually engaged in deep science learning when they find it relevant to their daily lives. Selection of the *Framework's* Disciplinary Core Ideas, which you will read more about later, was based on an understanding of the common conceptions that students bring with them to school and the kinds of questions they ask, as well as the scientific importance of these ideas (NRC, 2012). In the NGSS document, the Disciplinary Core Ideas (DCIs) are used to organize the learning by grade levels and by topics. Additionally, Appendix E (Achieve, 2013) includes learning progressions based on the progressions identified by the *Framework*. In the NGSS, short narrative descriptions are provided for each DCI and were used in the college- and career-readiness review to determine the desired depth of understanding expected by grade 12.

Equity for all students A commonly stated philosophy of education in the United States is that "All children can learn." The opportunity to learn about science and engineering should and must not be reserved for a privileged few. Moving toward equity involves providing, for all students, access to quality instructional settings and materials, well-trained effective teachers, and adequate time devoted to science learning. Rigorous learning standards and high expectations for all students also promote equity.

Since our nation is so diverse, research into the impact of culture, customs, and environment on learning is important for achieving the goal of equity. For example, studies have shown that rural students, with extensive, ongoing experience with plants and animals, develop a more robust understanding of some biology and ecology concepts than their urban and suburban peers. By better understanding the reasons for such differences in achievement, educators can effectively design instructional opportunities to minimize those differences.

After considering these guiding principles, the committee charged with developing the *Framework* recommended that K–12 science education in the United States should be organized around three unified dimensions. Note that the edges of the cube within the *Framework* circle in Figure 1.2 represent these dimensions: Scientific and Engineering Practices (SEPs), Crosscutting Concepts (CCs), and Disciplinary Core Ideas (DCIs). Each of these dimensions is composed of a limited number of elements, which are presented in Table 1.5.

Listen to Tom Jenkins, a STEM Educator, talk about **the value of STEM learning** for his students. What disciplines are integrated in a STEM lesson? Of what value are STEM lessons for students? What qualifications do teachers need to engage students in STEM lessons?

TABLE 1.5   Elements of the Three Dimensions of *A Framework for K–12 Science Standards*

Dimension 1—Scientific and Engineering Practices

1. Asking questions (for science) and defining problems (for engineering)
2. Developing and using models
3. Planning and carrying out investigations
4. Analyzing and interpreting data
5. Using mathematics and computational thinking
6. Constructing explanations (for science) and designing solutions (for engineering)
7. Engaging in argument from evidence
8. Obtaining, evaluating, and communicating information

Dimension 2—Crosscutting Concepts

1. Patterns
2. Cause and effect: mechanism and explanation
3. Scale, proportion, and quantity
4. Systems and system models
5. Energy and matter: flows, cycles, and conservation
6. Structure and function
7. Stability and change

Dimension 3—Disciplinary Core Ideas

Physical Sciences
PS 1: Matter and its interactions
PS 2: Motion and stability: Forces and interactions
PS 3: Energy
PS 4: Waves and their applications in technologies for information transfer

Life Sciences
LS 1: From molecules to organisms: Structures and processes
LS 2: Ecosystems: Interactions, energy, and dynamics
LS 3: Heredity: Inheritance and variation of traits
LS 4: Biological evolution: Unity and diversity

Earth and Space Sciences
ESS 1: Earth's place in the universe
ESS 2: Earth's systems
ESS 3: Earth and human activity

Engineering, Technology, and the Applications of Science
ETS 1: Engineering design
ETS 2: Links among engineering, technology, and science, and society

Source: NRC, 2012, p. 3.

Scientific and Engineering Practices   The interests of scientists are very diverse. An astronomer might search the galaxy for more life-sustaining planets orbiting around distant stars, hoping to find a "Goldilocks" planet, one that is the appropriate distance from its sun to have a climate that is not too hot, not too cold, but just right for life (Johnson, 2011). Microbiologists might investigate ways to synthesize an antibiotic that kills bad microbes while sparing good ones that keep human microbiomes healthy. (Sofia, 2016). Physics researchers might show mathematically that the equation, thought for 60 years to explain surface tension on solids, is incompatible with thermodynamic theory (Technical Research Centre of Finland, 2012).

Yet all of these scientists and those in other disciplines use some common Practices in their work. All true scientists are committed to using data and evidence to support the claims they make. As scientists investigate, develop models, and improve explanations, they engage in argumentation that involves critical reflection on their own current knowledge and that of others in the field (NRC, 2012).

In order to help students understand what scientists and engineers do and how scientific knowledge and engineering solutions develop, the first dimension of the *Framework*, Scientific and Engineering Practices, focuses on eight Practices, which are listed in Table 1.5 and explained in more detail later. By engaging in the Practices while investigating ideas and concepts, students' competency with the Practices is expected to increase along with knowledge and understanding. The Practices expose students to the wide range of approaches that are used to investigate, model, explain phenomena, and develop technologic solutions for human needs and wants, as well as the links between science and engineering.

The *National Science Education Standards* (NSES) (NRC, 1996) emphasized a focus on **inquiry** for science learning, but unfortunately a common understanding of the elements of inquiry did not emerge. Since the term *inquiry* meant different things to different people, some important things that scientists do in their work were often not emphasized or were overlooked completely when educating students. The Practices are basically an unwrapping of the elements of scientific inquiry, an attempt to be explicit about the various major components of doing science. Those of you already familiar with the elements of inquiry will recognize them in the Practices. The Practices were developed to include important aspects of doing both science and engineering, also differentiating this new approach of the *Framework* and NGSS from the focus on inquiry in the NSES. The Practices are also quite interrelated, as you will see when you consider Table 1.6.

> Seventh-grade teacher, Katy Jo Brown, has students participate in an afterschool robotics program. As you watch students learn to **program their robots**, determine the Science and Engineering Practices they employ to help them with their tasks.

TABLE 1.6 Dimension 1: Scientific and Engineering Practices

Scientific and Engineering Practices	Why is this Practice basic and important?	What should students be able to do as this Practice develops over time?
Asking questions and defining problems	• Scientists begin their investigations with questions. • Engineers begin their work with problems to solve.	• Ask questions of others about things and events they observe and wonder about. • Tell the difference between questions and problems. • Distinguish investigable questions from noninvestigable questions. • Formulate investigable questions (those that can be answered empirically). • Ask questions to clarify the problem, determine criteria, and identify constraints. (Engineering).
Developing and using models	• Scientists often create and use models to help develop explanations that answer questions about the natural world. • Engineers often create and use models to analyze existing systems, test possible solutions for a problem, and to identify strengths and weaknesses of a design. • Models enable investigators to study phenomena that are difficult to study in the natural world (too big, too small, too dangerous, too slow, too fast, too far away, too expensive).	• Be aware that things and events can be represented by many kinds of models: pictures, diagrams, drawings, 3-D models, simulations, equations, etc. • Develop and/or use models to represent things and events, both seen and unseen. • Use models to test predictions and possible explanations. • Use models or simulations to generate data that could lead to explanations or technological solutions. • Realize that all models have limitations.
Planning and carrying out investigations	• Scientists plan and carry out many kinds of systematic investigations to answer the questions they pose. • Engineers conduct investigations to get data needed to specify criteria (i.e., effectiveness, efficiency, and durability) and to test proposed designs under different conditions. • Both clarify what counts as data, identify relevant variables, decide how to measure them, and collect data for analysis.	• Plan and carry out "fair tests" and other kinds of investigations. • Use different technologies to collect data. • Consider the variables involved in an experiment or other type of investigation. • Decide what type of investigation is appropriate based on the question or problem being addressed.

(Table 1.6 continued)

(Table 1.6 continued)

Scientific and Engineering Practices	Why is this Practice basic and important?	What should students be able to do as this Practice develops over time?
Analyzing and interpreting data	• Data from investigations must be analyzed to be meaningful. • Scientists answer their questions based on their data. • Engineers use data from tests of designs to determine which design best solves the problem.	• Record and share data they have collected (drawing, writing, numbers, oral/written reports). • Use tools including tables, graphs, and statistical analysis to make sense of data. • Consider possible sources of error. • Find relationships and patterns in data. • Distinguish between correlation and causation.
Using mathematics and computational thinking	• Scientists use mathematics and computation to represent variables and their relationships. • Mathematics and computation are used to predict behaviors of systems, test those predictions, identify significant patterns, and establish correlational relationships. • As part of the design process, engineers use mathematics and computation, often in simulations, to analyze designs in terms of various criteria.	• Use appropriate measuring tools and units when collecting data to answer scientific questions or solve engineering problems. • Use computer probes to collect and display data from investigations. • Use computers to analyze data sets. • Use statistics to express significance of the data and patterns in the data.
Constructing explanations and designing solutions	• The goal of science is constructing theories to explain the natural world. • The goal of engineering is to design solutions that address human needs and wants.	• Use evidence to construct logical explanations of phenomena and to support a proposed solution for an engineering problem. • Use current scientific knowledge and models when constructing explanations.
Engaging in argument from evidence	• Scientists use reasoning and argument to clarify the pros and cons of a line of evidence and to identify the best explanation for a natural phenomenon. • Engineers use reasoning and argument to find the best solution to a problem.	• Decide which of two explanations for an observation is better supported by evidence from the data. • Ask each other to support their claims with evidence. • Identify claims and defend them with evidence. • Differentiate between data, evidence, and claims. • Use logical reasoning in presentations. • Collaborate with peers in order to find the best explanation or solution.
Obtaining, evaluating, and communicating information	• Scientists must clearly and persuasively communicate ideas and the results of inquiry so others can learn about them and science can advance. • Engineers must communicate clearly and persuasively about the advantages of their designs in order to design new or improved technologies.	• Share information about science and technology. • Effectively present information and ideas orally, in writing, and through tables, graphs, drawings, models, equations, etc. • Engage in respectful discourse with peers. • Read and comprehend various texts, reports, and articles written by other students, scientists, and engineers in order to evaluate their claims or solutions and appropriately apply their ideas to future research or design.

The general progression of the development of the Practices across grade levels is described in the *Framework* and further elaborated in the *Next Generation Science Standards*. For example, observation and explanation of direct experiences are stressed at the primary level. In upper elementary, the concentration shifts to introducing simple models that help explain observable objects, systems, and events. By middle school, there is a transition to more abstract and more detailed models and explanations.

During the development of the *Next Generation Science Standards,* the writing team added specificity to the progression of the Science and Engineering Practices from kindergarten to grade 12. It created a "Practices matrix" of statements that describe the components of each Practice expected to be mastered by students by the end of different grade level bands (Achieve, 2013b).

A Framework for K–12 Science Education: Practices, Crosscutting Concepts, and Core Ideas (NRC, 2012) recommends that the Science and Engineering Practices be integrated with the other two dimensions in performance expectations in the *Next Generation Science Standards.* The *Framework* emphasizes the inclusion of the Practices because educational research suggests that:

- students learn key concepts in science more effectively when they engage in the Practices,

- the best way to learn about the nature of evidence, the role of models, and the features of a sound scientific argument is through engagement in these Practices, and

- opportunities to engage in Scientific and Engineering Practices increases participation of underrepresented minorities in science. (NRC, 2012)

Crosscutting Concepts   The second dimension of the *Framework* is composed of big ideas, known as **Crosscutting Concepts**, which are relevant across all science disciplines and engineering fields. This dimension is intended to explicitly encourage educators and students to realize connections between Disciplinary Core Ideas and develop a coherent and scientific view of the world. Seven Crosscutting Concepts (see Table 1.7) were selected for inclusion in the *Framework* because they are fundamental to an understanding of science and engineering. In the *Framework*, they are reminiscent of the "common themes" identified by *Science for All Americans* (AAAS, 1989) and *Project 2061: Benchmarks for Science Literacy* (AAAS, 1993) and the "unifying concepts and processes" presented in the *National Science Education Standards* (NRC, 1996), which were seen as pervasive, powerful ideas that are ways of thinking applicable to the work of all scientists and engineers. Table 1.7 illustrates the evolution of these overarching ideas over time.

The general progression of the development of the Crosscutting Concepts across grade levels is described in the *Framework*. As they did with the Practices, the writing team for the *Next Generation Science Standards* added specificity to the progression of the Crosscutting Concepts from kindergarten to grade 12 (Appendix G). It created a "Crosscutting Concepts matrix" of statements that describe the components of each Crosscutting Concept expected to be mastered by students by the end of different grade level bands (Achieve, 2013c).

Relevant Crosscutting Concepts are included in each of the performance expectations in the *Next Generation Science Standards,* which guide instructional, curricular, and assessment development where and when they are adopted. The Crosscutting Concepts are not intended to be studied in isolation but in the context of Science and Engineering Practices and Disciplinary Core Ideas over the student's educational career (NRC, 2012; NGSS Lead States, 2013). After you have reviewed Table 1.7, take time to do Exploration 1.3 to enhance your understanding the Crosscutting Concepts.

Visit www .nextgenscience.org/ to read Appendix F, Science and Engineering Practices, in the NGSS to find out more about this dimension and examine the **Practices matrix.**

Kindergarten teacher, Sheri Geitner, explains how the three-dimensions intertwine in their Pushes and Pulls unit. Look for students' engagement with the Crosscutting Concept of cause and effect during the classroom scenes.

Visit www .nextgenscience.org / to read Appendix G, Crosscutting Concepts, in the NGSS to find out more about this dimension and examine the **Crosscutting Concepts matrix.**

TABLE 1.7   Comparison of Science Overarching Ideas over Time

Common Themes	Unifying Concepts and Processes	Crosscutting Concepts
Science for All Americans (AAAS, 1989) *Project 2061: Benchmarks for Science Literacy* (AAAS, 1993) - Systems - Models - Constancy and change - Scale	*National Science Education Standards* (NRC, 1997) - Systems, order, and organization - Evidence, models, and explanation - Constancy, change, and measurement - Evolution and equilibrium - Form and function	*A Framework for K–12 Science Education: Practices, Crosscutting Concepts, and Disciplinary Core Ideas* (NRC, 2012) and *The Next Generation Science Standards* (NGSS Lead States, 2013) - Patterns - Cause and effect: Mechanism and explanation - Scale, proportion, and quantity - Systems and system models - Energy and matter: Flows, cycles, and conservation - Structure and function - Stability and change

EXPLORATION

1.3

Considering the Crosscutting Concepts

Spend a few minutes examining Table 1.8. Notice that for each Crosscutting Concept there is a brief explanation of its importance and a related example activity. Working with a partner or a small group of your peers, discuss:

- how the bulleted points in the "Importance" column relate to science,
- whether the example activities are well aligned with the Crosscutting Concepts, and
- other science activities that would be good examples for each Crosscutting Concept.

Reflection Questions:

1. Select two of the bulleted points that you feel are important in science; then explain why you think they are so important.
2. Identify the example activity that, in your opinion, is best aligned with its Crosscutting Concept and explain your thinking.
3. Write additional example learning activities for three of the Crosscutting Concepts.

TABLE 1.8   **Dimension 2—Crosscutting Concepts**

Crosscutting Concept	Importance	Example of a Learning Activity in Which This Crosscutting Concept Is Evident
Patterns	• Guide organization and classification. • Stimulate questions about relationships and factors that influence them.	• Using climate data from various cities, students look for patterns in the variation of average monthly temperature over time.
Cause and effect: Mechanism and explanation	• Events have causes. • Recognize causality vs. correlation. • Find out "what makes" or "why" something happened and "how" it happened.	• Students investigate factors that might explain the variations in monthly temperature they observed in the climate data and argue from evidence to support their claims.
Scale, proportion, and quantity	• Relative size (time, energy) matters when considering a system's structure or performance.	• Students wonder about variations in average temperature over different time scales: hourly temperature over a week, daily temperature over a month, yearly temperature over a century. Then they design investigations to enable them to address their questions.
Systems and system models	• Systems are often too complicated to be studied or understood without specifying boundaries or considering their component parts in isolation.	• Students create a model or use a computer simulation illustrating the motion of the sun across the sky in different months to explain the patterns they observed in the monthly average high temperature data for their city.
Energy and matter: Flows, cycles, and conservation	• Possibilities and limitations of systems are easier to understand when you know how matter and energy move into, out of, and between systems.	• Students create a model to investigate how the length of the day and the angle of the sun relate to the amount of energy from the sun striking an area on Earth's surface and the resultant change in air temperature.
Structure and function	• The shape of an object, living thing, or system is related to what it does, how well it does it, and how it works. • The overall structure of an object, living thing, or system is often related to its substructure.	• Students investigate how the shape of a translucent container placed in direct sunlight affects the rate of heating of its contents. Then they try to design a container that minimizes the temperature change of its contents when placed in direct sunlight.
Stability and change	• Systems change or remain stable, but the time frame of the study is important. • Rates of change matter. • When a system is stable, competing effects balance each other.	• Students explore the literature about climate change, then present an evidence-based argument supporting their conclusion about whether or not global warming is occurring and if it is human caused.

Disciplinary Core Ideas   Think about all of the new information generated each day through discovery, research, and invention. It doesn't simply take the place of all of the old knowledge; it piles up on top of it! And many believe that in the information age (our current era), the rate of generation of new science knowledge is increasing, implying that the amount of knowledge is piling up faster and faster over time.

Now that there is much more knowledge in the pile, is it really fair for us to expect the students we teach to learn it all? Of course not! Teaching all of the facts is no longer a reasonable goal for science education. A more realistic goal is to ensure that students learn enough about the core ideas in science so that they can continue to learn and use scientific knowledge on their own throughout their lives. That is why the third dimension of the *Framework* identifies a limited set of **Disciplinary Core Ideas** (DCIs) for K–12 instruction. The science ideas discussed in the *Framework* document were reviewed and revised, and the final Disciplinary Core Ideas comprise the third dimension of the *Next Generation Science Standards*. The DCIs are listed as the third dimension to remind teachers that they must be linked to dimensions one and two and are not stand-alone science ideas.

The authors of the *Framework* used four criteria to select the core ideas to be included. To "make the cut," a core idea had to meet at least two of the following criteria. They preferred core ideas that met three or even all four of the criteria described here:

1. It has broad importance across multiple science or engineering disciplines or is a key organizing principle of a single discipline.

2. It is an important tool for understanding or investigating more complex ideas and solving problems.

3. It is relevant, either by relating to students' interests and life experiences or to societal or personal concerns that require scientific or technical knowledge.

4. It must be broad enough to be meaningfully taught and learned at increasing levels of depth and sophistication over a student's K–12 educational career.

As you can see in Table 1.5, within the third dimension of the *Framework*, the Disciplinary Core Ideas are organized into four major domains: the physical sciences, the life sciences, the earth and space sciences, and engineering, technology, and applications of science. These domains represent the three science disciplines typically taught in K–12 schools in the United States, plus engineering and technology. By including core ideas specifically related to engineering and technology, the writers of the *Framework* highlight the importance of understanding the human-built world and advocate for teaching Science, Technology, Engineering, and Mathematics (STEM) through an integrated approach to learning.

The integration of the fourth domain of the Disciplinary Core Ideas was greatly influenced by feedback from the public reviews during the development of the NGSS. Engineering design is found throughout the NGSS from kindergarten to grade 12. There are standards for which students are expected to apply engineering design Practices in order to demonstrate their understanding of a science concept and others at each grade level band that are specifically standards for engineering design (Achieve, 2013d).

In the *Framework*, the 13 Disciplinary Core Ideas are subdivided into **component ideas**. Each core idea and component has a discipline-related code, a descriptive title, and a related question. An overview of these features of the Disciplinary Core Ideas is provided in Appendix A (NRC, 2012).

Descriptions of the content included in each of the core ideas and components are part of the *Framework* document. Also, for each component idea, the *Framework* presents a set of **grade band "endpoints"** to specify what students should understand by the end of second, fifth, eighth, and twelfth grades, based whenever possible on research on learning progressions related to that component.

The authors of the *Framework* intentionally kept the number of Disciplinary Core Ideas in science and engineering low so that teachers and students could and would spend enough time to explore each of them in depth and actually understand them. The core ideas identified in the *Framework* were integrated, along with the other two dimensions, into the performance expectations in the *Next Generation Science Standards*. The organization of the standards requires some getting used to, and different components of the documents have language that is different from what has just been described for the *Framework*. If your state has adopted the *Next Generation Science Standards*, then you will want to spend time familiarizing yourself with the documents. For this course we will continue to refer to the narrative information from the *Framework* and with the activities provided, and throughout the chapters, links to the NGSS will be featured.

Visit www
.nextgenscience.org/
to read Appendix E,
Progressions within
the *Next Generation
Science Standards*,
to find out more about
the arrangement of
Disciplinary Core Ideas
through the grade levels.

Visit www
.nextgenscience.org/
to read Appendix I,
Engineering Design
in the NGSS, and
Appendix J, Science,
Technology, Society,
and the Environment, to
learn more about how
Engineering, Technology,
and Applications of
Science—the fourth
domain of the Disciplinary
Core Ideas identified
in the *Framework*—is
included in the NGSS.

A Framework for K–12 Science Education (NRC, 2012) did not present standards, but it offered guidance to the developers of the *Next Generation Science Standards*. These recommendations led the writers to create a limited number of clear and concise "standards" that emphasize all three dimensions of the *Framework*: Scientific and Engineering Practices, Crosscutting Concepts, and Disciplinary Core Ideas.

The NGSS are different from previous science standards in many ways. The conceptual shifts they bring include:

- K–12 science education should reflect the interconnected nature of science as it is Practiced and experienced in the real world.

- The NGSS describe student performance expectations—*not* curriculum.

- The science concepts in the NGSS build coherently across the grade levels.

- The NGSS focus on deeper understanding of content as well as application of content.

- Science and engineering are integrated in the NGSS at all grade levels.

- The NGSS and *Common Core State Standards* (English Language Arts and Mathematics) are aligned (Achieve, 2013e).

The NGSS also look very different than previous science standards in the way they are presented. To make interpretation and "unpacking" of the standards unnecessary, the NGSS are full of information and may seem overwhelming at first glance. Completing Exploration 1.4 should help you better understand how to read the Next Generation Science Standards. The NGSS are organized into three sections, including **performance expectations**, **foundation boxes**, and **connection boxes**. Though the NGSS can be printed as a document, a variety of features available when viewing them online makes them really come alive.

EXPLORATION

1.4

Learning How to Read the *Next Generation Science Standards*

To access the NGSS online, visit www.nextgenscience.org/. Explore the website, which includes instructions about how to read the NGSS in a section called "Structure of the NGSS" (Achieve, 2013f), a glossary to the many codes used in the document, and ways to search for standards by grade level and science discipline.

Select a standard at a grade level you plan to teach. Starting with the assessable component at the top of the page, try running your cursor over the text of the performance expectations to see what pop-ups appear. Explore the color coding that is available for the performance expectations. Consider the usefulness of assessment boundary statements and clarifications. Look for engineering and design performance expectations.

Notice how the text in the foundation boxes relates to the performance expectations. Move your cursor over this text to see what happens. Look for references to the nature of science and engineering, science, and technology in the dimensions represented in this section.

Finally, examine the connection boxes, the final section, which is intended to support a coherent vision of the standards—making connections within this grade level, across other grade levels, and with standards in other subject areas.

Reflection Questions:

1. Which features of the NGSS website do you find most useful in helping you understand the standards? Why?
2. To what extent does the standard you explored provide a clear idea of what students are expected to know and be able to do? Give evidence to support your claim.
3. What is the difference between assessment boundary statements and clarification statements?

☑ **CHECK YOUR UNDERSTANDING 1.3**

Click here to gauge your understanding of the concepts in this section.

Getting Started with Inquiry-Based Teaching and Learning

Young children are naturally curious and can learn science. When teachers nurture students' interest, foundational understanding, and thinking skills from the earliest years, students are more likely to pursue and succeed in science in high school and beyond.

In the book *Ready, Set, Science! Putting Research to Work in K–8 Science Classrooms,* the authors provide us with some key recommendations as you start your journey to engage students with science ideas (Michaels, Shouse, and Schweingruber, 2008). Students come to class with their own ideas about how science works so developing lessons that seek to develop understanding using a process of conceptual change can occur when implementing inquiry-based instructional practices. Science lessons should be organized around core science concepts where students can engage in doing science to make sense of science phenomenon. To foster learning, we will want to start with experiences and investigations that prompt student thinking, and it is our job to make student thinking visible using modelling, talk in the classroom, and ultimately engaging in arguing from evidence. Even very young students are taught how to make claims, gather data, and determine evidence, and develop reasoning and explanations (Zembal-Saul, McNeill, and Hershberger, 2008). In essence, we want students to learn from science investigations and inquiry-based teaching. This may sound like a lot to understand but don't worry. We will take the learning a piece at a time as you build your mental model of what is needed to provide effective inquiry-based instruction.

At the start of this chapter we invited you to develop your own definition of science and took you on a journey to discover the transitions in science education initiatives in the past that have led to the current guidance documents. In the previous section you learned about the current national emphasis on three-dimensional science teaching and learning (Science and Engineering Practices, Crosscutting Concepts, and Disciplinary Core Ideas). It's now time to "get started" as you develop your proficiencies as a teacher of science. Once you put all the pieces together and incorporate the ideas from the rest of the course with what you know already, you will be able to join the ranks of science educators able to move research-based approaches into Practice. The next chapter will feature what is needed to do inquiry-based science.

✓ CHECK YOUR UNDERSTANDING 1.4

Click here to gauge your understanding of the concepts in this section.

 ## CHAPTER SUMMARY

What is Science?

The current view is that science is both an evidence-based approach to better understanding the natural (as opposed to the supernatural) world and the resulting body of knowledge that is continually being extended, refined, and revised. Adjectives including *testable, replicable, reliable, tentative, collaborative,* and *evidence-based* are used to describe the *nature of science.* Scientists exhibit certain attitudes or *habits of mind* such as curiosity, honesty, and willingness to be persuaded by evidence. In science, common words such as *theory, law, fact, evidence, claim,* and *data* have specific meanings that differ from use in everyday language.

Science Education in Elementary and Middle Schools

Science literacy is considered to be an important goal for all citizens of the twenty-first century. When they grow up, some students will enter the STEM workforce, but all will need to use science knowledge and thinking to make decisions and solve problems in their daily lives. Federal and state legislation (No Child Left Behind and state standards) and science education associations advocate for the inclusion of science in the curriculum from the earliest years. Our quality of life, economy, national security, and global competitiveness depend on the Science, Technology, Engineering, and Mathematics (STEM) preparedness of our workforce. Project 2061, an initiative of the American Association for the Advancement of Science (AAAS), published *Science for All Americans,* which pointed out the need for scientific literacy and emphasized the societal importance of science and technology in our society; then it produced *Benchmarks for Science Literacy* and the *Atlases of Science Literacy* as resources to guide the science education reform effort. Several years later, the National Research Council (NRC) released the *National Science Education Standards,* a science education reform document that proposed standards for many aspects of science education, focused on inquiry as a method of teaching and learning. *Benchmarks* and the *National Science Education Standards* influenced the development of state science content standards, to which state science assessments required by No Child Left Behind were aligned. While states' science standards were based on the same science reform documents, there was a great deal of variation in format, content emphasis, and grade-level placement of specific concepts. Due to the influence of high-stakes testing, the science taught was highly influenced by existing state standards and lacked uniformity across the country. Appropriate science instruction fosters increased student achievement in language arts and mathematics.

K–8 Science Education in the Present and Future

Since the release of the *National Science Education Standards*, our understanding of how children and adolescents learn science and what it means for them to be proficient in science has changed. The report *Taking Science to School* (NRC, 2007) suggested the need for a new set of science content standards for the United States. *A Framework for K–12 Science Education: Practices, Crosscutting Concepts, and Core Ideas* was publicly released by the NRC in July 2011. The *Framework* describes three dimensions: Scientific and Engineering Practices, Crosscutting Concepts, and Disciplinary Core Ideas, and it presented advice to the developers of the *Next Generation Science Standards* (NGSS) as they developed a coherent approach to K–12 science education in the United States. The NGSS are a guide for science education in many states and will impact others in the near future. The Science and Engineering Practices included in both documents already form the basis of teaching and learning nationally.

Getting Started with Inquiry-based Instruction

To become proficient teacher of sciences, we have to first understand what science is and isn't. This links to how science knowledge is developed and what students are expected to know, understand, and be able to do as a result of science education. It is up to us as educators to know how to help students develop conceptual understanding of science phenomena. Building an internal mental model of effective inquiry-based instructional approaches is needed before we can design and implement lessons that engage students with inquiry and investigations just like scientists would.

DISCUSSION QUESTIONS

1. What is unique about science as an approach to finding answers and as a body of knowledge?

2. What is the most important reason that science instruction should be a core feature of K–8 teaching and learning?

3. How was elementary and middle school science teaching and learning impacted by the science education reform efforts of the late twentieth century? Why did this happen?

4. In what ways do you expect *A Framework for K–12 Science Education: Practices, Crosscutting Concepts, and Core Ideas* and the *Next Generation Science Standards* to change K–8 science education?

5. What is essential for you to understand about science and science education to inform your journey to become a teacher of science?

PROFESSIONAL PRACTICES ACTIVITIES

1. Interview at least three teachers and five students (K–8) at your field placement school to find out their opinion of "what science is" in general and at their school. Analyze their responses; then compare and contrast their opinions with yours. Use a graphic organizer (i.e., table, Venn diagram) to present your findings.

2. Ask at least three teachers and an administrator at your field placement school if they think teaching/learning science is important at their grade level. Analyze their responses and present your findings in a one-page report.

3. Go online to find the current state science standards for your state. Be sure to read any introductory material and examine the standards for your favorite grade level (K–8). Summarize the process by which your state's standards were developed, how they relate to state science testing, and their organization and areas of focus.

4. Find out what your cooperating teacher knows about *A Framework for K–12 Science Education: Practices, Crosscutting Concepts, and Core Ideas* and/or the *Next Generation Science Standards*. If it isn't very much, invite him or her to check out the NRC website or watch an archived webinar with you, and then talk with each other about your new learning.

Getting Ready for Inquiry Instruction

LEARNING GOALS

After reading this chapter, you should understand that . . .

1. Learning goals aligned to standards identify what students should know, understand, and be able to do at their grade level.

2. When getting ready for instruction, teachers must first select the science concepts, procedures and skills they will use during inquiry learning.

3. Units of instruction, curriculum maps, or guides along with a variety of resources assist with pre-planning for instruction and creating content storylines.

4. Familiarity with aspects of "doing science" (process skills and Practices) is needed prior to planning inquiry-based instruction.

5. Determination of the appropriate type of investigation in which to engage students is dependent on the question that is asked.

What is the difference between getting ready to deliver curriculum and instruction and actually planning and then working with students? Let's start by clarifying terminology. You are probably used to hearing these two terms—curriculum and instruction—in conjunction with each other. When you think about the term *curriculum*, what are the first three things that come to your mind? Record your ideas through words or drawings. Repeat this activity when thinking about *instruction*. How are the two ideas connected to each other?

Clearly, curriculum and instruction are linked to one another and also to assessment—determining if students actually learned the delivered curriculum. Part of getting ready involves linking these three components. We will focus on curriculum and instructional preparation in this chapter and you will learn more about assessment in Chapter 7. Jumping right into an existing written curriculum and teaching lessons that someone else has created rarely works. Veteran teachers will quickly suggest that it is not a good idea to use any curricular activities without trying them out yourself. Additionally, you won't want to jump into instruction with students without getting ready and spending time pre-planning. Consider again your reflections on your current thoughts about these two terms. The ideas developed in this chapter will acquaint you with the process of getting ready to implement an inquiry-based curriculum and the instructional strategies you can use when you are ready to actually plan instructional units.

In the twenty-first century, it is essential that teachers who are responsible for helping students learn science ideas understand the nature of curriculum and instruction designed to guide science teaching and learning. This chapter presents information and ideas to help you think about these important understandings so that you will be prepared to teach science well. *A Framework for K–12 Science Education* (NRC, 2012) refers to *curriculum* as "the knowledge and practices in subject matter areas that teachers teach and that students are supposed to learn" (p. 246) and to *instruction* as "methods of teaching and the learning activities used to help students master the content and objectives specified by a curriculum" (p. 250). Think about the ideas you recorded. How do these definitions match your initial ideas? What do you still wonder about? If you are clear about the distinctions about these terms, then you are ready to move right into the work that needs to happen prior to instruction.

Even though this chapter is about getting ready for inquiry instruction, we won't yet be "ready" to tackle creating a science lesson plan. In this chapter our goals focus on a the process of getting ready to help you prepare for inquiry instruction, so this is more about the pre-planning that is needed prior to planning and implementing a lesson with students. Ask yourself this question, "What do I need to do to prepare for inquiry-based instruction?"

Identify Learning Goals Aligned to Standards

The No Child Left Behind Act required all states to establish science standards by the academic year 2005 (National Science Board, 2004). The publishing of state standards made the development of statewide assessments possible. Since state standards define what students need to know to be successful on high-stakes state science assessments, understanding them is an important step in deciding what content to teach. Exploration 2.1 is designed to help you learn about your state science standards.

Most of the initial state science standards were based on two widely accepted sets of national standards in science education, the *Benchmarks for Science Literacy* (American Association for the Advancement of Science, 1993) and the *National Science Education Standards* (NSES) (National Research Council, 1996). Both *Benchmarks* and the content standards of the NSES specify how students should progress toward science literacy by recommending what they should know, understand, and be able to do by the time they reach certain grade levels. These complementary documents specified broad learning goals (science concepts), but did not inform teachers specifically of what to teach. Their intent was to provide guidance to states as they developed their unique set of science standards. Most states have revised their standards at least once in the last 20 years, and the original and revised documents were, in general, highly aligned with the two reference sets of national standards. Understanding how they link to state assessments and curriculum documents is an important first step when pre-planning for your curriculum and instruction.

The *Next Generation Science Standards (NGSS): For States, By States* (NGSS Lead States, 2013), represent a new set of science "standards" (this term is not actually used in the document) that states can use as a guideline when revising their standards. Some states have adopted the NGSS rather than generating new sets of state standards. As a reminder, these documents are not a curriculum and are not meant to be used that way. Rather, they inform development of curriculum Frameworks created at state or district levels. The Disciplinary Core Ideas (DCIs), one of the three dimensions of the NGSS, are similar to the content standards in the NSES, but within the NGSS they are not meant to be addressed in isolation but always intertwined with the other two dimensions: Science and Engineering Practices and Crosscutting Concepts. Each state has identified a cycle for review of standards, and many may revise their science standards to align with NGSS. Check to see when your state standards are scheduled to be revised and if they are currently based on the NGSS documents.

Another valuable resource found in the NGSS is a document showing the learning progressions for each broad learning concept as it takes students from being novice learners to mastery of the concepts. Similar progressions are also provided for the Science and Engineering Practices and the Crosscutting Concepts that identify student expectations as they progress toward mastery of the Concepts and Practices. Before you work

Examining Your State Science Standards   **EXPLORATION**

2.1

It is a good idea to become familiar with your state's science standards early in your teaching career. They are likely to be available on the website of your state's department of education. Take some time to access your state's current state science standards, read the introductory material, and examine how they are structured. Select a grade level that you hope to teach, and examine that grade level's standards in detail.

Reflection Questions:

1. What are the two most important things you learned by reading the introductory information about your state science standards? Why do you consider this information important?
2. How would you explain the structure and/or organization of your state science standards to a peer who had not yet looked at them?
3. Content as it is described in the *Next Generation Science Standards* (NGSS) includes science Disciplinary Core Ideas (DCIs), Science and Engineering Practices (SEPs), and broad Crosscutting Concepts (CCs). Based on your state science standards, what science content are the students in the grade level you selected expected to learn? How familiar are you with this content?
4. What might you do to become better prepared to teach this content?

on your unit planning, you should locate the guidance documents already existing in districts to help identify the curriculum that should be taught at each grade level and the standards on which they are based. You may need to, usually with the help of colleagues, develop unit-level learning progressions to connect individual ideas and practices into a content storyline allowing you to connect one idea and appropriate practices to the next idea. District curriculum specialists and/or state curriculum specialists often provide documents where the progressions have been created for teachers. Part of this process may involve identifying *science phenomena* – interesting, natural or human-caused events that stimulate curiosity. Phenomena don't have to be phenomenal like an erupting volcano, a solar eclipse, a giant redwood tree, or a rocket launch. Even common, every-day occurrences, such as a puddle drying up, a bird flying, a seed sprouting, or riding a bike can be appropriate science phenomena since they may also lead to questions that can be scientifically investigated.

Because school districts develop science curriculum documents that are aligned with the science standards of their state, your district's curriculum should include clear statements identifying what your students are expected to learn—know and understand (CCs and DCIs)—and be able to do (SEPs). It is then up to you as the classroom teacher to plan the lesson sequence that connects the learning experiences and targeted ideas before you select the teaching strategies and instructional materials most suitable to enable students to master the required content.

✅ **CHECK YOUR UNDERSTANDING 2.1**

Click here to gauge your understanding of the concepts in this section.

Getting Ready for Inquiry-based Instructional Planning

Getting ready to plan lessons involves selecting essential <u>content</u> (for our purposes this is content that includes DCIs, SEPs, and CCs), selecting instructional strategies that help students develop conceptual and procedural <u>understanding,</u> and promoting positive classroom <u>environments</u> that are student centered (Tweed, 2009). You will learn more about planning for procedural understanding later in this chapter with the introduction of science process skills. Promoting positive classroom environments will be developed further in Chapter 3.

In pre-planning for teaching and learning, there are two important parts to the instructional planning Framework. In the first part of the planning Framework, you must translate the content that you have selected to teach into instructional units so you are clear about the essential content you want to teach. In the second part of the instructional planning Framework, you will determine, with the help of a variety of resources, how to implement instruction focused on student learning. We now know that before selecting appropriate instructional strategies, clear **learning goals** (broad science concepts and Practices that guide a unit of study) need to be identified and then must be broken down into smaller **learning targets** (daily student-friendly learning expectations), which will guide your selection of instructional activities and appropriate teaching approaches. The NGSS documents can help with the process of identifying learning goals since they are organized with the perspective of Disciplinary Core Ideas and the corresponding Crosscutting Concepts and Practices that are already written as learning goals. Daily learning targets serve as a guide in the process of teaching and facilitate the assessment of student learning. When the learning targets are sequenced into a content storyline, you will be able to connect the learning from one day to another and build student understanding of the broader learning goals and develop proficiency with Concepts and Practices. A key instructional strategy is to share and discuss with the students the learning targets and also clarify Concepts and the expected lesson-level learning performances.

Before you can communicate learning goals to students, you will need to write learning goals. A learning goal is not an activity, phrase, or topic. Rather, a learning goal is focused on a specific understanding or Practice that students should develop or knowledge that they will acquire. You may remember from your own experiences in classrooms that teachers provided "Students Will Be Able To" statements that teachers called **SWBATs** for short. These represented behavioral objectives and related to what students would be able to do. From video studies of science and math classrooms (TIMSS Video Study, 1997), observations showed that even though students knew what activity they were meant to do, they generally did not know what content they were expected to learn. Lessons for the most part did not focus student learning on phenomena related to science concepts nor did they emphasize the importance of science

 Watch this video to learn how the NGSS helped two elementary teachers identify learning goals for their units.

Practices to develop understanding of science ideas. This approach is now a central goal of the NGSS document. Teachers are expected to be able to identify clear learning goals, and that skill has replaced the practice of simply writing behavioral objectives. An example of a Disciplinary Core Idea specified for fourth graders is that students should develop an understanding that plants and animals possess internal and external structures that function to support survival, growth, behavior, and reproduction. As you can see by this example, a Disciplinary Core Idea—a broad learning goal--combines many individual ideas together. Students will struggle with such a complex set of ideas, so it is up to us as teachers to identify the smaller learning targets that become the focus of daily lessons. Possible learning targets would include:

- I understand that plants have external structures that support their survival and protect them from being eaten (e.g., bark on trees, thorns on cactus).

- I understand that plants can store food to use for growth in a variety of structures including specialized roots, stems, leaves, and fruits.

- I know the role that flowers play to support reproduction.

- I understand that animals have internal organs that work together to keep them alive.

These are just a few examples of learning targets that would guide student inquiries. In this example you would want to check to see what learning goals came before this goal in earlier grades and what goals follow in later grades. Instructionally this will help you to focus on the essential understandings and knowledge appropriate for your students. A student expectation—known as a lesson-level learning performance in the NGSS documents—typically contains the performance *behavior* we expect from students to provide the evidence that they have met the learning target. Some recent literature refers to this as the "success criteria" (Heritage, 2010).

The *behavior* identifies the specific type of performance that will be expected of students and what actions they will be expected to take. Action words such as *compute, compare, identify, demonstrate,* and *predict* identify specific behaviors students will demonstrate. They also represent the levels of rigor you will expect from students. Instructionally, these action words can be used to ensure that your performance expectations are written at a variety of levels. Students often struggle with what we expect them to do, and it is important to realize that we may need to teach these procedures to students. One approach is to work with other teachers and determine which terms (e.g., *describe, classify, analyze, explain,* etc.) should be emphasized at each grade level. You will need to be clear yourself about what the terms found in Bloom's taxonomy require students to do. Bloom's taxonomy has been used in education since the 1950s to help teachers challenge students. In 2001, it was updated by Anderson and Krathwohl. Table 2.1 defines several action

TABLE 2.1 Action Verbs for Demonstrating Science Knowledge and Understanding

Revised Bloom's Level (from Lowest to Highest)	Action Verbs for Science for Lesson-Level Learning Performance
Remembering—Recalling or recognizing information from memory	Record, tell, recognize, define (recall), repeat, name, reproduce, list
Understanding—Explaining their comprehension of information and concepts; constructing meaning from data and evidence	Interpret, represent, change, expand, identify, distinguish, compare, give examples, depict, generalize, summarize, infer, classify
Applying—Using information in a new way or in a new context	Model, construct, demonstrate, predict, solve, Practice, interpret, examine, implement, illustrate
Analyzing—Distinguishing different parts of a whole; and determining how they relate to each other	Diagram, outline, diagnose, differentiate, conclude, examine, investigate, deduce, dissect, categorize, discover, distinguish, sequence, organize
Evaluating—Defending a concept or idea; making judgements based on evidence	Conclude, defend, recommend, decide, critique, prioritize, recommendation, assess, rate, judge
Creating—Creating something new	Combine, integrate, construct, design, formulate, reorganize, devise, modify, plan, generate, produce, expand

words based on the revised taxonomy that are particularly useful for science instruction. This list has been revised many times most recently in 2013.

In our previous fourth-grade example, the broad performance expectation identified in the NGSS is that students who demonstrate understanding can "Construct an argument that plants and animals have internal and external structures that function to support survival, growth, behavior and reproduction." To gather evidence to use in their arguments, lessons need to be provided that engage students with opportunities to gather data, cite evidence, and create and use models. You will want to check with the district where you will be working to find out if they are using Bloom's or revised Bloom's. They may expect you to implement Webb's depth of knowledge to increase student rigor or Hess's cognitive rigor matrix that correlates Bloom's cognitive process dimensions in science with Webb's depth of knowledge levels to guide their student expectations. In all of these models, you will need to be familiar with the action words and the level of cognitive demand they represent so that you can develop the success criteria (performance expectations) aligned to the learning goals.

 CHECK YOUR UNDERSTANDING 2.2
Click here to gauge your understanding of the concepts in this section.

Using Resources to Develop Content Storylines

Determining the science content you will teach is basically a two-step process. First, you have to decide *what* to teach using the procedure previously discussed, and then you have to decide *how* to sequence the learning to develop content storylines. To help you get started, Figure 2.1 provides a diagram showing the relationship between a learning goal, a lesson in the unit, and the individual activities that link to the smaller learning targets. Because students are novice learners, it is important to break the content down into smaller learning targets (individual ideas, skills, and components of the broader concepts) that connect from one activity to the next. Only by making connections can students develop science process skills and understand the concepts that explain phenomena.

FIGURE 2.1 **Developing a Content Storyline**

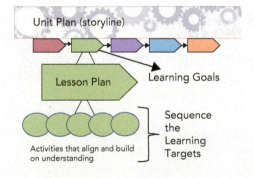

You can access the NGSS, along with supporting materials, at www.nextgenscience.org/, where learning progressions linked to the Disciplinary Core Ideas, Science and Engineering Practices, and Crosscutting Concepts will help you plan your own content storylines.

Your completion of Exploration 2.1 should help you figure out the *what*; more will be coming on the *how* later. Science content should be taught using instructional strategies that allow students to be very active, as your students should be doing science to develop understanding and make sense of the many activities in your class. Returning to the *what*, most likely, there are even more resources that can help you determine what to teach. Your state, district, or even school may have more detailed guidelines available in documents known as curriculum guides. In such documents, you will likely find your state's standards broken down from broad learning goals into even smaller and more detailed parcels of content—discrete science ideas—identified as learning targets, which were mentioned previously. A committee composed of teachers and perhaps a science or curriculum coordinator often works over the summer to develop the curriculum guide. During this process, they may "deconstruct" or interpret the state standards to clarify what they believe to be the most important content—learning goals—to be learned. District or school curriculum documents, sometimes known as unit maps, often include essential questions, correlations to state standards, a list of priority standards, common assessments, core/assured learning experiences, instructional resources, and even key vocabulary. You may also find a guide, known as the science scope and sequence, that specifies the length of time to spend on each broad set of science ideas, as well as the time of the year to cover it. This will ensure that students have sufficient opportunity to learn the ideas.

As you are deciding on what to teach, you need to feel confident in your knowledge of the science content that includes all three dimensions in the NGSS, though you may not consider yourself a science specialist. You do not need to be a science major to teach science effectively. Truth be known, the old adage "you don't really know something until you teach it" is true, and many experienced teachers of science began to really understand science skills and concepts only after teaching them.

To develop your own background knowledge on a science topic you will be teaching, and to identify the student misconceptions associated with the topic, you should:

- Read widely, including textbook chapters, teachers' guides from nationally funded science projects, and especially books written for children; however, be aware that children's books sometimes provide inaccurate information so if possible check the book reviews.

- Use an internet search engine, such as Google, to locate appropriate science content discussions and reveal common student preconceptions (these are students' ideas that they have before learning about the science ideas).

- Talk to other teachers and science education specialists.

- Attend college courses, workshops, and institutes for teachers.

- Attend relevant sessions at national, regional, and state science conferences.

- Visit websites of science education professional organizations such as www.nsta.org, which has a very useful professional development feature known as the NSTA Learning Center.

When you have selected the standards-based science content (DCIs, CCs, and SEPs) you will teach and have developed a deep understanding of that content yourself, you are ready to start preparing your content storyline. The format you use when writing learning goals and their learning targets will likely depend on the school district where you are working. Some schools may prefer learning targets in particular to be written as, "I know or I understand . . . ." Some schools may prefer learning targets that are written as Know, Understand, Do **(KUD)** as the target relates to procedural knowledge such as knowing how to focus a microscope. For unit planning, typically you would have just one or two learning goals—main ideas as Understand, and then many things listed under Know and Do. In science, the Do category is particularly important, as you want your students to be "doing" science as much as possible. And just like the learning goals and associated learning targets, you will need to set learning targets for the Do category.

Table 2.2 shows examples of some selected science content with corresponding lesson-level learning performances. This particular example does not reflect the three dimensions you would find in the NGSS as it doesn't include learning targets for the Science and Engineering Practices and the Crosscutting Concepts. Exploration 2.2 presents tasks and questions related to these examples.

The learning targets and lesson-level performance expectations for a fourth grade sound unit, outlined in Table 2.2 , are aligned with the *National Science Education Standards*. If you are using the *Next Generation Science Standards*, the ideas that sound can make matter vibrate and vibrating matter can make sounds are now introduced at Grade 1 (1-PS4-1). To align with the three-dimensional learning that is featured in the document, students should also understand that simple tests can be designed to gather evidence about causes (Crosscutting Concept: cause and effect). In order to plan and conduct the tests, collaboratively with

This video clip lets you listen to 2nd grade teacher, Nancy Michael, discuss ways she developed science teaching and planning skills throughout her career. (FYI – MSP stands for Math Science Partnership)

As you watch this video, identify the content storyline this teacher is describing and then write out the broader learning goal that connects all of these ideas into one concept."

In this video, fifth grade teacher, Nicole Bay, explains the storyline for her sound unit. Based on the video from her classroom, try to figure out where the students are in the planned learning sequence.

TABLE 2.2 Science Content (Learning Targets) and Objectives (Lesson-Level Learning Performances)

Science Content Learning Targets	Lesson-Level Learning Performances
1. Characteristics and Causes of Sound	Students will be able to:
• Objects can be identified by the sounds they make when dropped. • Sounds have identifiable characteristics. • Sounds can convey information. • Sound is caused by vibrations. • A sound source is an object that is vibrating. • A sound receiver detects sound vibrations.	• *Describe* sounds made by objects when dropped. • *Communicate* with others using a code. • *Compare* sounds to develop discrimination.
2. Pitch and Vibrating Sources	Students will be able to:
• Sound originates from vibrating sources. • Pitch is how high or low a sound is. • Differences in pitch are caused by differences in the rate at which objects vibrate. • Several variables affect pitch, including size (length) and tension of the source material.	• *Demonstrate* that sound originates from a vibrating source. • *Compare* high-, low-, and medium-pitched sounds. • *Record* observations on sound. • *Relate* the pitch of a sound to the physical properties of the sound source.

(Table 2.2 continued)

(Table 2.2 continued)

Science Content Learning Targets	Lesson-Level Learning Performances
3. How Sound Travels	Students will be able to:
• Sound vibrations need a medium to travel. • Sound travels through solids, water, and air. • Sound that is directed travels better through air. • Our outer ears are designed to receive, focus, and amplify sounds.	• *Describe* evidence that sound travels through solids, water, and air. • *Compare* how sound travels through different mediums. • *Record* observations on sound.
4. Sources, Mediums, and Receivers of Sound	Students will be able to:
• Several variables affect pitch, including size (length), tension, and thickness of the source material. • Sound can be directed through air, water, or solids to the sound receivers. • The medium that sound passes through affects its volume and the distance at which it can be heard.	• *Describe* the outer ear and *explain* that it is designed to receive sounds. • *Compare* different ways of amplifying sounds and making them travel longer distances. • *Record* observations of how sound travels. • *Report* findings in a class presentation.

Source: Adapted from FOSS® (Full Option Science Systemreg) Physics of Sound, Overview. © The Regents of the University of California and published by Delta Education. Adapted with permission.

EXPLORATION

2.2

Depth of Knowledge of Lesson-Level Learning Performance

Examine the Lesson-Level Learning Performances listed in Table 2.2. At what level is each expectation on the revised Bloom's taxonomy? Are there expectations at all the levels? Which levels need more coverage?

The objectives in Table 2.2 are written in the "students will be able to" format. Rewrite and organize them as know, understand, and do learning target statements (KUD).

Reflection Questions:

1. How do the KUD statements guide student learning?
2. Why should they be communicated and discussed with students?
3. How would you sequence the learning into a content storyline? Why?
4. Have you seen other formats for writing learning goals (objectives or outcomes) in your school experiences? How do they compare?

---

others, your students should be able to gather data that can be analyzed to determine evidence that they can use to answer questions about vibrating materials and sounds that can make materials vibrate (Science and Engineering Practice #3—Planning and carrying out investigations.) With these science content learning targets, you will want to plan for the lesson-level performance expectations to align with all three dimensions of the lesson. Examples and clarifications are provided in the NGSS document (www.nextgenscience.org/dci-arrangement/1-ps4-waves-and-their-applications-technologies-information-transfer).

✓ CHECK YOUR UNDERSTANDING 2.3

Click here to gauge your understanding of the concepts in this section.

Aspects of "Doing" Science and Engineering

Your learning targets and corresponding lesson-level learning performances should specify more than what students need to know. They should also indicate what students should be able to *do* as they try to figure out and solve problems in the world around them. Complete the Exploration 2.3 to recall

the strategies you used to figure out how the world works when you were younger. "The actual doing of science or engineering can pique students' curiosity, capture their interest, and motivate their continued study" (NRC, 2012, p. 43).

Science Process Skills

During the 1960s, science educators identified a set of discrete skills called **science process skills**. They thought that science was best learned by doing science; that children should learn processes, not memorize facts; and that if students practiced and mastered individual skills, they would be able to use them to develop scientific understanding. Science process skills were considered a set of broadly transferable abilities, including both procedural and thinking skills used by scientists in many different disciplines. At the same time, the processes that supported inquiry-based instruction were identified and included in a variety of innovative elementary and secondary curricula. Over the years, science education experts and new curriculum projects added additional skills, considered necessary for the process side of science learning.

> In this video of a kindergarten classroom, how are the students learning and practicing process skills?

Science process skills typically included in elementary and middle school science curricula are listed and described in Table 2.3. To provide a context for the process skills, examples related to water in its various states and what causes it to change states appear in the right column of the table.

Many of the science process skills intertwine and depend on each other; they often occur together or in sequence. For example: Observations may be quantified by measuring, both inferring and classifying depend on observing, and experimenting includes controlling variables and analyzing data.

For many years the first chapter of science textbooks introduced and differentiated among science process skills. Current thinking suggests that science process skills should no longer be taught in isolation, in a separate unit at the beginning of the school year. Instead, they should be introduced, reinforced, practiced, and applied throughout the year in the context of developing conceptual understanding when making sense of science phenomena.

Teaching science process skills in isolation (separated from concepts) did not result in students learning to think like scientists or being able to discover science concepts on their own. Science education researchers began to suggest using science process skills as tools in the context of the "inquiry approach" that was central to the *National Science Education Standards* (NSES) published in 1996. The NSES recommended a shift toward integration of all aspects of science content, teaching the science process skills in the context of science concepts, and using multiple process skills to accomplish inquiry tasks.

Still, there are several reasons you should be familiar with individual science process skills. They still appear in many current state Frameworks of science standards, teacher candidates' understanding of them is assessed on many certification exams, and they are useful tools for accomplishing inquiry tasks during the practice of science. The science process skills are still useful procedures that are important elements of doing science. When "doing" science, both scientists and students use selected science process skills as they engage in Science and Engineering Practices in the context of various types of investigations.

Appendix A presents more details about specific science process skills. There you will find definitions, classroom examples, and teaching strategies related to commonly used science process skills.

TABLE 2.3   Science Process Skills Emphasized in Elementary and Middle Schools

Science Process Skill	Description	Example of the Use of the Process Skill
Observing	Gather information using appropriate senses, which may involve instruments that extend the senses.	• Watch a melting ice cube as it changes from a solid to a liquid. • Feel the water to determine its coldness. • Use a hand lens to watch a snowflake melt.
Measuring	Quantify variables using appropriate instruments and units (standard or nonstandard).	• Use a ruler to determine the length, height, and width of an ice cube. • Use a balance to find the ice cube's mass. • Use a thermometer to monitor water temperature as an ice cube melts over time.
Inferring	Draw a tentative conclusion about objects, organisms, or events based on observations and prior knowledge.	Infer that when a wet towel is left overnight and is dry in the morning that the water evaporates, meaning it goes into the air.
Classifying	Group objects or organisms according to one or more common properties.	Classify ice as a solid, water as a liquid, and steam as a gas.
Questioning	Ask questions that can be answered through scientific investigation.	Form questions that are investigable such as: At what temperature does water freeze? How does the size of ice cubes affect how fast they melt?
Communicating	Record observations, measurements, inferences, experiments, conclusions, etc., and present them to others.	• Draw pictures of, write, and give an oral report about melting ice cubes. • Use a data table and/or a graph to present information about the temperature changes in a glass of ice water over time.
Analyzing Data	Making sense of data by looking for patterns and trends, and using statistical tools.	Use line graphs of temperature over time to compare cooling rates of water when different amounts of ice are added. Find the average time for an ice cube to melt when the room temperature is 70°F.
Predicting	Make a forecast based on patterns in data.	Based on the data, I predict the temperature of the water in the glass will be 10°C in 30 minutes.
Hypothesizing	Make a statement to guide an investigation of a question.	The greater the amount of water in the glass, the less its temperature will change when an ice cube is added.
Experimenting	Investigate by deliberately manipulating one variable at a time and observing the effect on a responding variable, while holding all other variables constant.	• Determine the effect of the amount of water in the glass on the change in temperature of the water when ice is added. • Vary the amount of water initially in the glass. • Measure the temperature of the water over time. • Keep initial water and air temperature, number, and size of ice cubes added, and the time for measuring water temperature the same.

Abilities Necessary to Do Scientific Inquiry

The *National Science Education Standards* (NRC, 1996) described *abilities necessary to do scientific inquiry* (learning targets for Science and Engineering Practices) as the skills that provide the basis for scientific knowledge. Thus, scientific inquiry and conceptual knowledge in science are intimately linked. Over time, with appropriate teacher guidance and support, students can develop the abilities necessary to do scientific inquiry:

- *Asking questions*—In elementary and middle school science, questions should come (insofar as possible) from the experiences and activities of learners. Children need ample time to simply watch and wonder about the world around them—to observe and compare leaves, tend to mealworms, watch ants in their underground homes, find out about air, observe weather changes, and on and on. Such rich, accessible experiences tend to generate interesting and productive questions about the natural world.

- *Planning and conducting investigations*—When inquiring scientifically, children investigate to gather evidence to use in answering their questions. In their investigations, children observe what things are like or what is happening within a system, collect specimens for analysis, or do experiments (American Association for the Advancement of Science, 1993). Examples of various types of investigations are provided later in this chapter.

- *Gathering and analyzing data*—As students investigate, they use simple tools (such as thermometers, rulers and meter sticks, and hand lenses) and practice simple skills (such as observing, measuring, recording data, graphing, inferring, and predicting).

- *Developing data-based, evidence-based explanations*—As they develop explanations to answer their questions, children reflect on the evidence they obtained and draw on existing and developing scientific knowledge to support their thinking. Most children have personal theories and explanations of objects, organisms, and events but will need some guidance from teachers in constructing scientific explanations.

- *Communicating about investigations*—Throughout the inquiry process, students engage in discourse with one another and their teachers about questions, investigations, findings, and explanations. Students should use different means, including speaking, writing, and drawing, to represent and communicate their procedures, observations and data, and explanations to others.

You can think of the abilities necessary to do scientific inquiry as a cycle, as illustrated in Figure 2.2. Though inquiry often progresses clockwise through this cycle, there is no fixed set of ordered steps that scientists or students always follow in doing science, no single path that always leads to scientific knowledge (AAAS, 1990). This inquiry cycle should not be interpreted as "the scientific method." Contrary to what you may have been taught, science is not practiced by scientists in a rigid, step-by-step way. Please do not teach your students that there is just one "scientific method" followed by all scientists all the time!

Figure 2.2 presents common characteristics of scientific investigations in a logical progression but does not imply a rigid approach to answering questions or solving problems. In Exploration 2.4 you are asked to reflect on your experiences with abilities necessary for doing scientific inquiry. Like inquiry in

> Watch this video clip to see Ashley Welsh review learning goals and mention abilities needed for students to do scientific inquiry after her 4th graders explore erosion and weathering at several activity stations. Which of the abilities does she emphasize with her class?

FIGURE 2.2   Inquiry Cycle

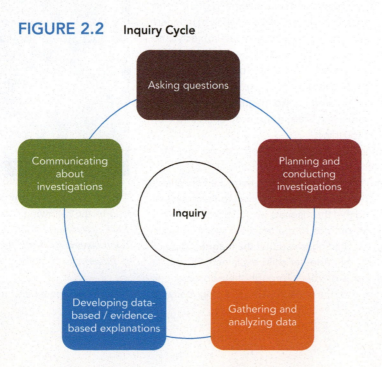

EXPLORATION 2.4

The Relationships between Your Experience and the Abilities Necessary to Do Scientific Inquiry

Reconsider the aspects of "doing science as a child" that you identified previously. Think about how they relate to the abilities necessary to do scientific inquiry presented in Figure 2.2. Starting with the abilities necessary to do scientific inquiry, create a graphic organizer that shows the relationships you identify. You may need to include a section labeled "other" so you have a place for all of your aspects of "doing science as a child."

Reflection Questions:

1. What does the graphic organizer you created reveal about your childhood science experiences?
2. What other memories of "doing science" as a child does each of the abilities necessary to do scientific inquiry bring to mind?
3. With which of the abilities necessary to do scientific inquiry do you have the most experience? The least experience? How did that affect your science learning?

scientists' studies of the natural world, inquiry in elementary and middle school science classes takes many forms, but each form generally involves some use of each of these inquiry tasks.

The inquiry lesson on magnetism presented in Exploration 2.5 incorporates each of the abilities necessary to do scientific inquiry, previously identified in the boxes in Figure 2.2.

EXPLORATION 2.5

Magnetic Interactions

Read the following vignette to experience a second-grade lesson about magnetic interactions. As you read, look for the abilities necessary to do scientific inquiry illustrated in Figure 2.2.

To begin a lesson on magnets, Julie Clark arranged her second-grade class in cooperative learning groups and gave each group sets of materials consisting of magnets and an assortment of metal and nonmetal objects. She challenged the students to find out how magnets interact with each other and with the various objects.

The curious children eagerly explored the magnets and materials. Holding up two magnets, one surprised child said, "Look, Ms. Clark, these push apart and they are not even touching."

Another child noted, "Put them like this and they come together."

"It won't pick this thing up," a third child observed.

Going beyond the materials given to them, several children found that the magnets would stick to the metal filing cabinet, but not to the teacher's wooden desk. One surprised child observed that the magnets did not attract a cola can. Another child explained, "The cola can is not made of iron." Through their observations and descriptions, the children were learning many new *facts* about magnets and magnetic interactions.

Michael Chamberlin / Shutterstock

The phenomenon shown could lead to the following conversation: *Look at this magnetic interaction! Why is this happening? Would this still work if I changed parts of the system?*

Ms. Clark then asked the children what they wondered about magnets and what they wanted to find out about them. Among the things the children wanted to know were: What are magnets? Why do they stick to some things? From the children's watching and wondering, Ms. Clark helped them form a question that they could investigate: "How do magnets interact with one another and with other materials?"

To address this question, the children decided they should test all of their various materials to find out if they were attracted to a magnet. While the children worked on this question, Ms. Clark circulated among the small groups, asking and answering questions, supplying terms, and suggesting some procedures. To help the students organize their findings and communicate them to others, she challenged them to sort their materials into groups according to how they interacted with magnets. As she went about the room, she asked each group of students to explain how they had sorted the objects. Some children had grouped the objects by color or size. After some prompting, these children began to understand how to classify the objects, not by their more obvious attributes but by the ways they interacted with the magnets. Most children ended up with two piles: things that were attracted to a magnet and things that were not attracted to a magnet.

In a whole-class discussion, Ms. Clark asked the children to report what they had found out. Collectively, the children's knowledge from their explorations of magnets and magnetic interactions was quite complete. To summarize the children's observations and discussion about how magnets interact with other magnets and with various materials, Ms. Clark wrote these "magnet rules" on the chalkboard:

1. Two magnets can *attract* (pull) one another, but they can also be made to *repel* one another (push one another apart).
2. Magnets will not attract nonmetal objects.
3. Magnets attract some metal objects but not all.

Each of the magnet rules was based on observational evidence the children had discovered as they investigated. Through the magnet rules, the teacher introduced some new *concepts*, including *attract* and *repel*. The rules themselves were *principles*, because they showed how concepts were related to one another.

To help the children remember and understand the rules, Ms. Clark pointed to each rule in turn and asked the teams to search for and hold overhead one example of objects that fit each rule. In each case, the class decided whether the objects selected were correct examples. This "game" continued until every object of every team had been held aloft. To further help children to understand and apply the rules of magnetism, children moved around the room making predictions and then testing them with different materials.

Reflection Questions:

1. Were you able to identify the abilities necessary for inquiry as you read this lesson?
2. Was each ability to do inquiry (the boxes from Figure 2.2) included in the vignette? Give examples.
3. Do your ideas agree with the following analysis?

First, a question about magnetism was asked (top box). Then, an investigation plan was formulated to address the question, and the students followed the plan to gather observational data relevant to the question (boxes at 3 and 5 o'clock). Observations were then used as evidence in formulating rules and generating explanations to answer the initiating question (box at 7 o'clock). In the course of the investigation, the students discussed their investigation results and conclusions with the teacher and other class members (box at 9 o'clock).

According to NSES, students should develop the abilities necessary to do scientific inquiry as they progress through school. Table 2.4, based on the NSES Content Standards for Science as Inquiry, shows how fundamental abilities necessary to do scientific inquiry change from the primary grades through middle school.

TABLE 2.4   Science as Inquiry Content Standards in the National Science Education Standards

Grades K–4	Grades 5–8
Ask a question about objects, organisms, and events in the environment.	Identify questions that can be answered through scientific investigations.
Plan and conduct a simple investigation.	Design and conduct a scientific investigation.
Employ simple equipment and tools to gather data and extend the senses.	Use appropriate tools and techniques to gather, analyze, and interpret data.
Use data to construct a reasonable explanation.	Develop descriptions, explanations, predictions, and models using evidence.
	Think critically and logically to make the relationships between evidence and explanations.
	Recognize and analyze alternative explanations and predictions.
Communicate investigations and explanations.	Communicate scientific procedures and explanations.
	Use mathematics in all aspects of scientific inquiry.

Source: NRC, 1996, pp. 122, 145, 148.

Exploration 2.6 is an activity designed to engage your thinking about the nature and role of engineering design.

EXPLORATION

2.6

A Design Challenge

You are locked in the copy room. You are very thirsty. There is water in the water cooler, but the cup dispenser is empty. It is impossible to get your mouth under the spigot of the water cooler, and your hands are too filthy to drink from. You need to design a cup, but the only materials you can find to make it from are three sheets of copy paper. Be an engineer. Solve your problem. You might consider the steps in the engineering design cycle summarized in Figure 2.8.

Reflection Questions:

After you have quenched your thirst, reflect with others about this problem-solving experience. These questions should guide your discussion.
1. What was your problem?
2. How did you solve it? Think about the steps in the process you used.
3. What do engineers do?
4. What is technology? What technology did you develop in this activity?
5. What technologies do you interact with on a daily basis?

Engineering Design Connects to Scientific Inquiry

Science and engineering are closely related, but their goals differ. Technology is the product of engineering design. The goal of *science* is to explain the natural world, while the goal of *engineering* is to solve problems in order to meet human needs and wants.

In *A Framework for K–12 Science Education: Practices, Crosscutting Concepts, and Core Ideas* (NRC, 2012), the Disciplinary Core Idea *ETS1: Engineering Design* relates to how engineers solve problems and spans all grade levels from K–12. Its component ideas include: identifying a problem to be solved, establishing *criteria* for successful solutions, and recognizing *constraints* that must be considered; developing and testing possible solutions (technologies); comparing solutions to determine which is best and striving to continuously improve the technology that was designed.

FIGURE 2.3 An Engineering Design Cycle

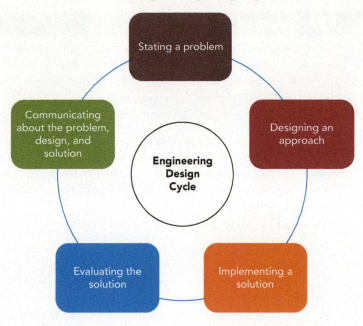

Paralleling the five abilities necessary to do scientific inquiry (presented previously in Figure 2.2), the abilities necessary to do engineering design (summarized in Figure 2.3) that students should learn include:

- *State a problem*—Students identify a specific need, problem, or task and explain it in their own words.

- *Design an approach*—Students should make proposals to build something or to make something work better.

- *Implement a solution*—Children should work individually and collaboratively and use simple materials, tools, techniques, and appropriate quantitative measurements when solving the problem.

- *Evaluate the solution*—Students should evaluate their own results or solutions as well as those of other children by considering how well a product or design met the challenge to solve a problem. The evaluation process is often a controlled experiment, thus the application of scientific inquiry.

- *Communicate the problem, design, and solution to others*—Students should prepare oral, written, and pictorial communication of the design process and products. The communication might involve show-and-tell, group discussions, short written reports, pictures, or multimedia computer presentations.

Implementing the engineering design cycle may require that students observe, measure, infer, make hypotheses and predictions, conduct controlled investigations (experiment), and apply scientific knowledge. Like inquiry, engineering design typically includes certain abilitiesbut they don't necessarily occur in a set order.

Several curriculum projects that focus on a version of the technology design process and engineering are described in Table 2.5 along with their website URLs.

Visit www .nextgenscience.org/ to read Appendix I, Engineering Design in the NGSS, to learn how the *Next Generation Science Standards* incorporate engineering design.

TABLE 2.5 Several Curriculum Projects That Feature a Technology Design Process

Project	Description
Engineering is Elementary www.eie.org	K–6 research-based, standards-driven, and classroom-tested curriculum units that integrate engineering and technology concepts and skills with elementary science topics. Uses a five-step engineering design process: Ask, Imagine, Plan, Create, and Improve. Units follow 5E instructional model, highlight various engineering careers, incorporate multiculturalism, and also connect with literacy and social studies.

(Table 2.5 continued)

(Table 2.5 continued)

Project	Description
A World in Motion www.awim.org/	K–12 design challenges focusing on toys that move, model vehicles, and related electronics. Students, working together as teams, experience design in an engineering context and gain some understanding of the design process and how the products they use have come to be. Developed by the Society of Automotive Engineers.
NASA eClips Elementary School Design Packet www.nasa.gov/pdf/324205main_Design_Packet_I.pdf	Open-ended packet applicable to any design project, for students in kindergarten through grade 5. Developed to accompany NASA Our World, a curriculum unit about the natural versus the designed world. Introduces a five-step design process: Ask, Imagine, Build, Evaluate, and Share. Presents questions about each step of the design process. Includes rubric to assist with evaluation. Developed by NASA eClips.
NASA eClips Middle and High School Design Packet www.nasa.gov/pdf/324205main_Design_Packet_II.pdf	Open-ended packet applicable to any design project, for students in middle or high school. Developed to accompany NASA Real World Mathematics (6–8) and NASA Launchpad (9–12). Introduces an eight-step design process: Identify the problem, Identify criteria and constraints, Brainstorm possible solutions, Select a design, Build a model or prototype, Test the model and evaluate, Refine the design, and Share the solution. Presents a detailed outline to guide student through the steps of the design process. Includes rubric to assist with evaluation. Developed by NASA eClips.

Science and Engineering Practices

With the introduction of the *Next Generation Science Standards*, the Science and Engineering Practices have become the "new" terms used to describe the "doing" of science. You were introduced to the eight Practices in Chapter 1. "The NGSS Practices represent the multiple ways of *knowing* and *doing* that scientists and engineers use to study the natural world and the design world" (p. 5). The NGSS use the term *Practices* rather than *science processes* or *inquiry tasks* to emphasize that engaging in scientific investigation requires not only proficiency in doing, but also knowledge that is specific to each Practice. It is as important for students to develop an understanding of the Practices of science and engineering as it is for them to understand science knowledge and concepts (NRC, 2012). If your state has adopted the Science and Engineering Practices identified in the NGSS, you can find information in Appendix F at the following link: www.nextgenscience.org.

The current view is that students learn science best through active engagement in the practices of science (NRC, 2007), which were introduced in Chapter 1, and that scientific inquiry is a particularly important form of scientific practice (Michaels, Shouse, & Schweingruber, 2008).

 CHECK YOUR UNDERSTANDING 2.4
Click here to gauge your understanding of the concepts in this section.

Science Investigations for Elementary and Middle School Students

Now that you've learned about various aspects of doing science, think again about scientific inquiry—"the diverse ways in which scientists study the natural world and propose explanations based on the evidence derived from their work. Scientific inquiry also refers to the activities through which students develop knowledge and understanding of scientific ideas, as well as an understanding of how scientists study the natural world" (NRC, 1996, p. 23). According to the National Science Teachers Association's

TABLE 2.6   Development of Understandings about Scientific Investigations

Grade-Level Band	Understandings
K–2	• Science investigations begin with a question. • Science uses different ways to study the world.
3–5	• Science methods are determined by questions. • Science investigations use a variety of methods, tools, and techniques.
6–8	• Science investigations use a variety of methods and tools to make measurements and observations. • Science investigations are guided by a set of values to ensure accuracy of measurements, observations, and objectivity of findings.

Based on Appendix H of the *Next Generation Science Standards* (NGSS Lead States, 2013).

Position Statement on Scientific Inquiry, "Inquiry is a powerful way of understanding science content. Students learn how to ask questions and use evidence to answer them. In the process of learning the strategies of scientific inquiry, students learn to conduct an investigation and collect evidence from a variety of sources, develop an explanation from the data, and communicate and defend their conclusions" (NSTA, October, 2004).

But what are these "investigations" that your students are supposed to conduct? Clearly, investigations are important since the third NGSS Science and Engineering Practice is *Planning and carrying out investigations*. In addition, one of the categories of understandings about the nature of science embedded in NGSS is *Scientific investigations use a variety of methods*. The related K–8 learning progression (what students should understand by the end of different grade-level bands) is shown in Table 2.6.

"There simply is no fixed set of steps that scientists always follow, no one path that leads them unerringly to scientific knowledge" (AAAS, 1990, p. 26). However, there are some specific types of investigations that children should experience; they are listed in Table 2.7.

It is true that science educators sometimes use the terms *inquiry investigation* or *inquiry-based investigation* to refer to an investigation that is based on a question (though they may seem redundant, since inquiry and investigation are synonyms). Therefore, the types of investigations included in Table 2.7 might also be considered "inquiry investigations" or "inquiry-based investigations."

Your reflection has probably led you to an important understanding about scientific inquiry mentioned in the *National Science Education Standards*—certain questions suggest certain kinds of scientific investigations to answer them (NRC, 1996). This is further illustrated in the classroom-based examples that follow.

TABLE 2.7   Types of Investigations Appropriate for K–8 Students

Types of Investigations	What Students Do
Descriptive *	Gather observational and measurement data to answer questions about the properties and actions of objects, organisms, events, and systems.
Classificatory *	Use classification processes to organize objects, organisms, events, and systems by sorting and grouping them or data about them according to one or more properties.
Experimental *	Design and carry out a "fair test"; investigate patterns or relationships between variables; conduct controlled experiments to provide evidence needed in forming and testing hypotheses and generating explanations.
Modeling *	Use a model or representation to investigate properties and actions of objects, organisms, events, and systems.
Engineering **	Identify the effectiveness, efficiency, and durability of designs under different conditions.

* These types of investigations were recommended in the *National Science Education Standards* (NRC, 1996, pp. 123, 148).
** This type of investigation is described in Appendix F of NGSS (NGSS Lead States, 2013).

EXPLORATION	**Questions Suggest Types of Investigations Needed to Find Answers**
2.6	

Suppose you were put in charge of your school's new outdoor learning space. How would you find out:

1. Where should a new flowerbed be placed on the school grounds to maximize the amount of sunlight it receives?
2. What species of birds visit the school's new bird feeder and which type is the most frequent visitor?
3. What type of bird feeder is best (and able to keep the squirrels from stealing the bird seed)?
4. How does soil composition affect how long tulips bloom?
5. How does groundcover limit soil erosion on a hillside?

Given these questions for investigation, jot down how you would go about answering them. Please suggest investigations you and your students could carry out rather than options such as "ask the audience" or "phone a friend."

Reflection Questions:

1. Which of these questions suggests one or more of the types of investigations listed in Table 2.7? Explain your reasoning.
2. How appropriate is it to apply the same investigation strategy to all of the questions presented? Why?

Mealworms

Mealworms are commonly used in classrooms during the study of life cycles of organisms, a core idea introduced in third-grade according to NGSS. An investigation titled "What are the stages in an insect life cycle?" is included in the activities section of this book. Take a look at it (Activity 34) and try to identify type(s) of investigation(s) it involves.

While you have the mealworms in your classroom it is likely that your class will have additional questions about these creatures. Learning about mealworms can involve several types of investigations depending on the questions asked. Some questions that might come up during a study of mealworms include:

1. What are the main body characteristics of mealworms?
2. How many legs does your mealworm have? Where on the body are the legs located?
3. Do mealworms have the general characteristics of insects? What are the similarities and differences between mealworms and other insects?
4. How does a mealworm move? How do its legs work together when it moves? How does it turn corners?
5. What kinds of food do mealworms eat most often?

For each question, decide which type of investigation from Table 2.7 is most suitable for answering it. Then, reflect on your reasoning before reading on.

To answer questions 1 and 2, students must observe the mealworms carefully, including observation with a magnifying lens. They can observe that mealworms have a segmented body with six legs attached to the body. Two antennae are attached to the head. Children might communicate this information through labeled drawings (see Figure 2.4). These activities are part of a descriptive investigation about the body characteristics of mealworms.

Students might learn from their teacher or through their textbook, a trade book, or the Internet (or already know) that insects have three main body parts, six legs, and two antennae. By comparing their observations of the characteristics of mealworms with their findings from outside sources or their prior knowledge, they can conclude that mealworms should be classified as insects. So question 3 suggests a classificatory investigation.

To answer question 4, students might work together to discover different ways the six legs of a mealworm might be used in moving (see Figure 2.5). Through observing whether mealworms actually use their legs in the proposed ways, students can test the different models of mealworm movement. The psychomotor involvement of the students helps them to understand the complexity and appreciate the wonder of mealworm movement. Question 4 calls for both descriptive investigation and modeling.

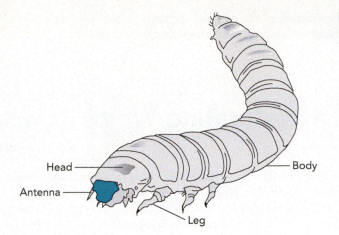

FIGURE 2.4   **What Are the Main Body Parts of a Mealworm?**

FIGURE 2.5   **How Do Mealworms Use Their Legs When They Walk and Turn Corners?**

One way to investigate question 5 is for student teams to draw a small circle (about 5 cm in diameter) in the center of a paper plate and draw four equally spaced lines straight from the edge of the inner circle to the edge of the plate. Different foods, including bran, apple, lettuce, and potato are then placed equidistant from the center within the four segments created by the four lines. A number of mealworms are then placed in the inner circle. Students can observe how many mealworms move to each segment and note whether they eat the food. Question 5 can be addressed with an experimental investigation. What is the manipulated independent variable in this experiment? What is the responding dependent variable? What variables should be controlled?

Mystery Powders

In classificatory investigations, students find out more about objects and organisms by discovering ways of grouping them according to their properties or traits. By focusing on properties, classificatory investigations tend to incorporate descriptive inquiry procedures. Vignette 2.1 takes you into a class of fifth graders who are learning about matter and its properties through descriptive and classificatory investigations of common white powders, including sugar, table salt, baking soda, and cornstarch.

The descriptive and classificatory investigations that occurred in Miss Garza's classroom helped her student-scientists develop well-structured and grade-level-appropriate knowledge about matter. These children were working toward the NGSS performance expectation *5-PS1-3: Make observations and measurements to identify materials based on their properties.* In addition, the students practiced a variety of science process skills and engaged in the Practices of planning and carrying out investigations, analyzing and interpreting data, constructing explanations, and engaging in argument from evidence.

Vignette 2.1   Investigating White Powders

Small groups of goggle-wearing third-graders cluster around labeled vials of white powders and several liquids. At one table, Sloane sprinkles a little power from one vial onto a square of black construction paper. Then Molly and Leah use their hand lenses to examine the powder carefully.

Molly comments: "Oh! The pieces of this powder look like little blocks!"

Miss Garza places a recording sheet on the table, and says, "Remember that scientists keep accurate records of their data so they can refer to it later. This table has the different powders listed across the top and the different tests listed down the side. You can use it to organize your findings."

William asks, "Which powder are you looking at, Sloane?" She replies, "It is table salt."

William finds the proper cell on the group's data table and records their description of the magnified salt crystals.

Soon the children discover that although the white powders look nearly the same in the vials, their properties are quite different. Through testing, the group notices that three of the powders seem to disappear when mixed with water, but that cornstarch just makes the water cloudy. They also discover, with much giggling, that when vinegar is poured onto baking soda, it fizzes. Table 2.8 summarizes their findings.

Miss Garza tells the class, "I'm going to give each group a mystery powder that is a mixture of two of the powders you have tested. Your challenge is to figure out what your mystery powder is made of."

Leah asks, "May we do the same tests on the mystery powder that we did before?"

Miss Garza replies, "You may, and you may also use the chart of the properties of the original white powders."

William pours a little of the mystery powder onto a square of black construction paper.

Molly says, "The grains in this powder are fine. Not as big as the grains of salt from before."

Leah touches the powder and agrees, "Yes, the powder feels smooth, so the grains must be small."

Sloane suggests, "I think cornstarch and baking soda are mixed together in this new powder, because the grains look so small and it feels so smooth."

William says, "I'll try the vinegar test." He makes a small pile of the powder then adds a few drops of vinegar from a small squeeze bottle.

Sloane says, "It's fizzing a little!"

William says, "There's definitely baking soda in there."

Pointing to the cell at the intersection of the baking soda column and the vinegar test row, Molly adds, "That's the only powder we had that fizzed with vinegar."

Leah suggests, "If it turns blue, the iodine test will show if the other powder in the mixture is cornstarch like we thought."

Molly squeezes a drop of iodine onto a small pile of the mystery powder, then exclaims, "Yes! It turned blue so there's cornstarch in the mixture, too!"

William raises his hand to get Miss Garza's attention. She asks, "Do you know what your mystery powder is made of?"

TABLE 2.8   **Properties of White Powders**

Observations	Powder 1 Granulated Sugar	Powder 2 Table Salt	Powder 3 Baking Soda	Powder 4 Cornstarch
Visual (Magnifying Glass)	White crystals	White box-shaped crystals	Fine white powder	Fine yellowish-white powder
Water Test	Dissolves in water	Dissolves in water	Forms milky mix	Makes water cloudy
Vinegar Test	Dissolves in vinegar	Has no reaction with vinegar	Fizzes with vinegar	Gets thick, then hard with vinegar
Iodine Test	Turns yellow with iodine	Has no reaction with iodine	Turns yellow-orange with iodine	Turns red, then black with iodine

Vigenette 2.1 (*continued*)

William replies, "Yes, it's made of baking powder and cornstarch."

Making eye contact with each member of the group, Miss Garza says, "So you claim your mystery powder is a mixture of baking powder and cornstarch. What is your evidence?"

Sloane answers, pointing to the data table as she speaks, "Both cornstarch and baking soda are fine grained, and so is our mystery powder. The iodine made our mystery powder turn blue, and that's what happens to cornstarch. Vinegar made our mystery powder fizz, and that's what happens to baking soda."

 CHECK YOUR UNDERSTANDING 2.5

Click here to gauge your understanding of the concepts in this section.

 # CHAPTER SUMMARY

Identifying Learning Goals Aligned to Standards

The *National Science Education Standards* have been used to help frame many current state standards. The *Next Generation Science Standards* will be adopted by many states, and other states will write new state standards influenced by the suggestions found in *A Framework for Science Education: Practices, Crosscutting Concepts, and Core Ideas* and the *Next Generation Science Standards*. State documents are transformed by school districts to create curriculum guides at the district level. These curriculum guides will have the greatest impact on deciding what to teach in your classroom. Some school districts will include pacing guides, or scope and sequence documents, with the curriculum to help you decide how long to spend on a given topic and in what order to present the topics. All of this will help you as a teacher decide what to teach; you will have much greater freedom in deciding how to teach it. Ultimately, as you plan your units, the curriculum, instruction, and assessments must be aligned to state standards.

Getting Ready for Inquiry-based Instructional Planning

Once you have determined what to teach in science lessons—the learning goals—it is time to determine the strategies that are most effective to foster student knowledge and understanding, the Know, Understand, and Do. Students are novice learners, so it is up to teachers to identify the smaller lesson-level learning targets from the learning goals. Teaching students procedures around the processes and Practices needed to do science means that action verbs identified in Bloom's taxonomy must be selected. Instructionally, teachers must focus on the essential understandings and knowledge appropriate for their students and make sure to communicate the goals and lesson-level learning performances with students.

Using Resources to Develop Content Storylines

Your learning goals and smaller learning targets detail what you want your students to learn from your daily lessons. Although they can be written in many forms, you should always keep in mind that they need to be communicated to students and written in student-friendly language. Once they are identified and sequenced into a content storyline, you can identify the lesson-level performance expectations that will determine what students must demonstrate to provide evidence of learning, and the conditions that will lead to student success. Science content should be taught using instructional strategies that allow students to be very active, as your students should be doing science to develop understanding and make sense of the many activities in your class. When you identify the lesson-level learning performance, use verbs based on the revised Bloom's taxonomy to ensure you are promoting higher-level thinking skills. Remember that with alignment to the *Next Generation Science Standards*, you will want to identify the progressions of the Science and Engineering Practices, the Crosscutting Concepts, and the Disciplinary Core Ideas that are part of your unit plan. Using resources from the district, the activities provided in this course or any other quality online lessons, you can determine your content representations and investigations and develop the success criteria for each learning target.

Aspects of "Doing" Science and Engineering

When planning inquiry instruction, think about how you will involve students in "doing science." Reflection on your "doing" of science as a child provides context for the evolution of this aspect of science learning. Over the decades, the terminology used to describe the components involved in doing science has evolved. Starting in the 1960s, science educators thought students could learn science content if they just mastered a set of science process skills. At that time, science learning was seen to be a dichotomy of process and content—doing and knowing. Science process skills, thinking skills and abilities used when doing science, include observing, classifying, inferring, measuring, predicting, experimenting, etc. In the 1990s due to the emergence of national science standards, the focus of "doing" science shifted to inquiry. The process skills did not vanish, but a more holistic idea about the process side of science learning emerged. Abilities necessary to do scientific inquiry were identified and shown in a cycle: asking questions, planning and conducting investigations, gathering and analyzing data, developing data-based/evidence-based explanations, and communicating about investigations. Meanwhile, an engineering design cycle illustrated the steps involved in solving problems to meet the needs and wants of humans. A fairly simple engineering design process might include: stating a problem, designing an approach, implementing a solution, evaluating the solution, and communicating about the problem, design, and solution. Because inquiry was such a broad term, often misused or misinterpreted, when the NGSS were released, Science and Engineering Practices became the new set of terms for "doing" science. To achieve the goal of three-dimensional teaching and learning, the Practices must be integrated with the other two dimensions of science—Crosscutting Concepts and Disciplinary Core Ideas in curriculum, instruction, and assessment.

Science Investigations for Elementary and Middle School Students

Investigations are carried out to answer scientific questions or solve problems. The appropriate type of investigation depends on the question asked. *Planning and carrying out investigations* is one of the eight Science and Engineering Practices described in NGSS. While sometimes science educators speak broadly about inquiry investigations, there are some types of investigations that K–8 students should be able to plan and carry out given adequate scaffolding, including descriptive, classificatory, experimental, modeling, and engineering.

DISCUSSION QUESTIONS

1. How will you determine what science content to teach when you have your own classroom?
2. What steps will you take to develop effective units of science instruction?
3. What are the key points you should keep in mind when developing science learning goals and smaller learning targets?
4. In what ways do the various science terms describing "doing" science relate to each other?
5. How do the types of investigations differ? How do you decide which type is appropriate for your class?

PROFESSIONAL PRACTICES ACTIVITIES

1. Read the various national science standards for the content and grade level you are expecting to teach.
2. Look at some existing instructional units for science. Analyze them for alignment with standards, and for clarity of the learning goals and targets they include.
3. Ask your cooperating teacher about the strategies he or she uses to ensure that students learn science concepts and procedures.

4. During your field experience in a school, observe a science class. Watch for and identify the science process skills, abilities necessary to do inquiry or engineering design, and/or Science and Engineering Practices that students are using during the lesson. With your mentor teacher, discuss which are emphasized at that grade level and how your mentor helps students to develop abilities for "doing science."

5. Ask your cooperating teacher to share his or her unit plans with you. Analyze the plans to find out which types of investigations are used. Discuss whether the class is better at some types of investigations than others and why that might be.

Creating a Positive Classroom Environment

Steve Debenport/E+/Getty Images

LEARNING GOALS

After reading this chapter, you should understand that . . .

1. Positive classroom environments exist when teachers plan for the physical and social/emotional environment of students, where students find the learning rigorous and engaging, trust is evident and everyone (teachers and students) believe that they can learn.

2. Designing a positive classroom environment is essential to promote active inquiry learning.

3. Procedures for maintaining student safety must be planned prior to doing science with students.

4. Teaching procedures will help you manage student behavior.

When asked about your favorite science teacher or favorite class where you learned science, most of can think of a classroom that we really enjoyed. People frequently say that the teacher made it fun to learn. Because of those experiences, you may even have decided to pursue teaching as a career. When you envision that positive classroom environment, what did it look like? What was the teacher saying and doing? How about the students? If you have visited a classroom that you thought was well-structured, or were lucky enough to experience one when you were a student, what made it so positive? Take 5-10 minutes to generate a two column list of characteristics of classrooms that had positive learning environments, and ones that were not positive or engaging to students. . Don't forget to include characteristics of the physical environment in the classroom along with the characteristics related to the student-to- student and student-to-teacher interactions.

The following chapter provides research and implementation strategies from experts in the field to help you reflect on how you can create a positive science learning environment in which students are active partners in their own inquiry learning. Additionally, this chapter will help you to reflect on aspects of planning that you will need to bring together as you develop your own positive science classroom environments.

Characteristics of a Positive Learning Environment

Planning for inquiry learning requires teachers to create a classroom in which students are active participants in the learning process. In this type of setting, students feel encouraged to ask questions, take risks, and receive and give feedback. Creating this environment requires planning the layout of the physical environment, building productive relationships among the students and between students and teacher to support the social and emotional environment, and developing student interaction skills using numerous teaching procedures. In science, this also includes taking precautions to maintain safety.

Critical to establishing a positive, inquiry-based science learning environment is the teacher belief that all students can learn. We can expect to have a variety of students in our classrooms, so we need to behave in ways that support learning for all by meeting the needs of individual students.. In a self-fulfilling prophecy (Rosenthal, 1998), you form an expectation of a student, which is communicated nonverbally through your behavior. The student then responds to your behavior, behaving in ways that conform to your expectation. The expectation then becomes reality. Self-fulfilling prophecies can be positive or negative. High expectations lead to high student performance, and low expectations lead to low performance. Whether we like it or not, we all make split-second judgments about people—and in teaching, our students—that are affected by physical characteristics, speech, name, and socioeconomics.

Rosenthal (1998) also proposed the four factor model to help explain how teachers convey their expectations to students. The four factors are

1. **Climate.** Climate is communicated nonverbally by smiling and nodding (or frowning and shaking your head), eye contact, and body position. Climate is the tone you set in which all the teacher-student interactions take place.

2. **Feedback.** Feedback is both affective (e.g., praise or criticism) and cognitive (e.g., the content, its detail and quality). Feedback is your response to a student action or communication.

3. **Input.** Input is the quantity and quality of information you provide the student. Teachers actually teach more (provide greater input) to students of whom they have high expectations.

4. **Output.** Output is the responsiveness of the student. You encourage greater or lesser responsiveness through verbal and nonverbal cues.

Keep these four factors in mind as you plan for and create science lessons that support creating and maintaining positive learning environments for all of your students.

What do we mean when we talk about the learning environment? In *How People Learn* (NRC, 2000), the researchers' synthesis of numerous studies includes advice on designing effective learning environments with four specific perspectives in mind. As "lenses," these design characteristics can be used to describe the components of a science learning environment.

The "*learner-centered*" lens encourages attention to preconceptions and begins instruction with what students think and know.

The "*knowledge-centered*" lens focuses on what is to be taught, why it is taught, and what mastery looks like.

The "*assessment-centered*" lens emphasizes the need to provide frequent opportunities to make students' thinking and learning visible as a guide for both the teacher and the student in learning and instruction.

The "*community-centered*" lens encourages a culture of questioning, respect, and risk taking.

The learner-centered, knowledge-centered, and assessment-centered perspectives overlap, and all three are held within the circle of community. The four interrelated perspectives influence one another and need to be aligned in order to improve the classroom learning environment—and, ultimately, student achievement.

In a subsequent book written by the National Research Council, *How Students Learn: History, Mathematics and Science in the Classroom* (NRC, 2005), the research summarized the findings related to the four lenses, and the writers emphasized the importance of determining the ideas and understanding that students bring to the classroom (*learner-centered*). Only by engaging students' ideas can you help students think about the content and what it means to do science. With a focus on *knowledge-centered learning,* opportunities for inquiry are not just activities that are added to a unit of study but are the method for learning the content. Having students follow step-by-step procedures probably introduces more misconceptions than it clears up for students. When planning instruction, our goal should be to emphasize both what scientists know and how they know it. As learning progresses, students need opportunities to assess the quality of their hypotheses, models, methods, and explanations. These types of formative assessment activities (*assessment-centered*) lead to ongoing feedback between students and teachers with students being invited to revise their thinking. Last, developing a culture of respect, questioning, and risk-taking (*community-centered*) is needed to allow student discussion in a safe and orderly classroom environment. When studying science phenomena in their classroom—just like scientists—students need to learn how to argue using evidence with grace and respect. Developing a community of learners takes Practice and teachers willing to continually work to create positive classroom environments.

Procedures and expectations for classroom interactions need to be taught, and establishing norms and modeling interactions and behaviors should be part of a teacher's lesson plan. With a classroom of students focused on learning for all, intellectual rigor can be reinforced and maintained. This doesn't happen unless there is a climate of mutual trust within a safe and orderly classroom.

A study by Horizon Research, called *Looking into the Classroom* (Weiss, et al., 2003), identified classroom culture as an important component for delivering high-quality science instruction. According to this study, a positive learning environment has the following characteristics:

- Teachers and students share responsibility for learning.
- Teachers establish and model norms for positive interactions.
- Supportive, collaborative relationships are in place.
- There is mutual trust among teachers and students.
- There is a community of practice focused on learning for all.
- A focus on intellectual rigor, constructive criticism, and challenging of ideas exists.

When planning for positive learning environments, you need to keep in mind that students need structures that support learning but in a setting that is not constricting. The opportunity for student-centered learning needs to be encouraged. Letting students ask and investigate questions that are interesting to them is key to developing their **metacognition** (thinking about their thinking). Teachers generally start with planning for the physical environment in the classroom, which includes the arrangement of desks, placement of learning centers, resources posted on the walls, and interesting science materials around the classroom. Consider these recommendations for the **physical environment**:

- Selected table grouping configurations should support different kinds of activities.
- Equipment and materials need to be accessible.
- Students should be involved with the management and organization of the classroom.
- Resources posted around the room are selected to support student learning.
- Procedures for where to find late work, turning in papers, etc., are understood by all.

What are others that you think should be included?

Supporting a positive *social/emotional environment* involves relationship building, another critical component of positive environments. Teachers and students are involved in asking and answering questions within an atmosphere of mutual respect. All students are active in the process. Consider these recommendations for the social/emotional environment:

- Model and provide guided practice for desired interactions.
- Build and promote positive relationships between/among students and teachers (frequent interactions, inviting student participation).
- Plan and manage time effectively.
- Provide a strong focus on continual reflection.

In Exploration 3.1, look for evidence that the teacher is promoting a positive classroom environment to support science instruction.

What Does a Classroom with a Positive Climate Look Like?

EXPLORATION

3.1

It is a good idea to become familiar with strategies teachers use to develop positive classroom climates. You can make observations in actual classrooms or watch videos of classrooms in action, such as the one you can access through the link on this page. Use the characteristics of a positive classroom environment and determine which characteristics are evident in the video you watch or in the classroom you observe. Respond to the following reflection questions:

Reflection Questions:

1. How did the teacher arrange the classroom to support science learning? What worked and what didn't work?
2. How would you describe the interactions between teacher and students and between the students themselves?
3. Based on your observation, what did the teacher and students do and say to indicate that there was a community of practice that supported learning for all?
4. What might you do to become better prepared to create a positive classroom climate with students?

What are other things you think should be included? We will return to classroom management later in this chapter. Beginning teachers spend much of their first three years of teaching finding out what works with students to develop a positive social/emotional environment.

In support of **cooperative learning**, the positive classroom environment must provide clear learning goals that everyone works to achieve. Cooperative learning is not the same as collaboration. Collaboration describes bringing students together in groups; cooperative learning occurs not just when students are in groups but when students work together to achieve a common learning outcome. Even though cooperation to achieve the learning goals is part of an effective classroom climate, individual accountability is also necessary. Students need to individually be prepared to provide evidence that they can meet the learning goals that are the focus of classroom work.

Consider these recommendations that students need to work toward in a student-centered environment that *encourages individual accountability* for learning:

- Engage in reflection.
- Set individual learning goals (proximal and long-range).
- Take action to further their own learning (go to others, use materials).
- Engage in metacognition and learn how to self-assess.

What are others you might include?

CHECK YOUR UNDERSTANDING 3.1

Click here to gauge your understanding of the concepts in this section.

Designing the Learning Environment

In Chapter 2, we talked about how to plan for the content students must master. This included aligning learning goals with standards and writing clear instructional targets that you communicate with students.

Certainly you will need a variety of instructional strategies to help your students meet the four strands for proficiency in science as reported in *Taking Science to School* (NRC, 2007) and echoed in the new *A Framework for K–12 Science Education* (NRC, 2012):

1. Knowing, using, and interpreting scientific explanations of the natural world
2. Generating and evaluating scientific evidence and explanations
3. Understanding the nature and development of scientific knowledge
4. Participating productively in scientific Practices and discourse

However, you must also develop a positive classroom environment where you will effectively engage students with appropriate learning activities. When designing lesson activities, teachers determine what specific learning experiences relate to the content, lead to the attainment of specified learning targets, and promote interest and understanding.

Good lessons begin with engaging experiences that invite students to wonder. The experience starts the thinking process as they consider what they think they know already when studying a science phenomena. Starting off right is critical for the entire class lesson. When the students are excited and interested about what they will learn from the very beginning of the lesson, other issues, such as motivation and classroom management, tend to take care of themselves. Introductory activities should be designed to engage the students in generating questions that will link to the lesson. Activities for the engage phase of a 5E lesson should be designed with the following in mind:

- Create a "hook" that draws in the students.
- Relate conceptual academic knowledge to familiar experiences.
- Motivate students.
- Assess prior knowledge and identify current conceptions.
- Most importantly, engage students in a question that can be investigated.

In Exploration 3.2 you will learn more about programs designed to support positive classroom environments.

Establishing a Positive Classroom Climate   **EXPLORATION**

3.2

To establish a positive culture in your classroom, talk with two other colleagues and discuss where you would start and strategies you could use to make your classroom a safe place for student learning. Investigate any initiatives that you are aware of from districts in your area or select one of the following programs to research further. Search the Internet for any of the following:

Program	Description
PBIS (Positive Behavioral Interventions and Supports)	An all-school initiative that supports positive climate
How Full Is Your Bucket?	An approach that addresses the social/emotional environment related to student interactions
Dimension 5 "Habits of Mind" from Dimensions of Learning (Wiggins and Pickering, 1997)	A set of teaching and learning strategies that features productive mental habits of students that, along with attitudes and perceptions, can enhance students' learning of academic content; including critical thinking, creative thinking, and self-regulated thinking.

Each of these initiatives can be used to create a culture in the classroom and the school that encourages the development of a positive classroom environment. To help your discussion, consider the following reflection questions:

Reflection Questions:

- Think about a classroom you think is well structured for a positive climate. What structures are evident to support science inquiry?
- Now think about a classroom you think is not well structured for a positive climate. What advice could you give to the teacher to improve the student interactions when engaged in inquiry?
- Now think about the classroom environment you want to create. What environmental structures would you like to focus on to make your classroom more positive where students are safe to take risks when sharing science explanations?

After viewing this video clip, identify aspects that you think support the claim: the classroom featured in this video has a positive climate.

Don't worry, you will learn more about the 5E inquiry-based instructional model in Chapter 4. Your engage activity may not address all of these bullets, as introductory activities should be brief.

A variety of engage activities can be designed for science lessons. For example, to introduce lessons on weather, you might show brief segments of videos illustrating different weather conditions, including rain, snow, and violent winds. You could include a video segment of a person measuring and recording weather factors and conditions in addition to a segment of a TV weathercast. One purpose of using video segments is to make abstract topics interesting and relevant for students.

If video is not available, you could start a discussion and ask questions such as: What factors cause tornadoes to form? What conditions are important in changing the weather? How are these various factors measured? How are they used in predicting the weather? In guiding the discussion, be generally accepting of students' answers, recording them in your own notes and/or on the chalkboard to validate their responses. Remember that the purposes of the introductory activities are to engage the students in thinking about the content and skills to be learned, to create interest, to motivate, to determine prior knowledge, and to establish a question for investigation. There will be plenty of opportunities in later activities for students to confront and clarify misconceptions—or preconceptions if this is their first time learning about the phenomena—and to construct new knowledge and understandings.

Engaging students is all about fostering intrinsic motivation so that students want to learn! One way to motivate students is with science mysteries. They fascinate students and you will be able to probe what students already think they know. Discrepant events are one type of science mystery that can be an excellent introductory activity. A **discrepant event** is some scientific phenomenon that surprises, puzzles, or astonishes the observer; one in which the unusual outcome is contrary to typical predictions. Discrepant events may be demonstrated by the teacher, presented through video, or embedded within student activities. Vignette 3.1: "Do Heavier Objects Fall Faster Than Lighter Objects?" features discrepant events. The key is to help students develop an understanding of the phenomena, so planning time for students to investigate further is essential. With a little research you can find a wide variety of discrepant events to consider when planning a unit.

Vignette 3.1   Do Heavier Objects Fall Faster Than Lighter Objects?

Mr. Rodriguez is getting ready to introduce the concept of gravity to his fifth-grade class. By the end of this physical science unit, he wants his students to show competence with the NGSS Performance Expectation 5-PS2-1: Support an argument that the gravitational force exerted by Earth on objects is directed down. *Clarification Statement:* "Down" is a local description of the direction that points toward the center of the spherical Earth. *Assessment Boundary:* Assessment does not include mathematical representation of gravitational force.

To engage the students, he has designed a discrepant event demonstration. Off to the side, he has placed a single penny, ten pennies taped in a stack, a single coffee filter, and ten coffee filters in a stack. All of these materials are near at hand but out of sight of the students.

Mr. Rodriguez begins class by asking a simple question, "Do heavier objects fall faster than lighter objects?" (If you have already introduced the concept of mass, then say "more massive" rather than heavier.) This appears to be a simple question but is intentionally more complicated than it seems. After asking the question, Mr. Rodriguez provides time for students to discuss their ideas. Without suggesting any right or wrong answers, he simply tries to lead the class to a make a prediction, or decide what the majority of the students think the answer should be. At this point in the discussion, the accuracy of the students' answers is not important.

On this day, Mr. Rodriguez's class has predicted that heavier objects fall faster than lighter objects. Mr. Rodriguez is now going to challenge their ideas. He steps aside and picks up the single penny and the stack of ten pennies (taped together). He asks the class if the ten pennies are heavier than the single penny. The class agrees they are. Mr. Rodriguez then tells the class that, based on their prediction, the ten pennies will hit the ground before the single penny if they are dropped at the same time from the same height. For dramatic effect, Mr. Rodriguez stands on his desk and holds his hands straight out with the ten pennies in one hand and the single penny in the other. He lets them drop and asks the students what they observed. Contrary to their initial ideas, both the ten pennies and the single penny hit the ground at the same time.

Now Mr. Rodriguez gives the class a chance to revise their thoughts on whether or not heavier objects fall faster than lighter objects. After a brief discussion, the class agrees that objects fall at the same rate. Mr. Rodriguez now picks up the single coffee filter and the ten coffee filters. Once again, he stands on his desk with the single filter in one hand and the stack of ten in the other. Before dropping them, he confirms with the class that they now think objects made of the same material fall at the same rate so the filters will hit the ground at the same time. The class agrees and Mr. Rodriguez drops the filters. Much to the class's amazement, the ten filters hit the ground long before the single filter.

This prompts a great deal of discussion among the students. Now, Mr. Rodriguez has a class that is ready to learn about gravity for the rest of the class period.

Now that you have read the vignette, try Exploration 3.3.

When you are planning your inquiry-based lessons you may be concerned that every day will be essentially the same, but they should not be. Activities are learning experiences that enable students to attain the specified learning targets. When selecting or designing inquiry-based activities to include in a lesson, their placement in a specific order within the lesson is an important decision. The same basic activity could be slightly tweaked to make it appropriate for use in the engage or explore part of the lesson, as the basis for student explanations, and/or used to elaborate on the learning and link to further investigations.

Discrepant Events

Go and get 11 pennies and 11 coffee filters and some tape so you can try Mr. Rodriguez's demonstration yourself. Observe what happens when the single penny and the taped-together stack of 10 pennies are dropped at the same time. Repeat this penny-drop test several times until you are convinced of the outcome.

Then, observe what happens when the single coffee filter and the taped-together stack of 10 coffee filters are dropped at the same time. As before, repeat this filter-drop test until you are convinced of the expected result.

Make a claim about each of the phenomena you observed. Identify evidence that supports your claims. Draw labeled models that could help explain your thinking to others. Indicate the forces you think are acting on each system.

Reflection Questions

1. If Mr. Rodriguez's class had decided that objects fall at the same rate, what would he have dropped first? Why?
2. How could you incorporate the video from the moon into this demonstration?
3. Write a learning target for this part of the lesson.
4. How does this compare to starting a lesson by having the students read a textbook section on gravity aloud? Which is more likely to lead to student understanding? Why?

> Follow this link to view video of astronauts dropping a feather and a hammer on the moon. Observe what happened when these objects were dropped in the airless environment of the moon. https://www.youtube.com/watch?v=5C5_dOEyAfk

There are many sources of ideas for effective science activities that you can consult when planning lessons. The Activities Section of this book, in fact, is an excellent source as it contains many mini-lessons related to a wide variety of science topics. Elementary textbook series, kit-based science programs, other books and documents, the National Science Teachers Association (NSTA) Learning Center, and advice from your fellow teachers also provide access to a wide range of activities.

In addition, there are thousands, if not millions, of activities available on the internet. But a word of caution is in order. Many of the internet science activities, and some published traditionally, are merely "show and tell" or "vocabulary drill" activities and become just activities for activities sake. They are not designed to lead students to develop conceptual understanding and inquiry abilities. However, you can modify almost any science activity to make it more inquiry and constructivist oriented, or to address the suggestions found in *A Framework for K-12 Science Education: Practices, Crosscutting Concepts, and Core Ideas* (NRC, 2012) by interweaving the three dimensions into the lesson.

Although hands-on inquiry activities are essential in science learning, this does not mean that every science lesson activity must have students handle science materials and generate new data. Your inquiry lesson activities should include a variety of teaching and learning approaches, including listening and speaking, reading and writing, research in books and on the internet, and observing as well as doing investigations. Films and videos, books, research reports, use of internet sources, existing data sets, and field trips (including virtual field trips presented through websites) can also provide excellent learning opportunities for students.

However, over the long term, be sure that your lesson plans provide opportunities for students to learn and use Scientific and Engineering Practices through their own activities to better understand the nature of science and scientific inquiry.

Exploration activities that incorporate descriptive, classificatory, and/or experimental investigations are ideal for developing inquiry abilities and Scientific and Engineering Practices. But almost any activity that follows an inquiry teaching approach can build inquiry abilities as well as conceptual understanding.

Open inquiries represent another type of activity that might be included in a lesson. In open inquiry, the teacher may provide the problem and materials for students, but then allow them time and freedom to simply "try things out" and make initial observations that will lead to other questions. In the 5E inquiry-based instructional model, as mentioned earlier this typically occurs in the explore stage. For example, you might give cooperative groups of students (with a shared learning target), soda bottles and pitchers

The URL is: http://ngss.nsta.org/Default.aspx This should be a margin link. Hub is a site that provides teacher resources when planning for three-dimensional learning to address the performance expectations included in the Next Generation Science Standards (2013).

of water (and newspapers and plenty of paper towels to mop up spills). You might then ask the groups to discover what they can do to change the pitch of the sounds that can be produced with the bottles. In producing sounds, some groups might try to strike the bottles with a wooden object. Others might blow across the open ends of the bottles. As they try different things, students may discover that putting different amounts of water in the bottles changes the pitch produced by their actions on the bottles.

Science explorations typically involve a variety of materials that must be managed. Careful planning and preparation as well as explicitly teaching students procedures for getting, using, and cleaning up materials can help eliminate the stress of involving your class in hands-on activities.

In classrooms where students actively engage in inquiry, learning centers or stations are a good way to present multiple activities that may test different variables, or allow observations of different phenomena, especially in the lower grades. Learning centers are created and directed by the teacher and contain independent activities for students. They can motivate, guide, and support the learning of individuals and small groups. Science learning centers allow teachers to meet individual needs and provide students with self-directed learning opportunities. They also encourage student responsibility.

There are various types of science learning centers. A guided discovery learning center involves students in developing a better understanding of specific science concepts. For example, place materials in shoeboxes with a series of guiding questions on cards for students to read. An example of a question to guide learning center activities on light is: "How can you use a flashlight and the cards in the box to show that light appears to travel in a straight line?" Include a flashlight and a number of blank index cards with 1-cm holes punched in the center of each card. Children should discover that light from the flashlight will pass through the holes in the center of the cards only if they are all aligned. This provides evidence that light travels in straight lines.

In developing lesson plans, engaging students and designing activities is important, but you must have a way to know if your students are learning from these experiences. You should use both formative (ongoing assessments) and summative (end of lesson) assessments. Formative assessment involves gathering assessment information during the process of instruction. A main function of formative assessment is to serve as a basis for adjusting instructional strategies to improve learning. More about assessment will be included in Chapter 7. It is just a reminder here that formative assessments incorporate feedback loops, which are one of our important characteristics of positive classroom environments. For example, information from formative assessment is important for teachers to determine what kinds of scaffolding assistance students need. Formative assessments can be very quick and easy. It can be as simple as asking your class for a "thumbs up" or "thumbs down" to represent how they are doing on an activity.

Summative assessment is assessment at the end of lessons or instructional units that provides important information for determining what the students learned and did not learn as a result of instructional activities. Summative assessment provides a basis for both feedback to students and for grades and accountability. Summative assessments should also guide your instruction. They will alert you to material that needs to be retaught and will provide direction for how to change your instruction for the next time you teach that content. From the work of Wiggins and McTighe in *Understanding by Design* (2005), when planning, begin with the end in mind. Then you can directly link the learning experiences to the learning targets.

Rubrics are often used in assessment of inquiry learning. A **rubric** defines several different levels of student performance and includes the knowledge and understanding in specific terms. Thus, teachers can use rubrics to specify the ideal levels of learning performance on learning targets and then assess the actual level of student attainment. The number of levels in a rubric should be based on the needs of your class and your observations of what your students are actually doing in science activities. Four-level rubrics are frequently used:

- Level 4: Advanced, Excellent, Exceeds Expectations
- Level 3: Proficient, Satisfactory, Meets Expectations
- Level 2: Basic, Below Expectations, Lacks Conceptual Understanding
- Level 1: Learning Is In-Progress with Some Factual Knowledge

In this video, watch student groups rotate through multiple inquiry stations and find out why teachers might select this organizational approach for hands-on learning activities.

 CHECK YOUR UNDERSTANDING 3.2

Click here to gauge your understanding of the concepts in this section.

Planning for Classroom Safety

Safety in the science classroom is critical. As a teacher, you are legally responsible for the safety of students in your classroom (Gerlovich, 1996). But the law does not require you to be superhuman in your efforts. It is only expected that you are reasonable and prudent in your judgment when performing your duties with students. You must attempt to anticipate hazards and then eliminate or address them. Consider possible safety hazards while selecting or designing activities for your class; safety issues are often noted in lesson plans or teacher's guides. Always do a "dry run" without students around to become aware of embedded safety concerns.

The responsibility for ensuring a safe environment for science learning in schools must be shared by the entire school community: administrators, teachers, support staff, parent volunteers, and students. The establishment and maintenance of safety standards should involve both school district authorities and teachers; so discuss safety issues with your fellow teachers, principal, and/or district science coordinator. Check with school medical personnel at the beginning of the school year to identify student medical conditions such as allergies, epilepsy, etc., and be prepared to take appropriate actions.

Safety in the science classroom is often closely tied to class size, teacher to student ratio, and the room's size and arrangement. As you arrange your room, think about patterns of student movement and avoid overcrowding any areas. Floor space and work space should be kept uncluttered; backpacks on the floor are often tripping hazards. Limit the size of student working groups to a number that can safely perform the activity without causing confusion and if you work with students with physical disabilities, for example students who are wheelchair bound, consider their special needs for movement in the room when you arrange the furniture and set up supply stations. Your entire classroom should be accessible to all of your learners, so that getting resources, equipment, or other materials does not slow down the process of learning.

You should be familiar with your school's fire regulations, evacuation plans, and the location and use of fire-fighting equipment. Post and discuss with your students the class emergency escape and notification plans.

At the beginning of the school year, you should generate, post, model, and enforce a list of safety rules that students should always follow. Review these rules as appropriate and make relevant additions throughout the year, especially targeting rules that apply to the current lab activity. It is highly recommended that students and their parents sign safety contracts at the beginning of the year that specify safety rules. Many publishers and science suppliers have standard forms that you can use or revise. Flinn Scientific™ has a comprehensive set of safety contracts, videos, and tests in addition to activities that feature safety issues that can arise in the classroom. At the middle school level, they also have the tests and contracts available both in English and Spanish. Use of goggles is critical at all levels when handling any liquids.

Also, post emergency contact numbers such as the extensions of the school nurse and principal, the poison control center, fire department, and of course, 911. Directions for what to do in an emergency situation should be listed in a teacher/staff handbook for your school. Chemicals including laboratory grade salt and sugar will have MSDS (Materials Safety Data Sheets) documents to alert teachers to potential hazards of the materials and indicate the proper storage of solids and liquids. The safety data sheets can be found online, and teachers should print copies of the information for any materials that they use with students including readily available materials like flour and vinegar.

Once again, it is a good idea to create a science safety contract appropriate to your grade level that both students and their parents or guardians sign. The contract should include your expectations for students' actions when working on science activities, in labs, and on field studies around or away from the school grounds. You should go over the document with your students to assure that they understand what it says, and they should explain the contract to their parents and ask them to sign to indicate it was discussed with their child. Most importantly, remain consistent with your enforcement of science safety rules and the policies included on the safety contract. Remember that you need to follow the same safety rules as your students: wearing goggles, no eating or drinking in the lab, etc. With more student allergies, the care and handling of living organisms can be a significant safety concern. Be sure you are aware of your district policies regarding safety expectations and refer to the guidance from veteran teachers and safety officers. One hazard that is often overlooked is high-powered batteries, which can interfere with electronics. One example of a safety list is presented in Table 3.1.

The National Science Teachers Association accepted a new NSTA Position Statement for Safety and School Science Instruction in 2015. Follow this link to read their recommendations. http://www.nsta.org/about/positions/safety.aspx

TABLE 3.1   Elementary Science Safety Rules for Students

Always:	Never:
Read and follow all directions for the activity	Eat or drink while conducting an experiment
Read all warning labels on all materials being used	Touch material to your eyes, mouth, or nose
Wear eye protection as directed	Experiment on your own
Follow safety warnings or precautions	
Use all materials carefully and as they were intended	
Clean up your area and dispose of materials properly	
Wash your hands well after every activity	
Immediately report any spills, breakage, accidents, or injuries to your teacher	
Tie back long hair to keep it away from chemicals, flames, and equipment	

Source: Adapted from the American Chemical Society.

The kinds of activities done in middle school science laboratories tend to be quite different than those that can be safely conducted in elementary science classrooms. Still, the basic safety rules and procedures apply to all grade levels. The following list, based on recommendations of the Council of State Science Supervisors, provides guidance to you as a teacher of science.

- Know district and state policies concerning administering first aid. Maintain and have immediate access to a first-aid kit for emergency treatment (if local and state policies allow), as well as biohazard and chemical spill kits/materials.

- Report all injuries, including animal scratches, bites, and allergic reactions, immediately to appropriate personnel.

- Make certain that you, your students, and all visitors are adequately protected when investigations involving glass (not recommended), heat, chemicals, projectiles, or dust-raising materials are conducted. Permanent or movable eyewash stations and fume hoods should be accessible to teachers and to students when working with chemicals.

- Do not use or let your students use mercury thermometers. Any mercury thermometers still in schools should be disposed of properly following an appropriate hazardous waste protocol. (Let your district's science coordinator or chemical safety officer know; he or she will take care of it.)

- Use only equipment that is in good working order; inspect equipment before each use.

- Use unbreakable plastic equipment whenever possible; maintain a separate waste container for broken glass; sweep up broken glass with dustpan and brush.

- Tie back long hair; secure loose clothing and dangling jewelry; do not permit open-toed shoes or sandals during lab activity. Clothing should cover upper and lower body.

When selecting science activities for your class you must consider the safety equipment that is available in your classroom or laboratory. While the following items should be easily accessible in elementary and middle school science classrooms, classrooms with labs, and science resource rooms, if safety equipment needed for an activity is not available, don't do that activity in that teaching space.

- Appropriate-size chemical splash goggles that are American National Standards Institute (ANSI) Z87 or Z87.1 coded and of type G, H, or K only. These must be worn when working with liquids that could splash, solids that might shatter, heat, fire, projectiles, chemicals, including common house-hold chemicals such as vinegar or ammonia. If goggles will be shared (not always worn by the same student), implement a goggle sanitation plan to limit transmission of bacteria or lice. Soaking them between uses in a 10 percent solution of chlorine bleach and water, then rinsing in water and letting them air dry is sufficient. Disinfecting cabinets that use ultraviolet light to sanitize may also be used; the goggles must be exposed to the UV rays for about 15 minutes.

- Non-allergenic (no latex) gloves. These are typically used to protect hands from chemicals, germs, and rough surfaces.

- Nonabsorbent, chemical-resistant protective aprons. These are designed to protect from spills and splashes.

- Eyewash units. These are used when chemicals splash or particles fly into someone's eyes.

- Safety spray hoses/shower. These are used to wash chemicals off of clothing and skin.

- ABC tri-class fire extinguisher(s). In case of fire, this is an important safety device; however, it is important that you are trained in its use.

- Flame retardant–treated fire blanket. This is used to smother a fire. If someone's clothes catch on fire, wrapping them in a fire blanket puts out the flames.

The use of chemicals in science activities also varies greatly across the grade levels. Typically, elementary activities utilize chemicals that are relatively safe to work with compared to those needed for some middle school activities. It is important that you understand the possible reactions and the storage needs of any chemical you use in science class. A well-written activity will mention any potential safety issues, but all activities aren't well written!

As mentioned earlier, Material Safety Data Sheets (MSDS) are provided when you order supplies from a scientific materials supplier. Remember, you need to be aware of potential safety hazards for any chemical you use in a science class. Soda, like Coke, is considered a chemical (contains citric acid) when used in science classrooms, even though it is a common beverage and you and your students may not consider it dangerous. You should have an MSDS on file for every chemical you use in your science classroom. Consult the MSDS and the container label before using chemicals each time in the classroom.

Some other things to keep in mind if you are working with chemicals in your science class include:

- Do not store, under any circumstances, chemicals and biological specimens in the same refrigerator used for food and beverages.

- Prevent contamination; do not return unused chemicals to the original container.

- Label and date all storage containers of laboratory chemicals and preserved specimens upon receipt. Properly label all secondary chemical and specimen (set-out) containers.

Animals can be a wonderful addition to your science classroom. Your students can learn about the animals themselves while developing the responsibility that is required to care for animals. In addition, the animals can provide a welcome break and reward in helping you to manage your classroom. In its 2005 position statement on *Responsible Use of Live Animals and Dissection in the Science Classroom*, NSTA supports including live animals as part of instruction in the K–12 science classroom because observing and working with animals firsthand can spark students' interest in science as well as a general respect for life while reinforcing key concepts as outlined in the *National Science Education Standards* (NSES) and in Disciplinary Core Ideas in the NGSS. NSTA encourages districts to ensure that animals are properly cared for and treated humanely, responsibly, and ethically. Ultimately, decisions to incorporate organisms in the classroom should balance the ethical and responsible care of animals with their educational value.

Always insist that students wash their hands before feeding the animals and after they have handled the animals or touched materials from the animals' cages. They should research information about animal identification, characteristics, feeding habits, and values.

Great care should be taken in choosing an animal to keep in your classroom. Some of the biggest concerns are possible student allergies and how to care for the animals when school is not in session. Small caged animals that are easy to handle such as gerbils, mice, small snakes, and finches are some examples of good selections. Fish, insects, frogs, and salamanders are also good choices but should only be observed by students, not held. Though students might want to bring in animals they find in the natural environment of the schoolyard or the woods, discourage them from doing so. Some of the critters, bugs, and baby birds students find might be diseased, carrying parasites, or aggressive. Safety issues aside, it is often very difficult to keep animals from the local environment alive for the long term. These animals should be returned to their natural habitats as soon as possible. All long-term classroom animals should be purchased from a pet store or a science supply company that sells living organisms.

✓ CHECK YOUR UNDERSTANDING 3.3
Click here to gauge your understanding of the concepts in this section.

Managing Student Behavior

Classroom management is the number one issue of concern cited by pre-service teachers, and the area of largest frustration for current teachers. It is also one of the top reasons teachers leave the classroom. So how can you avoid having classroom management as an area of stress in your classroom—especially when trying to encourage your students to be up and active? Surprisingly, having your students up, active, out of their seats, and doing science won't make your classroom management more difficult. Despite what you might think, it will actually make it better as long as you have established procedures to quickly refocus their attention on you! Your students will be engaged and busy learning for understanding throughout the class period and won't have the downtime that leads to most behavior problems in the classroom.

Listen to what this veteran teacher has to say about classroom management and procedures for regaining students' attention. What are two important ideas that you want to remember as you consider your strategies for maintaining positive classroom environments?

The second strategy is to teach students procedures. When they know what is expected of them, they feel a sense of comfort and order that will eliminate many of the behavioral problems that arise. If students don't know what they are supposed to do, they quickly get off track and may believe that they can't do what is being asked. This is very different from lacking the skill to implement a procedure. Remember that this relates to skills beyond the science process skills mentioned in Chapter 2. In both elementary and middle school classrooms, students need clear procedures to understand how to communicate in sense-making discussions, procedures to move into different grouping configurations, procedures for analyzing data, and how to generate evidence from data. There are many resources to help teachers teach procedures including *Classroom Instruction that Works,* 2nd Edition (Dean, et al, 2013), *Teaching Reading in Science* (Barton & Jordan, 2001). You will probably want to start creating an online or physical library of resources that you can refer to when gathering materials to help with positive classroom management.

Establishing a classroom learning environment focused on learning through inquiry is a critical factor for effective science classroom management. Giving your students ready access to the resources they need in order to investigate and communicate helps establish a climate of student-centered learning. Those resources include: measuring devices, drawing media, chart paper, computers with access to the Internet, reference and trade books, cameras, topic-related specimens, samples, and other materials.

Identifying **cooperative group roles and responsibilities** can be an effective way to manage inquiry activities. What roles and responsibilities of group members does this fourth-grade teacher identify for students in a lesson on "building skimmers"?

Research indicates that learning with understanding is enhanced when students are grouped in ways that provide them with opportunities to discuss their investigations, findings, and conclusions with one another and with the teacher (NRC, 2007).

Expert teachers use a variety of classroom arrangements for science and other subjects. These include (Lowery, 1998):

- Whole class structure (e.g., the teacher lectures, demonstrates, or guides the whole class in discussion);
- Cooperative group structure (e.g., students in small groups collaboratively collect data, organize it, exchange ideas, and arrive at individual understanding of the learning targets);

- Pair structure (e.g., two students work together to construct an explanation of some action in a demonstration); and
- Individual structure (e.g., each student works individually on an investigation, collecting data, recording it in a science journal, generating explanations, and answering relevant questions).

Whole class structure is exactly what it appears to be. The class is acting as a single group with the teacher leading the activity or discussion. In a science class, this is often an effective way to do demonstrations that are fun for the students to watch but too dangerous for them to do themselves as an investigation. This can also be a method to show a demonstration when materials are very limited. This presents opportunities to incorporate technology such as an interactive whiteboard, which will help keep the students active and engaged. Interactive simulations can also be provided in a whole class structure if computers in the classroom are limited to one.

Whole class instruction can also be led by the students. Teachers can enhance student learning by bringing the whole class back together and giving groups opportunities to make presentations of their work. Deeper understanding is attained when students explain, clarify, and justify what they have learned (NRC, 1996, p. 30). As the students communicate their findings and explanations based on evidence, they should be encouraged to accept and respond to the constructive criticism of others. Communication of investigations and findings to others typically occurs during the explanation part of the inquiry-based instructional model with the intention of helping students make sense of the science phenomena.

Cooperative groups—small groups of students working cooperatively—are especially important in upper elementary and middle school science classrooms. At the primary level, pairs are often more appropriate than small groups.

Whether working cooperatively or in small groups, students consider problems and assignments together, verbalize what they know, consider the multiple viewpoints of group members, collect data together, learn from one another, and come up with group solutions to problems. These group processes are the kinds of student interactions that help establish communities of learners in which students have opportunities to learn from and teach each other. Kagan (1994) has suggested that cooperative learning structures can increase student achievement. In his research he found that cooperative groups work best when there is positive interdependence (all working toward the same goals), there is individual accountability (every student needs to show mastery of the concepts), there is equal participation of all members of the group, and class time is structured to allow for multiple interactions between students.

Cooperative groups can be formed in many ways. Sometimes it is simple and effective for children who sit near one another to be in a group. At other times it may be more beneficial to form either heterogeneous or homogenous groups. Students may also be allowed to choose their own groups. All of these methods are used frequently, and there is not necessarily a right or wrong way to form the groups. The type of groups used often depends on the activity being completed. Whatever method of grouping you choose, the groups and the method of selection should be varied throughout the school year. You may be familiar with the grouping example called **Think-Pair-Share** where the cooperative group is two students working together to think and then share their ideas. Other common group structures include the following:

Hand Up Stand Up Pair Up The teacher poses a question, and the students when they have an answer stand up and put their hand up until they find another student also standing, and then they pair together to discuss the answer. The teacher after one to two minutes repeats the process and the students pair up with another student to discuss their answer. After two or three rounds, the students return to their original groups and discuss what they found out during the activity.

Showdown Students write their answers on their individual response boards. When everyone in the group is ready, the leader says "Showdown" and team members compare and discuss their answers.

Teammates Consult Students all have their own copy of the same worksheet or assignment questions. A large cup or beaker is placed in the center of each team, and students begin by placing their pencils in the cup. With pencils still in the cup, they discuss their answers to the first question. When all team members are ready, they remove their pencils from the cup and write their answers without talking. They repeat this process with the remaining questions.

There are dozens of strategies to group students and with each one you will want to go over the procedure with students, practice the strategy designed to support cooperative interactions, and then at the end of the discussion period talk to the students about how the procedure worked and what might be done to improve the strategy the next time it is used in class. Implementation of the cooperative discussion strategies should include clear guidance about how much time students have to talk with one another. The teacher can always be the timekeeper and let students know when to shift either to another group or back to their original group. Learning is hard work, and these social interactions that allow students to talk freely about their ideas and clarify their thinking are an essential part of classroom work. Without the emphasis on teaching the procedures, student behavior may not match a teacher's expectations. To reinforce these practices, remember that the sequence to follow is to explain the procedure, model the practice, practice it with students, and then reinforce what worked well and adjust for what didn't work.

Cooperative grouping is greatly enhanced if your classroom is equipped with tables instead of desks. With the research on mixed ability groups, it is becoming apparent that pairing your most able students with your least able students may not help the struggling students learn. What generally happens is the higher-performing student just tells the struggling student the answer or shows them how to do it. They are not teachers, so your best students should not be put in that role. It is better to put together flexible groups based on formative assessment data so that the cooperative groups can be working on the learning targets that are appropriate for them. As the teacher you will probably want to work directly with the students who are having the greatest difficulty.

In cooperative groups, the biggest struggle is to keep all of the students engaged in the learning activity. Assigning group roles is a helpful way to prevent potential management issues. This is particularly important with younger students who have not had experience working together. As the teacher, you would explain specific tasks or rules for each member of the group. You may want to consider having these written down and posted so that students can refer to them often. The roles you create will likely depend on the number of students in each group. It is common practice, for example, to assign one student from each group as the one who collects the materials needed for the group in order to limit the number of students who are out of their seats at a given time. Other roles that might be assigned include leader, data recorder, timekeeper, equipment manager, researcher, and illustrator. It is important that you establish the roles and group structure early in the school year so that they become a part of your classroom routine. Throughout the year, each student should have an opportunity to assume the responsibilities required of each of the cooperative learning jobs. Cooperative groups are typically used during the explore and/or elaborate phases of the 5E inquiry-based instructional model. Remember that for learning to be truly cooperative, you would not want to assign a group "grade" for the learning. Students must still be responsible for providing evidence that they have met the success criteria provided. Think about ways that all students share responsibility for reporting out for their group when asked. Some teachers use a random number generator to call on students. You can also number the students in a group and then roll a dice to see who will communicate to the rest of the class. Consider what you could do if a student is afraid to be wrong and doesn't want to present to the rest of the class. Remind them that if the reporter who is selected gets stuck they can always call on the rest of their group to add to the discussion.

Pair structures often provide for more interaction between students. Pairing students to work on an activity is an excellent choice when it is practical. Often, limited materials or space make it difficult to allow students to work in pairs very often. Working in pairs can be better than larger groups as there is less likelihood that students do not participate or are not accountable for their role. The downside of working in pairs is that there are fewer people contributing ideas, and it can be easier for one person to dominate the pairing. Choosing the partner groups can follow the same methods as choosing cooperative groups. When it is time to discuss the pair explanations and supporting evidence, you may want to get two pair groups to work together.

Having your students work individually is another method often employed effectively in elementary and middle school science classrooms. When the materials for an activity are plentiful and space is available, having students work individually can be effective. This allows students to really think through problems on their own and forces them to consider the whole problem without relying on others. This is also a good opportunity for students to record their own data in a science notebook. One downfall, however, is that students who become stuck or frustrated with the activity do not have a partner or a group to help them think about solutions to the question or problem being solved. When making sense of an activity, moving students from individual work to small groups is recommended. Learning is a social activity and students need to be able to rehearse their ideas out loud with others and then discuss the pros and cons of explanations in light of the evidence generated and being aware of the limitations of the data or the models being studied.

Used thoughtfully and strategically, different types of grouping arrangements can be effective tools for promoting cooperation and discourse, improving learning and instruction, and maintaining an orderly inquiry-learning environment. During inquiry, students are naturally active—getting materials, performing investigations, discussing procedures and results with one another and with you, and moving into different group structures. Still, you must establish rules for behavior, monitor students' activities, and enforce disciplinary consequences when necessary. Don't forget to have a procedure for cleanup and get students to help monitor whether materials have been checked in and are ready for other students to use.

Keep in mind that all misbehavior is not equal. Classify misbehavior as off task (attention wandering, failing to attend to the task at hand), inappropriate (doing something that is against the agreed-on rules), or disruptive (inappropriate behavior that prevents learning or is potentially dangerous). Deal with each case in an appropriate way, such as regaining attention indirectly or stopping inappropriate behavior and cautioning the student.

To provide a safe and supportive classroom environment, students need to have procedures in place so that they know what is expected of them. This means that there are structures that determine classroom organization, interactions, and expectations without constricting student learning experiences. Even the grouping structures described earlier in this section are procedures that need to be taught to students, modeled, and then practiced. As teachers we often have expectations of students that they fail to meet. Frequently it is due to a lack of understanding around the expectations. For example, if we want students to be able to summarize, think about whether they know what they need to do to generate a summary. If not, then teach them the procedure and reinforce the process when you ask them to do it in the future.

Harry and Rosemary Wong in their book, *The First Days of School: How to Be an Effective Teacher* (2009), emphasize the importance of clear classroom procedures. Knowing what is expected of them motivates students to try in class. When they have the resources they need, understand tasks and what help is available, and know how the classroom functions, then their physical environment supports teaching and learning.

Fred Jones in his book, *Tools for Teaching* (2000), suggests that fewer rules are better and determining expectations with input from students positively involves them in the process. More important than many classroom expectations is to provide consistent consequences to a few rules.

Monitoring the behavior of individuals or groups is critical in science classrooms. This is important for classroom management and safety. Some students, for example, may be too immature for group work. You may need to work with them individually while the rest of the class works in groups. The goal is to help each student develop strategies for following class rules and participating in activities effectively. We do not get to choose the students we have in class and it is up to us to provide learning opportunities for all our students using strategies to meet their needs. Students are quick to pick up on our verbal and nonverbal communication so it is important for us to show by our actions that we believe that they can learn. Do not give up on students who present obstacles, but rather find the appropriate strategies to meet their needs.

If there is a chronic offender in your class, you might talk with the student and ask for the student's perceptions of the problem. If that doesn't help solve the issue, call the parents to develop a plan or, if necessary, schedule a conference. Finally, if you are still having consistent problems with a student, make use of the resources in your school: Invite the principal, school psychologist, social worker, or other professional to observe the behavior of the student in the classroom.

Being clear and consistent with disruptive students is essential to enable all students to learn science effectively in inquiry settings. By setting high expectations and consistently enforcing these expectations at the beginning of the year, you can establish routines that will lead to a successful year of learning science. Here are some special actions you might consider:

- Prepare contingency plans for problem situations; for example, deliberate damage to science supplies or explosive student behavior (fighting and pushing).
- Consider beforehand the pros and cons of various methods of discipline, such as removing a student from the situation, so you can use the methods effectively if necessary.
- Consider developing routine procedures for handling improper actions so students understand beforehand the consequences of bad behavior.

> This video segment presents reflections about working with students with challenging behaviors. Which of these ideas do you find most meaningful?

If you feel that you are losing control of a lesson, don't hesitate to end it, especially if the behavior problem may lead to a safety problem. Assess what went wrong and plan the next lesson to eliminate the problem.

Despite your best efforts, some students may exhibit disruptive or asocial behaviors, and you may be dealing with students diagnosed with serious emotional disorders. Because students with emotional disorders may be included in your classroom, suggestions for working with such students may be helpful. You will likely have other kinds of high-needs students in your classroom also. Marzano and Marzano in their article "The Key to Classroom Management" (2003) also provide recommendations for working with students who are passive, aggressive, perfectionists, attention getters, or are socially inept. Consider learning more about each of these types of high-needs students and review the suggestions for how to interact with them in ways that help you to maintain a positive classroom environment.

As you work with students who have emotional or behavioral disorders, remember that your utmost concern is to provide a safe and supportive learning environment for all of your students. To work successfully with students whose conduct is often disorderly, try viewing their deficit in appropriate social behaviors just as you would academic deficits—skills that need to be taught. Don't condone inappropriate behaviors; teach alternative, appropriate ways to interact. With your patience and guidance, students can learn appropriate social behaviors just as they can learn to be more successful academically.

The most important thing to remember in your science classroom is to establish an atmosphere of respect. You need to respect your students and their appropriate ideas and opinions, while your students need to respect you, their classmates, and the science materials that they use throughout the year.

CHECK YOUR UNDERSTANDING 3.4

Click here to gauge your understanding of the concepts in this section.

CHAPTER SUMMARY

Characteristics of a Positive Learning Environment

To achieve a positive classroom climate, teachers plan for a physical environment that meets the learning needs of students, structures and procedures are in place to support the social/emotional needs of students, and classrooms are student centered— so that students learn how to be metacognitive and can self-regulate their learning. When observing a classroom with a positive classroom climate, the following characteristics would be evident:

- Respect for students' ideas, questions, and contributions is evident.
- Active participation of all is encouraged and valued.
- Interactions reflect positive working relationship between teacher and students.
- Interactions reflect effective working relationships among students.
- Students are encouraged to generate ideas and questions.
- Intellectual rigor, constructive criticism, and challenging of ideas are evident in a safe and respectful way.

To effectively teach science requires careful planning and implementation. You must design your lessons with an implementation plan in place for distributing and collecting the necessary materials. You need to establish a procedure for gaining the students' attention, such as flicking the lights, to make announcements and provide directions and clarifications throughout the lesson. Be sure to move around the classroom and check each group for understanding of the activity. Don't forget that student attitudes about learning can be influenced by four factors, which include climate, feedback, inputs to students, and outputs—our responsiveness to students' needs. We are directly in control of these four factors and can change our practices to help all students learn. Positive classroom environments do not happen without careful planning and implementation.

Designing the Learning Environment

The learning environment and experiences for your students are highly dependent on your ability to motivate student learning, provide opportunities to intellectually engage with science phenomena, and work collaboratively using ongoing feedback to move learning forward. How well you start your science lesson each day has a direct impact on the learning environment. Increasing student anticipation for learning will increase their reception of your lesson plans. After students are ready to learn, you need to have activities that will help channel their excitement. This exploration portion of your lesson plan should be varied each day, using the myriad of sources available to find activity ideas. In inquiry-based investigations, when students develop explanations, establishing and maintaining a positive climate where all ideas are accepted requires constant monitoring. Assessing your students formatively helps shape your future lesson planning and establishes an ongoing cycle of feedback with students.

Planning for Classroom Safety

The safety of your students in science class always comes first, but it should not prohibit you from doing inquiry-based science lessons. You should be prepared for accidents that could happen in your classroom and how you would respond. Be sure to review the safety rules with your class often and follow commonsense guidelines. Special care needs to be taken when deciding if you will keep animals in your classroom.

Managing Student Behavior

In science class, managing student behavior often means managing students working in groups. The most common grouping structure is to have students work in cooperative groups of three or more. Assigning roles to the students in each group helps keep all group members on task. When dealing with student misbehavior in your classroom, you must be firm, fair, and consistent. Have clear guidelines established and posted in your classroom. Don't forget to teach students procedures so that they know what is expected of them, and they are confident in their abilities to accomplish the tasks. Establish a positive environment by praising students' effort and groups who are working hard and behaving appropriately. Students who are consistently causing behavior problems may fall into the category of high-needs students who require appropriate interactions with the teacher. If all students can learn then we must show by what we say and do that we believe this is true.

DISCUSSION QUESTIONS

1. How does the set-up of the physical environment in a classroom support the social/emotional environment?
2. When planning for a positive classroom environment, where do you think you should begin?
3. How can you effectively communicate the importance of safety in the science classroom to your students and their parents?
4. What aspects of classroom management for science are you most concerned about? Why?
5. Why is teaching procedures to students an important part of positive classroom culture?

PROFESSIONAL PRACTICES ACTIVITIES

1. Read the various resources related to classroom management. What role should students play when setting classroom expectations and maintaining positive classroom behaviors? Discuss your ideas with current teachers at the grade level you are interested in teaching.
2. Ask a local school district what method they use to develop schoolwide procedures for students (i.e., homework policies, grading policies, later work policies, etc.). What is the impact on students? Parents? Teachers? If they don't have consistent policies, why not?
3. Go online and find a number of sites that have motivating engage and explore activities. Keep these bookmarked to help you plan throughout your career.

4. Find examples of science safety contracts and modify them to fit your classroom.

5. Ask some classroom teachers for their posted classroom rules and use those as a basis to create guidelines for your science class.

6. Generate a list of procedures that you think are important to teach to students. How would you determine if students have already learned a procedure or if you need to teach it? Work with another teacher to plan a lesson where teaching a procedure is part of the lesson.

Learning Science with Understanding

Pearson Education, Inc.

LEARNING GOALS

After reading this chapter, you should know and understand that . . .

1. Knowing science facts involves memorizing information that can be recalled, while understanding science ideas means being able to explain, to interpret, to apply and adapt knowledge.

2. A child's ability to construct learning depends on age and experiences.

3. Students can be led to deeper understandings of science concepts using a variety of approaches.

4. Students' alternative conceptions of science concepts can be changed using a conceptual change model.

Think back to when you were in grades K–8 and the science you learned. You learned the names and order of the seasons. Did you also learn and understand what causes the seasons? You learned about the phases of the moon, but did you understand what causes the phases? Your reflections will provide a context for the ideas developed in this chapter.

Effective teachers of science have learned what it means to teach science for conceptual understanding—understanding the science ideas associated with science phenomena. This chapter presents information and ideas to help you synthesize what it means to teach children to learn science with understanding.

Knowing vs. Understanding

Vignette 4.1   The Best-Laid Plans

Mrs. Thomas spent two hours of her Sunday afternoon planning a lesson on the difference between conductors and insulators for her fourth-grade class. She found an array of materials—batteries and battery holders, alligator clip wires, and small light bulbs. From these items students could set up an open circuit, insert a variety of objects to close the circuit, and see whether the bulb would light. They would then sort the objects into two categories: those that lit the bulb and those that did not. Afterwards, students would describe similarities and differences between the two piles. As her students would explain what they did and how they categorized the materials, Mrs. Thomas planned some probing questions to make sure she would get them to discuss the similarities and differences in the objects. After being assured that each group had their objects properly sorted, she would introduce the words *insulator*

and *conductor*, ensuring that her students would have the academic language in their minds to connect with the explanations.

On Monday morning, Mrs. Thomas is ready and excited for her class to walk through the door and complete the science lab. As students take their seats in small-group tables, the materials are already out and ready to go. Just as she is about to get started, one of her students exclaims, "Oooh! We must be doing insulators and conductors today. We know what those are from third grade!"

Mrs. Thomas freezes in her tracks with thoughts running through her brain. *What now? Should she jump to Tuesday's lesson since the students already know about conductors and insulators?* She stops and thinks, "*Maybe they know the words, but do they understand the conceptual difference between the two?*"

Now that you have read Vignette 4.1, if you were Mrs. Thomas, what would you do? For starters, we hope that you would not start a unit without giving students a pre-assessment activity first—but you'll learn more of this later. Take a minute before deciding what you would do, and think about the past 15 or more years that you have been a student. How many times have you been in a class and thought, *Oh no! I know this already!* Do you mentally check out at this point? Of course not! Successful college students still listen attentively and/or participate in the activity, hoping to gain further insight into the concept.

Is there a difference between knowing and understanding? In general language, there is some difference. **Knowing** generally relates to facts, things that can be directly observed, while **understanding** normally involves making sense of things or comprehending them. In educational terms, there is a significant difference. In the chapter on content knowledge for K–12 students in the *National Science Education Standards* (NRC, 1996) there is a direct reference to changing practice. They suggest putting less emphasis on "knowing scientific facts and information" and more emphasis on "understanding scientific concepts and developing abilities of inquiry" (p. 113). Likewise, *A Framework for K–12 Science Education: Practices, Crosscutting Concepts, and Core Ideas* (NRC, 2012) states, "The *Framework* is designed to help realize a vision for education in the sciences and engineering in which students, over multiple years of school, actively engage in scientific and engineering practices and apply crosscutting concepts to **deepen their understanding** of the core ideas in these fields" (pp. 8–9) (emphasis added).

"When students have an understanding of a concept, they can (a) think with it, (b) use it in areas other than that in which they learned it, (c) state it in their own words, (d) find a metaphor or an analogy for it, or (e) build a mental or physical model of it. In other words, the students have made the concept their own. This is what we call conceptual understanding" (Konicek-Moran, & Keeley, 2015, p. 6).

Perhaps you are wondering what instructional strategies best lead to understanding. Exploration 4.1 is designed to encourage you to think deeply about your experience as a learner who learned with understanding.

> Fifth grade teacher, Nicole Bey, explains how she recognizes when her students are learning science with understanding. Which of the student proficiencies related to conceptual understanding suggested by the quote from Konicek-Moran and Keeley do you think Nicole describes?

Which Instructional Strategies Best Lead to Understanding?

EXPLORATION 4.1

During science classes you may have experienced the following instructional activities:

- Defending your thinking in a discussion
- Designing and carrying out an investigation in a small group of your peers
- Filling out a worksheet
- Following the teacher-provided procedure for a hands-on activity
- Listening to a lecture
- Reaching consensus about an explanation through classroom discourse
- Reading a section of the text and answering the related questions at the end of the chapter
- Watching a demonstration conducted by the teacher

Reflection Questions:

1. Which of these actively involve your thinking? Explain your choice(s).
2. Which of these passively involve your thinking? Explain your choice(s).
3. Considering the criteria for conceptual understanding presented prior to this exploration, which of these strategies are most likely to result in your learning with understanding?
4. Do you notice a pattern in your responses? If so, what is it?

Considering the ideas you uncovered in Exploration 4.1 return to the question of what Mrs. Thomas should do. At least one, and probably most, of her students know (are aware of) the terms conductor and insulator. But do they understand (grasp the meaning of, have thorough acquaintance with) the difference between them? It's hard to say. So Mrs. Thomas, after her panicked moment, relaxes and lets her educational training take over, making a slight modification to her lab for the day. Instead of providing each of the groups with the materials that they will test, she instructs each group to look around the room and make a list of at least five objects that they predict to be conductors and at least five objects they predict to be insulators. Groups then justify their choices as they create a class list of predictions to be tested. She instructs the groups to test those objects and informs them to be ready to discuss their findings when the class comes together for a meaning-making discussion, and possibly why some objects may have interacted differently than they predicted. She expects that they will make claims and present evidence to support their claims, and that some of the claims may be accepted by the rest of the class and others may be disputed through polite argumentation. Mrs. Thomas also plans to ask the students if the brightness of the bulb was the same with each conductor and what claim can be made about that phenomenon. These questions will allow her to help the class dive more deeply into the concept being investigated. Her students may even be ready to rank all of the objects in their conductor pile in order of brightness to determine a pattern.

Mrs. Thomas worked to move her students from knowing what insulators and conductors were to understanding the differences between them. When she figured out her students knew (were aware of the factuality of) insulators and conductors, she was able to transform her lesson to help her students understand (grasp the meaning and make sense of) insulators and conductors. Mrs. Thomas was also aware this did not simply imply making the lesson more difficult.

CHECK YOUR UNDERSTANDING 4.1

Click here to gauge your understanding of the concepts in this section.

Constructing Science Learning

You have a strong desire to know how to teach children about science, but before you can learn more about that, you need to remember what you already know about how children learn. When we talk about how children learn science, the most widely accepted view is that children learn through **constructivism**. It is important to remember that *constructivism* is a learning theory, not a teaching method or philosophy. While it should influence how you teach (again, more on this later), it is solely focused on how children learn—or specifically, how they construct their understanding.

The traditional view of learning is that knowledge is discovered through the manipulation of objects or acquired from others when learners listen to what they say. We now accept, however, that learning is more complex. Knowledge cannot be passed directly from a teacher or book to a learner (for example, listening to or reading about someone else's ideas) nor is it simply discovered in the real world. Students can't learn all scientific knowledge and concepts by reading about what others have discovered. Practical experience shows that direct teaching of concepts does not result in student learning beyond the definition level. Students must *construct* new knowledge for themselves.

In the constructivist perspective, new knowledge is always based on the prior or existing knowledge that learners bring to learning situations. Students take in information from many sources, but in building their own knowledge, they connect information to prior knowledge and experiences, organize it, and construct meaning for themselves (Loucks-Horsley et al., 1998). Without an adequate level of prior knowledge, new learning and its transfer to new situations cannot be expected (Bransford, Brown, & Cocking, 1999). What learners already know influences what they attend to, how they organize input, and how they are able to integrate new constructions to expand their knowledge bases.

The NRC document *A Framework for K–12 Science Education: Practices, Crosscutting Concepts, and Core Ideas* (2012) reminds readers that young children are able to reason in a much more sophisticated way than Piaget's developmental stages (preoperational, concrete operational, and formal operational) presumed. The *Framework* is built on the notion of learning as a developmental progression. "It is designed to help children continually construct and revise their knowledge and abilities, starting from their curiosity about what they see around them and their initial conceptions about how the world works" (p. 11).

For each Component Disciplinary Core Idea (DCI), the *Framework* describes what learners should understand about that concept by the end of various grade bands. Reading these progression descriptions can help you as a teacher to determine the depth of knowledge you should aim for at your grade level. Appendix E of the NGSS presents these elements of the DCIs in a matrix. Figure 4.1 shows only part of the matrix for life science ideas.

Notice that the DCI Component Ideas – written as broad statements of understanding -- build on each other from left to right as the grade-level bands are higher. Based on the progression for LS1.A: Structure and Function, would you expect eighth graders to understand that there are organs in their bodies that enable them to digest food? (Certainly, they should have learned about the digestive system in

FIGURE 4.1   **Excerpt of Appendix E: K–8 Life Science Progression**

INCREASING SOPHISTICATION OF STUDENT THINKING

DCI Component Idea	K-2	3-5	6-8
LS1.A Structure and Function	All organisms have external parts that they use to perform daily functions.	Organisms have both internal and external macroscopic structures that allow for growth, survival, behavior, and reproduction.	All living things are made up of cells. In organisms, cells work together to form tissues and organs that are specialized for particular body functions.
LS1.B Growth and Development of Organisms	Parents and offspring often engage in behaviors that help the offspring survive	Reproduction is essential to every kind of organism. Organisms have unique and diverse life cycles.	Animals engage in behaviors that increase the odds of reproduction. An organism's growth is affected by both genetic and environmental factors.

upper elementary.) Based on the progression for LS1.B: Growth and Development of Organisms, at what grade-level band would a unit on butterfly metamorphosis be most appropriate? Why? (Did you select upper elementary since life cycles are mentioned in that column?) Do you see how the ideas developed in the primary grades form the foundation of future learning? Do you now understand the importance of a well-structured science program with clear learning goals in the primary grades?

The *Framework* and the *Next Generation Science Standards* (NGSS) also present progressions for cognitive development related to the other two dimensions of science. Chapter 3 of the *Framework* and Appendix F of the NGSS show how understanding of the Scientific and Engineering Practices is expected to develop. Chapter 4 of the *Framework* and Appendix G of the NGSS show how students' conceptions of the Crosscutting Concepts should grow through their years in school. Remember science learning should no longer just be about learning scientific facts and ideas, but about learning in all three of the dimensions: Practices, Crosscutting Concepts, and Core Ideas.

Contemporary research on child development and brain research related to learning has altered our understanding of the ways in which children progress and what they are able to learn. A child's development depends not only on age but also on experiences—this includes socioeconomic and ethnic backgrounds. Children's conceptual abilities vary greatly within a classroom of same-aged children; therefore, as a teacher, you can design activities to increase students' ability to reason without having to wait for all students to "mature." Activities should be designed to provide structure yet push students to think abstractly and foster higher-order reasoning in students of all ages.

Jirout and Klahr (2011) studied the development of scientific reasoning in children from a psychological perspective. They stressed that instructional methods implemented in a classroom must match the cognitive capacity of those children. Effective science instruction must find a way to balance open-ended instruction with the structure necessary to facilitate learning. The materials, goal setting, physical manipulation of materials by students, design of each experiment, probing questions, explanations, summary, execution of experiments, and observation of outcomes should be clearly defined and uniformly used. Clear and thorough explanations of science in the classroom lead us to substantial advances in science education.

A succinct summary of how these new ideas apply to science teaching appears in the book *Taking Science to School: Learning and Teaching Science in Grades K–8* (NRC, 2007, pp. 2–3):

- Children entering school already have substantial knowledge of the natural world, much of which is implicit.

- What children are capable of at a particular age is the result of a complex interplay among maturation, experience, and instruction. What is developmentally appropriate is not a simple function of age or grade, but rather is largely contingent on their prior opportunities to learn.

- Students' knowledge and experience play a critical role in science learning.
- Race and ethnicity, language, culture, gender, and socio-economic status are among the factors that influence the knowledge and experience children bring to the classroom.
- Students learn science by actively engaging in the Practices of science.
- A range of instructional approaches is necessary as a part of a full development of science proficiency.

The children that you are teaching are not just developing their reasoning skills and growing physically. Their brains are also changing and growing. All of the learning that you are stimulating is actually causing real change in their brains. New learning creates new synapses and neural pathways in the brain. The more these synapses and pathways are used, the more likely they are to become permanent.

As children age, their brains develop with them. At birth, the brain has only a small fraction of the synapses and pathways that will be developed over a lifetime. Several times during childhood, the brain will go into overdrive and produce extra synapses and pathways and then cull the unused pathways. The last major occurrence of this happens during adolescence. Continuous use of the newly developed synapses and pathways prevents them from being lost. You really must exercise your brain to keep it as active as possible! The brain and its function can be kept healthy and active by following many of the same guidelines and suggestions for general healthy living—be active, eat right, be social, sleep well, and eliminate stress.

Constructivism is not hard to grasp, especially since the name of the theory is so closely related to a useful analogy for explaining the theory. *Learning,* as defined by constructivism, is very much like the work done at a construction site. The bricks or boards go together when making a structure. These materials represent bits of knowledge that fit together to create an understanding.

An additional layer to add to this analogy is the construction workers. If you close your eyes and picture a construction site in your head, you will likely include a crew of workers rather than a single person completing all the work (that is, if you can leave aside any jokes about how on most construction sites it appears one person is working while everyone else is watching). The same idea holds for the construction of knowledge and understandings in a child's head. In the school setting, a child is almost never constructing new knowledge and understandings in an isolated, individual setting. In most cases, other children and the teacher are present and adding to the learning. This layer of social interaction with peers and teachers during the learning process is valuable. It is also why the term **social constructivism** is often used in place of simple *constructivism* to best describe the learning that should be taking place in your science classroom.

Vygotsky found that students can learn at higher levels when working in cooperation with others than when working alone (1962). Thus, learning is enhanced when teachers work to establish a shared understanding of a learning task among a **community of learners** (Hogan & Pressley, 1997). According to Brown and Campione (1998):

> A community of learners reflects a classroom ethos different from that found in traditional class-rooms. In the traditional classroom, students are perceived as relatively passive learners who receive wisdom from teachers, textbooks, or other media. In the community of learners classroom, students are encouraged to engage in self-reflective learning and critical inquiry. (p. 153)

One role of a teacher within a community of inquirers is to organize the learning environment to encourage an underlying cooperative culture centered on thinking. Just as communication among scientists is central in the construction of scientific knowledge, communication between students fosters learning by talking among themselves, writing about their ideas, and formally presenting them. Teachers, as part of the classroom community of learners, make students' ideas more meaningful by providing feedback and asking students to clarify, expand, and justify their own emerging conceptions while engaging with the thinking revealed by others. Conversational partnerships with the teacher allow students to build on and use the teacher's thinking strategies to support their efforts to think in more flexible and mature ways. In addition, the give and take among learners in a learning community enables them to scaffold one another's learning. Such discussions are often referred to as *classroom discourse.*

Exploration 4.2 presents a lesson plan for you to analyze in terms of expected prior knowledge, appropriate grouping strategies, and learning outcomes related to knowing and understanding.

▶ Watch this video to see students talking in their small groups about the phenomenon of touching a suspended ping pong ball with a vibrating tuning fork. Then find out why their teacher considers such science discourse to be so important for learning with understanding.

What Is a Switch and How Does It Work?   **EXPLORATION**

4.2

Though this activity does not explicitly state that students should be in groups, keep in mind that practicing and rehearsing their ideas out-loud with others helps learners learn. Given the importance of the social aspect in constructivism, as you read the investigation, think about the point at which it would be natural to group students. Also consider what type of grouping would be most effective for this investigation.

Materials:

- Heavy cardboard
- Brass paper fasteners
- Paperclips
- Electric circuits, each consisting of a D-cell in a battery holder, a flashlight bulb in a bulb holder, and three wires.

Instruction:

Present a familiar phenomenon to the class. Slowly flip the light switch in your classroom on and off several times.

To initiate discourse, ask: What's happening? Which Crosscutting Concepts seem to be obviously related to this phenomenon? (Cause and Effect, Patterns). Why? What questions do you have about this phenomenon? (Display the list[s] of questions generated by the students.)

Add the questions, "What do switches do?" and "How could we make a switch?" if students haven't raised these questions or something similar.

After some discussion about which questions could (and should) be investigated, challenge your students to make an electrical "switch" using a 10-cm by 10-cm piece of corrugated cardboard, two brass paper fasteners, and a paperclip. Encourage and provide necessary scaffolding for the students to identify both the criteria and constraints of this design project. Then urge each student team to build their prototype and test it in a battery-powered circuit. If their prototype does not function as a switch (i.e., meet the criteria), they should rearrange the components of the system until it does.

Then bring the class together for a meaning-making discussion. You could start the whole-class conversation by simply asking: "What did you figure out?"

The children should note that when the switch is closed, a complete circuit is formed and the bulb lights. When the switch is open, the circuit is broken and the bulb does not light. Take time for children to identify and talk about the electrical switches in the classroom.

Reflection Questions:

1. What knowledge and conceptual understanding from Mrs. Thomas's lesson on conductors and insulators would the students be building on for this activity?
2. Is this an activity that should be completed by individuals or in a group? What would be the advantages to having the students do this as a group?
3. What would you expect the students to know after completing this lesson?
4. What would you expect the students to understand after completing this lesson?

 CHECK YOUR UNDERSTANDING 4.2
Click here to gauge your understanding of the concepts in this section.

Instructional Strategies for Deeper Understanding of Science Concepts

At this point, you should be thinking about how kids learn and recognize that social constructivism makes the most sense for explaining how children should experience learning in your science class. Now that you are armed with that knowledge (or is it an understanding?), what are you going to do with it? How is that going to influence how you plan your instruction?

One way the analogy between a physical construction site and building science knowledge and conceptual understanding breaks down is that at a construction site, the first step is usually to clear and level the ground so that construction can begin with a clean, blank space. Children, however, are not clean, blank slates when they come into your classroom. They will inevitably have some prior knowledge. It is important that you as a teacher find out what that prior knowledge is to best inform your instruction.

In the beginning of the chapter, Mrs. Thomas planned a lesson but forgot to check on the prior knowledge of her students. She could have easily prevented her moment of panic in the classroom by pre-assessing the students about conductors. Ideally, Mrs. Thomas would have given students a formative task about conductors and insulators on the Friday before she did her lesson for two reasons. First, it would have let her know how prepared her class was in terms of knowing about and understanding conductors and insulators. Second, it would have the class thinking about conductors and insulators so that on returning to class Monday, students would have an idea of the concepts they would be trying to figure out.

Getting students to think about their prior knowledge of a topic is important. Students may have learned particular knowledge of concepts, principles, and strategies in the past, but fail to access and use this knowledge when necessary. Teachers can use a number of strategies to gain access to prior knowledge—one is finding ways to help students recall what they already know.

Another way to enhance access to prior knowledge is through frequent review in the form of rehearsal. **Rehearsal** is often contrasted with **practice**. *Practice* means to do something over and over again the same way to improve a performance (Ormrod, 2004). What is learned in practice is an item of knowledge or a specific skill applicable in a specific context. *Rehearsal,* however, takes place "when people do something again in similar, but not identical ways to reinforce what they have learned while adding something new" (Lowery, 1998, p. 28). When the focus is on rehearsal rather than just practice, children's knowledge and conceptual understanding is less likely to be bound to specific tasks and more likely to become transferable and useful in a variety of ways (Lowery, 1998).

But where does all of this knowledge and understanding that your students are gaining in your science class go? Well, we could really stretch the construction analogy; if each bit of knowledge or new understanding is like a brick or board, you would expect all of the new bricks and boards to be placed in an orderly fashion. All the bricks and boards about life science form one wing of a building of knowledge and understanding, while all the bricks and boards about physical science form another wing of knowledge and understanding. A better picture of the sum of your knowledge is to think of everything that you know as one giant concept map or schema (think 3D spiderweb). As you may already know, in concept maps, each bit of information can be connected to many other bits of information. This is a good representation of your students' knowledge. The younger they are, the smaller their concept map will be. It is your job as a teacher to help them add to that concept map and stretch it. Simply adding new bubbles of information to the concept map is not all that useful. You need to help your students create bubbles of information that are connected, and connected correctly, in as many ways as possible.

The NSES stressed placing less emphasis on individual areas of science—biology, chemistry, physics, earth science—and more emphasis on learning science concepts in a context that combines the traditional disciplines. This means that each new bubble should have connections outside of a single discipline. In the NGSS, the Crosscutting Concepts have application across all domains of science, so they are a way of linking the different domains of science. "The NRC *Framework* emphasizes that these concepts need to be made explicit for students because they provide an organizational schema for interrelating knowledge from various science fields into a coherent and scientifically based view of the world" (NSTA, 2014).

Take a moment to close your eyes and picture the three-dimensional (more realistic) concept map that is everything you know (you don't even need the special glasses!). Next, place your mind's cursor somewhere on this huge concept web. This is your consciousness, or what you are thinking about in a given moment. Now put yourself in the classroom: Your teacher asks you a question, and you know that the answer is somewhere in your web. You move your cursor across your web to the right answer as quickly as possible, staying on the connected path. If the right answer is only connected in one way, then there is only one correct path for you to arrive at that answer. Ultimately, this will slow you down, and your cursor may get lost. If that correct answer, however, is connected to many other ideas, which are connected to even more ideas, then your cursor can move quickly across the web and access the answer. This is why it is so important to attach each new piece of information to as many existing ideas as possible when adding new information to students' schema.

If you don't know any of the content already existing in their schema, how are you going to attach the new information? Don't worry, we'll return to the construction site. You have likely witnessed a building under construction in which the construction workers place scaffolding to work on different areas and move freely. The scaffolding allows them to reach above what is in place and connect the new materials to the existing structure. This is exactly what you have to do as a teacher—provide support to students so they can push beyond what they already know, add new information, and synthesize the materials into a new, complete structure. This is a cyclical process that occurs each time students engage with new material.

Vygotsky referred to the difference in what children can do with assistance and what they can do on their own as the **zone of proximal development**. For Vygotsky, the goal of instruction is to assist all children to reach their potential as defined by this zone. "What the child can do in cooperation today," he concluded, "he can do alone tomorrow" (p. 104).

Thus, for Vygotsky, instruction needs to be challenging, running ahead of the actual level of knowledge of the learner. If students are to learn with understanding, while instruction runs ahead of their level of knowledge, they will need varying degrees of teacher and peer assistance, or scaffolding. To consider the need for scaffolding in context, read Vignette 4.2

To scaffold the learning process for students, inquiry teachers might provide suggestions, questions, prompts, or hints. They might also guide students to clarify, elaborate, or justify their investigation

> Watch fourth-grade teacher, Glen McKnight, **scaffold student thinking** to test a variable during an investigation. How, specifically, did Mr. McKnight help students set up a meaningful, investigative task?

Vignette 4.2   The First Inquiry Lesson

Casey is a senior in her elementary education program, and she is currently taking a science methods course along with a practicum course that places her in a local fourth-grade classroom twice a week during their science time. Casey held a relatively traditional view about teaching elementary school until this semester. The more she learned about teaching through inquiry and teaching for understanding, however, the more excited she became. She knew that putting students into groups and having them design and create experiments to find answers to real-world questions would be so much more effective than reading sections out of a textbook, lecturing about those sections, and answering questions from a worksheet.

Unfortunately, her cooperating teacher at the local elementary school did not share these beliefs. She had been teaching for 22 years and taught in traditional ways. Her class was neat and orderly, her students well behaved. Due to this compliance, her principal considered her a model teacher in the building. Casey spoke with her several times about what she was learning in her science methods class and the wonders of inquiry-based teaching. Her cooperating teacher, however, seemed indifferent, going so far as to say that those methods wouldn't work in her classroom.

The day was finally approaching for Casey to teach her lesson in the practicum placement. She planned an outstanding 5E inquiry-based lesson (more about this instructional *Framework* is included in Chapter 5) that would place the students in groups and challenge them to think critically; she was excited for this opportunity! Casey was going to give students these materials: beakers, soil, thermometers, plastic wrap, etc. The students were going to design and create a model that would simulate the effects of greenhouse gases. In her mind, each group would decide to place the soil in two beakers with a thermometer. They would then cover one beaker with plastic wrap and leave the second beaker open. Both beakers would be placed under a light or taken outside, weather permitting, and students would take temperature readings for 10 to 15 minutes, finding that the covered beaker, representing greenhouse gases, heated much more quickly.

On the day of her lesson, Casey set the needed materials out, had the students rearrange their desks into small groups instead of rows, and set out the challenge for them to design and create their investigation. Instead of the groups jumping into discussion and laying out a plan of action, most just sat and stared at Casey. Those who didn't stare began to talk to their group members about anything other than science and greenhouse gases. The 40 minutes of science class were some of the most frustrating Casey ever experienced. She found herself running from group to group trying to prod them into thinking of how to set up the experiment. Every time she started to help one group, the others would spin out of control. By the end of the day, none of the groups recorded more than five minutes of data before cleaning up. There was no time for discussion or explanations of what they did and how it related to greenhouse gases. Casey left on the verge of tears. Her cooperating teacher simply said, "This is why *I* do not do inquiry."

procedures and findings. Teachers might even choose to provide necessary terms, concepts, and principles to students through formal, direct instruction. Textbooks, videos, the internet, and other means might also be used to help students develop knowledge needed to support understanding.

Just as scaffolds in a building project are designed to be taken down when the building walls are strong, scaffolding support in teaching should be gradually removed or "faded" (Ormrod, 2004) as students gain facility with science knowledge and inquiry processes.

So what went wrong for Casey? Did her science methods professor lie to her about the wonders of inquiry? Should she revert to teaching by lecture? No. This issue is almost entirely related to scaffolding. Casey attempted to build something on the fifth floor of a building that was only one story high. Earlier you learned about the skills and components needed to do inquiry. The students in Casey's class had none of these skills. The closest they had come to doing an inquiry-based laboratory activity was following some very prescriptive directions on a handout. They didn't have the experiences of designing and carrying out an experiment on their own. They didn't have the experience of working with a group, taking roles, and talking through problems.

Casey did have a solid lesson planned. She was prepared to help her students not just know about the greenhouse effect, but she was also going to help them understand how it works. Her lesson ideas did indeed have the necessary elements to develop this understanding. She was going to challenge them with a question on the greenhouse effect, and students would have worked in teams to design an experiment. The students would have collected data, leading them to the correct conclusions about the causes of the greenhouse effect. All of these ideas were excellent for moving the students to understanding the greenhouse effect, but the students simply were not ready. Basically, she had not taught them a procedure for how to design an investigation and how to come up with a testable scientific question.

Teaching through inquiry has to be established from the beginning of the year. Students need to be coached on what to do when placed into groups, how to assign roles, and how to constructively talk through problems and issues. Students need practice in setting up simple experiments and designing procedures that either have a control or only change a single variable. If this had been Casey's classroom from the beginning of the year and she had created the classroom environment where all of these things were practiced expectations, then her lesson incorporating the desired well-planned elements of group work, experimental design, and sharing of ideas to reach a conclusion would have been successful!

Table 4.1 summarizes many of the ideas discussed so far in the chapter. It offers strategies to help build your students' schemas in a strong and organized manner.

TABLE 4.1 Strategies for Enhancing Learning with Understanding and Why They Work

Teaching Actions That Enhance Learning	Description and Rationale
Provide for access to prior knowledge.	• Students take in information from many sources. In building new knowledge and conceptual understanding, they connect information to relevant *prior knowledge*, organize their developing knowledge and understanding, and construct meaning for themselves. • Failure to access prior knowledge and conceptual understanding interferes with new learning. Reminding students of what they already know and understand is one way to provide access to prior knowledge.
Provide for the transfer of new knowledge to new situations.	• Using new knowledge and conceptual understanding in new situations enhances its transferability and access. • Constructed knowledge is refined, expanded, and elaborated as learners transfer it to new situations in trying to understand the world. • Teachers should provide many opportunities for students to transfer their developing knowledge and understanding to new situations.
Provide for knowledge organization. (Build connections between the bubbles!)	• The size of cognitive structures, the number of connections between items in the structures, and the organization and richness of the connections are important for accessing prior knowledge and conceptual understanding, processing information, constructing meanings, and solving problems. • Using and teaching students to use graphic organizers, such as spider maps, Venn diagrams, and concept maps, promotes organization of knowledge and understanding.

(Table 4.1 continued)

Teaching Actions That Enhance Learning	Description and Rationale
Provide scaffolding support.	• Scaffolding the learning process for students effectively reduces the complexity of knowledge construction to help build understanding and enables students to learn at higher levels. • In scaffolding, teachers might provide suggestions, questions, prompts, or hints; guide students to clarify, elaborate, or justify their investigation procedures and findings; or provide necessary terms, concepts, and principles to students through formal, direct instruction or the use of textbooks, videos, the Internet, and other means.
Build learning communities; utilize social constructivism.	• Being a member of a collaborative community allows students to cooperatively work and think together and to scaffold one another's learning. • You can support learning communities by encouraging cooperative learning and teaching students how to work cooperatively. • Arranging for students to investigate in small groups is another way to promote learning communities.

Table 4.1 provides a summary of general instructional strategies that help students develop deep understanding of science concepts and recommendations for teacher Practices. These same strategies should be used regardless of the content being taught. Additionally, for science instruction, you need to think about what instructional strategies to include to make your science lessons effective.

From a synthesis of the research on effective science instruction, Banilower, Cohen, Pasley, and Weiss (2010) provide another perspective on how to lead students to a deeper understanding of science. They define science understanding as understanding how the world works, how to create knowledge, and how life in the world creates a working understanding. They identified *elements of effective science instruction*, listed in Table 4.2, that should be used to help students internalize the big ideas of science.

TABLE 4.2   Elements of Effective Science Instruction

Element of Effective Science Instruction	Description
Eliciting prior understanding	• Students bring ideas that either help or hinder their learning. • Provide opportunities to confront and formulate new ideas in the light of evidence. • Reflect on how ideas have evolved.
Intellectual engagement with relevant science phenomena	• Provide engaging experiences for students with scientific ideas (not just materials). • Activities must connect directly to learning goals. • Students must understand the purpose of the lesson.
Use of evidence to critique claims	• Instruction must provide numerous opportunities to make assertions and inferences that are evidence based. • Evidence must also be used to evaluate other students' claims.
Sense-making	• Provide opportunities for students to make sense of the ideas they have been formulating to draw suitable conclusions. • Opportunities may take the form of closure activities, reflection, metacognition, or application in new situations.

Motivation	• There are two types of motivation:
	  • Extrinsic: deadlines, competitions, tests, grades.
	  • Intrinsic: curiosity, personal interests/experiences, interest in resolving discrepant events or cognitive conflict.
	• However well-designed the instruction, students are unlikely to learn if they do not have a desire to do so. Instruction needs to "hook" students by addressing something they have wondered about, or can be induced to wonder about, possibly, in a real-world context.

☑ **CHECK YOUR UNDERSTANDING 4.3**
Click here to gauge your understanding of the concepts in this section.

Alternative Conceptions about Science

Even before they enter school, young children have figured out many things about how the world works based on their everyday experiences. Through play and routine activities, they probably already expect a dropped object to fall down, a heavy object to sink in water, an ice cube in a glass of water to disappear over time, to see their shadow when they are outside on a sunny day, etc. Such ideas have been called *preconceived notions*, *preconceptions*, or *naïve conceptions* to denote student understanding prior to learning. The terms **alternative conceptions** and **misconceptions**, often used synonymously, also refer to non-scientific conceptions or partially correct ideas held by learners even after they have been taught about the concepts in school. Some researchers prefer the term *alternative conception* since it sounds less negative than *misconception*.

Over the K-8 school years, the changes in children's scientific knowledge and understanding are neither uniform or universal. Multiple factors impact the conceptions students hold, including; cognitive development during the first five years of life, educational experiences in and outside of school, and explicit instruction. Over this period there tend to be improvements in children's scientific knowledge and understanding, but the rates of conceptual change vary among individual learners and learning contexts. Not all conceptual change results in understanding that matches accepted scientific explanations. These alternative concepts (misconceptions) can resolve themselves with time and experience or be quite persistent and resistant to change. It is important to realize that simply growing older does not ensure conceptual change resulting in increased knowledge and understanding (NRC, 2007).

Taking Science to School (NRC, 2007) suggests, "misconceptions should be seen as attempts by children to make sense of the world around them, often building on more correct notions that also coexist with the misconceptions. . . . they can be seen as necessary conceptual stepping stones on a path toward more accurate knowledge" (p. 98).

It is important to access students' prior knowledge so you can build on their early conceptions, but keep in mind that their naïve notions may or may not align with correct science ideas. When they hold misconceptions it is important that you as the teacher help the student understand why their conception is not correct and help the student rebuild that idea correctly. However, you need not feel committed to changing that "wrong" idea as quickly as possible. Remember, telling students that their alternative conceptions are wrong, won't make them change their minds (though they might remember what you told them so they can get a good score on the test). Instead, create a safe environment in the classroom to encourage dialogue and argumentation, listen as carefully as possible, and question students to find out where the ideas originated and how deeply they are committed to them. Showing students how interested we are in how they think encourages them to consider their own thinking—to engage in metacognition (Konicek-Moran & Keeley, 2015).

Some of these misconceptions are held onto very tightly (picture the misconception with many connections in their concept map of knowledge) and will need careful deconstructing and rebuilding. Consider how difficult is for some children to let go of the idea of Santa, even with strong evidence that he is a myth.

In addition to discovering what your students know by accessing their prior knowledge, it is a good idea to be familiar with general misconceptions that have been identified through research that are held by many students. Table 4.3 presents some examples of common misconceptions followed by the correct scientific conception.

Teaching children with no prior knowledge of a topic is challenging because you have no foundation from which to build. Teaching children with correct prior knowledge and conceptual understanding is relatively easy because the proper building blocks are already there. Teaching children with misconceptions, however, is by far the most difficult. For conceptual change to occur, students must be challenged to recognize that their personal theories and explanations are in conflict with accepted scientific views. As Roth (1991) explained, "They need to be convinced that their own theories are inadequate, incomplete, or inconsistent with experimental evidence, and that the scientific explanations provide a more convincing alternative to their own notions" (p. 49).

TABLE 4.3   Common Misconceptions and Correct Scientific Ideas

STEM Content Area	Common Misconceptions	Scientific Conceptions
Biology	• Animals are living because they move, but plants are nonliving.	• Living things are composed of cells that carry out life processes such as the extraction of energy from nutrients and energy release. • Plants and animals are living organisms, composed of living cells.
Physical Science	• Anything that pours is a liquid, including powders. • When liquids evaporate, they just disappear. • Electric current is used up in bulbs, and there is less current going back to a battery than coming out of it. • Light rays move out from the eye in order to illuminate objects. • Loudness and pitch are the same thing. • Suction causes liquids to be pulled upward in a soda straw.	• Powders are solids, composed of individual solid particles. • In evaporation, molecules in a liquid break free from molecular bonds and go into the surrounding air and are in the gaseous state. • Electric current is the same throughout a continuous series circuit. • Light from other sources reflects off objects to our eyes, enabling us to see them. • Loudness and pitch are different variables associated with sound. • When the air pressure at the top of a soda straw is reduced, atmospheric pressure pushes liquid up into the straw.
Earth and Space Science	• Planet Earth is flat, like a pancake. • The phases of the moon are caused by Earth's shadow falling on the moon. • Seasons are caused by the changing distance of the Earth from the sun (closer in the summer, more distant in the winter).	• Planet Earth is spherical, as is shown by lunar eclipses and photographs from space. • The sun illuminates half of the moon at all times. Phases of the moon result from the way light from the sun reflects off the moon to the Earth. • We experience seasons on Earth because different parts of the Earth receive more energy from the sun at different times of the year. The position of the sun in the sky affects the concentration of its energy striking parts of Earth's surface. When it is summer in the northern hemisphere, it is winter in the southern hemisphere because the angle of the sun's rays impacting the surface differs.
Engineering, Technology, and Applications of Science	• Only things requiring electricity are technology.	• Technology is broadly defined as the application of scientific knowledge for practical purposes.

Convincing children that their conceptions are incorrect is not a result of "telling" them what is right or threatening them. To change their beliefs, as Roth proposed, students need repeated opportunities to struggle with the inconsistencies between their own ideas and scientific explanations, to reorganize their ways of thinking, and to make appropriate links between their own ideas and scientific concepts. In other words, students must experience what is conceptually correct to truly understand it. These approaches are part of conceptual change strategies which require careful planning to support the student thinking needed to revise their strongly held conceptual ideas.

Anderson (1987) proposed an instructional model for **conceptual change**. For conceptual change to occur, he suggests that teachers must do the following:

- Recognize students' current misconceptions
- Help students become dissatisfied with them
- Present scientific conceptions as alternative to their preconceptions
- Enable students to apply and integrate the new concepts into their thinking

▶ A first-grade teacher conducts a demonstration for her class on one of the **properties of air**. Why do some students struggle with understanding why water does not go into the cup? What might convince them that air takes up space and keeps water from entering the cup until the cup is tipped?

An inquiry approach to science is especially compatible with this *conceptual change strategy*. As described in Exploration 4.3, inquiry teachers have many opportunities to interact with students, observe and listen to their thoughts, and recognize their conceptions that are incomplete, inadequate, and in need of further development. By understanding students' misconceptions and naïve theories, teachers are better prepared to "structure learning experiences that assist the reconstruction of core concepts. New constructions can then be applied to different situations and tested against other conceptions of the world" (Trowbridge & Bybee, 1996, p. 214).

EXPLORATION
4.3

Moon Phases

The causes of the visible Moon phases are one of the most misunderstood concepts in science on all academic levels. In the *Next Generation Science Standards*, the concept of Moon phases is address in middle school. There are several explanations for the phenomenon of Moon phases that are routinely offered when people (from elementary students through adults) are asked: "What do you think causes the phases of the Moon?" Of course for this question to make any sense at all, they must know that the Moon doesn't always look the same in Earth's sky and that the lit-up part of the Moon visible from Earth's surface is called a *phase*. A few of the more common answers to the question include:

- The Earth's shadow falls on the Moon.
- Different parts of the Moon's surface are giving off light.
- Visible part of the lit-up Moon's surface changes.
- Clouds cover part of the Moon.

A. Which response would you give?

B. Either individually or working with others who selected the same response as you, create a visual model to explain your thinking. You may draw a sketch, make a three-dimensional model or demonstrate with balls and a light source to make your thinking visible.

C. Use your model to try to convince others with different ideas that your idea about the cause of moon phases is correct; then those others will try to convince you that their ideas are actually true.

D. Watch Video 4.5. Prior to this scene, these students observed and kept records about the moon for about a month and have been working with this model with scaffolding from their teacher for about 15 minutes.

▶ This video shows a fifth grade class during a lesson about the cause of Moon phases. Which part(s) of Anderson's conceptual change model is/are represented in this clip?

Reflection Questions:

1. At the beginning of this exploration, why did you select the response you did to the question: "What do you think causes the phases of the Moon?" Would you have given the same response when you were a child? What would your answer have been then? Why?

2. What would you expect learners who held a misconception about the cause of Moon phases to uncover as they try to construct a model that supports their thinking and convince others that their idea is correct?

3. How do to the actions suggested in Exploration 4.3 relate to the parts of Anderson's model for conceptual change (described earlier in this chapter) and to the Conceptual Change Model described in Table 4.4?

4. After completing all steps (A-D) of Exploration 4.3, how would you explain the cause of Moon phases?

TABLE 4.4 **Conceptual Change Model**

Stage One: Students *become aware of their own preconceptions* about a concept by thinking about it and making predictions (*committing to an outcome*) before any activity or investigation begins.

Stage Two: Students *reveal their ideas and beliefs* by sharing them, initially in small groups and then with the entire class.

Stage Three: Students *confront their ideas and beliefs* by making observations, gathering data, testing their ideas, and then discussing them in small groups.

Stage Four: Students work toward *resolving conflicts* (if any) between their ideas (based on the revealed preconceptions and class discussion) and their observations, thereby *accommodating the new concepts* and revising their thinking to align with a scientific or mathematical explanation.

Stage Five: Students *extend the concept* by trying to *make connections* between the concept learned in the classroom and other situations, including their daily lives.

Stage Six: Students are encouraged to *go beyond*, pursuing additional questions and problems related to the concept.

Sources: Based on the research of Posner, Strike, Hewson, & Gertzog (1982) and Strike and Posner (1985) and revised from the work provided in *Targeting Students' Science Misconceptions: Physical Science Concepts Using the Conceptual Change Model* (Stepans, 2003).

 CHECK YOUR UNDERSTANDING 4.4

Click here to gauge your understanding of the concepts in this section.

 ## CHAPTER SUMMARY

Knowing vs. Understanding

The terms *knowing* and *understanding* both relate to what has been learned. Knowing often deals with a fact that is memorized; understanding is more complex, richer, usually dealing with a concept and idea that can be explained and applied. A student might know that another word for sweat is perspiration, but not understand that sweating, and the evaporation of perspiration, helps maintain a safe internal body temperature in humans; indicating that they know some information—vocabulary—but don't understand the concept of perspiration as it relates to the regulation of body temperature.

Constructing Science Learning

Students learn science through a process of constructing their own knowledge and understanding. This construction process can be aided by working in a group where students make their thinking visible. Student knowledge and understandings can be thought of as a giant concept map, or schema. Each new idea needs to be correctly connected to as many other ideas as possible to make the idea more available to the learner. Learning progressions in the NRC *Framework* and the NGSS illustrate how complexity of understanding builds through the grade levels.

Instructional Strategies for Deeper Understanding of Science Concepts

Contemporary learning theorists emphasize the importance of enhancing learning through providing students ways to access prior knowledge, promoting the organization of knowledge, providing opportunities for transfer and scaffolding support, using formative assessment of student understanding, and establishing communities of inquirers. To scaffold student learning, do the following: set challenging and interesting learning tasks; simplify tasks for students that need more support and then withdraw the scaffolding; facilitate student conversation in different settings; ask meaningful questions; lead students to clarify, elaborate, or justify their responses; and supply necessary information, concepts, and principles for learners.

Alternative Conceptions about Science

Students often come to science classes with pervasive misconceptions about how the world works. If students are to learn with understanding, teachers must help them recognize and deal with their incomplete and naive ideas and conceptions. Students should confront their misconceptions and find inconsistencies within them—this leads to the construction of scientific understandings. Using conceptual change models, the student learning experiences makes student ideas explicit, confronts their misconceptions and provides sense-making opportunities for student to change their ideas to scientifically-based explanations of phenomena.

DISCUSSION QUESTIONS

1. What is something that you know but don't understand? How would you go about developing understanding of that concept?

2. What is another analogy, besides the construction site, that could be used for constructivism?

3. How do you incorporate the social aspect of learning in your classroom in a manner that still promotes a positive classroom environment?

4. What is a misconception that you held onto for a long time? How did you change your conception to the correct scientific explanation?

PROFESSIONAL PRACTICES ACTIVITIES

1. Read the Next Generation Science Standards for the grade or grade-level band that you hope to teach. Pick one Disciplinary Core Idea and describe a lesson that would help your students know and understand the concept.

2. Examine Appendix E: Progressions Within the *Next Generation Science Standards*, on the NGSS website to see how a concept or Disciplinary Core Idea develops for students over the years.

3. Pick a Disciplinary Core Idea from the *Next Generation Science Standards* for your grade or grade-level band. With this concept in the center, draw a concept map (your schema around the concept) of all the related ideas.

4. Identify some children's literature books that perpetuate science misconceptions. Design an activity for your class to use the book to change the students' understanding to the scientific conception.

Engaging in Inquiry-Based Instruction and Using the 5E Model

Pearson Education, Inc.

LEARNING GOALS

After reading this chapter, you should understand that . . .

1. Inquiry-based instruction features Practices needed to ask and try to answer a scientific question.

2. Research says that inquiry-based instruction refers to the diverse ways in which students study the natural world and propose explanations based on the evidence derived from their work.

3. The essential features of classroom inquiry include engagement with scientific questions, collect evidence, formulate explanations, evaluate explanations, and communicate and justify explanations. The levels of inquiry vary depending upon the degree to which students make the decisions or teachers scaffold and guide the inquiry.

4. Instructional models that support inquiry-based instruction in science differ from the models used to design lessons in other content areas.

5. The 5E model of science instruction includes five phases where students are intellectually engaged in learning about science phenomena that leads to explanations based on evidence.

6. Each phase of the 5E model (engage, explore, explain, elaborate, and evaluate) of science instruction supports science learning.

Before reading this chapter, take this quick survey. Use the following scales to quantify your current feelings.

How do you feel about teaching science through inquiry in your future classroom?

	1	2	3	4	5	
Unprepared						Prepared
Inexperienced						Experienced
Afraid						Eager
Skeptical						Confident
Clueless						Well informed

Talk with a colleague about your responses and why you feel this way.

After studying this chapter, you can retake the survey to see how your feelings about teaching using inquiry-based instruction have changed.

Good teachers select instructional approaches and specific teaching strategies based on what they want their students to learn. In the language of NGSS, *three-dimensional teaching and learning* is an inquiry approach that involves students in using Scientific and Engineering Practices as they learn Disciplinary Core Ideas and consider them in the context of Crosscutting Concepts; this is a powerful teaching strategy that you should master. This chapter is designed to help you learn how, why, and when to use this important teaching strategy.

Inquiry-Based Instruction

Consider Exploration 5.1. Talk about your response and reasoning with a colleague if you have a chance. If you've ever examined science textbooks or instructional modules, units, or software (or even just looked at ads for them in teacher magazines), you may have noticed that many of these products are identified as **inquiry-based**. The sheer number of references to this quality probably makes it obvious that inquiry-based instructional materials are certainly what you need to teach science effectively. But you may still

What Do You Think About Inquiry-Based Instruction?

Several teachers are discussing their understanding of inquiry-based science instruction.

Meg says, "For my students to be involved in inquiry-based instruction, they must develop their own questions to investigate."

Irene says, "Inquiry-based instruction is the only way we should teach science in elementary and middle school."

Maria says, "Since my class is often doing hands-on activities, I'm using inquiry-based teaching methods."

Ashley says, "When I use inquiry-based instructional methods, the order of the lessons in the unit doesn't matter much."

Reflection Questions:

1. With which of these teachers do you agree? Why?
2. With which of these teachers do you disagree? Why?

wonder: *What is inquiry-based instruction anyway? As a new teacher, why do I need to know about it? Are all of these products really inquiry-based as they claim to be?*

The multifaceted nature of inquiry in science education includes: inquiry as a process of finding out, inquiry as a Practice to learn about, and inquiry as an instructional method (NRC, 1996). This chapter focuses on the third facet, which is sometimes referred to as inquiry-based teaching and learning.

Inquiry is central to the Science Teaching Standards presented in the *National Science Education Standards* (NRC, 1996). Teaching Standard A, which focuses on planning, begins, "Teachers of science plan an *inquiry-based* science program" (p. 30). Science Teaching Standard B, which focuses on instruction, states:

To guide and facilitate learning, teachers should

- focus and support *inquiries* while interacting with students;

- orchestrate discourse among students about scientific ideas;

- challenge students to accept and share responsibility for their own learning;

- recognize and respond to student diversity and encourage all students to participate fully in science learning; and

- encourage and model the skills of scientific *inquiry,* as well as the curiosity, openness to new ideas and data, and skepticism that characterize science. (p. 32, *emphasis added*)

As a result of these teaching standards, inquiry-based instruction became a strongly recommended science teaching strategy during the past two decades. However, during that time many interpretations of the nature of inquiry-based instruction emerged. Some clarifying statements about inquiry-based teaching and learning include:

- Inquiry is just one of many varied instructional strategies that should be used when teaching science.

- Learners need not generate and pursue their own questions in order to be involved in true inquiry.

- Teaching through inquiry requires a skilled teacher aware of the nature of inquiry-based instruction. Even the use of the best instructional materials does not ensure effective learning.

- Inquiry-based teaching and learning requires more than student involvement in hands-on activities.

- Inquiry-based instruction must occur in the context of science content. (NRC, 2000)

Inquiry-based instructional approaches help students actively develop their understanding of science through engagement with both scientific knowledge and with reasoning and thinking skills. In inquiry-based instruction, students build conceptual understandings, investigation skills, and understandings of the nature of science through inquiry procedures that mirror methods used by scientists. During inquiry-based instruction, learners interact with and describe objects and events, ask questions, construct explanations based on evidence, test those explanations against current scientific knowledge, and communicate their ideas to others. They identify their assumptions, use critical and logical thinking, argue using evidence and

Listen to second grade teacher, Nancy Michael, who has been trained in inquiry-based teaching, talk about how she makes inquiry work in her classroom.

consider alternative explanations. Ideally, as inquirers, learners assume major responsibility for constructing their own knowledge and understanding.

During inquiry-based instruction, teachers share in and facilitate student inquiry, guiding children as they ask questions, conduct investigations, and use observational evidence and scientific knowledge to develop explanations and answer their questions. The teacher's role in an inquiry-based learning environment is less involved with direct teaching and more involved with modeling, guiding, facilitating, and continually assessing student work (NRC, 2000). To effectively implement inquiry-based instruction in the classroom, teachers must thoroughly understand the nature of scientific inquiry, understand the concepts and relationships of the science being taught, and effectively use inquiry-based teaching strategies (Bybee, 2000). For a traditional lesson, the teacher might be "the sage on the stage" while for an inquiry-based lesson, the teacher should be "a guide on the side." Teachers who effectively use inquiry-based instructional approaches realize that they must be very well prepared, but that it is fine to tell their class, "I don't know. How could we find out?"

Not all inquiry-based instruction looks alike. This makes it challenging to define. To compound the problem, the terms *inquiry* and *inquiry-based* are sometimes used inappropriately to describe certain types of teaching and learning; for example, when curriculum developers claim that their materials are inquiry-based just because they include hands-on activities for learners to do. But don't worry, a more specific explanation of the nature of inquiry-based instruction and how to recognize it appears later in this chapter, in the section titled: "The Essential Features of Classroom Inquiry".

A myth emerged that all science lessons should be inquiry-based. This was never the intention of the *National Science Education Standards* (NRC, 1996). The emphasis on inquiry was not meant to recommend that a single approach to science teaching be used to develop knowledge, understanding, and abilities described in the NSES content standards. Inquiry-based learning should be included regularly because inquiry is the approach scientists use.

As you embark on your teaching career, it is likely that you will see a shift from inquiry-based instructional materials to new resources more broadly focused on the three dimensions introduced in *A Framework for K-12 Science Education*: *Scientific and Engineering Practices, Crosscutting Concepts, and Disciplinary Core Ideas* (NRC, 2012). But please realize that in the context of recent science reform efforts, scientific inquiry is considered a particularly important form of scientific practice (Michaels, Shouse, & Schweingruber, 2008).

✓ CHECK YOUR UNDERSTANDING 5.1

Click here to gauge your understanding of the concepts in this section.

Research on Inquiry-Based Instruction

So how do we know whether an inquiry-based instructional approach is appropriate and better than another approach, such as lecturing, using a textbook, viewing a video, or involving students in isolated hands-on activities? Of course, we consider the educational research!

A key question asked in many research studies on learning and instruction in science has been: *What is the relative effectiveness of different approaches to teaching science?* Haury (1993), the National Research Council (NRC, 2001), and Duschl and colleagues (NRC, 2007) have reviewed a large number of research studies on the effectiveness of different approaches to teaching science. Although definitions of inquiry vary from study to study, research data indicate that inquiry instruction is effective in fostering problem solving, creativity, and independent learning and in improving reasoning, observing, and logical analysis. Research also shows that students exposed to inquiry methods in science typically perform better than their peers in more traditional classes on measures of general science achievement, process skills, analytical skills, and related skills found in language arts and mathematics. Studies consistently found that, when compared with students in more traditional, textbook-oriented science programs, students engaged in inquiry activities found science more exciting and interesting, had greater feelings of success, and had a more positive view of science and scientists. In many studies, data on **cognitive** (related to knowing or understanding) and **affective** (related to attitudes) variables support the advantages of inquiry-based instruction over other methods. Yet many important things that students learn through an inquiry approach are challenging to quantify, such as how well learners ask investigable questions, place a priority on evidence, and use observable data, knowledge, and clear reasoning to arrive at explanations and evaluate claims.

There are also studies that indicate that the advantages of inquiry-based instruction also extend to special student populations. For example, English language learners (ELLs) and students with learning disabilities can successfully engage in inquiry and learn science concepts through inquiry-based instruction (NRC, 2007).

There are researchers who are not proponents of the inquiry-based approach. An article by Kirschner, Sweller, and Clark (2006) titled, "Why Minimal Guidance During Instruction Does Not Work: An Analysis of the Failure of Constructivist, Discovery, Problem-Based, Experiential and Inquiry-Based Teaching" asserts that for novice learners, instructional approaches that emphasize guidance of the learning process are more effective and efficient than unguided or minimally guided approaches. The researchers' claims are based on knowledge of cognitive architecture of the human brain, expert–novice differences, and cognitive load (total amount of effort being used in the working memory during instruction), as well as from empirical studies over 50 years. Throughout their article, the diversity of definitions applied over the years to inquiry-based instruction becomes amazingly obvious. Their findings support the importance of teacher guidance during instruction, but they fail to recognize that such scaffolding is a vital part of inquiry-based instruction when it is done correctly.

The results of another study, Klahr and Nigam (2004), may seem at first glance to challenge the appropriateness of inquiry-based instruction. These researchers compared two models of instruction, but used names for the models that did not really align with conventional science education terminology. **Discovery instruction** was defined in terms of a very open inquiry approach, with essentially no teacher guidance or scaffolding during the lesson. **Direct instruction**, as defined in this study, involved considerable hands-on activities, with appropriate teacher scaffolding which would be a **guided inquiry** approach. It was quite different than Hunter's lesson design, described later in this chapter as an example of a direct teaching instructional model.

In Klahr and Nigam's study, two groups of students were involved in designing and constructing controlled investigations related to balls rolling down ramps. One group received discovery instruction; the other group received direct instruction, as defined by the researchers. Tests assessed *near transfer* (students' abilities to design experiments related to the balls and ramps problem, but requiring the testing of different variables) and *far transfer* (students' abilities to design totally new experiments). On average, the direct instruction group scored significantly better on measures of both near and far transfer than the discovery instruction group. Results of the study by Klahr and Nigam strongly favored direct instruction (with guided inquiry incorporating hands-on activities) over discovery (open inquiry with no teacher input) for both near and far transfer (Klahr and Nigam, 2004). It is important to recognize that the term—direct instruction—in their study, had a meaning that differed from the usual interpretation in educational research.

The critical importance of teacher input in instruction was supported by this study. In the discovery approach tested, there was little if any scaffolding and no "direct instruction" on how to design and set up controlled investigations. In contrast, teacher scaffolding, including teacher instruction about controlled experiments and experimental design, was a critical part of the researchers' "direct instruction" approach.

The discovery condition in the Klahr and Nigam study omitted the critically important 5E phases of explain and elaborate. In contrast, the direct instruction approach emphasized the importance of teaching explicit concepts and skill in the explain phase of the model. Thus, the study by Klahr and Nigam indirectly demonstrates the value of the 5E approach in learning and instruction that you will read about later in this chapter.

 CHECK YOUR UNDERSTANDING 5.2
Click here to gauge your understanding of the concepts in this section.

Essential Features of Classroom Inquiry

Four years after the release of the *National Science Education Standards* (NRC, 1996), a companion work, *Inquiry and the National Science Education Standards: A Guide for Teaching and Learning* (NRC, 2000), was published in an effort to clarify the nature of inquiry and inquiry-based instruction. When faced with the task of defining *inquiry-based instruction*, the authors encountered a challenge similar to one you might face when trying to write a definition of a beautiful day. Rather than defining, you might develop a list of descriptors of a beautiful day, such that, if all were present, everyone would agree that "beautiful-dayness" was achieved. This list might include the following essential elements of a beautiful day:

- The temperature is comfortable for most people wearing standard business clothing.
- The wind is intermittently blowing at less than 4 mph.
- The relative humidity is such that people's skin neither feels clammy nor parched.
- No more than 25 percent of the vivid blue sky is filled with interesting cloud formations.

For the day to be considered fully beautiful, all of those essential elements must be in place.

So rather than creating a definition of *inquiry*, the NRC identified five Essential Features of Classroom Inquiry:

- Learners engage in scientifically oriented questions.
- Learners give priority to evidence, which allows them to develop and evaluate explanations that address scientifically oriented questions.
- Learners formulate explanations from evidence to address scientifically oriented questions.
- Learners evaluate their explanations in light of alternative explanations, particularly those reflecting scientific understanding.
- Learners communicate and justify their proposed explanations.

Classroom inquiry is happening if during an instructional segment (i.e., a lesson, a unit, a module) students are involved in each of these essential features. An inquiry lesson does not need to begin and end in a single class period. In fact, inquiry lessons often extend over several days or even several weeks. The involvement with each of the essential features of inquiry happens on and off during instruction, rather than continuously throughout the lesson, unit, or module. There are times when learners develop scientific questions or think about ways to find answers to them. During parts of the inquiry experience, learners use evidence, rather than beliefs or hunches, to come up with explanations related to their questions, then they consider how their explanations hold up to those of others. At other times, learners talk with each other about their ideas or write reports to communicate their findings.

Though it might seem redundant, the term **full inquiry** is used when all five essential features of classroom inquiry occur in a lesson. Some educators would argue that unless all five of the essential features are present, the lesson is not an inquiry lesson at all. But others say that if one or more of the essential elements are omitted from the instructional segment, the lesson or unit should be called **partial inquiry**. For example, a partial inquiry lesson might focus on helping students master just one of the essential features, such as learning the difference between investigable and non-investigable questions. These disagreements about appropriate terminology just confirm the variety of meanings inquiry-based instruction has.

Exploration 5.2 provides an opportunity for you to distinguish between full and partial inquiry.

EXPLORATION

5.2

Recognizing a Full Inquiry Lesson

Read Vignettes 5.1 and 5.2. Look for the essential features of classroom inquiry in each of them. Consider how they differ in terms of learning outcomes. Then, after jotting down your responses to the reflection questions, discuss your ideas with a colleague.

Reflection Questions:

1. Which of the vignettes describes a full inquiry lesson? What is your evidence?
2. Which of the vignettes describes a partial inquiry lesson? What is your evidence?
3. Which lesson better promotes conceptual understanding? Explain your thinking.
4. How could you modify the partial inquiry lesson to incorporate all the features of classroom inquiry?

Vignette 5.1   Melting and Methods

Mrs. Day held up a box of crayons. When she opened it in front of the class, they were surprised. Instead of 64 pointed wax rods, the box contained a multicolored wax block with some cylinders of paper sticking out. As she peeled away the outside cover of the box, with a look of shock on her face she asked the class, "What happened to my crayons?"

What happened here? What evidence supports your claim?

"They melted," "They got too hot," "You left them in the sun," the students suggested.

Mrs. Day said, "You all seem to agree that somehow they melted, but are they melted now?" A chorus of no's filled the classroom. "So what do you think happened?" Mrs. Day asked. As children responded, Mrs. Day encouraged them to explain their evidence for their ideas. Then Mrs. Day commented, "So most of you seem to agree that somehow the crayons melted and then became solid again. Can you think of some other things that might melt and then get solid again?" The students' brainstormed list included ice cream, ice, butter, bacon fat, wax, etc.

While opening a bag of chocolate chips, Mrs. Day announced, "Today you'll have a chance to explore ways to melt chocolate and turn it back into a solid again. I've put out thermometers, oven mitts, tongs, warming trays, hair dryers, heat lamps, containers for hot or cold water from the faucets, and a supply of ice for you to use. I want you to work with your partner to find ways to melt the chocolate and then have it turn back into a solid. Remember to be very careful with anything that is hot, so that you don't get burned (I.e., go over the safe operation of the equipment). Make predictions

before trying each approach and record your findings in your journal in as much detail as possible. We'll come back together in about 30 minutes to talk about your discoveries."

As the students worked, their teacher walked around noticing the methods they used, monitoring for safe Practice, and reminding pairs of students to record all of their findings. About 25 minutes into the activity, she told the class to clean up their workspace and return to their seats.

Mrs. Day encouraged the students to share what they did and what they found out. There was some disagreement over the meaning of *melted,* so she helped the class develop an operational definition for the term, so that they were all using it to mean the same thing. After comparing methods and results, the class reached consensus that for chocolate to melt it must be warmed, and that it must cool to become solid again.

"Now I want you and your partner to decide on a question about melting that you want to investigate tomorrow. I suggest you use the procedure for asking an investigable question that we Practiced last week. You may pick the substance you investigate. The same heat sources and ice buckets will be available for you to use. Give me your questions before you leave today, so I can look them over tonight. You'll have until the end of class on Thursday to complete your investigations. Then, on Friday, you'll present your findings at our scientific conference about melting. Here is a rubric that explains my expectations for your presentation."

The next day, the student pairs got their questions back, either approved or with some suggestions they needed to address before starting their investigation planning. Questions included: *Does shortening from a can melt faster than butter? How does the size and shape of the chocolate piece affect the time it takes to melt? How does location in the classroom affect how much water falls from an ice cube in one minute?* Before students got their materials, they had to show their procedures to Mrs. Day and explain to her how the data they planned to collect helped them answer their question. Soon, the class was involved in their investigations. Some students revised their questions and methods during their work but were sure to note those changes in their notebooks.

On Friday, the classroom walls were covered with posters displaying questions, pictures, and descriptions of procedures used, and charts and graphs of the data that students then used to determine their evidence. As each pair of students presented their investigations and findings, the rest of the class listened with interest and asked insightful questions of the presenters. Mrs. Day also listened carefully as she used the rubric that the class was given earlier to guide her evaluation of their understanding of the concept of melting and the inquiry processes they used.

Vignette 5.2   Studying the Solar System

"Your homework last night was to read Chapter 7 in your science book and look up the meanings of these words," Mr. Wu told the class, while pointing at four terms (*solar system, sun, planet,* and *orbit*) on the board. "We'll use these words and information from the chapter in today's lesson. By this afternoon, you should be able to name the planets in our solar system in order from the sun."

To get ready for this lesson, Mr. Wu had made a sign with the name and a downloaded image from NASA.gov for each solar system body he planned to discuss.

"Class, please look at the drawing of the solar system in your textbook. We'll use it to learn how the sun and the planets' orbits are arranged."

"José, where is the sun on this drawing?" Mr. Wu asked.

"The sun is in the middle of the planets' circles," replied José.

"That's right. The sun is in the center of the solar system, and the planets orbit around it." Then Mr. Wu taped the "Sun" sign at the far left side of the board.

"Now, Ann, what planet is nearest to the sun? You may look at the drawing in your book to help you decide."

"Mercury?" Ann replied tentatively.

"That's right!" said Mr. Wu as he taped the "Mercury" sign directly below the word *My* in a sentence that read: My very educated mother just served us noodles. "Jim, what planet is the second farthest from the sun?"

"Venus." Jim answered as Mr. Wu posted the "Venus" sign beneath the word *very*.

Questioning continued in this manner until all eight planet signs were in order on the board.

"Did anyone notice the hint I wrote on the board to help you figure out the planets' order?" the teacher asked the class.

Quizzical looks flashed across the students' faces. Finally, Max raised his hand and said, "Do you mean that weird sentence that is written up there?"

"Yes, how could that be a hint?" responded Mr. Wu.

Shannon said, "Oh, I see. The first letters match."

"That's right. The first letter of each word in the sentence is the same as the first letter of the planet's name," explained Mr. Wu while pointing to pairs of letters. Then he took down the planet signs and randomly placed one on each of the eight tables in the classroom. "Work with your tablemates to find at least three facts about the planet on the sign you received. You have five minutes to find your facts!" Students began to flip the pages of their books to find the information they needed.

When the five minutes was up, Mr. Wu announced, "Now, let's Practice the planet order while we learn some facts! One person from each table bring your sign and stand by the board. Line up to show your planet's place in the solar system." Eight students with planet signs sorted themselves into an ordered line with assistance from their classmates. A few of the students glanced up at the sentence of the board for a hint. Once their order was correct, Mr. Wu asked the standing students to say the name of their planet and tell one fact about it.

Ed said, "Mercury has no atmosphere."

Jesse said, "Venus has thick clouds covering its surface."

Maya said, "Earth's oceans cover two-thirds of its surface."

Tyler said, "Scientist have found visual evidence of flowing water on Mars."

Nick said, "Galileo used a telescope to discover Jupiter's four largest moons."

Irma said, "Saturn is the second largest planet in our solar system."

Chris said, "Uranus is classified as a gas giant."

Tanisha said, "When passing Neptune, the space probe, *Voyager 2*, sent back pictures showing a faint ring system around Neptune and a 'dark spot' in its atmosphere."

Mr. Wu noticed the variety and sophistication in the types of facts presented, and then he told the standing students to give their signs to one of their tablemates. Another set of students found their places in the solar system and shared planet facts. Eventually all students took a turn at being a planet.

During music class, Mr. Wu typed in the URL for "Schoolhouse Rock" and selected "Interplanet Janet." After listening to the song several times, the class began to sing along.

Later, Mr. Wu distributed activity sheets, glue, scissors, and crayons to the class and explained, "Use the facts beneath each picture to help you identify each solar system object. Write its name in the blank. Then cut apart the sections. Glue them in the proper order on the sentence strip. Be sure to put the sun at the far left end of the strip. If you have time, color the pictures realistically."

Mr. Wu assessed his students' mastery of the order of the planets and their general characteristics by checking for proper identification and order of the planets on their sentence strips. Based on neatness, he selected five of the correctly completed strips to display on the bulletin board.

According to the *National Science Education Standards* (NRC, 1996) all elementary and middle school students should have opportunities to learn science in the context of inquiry-based activities. As a teacher of science at any grade level from pre-K through 8, you should strive to involve your students in full inquiries several times each year, as well as involving them in many partial inquiry lessons. Please note, this does not mean that every daily lesson should be an inquiry lesson! Some things, such as teaching eighth graders how to safely light a Bunsen burner, are just not appropriate to teach through an inquiry approach.

Teachers should serve as "facilitators of learning" in inquiry-based classrooms, guiding students through the inquiry process. The amount of direction, guidance, or scaffolding by the teacher can (and probably should) vary during an inquiry lesson. When planning and carrying out an inquiry lesson, it is very important to consider how much scaffolding your students will need to successfully reach the learning goals. Some teachers hold the misconception that teaching through an inquiry-based lesson/investigation means letting the students take over the classroom. Instead, good inquiry-based instruction requires careful planning and constant monitoring and adequate teacher direction so that learners aren't lost and confused, but are supported just enough to enhance their skills and understanding. As a result, most teachers have found that starting with scaffolded or guided, full inquiries is a good place to start.

Table 5.1 presents variations on the teacher-directed/learner-directed spectrum for each of the essential features of classroom inquiry. Notice that the columns showing the variations of instruction change from very learner centered on the left to very teacher centered on the right. The arrows at the bottom of the table show that the amount of learner direction is inversely related to the amount of teacher or material direction; that is, for a given feature, when there is a lot of teacher direction, there is little student direction, and vice versa.

TABLE 5.1   **Essential Features of Classroom Inquiry and Their Variations**

Essential Feature	Variations			
	1	**2**	**3**	**4**
1. Learner **engages** in scientifically oriented questions.	Learner poses a question.	Learner selects among questions, poses new questions.	Learner sharpens or clarifies question provided by teacher, materials, or other source.	Learner engages in question provided by teacher, materials, or other source.
2. Learner gives priority to **evidence** in responding to questions.	Learner determines what constitutes evidence and collects it.	Learner directed to collect certain data.	Learner given data and asked to analyze.	Learner given data and told how to analyze.
3. Learner formulates **explanations** from evidence.	Learner formulates explanations after summarizing evidence.	Learner guided in process of formulating explanations from evidence.	Learner given possible ways to use evidence to formulate explanations.	Learner provided with evidence and told how to use evidence to formulate explanations.
4. Learner connects **explanations** to scientific knowledge.	Learner independently examines other resources and forms the links to explanations.	Learner directed toward areas and sources of scientific knowledge.	Learner given possible connections.	
5. Learner **communicates** and justifies explanations.	Learner forms reasonable and logical argument to communicate explanations.	Learner coached in development of communication.	Learner provided broad guidelines to use and sharpen communication.	Learner given steps and procedures for communication.

<More . . . . Learner Self-Direction . . . . Less
<Less . . . . Direction from Teacher or Material . . . . .More

Source: NRC, 2000, p. 29.

Exploration 5.3 provides you with the opportunity to apply the information presented in Table 5.1 to Vignettes 5.1 and 5.2. Please take the time to complete Exploration 5.3 before reading on.

EXPLORATION

5.3

Considering Variations in Learner and Teacher Direction

Look back at the vignette you identified in Exploration 5.2 as describing a full inquiry lesson. Consider the information presented in Table 5.1; then decide which variation in each row best describes the extent of learner and teacher direction for each of the essential features. Discuss your ideas and the evidence that supports them with a colleague.

Reflection Questions:

1. Which variation in each row did you select for each of the essential features of classroom inquiry?
2. What are some possible reasons that the teacher of this lesson decided to use these levels of direction for this inquiry lesson?

So far in this section you've been introduced to the five essential features of classroom inquiry, tried to identify them in vignettes of lessons, differentiated between full and partial inquiry, and learned that the teacher- or student-centeredness of each essential feature may vary independently. Perhaps now is the time to revisit the essential features of classroom inquiry in more detail through the lens of scaffolded instruction.

1. *Learners engage in scientifically oriented questions*

    Throughout an inquiry lesson, students should be asking questions about objects, organisms, and events in the real world. An early stage in the inquiry process is the formulation of questions for investigation. There will be times when you should formulate the question or problem for the inquiry because of time constraints or the need to focus on a specific learning outcome. Ideally, students would generate questions from their own real-world experiences. Many students, however, will need your assistance in learning to form questions that can be investigated scientifically. To enhance your students' competence with this over time, you should select the left-most variation that you think would meet the needs of you and your class.

2. *Learners give priority to evidence in responding to questions*

    In inquiry approaches, students use or devise ways to gather evidence to answer their questions. With varying degrees of assistance, shown in the second row of Table 5.1, students determine what data might be relevant and decide how to collect the data, how to represent it, how to organize it in useful ways, and how to analyze it. Students may use a variety of investigational approaches to gather evidence, including descriptive, classificatory, and experimental investigations, as well as library and online research. You may need to introduce your class to ways to verify the accuracy of their evidence, such as checking measurements, doing multiple trials, gathering different kinds of data related to the same phenomenon, and recognizing reliable sources.

3. *Learners formulate explanations from evidence*

    In science, explanations must be based on reason and consistent with the observations and evidence collected. Scientific explanations provide causes for effects and establish relationships based on evidence. This feature of inquiry provides opportunities, through reflection and discourse, for students to build new ideas on their current knowledge, since explanations are ways to learn what is unfamiliar by relating what is observed to what is already known. When your students are just beginning to create explanations, you may need to use the most teacher-directed variation on this feature of inquiry. (See the far right cell in the third row of Table 5.1.) As their understanding of how explanations are formulated increases, you should select variations with less teacher direction and more student direction. This gradual movement toward the left side of the table should result in your students becoming more independent in their scientific reasoning. Since new evidence may challenge the validity of old explanations, you can also help students develop a deep understanding of the tentative nature of science ideas.

4. *Learners connect explanations to scientific knowledge*

    In inquiry instruction, it is important that students make connections between their results and accepted scientific knowledge. You can help them do this by asking the class questions such as these: Does the evidence support the explanations provided in the textbook? Can other reasonable explanations be derived based on our evidence? Do we need to change our explanation now that we have this additional evidence? The variation on this feature of inquiry that you select as a teacher should depend on the complexity of the concept and the experience and abilities of the class.

5. *Learners communicate and justify explanations*

Children love to talk about their experiences. Inquiry-based science provides a rich context for all students to develop language and thought (Rowe, 1973), including students with special needs and English language learners (ELLs). Communicating and justifying scientific procedures, collecting, recording, reporting, and reflecting on evidence, and generating interpretations focus the students on *what* they know, *how* they know it, and *how* their knowledge connects to the knowledge of other people, to other subjects, and to the world beyond the classroom (NRC, 1996).

Inquiry provides an appropriate context for students to communicate like scientists, in enough detail that their results can be reproduced. With appropriate scaffolding, over time your students will learn to clearly articulate their research questions, procedures, evidence, and proposed explanations. By selecting the appropriate variation on this feature of classroom inquiry, you can challenge your class as they practice science communication skills, but not overwhelm them.

Having students share their observations and explanations through classroom discourse gives others opportunities to ask questions, examine evidence, identify faulty reasoning, point out statements that go beyond the evidence, and suggest other explanations for the same observations. With your guidance, they can learn to resolve contradictions and solidify an empirically based argument.

The complex process of tending to the five essential features of inquiry while teaching a classroom of students can be a daunting task. However, Inquiry-based instruction can be considerably simplified through use of the 5E model of instruction, which will be introduced later in this chapter.

 CHECK YOUR UNDERSTANDING 5.3
Click here to gauge your understanding of the concepts in this section.

Levels of Inquiry

Inquiry in the classroom can take many forms. Inquiry-based instruction can be highly directed by the teacher so that students proceed toward known outcomes, or it can encompass free-ranging explorations of unexplained phenomena. The form that inquiry teaching takes depends to a great extent on the goals of the lesson, and because of the diversity of instructional goals, a range of inquiries, from highly structured to very open-ended, are appropriate in science classrooms (NRC, 2000).

The idea of **levels of inquiry** has been around for nearly 50 years. One current model, presented in Table 5.2, identifies four levels based on how much information is provided to students (Bell, Smetana, & Binns, 2005).

TABLE 5.2 **Levels of Inquiry**

Name of Level	Description	Problem/ Question Provided by:	Procedures Provided by:	Results Provided by:
Open Inquiry	Student-developed procedure used to answer an investigable question developed by one or more students	Student	Student	Student
Guided Inquiry	Procedure prescribed by teacher or instructional materials to answer an investigable question also given by the teacher or instructional materials	Teacher	Student	Student
Structured Inquiry	Cookbook lab to answer an investigable question with procedure specified by the teacher or instructional materials	Teacher	Teacher	Student
Confirmation Lab	Cookbook lab (procedure specified by teacher or instructional materials) to verify results that are known in advance	Teacher	Teacher	Teacher

FIGURE 5.1   Graphic Representation of Levels of Inquiry

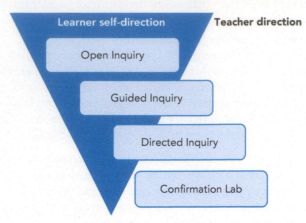

The levels of inquiry can also be displayed as a continuum, from very learner-directed to very teacher- or instructional materials–directed. This sequence is illustrated in Figure 5.1. In this graphic representation, the blue triangle represents learner self-direction in the lesson, while the surrounding white areas represent teacher direction. The labels are placed to show the relative proportion of direction at each of the levels.

Open inquiry requires the least amount of teacher intervention and is student led. Students often work in groups and plan all phases of the investigations, determining the question or problem, determining the procedures, and finding and communicating results. Because students develop the question to be investigated at this level of inquiry, open inquiry is sometimes called **student-initiated inquiry** (Vasquez, 2008). This is the purest form of inquiry conducted in science classrooms; most like the work of scientists. Some educators believe that open inquiry is the only form of inquiry worthy of the title of inquiry. Open inquiry requires the most scientific reasoning and highest level of cognitive demand from students. As shown in Table 5.2, in open inquiry, students provide the question or problem to be investigated and the methods of investigation, and they determine the results and conclusions. This highest level of classroom inquiry is an opportunity for students to really act like scientists, but their teachers should still be actively involved in the learning process, providing appropriate scaffolding as needed (Banchi & Bell, 2008). If an open inquiry lesson were analyzed considering the essential features of classroom inquiry (Table 5.1), most of its descriptors would be on the left side of the variations chart. The instructions given for an open inquiry of pendulums might be: "Now that you've seen different pendulums and other things that swing, what questions do you have about them? Select one of your questions that is investigable or write a new question that is investigable, then show it to me for approval. Then work with your group to plan and write your procedure. Once I've approved your procedure, carry out your investigation and find your results. Then prepare a five-minute presentation to share your work with your classmates."

When looking at science lessons or units in journals or online, you may notice that sometimes the term *full inquiry* is used to refer to *open inquiry* as it is defined here. Just remember that full inquiry describes a lesson that includes all five of the essential features of classroom inquiry, while open inquiry more specifically describes a full inquiry lesson that is very student directed.

In **guided inquiry**, students are given the opportunity to plan their own investigations and write their own procedures as well as being responsible for determining results. At this level of inquiry, only the question or problem is still provided by the teacher, as shown in Table 5.2. Because students are responsible for so much more in guided inquiry than they are in the lower levels of inquiry, they tend to be more successful when they have had many opportunities to learn and Practice different ways to plan experiments and record data. Though learners design their own procedures at this level of inquiry, the teacher's role in instruction is still that of active facilitator. Students will need encouragement and guidance as to whether their plans make sense (Banchi & Bell, 2008). The instructions given for a guided inquiry of pendulums might be: "Write a procedure for an experiment that would help you answer the question, 'Which variable (length, mass, or release height) has the greatest effect on the frequency of a pendulum?' Once I've approved your procedure, you may complete your investigation." To prepare students to write procedures for guided inquiry, students frequently engage in preliminary observation inquiries with set procedures to learn a testing protocol, use of equipment or to gather sufficient information from which to have the class or teacher generate the testable question(s).

Structured inquiry, sometimes known as **directed inquiry**, is commonly seen in science classrooms in the form of laboratory exercises. The teacher sets up the inquiry by giving the research question or problem, along with the procedures the students should follow to find the results themselves. Look at how this level is represented in Table 5.2 and Figure 5.1. If a structured inquiry lesson were analyzed considering the essential features of classroom inquiry (Table 5.1), most of its descriptors would be on the right side of the table. The instructions given for a structured inquiry of pendulums might be: "Follow the procedures given on the lab sheet to find out which variable (length, mass, or release height) has the greatest effect on the frequency of a pendulum."

Confirmation activities are entirely teacher- or instructional material–directed. These are the labs that are typically completed to verify what has already been taught in the textbook or through lecture. As shown in Figure 5.1, there is no student direction in confirmation activities. In a confirmation activity, the teacher or teaching material selected by the teacher provides the research question (if there is one), the procedure students are expected to follow, and the expected results, as illustrated in Table 5.2. Though confirmation activities are "hands-on" for the students, they are not really "minds-on." Many science educators do not consider confirmation activities inquiry at all! The instructions given for a confirmation activity about pendulums might be: "How does the pendulum's length affect its swinging frequency? Follow the procedure given on the lab sheet to prove that the shorter the pendulum, the faster it swings back and forth."

You might be wondering which level of inquiry effectively helps students develop understanding and apply that learning to new situations. The general consensus is that any form of inquiry can be useful to students when taught appropriately and well. You will need to decide which level of inquiry is the one that is appropriate for your class, or if you are differentiating instruction, for small groups within your class. Your understanding of your students' inquiry abilities should inform your decision about which level of inquiry to use. If you find a guided inquiry lesson that you want to use, but your class is still unable to write usable procedures in small groups, modify the lesson to make it more structured. You could simply change it to a structured inquiry, by giving the students the procedure. Then to enhance their procedure-writing abilities, you could lead a class discussion about that procedure and what is good about it. Or you could lead the class in a collaborative writing exercise, so that all the children could contribute ideas as you support their organization and style. Over the course of the school year you should keep track of the different inquiries you provide and vary the opportunities for your students. Even when you scaffold the experiences for students, eventually you will want to withdraw your support as students become more self-directed when engaged with inquiry-based investigations.

Teachers and classrooms new to inquiry often begin with structured inquiry activities and transition to more open inquiry activities. Moving gradually from structured classrooms to open inquiry classroom environments is often less overwhelming. Radical changes can be frustrating and upsetting to some students, particularly because inquiry-based classrooms are typically more student-centered. Students in inquiry-based settings are more actively involved in their discovery and subsequently more responsible for their learning. Teachers using inquiry-based instruction play more of a "facilitator of learning" role than teachers in traditional settings where the teacher tells students about science ideas and explains science phenomena. Teachers and students may need practice to get comfortable with learning experiences that require less guidance and fewer teacher interventions (The Access Center).

If your goal is to model your inquiry instruction after the practice of professional scientists, remember that while they are involved in open inquiry, they do not work alone. Most scientists experience quite a bit of guidance, direction, and structure from their colleagues, their company or institution, and the government. So when you plan a structured or guided inquiry lesson for your class, don't feel that they aren't really being scientists! However, please don't use this reasoning as an excuse to avoid the richness of open inquiry when it is appropriate. To do so would rob your students of the joy of following their curiosity from the creation of a question to an evidence-based answer.

CHECK YOUR UNDERSTANDING 5.4

Click here to gauge your understanding of the concepts in this section.

Instructional Models and How to Select One

Before diving into this section, please take the time to do Exploration 5.4

EXPLORATION

5.4

Does the Order of Learning Experiences Matter?

Your cooperating teacher asked you to design a lesson for her seventh-grade class. The lesson, about dissolving, is part of their unit on physical changes. She wants her students to *understand* that mass is conserved in physical changes and that dissolving is an example of a physical change. You found many lesson segments you might include in your lesson plan. They appear in Figure 5.2 below. Select the lesson segments you want to include and put them in an order that will help students understand the concept being developed. You do not need to include all of the lesson segments.

Reflection Questions

1. Why did you select the lesson segments that you did?
2. Why did you order the lesson segments the way you did?
3. Explain why the order of your lesson segments matters.

FIGURE 5.2   **Lesson Segments**

Find out what students already know about dissolving.

Have students look up the definition of dissolving in the glossary.

Ask the class to read the chapter in their textbook about solutions.

Demonstrate what happens when salt is poured into a clear beaker with water.

Ask the class what other questions they have about the idea of dissolving.

Give the class clear containers, a balance, salt, and water. Let them explore with these materials.

Ask the class to give examples of dissolving in their everyday lives.

Place a clear container of water on the overhead projector. Turn on the projector and have the students look at the screen. Encourage students to observe what happens when you pour in a tablespoon of sugar and then stir the liquid.

Have students complete the following writing prompt: What factors do you think affect the rate of dissolving when you put salt in water? How could you find out?

Work with the group to answer your questions about dissolving.

You just used your experience and intuition to plan the order of instruction in a lesson, but there are research-based formats that can assist in your lesson planning. You can use organizational structures known as models of instruction or **instructional models**. Novice teachers often use instructional models as templates for lesson planning. Experienced teachers apply instructional models without having to refer to them. Just as with any procedure you teach to students, it takes 20-24 experiences with a procedure like an instructional model before it becomes routine. So with practice, you and your students will get there.

Instructional models involve some arrangement of phases, steps, actions, or decision points for teaching and learning. Instructional models may be appropriate for lesson, unit, and/or program planning. Different instructional models in science build on different points of view about the nature of inquiry, processes of science, scientific knowledge and understanding, and goals of science learning. They also incorporate different principles from research on learning and development. Good instructional models are based on learning theories that are accepted at the time of the model's development. Instructional models, like science itself, are tentative. When new evidence of how students learn is discovered, instructional models are modified in response to the new theories of learning.

There are many things to consider when selecting an instructional model, such as: the local curriculum, accepted school or district instructional strategies, professional learning community decisions, and your personal preferences (Bell & Shouse, 2015). When planning and delivering instruction, you cannot just import an instructional model, follow prescribed procedures, and expect students to attain understanding of complex subject matter. Your use of a model must reflect the viewpoints and principles on which it is based (Brown & Campione, 1994). Before selecting an instructional model, you must first know what learning outcomes you expect. For example, when introducing basic skills or teaching facts for recall, direct instruction models, such as Madeline Hunter's lesson design that was popular in the 1980's, are particularly useful. They are appropriate models to use when teaching about math algorithms, grammar rules, operation of equipment, etc.

The desired learning outcomes in science are often quite different than those in other subjects. The goals of science instruction emphasized in the *National Science Education Standards* were conceptual understandings in science, ability to carry out scientific inquiries, and understandings about the nature of science in scientific inquiry (NRC, 1996). These proficiencies are also reflected in most current state science standards.

The goals of science instruction emphasized by the *Next Generation Science Standards* (NGSS) involve three-dimensional teaching and learning, through integrated understanding of Science and Engineering Practices, Crosscutting Concepts, and Disciplinary Core Ideas. There are multiple Practice-focused instructional models that can be productively used to implement the NGSS learning goals including: modified inquiry kit instruction, challenge-based instruction, the 5E (and 7E) instructional model, project-based instruction, place-based instruction, etc. (Bell & Shouse, 2015).

When you plan a lesson that has a goal of understanding science concepts, it is important to use an instructional model designed for that purpose. The 5E model of instruction is a good example of an adaptable teaching and learning sequence designed to help students understand scientific explanations in the context of inquiry and three-dimensional teaching and learning. For this reason, we have chosen to emphasize the 5E instructional model for science instruction in this text.

 CHECK YOUR UNDERSTANDING 5.5

Click here to gauge your understanding of the concepts in this section.

The 5E Model of Science Instruction

The **5E instructional model** is a series of instructional steps designed to result in students learning science concepts with understanding. It is a useful tool for planning units and lessons that support inquiry-based learning in the classroom. The 5E model consists of five teaching phases: *engage, explore, explain, elaborate,* and *evaluate.* So, its name is actually quite logical! Details about the instructional functions of each phase are presented later in this chapter.

The 5E model also facilitates the implementation of the research-based factors that influence learning with understanding, including accessing prior knowledge (at the engage phase), scaffolding (at every phase), building learning communities (in preparation for lessons and throughout the 5E lesson phases), transfer (especially at the elaborate phase), and continual assessment (at every phase).

Hear directly from Dr. Bybee as he answers questions about science education and the 5E instructional model. https://www.youtube.com/watch?v=boAnWI3vu3Y

This video clip describes the use of the 5E instructional model in a free unit, titled Hot Wheels Speedometry, developed for fourth grade by Mattel. You can download the lesson plans and find additional information at https://www.youtube.com/watch?v=W_xZrRWwe_g

The 5E model was developed by Dr. Rodger Bybee for the Biological Sciences Curriculum Study (BSCS) during the 1980s. Since that time, BSCS has used the 5E model as the organizing structure for the science programs it has published for elementary, middle, and high school use.

Currently, the 5E model is a widely accepted instructional model for inquiry-based instruction when conceptual understanding is the desired learning outcome. You'll find the 5E model used to sequence instruction in various science curriculum projects, textbooks, journal articles presenting lessons or units, and even state-developed curriculum-embedded tasks. We've even used it to organize most of the lesson plans in this book.

The 5E model aligns well with the aims of the *Next Generation Science Standards* (Bell & Shouse, 2015; Bybee, 2013, 2014, 2015). This instructional model, which takes students through the phases of engagement, exploration, explanation, elaboration, and evaluation in order to facilitate conceptual change, enables the inclusion of Scientific and Engineering Practices in most of its phases and is designed to focus on sense-making during the explain phase (Bell & Shouse, 2015).

Teaching models with goals similar to the 5E model are not new. In fact, the 5E model is an expansion of an earlier model of inquiry-based science instruction, known as the Learning Cycle, developed in the 1960s by Atkin and Karplus for the Science Curriculum Improvement Study (SCIS) program. This classic inquiry-based science instructional model had only three phases of instruction:

- *Exploration*, when learners are involved in self-directed, unstructured exploration
- *Invention*, when new, integrating concepts, previously invented by scientists, are introduced, often formally by a teacher
- *Discovery*, when learners construct new understandings by applying their discovered and acquired knowledge to new situations (Kratochvil & Crawford, 1971)

These phases were later renamed *exploration, term introduction,* and *concept application.*

The three phases of the SCIS learning cycle evolved into the middle three Es in the 5E model as shown in Table 5.3. The 5E model added an initial phase, *engage,* in response to findings in cognitive science related to the importance of eliciting prior understandings and getting students interested in and thinking about the concepts being developed. It also added a final phase, *evaluate,* in response to the importance of both formative and summative assessment in the learning process.

Though the 5E model is still widely used, an expanded model known as the 7E model was proposed by Dr. Arthur Eisenkraft in 2003. He thought it was important to ensure that instructors include all crucial elements for learning in their lessons. So he split the *engage* phase of the 5E model into two phases—*elicit* and *engage*—to ensure that teachers elicited learners' prior knowledge *and* engaged students in the learning. He also expanded the last two phases of the 5E model (*elaborate* and *evaluate*) to three phases—*elaborate, evaluate,* and *extend*—in the 7E model. These modifications, illustrated in Table 5.3, emphasize the importance of transfer of learning (Eisenkraft, 2003).

The BSCS 5E model continues to impact teaching and learning around the world. In 2009, the Department of Education for the State of Victoria in Australia launched the e^5 *Instructional Model* as a reference

TABLE 5.3 Comparison of Several Instructional Models That Develop Science Conceptual Understanding

Learning Cycle	5E Model	7E Model
		Elicit
	Engage	Engage
Exploration	Explore	Explore
Invention (Term Introduction)	Explain	Explain
Discovery (Concept Application)	Elaborate	Elaborate
	Evaluate	Evaluate
		Extend

Source: Eisenkraft, 2003.

point for high-quality teacher practice that engages students in intellectually demanding work. The BSCS 5E model was used as the starting point for the development of the e^5 *Instructional Model*.

There are various graphical representations of the 5E model based on subtly different interpretations of the flow of its phases. Figure 5.3 illustrates these.

Notice that the order of the phases of the 5E model is the same in representations A and B shown in Figure 5.3. In both cases, the phases follow in the same order: engage, explore, explain, elaborate, and evaluate. The order of the phases is an important research-based feature of the model, because the sequence of instructional phases matters! The sequence supports conceptual change.

Consider Representation A. It shows the original conception of the model as a sequence of instructional phases with a distinct beginning and end. This representation presents the instructional sequence for a stand-alone lesson or isolated unit designed to teach about a phenomena linked to a specific concept. The teacher starts the lesson by engaging and pre-assessing the learners, provides time for exploration, facilitates sharing and discussing of explanations, encourages application of the new learning in the elaboration phase, and then evaluates (assesses) learning in the final phase.

Notice that Representation B shows a cycle of phases. It better illustrates science learning building on previous experiences and one lesson or unit leading into another. This model suggests that after a concept is developed during one cycle through the phases, another concept, often related to the previous concept, is then developed during another cycle through the phases, and so forth.

Look at Representation C. It illustrates that evaluation of learning need not only happen at the end of a 5E lesson. Summative assessment should happen during the final phase of the model as a basis for evaluating the students' conceptual understanding, use of inquiry abilities, and understandings of the nature of science and scientific inquiry, but formative assessment should be continuous throughout instruction

Hear from Australian educators who use an elementary science curriculum called Primary Connections. Their units are organized according to the 5E instructional model. https://www.youtube.com/watch?v=OSo5R3sDXAc

FIGURE 5.3 **Various Representations of the 5E Model**

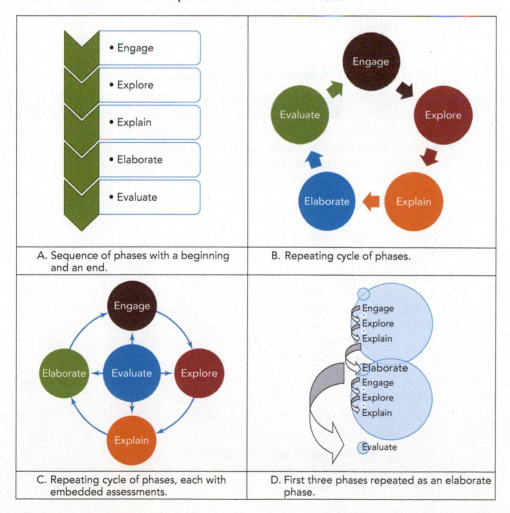

A. Sequence of phases with a beginning and an end.

B. Repeating cycle of phases.

C. Repeating cycle of phases, each with embedded assessments.

D. First three phases repeated as an elaborate phase.

See the Australian students and teachers as they use the 5E model in their classrooms.https://www.youtube.com/watch?v=v7-C_5rBh1Q

activity to obtain information for improving learning and instruction. Details about what assessment looks like at each phase appear later in this chapter.

Study Representation D, which shows a sequence of lessons within a 5E unit. Each individual activity involves the first three phases in the 5E model—engage, explore, and explain. Thus, explanation is implemented within each activity, rather than letting the data from exploration accumulate across different activities before the explain phase is introduced. Basically the elaboration is a second set of the first three phases that require the transfer/application of previously learned ideas to new situations or develop additional concepts, principles, and explanations. The diagram could be expanded downward to include more elaborates (with embedded engage, explore, and explain) before the final evaluation.

By now you probably realize that interpretation and application of the 5E model varies. The important thing to remember is that the order of instruction matters. A lesson plan that includes the headings of Engage, Explore, Explain, Elaborate, and Evaluate in that order might be a 5E lesson, but only if the activities in each phase carry out the intended function of that phase. Sometimes a template is completed incorrectly because the writer does not understand the intent of the phases. You might also find a lesson that claims to follow the 5E format, but the phases are not in the proper sequential order (e.g., the explain phase comes before the explore phase). Remember that though all of the headings for the segments of the lesson start with the letter "e," it's not necessarily a 5E lesson.

 CHECK YOUR UNDERSTANDING 5.6

Click here to gauge your understanding of the concepts in this section.

How Each Phase of the 5E Model of Science Instruction Supports Science Learning

After watching this video clip of Nancy Michael's second grade class, use the information in Table 5.4 to help you identify which phase of her 5E lesson is shown. Give evidence to support your claim.

TABLE 5.4   **The Phases of the 5E Model of Instruction and Their Functions**

Phase	Functions
Engage	• Promote learners' curiosity about and interest in the topic of study. • Involve learners with the expected learning outcomes of the lesson. • Elicit learners' prior knowledge and understanding about the concept. • Make connections between past and present learning activities.
Explore	• Provide learners with common experiences related to phenomena or the topic of study. • Offer learners time to apply their current concepts and skills, try out ideas, address possibilities, and pose new questions. • Allow learners to design and conduct preliminary investigations and collect data.
Explain	• Focus learners' attention on important aspects of their experiences in prior phases. • Provide opportunities for learners to share their findings from the exploration phase and discuss their developing understanding of the concept being studied. • Enable teachers to directly introduce a concept, process, or skill. • Guide learners to develop deeper understanding of concepts through strategic explanations by teachers or instructional materials.
Elaborate	• Enable learners to apply their new learning through additional activities and/or use it to answer new questions or solve innovative problems. • Challenge, deepen, broaden, and extend learners' knowledge, conceptual understanding, and skills.
Evaluate	• Encourage learners to self-assess their learning. • Provide opportunities for teachers to evaluate student progress toward achieving desired learning outcomes.

Source: Adapted from Bybee et al., 2006.

To practice recognizing the phases of a 5E lesson, please complete Exploration 5.5 before reading further.

Finding the Phases

EXPLORATION

5.5

Look over the instructional plan "Lighting the Bulb" and read Vignette 5.3, about the science lesson, "Let There Be Light!." that follows. Work individually or with a colleague to try to identify the parts of the lesson that correspond with each of the phases of the 5E model. Use the information in Table 5.4 to help you complete this task.

Reflection Questions:

1. What happens during the engage phase of this lesson? How do these activities relate to the function of the engage phase?
2. What happens during the explore phase of this lesson? How do these activities relate to the function of the explore phase?
3. What happens during the explain phase of this lesson? How do these activities relate to the function of the explain phase?
4. What happens during the elaborate phase of this lesson? How do these activities relate to the function of the elaborate phase?
5. What happens during the evaluate phase of this lesson? How do these activities relate to the function of the evaluate phase?
6. Is the lesson "Let There Be Light!" a good example of a 5E lesson? Why or why not?

Instructional Plan: Lighting the Bulb

Grade 4

Working toward:

NGSS Performance Expectation: 4-PS3-2 Make observations to provide evidence that energy can be transferred from place to place by sound, light, heat, and electric currents.

Learning Target Electric currents can flow through closed circuits and cause a light bulb to light.

Success Criteria The students will:

Light a bulb using just one wire and one D cell and be able to explain why this occurs.

Differentiate between visual representations of open and closed circuits.

Planned sequence of teaching:

1. Tell the elevator story. Remember to use props in tote bag.
2. Ask questions to encourage student discussion of predictions and ideas.
3. Present question they will investigate.
4. Tell them who they will work with and what materials they will need.
5. Explain expected notebook entries.
6. Distribute materials.
7. Circulate through the class and facilitate collaborative student work.
8. Announce cleanup time when most groups have lit the bulb and recorded some findings.
9. Distribute yellow and blue index cards.
10. Display and go over instructions for use of index cards. Yellow: Draw arrangement for the bulb that lights. Blue: Draw arrangement for the bulb that does not light.

11. Five minutes for students to complete drawing on their card.

12. Post instruction sheets on two bulletin boards. Send students with yellow cards to one bulletin board and those with blue cards to the other.

13. Tell them they have five minutes to complete the tasks described on their instruction sheet. Remind them to follow the discussion norms already posted in the room.

14. Listen in on their small-group discussions.

15. Prompt students to return to their seats after five minutes or when tasks are completed.

16. Start discussion about what they've learned about lighting a bulb.

17. Ask students how the arrangements on the yellow cards differ from the blue cards.

18. Introduce the concept of a circuit.

19. Differentiate between the terms *complete circuit* and *incomplete circuit*.

20. Generate rule for building a complete circuit through group discussion (a group write).

21. Distribute prediction sheets.

22. Table groups collaborate to complete their prediction sheets. Then check their responses by building those arrangements.

23. Turn on interactive white board, and open the quiz program. Distribute learner response devices.

24. Students enter their response for each item on the quiz.

25. Analyze spreadsheet.

Vignette 5.3   Let There Be Light!

The fourth graders listened attentively as Ms. Brown told them a story. "Once, about a year ago, I was in an elevator when the power went out. All of a sudden we stopped and the elevator was totally dark. Pushing the elevator buttons had no effect. We were trapped! Several of the other passengers were frightened, and one child began crying because he was very afraid of the dark. I remembered that I had my science tote bag with me. Though I wouldn't be able to restart the elevator, I realized I might be able to help the crying boy."

Reaching into her tote bag, Ms. Brown pulled out and showed the class several items as she continued her story. "I rummaged through my bag until I found a D-cell, a flashlight bulb, and a large paperclip. Who thinks I was able to use just these items to help the boy feel better?" Several of the children raised their hands. Ms. Brown asked one of them, "So what do you think I did?" "You lit the bulb so it wasn't so dark in the elevator," Sam said. Ms. Brown asked, "Who thinks they could produce light with just these three items from my bag?" Again, some hands went up; other students weren't so sure. "I suppose you should try it yourselves to find out. Please take out your scientist's notebooks. Today you'll work with your elbow-partner at your table to answer the question: *How can*

you produce light using only one D-cell, one large paperclip, and one flashlight bulb?"

Ms. Brown told the class, "Soon, you and your partner will get a bag of materials to use in your investigation. Then, you'll work with your partner to find what happens when you connect the items in your bag in different ways. Record your discoveries in your scientist's notebook. On your next blank spread, at the top, label the left page: *Ways the bulb lights*; label the right page: *Ways the bulb doesn't light*. As you see what happens with different arrangements of the three items, draw detailed diagrams on the appropriate page."

The class materials-manager gave each pair of students a plastic bag containing one 1.5-volt D-cell, one flashlight bulb, and one large paperclip. Getting right to work, most students used trial and error; others thought about possibilities, made hypotheses and predictions, and tried out their ideas. As Ms. Brown circulated through the tables of budding scientists, she reminded them to record both arrangements that light and those that don't. Sometimes Ms. Brown asked students to explain what they were doing and what they had found out so far, but she resisted the temptation to give any hints about how to light the bulb. If she noticed that someone's drawing did not effectively show what they did to light the bulb, she asked a few questions to encourage them to observe more carefully or to add detail to their drawings.

Children freely exchanged information and ideas as they worked. Some student pairs lit the bulb within a few minutes; others took considerably longer. When Ms. Brown noticed that a few children were becoming frustrated because they couldn't light the bulb, she encouraged them to watch other groups to get some new ideas.

When students successfully lit a bulb, Ms. Brown acknowledged their success with a little cheer, a word or two, or a smile or gesture; reminded them to record; then challenged them to find another way to light the bulb. Once all the students found and recorded at least one way to light the bulb, she got the class's attention and told them to put their D-cells, bulbs, and paperclips back into their bags and set them aside. While cleanup was occurring, the materials-manager gave each pair of students a blue and a yellow index card.

When Ms. Brown regained the class's attention, she announced, "Everyone, please pick up an index card." She paused as students selected their cards and then projected a slide on the whiteboard. It showed two rectangles: one was yellow and contained the words *Your drawing of an arrangement that lights*; the other was blue and contained the words *Your drawing of an arrangement that does not light*. Ms. Brown continued, "If you have a yellow card, draw one arrangement that *lit* the bulb. If you have a blue card, you should draw one arrangement of the items that *did not* light the bulb. Please use a dark marker and make your drawing large and neat so we can see it from across the room. You have five minutes to complete your drawings."

Ms. Brown sent the students with yellow cards to one bulletin board and those with blue cards to another. An instruction sheet was posted at each location. It said:

Work together as a group. Follow regular discussion norms.

- Look at all the cards on your board.
- Put drawings that show the same arrangement together in a cluster.
- Questions to discuss:

  - How many different (unique) arrangements does your group have?
  - In what ways are your groups' arrangements similar?
  - What might those similarities have to do with lighting the bulb?
  - Then she announced, "You'll have five minutes to work."

After five minutes, Ms. Brown asked the students to return to their seats. She started the discussion by asking, "What did you find out about how to light the bulb? Remember to speak clearly so everyone can hear your ideas." After many students shared their discoveries, their teacher asked, "How are the arrangements on the yellow cards, which lit the bulb, different from the arrangements on the blue cards, which did not light the bulb?"

Mia suggested, "The arrangements on the yellow cards are like loops; everything is connected, like in a circle."

Bryan said, "But some of the drawings on the blue cards have everything connected in a circle, but the bulb still didn't light."

Evelyn said, "Maybe there are special places on the bulb and battery that need to be connected."

Ms. Brown decided it was time to formally introduce the concept of a circuit. She explained, "Scientists have a term for the idea of connectedness you are talking about." She wrote the word *circuit* on the board, and then said, "When you connected the D-cell, flashlight bulb, and paperclip together, you made circuits. This circuit is called a *complete circuit* if the bulb lights. If the circuit is complete, there is an unbroken pathway around the circuit through which electricity flows. When the bulb does not light, the arrangement of the parts is called an incomplete circuit."

"Let's try to write a rule for making a complete circuit from only one D-cell, one large paperclip, and one flashlight bulb. We have lots of data on the index cards and in our notebooks that should help us write that rule."

After examining the drawings of complete circuits on the yellow cards and in their notebooks, a group discussion led to consensus on the following rule for making a complete circuit from just these three components:

In order for the bulb to light, the tip or the screwy part of the bulb must touch the top or base of the D-cell, one end of the paperclip wire must touch

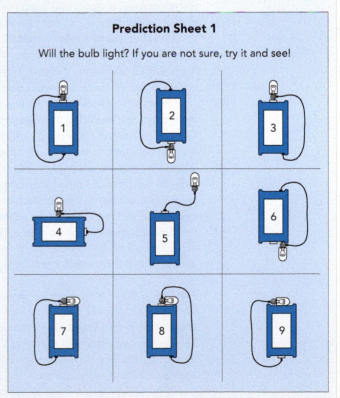

Prediction Sheet 1

Will the bulb light? If you are not sure, try it and see!

(continued)

(continued)

the other part of the bulb (tip or screwy part), and the other end must touch the other end (top or base) of the D-cell.

"Now that we have a rule, let's see if it really works. Use it to decide which of the circuits drawn on the prediction sheet are complete circuits and which are incomplete circuits. Then use your materials to build each circuit on the sheet to test whether your prediction is correct."

Working in table groups, the children applied their new rule to each frame on the prediction sheet, noting which circuits must be complete ones and identifying why other circuits pictured might not provide complete paths for the electricity.

The students, each holding their learner response device, sat facing the interactive whiteboard. As a final assessment of their ability to recognize open and closed circuits, students entered their responses as Ms. Brown projected a series of photographs of circuits made with just one bulb, one battery, and one paperclip and drawings similar to those included on the prediction sheet. Later, Ms. Brown examined the automatically generated spreadsheet to look at the students' responses and quiz scores. She was able to determine which students had not yet mastered the concept of open and closed circuits and was even able to tell which quiz items they missed. She then planned ways to differentiate further instruction for those students who were still confused.

Engage   During the engage phase of her lesson, Ms. Brown told the dark elevator story in order to help her students become engaged with the new concept. She hoped the story and the props in her bag would generate initial interest and curiosity about how to light a bulb in a context that most students would understand. By doing this, she was addressing the *motivation* element of effective science instruction, specifically, trying to create some intrinsic motivation in her class.

Additionally, during the engage phase, she addressed the *eliciting students' prior knowledge* element of effective science instruction by asking students if they thought they already knew how to light the bulb with only the props from her bag. Her question helped her identify who thought the challenge was possible. If she wanted to know more about how students would light the bulb, she could ask an open-ended question, such as "What would you do to produce light?" However, she didn't want just one student to provide a solution at this point; she wanted everyone to have a chance to be intellectually engaged with the question during the upcoming explore phase. She had planned her engagement activities so that once the problem had been introduced and curiosity was high, students could begin to *explore* immediately, manipulating materials and making observations. The story helped the students comprehend and maintain focus on the task.

Another way to uncover students' ideas throughout a lesson is to have the class make a K-W-L chart, where K stands for what they know, W stands for what they want to know, and L stands for what they've learned. In a 5E lesson, the brainstorming for the K and W columns would probably happen during the engage phase of the lesson, while the class would complete the L column as part of the evaluation phase.

Formative assessment probes are also great tools for uncovering student ideas, so they are quite appropriate to use during the engage phase of a 5E lesson. A collection of formative assessment probes focused on science concepts that have been identified as difficult for students to learn, because of their abstract or counterintuitive nature, appears in a series of books, *Uncovering Student Ideas in Science* (2005–2012). These formative assessment probes are designed to determine what learners think about particular foundational concepts identified in national standards and cognitive research literature. Their use during the engage phase is recommended because they can provide information about ideas that students have before instruction and about how ready individual students are for instruction (Keeley, Eberle, & Farrin, 2005).

Encouraging students to raise questions of their own also brings their ideas to the surface so that students themselves are aware of them and able to build on them. Often at the engage phase, the question for investigation is formulated or presented in order to focus learners' thinking on the expected goal of the lesson.

Explore.   During the explore phase of her 5E lesson, Ms. Brown provided hands-on materials and supported students as they devised ways to gather evidence to answer their question. Instead of providing students with answers, her scaffolding pushed them toward *intellectual engagement* through questioning. As Ms. Brown circulated and monitored conversation, she learned more about students' ideas about how to light a bulb. She also encouraged ongoing *motivation* by praising success and challenging them to find additional bulb-lighting methods.

During their exploration of various arrangements of the circuit components, as students collected and recorded their discoveries, they were *intellectually engaged with relevant phenomena* that were well aligned with the learning goals. The focus on this element of effective science instruction continued as the class shared, compared and contrasted, organized, and analyzed their index cards with drawings of arrangements that light and those that don't. During that final part of the explore phase of Ms. Brown's lesson, students began their involvement with the *use of evidence to make and critique claims* and *sense-making.*

Generally, during the explore phase, students use a variety of observational and experimental investigational procedures to gather data. In planning investigations, students may consider whether descriptive, classificatory, experimental, or some other approach to investigations would be most appropriate. While gathering data, students practice process skills such as how to observe, measure, infer, and predict. They also might practice fine motor skills such as how to cut, connect, switch, pour, tie, hold, and hook. Beginning with simple instruments, students learn to use rulers, thermometers, watches, spring scales, and balance scales to measure important variables. They learn to use magnifiers and microscopes to see finer details of objects and organisms (NRC, 1996).

Students should be encouraged to record their discoveries during the explore phase. One useful format for accomplishing this task and supporting future inquiry is the *I Notice/I Wonder* chart. The left column of this two-column chart should be labeled "I Notice." In this column students write their observations and discoveries as they explore with the materials. The right column should be labeled "I Wonder." In this column students write questions that come to mind as they are exploring. These questions can lead to further inquiry investigations. Keeping records helps children to organize their findings and to remember them when they are needed in reflection or during the explain and elaborate phases.

The explore phase of inquiry involves largely guided discovery by the students. It is in the explain and elaborate phases that the 5E model goes beyond discovery approaches to learning with understanding.

Explain.   To begin the explain phase of her 5E lesson, Ms. Brown asked her class to share what they noticed during the explore phase, reflect on their observations, and give their own hypotheses and explanations that make sense of the observational data. Then, building on the activities and discussion of students, she used direct instruction to formally introduce several scientific terms. Finally, she facilitated class discussion that led to a rule about making a complete circuit generated by the students. Ms. Brown used student input and discussion to maintain their *intellectual engagement* during the explain phase. The main purpose of the explain phase of the 5E model is *sense-making,* which she facilitated while helping the class *use their evidence to make and critique claims.*

It is during the explain phase that you would be most likely to use direct teaching methods, including lectures, readings from the textbook, or videos. At some point during the explain phase, you might provide an explanation for the students. In presenting science knowledge, you should strive for students' understanding of the natural world rather than just acquisition of terminology and facts. Your goal in this phase is to assist students to use the new knowledge and the evidence from the explore phase to examine their initial conceptions and then to build accurate scientific explanations that help to answer the initiating question.

Elaborate.   It is not enough just to have knowledge. In developing understanding, learners must be able to access their knowledge and use it in new learning and problem solving. Failure to access knowledge at the appropriate time can severely constrain new learning and transfer (Bransford, Brown, & Cocking, 1999).

Mary Budd Rowe (1973), a distinguished science educator, has suggested that concept application is too often the neglected ingredient in science teaching. It is through concept application that understanding is generated. Rowe emphasized that children need to learn to view knowledge as procedures to be applied rather than just as information to be memorized and recalled. Once they have been introduced, concepts, principles, and explanation must be applied or transferred to new situations to be understood.

Concept application takes place at the elaborate phase of 5E instruction. At this phase, learners are presented with new learning tasks and called on to use their developing knowledge to negotiate the new task.

During the elaborate phase of Ms. Brown's lesson, the prediction sheet activity provided an opportunity for students to apply their new knowledge and the rule the class generated from it. Having access to the materials again to check their predictions helped maintain student *motivation* and *intellectual engagement.*

Evaluate.   Ms. Brown used technology to facilitate the evaluate phase of her 5E lesson. The use of the student response devices and the interactive white board may have been *motivational* and *intellectually engaging* for many of her students. This final phase of the lesson acted as a quiz on the concepts of circuits, both complete and incomplete. Her lesson was brief and focused, so the interactive quiz she developed was sufficient to determine if her instructional goal was reached.

Throughout the other phases of the lesson, she was continuously assessing students' ideas and making decisions about what she needed to do next in the lesson to maximize *intellectual engagement* and student learning. She informally monitored students' performances during investigations, examined their products, such as drawings and notebook entries, and listened to their discourse.

Self-assessment is an important aspect of the evaluation process. Brown and Campione (1994) argued that students should be taught metacognition strategies for planning, executing, monitoring, and adjusting their processes and products of learning.

As a summary view of the 5E instructional model, Table 5.5 provides a chart that identifies teacher actions and student behaviors consistent with each phase of the model.

TABLE 5.5　Applying the 5E Instructional Model

Stage of the Instructional Model	What the TEACHER Does	
	That Is Consistent with This Model	That Is Inconsistent with This Model
Engage	• Creates interest • Generates curiosity • Raises questions • Elicits responses that uncover what the students know or think about the concept/topic	• Explains concepts • Provides definitions and answers • States conclusions • Provides closure • Lectures
Explore	• Encourages students to work together without direct instruction from the teacher • Observes and listens to students as they interact • Asks probing questions to redirect students' investigations when necessary • Provides time for students to puzzle through problems • Acts as a consultant for students	• Provides answers • Tells or explains how to work through the problem • Provides closure • Tells students that they are wrong • Gives information or facts that solve the problem • Leads students step-by-step to a solution
Explain	• Encourages students to explain concepts and definitions in their own words • Asks for justification (evidence) and clarification from students • Formally provides definitions, explanations, and new labels • Uses students' previous experiences as the basis for explaining concepts	• Accepts explanations that have no justification • Neglects to solicit students' explanations • Introduces unrelated concepts or skills
Elaborate	• Expects students to use formal labels, definitions, and explanations provided previously • Encourages students to apply or extend the concepts and skills in new situations • Reminds students of alternative explanations • Refers students to existing data and evidence and asks: "What do you already know?" "Why do you think . . . ?" (Strategies from explore stage apply here also)	• Provides definitive answers • Tells students they are wrong • Lectures • Leads students step-by-step to a solution • Explains how to work through the problem
Evaluate	• Observes students as they apply new concepts and skills • Assesses students' knowledge and/or skills • Looks for evidence that students have changed their thinking or behaviors • Allows students to assess their own learning and group-process skills • Asks open-ended questions, such as: "Why do you think . . . ?" "What evidence do you have?" "What do you know about x?" "How would you explain x?"	• Tests vocabulary words, terms, and isolated facts • Introduces new ideas or concepts • Creates ambiguity • Promotes open-ended discussion unrelated to the concept or skill

Stage of the Instructional Model	What the STUDENT Does	
	That Is Consistent with This Model	That Is Inconsistent with This Model
Engage	• Asks questions, such as: "Why did this happen?" "What do I already know about this?" "What can I find out about this?" • Shows interest in the topic	• Asks for the "right" answer • Offers the "right" answer • Insists on answers or explanations • Seeks one solution
Explore	• Thinks freely, but within the limits of the activity • Tests predictions and hypotheses • Forms new predictions and hypotheses • Tries alternatives and discusses them with others • Records observations and ideas • Suspends judgment	• Lets others do the thinking and exploring (passive involvement) • Works quietly with little or no interaction with others (only appropriate when exploring ideas or feelings) • Plays around indiscriminately with no goal in mind • Stops with one solution
Explain	• Explains possible solutions or answers to others • Listens critically to one another's explanations • Questions one another's explanations • Listens to and tries to comprehend explanations offered by the teacher • Refers to previous activities • Uses recorded observations in explanations	• Proposes explanations from thin air with no relationship to previous experiences • Brings up irrelevant experiences and examples • Accepts explanations without justification • Does not attend to other plausible explanations
Elaborate	• Applies new labels, definitions, explanations, and skills in new, but similar, situations • Uses previous information to ask questions, propose solutions, make decisions, and design experiments • Draws reasonable conclusions from evidence • Records observations and explanations • Checks for understanding among peers	• Plays around with no goal in mind • Ignores previous information or evidence • Draws conclusions from thin air • Uses in discussions only those labels that the teacher provided
Evaluate	• Answers open-ended questions by using observations, evidence, and previously accepted explanations • Demonstrates an understanding or knowledge of the concept or skill • Evaluates his or her own progress and knowledge • Asks related questions that would encourage future investigations	• Draws conclusions, not using evidence or previously accepted explanations • Offers only yes-or-no answers, memorized definitions, or explanation and answers • Fails to express satisfactory explanations in own words • Introduces new, irrelevant topics

Source: *Teaching Secondary School Science*, 6th ed. (pp. 218–219), by Leslie Trowbridge and Rodger Bybee, 1996, © Reprinted by permission of Pearson Education, Inc., Upper Saddle River, NJ.

 CHECK YOUR UNDERSTANDING 5.7
Click here to gauge your understanding of the concepts in this section.

CHAPTER SUMMARY

Inquiry-Based Instruction

Inquiry-based instruction is a teaching and learning approach based on constructivist learning theory. The *National Science Education Standards* (NRC, 1996) strongly recommend that inquiry-based lessons be prominent among the varied instructional strategies used for science teaching. Ideally, in inquiry-based instruction teachers facilitate learning rather than deliver it, and students assume responsibility for constructing their own knowledge and understanding.

Research on Inquiry-Based Instruction

Definitive educational research comparing instructional approaches is challenging to conduct. However, there are numerous studies that indicate the advantages of inquiry-based instruction over other instructional methods, such as a traditional textbook approach. Some of these advantages relate to cognitive variables, such as general science achievement, problem solving, independent learning, process skills, analytical skills, and even language arts and mathematics skills. Other advantages relate to affective variables, including level of interest and/or excitement in science class, feelings of success, and view of science as a career. Some studies find other instructional methods to be superior to inquiry-based approaches. Differences in the terminology used to describe the instructional methods being compared makes analysis of these studies challenging.

Essential Features of Classroom Inquiry

The essential features of classroom inquiry were identified by the National Research Council in 2000 in order to operationally define inquiry-based teaching and learning. They include:

- Learners engage in scientifically oriented questions.
- Learners give priority to evidence.
- Learners formulate explanations from evidence.
- Learners connect explanations to scientific knowledge.
- Learners communicate and justify their proposed explanations.

For a lesson, unit, or program to be considered "full inquiry," all five of these features should be present. There are variations in the amount of student and teacher direction for each of the essential features. This helps to account for the diversity of the nature of inquiry-based instruction.

Levels of Inquiry

Inquiry-based instruction can be described as a continuum based on how much information is provided to the students. Listed from most teacher directed to most student directed, the levels of inquiry are: confirmation, structured (or directed) inquiry, guided inquiry, and open (student-initiated) inquiry.

Instructional Models, and How to Select One

An instructional model is an arrangement of phases, steps, actions, or decision points for teaching and learning. They provide a structure for planning and organizing instruction. Developers of instructional models assume that the order of instruction matters. Learning theory, the nature of the subject being taught, and expected instructional outcomes are the basis of good instructional models. When selecting an appropriate instructional model, you must know your instructional goals.

The 5E Model of Science Instruction

The 5E model of science instruction is an instructional model designed to support concept development through inquiry instruction. It can be applied to lessons, units, and/or programs. It is composed of five phases, each of which begins with the letter E, that generally follow each other in a defined sequence. These phases are engage, explore, explain, elaborate, and evaluate.

How Each Phase of the 5E Model of Science Instruction Supports Science Learning

Engage—This phase is about motivation, eliciting learners' prior knowledge, and intellectual engagement. Brief, surprising, or interesting activities "hook" students' interest and set the stage for the learning to come. Activities to uncover students' current thinking about the topic assist teachers in instructional planning.

Explore—This phase is about discovery. Teachers facilitate experiences to provide a common base of activities related to the concept being studied. Learners collaborate and communicate while planning investigations to answer questions, manipulating materials to generate data, recording findings, etc.

Explain—This phase is about sense-making. Mental engagement of students occurs as they present, discuss, and defend their claims with evidence from the explore phase. Teachers facilitate discussion and may directly teach related terms, background information, and so forth, while helping students make cognitive connections.

Elaborate—This phase is about applying new learning to new contexts. Activities lead to deeper conceptual understanding. There are often opportunities for learners to find more evidence to support or refute their claims.

Evaluate—This phase is about assessing learning. Formative assessment should occur throughout the entire 5E lesson in order to inform instruction. Summative assessment occurs at the final phase as a measure of students' achievement of the learning outcomes.

DISCUSSION QUESTIONS

1. Describe inquiry-based instruction.
2. What are some of the advantages of inquiry-based instruction?
3. Is the lesson "Let There Be Light!" a full inquiry lesson? Why or why not?
4. Compare and contrast the levels of inquiry-based instruction.
5. Why are there multiple instructional models?
6. Why is the 5E instructional model useful when planning an inquiry-based lesson?
7. Are all 5E lessons inquiry-based lessons? Why or why not?
8. How does the varying role of the teacher during a 5E lesson help students learn with understanding?

PROFESSIONAL PRACTICES ACTIVITIES

1. Talk with your cooperating teacher about his or her thinking related to inquiry-based instruction.
2. Evaluate the extent to which several teachers use inquiry-based instructional methods by interviewing them and examining their lesson plans. Then survey or talk with students of each teacher to assess affective variables such as their interest/excitement in science class, their feelings of success in science class, and their view of science as a career.
3. Teach or observe a science lesson. Analyze it according to the essential features of classroom inquiry and their variations.
4. Look at the teacher's guide for a science textbook or kit. Identify the level of inquiry in several of the activities they include. Consider how you could modify the plan for the activity to move instruction toward more open inquiry.

5. Talk with your cooperating teacher about the instructional models he or she uses to plan and organize instruction, and how and why he or she uses them.

6. Find a 5E lesson that relates to the science unit your class is working on. Volunteer to teach that lesson or ask your cooperating teacher to teach it so you can observe its implementation.

7. Observe a class during a 5E lesson. Focus on the actions of both the teacher and the students during instruction. Use Table 5.5 to help you determine if the actions of the teacher and the students were appropriate during each phase of the lesson.

Effective Questioning

Shutterstock

LEARNING GOALS

After reading this chapter, you should understand that . . .

1. Asking the right question is at the heart of teaching and learning.

2. Different kinds of questions when used at the right time are important to move learning forward.

3. Different kinds of questions are needed to align with the different phases of the 5E model of inquiry-based instruction.

4. Teachers responses to questions will guide learning and classroom discourse.

5. Implementing science talk in the classroom will support conceptual change that results in student understanding.

What do you know about the role that questions play instructionally? Think about what you know already about questioning. Do you ask a lot of questions? How many questions do you ask on a typical day? Do teachers ask more or less questions than an average person? Why do you ask these questions? What kind of questions do you ask and why? Do teachers ask open-ended or closed questions? In what ways does asking questions make your life easier or better? Is there a "right" way to ask questions particularly if we want students to think scientifically? Does the way you word a question affect the response you get? Does discussion help you learn? What are you learning by considering these questions? Why do you think I am asking them at the beginning of this chapter? Did you figure out that I'm engaging you with some of the ideas presented in this chapter? Have you noticed that you already know quite a bit about questioning, even though you've just been responding to questions?

You may have already realized that questions are an integral part of science and science education. Questioning is included in many lists of science process or thinking skills found in elementary and middle school curricula from the 1970s and beyond. The Science as Inquiry Content Standards in the *National Science Education Standards* (NRC, 1996), include: for grades K–4, "Ask a question about objects, organisms, and events in the environment," and for grades 5–8, "Identify questions that can be answered through scientific investigations." In the *Framework for K–12 Science Standards* (NRC, 2012), "Asking questions (for science) and defining problems (for engineering)" is the first Practice of Dimension 1—Scientific and Engineering Practices. All of these references to questioning relate to investigable questions that drive science investigations. While questioning is an important Science and Engineering Practice, this chapter focuses instead on the questions teachers ask their students and the techniques used to encourage discourse or "science talk" in the classroom needed to help students successfully understand science ideas.

The Role of Teacher Questions

Asking the right question is at the heart of doing science. It is also at the heart of learning and teaching science as inquiry. Science teachers who use inquiry methods ask questions to focus investigations, probe prior knowledge, stimulate reflective thinking, shift the focus from observation to explanation, encourage creativity, and develop student understanding.

Just as important as asking the right question at the right time is the way you respond to students and promote student discourse. **Discourse**—expressing one's own questions, observations, concepts, ideas, and thinking, while listening to and reflecting on the ideas of others—is fundamental to the practice of science. It is also an essential part of children's inquiry. Making meaning from investigations and experiences requires that you guide student dialogue, encourage your students to make connections, draw conclusions, and ask new questions.

Questions are among the most important tools teachers have. They may also be the predominant instructional intervention used in classrooms (Tienken, Goldberg, & DiRocco, 2009). Teachers of science use questions for many purposes: to manage classroom activities; to initiate and support inquiry; to guide student organization of data; to encourage students to reflect on their data and use it as evidence in constructing explanations; to promote problem-solving, help when students get stuck; to help students reason and collectively make sense of science; and to assess student knowledge and understanding.

During inquiry-based instruction, effective teachers of science use questions to stimulate physical and/or cognitive actions by their students and to determine what learners know and understand. A properly worded question can encourage learners to observe carefully (What do you see in your drop of pond water?), develop a process or product (How will you do [or make] that?), and discuss ideas with peers (What do the others in your group think about that?)—all physical actions. Appropriately stated questions can result in intellectual acts by learners, such as reflective thinking (What happened in the experiment that led you to that conclusion?), creative thinking (What other ways could you do that?), and critical thinking where they make connections with prior experience (Does that remind you of something you have seen before?). Teacher questions can also be constructed to assess student current knowledge (What kind of tree produces acorns?) or understanding (Which trees in the schoolyard are deciduous? How do you know?) when asked either before, during, or after instruction.

Teachers' questions are widely accepted as crucial in helping students make connections and learn important science concepts. However, in a series of classroom observations of science teachers' questioning behavior, Weiss and Pasley (2004) found that effective questioning was relatively rare. As you observed in the video clip about creating compost, instead of teacher questioning that monitors learners' understanding of ideas and encourages deep thinking, the researchers found that during typical teacher questioning sessions students are quizzed though a rapid series of knowledge level, vocabulary-focused questions that emphasize knowing the right answer. This occurred 80 percent of the time and when students did not know the answer, the teachers often provided it themselves. Based on these findings, they recommended teachers plan and ask open-ended questions where interactive discussions were provided to help students with sense-making.

Though properly worded questions at the appropriate time in the lesson are extremely important in encouraging student thinking and learning, your entire pattern of interaction with your students impacts their learning. Aspects of this pattern of interaction include your words, your actions and pacing while asking the initial question, calling on students, listening to students' answers, and responding to students' answers (Olson, 2008).

Effective, lesson-embedded formative assessment generally relies on a teacher's use of well-chosen questions. As mentioned earlier, questions that teachers ask are just one part of the process, however. We expect the teacher's questions to prompt thinking and elicit students' answers, which teachers first consider and then respond to. Duschl and colleagues (NRC, 2007) described a *formative assessment scaffolding* "feedback loop" proposed by Furtak and Ruiz-Primo (2005). When using this interactive feedback loop in your classroom:

1. You ask questions to elicit levels of student understanding.

2. Students respond to the questions orally, in writing, or through diagrams and drawings.

3. You recognize and acknowledge student responses.

4. You provide scaffolds to improve learning and understanding including feedback that moves the learning forward with suggestions and recommendations for next steps.

When formative assessment strategies and scaffolding are applied together, continuous improvement in student understanding, as well as modifications in teaching approaches, can be achieved (NRC, 2007).

Teacher questions serve varied roles in science teaching, including evaluating student learning; focusing student thinking on targeted Science and Engineering Practices, Crosscutting Concepts, and Disciplinary Core Ideas; and encouraging appropriate science talk during elementary and middle school science lessons. Look at Figure 6.1 and consider the current thinking about the role that questions play to advance instruction.

Consider this analogy—tools are to master carpenters as questions are to effective science teachers. Tools have unique purposes. Carpenters use different tools to drive a nail, cut a board, or square off the end of a piece of lumber. The master carpenter plans ahead by keeping a well-stocked toolbox and becoming proficient in selecting and using each tool. Similarly, effective teachers need different questioning tools for specific educational tasks, such as setting the cognitive level of inquiry, eliciting observations and

Questioning plays an important role for science teachers. What is the purpose of the questions you hear the teacher ask in this video on **creating compost**? How might these questions be re-written from closed questions (seeking the right answers) to open-ended questions (with multiple points of view)? How can open-ended question help engage students in the inquiry-based investigation and prompt student thinking on this year-long study?

Use the simulation on Questioning Strategies to learn more about how to effectively incorporate questioning with students. After you finish the simulation, record at least two ideas that you want to remember that will help you to implement effective questioning strategies.

FIGURE 6.1 Think about the role that questions play. What questions might you ask your science students so you can check off items from this "to do" list?

Which ~~tool~~ *question* should I use?

predictions, promoting discussion by class members, stimulating deeper thought on the part of students, and building meaningful explanations that connect investigative evidence to what students already know. Teachers, like carpenters, need well-honed tools that they know when and how to use.

Taking the tool/question analogy a little further, consider various ways that tools can be classified. A carpenter might have a cabinet for hand tools and store power tools elsewhere—those with cords near an electric outlet, those with rechargeable batteries near their charger, and those with gasoline engines in the garage. Or the carpenter might keep all of the cutting tools (saws, planes, axes, and hatchets) in one place and all the fastening tools (screwdriver and screws, hammer and nails, and wrench and nuts and bolts) in another place.

Similarly, there are multiple ways that questions are classified. They can be productive, essential, open-ended or close-ended, person-centered or subject-centered, and/or equitable or inequitable.

 CHECK YOUR UNDERSTANDING 6.1
Click here to gauge your understanding of the concepts in this section.

Different Kinds of Questions

Productive Questions

In his article "The Right Question at the Right Time" (Elstgeest, 2001), Jos Elstgeest called teachers' questions that promote children's activity and reasoning **productive questions**. This term continues to appear in educational literature with basically the same meaning. Productive questions are considered useful tools for supporting constructivist learning. They can guide students to make cognitive connections between experience and understanding when asked at the right time. Productive questions are scaffolding tools; they are designed to move students forward in their thinking (Martens, 1999). Refer to Figure 6.2 to learn more about the characteristics of productive questions.

Elstgeest (2001) described six different types of productive questions. Table 6.1 is based on Elstgeest's descriptions and are summarized in the table. Other science educators continue to use these classifications of productive questions in their work (Martens, 1999). You should notice that the question starters can be used again and again. They aren't just for the teacher, either; students can use them when asking questions. Posting the question starters will help you and your students ask more productive questions.

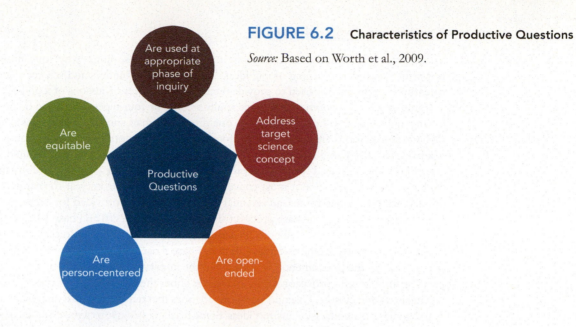

FIGURE 6.2 Characteristics of Productive Questions

Source: Based on Worth et al., 2009.

TABLE 6.1 Six Types of Productive Questions

Types of Productive Questions	Typical Question Starters	Learner Action Called For—Thinking Strategies
Questions that "hook" learners	Have you ever seen . . . ? What was it like?	Share prior experience/knowledge
	What do you notice about . . . ?	Observation, especially of significant detail
	What's happening here?	Observation/description of an event
	What do you hear, . . . see, . . . feel, . . . smell?	Observation with multiple senses
Measuring and counting	How many . . . ?	Quantify by counting, increase precision of data
	How heavy, . . . hot, . . . far?	Quantify by measuring, use measuring devices
	How often . . . ?	Determine frequency
Comparison	Which is longer? . . . heavier? . . . cooler?	Order by a certain property
	How much longer is . . . ?	Quantify difference in length
	How are . . . the same, . . . different?	Analysis, classification skills
Investigative	What happens when . . . ?	Design an investigation, try it out, find relationships between variables
	What will happen if . . . ?	Apply known relationships between variables, make a prediction, test it
Problem-based	Design a prototype . . . ?	Plan and implement solutions to a problem
	Can you find a way to improve a product . . . ?	Evaluate a challenge, develop possible solutions
	How would you accomplish your goal?	
Reasoning	Why do you think . . . ?	Metacognition; think about experiences and construct your initial ideas based on them
	How would you explain . . . ?	Apply skills of interpreting and analyzing data and drawing conclusions
	What evidence supports your claim?	Prepare to argue from evidence

Essential Questions

Of all the types of questions that prompt thinking and reasoning, "why" questions can be the most powerful for student learning of big ideas. To help students understand science phenomena **essential questions** are frequently used to provide the focus for a series of lessons or a unit of study (McTighe & Wiggins, 2013). Classroom questions generally are one of four types, which can be grouped into the following: questions that hook students (Is one diet better than another?); questions that lead the learning (What types of foods are in the different food groups?); questions that guide and prompt thinking (What is a balanced diet?); and essential questions (Why is food necessary and what should we eat?). Essential questions signal the need for inquiry learning about ideas that are puzzling or don't make sense initially. To be an essential question it must convey an idea that occurs from year to year and is foundational in science. In science classrooms, an essential question should be provided for each unit of study and then implemented using a four-phase process (McTighe & Wiggins, 2013). Phase 1 is when you use the question to design and develop an inquiry. Phase 2 starts by using the inquiry to elicit the widest possible array of student responses to the essential question. Phase 3 occurs when teachers introduce and explore new perspectives as the phenomenon is studied and the inquiry is extended. Phase 4 asks students to generalize their findings into provisional understandings about the content and processes as they reach tentative explanations and closure. Essential questions are ones that require personal understanding where students pull together isolated facts or abstract ideas. Some teachers struggle to write essential questions and refer to resources provided by their districts. By their very nature, essential questions require higher-order thinking, invite multiple responses, and require students to think about and discuss their initial ideas as they move forward with in-depth investigations leading to evidence-based argumentation. Exploration 6.1 gives you an opportunity to apply what you now know about essential questions and questions that don't meet the criteria for essential questions. You will learn more about questions used in discourse and argumentation later in this chapter.

EXPLORATION

6.1

Essential Questions—Is It or Isn't It?

To help you recognize and then write essential questions, start by reviewing the following sets of questions that are identified as "essential" and "nonessential."

Essential Questions:

1. Why is the sky blue?
2. How does the life cycle of a plant differ from the life cycle of animals?
3. Why are the seasons different from region to region around the world?
4. How is matter cycled in ecosystems?
5. How do we know if water is safe to drink?

Nonessential Questions:

1. Where does photosynthesis occur in a green plant?
2. What are some examples of animals that are adapted to their environment?
3. What does it mean to be warm-blooded?
4. Describe the three primary states of matter.
5. Where do parasites get their food?

After reviewing the questions that are essential, what do you think are some common characteristics? You may have noticed that essential questions are open-ended, and nonessential questions are closed questions—they have a right answer. What other characteristics did you notice? Discuss your responses with someone else. Did you also come up with the following characteristics for essential questions—intellectually engaging, lead to more questions that can be investigated, are broad, require the gathering of evidence, and promote higher-order thinking?

Reflection Questions:

Now, check your understanding. Read the following questions and decide whether they are essential and be prepared to support your answer.

Is It Essential or Isn't It?

1. How does the brain work?
2. What percentage of the air we breathe is nitrogen gas?
3. How are human activities impacting climate change?
4. How can you tell if an organism is living?
5. Who first identified the structure of DNA?

Closed vs. Open-Ended Questions

A **closed question** has a single correct answer, while **open-ended questions** can be answered in a number of ways (Texas A&M Center for Mathematics and Science Education, 2005, 2006). Both types of questions are important for assessing prior knowledge and promoting new learning, but in very different ways. Look at Exploration 6.2 to learn more about open-ended and closed questions.

Analyzing Some Teacher Questions   **EXPLORATION**

6.2

Imagine that you observed a seventh grade science class several times during a unit about the flow of matter and energy involved in plant growth. You recorded some of the questions that the teacher asked during your class visits. Ten of these questions (selected randomly) appear below:

1. How many of you read the chapter on photosynthesis last night?

2. For your investigation, which color of light resulted in the tallest plants?

3. Do you think plants need energy to grow? Please explain your reasoning.

4. What is the chemical formula that describes photosynthesis?

5. What can you tell the class about the results of your experiment?

6. How would you explain photosynthesis in your own words?

7. Where does most of the energy for plant growth come from?

8. How would you design an investigation to find out if plants always need light to grow?

9. What new questions do you have about the importance of energy for plant growth?

10. Why is it that a seed germinates even if no sunlight reaches it when it is planted underground?

- Create a four column chart as shown that includes a column for each question, a column for the teacher's purpose in asking the question (hook the students, lead the learning, guide thinking), a column for

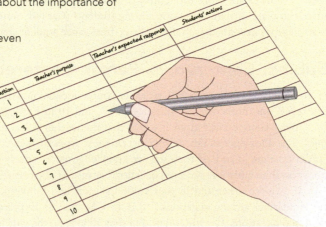

the teachers expected response and a fourth column for what students would do or say when asked the question.

- As you read each question, think about why the teacher asked it. In the appropriate column on the chart, jot down your ideas about the teacher's purpose in asking each question.
- Reread the questions, but this time note what you think the teacher expects students to do in response to each question.
- Reread the questions again. For each, consider what the students will be doing and say when responding to each of the questions. Record your thoughts on the chart.
- If possible, discuss your ideas with one or more of your peers.

Reflection Questions:

1. What general categories of questions did you identify in the Teacher's Purpose column?
2. Which questions do you think are best for finding out what students have memorized? Why?
3. Which questions do you think are best for finding out what students understand? Why?
4. If you were a student in this class, which three questions would you volunteer to answer? Why?
5. Which questions seem to lead to student understanding? What do they have in common that may make students engage in thinking about the science ideas?

In this video, how does the teacher use closed questions to help student learn about the characteristics of animals? After you have seen the video, write an open-ended question that the teacher could use to engage the students with the learning before they make their observations.

Closed questions require students to recall and reproduce knowledge—that is, to focus on a single scientific fact, define a particular term, or attend to specific objects or specific aspects of events. Closed questions often focus on specific observations and recall of prior knowledge and experiences. Questions that can be answered with a single word, especially yes/no or true/false questions, are typically closed questions. In Exploration 6.2, questions 1, 2, 4, 7, and 10 are examples of closed questions. Children's responses to closed questions help you assess their factual recall and observation skills and allow you to adjust your teaching accordingly.

In contrast, open-ended questions enable multiple students to make useful contributions to a discussion because they have more than one possible answer. Open-ended questions trigger thinking, in which children engage broad portions of their schemas and consider a wide array of possibilities based on prior experiences. A single word seldom is an adequate answer to an open-ended question; thus, the use of open-ended questions encourages verbal development and academic language acquisition. In Exploration 6.2, questions 3, 5, 6, 8, and 9 are examples of open-ended questions. Open-ended questions are broader questions that can engage students reflectively and build conceptual understanding.

In typical classrooms in every subject, the large majority of teachers' questions are closed, calling for factual knowledge and thinking with a focus on recall. In these classrooms, there is an emphasis on leading students to know the right answer rather than on being creative or thinking critically. Research indicates that even a slight increase in the percentage of open-ended questions by teachers yields a significant increase in intellectual engagement with science ideas by students; that is, a larger number of students respond, and their responses are more thoughtful and exhibit higher levels of thinking. These types of responses, in turn, stimulate further discussion among students (Carin & Sund, 1978). The climate in these classrooms is sometimes described as "safe" or "risk-free" since student sharing of ideas and thinking is encouraged.

Subject-Centered vs. Person-Centered Questions

If you are only concerned with whether your students know the correct answers, you may ask **subject-centered** questions. Review questions 4, 7, and 10 in Exploration 6.2. Notice that in these examples of subject-centered questions it seems that the teacher is leading students to the "right" answers to the questions. Don't get caught relying just on these types of questions. Students who see themselves as poor students or are unsure of their science knowledge are less likely to volunteer to answer a subject-centered question than a person-centered question because of the possibility their answer could be wrong.

If you are interested in your students' ideas and thinking, ask a **person-centered** question. Look for similarities among questions 1, 2, 3, 5, 6, 8, and 9 in Exploration 6.2. These are examples of person-centered questions. Do you notice that they all include the word *you* or *your* in their construction? They all clearly ask for learners' personal ideas without implying that there is a "right" or "best" answer. Remember that person-centered questions also support the climate of a safe or risk-free classroom since they encourage students to share their own ideas and make their own thinking visible to others without the fear of being wrong. Opportunities for students to interact with others are critical when sharing a person's ideas. From brain research we know that learning is a social activity or as Margaret Wheatley explains it, conversation is the natural way we humans think together (Wheatley, 2007) and opportunities for students to discuss their ideas, and not just answer the person-centered questions themselves, must be included in your teaching. Understanding science ideas is critical in the K–8 science classrooms where students learn how to learn. Think about the quote that follows and remind yourself that our students are novice learners and depend on us to help them move beyond recall and memorization skills to a climate where they learn with understanding.

> In times of drastic change, it is the learners who inherit the future. The learned usually find themselves equipped to live in a world that no longer exists. (Hoffer, 1973)

Equitable vs. Inequitable Questions

Equitable questions are inclusive, answerable by all students. They are based on experiences shared by the entire class rather than on the experience of just some of the students. For example, during a unit about flight after the class explores the flight paths of various paper airplanes, you might ask: *"What were the features of the paper airplane that flew the farthest?"* Any child who participated in the activity would be equally qualified to answer this question.

A question is **inequitable** if learners have not had the necessary experiences to contribute an answer. In the same unit, the question *"What is it like to fly in an airplane?"* is probably inequitable, since in most classes some children may have not flown in a plane. Because of the diverse nature of our student populations in most schools today, you should not assume that all your students have the same background experience. To be able to ask equitable questions, you must provide opportunities for the class to gain the relevant experiences they need.

Since the instructional activities and student experiences included in the seventh-grade unit mentioned in Exploration 6.2 were not described in much detail, it is not really possible to classify the questions presented as equitable or inequitable. That categorization is really dependent on the context in the classroom.

Questions Aligned with Learning Targets

Productive and effective questions must be on topic in order to encourage student thinking about specific science Practices, Disciplinary Core Ideas, and Crosscutting Concepts. It is important that you, as the teacher, have a clear understanding of the objectives of your lesson or unit so that the questions you develop to scaffold the learning and inquiry are focused on the intended topic. For example, during a unit about moon phases, the following questions would be appropriate because they relate directly to the topic of study:

- What did the moon look like in the sky while you were at recess?
- What pattern of change in the appearance of the moon do you notice when you look at your observation calendar for the last week?
- Which phase of the moon do you expect to see next Friday?
- If the moon is full, when do you expect it to rise? To be at its highest point in the sky?
- How much of the moon do you think is illuminated at a given time? Explain your reasoning.
- How would you describe the motion of the earth, moon, and sun over time?

During that same unit, the following questions would not be productive because they are not really focused on the topic of the unit:

- Why do you think the moon has craters?
- What do you know about the *Apollo* space missions?
- How would you explain the cause of a lunar eclipse?
- How much would you weigh on the moon?
- How do you think the moon was formed?

Notice that all of the questions presented in Exploration 6.2 seem to have the characteristics of productive questions. Most relate directly to the relationship between energy and plant growth, while the final question asks generally about the investigation results. Similar broad questions (e.g., *"What patterns or trends did you find in your data?"* and *"How is your claim supported by the evidence?"*) automatically focus on the topic of inquiry since they relate directly to the investigation. To help ensure that you are asking productive and effective questions, it is a good idea to formulate a list of questions to ask while you are writing your objectives. Scripting them ahead of time will ensure that you ask questions that prompt student thinking and discussions.

✓ **CHECK YOUR UNDERSTANDING 6.2**
Click here to gauge your understanding of the concepts in this section.

Questioning Aligned to the 5E Inquiry Model

Productive questions must match the phase of the inquiry in which they are used. It is important to ask the right question at the right time. Consider the phases of the 5E instructional model. Just as each phase of the lesson has a different purpose, the questions you use at each phase to focus student thinking and move learners through the inquiry process should differ, too.

Strategic questioning involves selecting and using specific types of questions with well-defined functions at the appropriate phase of a lesson. Table 6.2 focuses on asking questions strategically. The strategy follows the 5E model of inquiry-based instruction. It involves asking questions that can initiate inquiry discussion (engage), guide discussions of information and data obtained through observation and investigations (explore), assist students in making the transition from observation to explanation (explain), and apply new ideas in new situations (elaborate). Since the fifth E, evaluation, is typically embedded within each of the other phases for the purpose of formative assessment, the last phase of the 5E learning model

TABLE 6.2 Strategic Questions Throughout the 5E Model

Phase of 5E Model	Purpose of Question	Generic Question Prompt
Engage	Build interest and enhance motivation.	What do you think would happen if . . . ?
	Assess prior knowledge and conceptions.	Have you ever (seen or done) . . . ? What do you know about . . . ?
	Initiate and focus inquiry.	When observing this scientific phenomenon, why does this happen and what variables matter?
Explore	Focus students' thoughts on investigations, observations, and data.	How are you (or How is your group) addressing our question? What's happening? What data are you collecting?
	Guide students' analysis of data to prepare them to make inferences.	What do you notice about your data? Does it happen this way every time? What does your data suggest?
	Encourage identification of patterns and relationships in data and determine evidence from their analysis.	Did you collect enough data to draw conclusions? Can you analyze your graph and explain any trends or patterns? When you change . . . what happens to . . . ?
	Promote sharing of observations and data.	What did you (or your group) observe? How do your findings compare with those of other groups in the class?

Phase of 5E Model	Purpose of Question	Generic Question Prompt
Explain	Invite students to offer their thinking and explanations about what happened.	Why do you think . . . happened? How is your claim supported by evidence?
	Encourage examination and reflection on presented hypotheses and explanations.	Do you agree with . . . 's explanation? Why or why not? How is . . . 's hypothesis different from . . . 's hypothesis?
	Invite students to relate evidence to their prior and existing knowledge as they develop their reasoning.	Considering what happened, how has your thinking about this changed? How does this textbook passage relate to what we found in the investigation?
	Prepare the way for instruction on new scientific knowledge (facts and concepts).	What do you think you need to find out more about?
Elaborate	Encourage students to apply new learning in other situations.	Do you expect the same results if you use different materials or organisms? How would you use this method to . . . ? What else could this help us explain?

is not identified separately in Table 6.2. Once you are familiar with the information in Table 6.2 about strategic questions for the 5E Inquiry Model, refer back to the characteristics of productive questions from Table 6.1 and apply your learning to Exploration 6.3.

Which Types of Productive Questions Would You Expect to Find at Each Phase of a 5E Lesson?

EXPLORATION

6.3

Working individually or with a partner, consider Tables 6.1 and 6.2. Decide which types of productive questions are appropriate to use during each of the phases of an inquiry lesson based on the 5E model. Construct a table or other graphic organizer to display your ideas.

Reflection Questions:

1. For each phase of the lesson, why did you include the type(s) of productive questions you did?
2. Why does using "the right question at the right time" matter during instruction?

Instructional Plan for Engage Phase

Materials:

- Large steel sewing needle
- Styrofoam packing or 2-cm diameter circle cut from a clean Styrofoam meat tray
- Transparent 9-oz plastic cup filled nearly to the top with water
- Strong bar magnet

Classroom Organization:

Gather the class around so all can see the top surface of the water in the plastic cup when placed on the desk, an overhead, or under a document camera.

Instructional Sequence:

Place Styrofoam circle into the cup with water. It will float. Gently lay the needle horizontally on the Styrofoam circle.

> **Ask the class:** *"What do you see happening?"*

Accept multiple answers and allow brief discussion. Expected answers include: *"Nothing special,"* and, *"A needle is lying on a piece of Styrofoam floating in a plastic cup of water."*

To focus their observations, ask the class: *"What's happening to the needle?"* Expected answers include: *"The needle is staying in place on the Styrofoam, but the Styrofoam is floating around randomly."*

Remove the needle from the Styrofoam, then stroke it several times in the same direction with one end of the bar magnet. Lay the needle on the Styrofoam disk again.

> **Ask the class:** *"What do you see happening this time?"* Expected answers include: *"It's moving,"* *"It's turning,"* and *"The magnet changed what it does!"*

Pick up the needle and reorient it on the Styrofoam or turn the floating Styrofoam around and release it. Do this several times as the students look on. Regardless of how you orient the needle, it should always swing around and point in the same direction.

To maintain student focus on observing, ask the class: *"What do you notice about the behavior of the needle now?"*

Then, to encourage them to consider their accumulated observations, ask: *"Is there a pattern to what happens each time?"*

After a discussion of what is observed and the patterns that are emerging, ask: *"Where have you seen something like this before?"* or *"What do you think this might have to do with force?"* to learn more about students' previous experiences with similar phenomena and possible connections they already have made in a previous unit of study.

Refocus the discussion on what was puzzling here. Ask, *"What is unexpected or puzzling in the event observed?"* or *"What needs to be explained about this?"*

Engage: Using Questioning to Initiate Inquiry

In science inquiry, we want students to be intrinsically motivated to pursue a learning task and to engage in it for intrinsic reasons—they are engaged and want to learn—rather than because of grades or teacher approval, which is a part of extrinsic motivation. One very effective way to create intrinsic motivation in students is by surprising them and challenging their thinking with novel events, phenomena, or science mysteries. For example, why does a glass of ice water get slippery? Does this happen in all parts of the country and does the container have to be glass? Why does adding salt to ice cause it to melt?

Novel or discrepant events can be presented through a teacher demonstration using science materials, hands-on student investigations, or a video segment. The sample instructional plan for a discrepant event that follows might build interest and initiate inquiry about the Earth's magnetic field.

You have reached the end of the engage phase of this lesson. The purpose of the engage phase has been accomplished; the learners want to better understand the surprising phenomenon they just observed! Demonstrating discrepant events is certainly a good way to arouse curiosity and promote interest in the topic you plan for them to investigate. Next, they need time to explore.

This isn't the time to ask students to explain why this happened, nor is it the time to give a lecture to explain what happened and why. But for your information, the science behind this discrepant event relates to magnetism and Earth's magnetic field. In the demonstration, the needle was not initially a magnet. Therefore, it was not affected by Earth's magnetic field. However, stroking it with a bar magnet magnetized the needle. When the magnetized needle was placed on the Styrofoam, it swung around until it was oriented along the direction of Earth's magnetic field. The needle pointed along a magnetic north-south direction.

To help your students build and strengthen their scientific concepts, you must be aware of what they know or do not know at the start of any study. You might assess children's prior knowledge by simply asking them what they already know about a topic. The engage portion of the lesson, such as the magnetized needle demonstration, provides a natural context for you to discover what they already know. In the needle demonstration, children display their prior knowledge of magnetism as they talk about the event and respond to your questions.

When motivated by a good engage task, students are called on to observe objects and events, form a question about why something happens, and recall relevant knowledge to be used in explaining the event. As children conduct an investigation or watch a demonstration, they typically talk about what they observe and think. By listening and interacting with the students, you will be better able to assess their prior knowledge and conceptions.

When students are ready, ask questions or lead them to ask questions to initiate and focus the next phase of the lesson. Of course, the questions asked should be ones that students are able to investigate through their own inquiries.

Explore: Using Questioning to Guide Discussions of Observations

One way children seek answers to their questions is through using the senses or instruments that extend the senses to observe what happens in an investigation or demonstration activity. Observing what happens familiarizes children with the natural world and provides evidence for understanding it.

An important key to inquiry teaching is to lead children to think about their observations. You can guide children in thinking about their observations through the questions you ask. In general, observation questions should be open-ended. A broad, open-ended question such as *"What are some of the things you noticed during the demonstration?"* allows many students to contribute useful information during inquiry.

When working with small groups or the class as a whole, provide wait time until a number of responses have been collected. This approach not only gives more students a chance to enter into the discussion but also ensures that all students will have a variety of descriptive information from which to later build explanations. Class members' observations might be recorded by you or by the students on a flipchart, the chalkboard, or an interactive whiteboard. **Learner response devices**, or "clickers," are another great way to gather data for display and discussion. Since they enable students to anonymously and simultaneously input their own answers electronically without leaving their seats, even shy students can participate freely. If you don't have "clickers," you can ask students to put their responses on individual whiteboards and then hold them up for the teachers to see. Or you can have them share their responses with their table groups.

When getting responses from several students on the same question, it is generally not necessary to repeat or rephrase the question. After one student has supplied an answer, you may redirect the question to another student by asking a question such as, *"Juan, would you like to add anything else?"* or you might ask, *"Does anyone have another idea or something to add?"*

If you want your students to describe a certain aspect of the discrepant event or investigation, include those specifics in your questions. For example, if you want students to think about the equipment and materials used, ask: *"What objects were involved in the investigation (demonstration)?"* If you want them to focus on the events that occurred, ask questions such as:

- *What did you do?* (or *What did I do?*) *What did I vary?*
- *What happened in the experiment (demonstration)?*
- *What are some of the changes you noticed in the . . . ?*
- *What did you see that surprised you?* (*that confused you? that startled you?*)

By focusing on the aspect of an event that is puzzling, the last question begins to lay the groundwork for explanations.

Discussion about observations often occurs when children report their observations and data to the class. Rowe (1973) recommends asking them to answer these questions as part of their report:

- *What was observed?*
- *In what sequence did events happen?*

After each group reports, ask students to compare their observations:

- *Were the observations of all groups the same?*
- *Are the reported sequences the same?*
- *How are they alike? How are the observations different?*

Differences among groups in reports of what they observed or the sequence of events observed can lead to disagreements. To resolve these disagreements, students must think more carefully about their data and sometimes repeat an activity. Data itself is a record of observations that are both quantitative and qualitative. Once students analyze their data and determine if there are trends, then they can summarize their findings into statements of evidence. Discussions that emerge are examples of the NGSS Practice of *engaging in argument from evidence*. If students are unclear about what happened in an investigation, they will not have adequate evidence for constructing explanations for why it happened.

Discussing differences in the data reported by groups is the first step to clarify their findings before they can draw conclusions and determine their evidence. This also gives you an opportunity to discuss the nature of science with your students. According to the *Benchmarks for Science Literacy* (AAAS, 1993), by the end of second grade, students should know that science investigations generally work the same way in different places and that when people give different descriptions of the same thing, it is usually a good idea to make some fresh observations instead of just arguing who is right.

When the observations reported by groups include numerical data (quantitative observations), you can involve your students in the NGSS Practice of *using mathematics and computational thinking*. If you want the class to make and compare measurements, you might ask:

- *Which of the reported measurements is highest? Which is lowest?*
- *Why do you think there is variation (differences) in the class's measurements?*
- *What changes in the temperature of the water did you notice?*
- *Do you have enough data to draw conclusions?*

It is important that children spend considerable time at the *observation* level before beginning to search for *explanations* linked to the scientific question being investigated. Unless sufficient time is spent in developing an adequate foundation at the lower cognitive level, students are often not able to sustain discussion at higher levels of thought.

Explain: Using Questioning to Guide Discussions of Explanations

At some point in the discussion, you should shift the thinking of students from *observation* to *explanation*. Explaining is the counterpart of observing. In observing, students are directly involved with objects and events. Explanations require students to go beyond observations, to reason about their experiences, and make the meaning clear to someone else. Careful observations determine *what* happens. Explanation is concerned with *why* it happened.

When you are ready to shift instruction from an observation or exploration phase to explanation, let children help you decide which aspects of an investigation might need explaining. Find out what *they* want to know about the results of an investigation or why a puzzling event occurred. List the children's questions where they can see and think about them. Make sure that all children have a chance to frame their own questions.

In leading students to identify problems, you might ask:

- *What do you think needs explaining here?*
- *What is most puzzling to you?*

When attempting to focus thought on interpreting and explaining, a good approach is to start with the simpler problems that have been identified, gradually gather interpretative ideas, and build toward the more difficult problems.

The transition from observation to explanation can be a difficult process for students. One of your jobs in inquiry teaching is to facilitate the process of *making meaning* from data. To facilitate the meaning-making process, you might begin by asking students, *"Do you notice any pattern in your data (in your moon observations)?"* After some discussion, shift the thinking of students to making sense of the data and patterns in the data. You might begin to facilitate the process of explaining by asking: *"What ideas do you have about why this happened?"*

The *National Science Education Standards* (NRC, 1996) emphasize that in constructing explanations, students must think critically about evidence they identified from analysis of their data, considering which of their observations constitute evidence and which are irrelevant. They must also have adequate subject matter knowledge. Finally, they must be able to link their evidence with their prior knowledge in a reasonable way to explain why something happened.

Learners in grades K–2 observe the world using all of their senses and offer their personal "theories," which are just their ideas about why an event happened. Typically, learners in grades 1 and 2 do not construct consistent explanations of events in the world. It is not until late second grade or third or fourth grade that children begin to consistently distinguish between observations and interpretations (or inferences) and to construct simple explanations involving effects and their causes. Complex explanations involving chains of causes and effects are not formed until about grades 5 or 6. Yet learners at every grade level can profit from considering why an event happened and how the world works.

A first step in developing explanations is for students to organize their data or observations in some way. To *organize* means to fit individual parts into a whole. Discussion of data and organization might take place as groups build data tables or report their findings to the class or perhaps in a whole-class discussion.

Research suggests that understanding is enhanced when students actively integrate information in various ways. To help students see their data holistically, rather than as fragmented parts, teachers might ask them to:

- describe to others what they did and what they found out
- summarize their data
- organize their data/information into tables and graphs
- elaborate information by adding details
- generate relationships between the new material and information already in memory
- recognize patterns in observational data

For example, in developing ideas about relationships, ask such questions as:

- *How is this situation like (different from) the other one?*
- *What similarities (differences) do you see in these situations?*

Viewing data holistically is not enough, however. According to Duschl and colleagues (NRC, 2007), research evidence indicates that children and adolescents had particular problems in coordinating evidence and reasoning. Through strategic use of questions, science teachers can help children reflect on and represent evidence more completely, think at deeper levels, and connect evidence and knowledge more logically in explaining events in the natural world.

Students may need considerable scaffolding assistance in accessing prior knowledge to make sense of observations. To encourage students to think about scientific knowledge that might be involved in an explanation, ask such questions as:

- *What principles that we have learned do you think may come into play here?*
- *What do we already know that might help us here?*
- *What principles (rules, laws, concepts) do you think are needed in solving this problem or answering this question?*
- *How do you think the principles of floating and sinking apply to this problem?*

To get students to consider the possible cause of an event, ask questions such as:

- *What ideas do you have about why this happened?*

- *What suggestions (theories) do you have about the cause of this?*
- *Can you explain why it might have happened?*
- *What do you think is the cause of . . . ?*

Questions that focus on interpretation and explanation should be open-ended and prompt thinking and should be pursued for a sufficient time to get responses from several students or groups. This strategy helps to ensure that ideas and explanations at a variety of levels of abstractness are at hand for students of different abilities to consider.

Note the use of the personal pronoun *you* in the examples of explanation questions. Recall that productive questions are person centered, allowing children to respond at their own level of thought. An explanation question such as *"What ideas do you have about why?"* rather than *"Why did this happen?"* focuses more on the act of thinking than on correct answers. This questioning approach frees children from the burden of knowing in advance why something took place. It encourages them to think about possible reasons for the cause of a puzzling event and to offer suggestions or reasonable ideas to build on. Their initial responses need not be absolutely correct.

Through sensitive listening, careful and caring questioning, and appropriate scaffolding, you can help the class as a whole formulate a satisfying response that is age and grade level appropriate. Practical experience demonstrates that children can learn to go beyond their observations and construct scientific explanations for why things happen.

Elaborate: Questioning to Guide Discussions of Applications to New Situations

In building understanding, children need opportunities to apply or transfer new knowledge and understanding in many problem-solving situations (Bransford, Brown, & Cocking, 1999). Problems and questions can be generated in various ways. For example, you may plan the problem situations or provide the questions, or they may arise from students' creative ideas and interests. As they work on fresh questions and problems, students try out their recently learned ideas by transferring them to the new situations, thereby refining and extending their developing understanding. In a 5E model of instruction, the elaborate (application) phase of a lesson allows students to make new connections and construct more useful schemas from the knowledge they gained in previous activities.

To elicit thinking about how new knowledge and understanding might be extended to different phenomena, ask such questions as:

- *How do you think . . . applies to . . . ?*
- *In what ways does this idea compare/contrast with . . . ?*
- *How can we use this principle to explain . . . ?*
- *What new problems or questions does this suggest?*
- *What might happen if . . . ?*

Especially good questions or problems for the elaborate phase can be found from applications of science in technology. Application opens up the opportunity for students to explore the natural and technological world more deeply and to realize how extensively science and technology affect people.

 CHECK YOUR UNDERSTANDING 6.3
Click here to gauge your understanding of the concepts in this section.

Managing Classroom Discourse

Typically, after you ask your class a productive question, your students will think, and one or more students will answer you. The answers offered may be correct or incorrect, expected or surprising, but then what should you do to keep the discussion going? You might ask a new unrelated question or proclaim the answer right or wrong, but those options don't encourage deeper thinking about the concept addressed by your initial question; in fact, they tend to shut down student thinking. It also doesn't encourage all of your students to engage with the question. What are your options if you don't call on the first few students to raise their hands?

Elementary and middle school teachers often feel pressured to cover everything in the few hours that students are in the classroom each day. So it is no surprise that they try to rush through many of the things they do, even question-and-answer and discussion times. Rowe (1973, 1987) found that most teachers usually wait less than a second for a response after asking a question! Such very brief intervals, or **wait times**, encourage rote answers that are usually verbatim recall of textbook or teacher-made information. In contrast, inquiry requires time for students to reflect, make connections, and construct inferences and explanations.

What differences in student responses do you think were found with longer teacher wait times? Rowe found that when teachers waited three seconds or longer, student responses included greater speculation, conversation, and argument than when wait times were shorter. She also found that when teachers are trained to wait an average of more than three seconds before responding, the following positive student behaviors happen:

- The length of student response is between four to eight times longer.
- The number of unsolicited but appropriate responses increases.
- Failure to respond decreases.
- Confidence increases.
- The number of questions asked by students increases.
- Academically challenged students contribute more.
- The variety of types of responses increases. There is more reacting to each other, structuring of procedures, and soliciting.
- Speculative thinking increases by as much as seven times.
- Discipline problems decrease.
- Achievement improves in cognitively complex items on written tests.

Rowe also found that teachers trained to prolong wait time changed their teaching behavior in the following ways:

- The number of teacher questions decreased, because more students responded and the responses of students became longer.
- The number of teacher questions that called for reflection and clarification increased.
- Teacher expectations for student performance were modified. (Teachers were less likely to expect only the brighter students to reply and viewed their class as having fewer academically challenged students.)
- Teachers changed the direction of discussion from teacher-dominated to teacher–student discussion.

There are two types of wait time. **Wait time 1** is the pause that follows a question by the teacher. The students may answer quickly, but if they do not, the teacher waits. **Wait time 2** is the pause that follows a burst of responses by the students. The teacher waits before responding or asking another question to see if the students will continue to talk.

Of the two, Rowe (1987) indicated that wait time 2 is more important for a teacher to develop. She found that when teachers used wait time 2, student responses increased five to eight times. Furthermore, the responses from the academically challenged students increased significantly when teachers increased their wait time after student talk.

It can be challenging to increase your wait-time tolerance so your students have more opportunities to think, create, and fully demonstrate their potential. But by using wait time appropriately and learning to respond to your students' answers strategically, you can help them learn more science.

Not only is what you say important, but also how you say it. Tone of voice, body language, and facial expressions all matter when you are involved in question-and-answer sessions and discussions with your class. Even the pace of the discussion matters.

There are three main ways you can respond strategically to nurture and extend children's ideas during inquiry. You can **accept** or recognize student answers without judging them; you can **extend** student answers by adding something new to what was said; and you can **probe** student answers by asking questions based on their answers. Extending and probing represent two different ways to scaffold student understanding. Figure 6.3 shows some ways to apply these three teacher responses strategically.

FIGURE 6.3 Types of Teacher Responses to Student Answers

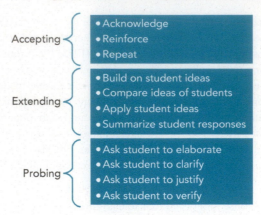

Accepting Student Responses

Your inquiry teaching repertoire should incorporate an attitude of initial *acceptance* of student ideas, even when they contain errors, mistakes, and alternative conceptions. Students should feel that they have the "right to be wrong." Because the practice of inquiry involves the challenge of investigating the unknown, sometimes it results in mistakes. The need to be always right, whether imposed by teachers, peers, or self, is a limiting and threatening position. In your role as a teacher, you have the responsibility to help students explore new experiences and new meanings without penalizing the mistakes and wrong turns that are certain to accompany the process of inquiring. By accepting children's ideas without initially judging or evaluating them, you can help establish a climate in which students feel they can risk to share their ideas.

You can show acceptance of your students' ideas by acknowledging, repeating, and reinforcing them. When *acknowledging,* you should refrain from evaluating students' responses. This leaves the door open for further discussion. Whether an answer is right or wrong, you might respond:

- *Thanks for answering.*
- *OK. Did anyone else have the same idea?*
- *Let's list your idea on the board.*
- *Let's keep your idea in mind.*

You might also use nonverbal behaviors such as a nod to tell students that their responses have been heard and accepted.

Simply repeating a student idea is another way to acknowledge and accept it. You can show that you accept a student's idea by repeating it almost verbatim or by paraphrasing the idea, without changing or adding to it significantly. For example:

Student: *Maybe it's the air leaking.*
Teacher: *OK. You think it may be the air leaking. [Repeating]; or*
Teacher: *OK. You think the bubbles may be caused by escaping air. [Paraphrasing]*

Blosser (1991) cautioned against the overreliance on repeating student responses. If students know you are going to repeat responses, they may tend not to listen to one another but wait for your repetition. If you think the whole class has not heard a response, you might say something like: *"That's an interesting idea. I don't think the whole class heard it, though. Would you say it again so everybody can hear?"*

Another type of accepting behavior is *reinforcing* student ideas. It is an established principle of behavioral psychology that a person's tendency to display an action is dependent on events that follow the action (Ormrod, 2004). These special events are called *reinforcements*. In order to encourage student participation in discussion, you might need to reinforce the act of responding. You might also wish to reinforce both good thinking and good ideas.

One way of reinforcing student responses is with praise. For example:

- *Good thinking*
- *All right!*
- *Excellent explanation!*

A stronger way of reinforcing children's responses is through praise followed by an explanation of the reason for the praise:

- *Great! I like the way you are contributing.*
- *Good job! Your idea is particularly helpful because it relates your explanation to your observations.*
- *Fine! I like the way you compared your idea to Celeste's idea.*

Praise is important, but it should not be given in such a way that students think the idea praised is the only possible one. You don't want other children to just give up on their own lines of thought. Even when the idea you are seeking is voiced by a student, reinforce the child but let the class know there is more to be done. You might say: *"Great thinking! Your idea is one we will have to consider."* Then, to the class, *"What other ideas do you have that are supported by your evidence?"*

Reinforcement is more effective if it follows an unpredictable schedule. If students can predict that you will say "very good" after every response, this form of praise loses its effectiveness. For best results, you should use intermittent reinforcement and it should focus on the work and the ideas, not comparing one student to another.

Reinforcement is, of course, more than a matter of what the teacher says. Both research and practice show that students are less inhibited about answering and show more productivity and achievement when their teachers tend to be approving, to provide emotional support, to express sympathetic attitudes, and to accept their feelings.

Extending Student Responses

When students give vague, incomplete, unorganized, or partially correct responses or when they are on the right track but need assistance, you might respond in a way that nurtures and extends their ideas. Perhaps the best reinforcement for students comes when they see their own ideas used by the teacher. Several techniques for extending student responses are described next.

To help move the discussion along, it is sometimes appropriate to focus on an idea suggested by one or more students and to build on it. For example, you might say: *"All right! I believe we are on the right track here. Let's think about what we learned last week in science. Remember . . . "*

To help clarify a student idea, you might restate the idea in simpler terms, reorganize the idea, or perhaps summarize it. For example, suppose a student has given an unclear and unorganized answer. You might respond:

- *In other words, the air takes up more space when heated.*
- *If I understand you correctly, you are saying that the air takes up more space when it is heated.*

When two or more students make suggestions that have significant similarities or differences, you might extend the ideas by comparing or contrasting them:

- *Your idea is similar to Jamal's in that . . . ?*
- *Notice the difference between Kenesha's idea and Sean's idea. Kenesha said the wire would expand when it was heated; Sean said it would expand when it cooled. Both are possibilities that we can test. How could we test these two hypotheses?*

There is uncertainty among teachers about how to handle incorrect ideas and misconceptions held by students. On the one hand, a student who is told that his idea is wrong may be reluctant to participate in discussions again. On the other hand, misconceptions left unchallenged can cause confusion and interfere with understanding. Teachers need tactful ways to help students confront their ideas using a conceptual change process. Sometimes you might decide to directly correct an incorrect notion and move on. In that case, then you might determine if part of the student's answer is correct and reinforce this part. For example: *"Yes, heat does play a part in the expansion of the copper rod, but melting does not take place. Remember, in melting, the solid rod would become a liquid. Is that what you observed? Can you revise your explanation?"*

Applying an idea suggested by a student in building an explanation is an excellent method of extending student ideas. However, you should be careful not to shift from extending student ideas to simply giving the desired information through lecture.

Don't forget that when asking a question to the class that requires them to justify their response, you can provide thinking and discussion time by telling the class that they have two minutes to discuss their ideas in their groups first. Students will be more comfortable sharing their initial ideas with other students. You can also stop in the middle of a discussion and review the two or three ideas provided by students and ask the group to discuss which ideas they agree with and why. Both of these strategies give students a chance to make their thinking visible during the table talk and then to revise their thinking to incorporate the ideas of others. To move the inquiry along, occasionally summarize the group's discussion and assess the various suggestions. This will not only extend students' ideas but also promote further inquiry. When the concepts involved are abstract or vague, when there are many responses, when student answers have been lengthy, or when some investigations have taken a great deal of time, you might briefly summarize what has been said or identify and restate the main ideas discussed.

Probing Student Responses

After a student has contributed an idea to a discussion, you might use a probing response to find out more about what he or she is thinking. Probing is a strategy in which the teacher reacts to student responses by asking penetrating questions that require students to go beyond superficial, first-answer responses. This takes some practice on the part of the teacher. To help students help each other, you can teach them to ask probing questions by providing some sentence starters that will work with their grade level. Even at the K–2 level, get accustomed to asking students probing questions like, *"I noticed . . . about your work. Can you tell me more about what you did?"* or *"I disagree with you. Did you try . . . ?"*

Probing differs from extending. In *extending,* the teacher does the clarifying, comparing, and contrasting of student ideas; in *probing,* the teacher asks students, or students ask other students to look more deeply at their own ideas or those of others. Descriptions of four probing techniques commonly used in science classes follow.

One good way to probe is to build on a student response by asking a question based on it to help students build confidence and to think scientifically. For example:

Teacher's question: *"Why do you think there is so much variation in the size and shape of bird beaks?"*
Student's answer: *"Because different kinds of birds eat different things."*
Teacher's probing response: *"In what ways does the size and shape of a bird's beak relate to its diet? Can you tell me more using examples?"*

You might also probe students' responses by asking them to clarify the response by giving more information, explaining a term used, or restating the response in other words. For example, during an investigation of what happens to various powders when they are poured into hot water, the teacher asks the class: *"What happened when you used sugar?"* A student answers: *"It melted."* Since that isn't the term the teacher wants to hear, she probes for clarification by asking one of the following questions:

- *What do you mean by melting?*
- *How could you restate that to make clearer what you mean?*
- *How could you explain that further?*

You can also probe to seek justification of student ideas. In asking a student to justify a response rationally, you might say:

- *What are you assuming here?*
- *Why do you think that is so?*
- *I'm not sure I follow your reasoning. Tell us how you arrived at that answer.*
- *What evidence supports your claim?*

Sometimes you might probe by asking students how they would test and verify ideas or confirm a theory. For example, you might say:

- *You have suggested that the heaping effect might involve both adhesive and cohesive forces. Can you think of a way to test your idea?*
- *What would you do to test your idea?*
- *What would it take for that to be true?*
- *What evidence (additional information, data) would we need to support your explanation (suggestion)?*
- *What experiment could we do to test your idea?*

Depending on the questions you ask, you can help students to share their progress, make sense of the science, make connections between ideas and applications, or even help students who are stuck to get unstuck. You can use the following probing questions to prompt student thinking and keep the learning moving forward.

- *How would you describe the problem in your own words?*
- *What data do you have?*
- *Would it help to create a diagram? Make a data table?*
- *Have you compared your work with anyone else?*
- *What have you tried? What did other members of your group try?*
- *What background information do you know that might help you?*
- *What about putting things in order?*
- *Could you try your investigation again?*

Vignette 6.1 Questioning Strategies in the Classroom: Properties of Air in Fourth Grade

Ms. Newhall is ready to help her fourth graders, who are anxiously gathered around her at the demonstration table, understand that "air" is a real material substance. In front of her are a fish bowl about three-quarters full of water and a small, transparent glass. To focus the children's attention and find out their prior knowledge about ways air and water interact, she holds the glass upside down above the surface of the water in the fish bowl, as shown in Figure 6.4, and begins a discussion:

TEACHER: I'm going to push this glass into the water until it is all the way under the water. What do you think will happen? [She pauses as many hands are raised.] Avery, what do you think?

AVERY: It's going to stay at the bottom . . . sink.

Ms. Newhall wants the students to focus on the air and the water rather than the glass. So, with a nod acknowledging Avery's answer, she turns to another student who has her hand up.

TEACHER: Samantha.

SAMANTHA: Me and my dad took a glass into the pool one time. We put the glass under the water. We kept it straight, and if you keep it straight, no water will come in. The air will stay in there, but if you tip it up, the water will come in.

TEACHER: Interesting.

Samantha's answer revealed that she had significant prior experience and knowledge about what would happen in the demonstration. Some of her knowledge came from personal discoveries. She had also acquired some knowledge from discussions with her father. Samantha used the term air appropriately, but Ms. Newhall was not sure what she really understood about

(continued)

(continued)

FIGURE 6.4   **Investigating the Properties of Gases**

the concept. Ms. Newhall acknowledges Samantha's answer and files it away for later use. But she wants to know what the other children know about air and what they think will happen in the demonstration. So she turns to the class again.

TEACHER: Is there anybody else who thinks if you put this whole glass under the water, nothing is going into the glass? [She pauses for several seconds.] What do you think, Michelle?

MICHELLE: Water may go in the glass.

After giving the rest of the class time to offer opinions, Ms. Newhall polls the students to see which of the two ideas they support. There is about equal support for Samantha's idea that water would not come into the glass and Michelle's idea that the glass may fill up with water.

TEACHER: OK. We have two ideas. Let's test these ideas.

Ms. Newhall calls on a student to help her with the demonstration. First, she asks the student to check to make sure the glass was dry. To encourage careful observation, she tells the class, "Make careful observations with your eyes." Then she pushes the glass, open end down, all the way under the water. Most students notice that the water did not go into and fill the glass, but one student is not sure.

After drying the glass carefully, Ms. Newhall crumples a paper towel and inserts it into the bottom of the dry glass. She pushes the glass with its open

end down under the water again. When she removes the glass from the water, she asks a child to examine the paper towel. The child observes and announces that it is dry. In order to shift the students' thoughts from observation and description to the higher cognitive level of explanation, Ms. Newhall continues the discussion:

TEACHER: Why did it stay dry? [She pauses and considers which student to call on first.] What do you think, Jessica?

JESSICA: Because it was inside that glass which protected it from the water outside.

TEACHER: But what kept the water out? [Pausing briefly.] Anthony?

ANTHONY: A water seal. There was water on the bottom of the open glass, but not on the inside.

TEACHER: But if there's all that water around the outside, why didn't it go in here? [She points to the inside of the glass and pauses again to let everyone think.]

BLAIR: Because the air was in there.

TEACHER: The air. . . . Oh . . . is that what kept the water out?

The initial answers to Ms. Newhall's question about why the paper towel stayed dry indicate that many children do not yet have a good understanding of air taking up space. Although they know the term air and in previous lessons had connected it to some physical situations such as wind and breathing, they still have difficulty applying the concept in interpreting the demonstration. Because of Blair's answer, Ms. Newhall decides to extend Samantha's earlier contribution.

TEACHER: Samantha said something earlier. In the pool, when she put the glass down straight, the glass did not fill with water, but when she pushed it down and tipped it, it did.

Ms. Newhall then demonstrates that when she tilts the glass, bubbles come from the glass and rise in the water. She tries to get the children to describe the bubbles as bubbles of air. However, the children describe the bubbles as "water bubbles" and in other ways, but no one uses the term air bubbles. So, the discussion continues:

TEACHER: In the bottom half of the glass is water; in the top half of the glass is . . . ?

KATE: Dry.

TEACHER: What is in there?

The children just look at her quizzically, obviously confused. So, demonstrating again:

TEACHER: When I tip it (a small amount), the water keeps the air in. When I tilt it far enough, the air can come out.

Ms. Newhall realizes the class is now ready to move into the explore section of the lesson. So she provides clear tubs and plastic glasses for pairs of students to further investigate as she monitors their work and guides their thinking through additional questioning.

Source: Based on a segment of a video produced by Merrill Education.

There is much for you to learn about questioning from the teacher in this lesson. She strategically used some exceptional science questioning techniques:

- First, she asked questions to ascertain the students' prior knowledge.

- Then, she asked observation questions to get the children to focus on what happened and to help them improve their observational skills.

- Only after sufficient evidence had been introduced into the discussion did she ask explanation questions, focusing on why the events happened.

- She did not immediately acknowledge that Samantha's initial answer was correct but kept the discussion open so that all students could enter in and possibly construct knowledge about air for themselves.

- Also, she asked her questions before calling on a student by name, thus helping to ensure that all students would have to listen to and think about their answers to the questions.

- She called on a diversity of students, making sure she included both boys and girls and children of all ability levels.

- She also used appropriate wait time, though that is difficult to know by just reading the vignette.

Despite Ms. Newhall's use of model teaching techniques, many of the children still had difficulty constructing notions about air and its properties that are useful in *understanding* why the paper in the glass remained dry. That is, some children still had problems in *applying* their knowledge to *explain* or make sense of the demonstrations involving air. Nevertheless, through their discoveries and discussion, the children are building knowledge to apply in future knowledge construction experiences.

 In this video, third-grade teacher, Nancy Michael, reflects on her efforts to guide student sense-making with questioning. What was her message to herself and to other teachers?

✓ CHECK YOUR UNDERSTANDING 6.4

Click here to gauge your understanding of the concepts in this section.

Implementing Science Talk in the Classroom

Student talk in your science classroom should go beyond answering the questions that you pose as the teacher. Though the traditional vision of a well-managed classroom often involves children working individually—reading, writing, studying—in near silence, remember Vygotsky's work in social constructivism. As a new teacher, please do not equate a silent classroom with an effective classroom. Instead, help your children use accountable science talk with each other in pairs, small groups, and in the whole group by establishing norms for discussion; modeling and teaching how to ask productive questions, listen carefully, and respond thoughtfully; and allowing plenty of time for them to practice communicating like scientists. Of course, this doesn't mean that if your classroom is noisy that it is necessarily effective either!

According to the Institute for Learning at the University of Pittsburgh, **accountable talk** is discourse that promotes learning and sharpens student thinking by reinforcing student ability to use knowledge appropriately. Such talk is accountable to the following:

- *The learning community*—by actively listening to each other, building on one another's ideas, requesting clarification, disagreeing respectfully, and challenging claims (not the person making them).

- *Accurate knowledge*—by getting the facts straight, reporting observations that are both relevant and specific, making claims that are supportable, questioning unsupported claims, and avoiding the introduction of falsehoods, rumors, opinions, or irrelevant concepts into the discussion.

- *Rigorous thinking*—by using data from investigation as evidence to support claims, basing claims on a variety of valid sources, reasoning logically, examining assumptions, clarifying ideas, and building sound and cogent arguments (Michaels et al., 2010).

Based on Exploration 6.4, think about what you would expect teachers and students to be saying when engaged in accountable talk.

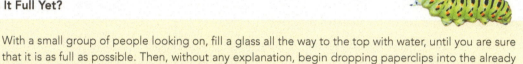

| EXPLORATION 6.4 | Is It Full Yet? |

With a small group of people looking on, fill a glass all the way to the top with water, until you are sure that it is as full as possible. Then, without any explanation, begin dropping paperclips into the already full container. Observe what the onlookers do and say as you continue adding paperclips until the water finally overflows.

Reflection Questions:

1. How did the onlookers react to what happened in your demonstration?
2. If there was conversation about what happened, who talked to whom? Did certain roles emerge?
3. If predictions were made, questions were asked, and/or explanations were suggested, what were they? How did others react to them?
4. If claims were made, what were they? And what evidence was given to support those claims?
5. How do you think the onlookers would have reacted if they were asked not to talk during and after the demonstration? How could you find out?

Currently, most classroom talk is in the form of recitation and question-answer-response interactions between teachers and individual students. It is the kind of discussion that most students have come to expect in school. This form of communication is useful for review of prior knowledge, assessment of what students know, and vocabulary drill, but it is not particularly productive in terms of helping students construct knowledge and understanding. Developing explanations and reasoning skills occurs when students are encouraged to have conversations about their ideas.

The first part of this chapter focused on how to improve this discussion pattern through the use of productive questioning and appropriate wait time, listening actively to students' answers, and responding effectively. The current trend in science education is to shift talk in the science classroom from recitation to student discourse modeled on the oral communication of practicing scientists and engineers. In *Taking Science to School: Learning and Teaching Science in Grades K–8* (NRC, 2007), the fourth of the science proficiencies students should exhibit is: "Participate productively in scientific practices and discourse." Also, science talk is integral to at least two of the Science and Engineering Practices from *A Framework for K–12 Science Standards* (NRC, 2012): *Engaging in argument from evidence,* and *Obtaining, evaluating, and communicating information.*

Unfortunately, accountable or productive science talk is generally absent from science lessons in elementary schools. Since instructional time for science is so limited, many teachers focus on hands-on activities and lack adequate time for whole-group discussion that could enable students to make sense of what they observed during their direct experience (Winokur, Worth, & Heller-Winokur, 2009).

Various researchers have found many benefits of productive classroom science talk. According to Michaels and colleagues (Michaels, Shouse, & Schweingruber, 2008), the benefits include deeper learner engagement with the content being discussed, higher-level reasoning about complex and subject specific ideas, and more involvement in discussion by all learners. They suggest the following reasons for the effectiveness of productive classroom talk.

- Student ideas surface, enabling teachers to assess student understanding.

- By talking about their thinking, students have more opportunities to reflect on, participate in, and build on scientific thinking.

- Learners become aware of discrepancies between their own thinking and that of others (including the scientific community).
- It provides a context in which to develop mature scientific reasoning.
- Learners are motivated when considering peers' claims and positions.
- Such discourse provides opportunities for students to improve their logical reasoning skills and enhance their ability to build scientific arguments.

According to Karen Worth and her colleagues (Worth et al, 2009b, p. 123), "Science talk promotes both science understanding and language learning." In order to talk about an idea, a speaker must first think about it and then articulate it. When students orally share something in their own words, they have a reason to reflect on what they understand and what still confuses them. In addition, using the precise language of science in a discussion helps children understand the difference between science-specific and common language use of terms.

Scientists depend on discussion and debate with peers as they refine their procedures, evaluate data, test the strength of their conclusions, and present their findings to others for review. Participating in similar conversations with their peers about investigations helps students better understand how scientific knowledge is generated. It is part of the jobs of scientists to argue about the evidence, and it is part of our role as teachers to teach students this practice.

Talking something through with others promotes cognitive development when students clarify their ideas or check their reasoning in response to the ideas brought up by others. They rehearse, rethink, and revise ideas. When preparing to talk, learners consider what they already know, examine prior experiences, try to make sense of data, defend their reasoning, and entertain new ideas and perspectives. After hearing others' comments, students compare ideas with ideas of others, challenge what others are saying, and modify their own ideas if necessary.

Science talk is a new language for most students, unless they've grown up in a family of scientists and engineers who bring this talk format with them to discourse around the dinner table. Unlike classroom chatter about clothes or after-school plans, accountable science talk needs to be taught. Students can Practice science talk in many ways: through dialog with a partner, by speaking with members of their small group, and/or by engaging in a whole-class discussion. Each of these talk formats has its own protocol for participating and taking turns and is useful in certain teaching situations and to accomplish specific goals.

Partner talk maximizes the number of students talking at the same time, thus providing the most Practice. It also is less intimidating for most students to speak with just one other person.

When working in small groups, talk is most successful when students know what expectations you have of them. It is less intimidating for many students to share, argue, and defend ideas with a few of their peers than with the whole class. You should listen in as you circulate through the class during small-group discussion. You can contribute productive questions or appropriate responses when needed to keep a group's conversation on track and moving forward.

Whole-class discussion can be made effective as well. Some suggestions based on Douglas et al. (Douglas, Klentschy, & Worth, 2006) and Worth et al. (Worth et al., 2009a, b) follow.

Arrange your students and yourself in a circle for discussion so that everyone else can look at the person speaking by simply turning their heads. The circle arrangement engages all students equally, makes listening easier, and lets you facilitate without dominating—think King Arthur and the Knights of the Round Table.

Have class norms for science talk that everyone understands and agrees to follow. These student expectations typically involve being respectful, open to new ideas, and willing to participate by asking questions, contributing ideas, and responding to the ideas of others. In addition to these students' rights (norms) to share their ideas in a respectful environment, students should also be provided with student obligations, which include:

1. You are obligated to speak loudly enough for others to hear.
2. You are obligated to listen for understanding.
3. You are obligated to agree or disagree (and explain why) in response to other people's ideas.

If you have general discussion norms already in place as part of your classroom management plan, use them as a foundation to build on. If not, either negotiate with your students to generate norms or present expectations you've already developed to the class, then ask students to explain them in their own words and tell why the rules are appropriate. Consistently enforce the norms and reteach discussion skills when necessary. One implementation strategy you can use is the stoplight method. During discussions when

Preparing your students for science talk in the classroom requires teachers to teach procedures and establish norms for student interactions. How does this teacher prepare her students for science talk? How did this help her establish a positive environment?

Now that we've talked about the investigation, our results make more sense.

all of the norms are being met, a green card is showing. When someone violates a norm, then they get a warning and with a repeat offense they get a yellow card. When someone breaks a norm, stop and discuss it with the class and reinforce the expectations. If additional infractions occur, then the student receives a red card, which requires a call home. It will take students awhile to get used to the procedures so be consistent. By doing so, you can transform your classroom into a safe place to have a scientific argument, a risk-free learning community in which learners make their thinking visible to themselves and others.

You might also need to teach some discussion skills, including taking turns, speaking loudly enough that everyone can hear, staying focused on the topic, disagreeing with an idea not with a person, looking at the speaker, and listening for understanding rather than just being quiet while someone else is talking. Pointing out that many science talk discussion skills are similar to those used in interactive read-alouds or literature circles might help your class apply skills they've learned in reading class to science discourse.

Encourage student-to-student interaction and natural conversational flow during the discussion. One approach, which many teachers find challenging, is to just be quiet so students have a chance to talk directly to each other.

In addition, don't require students to raise their hands in order to be called on to speak, especially in the older grades. Instead, teach them the skill of entering a conversation without being invited to do so. To teach this skill, you might create a script for role playing, model it yourself during discussions, and point out to the class what you did and how you did it, or when a student joins a discussion gracefully without raising his or her hand, celebrate that accomplishment and challenge the rest of the class to analyze how it was done.

If your students are having difficulty finding the "right words" to interact with each other politely during a formal discussion, post appropriate question and response starters on the classroom wall. Like a word wall, it can provide scaffolding for the learners who need assistance.

If your science discussions still seem awkward, have your class analyze a nonacademic conversation that occurred at school. Once students recognize the many elements and interactions in that kind of talking, they may be able to better include them in a classroom science talk, thus improving the natural flow of the discourse.

Science talk should be as inclusive as possible. One way to encourage everyone in your class to participate is to occasionally use extreme wait time. Preface your questions with a direction to your class to think for five to ten seconds before answering. This pause allows deeper thinking and can enable even reluctant speakers to compose an answer they are willing to share with the class. Other ways to be sure that even shy students have something to say to the whole group include providing time to talk with a partner or with members of their small group so they can try out their ideas and words, to check information recorded in their science notebook, or to do a quick write that they can refer to later. Sometimes, eager students who always have something to say simply need to be reminded that they should allow others a chance to speak. Remember that this will work best when you specify the time that they have for the discussion at their tables. For younger students give them one to two minutes; older students may need three to five minutes depending on the size of the groups and the question that you asked.

Staying on topic during a science discussion can be a challenge. You can help by reminding students that during science talk they should build on what others have already said instead of just reporting what they want to say. Sometimes you might need to redirect the conversation with a statement like: *"That's an interesting idea, but let's focus on our observations for now."* Students will soon learn to follow your lead and politely begin to keep the class focused. If the train of thought seems to get lost during a science discussion, students might just need to regroup. They could do that by referring to data or notes in their science notebook or by talking briefly with the members of their small group.

Some of the different types of whole-class discussion are as follows:

- *Gathering-Ideas discussions* (brainstorming webs) are most appropriate during the engage phase of a lesson. They focus on finding out what students already know about a topic or concept (Worth, 2009a, b).

- *Making-Meaning discussions* (use charts, graphs, and nonlinguistic representations) are most appropriate during the explain phase of a lesson. Its purpose is to enable students to share their views of what happened in the explore phase with the rest of the class. During this discussion, students present findings, use evidence to support claims, and defend their arguments concept (Worth, 2009a, b).

- *Position-Driven discussions* usually occur in the explain phase of a lesson, too. They involve two or three premises suggested by the teacher or developed by the class. Students are asked to select one of these claims to support using evidence from their investigation or reading (Michaels et al., 2008).

- *Discourse circles* usually occur near the end of a unit. After extensive study involving direct experiences and reading, the class is given a statement to consider. Working in pairs or groups of no more than four, students create arguments for and against this statement using evidence from multiple sources. Then in small groups composed of agreeing and disagreeing students, evidence is presented and positions are stated in an effort to reach consensus or an agreement to disagree. Finally, groups reflect on and share their small-group discussions as the whole class debriefs (Tilson, 2007).

Argumentation is a Science and Engineering Practice that is very important in the last three types of whole-group discussions given in the bulleted list. Your class needs to internalize the difference between respectful scientific argument and everyday argument, which may be confrontational and competitive. Figure 6.5 illustrates the similarities and differences between oral argumentation in science and in daily life. Students must realize that the goal of scientific argument is to reach a point of mutual understanding or consensus. Talking about evidence, models, and hypotheses that support a given theory helps students not only understand scientific outcomes and the concepts that support them, but also how one knows and why one believes. The terms *hypothesis* and *theory* have specific meanings in science, so help students use these terms correctly.

The idea that more than one scientific explanation for a phenomenon might be correct is difficult for elementary and middle school students to accept. They have become conditioned to think there is

FIGURE 6.5 Venn Diagram about Argumentation

ORAL ARGUMENTATION

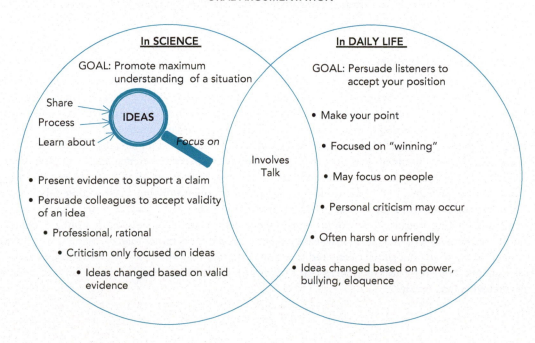

only one right answer to any question and expect the teacher or the text to tell them what it is. Alternative explanations should always be examined.

Not only should you allow science talk in your classroom, but you should also encourage it and perhaps even find ways to make it mandatory. Give priority to finding time to have whole-class discussions. One implementation strategy is to number the students in a group from 1–6 and then roll a die to determine who will be the one to share their ideas first. If the group has three people, then the first student will be the (1,4), the second student will be (2,5) and the third person will be (3,6). If the team has four people, then they will be the numbers 1–4, and if you roll a 5 or 6, just roll again. This protocol supports cooperative learning where all of the students are focusing on the same learning goal, and there is individual accountability for the learning because all students need to be prepared to respond. Some students will be hesitant to share their ideas so when you start this procedure, allow them to start out and then rely on their classmates to continue the explanations. Work toward becoming comfortable with facilitating discussion that is more than just starting out, even though such discussions can be unpredictable. Students need to become proficient at sharing ideas, debating, supporting ideas with evidence, and clarifying the ideas of others—all skills that can be developed through appropriate science talk.

CHECK YOUR UNDERSTANDING 6.5

Click here to gauge your understanding of the concepts in this section.

CHAPTER SUMMARY

The Role of Teacher Questions

In inquiry lessons, effective teachers use questions to motivate students to do things (physical actions) and to think in ways (cognitive actions) that move the inquiry along. Teachers also ask questions to find out what their students know and understand at various points in the lesson so they can decide what should happen next in order to deepen the learning. Properly worded questions can initiate inquiry, probe prior knowledge, focus attention, spur discussion, encourage reflection, shift the focus of a lesson, inspire creativity, guide data analysis, develop and assess student understanding, and help students make connections, test prototypes, defend their ideas, etc.

Different Kinds of Questions

Questions can be classified in many ways. Productive questions have the following characteristics: They are open-ended, person centered, equitable, aligned with targeted science learning, and appropriate for the part of the lesson they are used. Their purpose is to promote students' activity, engagement, and reasoning. Open-ended questions are worded in a way that invites many students to answer; they trigger higher-order thinking, encourage reflection, and build toward understanding. Essential questions are broad open-ended questions that lead to inquiries related to science ideas and phenomena. Their opposite, closed questions, have only one right answer and can often be answered in a single word. Closed questions call for factual knowledge and convergent thinking. Person-centered questions usually include the word *you* or *your* in their construction. They help teachers learn about students' ideas and thinking, because their wording makes them less threatening to answer than subject-centered questions. Person-centered questions clearly ask for personal ideas rather than the right or best answer needed to respond to a subject-centered question. Equitable questions are inclusive, answerable by all students. They refer to experiences that the whole class has had; everyone has a fair chance to be correct when answering.

There are six types of productive questions: questions that "hook" learners, measuring and counting, comparison, investigative, problem posing, and reasoning. The name of each type describes its purpose.

Questioning Aligned to the 5E Inquiry Model

During the *engage* phase, questions that build interest and motivate, assess prior knowledge and conceptions, and initiate and focus inquiry are appropriate. Teacher questions that focus student thinking on their investigation (procedure, design), their observations (techniques, tools used, communicating), and their data (recording, reflection, finding patterns and relationships, sharing) are appropriate for the *explore* phase. The *elaborate* phase calls for teacher questions that encourage students to apply their learning to novel situations. Teacher questions designed for formative assessment of student learning are appropriate in each of the first four phases, and those designed for summative assessment belong in the final phase, *evaluation*.

Managing Classroom Discourse

The three main ways teachers can respond strategically to nurture and extend children's ideas during inquiry are: (1) *accepting* or recognizing student answers without judging them, (2) *extending* student answers by adding something new to what was said, and (3) *probing* student answers by asking questions based on their answers. Extending and probing are ways to scaffold student understanding. Using appropriate wait time, body language, and facial expressions are also helpful.

Implementing Science Talk in the Classroom

Accountable or productive science talk is student discourse that encourages thinking and supports science learning. It involves active listening, building on ideas, clarifying, respectfully disagreeing, presenting accurate facts, making relevant and specific observations, stating supportable claims, challenging weak claims, using data as evidence to support claims, basing claims on multiple sources, reasoning logically, and building strong arguments. It is important because it parallels the practices of discourse and argumentation used by scientists and engineers. Teachers can implement it in the classroom by making time for discussion in pairs, small groups, and in the whole group; developing and using discussion norms; modeling good sentence starters; and facilitating, perhaps through teacher questioning, the right type of discourse at the right time in the lesson.

DISCUSSION QUESTIONS

1. Why should you plan some open-ended questions for use during an inquiry lesson before instruction begins?
2. What are the characteristics and types of productive teacher questions?
3. How do you know what teacher question to ask when?
4. What are the similarities and differences among the main types of teacher responses to student answers?
5. Why is student-led discourse preferable to question-answer sessions?

PROFESSIONAL PRACTICES ACTIVITIES

1. Include suggested teacher questions in an inquiry lesson plan you develop and teach to a group of students.
2. Make an audio or video recording of yourself or your cooperating teacher during an inquiry lesson. Create a list of ten of the teacher questions asked during the lesson. Classify the identified questions

as productive or unproductive and give reasons for the way each was sorted. Suggest a way to revise each unproductive question you identified to make it a productive question.

3. Select one phase of a 5E lesson plan. Develop five productive teacher questions that you might use when teaching that phase of the lesson and explain why you wrote the questions as you did.

4. Make an audio or video recording of yourself or your cooperating teacher during a teacher-led class discussion. Analyze at least five minutes of the recording to identify the types of teacher responses that occurred. Comment on the effect of various responses on the students.

5. Plan a lesson that gives students an opportunity to practice argumentation. Be sure to introduce appropriate norms and teach discussion skills before delivering the lesson.

Assessing Science Learning

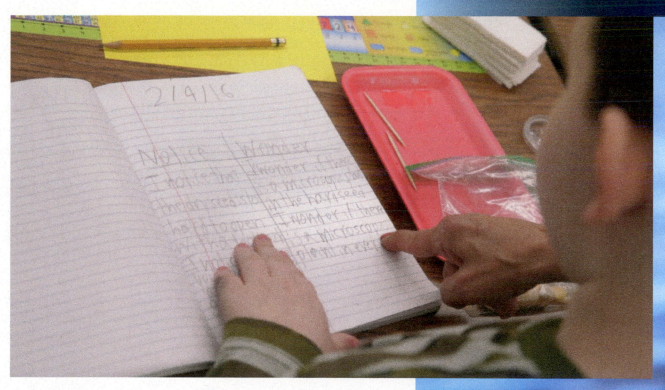

LEARNING GOALS

After reading this chapter, you should understand that:

1. Assessment processes provide opportunities to gather evidence of student learning (summative) or for student learning (formative) which can be evaluated to determine level of mastery of the identified learning goals.

2. Formative assessment processes when implemented as a part of effective teaching practices use feedback loops that helps move student learning forward.

3. Summative assessments provide evidence of student knowledge and understanding at the conclusion of a learning cycle.

4. Performance assessments can measure student understanding of several learning targets.

5. Large scale (state and national tests) assessments indicate the effectiveness of science programs at schools and are used to inform changes needed at the school and district level.

The science committee at a K–8 school was having an informal discussion one day after school. The topic turned to the question, "What is the purpose of classroom assessment?" Various opinions emerged:

- Amy, an enthusiastic fourth-grade teacher, said, "I use assessment to help all of my students learn."

- Steve, an experienced eighth-grade teacher, said, "Assessment allows me to assign grades fairly."

- Tina, who teaches all-day kindergarten, said, "When I assess, I gather data about what each child knows and can do."

- Bill, a sixth-grade teacher who is known as the faculty jokester, said: "I think it's obvious that the purpose of assessment is to keep teachers from having an active social life!"

- Glenda, who works with third and fourth graders with special needs, said: "By assessing my students based on their IEPs, I determine whether or not they have mastered grade-level science learning goals."

- Betty, a veteran fifth-grade teacher, said, "My assessments are designed to get my class ready to do well on the state science test that they take for the first time in fifth grade."

Since you have experienced educational assessment as a student for many years, you have probably developed your own opinion about its purpose. Which of these teachers do you agree with most? Why? If you were part of the discussion, what would you say about the purpose of assessment in science? Considering various views of the purpose of classroom assessment should help you engage with the assessment concepts presented in Chapter 7.

Assessment in the Science Classroom

In education, two terms are frequently used when discussing this topic, **assessment** and **evaluation**. Though these terms are often used as synonyms, some sources find it important to distinguish between these closely related concepts (Smouse, 2010; Kizlik, 2012; Duke ARC, 2012). The stated differences boil down to this: *Assessment* is a process of gathering information about student learning for decision making, while *evaluation* involves using that data in judging student performance and making decisions about learning and instruction. A document from Duke's Academic Resource Center (Duke ARC, 2012) summarizes the differences as follows: *Assessment* is ongoing, focused on how the learning is going, and used to identify what needs improvement for the purpose of improving learning. *Evaluation* is final, focused on what has been learned, and used to arrive at an overall grade or score for the purpose of judging quality.

But in general usage, the distinction between these terms seems to get lost, probably because assessment and evaluation should occur as a linked pair. So throughout the rest of this chapter, the common classroom jargon will be used, and you don't really need to analyze whether a technique, method, or strategy is called *assessment* or *evaluation*.

Think of classroom assessment as a tool or process used in the service of learning and instruction. By observing students while they work, asking key questions, examining the performance and products of students, and administering assessment tasks of various designs, teachers can ascertain students' conceptual understanding, ability to use inquiry strategies, and proficiency with Scientific and Engineering Practices.

Learning and assessment are closely linked in inquiry-based teaching. The interactive approach to teaching science as inquiry provides you with multiple opportunities to teach science for understanding, to assess student learning in ongoing ways, and to make reflective judgments based on concrete evidence of students' accomplishments.

Student participation is a key component of successful assessment. If students are to participate successfully in the process, they need to be clear about the learning goals and criteria for good work, to assess their own efforts in light of the criteria, and to share responsibility in taking action (NRC, 2001).

Assessment in inquiry science should be based on three guiding questions (NRC, 2001):

1. **Where are students trying to go?** This question relates to the learning standards and goals you want your students to achieve. In today's standards-based educational world, the state standards and the national standards on which they are based define the goals that should be achieved in science at different grade levels. It is the responsibility of district curriculum personnel and classroom teachers to determine the specific learning targets that will lead to the attainment of the goals set forth in the science standards. Teachers and districts develop specific learning targets designed to guide the learning process. Assessments of any kind must always be related to standards and lesson learning targets identified in the curriculum and have a clear purpose. The purpose of classroom assessment is to improve learning and instruction.

2. **Where are students now?** This question involves assessing your students' learning at various times during the lesson. Through a combination of formal (planned) and informal (on-the-fly) classroom assessment techniques, you can monitor various aspects of students' learning. It is important to select assessments that target what you want students to know, understand, and be able to do. For example, using multiple-choice items, just because they are easy to administer and to score, will not produce meaningful data unless they are aligned to the lesson's learning goals. For the assessment data collected about your class to be useful, you must also consider the third and final question . . .

3. **How are students going to get there?** This question relates to how you use assessment data to make decisions about scaffolding, learning strategies, feedback, and instruction. Based on information from the first two questions, you should plan and provide students with opportunities to move from where they are to where they should be going. Assessment results determine the teacher responsive actions, which include decisions about how to modify instruction and feedback that can help learners achieve agreed-on learning goals.

In the past, concern with assessment techniques took a back seat to learning theory and instructional reforms in science methods courses. Today, assessment is an integral part of the teaching–learning process. Perhaps the assessment standards for science that were proposed by the National Science Education Standards (NRC, 1996) helped to bring about this change. They envisioned the following shifts in what is emphasized in science assessment:

A shift from:

- assessing what is easily measured, ***toward*** assessing what is most highly valued
- assessing discrete knowledge, ***toward*** assessing rich, well-structured knowledge
- assessing scientific knowledge, ***toward*** assessing scientific understanding and reasoning
- assessing to learn what students do not know, ***toward*** assessing to find out what students do understand
- assessing only achievement, ***toward*** assessing achievement *and* opportunity to learn
- end of term assessment by teachers, ***toward*** students engaged in ongoing assessment of their work and that of others. (NRC, 1996, p. 100)

With the current climate of assessment and accountability that accompanies high-stakes state testing, it is important to remember that the role of assessment in the classroom is focused primarily on the learning of each student. This differs from the role of district interim, benchmark, and common assessments that provide evidence of program effectiveness and only when used formatively can identify groups of students or individuals that need extra support.

TABLE 7.1 Characteristics of Summative and Formative Assessments

SUMMATIVE ASSESSMENT	FORMATIVE ASSESSMENT
After instruction ends	During instruction after some learning
Every 3-4 weeks	At critical points
Samples content	Ideally, assesses every major concept
Tests general concepts	Non-graded
Can help revise course or program	Can determine future learning activities
Measures unit or course effectiveness	Results in feedback to students to move learning forward

The purposes of assessment also vary depending on the phase of a lesson or a unit in which the assessment occurs. Sterling (2005) suggests an assessment cycle in which assessments can be diagnostic (before teaching starts), formative (during teaching), summative (after teaching), and confirmatory (a while after the lesson or unit has ended.) A variety of assessment methods appropriate for one or more stages of the assessment cycle will be described later in the chapter. Please keep in mind that the type of assessment is determined by how (for what purpose) the teacher is using the data it yields, not by which assessment type is used. In the classroom, the two types of assessment processes used most frequently are summative and formative processes.

The characteristics listed in Table 7.1 reveal the differences between summative and formative assessment processes.

Diagnostic assessment, sometimes called *pre-assessment* or *pretesting,* is used before you start teaching a lesson or unit to discover needed information about your students' knowledge, interests, abilities, and preferences. Vignette 7.1 provides an example of diagnostic assessment.

Diagnostic questions asked and observations made at the beginning of a lesson (the engage phase of the 5E instructional inquiry model) help you identify what students already know about a topic, what misconceptions and alternative hypotheses they carry, and what they are interested in learning. Though some type of notation (IP—In progress, PP—Partially proficient, P—Proficient, and M—Mastery) might be recorded for future comparison to measure growth, grades should not be given for diagnostic assessments.

Vignette 7.1   Why Did That Happen?

Mr. Garza's sixth-grade class is just beginning a unit about flight. They look on as John grasps a piece of paper and blows steadily across the top of it as shown in Figure 7.1. Unexpectedly, the paper moves up rather than down. Exclamations of "Wow!" and "I didn't expect that to happen!" are heard. The students each draw a line down the middle of a page in their science journals. On one side, they list questions pertaining to the event that might be investigated; on the other side, they propose explanations about why the paper went up rather than down. Mr. Garza collects the science notebooks and scans the students' charts after class. By examining his students' work, he has a good idea of their prior knowledge about Bernoulli's principle and the effect of rushing air and changing air pressure.

FIGURE 7.1

Blow across top of paper

By using various assessment procedures diagnostically to elicit students' initial ideas before you begin teaching, you can decide what specific experiences will best encourage students' learning progress. Diagnostic data will help you adjust instructional strategies and scaffolding to students' individual differences and, therefore, serves as a useful differentiation tool.

Keeley and colleagues (Keeley, Eberle, & Farrin, 2005; Keeley, 2011; 2012) have written extensively about **formative assessment probes**. They are "formative" assessment items designed to uncover students' ideas in science. They were developed with extensive knowledge of science concepts and commonly held misconceptions and intended to be efficient classroom tools for informing instruction. Despite their name, formative assessment probes can be used at any phase of a lesson, if they are used purposefully (Keeley, 2011). If used at the beginning of a lesson or unit, then they are actually *diagnostic* assessment probes. Work through Exploration 7.1 to help you understand how formative assessment probes uncover students' ideas.

Trying Out a Formative Assessment Probe

EXPLORATION

7.1

A formative assessment probe is designed to uncover learners' ideas about technology. This type of formative assessment probe is known as a justified list (Keeley et al., 2005). Follow the instructions provided, then share your thinking with a small group of your colleagues.

Is It Technology?

Examples of technology and things that are not technology are listed below.
Put a check mark beside the things that you consider to be technology.

____ cup	____ telephone	____ pencil	____ flower
____ horse	____ laser	____ remote control	____ rock
____ telescope	____ electricity	____ book	____ television
____ automobile	____ carrot	____ cow	____ recipe
____ microwave oven	____ tree	____ pencil	____ candle
____ computer	____ chair	____ shoes	____ soap

On the lines below, explain your thinking. How did you decide whether something was technology or not? What "rule" did you use to distinguish between them?

_____

_____

_____

_____

_____

Reflection Questions:

1. How much agreement was there in your discussion group about which things could be considered technologies? For which items was there disagreement? How varied were the "rules" developed by members of your discussion group? Were you able to reach consensus on a rule for your group? What happened during that discussion?

2. What attributes of technologies did you focus on when deciding to make a check mark or not?

3. How do you think students at different grade levels would respond to this formative assessment prompt?

4. In what ways do the two parts of the probe help to make student thinking visible?

Through experience, you will realize that the terminology used to describe different purposes and types of assessment is not completely consistent. Colburn (2009) describes formative assessment as *diagnostic,* while others refer to pre-assessment as *formative assessment,* since it also informs instruction. The differences in the terminology when labeling assessments are not as important as your varied and strategic use of assessment in your classroom. To be consistent we will use the term *diagnostic* to mean pre-assessment as different from a formative assessment process.

The opening section of this chapter is formatted like a diagnostic type of formative assessment probe. Look back at it, and you will see that it first presents a scenario to set the context, then asks you to make a selection from possible responses, and finally asks you to justify your response.

✔ CHECK YOUR UNDERSTANDING 7.1
Click here to gauge your understanding of the concepts in this section.

Formative Assessment Processes

Formative assessment is integral to inquiry learning and instruction. Its primary purpose is to promote learning, so it is often referred to as assessment *for* learning (Keeley, 2012). In a 2005 book, *Preparing Teachers for a Changing World*, Lorrie Shepard et al. tackled this confusing terminology, defining formative assessment as "assessment carried out during the instructional process for the purpose of improving teaching or learning" (p. 5). What differentiates formative assessment from other classroom-based assessments (such as interim and benchmark assessments) is, first, that the evidence of student learning is not graded and, second, that the information is used immediately to inform instruction. Feedback is a critical part of the process and, after being provided with feedback, students are given time to use the feedback.

In a 2007 article in *Phi Delta Kappan* magazine, Margaret Heritage defines formative assessment not as a test or a task or a high-stakes standardized assessment, but as a process of feedback in which a teacher learns about a student's current level of understanding to determine the next learning steps for that student. Sounds simple enough. So, what makes this confusing? Formative assessment is a process that is part of best instructional practices in the classroom. The diagram in Figure 7.2 shows how this formative

FIGURE 7.2 **Formative Assessment Process**

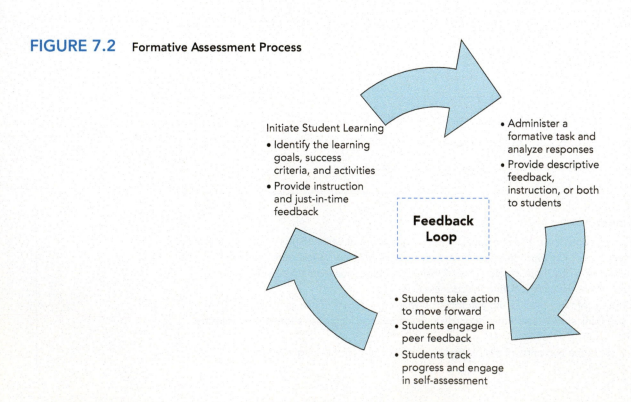

assessment process flows and how it is part of a continuous feedback loop between teachers and students and students and students.

Vignette 7.2 illustrates formative assessment in a classroom.

Vignette 7.2   Moon Phases

Ms. Westin's fifth graders have been watching and keeping records about the moon's appearance every night for two weeks. In class, her students respond to Ms. Westin's oral questioning about any patterns they think they have discovered in the data. While she encourages her class to share their findings and give evidence for their claims, she makes decisions about what kinds of scaffolding assistance might help them improve their understanding using descriptive feedback and individualized instruction.

Later in the moon-watching unit, the class takes a practice quiz (a planned-for formative assessment task) consisting of a few multiple-choice questions about moon phases and their causes. Instructions on the practice quiz sheet remind the students to justify their answers using drawings and by writing in the blank area below each item. When they finish, Ms. Westin studies the answers and explanations to determine whether any students still hold misconceptions that might interfere with their continued learning about lunar phases. She also uses the students' responses to decide which students need additional instruction on this concept and what feedback is needed for other students to advance their learning.

As illustrated in Vignette 7.2, teachers use formative assessment processes *during* lessons to support instruction and learning (NRC, 2001). Formative assessment involves collecting data on student learning during a lesson sequence and then making instructional decisions based on the data. An easy way to remember this term is that formative assessment *informs* instruction. Because formative assessment tasks and probes are not graded, but provide ongoing, perhaps daily, monitoring of student learning you will want to explain this process to students and practice it in the classroom. Since formative assessment can enable you to provide students with feedback on their learning, it is important to provide time for them to implement the feedback. One of the key findings from the meta-analysis of formative assessment research is that students who struggle the most in our classrooms, benefit the most from the feedback provided. This occurs because students find out what they are doing well, where their work differed from the expected, and have suggestions about what to work on next (Black & Wiliam, 1998a, 1998b).

In *Taking Science to School* (NRC, 2007), Duschl and colleagues emphasized the importance of linking formative assessment processes to scaffolding. A central theme in scaffolding is to make a process, concept, or principle more explicit for learners by enabling them to do something they could not do without some crucial element. For example, the crucial elements in the process of using evidence to formulate explanations include the claim, the empirical evidence in support of the claim, and the reasoning that connects the evidence and the claim (NRC, 2007). Assessment of what students understand and can do provides evidence teachers can use to determine the support they need to close the gap between their existing understanding and the desired level of understanding.

Scaffolding of these crucial elements might come through your actions as a teacher, instructional materials, or other students. Sometimes, explicit or direct instruction of concepts, principles, and strategies might be needed to improve learning. Explicit teaching of concepts and strategies can be a part of the explain phase of the 5E model of inquiry instruction when it is used to address misconceptions and is built around the students' explanations of the activity revealed during formative assessment.

A carefully designed and well-researched assessment component has been included in the recently released third edition of FOSS (Full Option Science System) modules for elementary grades. Each module includes a survey/posttest to be used at the beginning of the module (diagnostically) and at the end of the module (summatively). In addition, formative assessment is fully integrated with instruction through tools known as **I-Checks**, short for "I check my own understanding," that are used at the end of each investigation within the module. While field-testing the I-Checks, the assessment developers discovered that in some classrooms student achievement and students' attitudes toward assessment improved. In these classrooms, students took the assessments, and teachers reviewed the student responses and returned unmarked (not graded) I-Checks to the students as a resource for further discussion and peer and self-assessment activities. Students were eager to talk about their thinking and current ideas; they wanted to engage in discussion with the class and the teacher about what they understood and what they were still confused about. Instead of competing for the highest scores, students willingly helped each other find and actually understand the right answer. Their goal seemed to shift from getting good grades or points to learning deeply and effectively (Long, 2011).

Formative assessment tasks and strategies can also be described as formal or informal. Rather than considering these two descriptors as separate categories, it probably makes more sense to think of them as opposite ends of a continuum. Formative assessment processes are generally characterized as informal if they are administered "on the fly" (NRC, 2007) rather than at planned intervals, do not provide for standardized procedures of administration, and do not involve systematic ways to record, analyze, and report student responses. Informal formative assessment processes are often not paper and pencil based. **Formal formative assessments** are quite the opposite, the most formal likely being the various ones planned for formative assessment tasks or probes given in science classrooms.

Informal formative assessment includes asking students questions, listening to what they say during small-group work or whole-class discussions, watching what they do as they explore and investigate, and examining the products they create. You can also gather informal formative data through reading and analyzing what students have written on their record sheets and in their science notebooks. Checklists can be used as a guide in systematically watching and assessing students as they work. Though they can be used at any phase of a lesson or unit, informal formative assessment tends to generate feedback, and the tasks are not graded or given points. Students may even be unaware that they are being assessed when you are using informal formative processes, because it's the interactions that happen every day in their classroom. Some common methods used in informally assessing students' conceptual knowledge and understanding are described here.

> ▶ Much of what teachers use to assess science learning is informal. **Review the checklist** that fifth-grade teacher Donnovant Dahunsi uses for a math/science project on scale models. How can checklists be an effective, informal formative assessment tool?

Teacher Questioning. Teachers' questions are crucial in helping students make connections and learn important science concepts. As an example of how teachers' questions can facilitate understanding, consider how a simple question like "Can you use these materials (one wire, one battery, and one bulb) to make a bulb light?" engages the children in practical activities. By watching the children and listening to them, you can begin to informally assess the students' prior knowledge and current understanding. A follow up question like "Can you draw a picture of the circuit you made to light the bulb?" reveals the extent to which students understand what they did to light the bulb. As students work on a prediction sheet, which includes drawings of a variety of arrangements, the guiding question "In which of these situations will the bulb light?" discloses how the students conceptualize and generalize what they did to light a bulb. Such questions help to make students' thinking and understanding visible and provide a basis for the continual adjustment and improvement of learning and instruction. Open-ended questions like the ones in this example engage students' thinking and help to elicit their initial ideas.

Student Record Pages. Record keeping for all students may involve the use of simple data sheets formulated by students or teachers. Record keeping for older students can include brief descriptions of what they did, what they observed, and what they concluded. Prompts to guide investigation and thinking might be included on data sheets.

When your students learn how to give brief descriptions of what they did in groups, they are ready to start their own individual record keeping. You can design a page, such as the one in

FIGURE 7.3 Science Record Page

You have been working with things that sink or float. What did you do to find out which objects sink or float? Write a description and draw a picture.

We put objects in the bowl of water. If the object floated, we put it in box with the Float label. If it sank, we put it in box Sink. Then we tried all the objects in the Float box to check if they all floated. We did the same with the objects in the Sink box.

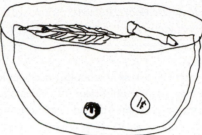

What did you find about which objects sink or float? Record your observations on the chart below.

OBJECT	SPECIAL FEATURES	LARGE OR SMALL	HEAVY OR LIGHT	SINK OR FLOAT
Penny		small	heavy	sink
Styrofoam ball		large	light	float

Figure 7.3, on which your students record their observations and thinking. To show their understanding, students might:

- *write* a description of what they did
- *draw* a picture of the activity, and/or
- *record* written observations in the chart

Once students become familiar with a particular thinking strategy, encourage them to devise their own observation formats. You can use this as a differentiation strategy to meet the needs of diverse learners. Be sure to provide time for students to share their personally developed approaches to recording and displaying data and their thinking so your students can learn from each other.

Science Notebooks.   Science notebooks are tools for students to grapple with scientific questions and help them make sense of what they have observed through using meaningful recording and organizing strategies. As an example, students often keep notes of their observations. Your examination of observation notebooks can reveal the students' developing knowledge about a topic. Student notes can take many forms, such as drawings, narratives, charts, and graphs. Students consider their notebooks as resources when they are used to advance learning, so once again they should be used to provide feedback and not be used for grades.

- *Technical drawings and diagrams with labels.* These are drawings based on careful observations of objects and organisms.
- *Notes and lists.* These are reports of observations used to record information quickly.
- *Charts, tables, and graphs.* These represent different ways to display and view data.
- *Written observations.* These are more detailed accounts of investigations and observations.
- *Additional questions about which students wonder.*
- *Personal judgments and feelings related to activities.*

An example of a student's entry in her science notebook is given in Figure 7.4.

FIGURE 7.4 Student Science Notebook Entry

> Today we used one wire and one battery to make a bulb light. At first, I didn't think I could do it, but I did! I made the bulb light on my own! I can't wait for more activities on electricity tomorrow. I feel really confident now and like this way of learning.

As you formatively assess notebooks, keep your learning goals in mind. Content learning may be your main goal, but it can also be important for students to learn to use different reporting and organizational strategies. You might teach reporting and organizational strategies in mini-lessons, perhaps in language arts classes, and use later lessons to assess student use of these skills. Provide feedback to improve reporting strategies whenever appropriate.

The *National Science Education Standards* emphasize that students must be provided opportunity to develop both conceptual understandings and abilities of scientific inquiry (NRC, 1996; NRC, 2000). In the *Next Generation Science Standards* (NGSS Lead States, 2013), you will also want to assess the Science and Engineering Practices that are appropriate for the grade you teach as part of assessing three-dimensional lessons. Assessing inquiry abilities formatively through informal formative assessment is an important part of science learning.

Checklists. A checklist is simply a list of the specific key elements that you plan to consider in judging a student performance or product. Teachers and students can work together to develop checklists that can be used to determine process related to success criteria. Scorers observe student performances and examine products and check *yes* or *no* for each element on the checklist. The check mark typically shows only whether the element is observed; no effort is made on a checklist to assess how well the skill is performed. However, space might be added to a checklist for teacher notes or student notes or comments. They help keep teacher observations focused. Checklists are easy, quick, and handy to use particularly when students are taught how to use them for peer assessment. Remember that you can help students to self-assess if you first ask them to peer-assess their classmates' work using checklists.

Checklists are particularly useful for monitoring the development of students' laboratory techniques. Figure 7.5 is a sample checklist for observing and assessing students' skills in using a microscope. Student results determined with checklists might be used both to provide feedback on learning and to adjust instruction. The design of this checklist requires that you keep a separate record sheet for each student, but it is not necessary that you assess everyone in your class on the same day. Using a feedback sheet that is included in the student's science notebook provides a location for you to share your notes and

Watch this video clip where the teacher is informally assessing student science notebooks. How does she do this and how is student learning impacted?

FIGURE 7.5 Checklist for Assessing Microscope Skills

Student's Name _____									
Behavior/Skills	Date	Yes	No	Date	Yes	No	Date	Yes	No
Is careful in handling microscope									
Cleans lenses properly									
Focuses instrument properly									
Prepares slides correctly									
Orients mirror for correct amount of light									

comments. Periodically you should meet with each student to assess and discuss his or her progress in specific skills.

Hands-on inquiry activities provide an authentic setting for assessing children's developing abilities to do scientific inquiry. Figure 7.6 displays a checklist that can be used to keep track of students' use of specific science process skills. Figure 7.7 shows a checklist for use in assessing investigation procedures. If your state has adopted the NGSS, you will want to revise this checklist to incorporate all eight Science and Engineering Practices. Checklists are best used as part of your informal formative assessment process since there are no standardized procedures for collecting and reporting this type of student information.

A critical part of understanding the nature of science and scientific inquiry is some knowledge of scientific habits of mind, the attitudes that characterize scientists. Although students should attain many affective goals in science, five main attitudes, values, and habits of mind are especially relevant to successful inquiry in elementary and middle school classrooms: (1) being curious, (2) insisting on evidence, (3) seeking to apply science knowledge, (4) being willing to critically evaluate ideas, and (5) working cooperatively.

FIGURE 7.6 Checklist for Assessing Science Processes

Student Name: _____

Process or Skill	Task or Behavior	Task Observed? Date	Task Observed? Comment
Observing	Uses several senses in exploring objects		
	Uses magnifying glasses and other instruments to extend the senses		
	Identifies details in objects, organisms, and events		
	Notices patterns, relationships, or sequences in events		
Inferring	Uses evidence and scientific knowledge in making inferences		
	Explains basis for inferences		
	Makes reasonable inferences that fit the evidence and scientific knowledge		
	Suggests how to test inferences		
Predicting	Uses evidence in making a prediction		
	Explains basis for predictions		
	Makes reasonable predictions that fit the evidence, whether accurate or not		
	Makes interpolations and extrapolations from patterns in information or observation		
	Suggests how to test predictions		
Communicating	Talks freely with others about activities and ideas		
	Listens to others' ideas and looks at their results		
	Reports observations coherently in drawings, writing, and charts		
	Uses tables, graphs, and charts to report investigation results		

FIGURE 7.7 Checklist for Assessing Investigation Procedures

Student Name:_____

Procedure	Task or Behavior	Task Observed?	
		Date	Comment
Questions	Asks a variety of questions, focusing on questions that can be investigated		
	Recognizes differences between questions that can be investigated and questions that cannot be investigated		
Places Priority on Evidence	Has some idea of what evidence to look for to answer the question		
Plans Investigations to Obtain Needed Data or Information	Chooses a realistic way of investigating, measuring, or comparing to obtain results		
	Plans descriptive, classificatory, experimental, and other investigation procedures		
Conducts Planned Investigation	Carries out investigation procedures carefully		
	Works cooperatively with teammates		
	Takes steps to ensure that the results obtained are accurate		
Explains, Interprets, or Make Sense of Data	Gives explanation consistent with evidence and scientific knowledge		
	Explains basis for explanations		
	Shows awareness that other explanations may fit the evidence		
	Asks questions about ways to test predictions and explanations made in activities		
	Suggests how explanations and predictions can be checked		
	Shows awareness that explanations are tentative and subject to change		

It is difficult to measure attitudes reliably, but attitudes cannot be improved without an understanding of students' existing attitudes (Shepardson & Britsch, 2001).

Figure 7.8 presents a possible checklist for assessing curiosity in a middle school science class. It is designed to record information about the entire class on one chart by placing check marks at the intersection of the row of a particular student and the column of the component behavior observed.

You might keep an attitude assessment checklist throughout the year, noting when you judge that the child has displayed the attitude or failed to display the attitude when it mattered. Information gained via the checklist should be used formatively and to praise and improve attitudes, rather than summatively for grading purposes.

In contrast to informal formative assessment, formal formative assessment tasks are assessment *events,* such as tasks and probes. Formal summative assessments (tests and quizzes) are usually preplanned and scheduled in advance, and students are expected to study or prepare for them. Formal summative assessments will be discussed in the next part of this chapter. They typically involve using traditional, paper-and-pencil items or performance tasks to determine where students are in the learning process. Formal formative assessment tasks may be used before or during instruction, but formal summative assessments should be given after instruction.

FIGURE 7.8   **Class Checklist for Assessing Curiosity**

Class Checklist for Assessing Curiosity
Component Behaviors of Curiosity Exhibited

Name	Notices and attends to new things and situations	Asks insightful questions	Independently seeks out resources of interest	Eager to learn new information	Exhibits interest through careful observation of details
Dora					
Felix					
George					
Hanna					
Ira					
Jennifer					
Ivanka					
Lynn					
Muhammed					

A Checklist to Assess Scientific Attitudes

EXPLORATION 7.2

Develop a checklist of component behaviors that you could use to informally assess your students on *one* of the other important scientific attitudes.

Reflection Questions:

1. Why did you format your checklist the way you did? Will you include students in the development of the checklist?
2. How did the grade level of the students for which you were developing the checklist affect your final product?
3. How will you introduce your checklist to your class? What will you tell your students about its purpose?

✓ **CHECK YOUR UNDERSTANDING 7.2**
Click here to gauge your understanding of the concepts in this section.

Summative Assessments

Most current commercial elementary and middle school science programs include resources for student assessment. Many such programs address diagnostic, formative, and summative assessment and, in addition, provide quiz and test items, suggest procedures for recording student scores, and have culminating projects at the end of their units. We will discuss summative assessments in this section of the chapter.

Vignette 7.3   Which Paper Towel Is Best?

Mrs. Brady's second-grade class has been learning about properties of materials and conducting a variety of "fair tests" for nearly a month. On the front table one day, there are rolls of three different brands of paper towels. Mrs. Brady tells her class: "Your job is to test these paper towel brands for a consumer magazine to determine which paper towel is best. What factors will you test? How will you determine the properties of the paper towel to determine which brand is the best?"

For several days, children work together in small groups to formulate their plans and carry out their investigations. As the students work, Mrs. Brady circulates among the groups, keeping notes and marking mastered skills on a checklist.

The class plans their upcoming "scientific conference." Mrs. Brady shares the rules for participating (this is really the scoring guide she will use that is based on the success criteria to assess the oral and visual components of their presentations). With the rules in mind, each group creates a poster summarizing their approach and conclusions and then presents a brief report of their research to the rest of the class.

Decisions about grades should be based on data from high-quality summative assessments. Summative assessments require more standardized instruments than are typically used in formative assessment and more systematic, uniform ways of evaluating and reporting student responses. This is why Mrs. Brady developed a scoring guide for the student presentations and explained her expectations to her class.

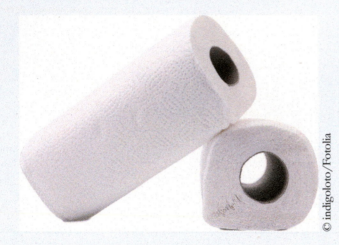

© indigoloto/Fotolia

Summative assessment should occur after instruction has been completed, after students have had adequate time and experience to achieve the learning goals of the lesson or unit. A way to remember this term is that summative assessments sum up student learning. Vignette 7.3 provides an example of summative assessment.

The goal of summative assessment is to determine a student's knowledge and conceptual understanding of the science ideas being studied. But summative assessments are only effective if they provide enough evidence to actually reveal that knowledge and understanding. So how can we assess for knowledge and will the same types of questions reveal understanding? There is a key distinction between knowledge and understanding. What do you think it is?

Teachers are often satisfied with apparent signs of student understanding, such as students being able to provide the right word, definitions, or recall factual information. Changing the question or terms may cause the students to reveal that they really do not understand the concepts at all. What they are able to recall represents what they know but it doesn't show conceptual understanding. Their answers may even show a variety of misconceptions.

If "correct" answers can result in insufficient evidence of understanding, then how can teachers assess students to know if they can transfer their learning to new contexts? To show understanding, students must be able to make sense of what they have learned. They need to be able to explain, to interpret, to apply and adapt knowledge, to have perspective, to ask relevant questions, to problem-solve new situations, to make claims based on evidence, and to have self-knowledge about their understanding. So understanding is really a group of related abilities.

Most teachers are not trained in psychometrics and rely on assessment items created by others. It is still important to understand the different types of assessments and when they should be used with students. To put together a summative assessment, you can begin by creating an assessment blueprint. Record the learning targets and skills you want to assess and then match them to the kinds of assessment items that you want to use. A traditional summative test should have about half of the questions that can be answered using selected response questions that focus on factual knowledge, vocabulary, and skills that are easy to

TABLE 7.2 Matching Assessment Types with Knowledge Targets

Target to Be Assessed	Best Assessment Matches	Not Good Matches
Vocabulary	Use multiple-choice, fill-in-the-blank, matching, true/false, or short answer and essays.	Performance assessment is not a good match.
Facts and Details	Use multiple choice, fill-in-the blank, matching, true/false, constructed responses	Performance assessment is not a good match.

Concepts
   Principles
      Generalizations
	Higher-order multiple choice, constructed responses, and performance assessments	Fill-in-the-blank, matching, and true/false are not a good match.

Skills and Reasoning Processes	Constructed responses and performance assessments	Selected responses are generally not a good match.
Attitudes	Open-ended questionnaires and some short answer/essay	Most selected-response types are not a good match.

demonstrate. The rest of the test should include short-answer and essay questions that link to the concepts in the unit. **Traditional assessment items** include multiple-choice, true-false, short-answer, essay items, and performance assessments. They can be useful and effective for assessing science knowledge, understanding, skills, processes, Practices, and attitudes. Each type of assessment question is best matched with certain knowledge types. Table 7.2 summarizes the recommendations for how to match assessment types with knowledge and understanding.

Multiple-choice, true-false, and matching items are sometimes called **selected-response items**, while short-answer and essay items are referred to as **constructed-response items**. Traditional assessment items are useful for assessing students' knowledge, understanding, and abilities to inquire. They have the advantage that they are quicker to construct, administer, and score than performance assessments.

Selected-response items are easy to administer and score, but writing good (meaning **valid** and **reliable**) selected-response items is time consuming and requires a thorough understanding of the concept being assessed. Of course, some multiple-choice items are easier to write than others. It is much easier to develop an item asking students to select the definition of a term than to construct one that reveals whether they truly understand a concept.

Selected-response items also enable you to measure a wide range of knowledge over a short period of time. Because they are quick to score, especially if you use electronic or computer-based scoring systems, it is possible to promptly provide feedback on student performance. However, these items do not usually require students to show their reasoning. Further, traditional selected-response items measure more than just knowledge. The reading level, language ability, and vocabulary of students can also affect their choices of answers. So a below-level reader may understand the science concept the item is designed to measure but get the item wrong because of poor reading skills.

Multiple-Choice Items.   Basic multiple-choice items have three parts:

- *Stem:* presents the task or question to your students
- *Distractors:* incorrect responses
- *Correct response*

Multiple-choice items are frequently used to measure retention of science knowledge, such as being able to select the term that corresponds to a given definition or description or vice versa. Figure 7.9 provides examples of this type of item.

Traditional assessments can be used to go beyond simple recall to assess student understanding of science concepts and principles. Standard multiple-choice items and justified multiple-choice items can be designed that require students to integrate information and to use knowledge in thinking and problem solving.

FIGURE 7.9 Examples of Multiple-Choice Items That Measure Recall of Science Knowledge

The most abundant gas in Earth's atmosphere is:
A. Hydrogen
B. Oxygen
C. Nitrogen
D. Carbon Dioxide

What is a herbivore and how does it eat?
A. A plant that makes it own food to eat
B. An animal that eats only plants
C. An animal that eats only animals
D. An animal that eats both plants and animals

Which part of the plant is the hand touching?
A. Root
B. Stem
C. Leaf
D. Flower

Figure 7.10 is an example of a multiple-choice item that measures understanding rather than mere recall.

FIGURE 7.10 Example of a Multiple-Choice Item to Assess Science Understanding

Beans and coal both have stored energy.

Where did the energy come from that is stored in beans and coal?

A. from the earth's gravity
B. from the sun's light
C. from the heat in the arth's core
D. for the carbon dioxide in the air

Source: 2000 National Assessment of Educational Progress (NAEP), fourth-grade level released item.

This item assesses understanding because it requires students to think about two different examples of stored energy and then to examine each possible source of energy to find one that fits both samples. The item was designed by the NAEP (National Assessment of Educational Progress) project to be used on a national assessment, but it can be used formatively if teachers analyze it quickly, give immediate feedback, provide opportunity for students to learn from their mistakes, and use the assessment results to modify instruction. Checks for understanding questions or practice quizzes are two examples of strategies to use the questions formatively.

Constructed-response items can assess both the knowledge and understanding of students. These items have the advantage of requiring students to generate information in their own words, rather than to just recognize correct answers. Such items can also provide you with information about how the student arrived at the answers. A disadvantage of constructed-response items is that poor writing skills can mask the student's science understanding. While writing an essay question may be quicker than writing a good multiple-choice item, the time needed to read and evaluate the essay will certainly take longer than checking the multiple-choice item.

Completion and Short-Answer Items. Short-answer and completion items require students to generate, not just recognize, correct answers, as is shown in Figure 7.11.

FIGURE 7.11   Examples of Knowledge-Level Completion and Short-Answer Items

List 3 forms of precipitation and describe each.

_____

_____

_____

A water molecule is composed of one atom of _____ and two atoms of _____.

Assessing Understanding from Written Responses.   Essays, which involve written responses, represent an important way for students to demonstrate understanding. Through an essay, a student might interpret data, describe and explain an event, or show relationships among facts, generalizations, definitions, values, and skills. Like all assessment devices, the written response or essay has disadvantages as well as advantages, as shown in Table 7.3.

TABLE 7.3   Advantages and Disadvantages of Essay Items

ADVANTAGES of Essay Items	DISADVANTAGES of Essay Items
They show how well the student is able to organize and present ideas.	Scoring may be subjective without firm answers unless you have a clear scoring guide.
They show varying degrees of correctness, because there is often not just one right or wrong answer.	Scoring is very time consuming. It is easy to infer that they understand, though there may not be enough evidence.
They assess abilities to analyze problems using pertinent information and to arrive at generalizations or conclusions.	Scoring is influenced by spelling, handwriting, sentence structure, and other extraneous items.
They assess deeper meanings, reasoning, and interrelationships rather than isolated bits of factual materials.	Questions or writing prompts may be either ambiguous or obvious unless you carefully construct them.

To offset the disadvantages of essays, you must carefully construct each essay question. Word the question so students will be limited, as much as possible, to the concepts being tested.

A sample essay prompt could be as follows:

A science fair judge asks you, "What is a controlled investigation?" Write out your answer.

Your scoring criteria for the item may include that the student's answer must show:

- a responding (dependent) variable and manipulated (independent) variable are selected;
- what is investigated is how the responding variable changes in response to changes in a manipulated variable; and
- all other variables are controlled or held constant.

You will be able to overcome or minimize subjectivity in scoring answers to written questions by preparing a rubric beforehand and scoring each question separately. The rubric would show the quality of the responses relative to each criterion necessary for the student to receive full, partial, or no credit. If you prepare a list of the important ideas you expect, before scoring, there is less chance for ambiguity while scoring. This list can be developed with your students or at least shared with them when they get the assignment.

Written response items may also be used to determine how well students can interpret data from an investigation and then apply concepts and relationships in a novel situation. An example of a series of items that accomplishes this is presented in Figure 7.12.

FIGURE 7.12   Cluster of Written Response Items about Ashley's Investigation

One hot, sunny day Ashley left two buckets of water out in the sun. The two buckets were the same except that one was black and the other was white. She made certain that there was the same amount of water in each bucket. She carefully measured the temperature of the water in both buckets at the beginning and end of the day.

Look at the shown results of Ashley's investigation, then write your answers for these three questions.

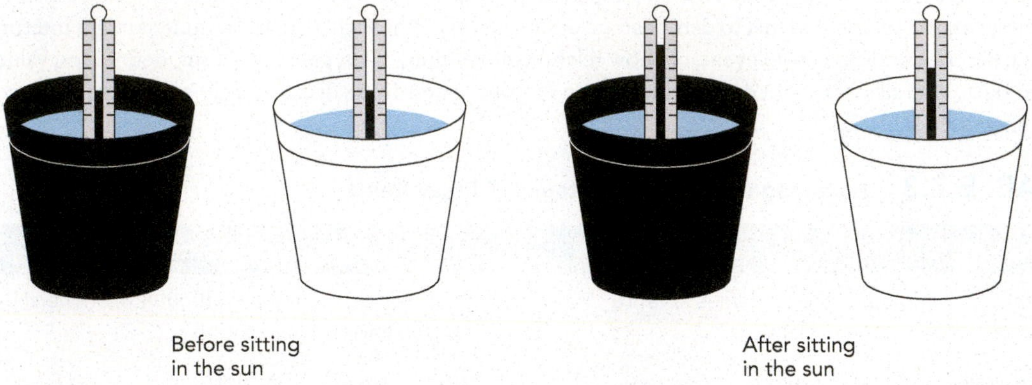

Before sitting
in the sun

After sitting
in the sun

1. What can Ashley conclude from her inquiry?

_____

_____

2. What is the evidence and reasoning for Ashley's conclusion?

_____

_____

3. How does the experiment help explain why people often choose to wear white clothes in hot weather?

_____

_____

The items included in Figure 7.12 are released items from the 2000 NAEP Science Test for fourth grade. Figure 7.13 shows the scoring guide used to evaluate responses for the final item. This item proved to be quite difficult for the national sample of fourth-grade students who took the NAEP science test in 2000. Only 12 percent of the national sample wrote complete explanations, 15 percent supplied partial explanations, while 73 percent gave unsatisfactory, incorrect, or off-task answers.

FIGURE 7.13 NAEP Scoring Guide for Essay Item 11

Score and Description

Complete
Student explains that white clothes reflect more heat from the sun than black clothes, or that black clothes absorb more heat from the sun than white clothes.
   A. Black clothes soak up the heat from the sun.
   B. The sun's rays reflect white clothes.

Partial Student explains that black clothes attract more heat or that white clothes do not attract as much heat.

Unsatisfactory/Incorrect
Student provides little or no explanation that is related to the heat-absorbing properties of dark-colored clothes and light-colored clothes, or gives unrelated answers.
   A. They stay cooler in white clothes.
   B. The sun likes dark clothes better.

Assessing Understanding with Justified Multiple-Choice Items. In justified multiple-choice questions, students first mark the best answer and then explain in several sentences why they chose that answer. A rubric might be used to assess students' explanations of their answers. This type of item includes both a selected-response component and a constructed-response component. An example of a justified multiple-choice item is shown in Figure 7.14.

FIGURE 7.14 An Example of Using a Justified Multiple-Choice Item to Assess Understanding of Investigative Procedure

John cuts grass for several different neighbors. Each week he makes the rounds with his lawn mower. The grass is usually different in the lawns. It is tall in some lawns, but not in others.

1. Which of the following is a suitable hypothesis he could investigate related to this situation?
    A. Lawn mowing is more difficult when the weather is warm.
    B. The amount of fertilizer a lawn receives is important.
    C. Lawns that receive more water have longer grass.
    D. The more hills there are in a lawn, the harder it is to cut.

2. Explain in a few sentences why you think your answer choice in item 2 is better than the other choices.

Complete answers to item 2 should note that:

- the variable of interest (responding variable) in the item stem is *length of grass;*

- length of grass is a variable only in answer choice C; and

- answer choice C implies a hypothesis/question that can be investigated: *What effect*

Assessing Investigative Procedures with Justified Multiple-Choice Items. Ability to apply scientific procedures can be assessed with standard multiple-choice items, especially if they are combined with essays, as shown in Figure 7.15.

Including traditional items in your plan for assessing the application of science processes and inquiry procedures can help to achieve balance in assessment. Such items are often easy to construct, are quick to score, and can provide the basis for immediate feedback for the improvement of learning.

Confirmatory assessment relates to long-term knowledge retention (Sterling, 2005). For example, confirmatory assessment happens when content taught and supposedly learned in September is included on the end of year final in June.

Traditional assessments are certainly effective for achieving many assessment purposes. When you use them, do so strategically, and be sure to follow through by giving feedback to students on their learning rather than just grading and forgetting them. Score all assessments as quickly as possible in order to give timely feedback to students about their work.

FIGURE 7.15 Justified Multiple-Choice Assessment

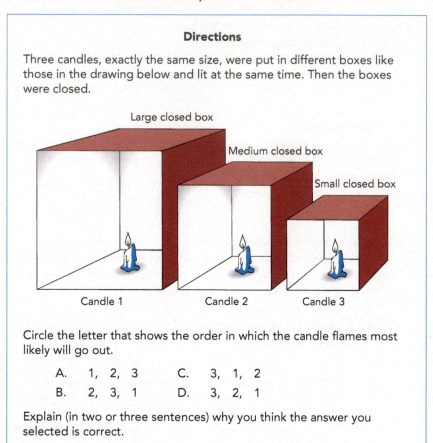

Directions

Three candles, exactly the same size, were put in different boxes like those in the drawing below and lit at the same time. Then the boxes were closed.

Large closed box

Medium closed box

Small closed box

Candle 1   Candle 2   Candle 3

Circle the letter that shows the order in which the candle flames most likely will go out.

A. 1, 2, 3   C. 3, 1, 2
B. 2, 3, 1   D. 3, 2, 1

Explain (in two or three sentences) why you think the answer you selected is correct.

Providing time for students to discuss what they are still confused about with you and their peers is also a good idea. Often students can better understand the explanations of other students than your own (Long, 2011).

 CHECK YOUR UNDERSTANDING 7.3

Click here to gauge your understanding of the concepts in this section.

Performance Assessments

More powerful methods of assessment have been developed to fit the expanded formative and summative purposes of classroom assessment. In recent years, there has been an increasing emphasis on **performance assessment**.

Performance tasks are rich tasks that require higher-order thinking. They provide students with opportunities to demonstrate what they know and, more importantly, their conceptual understanding. Sometimes, performance tasks are a natural part of the science lesson. At other times, you might design special performance tasks that require students to demonstrate their understanding in ways that require them to make sense of a wide range of facts and ideas.

When compared with traditional summative assessment measures, performance assessment offers students a wider range of options for communicating what they understand in science and what they are able to do with their knowledge. Students are generally more comfortable with performance assessments, because they are typically set in authentic contexts and often have the look and feel of regular, hands-on learning situations.

Students are introduced to a long-term performance assessment task in this video clip. How do they know what they will be expected to understand, and how will they provide evidence of understanding?

Performance tasks can be used to assess conceptual understanding and inquiry abilities. All performance assessment tasks have a performance that can be observed and/or a product that can be examined. Student performances in science assessment tasks might include such tasks as measuring, observing, collecting and organizing data, constructing a graph, making a visual or audio presentation, presenting an oral defense of work, interpreting data, or presenting a how-to explanation of a procedure. Products presented for assessment could include such tangible things as data tables, graphs, models, reports, and written explanations and problem solutions.

Creating a good performance task involves determining the *focus* of the task, setting the *context* for the task, writing *directions,* and developing a *scoring guide* (Kentucky Department of Education, n.d.).

Focus. The first step in developing a performance assessment is to decide what students are expected to learn and how they can demonstrate that they have learned it. This becomes the *focus* of the performance task. Focus is closely related to learning targets. In determining the focus, state precisely what you expect your students to know, understand, and be able to do. Once you have determined a focus for the assessment task, a context should be created. With the emphasis in the NGSS on Science and Engineering Practices, your focus may include a problem-based assessment task with students following an engineering design process to solve the problem that is proposed.

Context. The context of a performance assessment usually includes a background and a question related to the focus objective. The background may be presented in a variety of ways, including in written form and through hands-on activities. The focus question should center on a problem to which students will want to find an answer or solution. The background scenario and focus question represent the "hook" that draws students in and engages them in the task.

The scenario should be made as authentic, or as close to the "real thing," as classroom conditions will allow (Jarolimek & Foster, 1997). Authentic contexts better portray the nature of science, relate classroom learning to the real world, are more intrinsically motivating to students, and serve not only as assessments but also as interesting learning situations. If your performance tasks are focused on an engineering design process, then the context may relate to an actual community-based issue that they would solve.

Directions. Directions for performance tasks should explain what students are expected to do and should describe the final performance or product to be assessed. It is very important to make sure that the directions are clear. You should ask other teachers and some students to review the directions for clarity.

Scoring Guides. Performance assessments have been criticized as being too subjective, but when good scoring guides are used, consistent scoring can be obtained. A scoring guide is a means for judging the quality of the assessment performance or product. A **rubric** is a specific type of scoring guide; however, the terms *rubric* and *scoring guide* are often used interchangeably. You may generate several rubrics to correspond to the components of the performance task (communication, scientific understanding, and poster or model rubrics).

In an inquiry-oriented classroom, there are many opportunities to extend learning activities by making them the centerpiece of performance tasks for assessing science processes and procedures. The focus, context, and directions of the performance tasks are then derived directly from the learning activities.

A distinctive element of the *National Science Education Standards* (NRC, 1996) was the dual focus on students attaining science understanding and, at the same time, improving their abilities to inquire. Assessing these two aspects of science learning simultaneously, both formatively for learning improvement and summatively for accountability and grading, has been an important goal of elementary and middle school science programs and continues to be an important goal. Performance tasks are preferable to traditional assessment items when trying to reach the dual nature of this assessment goal.

The *Next Generation Science Standards* are stated as **performance expectations** that include each of the three dimensions of the *Framework*: Scientific and Engineering Practices, Crosscutting Concepts, and Disciplinary Core Ideas. These performance expectations are intended to be the assessable components used after instruction to summatively assess all three dimensions of science learning simultaneously (Achieve, 2013). It is not surprising that performance tasks will continue to be more effective than traditional assessment items for this purpose. In addition, new and innovative assessment procedures, perhaps involving computer-based simulations, are likely to be developed to meet the challenge of assessing the NGSS on state, multistate, and national tests. Technology-based questions have already been piloted as part of the NAEP Science Assessment.

Conceptual understanding of the natural world is a key goal of elementary and middle school science. When students understand, they are able to do something with their knowledge. Remember that demonstrating understanding really involves a host of skills that can be incorporated into well-crafted performance assessments. Students can interpret concepts and principles and use them along with observational evidence in inferring, predicting, analyzing, and explaining. Performance tasks are particularly suited to assessing understanding.

Performance Tasks and Rubrics.   Notice that in the performance task shown in Figure 7.16, students make predictions about what happens in an illustrated circuit when switches are either open or closed. Then they construct the circuit and use it to test predictions. Finally, they write explanations of what happens

FIGURE 7.16   **Electrical Circuits Task**

Performance Task:

A. PREDICT : Study the diagram of the electric circuit. Make a prediction about what will happen to each light bulb if switch 1 is closed and switch 2 is open.

My Predictions:
Bulb 1: Lit   Not Lit   (Circle Lit or Not Lit)
Bulb 2: Lit   Not Lit   (Circle Lit or Not Lit)
Bulb 3: Lit   Not Lit   (Circle Lit or Not Lit)

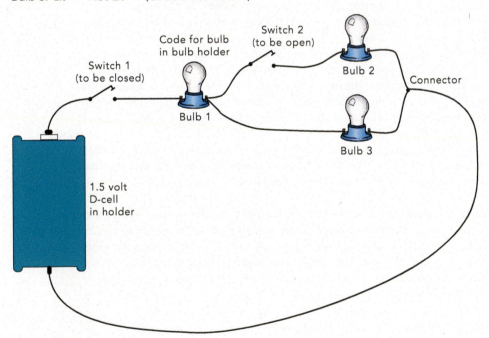

B. CONSTRUCT: Obtain a kit of materials from your teacher. Using the materials, build the circuit illustrated.

C. TEST : Use your circuit to test your predictions. Arrange the circuit so that switch 1 is open and switch 2 is closed. What happened to each bulb?

My Observations:
Bulb 1: Lit   Not Lit   (Circle Lit or Not Lit)
Bulb 2: Lit   Not Lit   (Circle Lit or Not Lit)
Bulb 3: Lit   Not Lit   (Circle Lit or Not Lit)

D. EXPLAIN: Use your knowledge of circuits to explain your observations of what happened to each bulb when you opened switch 1 and closed switch 2 of the test circuit.

My Explanation: (Write out your explanation here.)

_____

_____

_____

_____

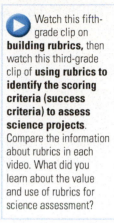

to each of the bulbs in the test based on their understanding of the concept and what happens when the variables are changed. This performance task gauges how well students solve a real-world scientific problem in a laboratory setting. Based on grade-level endpoints for Disciplinary Core Ideas from the *Framework for K–12 Science Education* (NRC, 2011, p. 125), by the end of grade five, students should understand that: "Energy can also be transferred from place to place by electric currents, which then can be used locally to produce motion, sound, heat, or light."

If you plan to use this assessment formatively, to informally check the understanding of your class about some concepts of circuits so you can decide what scaffolding is still needed, just observe your class as they work and look over their submitted papers. If you plan to use this assessment summatively, to formally assess your class's skill and understanding related to circuit concepts so you can grade their work, use a rubric to make your scoring as consistent and objective as possible. Two sample rubrics for the electrical circuits performance task follow. They represent two main types of scoring guides. In Exploration 7.3 you will have an opportunity to compare and contrast them.

Rubrics are **holistic** if teachers make judgments about task performance by assessing the task as a whole. Figure 7.17 is a holistic rubric for the electrical circuits task presented in Figure 7.16. To use this scoring guide, examine a student's work, select the description that best captures a summary of his or her level of achievement, then assign the corresponding point score. Notice that with holistic rubrics all factors expected to be part of a product or performance are considered simultaneously. The score range on this sample holistic rubric is between 0 and 4, and all scores should be whole numbers.

FIGURE 7.17   Holistic Rubric for Electrical Circuits Task

Score	Description of student's response
4	The responses are consistent with a sound scientific approach. They indicate that the student has a clear understanding of the problem and of how to predict, construct circuits, and use the circuits to test predictions. The scientific explanation may in some cases define additional aspects of the problem or include extensions beyond the requirements of the task. Some inconsistencies may be present, but they are overwhelmed by the superior quality of the responses.
3	The overall responses are largely consistent with a sound scientific approach. They indicate that the student has a general conceptual understanding of the problem, how to make predictions, how to construct a circuit, and how to use it to test predictions. The quality of the explanation provides some reasoning, although minor errors may be present.
2	The responses represent a limited attempt at applying a sound scientific approach to the problem. Although the responses exhibit errors, incompleteness, and/or omissions, the student demonstrates some expertise related to how to predict, how to construct a test circuit, and how to use the circuit to test predictions. Little scientific understanding of the concept of circuits is demonstrated.
1	The overall responses are inconsistent with sound scientific thinking and investigative procedures. The responses indicate the student has little or no understanding of the problem and of circuit ideas.
0	The student does not attempt to solve the problem and/or does not respond to the questions on the response sheet.

Rubrics are **analytic** if they identify separate performance criteria and provide descriptions for the levels of achievement for each. Figure 7.18 is an analytic rubric for the electrical circuits task presented in Figure 7.16. When using this scoring guide, for each student consider one criterion at a time; look first for the wording that best describes the level of prediction exhibited in this task; then select the descriptor for circuit building that best represents the student's work, etc. In this example, a score between 0 and 4 is awarded for each criterion, and only whole numbers are assigned; thus, the score range for the assessment is between 0 and 16.

The first step in creating the scoring guide is determining what a high-quality performance or product should look like. This obviously should be tightly aligned with your instructional learning targets. Then, decide whether you want the scoring guide to support formative or summative assessment. A checklist may be sufficient for a formative, ungraded assessment; while a rubric, which includes performance levels, is preferable if you plan to assign grades. Exploration 7.3 will provide an opportunity for you to compare holistic and analytic rubrics.

The next step is to decide how many performance levels are needed. Typically, between three and five levels are included. Levels might be labeled with terms like *Exceeds Expectations, Proficient,* and *Not Proficient*

FIGURE 7.18   Analytic Scoring Guide for Electrical Circuits Task

Analytic Rubric for Electrical Circuits Task					
Criteria	4	3	2	1	0
Predictions	Accurate	Generally accurate, not more than one error	Two or more inaccurate predictions	All inaccurate and/or missing	None given
Building test circuit	Well constructed, accurate, no flaws	Adequately constructed, serves the purpose	Partially complete, but a few flaws present	Limited attempt made, constructed circuit incomplete or inaccurate	No attempt made
Testing predictions with circuit	All tests completed, all observations accurate	Tests completed, but one observation is inaccurate	Tests completed, but more than one observation is inaccurate	Attempts to test unsuccessful, observations missing	No attempt made, no observations recorded
Explanation	Accurate, clear, detailed, convincingly supported by data, shows strong understanding of circuit concepts	Logical, basically consistent with data, shows basic understanding of circuit concepts	Confusing, lacks detail, poorly supported by data, understanding of circuit concepts not demonstrated	Missing or illogical, not supported by data, understanding of circuit concepts not demonstrated	None given

EXPLORATION

7.3

Comparing Holistic and Analytic Rubrics

Review the performance task presented in Figure 7.16 and evaluate its elements. Look over the alternate rubrics in Figures 7.17 and 7.18. Think about the advantages and disadvantages of each of these scoring guides. Talk about your ideas with a small group of peers, if possible. Decide which rubric you would use if you were scoring the performance task reports turned in by your class of 24 students.

Reflection Questions:

1. How would you describe the focus and context of this performance task?
2. Do you consider the directions on the performance task sheet adequate? Why or why not? How might you improve the directions?
3. Which rubric would you use to assess your students' work? Why did you select the one you did?
4. Would you provide or go over the rubric before your students did the performance assessment? Why or why not?

and/or with whole numbers representing a score. You must provide enough information about each performance level to communicate expectations to students and for scorers to distinguish differences in the quality of the students' performances and products. The number of levels you select should be based on the following factors: your needs, the ability to differentiate between levels of achievement when assigning grades, the grade level you teach, and your students' ability to understand the distinctions between levels.

It is a good idea to include your students in creating rubrics and in the process of scoring task performance. Most educators agree that rubrics and other scoring guides should be shared with and explained to students when the performance task is assigned. Sharing examples of work that meet expectations for generic rubrics will help students to ask good questions when trying to understand what they need to provide to meet the goals of an analytic rubric. When students know what is expected of them, they don't have to guess what "counts" in the assignment. Referring to rubrics before turning in a project or presenting a performance leads to reflection and self-evaluation by learners, often leading to improved work. Steer clear of rubrics that are based on the amount of work. Students use them as checklists and don't concentrate on demonstrating conceptual understanding. When students are involved in the assessment process, they become more aware of learning expectations and are enabled to take more responsibility for their own learning.

Oral/Written Pictorial Interpretations. You can gain insights into your students' understanding of concepts and principles by using assessments that ask them to respond to pictorial situations. You can assess for hidden meanings, underlying patterns, and explanatory schemas that bring coherence to the students' observations. Such an assessment is intended to determine students' abilities to communicate the trends and sequences of the pictorial situation.

In developing pictorial assessments, decide on the learning objective (the *focus* of the performance task). You might show a science pictorial situation (the *context*), then give *directions* for how to respond to the questions. This can be done orally for younger students or those with limited reading skills, or in written form for others. Figure 7.19 illustrates such an activity.

Teacher shows pictures and says to children:

What differences do you see in these three pictures?
Which do you think will happen first? Second? Last?
Why do you think the snowman is changing?

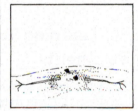

FIGURE 7.19 Pictorial Interpretation Assessment

Source: From Material Objects Student Manual, Section 5, Chapter 18, SCIS3, 1992, Hudson, NH: Delta Education, Inc. Copyright 1992 by Delta Education, Inc. Reprinted with permission.

An example of a *scoring guide* to assess students' responses to the snowman item in Figure 7.19 is given in Figure 7.20. The scoring guide relates to each of the three questions in the pictorial assessment. This scoring guide is similar to a checklist in that the teacher is to examine students' responses for specific criteria. However, points are to be assigned for each relevant response. Teachers must use their own experience to judge the quality of the response and to assign points.

FIGURE 7.20 Scoring Guide for Pictorial Interpretation Assessment

Element	0–8 Points
Differences among pictures	At least three key differences are clearly stated. Differences might relate to the snowman's height, size, position of arms, depiction of eyes. (0–3 points)
Ordering of pictures	Pictures arranged in correct order (picture 1, picture 2, picture 3). (0–1 point)
Reasons for changes	Judge how well the reasons for changes relate to the *evidence* in the pictures and to *knowledge* of heating and melting. Examples: The sun came out and melted the snowman; the longer the sun was out, the more the snowman melted. The snowman melted because he got hot. The snow changed to water because of the energy from the sun. (0–4 points)
Scoring	Outstanding 7–8 points Satisfactory 5–6 points Needs improvement 3–4 points Unsatisfactory 0–2 points

The pictorial interpretation assessment shown in Figure 7.19, with its accompanying scoring guide in Figure 7.20, could be used formatively to guide teachers to improve student understanding or summatively in assigning student grades.

Concept Maps. A **concept map** is a visual representation of a major concept and its connections to subsidiary concepts. Joseph Novak and others (Edmondson, 1999; Novak, 1995) have advocated the use of concept maps in assessing the science understanding of students.

By examining student concept maps before or during instruction, teachers can discover learners' conceptual understandings and their misconceptions. Students' concept maps can then be used by the teacher to provide feedback to students and as a guide to improve instruction. Concept maps are useful tools to assess science understanding. Psychologists theorize that learners organize their knowledge into connected networks called *knowledge structures*. The size of these structures, the number of connections between items of knowledge, and the organization and richness of the connections are all considered to be important for processing knowledge, constructing meanings, and solving problems (Rosenshine, 1997). By drawing a concept map, learners create a pictorial representation of their mental structures. They show the conceptual connection they have, basically making their thinking visible.

Concept maps can be used as assessment tools for diagnostic, formative, or summative assessment. Comparison between a concept map completed at the beginning of a unit and another one drawn at the end of the unit can indicate conceptual growth over time. When used summatively, students demonstrate their ability to synthesize and evaluate. Some procedures for counting concepts, subconcepts, and connections would be helpful in order to quantify change over time or, if the assessment was to be used summatively, to assign grades.

Assessing Multiple Learning Targets through Performance Assessments

Students can use previously acquired science knowledge and understanding to solve problems and create products in situations that are new or different from those in which they were taught.

Model Building. Physical models that illustrate students' understanding of natural objects, organisms, structures, and phenomena and that require abilities to use science inquiry processes and procedures are excellent products for assessment. In building models (physical, mental, mathematical, computer, etc.), students are required to research relevant information, discover what kind of models illustrate the scientific concept(s) to be shown, collect needed scientific supplies and equipment, plan and build the model, and explain it to the class and teacher. Students have successfully built physical models of the solar system, geological structures, physiological systems of the human body, and so forth. Drawings can be models, too; they are just two-dimensional instead of three-dimensional. Modeling is one of the Science and Engineering Practices, and it would be appropriate to have middle school students build computer models (climate change), graphical models (population studies) and mathematical models in additional to physical models. In many of the performance expectations found in NGSS, student are asked to create models that represent systems that interact with one another. These types of models prompt the development of questions and explanations and as they are revised, they are useful when communicating ideas to others. Although models do not correspond exactly to the real world, they contain approximations and assumptions and have predictive power. While helping students to develop conceptual understanding, models also have their limitations which are important for students to recognize.

© Ariel Skelley/Blend Images/Corbis

A model that represents a student's current thinking about a concept can be assessed.

Student Demonstrations. Students can demonstrate much of what they know and understand about scientific concepts and their interrelationships through planning, manipulating, and demonstrating with scientific supplies and equipment. The audience may be their own classmates and teacher, other classes, their parents, or other persons. Individual students or groups may give the demonstrations—such as showing how electrical circuits work, exhibiting static electricity in everyday situations, playing a musical instrument they designed, or demonstrating what happens when colored lights are mixed—and then explain the science behind the demonstration by sharing claims about why their demonstration did what it did and supporting those claims with evidence.

Student Presentation Projects. Student presentation projects may uncover much about students' understanding and thinking. Project assessments provide the teacher with insight into how well students have learned, recorded, and put their knowledge into practical use. You and your students should work out expectations of what the projects will encompass *before* students start their projects.

Primary grade students often make something as part of their science learning; perhaps each child makes one page for a class book about how the animal he or she selected to study moves and what body parts are involved in this behavior. Developing the rubric or scoring guide as a class would also be appropriate.

In the example of project assessment that follows, groups of students worked together to design an aquarium. Here is the students' task:

> **Performance Task:** You are a zoologist at a city zoo. Many people have suggested adding aquariums to the zoo. Your task as a zoologist is to (a) choose a type of water habitat; (b) choose three animals that can coexist in the water habitat; and (c) design an aquarium so that it is an appropriate habitat for the three animals.

The students would need to have explored the habitat and food needs of organisms in previous activities. In this activity, they use reference books and the internet to gather information on the habitat and animals selected. They will need to find information concerning the different components of the habitat (such as plants and rocks), the food that should be available for their animals, and what enables each of the animals to live in a water habitat.

Their aquarium design can be presented to the teacher and the class in the form of a Kid Pix or PowerPoint presentation or as an actual aquarium. As the teacher, you will be there to assess learning and provide scaffolding and instruction as needed. But do not give too much assistance—this is a student project.

A rubric is used to assess the students' aquarium designs and their performance in oral discussions. The rubric might include these three main criteria:

1. The student identifies and distinguishes between freshwater and saltwater habitats.

2. The student lists at least three animals that live in the chosen water habitat and gives information about each, including the food, shelter, and parts of the body that enable them to live in the environment.

3. The aquarium design includes an appropriate habitat for each of the three animals, including shelter and a source of food for each.

Developing Levels for a Rubric for the Aquarium Task

EXPLORATION

7.4

Take some time to develop the aquarium task rubric by writing quality descriptions for three levels: exemplary, proficient, and not yet proficient. Be sure that the wording for the rubric is accessible to students you plan to use it with. You may work individually or collaborate with one of your peers.

Reflection Questions:

1. How does the project call for the development of knowledge and understanding and of science processes and procedures?

2. In what order did you develop the level descriptors? Describe your procedure and explain why you did it that way.

3. What was the easiest part of completing this rubric? Why?

4. What was the most challenging part of completing this rubric? Why?

Science Fair Projects. Students in many elementary and middle schools are required to develop science fair projects. Projects are usually evaluated by external judges, using a common set of judging criteria. Figure 7.21 shows a composite of the judging criteria used in many science fairs.

The first step in creating a good science fair project is for the student to select an interesting, sufficiently narrow question to investigate. Three types of scientific investigations—descriptive, classificatory, and experimental—are generally included in elementary and or middle school curricula. Judging criteria often favor experimental investigations, with hypotheses, responding and manipulated variables, and adequate controls designed into the investigation. Because true experiments are difficult for younger learners, we suggest that school and district science fairs be for students from the fourth or fifth grade up. Younger students might be involved in descriptive and classificatory investigations and the construction of models and demonstrations. These might be displayed in their own classrooms.

In carrying out experimental investigations, students must perform a test to answer their research questions. If they are interested in earthworms, for example, they might perform a test to see if temperature has an effect on how earthworms move. Students would have to get some earthworms, find a way to vary the temperature of the soil in the earthworm container, and measure what happens, related to earthworm movement, at different temperatures.

FIGURE 7.21   Science Fair Judging Criteria

Source: Multiple science fair judging sheets found on the Internet.

Judging Criteria	Indicators
Creativity	• Creativity is shown in the selection of a problem to investigate. • Ingenuity in the design and development of the project is shown.
Scientific Thought	• The problem selected is appropriate. • The question and hypothesis are clear, well formulated, and sufficiently narrow to be investigated empirically. • Experimental variables are clearly defined, and appropriate controls are used. • Data are well organized and accurate graphs are shown. • Data collected serve as adequate evidence to support the conclusions formed.
Thoroughness	• The project shows thorough planning. • Review of background information is thorough. • All data are accurate. • All data collected were used in drawing conclusions. • A project notebook sufficiently documents the student's work from beginning to end.
Skill	• The project clearly represents the student's work. • The project is sturdy and well constructed. • The student clearly understands the equipment used. • The project shows continual attention to safety standards.
Clarity	• The student kept and displayed an original, bound logbook. • The project report was well done and easily understandable, with appropriate documentation. • The project display was eye appealing, with appropriate materials, posters, charts, and graphs. • Lettering, signs, and diagrams are neat and accurate. • Visual aids assist the reader or judge in understanding the project.

The question or hypothesis, background information, experiment design, and results might be recorded in a bound notebook. The data collected would be used as evidence to answer the question posed. Students would need to carry out the project with only a little help from parents, teachers, or friends.

The project should be clearly and dramatically displayed, perhaps using show boards. Finally, the students would explain the project in detail through an interview with a judge or team of judges.

For elementary and middle school students, downplay the competitive nature of projects. The goal is for students to improve in their abilities and understanding of science, not necessarily to "win." Thus, you should use the project assessment formatively to improve student learning, rather than summatively for grades. Science fair projects are fun. Students will learn a great deal, and the projects will display to others what students know and have learned.

Fitting Assessment Methods to Learning Goals

Remember that in science your selection of assessment strategies will depend largely on your reason for assessing.

- If you wish to make a quick assessment of where students are in science understanding, informal strategies might be used.

- If you wish to assess recall of factual or conceptual knowledge, traditional multiple-choice or short-answer items are often suitable.

- Traditional assessments might also be appropriate to assess student attainment of learning goals related to understanding of science knowledge, particularly if you use essay items or combine multiple-choice responses with written explanations of why a particular response was chosen.

- You might be able to probe deeper into student understanding and assess inquiry abilities more completely when you use performance assessments that enable students to demonstrate their understanding and investigative abilities during or after a learning task.

- Finally, performance methods are much more appropriate than traditional assessments when you wish to assess how well students can apply knowledge and plan and carry out inquiry procedures or solve engineering problems.

Please keep in mind that the example assessment items described in this chapter are *not* samples of possible assessment items on the large-scale assessments yet to be developed to assess mastery of the *Next Generation Science Standards*. They are simply examples of various item types that you might use informally or traditionally in your classroom, perhaps the start of a collection of assessment items that you develop over your teaching career. You can find many good assessment examples on the internet, in teachers' guides, and in the education literature. In most cases, it is necessary to modify examples from outside sources so that they fit your own learning targets and classroom situation, because if your assessment items are not aligned to your learning targets, they are probably not assessing what needs to be assessed. Released items are another good source of summative questions.

 CHECK YOUR UNDERSTANDING 7.4
Click here to gauge your understanding of the concepts in this section.

The Role of Large-Scale Assessments

Large-scale assessments administered at district, state, national, or international levels provide evidence needed to make fair, high-stakes decisions about students, teachers, and a district's need to modify its science program or redesign professional development opportunities for teachers (NRC, 2000). Large-scale assessments are usually not classified as formative or summative, because they do not provide information about individual students or apply directly to what has just been taught in the classroom. The nature of items typically used for large-scale assessments will be described in more detail later.

According to the No Child Left Behind legislation, all states were required to begin administering statewide assessments in science at the elementary, middle school, and high school levels by the 2007–2008 school year. Although they are ultimately based on similar standards, tests of science differ widely from state to state. It is hardly possible to generalize from such an array of tests and items.

Currently, state education agencies and local school districts typically provide in-service workshops to familiarize teachers with the tests designed for use in their states. Additionally, many states release test items from previous tests to assist teachers as they work with students to improve performance on the tests.

State assessments of science are designed, administered, and scored outside the specific context of classrooms. Currently most state science tests include multiple-choice and perhaps short-answer items. Usually answer sheets are machine scored, requiring students to bubble-in the answers; however, some states are piloting computer-based state testing. Results of these assessments are typically not available to teachers until near the end of the school year. Thus, statewide tests of science learning do not typically provide formative information to be used immediately in improving science learning and instruction, although the scores can be used to improve instruction from year to year in states that report detailed achievement data by specific standards. Nor are the statewide tests suitable as summative assessments to determine overall levels of understanding at the end of instruction. Rather, state measures of student understanding and performance are intended to provide a basis for policy makers to judge accountability and formulate new regulations. Statewide tests have standardized administration procedures and ways of using assessment results to reliably and fairly judge the levels of understanding of students.

At the elementary and middle school levels, statewide tests are typically administered at grades four or five and at grade eight. However, helping students prepare for these high-stakes assessments is an important task at every grade level, not just the grades at which the tests are administered. All teachers of science should become very familiar with the state standards and the related performance expectations at their grade level. One of the first steps in understanding test items used for large-scale assessment is to examine the specific standards on which they are based. In Exploration 7.5 you may practice this with standards and released items from the National Assessment of Educational Progress (NAEP) science assessment.

Test items on state assessments typically include:

- **Stand-alone test items.** Many released test items are stand-alone, multiple-choice items.

- **Items requiring written responses.** States also include many written response items in which students might write descriptions and explanations or plan investigations to answer questions. Detailed rubrics are typically provided to facilitate and standardize scoring.

- **Clusters of related test items.** Some states use clusters of items related to a scenario. Both multiple-choice and written responses are used with the clusters.

EXPLORATION

7.5

Matching Science Standards and Test Items

The items below were collected using the NAEP Questions Tool (nces.ed.gov). They all assess facts, concepts, laws, theories, or key principles that relate to weather, climate, or the atmosphere. In addition, each item is designed to assess one of the four science Practices identified by the NAEP *Framework*.

NAEP Science Practice	Cognitive Demands	Type of Knowledge
Identifying Science Principles	Knowing that	Declarative
Using Science Principles	Knowing how	Procedural
Using Scientific Inquiry	Knowing why	Schematic
Using Technological Design	Knowing when and where to apply knowledge	Strategic

The NAEP science assessment focuses on how effectively students can simultaneously use science content and Practices to learn about the world. Performance expectations that guide item development come from the intersection of science content and science Practices. Neither content statements nor science Practices are assessed in isolation on the NAEP.

As you read these items, analyze them to decide what science content and which Practice each item was designed to assess. Then discuss your ideas with a small group of colleagues.

1. Which tool is used to measure how much rain falls during a storm?

A.

Source: Beermedia/Fotolia

B.

Source: Meryll/Fotolia

C.

Source: Bigfoot/Fotolia

D.

Source: Alswart/Fotolia

(continued)

(Exploration 7.5 continued)

2. The diagram below shows four places on Earth. Places 1, 2, 3, and 4 are all at sea level.

A. Places on Earth

Which place has the coldest winters?

A. 1

B. 2

C. 3

D. 4

3. Why do mountain climbers at high elevations use oxygen tanks to help them breathe?

A. At high elevations the ozone layer draws oxygen out of the atmosphere.

B. The atmosphere is less dense at higher elevations so there is less oxygen available.

C. Oxygen is heavier than the other gases in the atmosphere and sinks to lower elevations.

D. Radiation from the Sun splits oxygen molecules into atoms, making the oxygen unbreathable.

4. Water evaporates and falls back to Earth as rain or snow. What is the primary energy source that drives this cycle?

A. The wind

B. The Sun

C. Air pressure

D. Ocean currents

The following 2 questions refer to the following diagram, which represents a portion of Earth's water cycle.

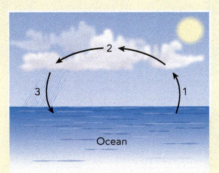

5. Using your knowledge of the water cycle, explain why rainwater is not salty, even though ocean water is.

_____

_____

_____

6. Which process is represented by 2?
   A. Liquid water evaporating
   B. Cool air warming as it rises
   C. Clouds blocking the Sun's energy
   D. Water vapor condensing

7. Burning coal, oil, and gasoline for energy releases gases into the atmosphere that can be harmful to the environment.
   What are two ways that people can reduce the amount of these gases released into the atmosphere?

   1. _____

   _____

   2. _____

   _____

8. Grace's class measured the temperature outside four times a day for four days in a row. Their results are shown below.

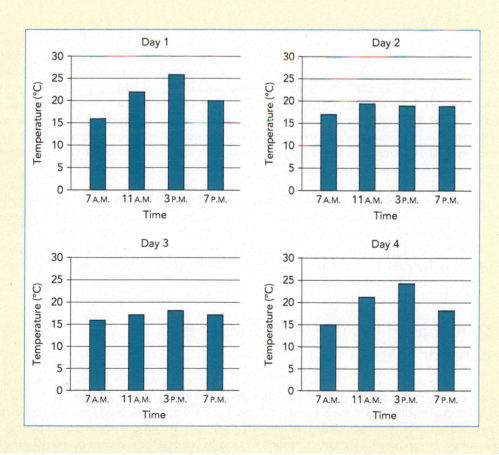

(continued)

(Exploration 7.5 continued)

Based on these data, choose two days that were most likely cloudy.

A. Day 1
B. Day 2
C. Day 3
D. Day 4

Explain why you chose these two days and why you did not choose the other days. Your answer should use the data in the graphs and your science knowledge about weather.

_____

_____

_____

Reflection Questions:

1. Which items were associated with each of the four NAEP Science Practices?
2. What specific science content did you need to know to respond correctly to each item?
3. Which items did you find to be easiest? Why?
4. Which items did you find to be most challenging? Why?

Several states are beginning to administer their high-stakes, standardized tests online using computers rather than using more traditional paper-and-pencil methods. Innovations in computer-based educational measurement may soon drastically change the look and experience of standardized state testing.

During the 2009 administration of the National Assessment of Educational Progress (NAEP) science assessment, fourth, eighth, and twelfth graders engaged in hands-on and interactive computer science tasks. These new approaches to standardized, large-scale testing revealed not only what students know, but also how they respond to scientific challenges and how well they can apply their learning to real-life situations. NAEP analysts have learned:

Students were successful on parts of investigations that involved limited sets of data and making straightforward observations of that data. Students were challenged by parts of investigations that contained more variable to manipulate or involved strategic decision making to collect appropriate data. The percentage of students who could select correct conclusions from an investigation was higher than for those students who could select correct conclusions and also explain their results. (National Center for Education Statistics, 2012, p. 1)

Using Released Items to Help Students Prepare for State Tests

The best way to prepare students to be successful on state science tests is to follow a coherent curriculum that is aligned with your state's standards. Preparing students for tests at a specific grade level, say fifth grade, is a responsibility of K-5 teachers, not just fifth-grade teachers. Science lessons from the earliest grades should be designed to build conceptual knowledge and understanding, as well as inquiry procedures. It is also the goal to prepare students mentally for the exams by building their confidence and reducing test anxiety. Students at both the elementary and middle school levels should have opportunities to practice with questions similar to what they will see on the large-scale assessments.

In many states, items are released from previous tests providing practice items for students and providing models for teachers developing classroom test items. A group of teachers from the same district might work together to study items released from their own state tests. The information gained through this process can then be used to plan instruction. Released test items from your own or other states can be directly used to help your students prepare for future statewide tests. One way to use the items is to break the test up into four- or five-item mini-tests and administer the mini-tests to your students periodically (only after the concepts or inquiry abilities to be assessed have been taught and mastery is expected). Have your students complete the mini-tests individually and turn in their answer sheets to you. Students keep a copy of their answer sheets. While you score answer sheets, students should work together in small groups to develop a "key" for the test. Record student scores on the mini-tests. Ask them to keep a copy of their answer sheets and compare their answers with yours. When students have developed answer keys that are satisfactory to them, go over the items one by one with them. Through this procedure, students have an opportunity to receive immediate feedback on their work, to think through their answers more completely, to learn from one another, and to better prepare for the high-stakes statewide examinations.

As tests are developed that are aligned with the *Next Generation Science Standards*, state assessments in states that adopt the NGSS will be similar or perhaps identical. The *Next Generation Science Standards* are written as performance expectations that intertwine the three dimensions of the *Framework*: Science and Engineering Practices, Crosscutting Concepts, and Disciplinary Core Ideas (Achieve, 2013). Thus, new science assessments must be developed to reflect the integration of the dimensions while functioning appropriately in a variety of contexts and for different purposes. The new assessment will need to be revolutionary to meet the goals of three dimensions simultaneously.

Extensive in-service training certainly must occur as new testing formats and procedures are developed for the NGSS. Some sample items have been developed and are being shared through webinars and professional development opportunities. If your district has adopted the NGSS, then check for opportunities in your region or through state and national science teacher associations.

Effective assessments in science require thorough planning, skillful execution, and careful, constant review and modification. Learning to use assessments effectively will help you become a better teacher and your students better learners. It is clearly worth the effort.

CHECK YOUR UNDERSTANDING 7.5

Click here to gauge your understanding of the concepts in this section.

CHAPTER SUMMARY

Assessment in the Classroom

Classroom assessment can be considered as a tool that teachers can use to improve both learning and instruction. In the science classroom, assessment should be happening continuously, the teacher always attending to the achievements and needs of the students and then using that information to plan his or her next instructional steps. Learning and assessment are closely linked in inquiry teaching. Assessment in inquiry science should emerge from three guiding questions: (1) *Where are students trying to go?* (2) *Where are students now?* and (3) *How are students going to get there?* The focus of assessment in science has shifted over the years from a narrow summative view to a more balanced view that includes the importance of formative assessment processes as well.

Formative Assessment

Since different phases of a lesson or unit have different purposes, the associated assessments should have different purposes, too. Diagnostic assessment is appropriate before instruction to determine learners' interests and current conceptions. Formative assessment processes are appropriate during instruction to inform teachers of what students know, understand, and can do so they can decide what feedback and instructional steps to use next. Informal formative assessment is the ongoing monitoring of student learning that good teachers do continuously. It includes actions such as asking questions, listening to students' science talk, watching students investigate, looking over written work on record pages or in science notebooks, etc. Checklists can help teachers stay focused while assessing informally, since it does not involve grading. Informal assessment should not be an event or something that is announced ahead of time, but rather it should just be part of the classroom culture.

Summative Assessments

Summative assessment occurs after instruction to evaluate what has been learned and to assign grades. Confirmatory assessment might occur a long time after a lesson or unit was taught to determine what students retain from their earlier studies. Traditional assessment items are the kinds of questions you would expect to find on a paper-and-pencil test. Summative assessment is used by teachers to assign grades. There are selected-response items, such as multiple choice, true-false, and matching. These are quick and easy to score but usually assess at the factual knowledge level. There are also constructed-response items, such as completion, short-answer, and essays. These take more time to score and may require scoring guides, but they can let you know what learners are thinking "in their own words." If you select traditional items from a bank of questions to use in a test or quiz, be sure that they are aligned with your instructional learning goals.

Performance Assessments

Performance assessments let students demonstrate what they know, understand, and can do by creating a product (concept map, model, poster, brochure, invention) or performance (demonstration, skit, presentation). Performance assessments look much like an instructional activity and are often authentic. They may be formative or summative depending on how the teacher uses the data. Scoring guides or rubrics are often used to make assessing performance tasks as objective as possible. Performance assessments can be used to assess conceptual understanding, Scientific and Engineering Practices (including inquiry skills), and the application of learning. Performance assessments typically have a focus, a context, directions, and a scoring guide.

The Role of Large-Scale Assessments

State science tests are intended to assess students' mastery of state science standards. They are high-stakes tests with standardized administration procedures, designed and scored at the state or regional level. Most are at least partially machine scored, requiring students to bubble-in their responses. Development of computerized tests is occurring in many states. Most states administer them once in each school level (elementary, middle, and high). Numerous state tests are being revised to align with the adoption of the *Next Generation Science Standards*.

DISCUSSION QUESTIONS

1. What does "using assessment in the service of learning science" mean to you?
2. In what ways do diagnostic, formative, summative, and confirmatory science assessments differ?
3. What are some advantages and disadvantages of using informal assessment in the science classroom?
4. When using traditional assessment items, what aspects of science learning are easy to assess? Difficult to assess? Why?
5. Why do you think performance assessment of science learning is now a focus of many classroom teachers?
6. How are state science tests impacting K–8 science programs? Please use evidence to support your claim.

PROFESSIONAL PRACTICE ACTIVITIES

1. Obtain a science assessment from a grade level you would like to teach. Analyze it in terms of the extent to which the shifts envisioned by the *Next Generation Science Standards* (NGSS Lead States, 2013) are apparent.

2. Examine an elementary or middle school science lesson from a text, kit-based program, your cooperating teacher, or the Internet. Identify any examples of diagnostic, formative, and summative assessment that you can find.

3. Volunteer to help your cooperating teacher informally assess the class on a science laboratory skill or a Scientific and Engineering Practice. Develop a checklist to guide your data collection, then use it to record information about the students' accomplishments.

4. For a science lesson you plan to teach or assist with, develop a short quiz composed of six traditional assessment items. Half of the items should be selected-response items, and the others should be constructed-response items. Be sure all items align with your instructional learning goals. Administer the quiz, score it, and analyze the results. If most of the class incorrectly answered or skipped the same question(s), talk to a few students to determine if they understood that question.

5. Develop an oral/written pictorial interpretation task. Suggested steps are described in this chapter. Try your task with several students and make any needed improvements.

6. Visit your state's Department of Education website. Find information about the elementary and middle school state science tests. Look for resources such as a Science Assessment Handbook, a collection of released items, and/or distribution of items by topic.

Using Technology Tools and Resources for Science Learning

Martin Shields/Alamy Stock Photo

LEARNING GOALS

After reading this chapter, you should know and understand that . . .

1. General educational technology to support science instruction in K-8 classrooms should minimally include a computer with internet access that is connected to a classroom projector.

2. Digital technologies for gathering scientific information, data collection and analysis by students, creating and using models of scientific phenomena, and communication support student engagement in specific Science and Engineering Practices.

3. Social media can be a useful resource to support science teaching and learning.

As a student, what technologies do you rely on to help you learn? List at least five examples. Review your list and try to prioritize it. Put your examples in order from the one you rely on the most to the one you really don't care about. Then look for patterns in your prioritized list. Reflect on what the list tells you about yourself as a learner. How did you learn to use these technologies? Which do you feel most confident using?

As a teacher of science, what technologies would you like to have in your classroom? How would you use them to help your class learn science? Are some of these technologies ones that you already use for your own personal learning? This chapter is designed to expand your understanding of instructional technologies that can help students learn and do science.

General Educational Technology in the Science Classroom

First, let's agree on what we are talking about when we say technology. Yes, it can be argued that technology is anything that has been designed and created to make a task easier. So, yes, your pencil is technology. No, that is not what this chapter is about. The computer being used to write this chapter is the type of technology we are talking about. Think of the technology that would have immediately jumped to your mind if we hadn't just defined technology—basically, the electronic instructional technology of today. With the variety of computer-based technology that now exist, the term "mobile devices" is often used to refer to all kinds of computers including desktops, laptops, notebooks, smartphones and tablets.

When you walk into your classroom for practicum, student teaching, or even your first job, the room will most likely have some technology available to use. At the very least, you will hopefully have a "teacher" computer that is connected to the internet. This computer is often used for many of the daily routines that are expected of you as a classroom teacher. For example, you may be expected to enter your attendance and your lunch count into the computer daily, and to enter student assessment data into a school or district database that generates report cards periodically. With any luck, this computer is a laptop that can go home with you at the end of each day and be checked out for use during the summer.

Your teacher computer hopefully provides easy access to your district's science curriculum documents and to units you are expected to teach at your grade level. It can connect you to ongoing professional development opportunities as well, which is especially important in this time of transition to the *Next Generation Science Standards* (NGSS) in many states. Webinars, listservs, videos, and blogs can help you learn from science educators who are NGSS experts and let you network with other teachers trying to implement three-dimensional teaching and learning. Two sites focused on the NGSS and their implementation that you should check out if you haven't already are NGSS@NSTA, also known as the *NGSS Hub* (http://ngss.nsta.org/) and Achieve's site, *Next Generation Science Standards: By States for States* (www.nextgenscience.org/). They are both well-organized websites that provide access to the NGSS, supporting materials such as appendices, evidence statements, sample assessment tasks, example storylines, etc. Additionally, the *Teaching Channel* (www.teachingchannel.org), a thriving online community where teachers can watch, share, and learn, has nearly 150 science-based videos focusing on lessons, instructional strategies, and implementing NGSS and provides opportunities to network with other teachers who are working to improve their practice.

Your teacher computer is also likely to be capable of being connected to several other pieces of general technology to help you teach the students in your room. These could include a projector, a document camera, an interactive white board, and speakers. Let's examine briefly how each of these could be used while teaching science.

The classroom education projector connected to your computer is probably the single most important piece of extra technology in your classroom. This is what allows you to turn your computer, a device that can be seen by one, or a few, into something that can be seen by many. The ability to project what is on your computer screen is a powerful teaching device. Student or group work that has been emailed to you can be shared and compared to support argumentation during discourse. Essentially, now anything you can see or do on your computer can be shown to your class. While this is great for allowing you to project all of the wonderful educational activities that you find online, it also means there is a flip side that you have to be careful about. As easily as you can project a video clip found online, you must review everything that you plan to share so that you do not show anything on your computer that your students should not see. Perhaps you were entering grades before class and then turn on the projector. Suddenly your gradebook is displayed to the class, and a student is being teased for either very high or very low grades. Worse yet, you could inadvertently project something inappropriate for young children. Ensuring that your computer is not set to "mirror" your display can prevent this. Instead, arrange the desktops so that the projector is an extension of your computer's desktop. Then to have something displayed to all, you have to purposely drag it to the space that is beside your own computer's screen. If you don't know how to do this, get help from another teacher or IT staff member, and be sure to practice the procedure.

A document camera is a device that is intended to do almost exactly what its name suggests. It has a camera, and likely some lights, that is connected to your projector and possibly your computer, and is intended to project the image of a document that is placed below it onto a screen or the wall. You could think of it as the next-generation overhead projector, except you don't need to make transparencies to use it. It is great for enabling students to display their work (i.e., a sketch of a natural object or organism, a data table or graph, or a two-dimensional visual representation to show their thinking) for the whole class to see and discuss. The cool thing about a document camera is that you can be creative with it, as it will project whatever is placed beneath it, not just documents. This is particularly useful in teaching science, as you can place small objects that are part of an activity beneath the camera so the class can see exactly what you are talking about. You can even use a document camera with a traditional microscope to enable students to see magnified specimens projected on a screen so the whole class can observe and discuss the same image.

> ▶ Middle school students are learning to use microscopes to make close observations. What are some advantages of pairing a microscope with a document camera instead of having students just use a traditional microscope?

If you are fortunate, your computer will be connected to a projector that is mounted on the ceiling. If you are really lucky, that projector will shine onto an interactive whiteboard, which is the generic term for a commonly used brand name, SMART Board, associated with the device (think Kleenex). The interactive whiteboard is a wonderful thing as it essentially turns your projected computer screen into a giant touchscreen. When the associated software is also used, a whole new set of functionalities are introduced. The software will have many built-in features that are inherently interactive in nature and take advantage of the touchscreen abilities. A science-specific example of this would be doing a virtual frog dissection on the screen. If you as the teacher demonstrate this for your class, however, you are missing the most powerful aspect of an interactive whiteboard. This is the ability to get students up, out of their desks, and interacting with the content you are projecting. Students should be the ones up at the board clicking, touching, dragging, and writing as much as possible. This will vastly increase the engagement level of the entire class, as the lure of interacting with the board is powerful.

The last item that is hopefully connected to your teacher computer is a set of external speakers. It is likely that at some point you will show a video on your computer to be projected for the class to see on the screen or on your interactive whiteboard. If there is any audio associated with that video, you'll need those external speakers. The impact of these speakers should not be underestimated. Think of going to a movie theatre; yes, it is great that the screen is giant and you feel somewhat immersed in the picture, but pay attention to how loud the soundtrack is within the movie; sometimes you can feel the music. This is a major part of the experience that makes watching a film in the theatre worthwhile. Even if you don't have a projector, speakers are still important as your computer can be used to play music in your classroom. This music can be directly related to content, like the songs found at symphonyofscience.com, or just used in the background during group activities as a part of your classroom management plan.

Even though most of the technologies already mentioned seem relatively simple there are some issues that you need to be aware of for their most effective use, such as:.

- **The physical location of your projector** – A ceiling mounted projector is preferable. If the projector is on a table, you and your students must be careful to not walk between it and the screen (which would block the projected image) and to not accidentally look into it (because of the intensity of the beam of light it projects).

- **The physical location of your interactive whiteboard** – A wall mounted projector is preferable to a portable version on wheels (which has a power cord that presents a tripping hazard and is hard to keep in alignment). The interactive whiteboard should be mounted so that you and your students can reach all parts of its surface, including the top part; yet high enough so that it is visible to students in the back of the classroom.

- **Managing cords** – Though high-quality Wi-Fi is becoming prevalent in classrooms, eliminating the need to have all components of a projection system to be physically connected, they still need to be connected to the electrical outlets in your room. With any luck, you won't be responsible for connecting all the cords, but you may have to find a way to put the cords out of the way as much as possible and to work around them. Learning how all the cords connect would serve you best in the long run. This ensures you are not "stuck" when technology help is unavailable and something gets disconnected right when you need to use it.

One technology that was previously mentioned was the use of video, and this needs to be explored a little more. There is no shortage of video programming that can be found online to show in your classroom. A major source of videos is probably one that you are very familiar with, YouTube. While YouTube is a great resource, there are many other sites; some that are free and others that require subscriptions. After checking your school's internet use policy, you may want to learn how to download video from YouTube for use in your classroom as YouTube may be blocked by your school's internet content filter, or you may just have a slow and unreliable internet connection at your school.

No matter the source of the video that you are showing, you should be aware that the days of showing a full movie or TV show in the classroom are gone. You should select the most appropriate clip to show in your class. Within reason, the shorter the clip the more effective it will be in your classroom. It is important that you find a way to seamlessly incorporate video clips into your instruction. It should not be a production of getting out the projector, turning off the lights, and turning on the speakers, simply to show a 30-second clip of someone pushing against a rock that doesn't move to demonstrate inertia. Most projectors now are bright enough that the lights do not need to be turned off, and they often contain a black screen button that allows them to be kept on without running down the bulb or displaying something you don't want seen. This way, including video during instruction can just be a matter of walking by your computer and hitting play on the cued-up video waiting on your desktop.

Video clips that present phenomena (interesting objects or events that can be observed in the natural or human-made world and are related to core ideas for students to investigate) are great ways to introduce an NGSS-aligned unit or lesson. This is especially true of phenomena that are difficult to replicate in the classroom or on demand, such as earthquakes, eclipses, or imploding tank cars. According to Brian Reiser (2013), the *Next Generation Science Standards* shift the focus from science classrooms as environments where students learn about science ideas to places where they explore, examine, and use science ideas to explain how and why phenomena occur. The *EQuIP Rubric for Science*, Version 3.0 (2016), a tool designed to evaluate lessons and units for alignment with the NGSS, states: "Lessons and units designed for the NGSS include clear and compelling evidence (that they are) designed so students make sense of phenomena and/or design solutions to problems by engaging in student performances that integrate the three dimensions of the NGSS... (and support) monitoring student progress in all three dimensions of the NGSS as students make sense of phenomena and/or design solutions to problems (p. 2)."

While showing video clips in the classroom is a great way to support instruction, the best use of video is to not only have students watch, but also to create their own. The number of low-cost devices capable of capturing video has exploded in recent years. In fact, you may be reading this on your smartphone or tablet computer. Students can easily capture video on their smartphones, iPads, or tablets and use a computer to edit and create short movies that explain a concept. iMovie and MovieMaker are free Mac and Windows editing programs that are great resources for such an activity. This application of video promotes learning by the students at a much deeper level than simply watching a pre-made video. Students can even make time-lapse videos that reveal changes over time.

Now that you have read about general ways that general technologies are used in classrooms, focus on science education applications by completing Exploration 8.1.

EXPLORATION
8.1

Applying General Technologies to Science

The technologies that we have discussed are likely found in any elementary or middle school classroom and are not specific to science. But that doesn't mean they can't be. Think about each of these technologies and describe an activity that uses the generic educational technology tool and applies it directly to the learning of science. No, you may not use the examples already given in the chapter!

- Computer or "mobile device"
- Classroom projector
- Document camera
- Interactive whiteboard
- Speakers

Reflection Questions:

1. What similarities do you find in all of the activities you came up with?
2. How do these activities differ?
3. Which technology do you find to be the easiest to apply to science? Why?
4. How would you rank these technologies for the importance of having them in your classroom? Why?

The International Society for Technology in Education (ISTE) developed a series of standards for the use of technology for students, teachers, administrators, coaches, and computer science educators. You can view the ISTE Standards at www.iste.org and learn how they work together to transform learning and teaching.

 CHECK YOUR UNDERSTANDING 8.1
Click here to gauge your understanding of the concepts in this section.

Specific Digital Technologies for Science Education

Science and technology hold a unique relationship with each other. Advances in science are often translated into new technologies. Sometimes these new technologies then fuel additional advances in science. Take a historical example; at some very ancient point in history, scientists discovered that crystal and glass could bend light (refraction). Eventually this knowledge was applied to the making of eyeglasses and then, as more was learned about how light was bent by glass, to the invention of a microscope in the late 1500s. The microscope then opened up a whole new world of study for science.

This chicken/egg relationship of science and technology is why technology is explicitly included in *A Framework for K–12 Science Education: Practices, Crosscutting Concepts, and Core Ideas* as the fourth domain of the Disciplinary Core Ideas: Engineering, Technology, and the Applications of Science. Disciplinary Core Idea ETS2 focuses on the links among engineering, technology, science, and society (NRC, 2012). It is important, therefore, to have technology included in the science curriculum. Though the technology that is featured in the fourth domain of the DCIs in the *Framework* is not specifically instructional technology, using instructional technology to teach science seems like an obvious application.

In 2006, Park and Slykhuis examined the uses of technology in science education and determined that virtually all applications could be placed in one of four categories.

> Using [instructional] technology as a tool for science inquiry by pupils in the school science classroom and laboratory is the central theme of the ASTE [Association of Science Teacher Education] position statement. This is congruent with the *National Science Education Standards* (NRC, 1996), which emphasized that science should be learned using inquiry methods. The methodologies related to using [instructional] technology tools in school science discussed in the ASTE document can be categorized into four broad groups: (a) gathering scientific information; (b) data collection and analysis by pupils; (c) creating and using models of scientific phenomena; and (d) communication (Park & Slykhuis, 2006, p. 2).

Gathering Scientific Information

A Framework for K–12 Science Education: Practices, Crosscutting Concepts, and Core Ideas (NRC, 2012) introduced eight Scientific and Engineering Practices. When students use digital technology to access information about core ideas related to phenomena or problems to be solved, they are engaging in the eighth Practice: *obtaining, evaluating, and communicating information.*

Scientific information may be collected firsthand through experiences and investigations in the natural or human-made world, or it may be gathered indirectly through reading reports that others have written. Before the digital age, libraries and archives were the repositories of this second kind of scientific information. The digital age brought with it new ways to store and access such information. Science facts, data, and diagrams that may have taken days to locate in the library system 30 years ago are now basically at your fingertips if you have internet access for your smartphone, tablet, or computer and a reliable search engine like Google or Bing.

There are a variety of ways that digital text can help to increase student engagement with scientific information. It's now possible to listen to text without asking someone to read it to you. New terms and complex vocabulary can be hot-linked to enable you to access definitions or examples with a single click, instead of consulting a dictionary or glossary. Still images have been replaced with video clips, which adds the dimension of time to the information provided. Learners can take virtual field trips. Complete Exploration 8.2 to find out how scientific information can be acquired through virtual travel. Google Earth serves as a virtual globe that lets you access images of places by clicking on a map. Layers in Google Earth allow you to select the information to be displayed, such as terrain, roads, borders, labels, and geographic

Gathering Scientific Information Through Virtual Field Trips

EXPLORATION

8.2

Field trips have been a traditional learning activity in science classes for years. Field trip destinations include museums, various habitats, factories, geological points of interest, etc.

Opportunities for field trips are often limited by distance, accessibility, and cost, but virtual field trips can overcome those constraints and take your students to places that can't be accessed by your district school buses. Follow these links to experience several types of virtual educational travel.

Type of Virtual Field Trip	Destination	URL
Museum Visits	Smithsonian: National Museum of Natural History	http://naturalhistory.si.edu/panoramas/
	Museum of Science: Boston	www.discoveryeducation.com/Live/mos.cfm
Industrial Tours	Copper Mining	www.digintomining.com/virtualfieldtrips
	How Everyday Things Are Made	http://manufacturing.stanford.edu/

(continued)

(Exploration 8.2 continued)

Type of Virtual Field Trip	Destination	URL
Natural Areas	Gorongosa National Park: Mozambique	www.hhmi.org/biointeractive/gorongosa-national-park
	The Virtual Cave	www.goodearthgraphics.com/virtcave/
Out of This World	Mars	www.youvisit.com/tour/ryan.lee/87131
	Moon	http://sservi.nasa.gov/articles/video-tour-moon/
Live Webcams	Blacktip Reef: National Aquarium, Baltimore	http://aqua.org/explore/baltimore/exhibits-experiences/blacktip-reef
	Hawaiian Volcano Observatory	http://hvo.wr.usgs.gov/cams/
Immersive Virtual Reality	Various (Expeditions Pioneer Program, Google Cardboard)	www.google.com/edu/expeditions/

Reflection Questions:

1. What features of virtual field trips do you think would be especially engaging to students at the grade level you plan to teach?
2. Which of these virtual field trips might you use to introduce an anchoring phenomenon to launch a three-dimensional learning unit aligned with NGSS? Identify the phenomenon and a related question for investigation. Explain why you selected the one you did.
3. Think of another destination for a possible virtual field trip that would help your class gather science information. Use your favorite web browser to search for a resource that could meet your needs. Give the URL for the site you identify and describe how and why you would incorporate the virtual field trip into your science instruction.

features. Street view lets you explore the Earth's surface as if you were walking or driving around at many locations. Related features let you explore beneath the oceans' surface, Earth's moon, Mars, and even compare how some places have changed over time by looking at archived images from the past.

Effective use of a web browser is a skill that must be taught and developed over time. Just typing in a topic descriptor may lead to so many web resources that the search is overwhelming. Expecting students who are novice internet users to conduct a productive search for science information may not only be ineffective, but may also be dangerous as they may stumble across inappropriate material that has managed to evade your school's content filter.

A way to introduce students who are inexperienced with conducting web searches is to pre-select appropriate websites specifically related to their unit of study. By providing links to only pertinent, grade-level-appropriate sites, students are less likely to get lost in the search or overwhelmed by the process. Young learners may be directed to only one or two resources, while as students progress through the grade levels, the list of links also expands.

Using Caution Online. Even when links for students to follow are already selected, the internet must always be used with caution. While the internet is undoubtedly the most powerful way you can find scientific information, it is not always a safe place for your students to be. As previously mentioned, it is likely that your school will have some kind of internet content filter in place to deny access to sites that would be inappropriate in a school setting. Do not rely on this filter to be 100 percent accurate; it will block sites that you want access and that are appropriate and will miss some sites that are clearly inappropriate. You must be diligent when your class is working online to ensure that they remain on task (always a good idea when you are teaching anything) and to be sure that they are not going anywhere they should not be. Often the easiest solution to this lies in how you physically arrange the computers in the classroom. If the computers are all around the outside of the room with the screens facing in, it is relatively easy for you, as the teacher, to stand in the middle and simply turn around to observe all the screens.

The internet serves as a giant library, searchable electronically rather than simply browsing the stacks, providing nearly instant access to huge numbers of publications. Students should be taught how to narrow their searches using key words and sites like Google Scholar. The sources students identify, whether physical books or online files, must be evaluated for their usefulness in their research. Before students can effectively use print or web-based resources, they must learn to evaluate them in terms of certain criteria; that skill relates to the "evaluating" part of Practice 8. Table 8.1 lists typical criteria used to evaluate both print and web-based publications.

TABLE 8.1   Criteria Used to Evaluate Print and Web-Based Publications

Criteria	Questions You Might Ask
Authority	Do the authors or posting organization seem qualified to write about the subject?
Accuracy	Is the information presented supported by evidence (including other references)?
Objectivity	Are underlying biases apparent?
	Does the publication express only one point of view without acknowledging other viewpoints?
Currency	How recently was it published or updated?
Coverage	How well does the site inform your research topic/question?
	What is the depth of knowledge of the information presented? (basic, substantial, or detailed)
Value	Did the site provide new information or confirm prior knowledge?
	Did it address all pertinent issues?
	Was it worth visiting/reading?

Source: Based on Henderson, 2016.

Data Collection and Analysis

When you think about scientists using technology to do science, this is probably the category of uses for technology in science education that comes to mind first. This may be a carryover from the classic caricature of a scientist using a hand lens or peering at a graph. Using digital technologies for data collection and analysis relates to a cluster of NGSS Science and Engineering Practices: *Planning and carrying out investigations, Analyzing and interpreting data,* and *Using mathematics and computational thinking.*

Probeware.   Probeware is a tool that enables sensors (probes) to be interfaced with software with microprocessors to collect data and display data. Most probes consist of transducers, which are devices that convert physical quantities into electrical quantities. There are probes to measure temperature, light intensity, sound level, force, air pressure, pH, salinity, humidity, voltage, etc. The data are usually reported both as a data table and as a graph. The truly amazing part is that this reporting happens in real time. As the investigation is happening and the probe is collecting data, a graph of those data is being created and displayed. That means that any point of interest in the investigation (the reaching of a maximum, a change in direction of the curve, etc.) can be seen by the students when it happens, allowing them to more easily connect the physical event that is occurring to the data being collected and displayed. With greater accuracy and speed, the often tedious and time-consuming processes of collecting, recording, graphing, and analyzing data are carried out by this useful technology.

The method for displaying real-time graphs has changed dramatically over time. Originally, probeware was used as part of a computer-based laboratory (CBL) or microcomputer-based laboratory (MBL). The probe was hooked to a box that interpreted the signal from the probe and then, in turn, fed that data to a desktop computer. This was a great system, but it required a computer at every lab station and for experiments to be completed in the laboratory. Realizing there is a lot of science can be learned outside the laboratory, manufacturers began to try to find ways to make probeware more portable. Systems have been created to connect probes to graphing calculators, smartphones, tablets, and to stand-alone devices that incorporate a display screen directly into the device. While not the only options, the two most common applications of this system are the LabQuest system by Vernier and the Spark system by Pasco. Both of these systems are essentially handheld devices that a myriad of probes can be connected to and have screens to display the data. They are battery powered and can be taken to where the science is actually happening, instead of being confined to the laboratory.

Probably the simplest and most common probe in elementary and middle school science is the temperature probe. So what opportunities are there for using a temperature probe instead of a thermometer? Take the example of a simple investigation requiring students to find either the boiling point or freezing point of water. For the boiling point, a beaker of water can be placed on a heating element and temperatures can be recorded. For the freezing point, a test tube of water can be placed in an ice and saltwater bath.

For students to complete this investigation with a thermometer, they would first need to learn how to read that very thin red line that is present in a thermometer. (If they are trying to read a very thin silver line, stop the experiment immediately! That is a mercury thermometer and should not be in a school!) This in itself can be a somewhat difficult process. Assuming they can read it properly, students must choose a time interval (every minute?) to read the thermometer and record the data. As the water in the beaker approaches the boiling point, they then have to be very careful about reaching for the thermometer and avoiding the hot water, especially as they try to read it without pulling it out of the water. As the water in the test tube approaches the freezing point, again students must try to read the thermometer. However, the point they are trying to see on the thermometer will be getting lower and lower and falling inside the test tube itself. This makes it extremely difficult to read the thermometer without removing it from the test tube, thus changing the temperature reading. Later, after all the data is collected, students must find a sheet of graph paper, decide on what the x and y axis should be, choose a system to mark the intervals along the axis, and then plot their points. This is not to say that graphing and interpreting graphs is not a necessary skill, merely that the graphs generated by the probeware provide more accurate data points. After all of this, they can then begin to try to interpret their graph to determine what happens to the temperature as water approaches its boiling and freezing point. Of course, this would most likely have to be during the next class period, given the time restraints.

Picture now the same investigation with a temperature probe. The probe is connected to a device and placed in the beaker of water being heated, being careful not to place the probe on the very bottom of the beaker. Now data collection has begun. The device can be set to collect data at almost any interval. For example, it could easily be set in this situation to collect a temperature reading every second. The graph of the data is then displayed in real time on the device as the temperature of the beaker increases. The students can watch the temperature increase right up to the boiling point and then level off as the water reaches a boil. Conversely, when finding the freezing point, with a temperature probe placed in the test tube, students can watch the graph of the temperature fall toward the freezing point and then level off as they watch ice begin to form in the test tube. Students will quickly be able to see and read the temperature at which boiling and freezing occurred. Then they may begin to question why the temperature did not continue to rise or fall during boiling and freezing. All of this could easily be accomplished during a single class period, as a result of the probeware system doing much of the work collecting and graphing the data during the experiment.

In elementary and middle school science classrooms, another popular probe is a motion detector. These can be used to record the position, velocity, and acceleration data for most objects in motion. If you have access to a motion detector, grab one and play with it. They work essentially as sonar, sending out pulses of sound, recording the time until the sound is returned, and translating that into distance, velocity, and acceleration.

This video clip shows some students using motion detectors. As you watch, consider how this activity helps students understand the relationship between the line graph on the monitor and the position, motion, and speed of a book in the real world. www.youtube.com/watch?v=iqgAUFVqtc0

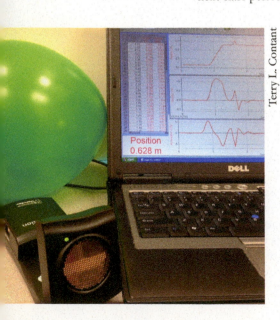

Terry L. Contant

Elementary and middle school students can successfully engage in similar investigations. Metcalf and Tinker (2004) found that middle school student learning was enhanced through the use of the probes and handhelds. They reported that students in their study experienced the physical correlation between phenomenon and modeling, which helped them to develop understanding and to confront misconceptions. In other words, one of the great things about using probeware is that students can connect what they physically see happen in the investigation to the graph that is created. This way, physical events and their representation on the graph are much more easily understood.

But what happens if a student is watching only the developing graph on the screen or only the phenomenon generating the data, or (and I am sure this won't happen in your class) what if one member of the group is absent and not able to watch either event? Don't worry; the investigation can be recorded on video, either by a built-in camera on a computer or on another device, and then imported into a computer. This video of the event can then be synchronized with the graph of the data, allowing the video and the graph to be displayed side by side on a computer screen. This enables students to review the graph and the investigation as many times as needed, skip to interesting points, and find new events they may have missed in real time. All of these uses of probeware and the associated software mean little or nothing if they are not used to support inquiry-based instruction in your classroom.

Digital Microscopes. Probeware is not the only way to collect and analyze data in science education. Another simple approach is the use of a microscope. There are also simple hand-help microscopes that have internal light sources that can magnify small objects and organisms to 30X life-size. A relatively common and low-cost alternative to the traditional microscope for elementary and middle school science classrooms is an electronic version of a microscope that can be connected to a computer via a USB connection or through Wi-Fi. This type of microscope is often much easier to use, especially for younger students, than a traditional look-through-an-eyepiece microscope. The object being studied is displayed on a much larger screen than looking though the eyepiece, a group instead of a single person can view it, and the image can be recorded and saved for further inspection later. When you and your class are observing the same magnified drop of pond water at the same time, it is much easier to have a discussion about what everyone is looking at on a shared display, than when each student is trying to find a paramecium on their own microscope slide. Often students think they have focused their optical microscope on a specific organism only to realize later that they are just noticing their eyelashes in the eyepiece.

Geographical Information Systems (GIS). Another technology that has made it easier for students to analyze data is Geographical Information Systems (GIS). While the students are not collecting their own data with this technology, they are analyzing large data sets that were not available before. GIS systems are available in many different shapes and sizes. They can vary from being commercial software aimed only at GIS in education to the use of free software such as Google Earth, Google Moon, and Google Mars. There are several advantages of using a system such as Google Earth to analyze data. First, it is cross platform, enabling use on any type of computer and also on smartphones and tablets. Second, it easily allows students to obtain a larger picture view of the world around them. For example, when studying glaciers, a tour can be constructed in Google Earth that starts at your home school and then "flies" around the world to see examples of glaciers. Instead of simply placing photographs of glaciers in a slide presentation, now students are able to easily see where the glaciers are situated in relation to themselves and the rest of the world, making the learning experience much more powerful. The significance of using these technologies is that it lets students ask questions that can then be answered using the data from the remote sensing technology.

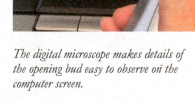

The digital microscope makes details of the opening bud easy to observe on the computer screen.

Creating and Using Models of Scientific Phenomena

This category for the application of technology is explicitly mentioned in *A Framework for K–12 Science Education: Practices, Crosscutting Concepts, and Core Ideas* (NRC, 2012) in the description of the second Science and Engineering Practice: *Developing and using models*. Computer simulations, an important type of model that can help both students and scientists test predictions and illustrate core ideas, are described in this section.

This fifth-grade class has been studying the phases of the moon. What evidence of the use of specific technologies do you see in this video clip?

The reasons for doing simulations are plentiful. You can simulate experiments that are too dangerous or too expensive to do in your classroom. In simulations, you can set parameters to extremes that would not be possible in the classroom. Simulations also run much more quickly than real-world investigations; there is limited setup and no cleanup. Simulations are also widely available online. Many are already within educational software, such as the software that accompanies interactive whiteboards, as well as apps on touchscreen tablets and smartphones. If they are readily available, cost so little, and are safe and easy to use, maybe all inquiry-based investigations in your classroom should be simulated? While simulations offer many advantages, they should not be used universally in place of investigations that can be completed in the classroom. Hands-on inquiry-based investigations allow students to learn how to use the tools and technology to gather data, adjust variables and there is some research that suggests that using both simulations and hands-on experiences reinforce the conceptual understanding of students.

An excellent example of the effective use of simulations is provided by a study by Randy Bell and Kathy Trundle (2008) on the software Starry Night. Starry Night is a software package that shows you the night sky on any given night. Randy and Kathy used Starry Night to have students explore the phases of the moon. Students were assigned one of three conditions: to go outside and observe the night sky and the moon every night for a month, to use Starry Night to observe the night sky and the moon every day for a month, or to go outside and make observations and to use Starry Night. The students who made observations outside had difficulty getting complete data sets. Many nights the night sky was filled with clouds obscuring the moon, or the moonrise was well beyond an appropriate time for them to be awake and observing the sky. The students who used the Starry Night software only were able to quickly make their observations and record their data, but it was not connected to the physical world right outside their window. Those students who used a combination of the two were able to make observations of the real world around them and then confirm those observations using the software. In addition, they could use the software to fill in any gaps that occurred in their data from poor visibility conditions or the time of the moonrise. Not surprisingly, on a posttest assessing the phases of the moon, students in the third condition performed the best of the three groups.

Exploration 8.3 will introduce you to a collection of science and mathematics simulations called PhET. These free, research-based programs are interactive models of scientific phenomena.

While simulations are prevalent online and other places, some care and preparation must still go into proper implementation in your classroom. Because a good simulation is interactive, meaning the user gets to control or change variables, the simulation is not like a static website. Therefore, they almost always require a little extra software to run, even if they are embedded on a website. This software could be Java, Flash, or an Applet, but it is critical that you as the teacher test the functionality of the simulation on the computers or device that the students will be using. Additionally, you will want to have them use the simulations to plan and conduct investigations or study models. It is important to move on to the other

---

EXPLORATION

8.3

Trying PhET Simulations

The next time you are near a computer, check out the massive library of simulations at the PhET website, http://phet.colorado.edu/. There you will find a wide variety of free simulations in every science content area, as well as teacher tips and lesson plans written by teachers from around the world.

Take a look at the PhET science simulations available for the grade levels you might teach. Consider the NGSS or state science standards you are likely to address in your classroom. Then select at least three simulations that seem to be aligned to core ideas in your chosen grade band and try them out.

Follow the links for "Research" and "Teacher Resources" to watch videos and read more about these topics.

Reflection Questions:

1. Which simulations did you select to try out? Why did you select those?
2. What are the variables that you can change and control in each of the simulations?
3. Which of these simulations would you want to use in your classroom? Why?
4. How would you use it/them (just the sim, the sim and a hands-on investigation, in small groups, as a whole class)? Why?

parts of an effective inquiry and include opportunities for students to make claims based on evidence and develop explanations that they communicate with others.

Another great site for finding science simulations appropriate for elementary and middle school students is ExploreLearning Gizmos (www.explorelearning.com/). That site states: "Gizmos use an inquiry-based approach to learning that has been validated by extensive research as a highly effective way to build conceptual understanding." Though there is a subscription fee for this collection of simulations, a 30-day free trial is typically available.

Desktop Manufacturing. If you teach at a school that emphasizes STEM (integrated science, technology, engineering, and mathematics expect to encounter a 3D printer. Affordable, reasonably-sized (desktop) versions of this technology have become popular tools for STEM classrooms. 3D printing or additive manufacturing is a process of making three dimensional solid objects from a digital file. Similar processes have been used in industry for decades to create prototypes research purposes and to manufacture custom parts for designs.

Desktop manufacturing provides a quick and easy way to create classroom models that you might not find in a supply closet. You simply make the shape that you need! You can easily manufacture the shapes and parts needed to create simple machines, create houses and buildings for an environmental landscape diorama. There are online sites with collections of ideas and files to print on your 3D printer. Visit www.thingiverse.com to explore the wide range of objects printed on a 3D printer and to network with others interested in effectively using 3D printers.

In upper elementary and middle school classrooms 3D printing is most appropriately used in the context of an engineering design project. Students identify a problem to be solved – maybe they want to create a stand to securely display an interesting fossil they found on a recent field trip. Considering the criteria and the constraints associated with the project, students may first draw a sketch or create a clay model that specifies the size and shape of a 3D object that could hold the fossil. Then, using solid modeling software, such as Blender or Tinkercad (which are free), they draw their 3D model on the computer. Alternatively 3D scanners can turn a real-world object into a file that can be replicated and/or scaled by a 3D printer. Next, the software "slices" the 3D model into hundreds (or thousands) of virtual horizontal layers in a file that is uploaded in a 3D printer; then the design is printed layer by layer, building up the three dimensional object. 3D printing can take a while, as it must lay down plastic, metal for each "slice" of the model. Students would then test their prototype to see if it functioned as a fossil holder as they had planned. If it doesn't, they would use the solid modeling program to tweak or redesign their model and 3D print the next version.

Communication

One important step in the scientific process that is often passed over in the school curriculum is the sharing of experimental results and meaning-making discussions based on the findings. *A Framework for K–12 Science Education: Practices, Crosscutting Concepts, and Core Ideas* (NRC, 2012), however, makes this step explicit. The Scientific and Engineering Practices: *Engaging in argument from evidence,* and parts of *Obtaining, evaluating, and communicating information,* address communication directly. Technology provides a quick and effective means to accomplish these tasks.

It is often mentioned that scientists will share their results for others to test and confirm or contest, but this process is rarely modeled in school. Given the plethora of communication options that currently exists, there is no reason for this trend to continue. One way for students to communicate their results was mentioned earlier in this chapter: through the use of video that they create. Students can record both their investigation and a discussion of their results that can be shared with the teacher and/or their peers.

Video, however, is only one of a myriad of ways that students can communicate their results. They can simply use a word processor to write a report, utilize a spreadsheet to create some graphs, or put together a slideshow to help them present the results in class. Another option is for each student to record individual results on the class wiki, discuss the results on the class discussion board, or share pictures of their experiment on the class photo stream. Many of these solutions that enable students to share their data have the added advantage of being online, allowing this activity to take place outside of the class.

There are some apps available that allow each student in your class with a computer or mobile device to interact with others in the class on the same screen. Small groups or whole classes can collaborate on the same document using Google Docs, Google Slides, Google Sheets, etc. These apps are especially useful for

▶ Watch this short video of a fifth-grade class using a Gizmo simulation about mineral identification. How do the students react to this instructional approach? www.youtube.com/watch?v=J6BHqO8Orfg

▶ This video presents many possibilities for using a 3D printer in your classroom and demonstrates the steps in the 3D design and printing process. How might you use this technology in your STEM teaching? https://www.youtube.com/watch?v=N9raogfvBdA

sharing individual or small-group data with the whole class or for a group writing activity. Exploration 8.4 presents several investigations about plants that produce data that classes might share and discuss digitally. Padlet, described as a virtual bulletin board, is another app that facilitates collaboration and sharing in the classroom. Your students can contribute their ideas, images, data, questions and answers to a shared empty sheet of online paper. This app is perfect for brainstorming without scribing students' ideas, because they can type them in from their own device. Contributed ideas can be moved around to categorize or prioritize by anyone in the class, and the created sheet can be saved for future reference, reducing your need for chart paper and easel. Many teachers use Edmodo to create a space for student learning groups, create digital libraries and embed videos, images and audio clips to spark class discussion online as well as providing a space for students and teachers to post messages and engage in micro-blogging.

Since most computers already have built-in webcams, the many free options for communicating, via videoconferencing, video chatting, or video calling, make it relatively easy for your class to share and communicate with other classes as well. In fact, one free and commonly used tool for video calling, Skype, has its own education community where teachers can post ideas and requests for collaborating with other teachers from around the country and the world. This project is called "Skype in the Classroom" and can be found at education.skype.com.

Collaborating with other classes from across the country or across the globe can provide an exciting and enriching experience for your students. However, coordinating details for communicating across large distances synchronously can be very difficult. Not only are your schools on different schedules, but you may also be in different (sometimes significantly different) time zones. For that reason, don't dismiss the idea of simply collaborating with other schools in your same district. Often the elementary schools within a district operate on similar schedules throughout the day. This makes it likely that two science classes on opposite sides of town will take place simultaneously. District pacing guides also increase the likelihood that both schools will cover the same content at the same time. Regardless of whether you're video calling across the town or across the world, students will still get the benefit of exposure to the technology tool.

EXPLORATION
8.4

Sharing Data

A common classroom investigation in both elementary and middle school involves comparing a variety of conditions for the growth of Wisconsin Fast Plants (*Brassica rapa*). These little relatives of turnip and mustard plants were selectively bred to go through an entire life cycle, from seed to seed, in four to five weeks. The seeds are often carefully observed and recorded and then planted under a variety of conditions (wet/dry, light/dark, etc.). Students monitor the growing plants over several weeks, keeping data as the plants develop. This investigation can take several forms. (1) One option is for each group to complete the investigation, tracking their own data all the way through. (2) Another is for the class to pool their data, using one of the many online methods previously mentioned. (3) And yet another possibility is for the class to share data with another class across town or even farther away. As you imagine these different scenarios:

Reflection Questions:

1. What similarities do you find among the three scenarios?
2. How would each scenario change what your students would learn from the investigation?
3. What elements of each method of sharing do you find most helpful? Why?
4. Which one of these methods of sharing would you want to use in your classroom? Why?
5. What information would you want your students to share to help them develop conceptual understanding?

✓ CHECK YOUR UNDERSTANDING 8.2
Click here to gauge your understanding of the concepts in this section.

Social Media

What is social media doing in a chapter on educational technology? It has become such a prevalent form of technology that it has applications for the classroom as well. First, what is social media? It is quite simply the technology that we use to share our lives with others, be they friends or followers. Which brings us to the two dominant forms of social technology today, Facebook and Twitter, which are both available to you on any platform and on any type of mobile device. They are certainly not the only forms; simply look at almost any news website and all the options for sharing that page to get an idea of the vast variety of social media.

So back to the original question, what is social media doing in a chapter on educational technology? Well, if you remember, the opening question of the chapter asked: "How can you keep up with all the changes in technology?" While the simple answer is you can't, the better answer is that you can use social media to keep as up to date as possible. Using Facebook, you can belong to groups that post about new technology and give you suggestions about how to use existing technology in new and innovative ways. While that is effective, this is an area in which Twitter really shines. By finding a few people who are experts in using and implementing technology, you can easily follow them and their updates. These experts will become part of your professional learning community (PLC).

You should construct a PLC to help keep yourself up to date in all areas of teaching, not just technology. Your PLC can include people on Twitter who are experts on technology, as well as other teachers on Twitter who recommend resources and lessons to use in your classroom. Your PLC should also include other teachers or technology experts whose blogs you subscribe to. Both following teachers on Twitter and subscribing to blogs transforms how you add to your knowledge base; instead of you searching for new information about teaching or technology, the new information comes to you. Table 8.2 suggests some websites that provide resources for your PLC.

In addition, you can use the hashtag (#) function in Twitter to bring information to you. A simple internet search for educational hashtags will return many worthwhile results. You will need to take just a little time to research what each hashtag will provide, and then you can use a Twitter aggregator, such as Tweetdeck, to compile all the tweets that contain the hashtag that you have chosen. Several hashtags that can link you to information about the *Next Generation Science Standards* and their implementation in classrooms include #ngsschat and #NGSS.

Using social media is not without its pitfalls. Whether you agree with it or not, you need to be aware that as a teacher, you will be held to a different standard of acceptability in your use of social media. You need to be aware that no matter how private you try to make your social media use, the chances are that anything you post online will be seen—possibly by someone who should not see it. There have been

TABLE 8.2   Some Suggestions for Starting Your PLC

Resource	Location
Cool Cat Teacher	www.coolcatteacher.com/ @coolcatteacher
TeacherCast	Teachercast.net @TeacherCast
Marc Anderson's Blog	Ictevangelist.com @ICTEvangelist
The Educator's PLN (Personal Learning Network)	Edupln.ning.com
National Science Teachers Association	@NSTA
Howard Glasser	@hglasser
Wired Science	www.wired.com/wiredscience @wiredscience
Hashtags	#education, #edchat

numerous stories of teachers being fired or suspended over what they have posted on Facebook. The easiest solution isn't to dive deep into Facebook's privacy settings, but instead, to refrain from posting anything that could be considered objectionable.

Besides being cautious about what you post online via social media, you should also be deliberate about posting online items that will contribute to your public presence in a positive and professional manner. Ideally, if a parent, student, or potential employer were to search your name online, they should find positive news about you. You can create this positive news by contributing professional items and suggestions to blogs or other sites that are public and searchable. By positively contributing online, instead of being worried about what people might find about you, you can be confident that your online reputation will help you.

 ## CHECK YOUR UNDERSTANDING 8.3
Click here to gauge your understanding of the concepts in this section.

 # CHAPTER SUMMARY

General Educational Technology in the Science Classroom

Your classroom is likely to be equipped with at least a computer and a projector. These are almost seen as necessities to teaching, and they can be applied to teaching science by what you as a teacher choose to show on them. Hopefully, your classroom will have additional technologies, such as a document camera, an interactive whiteboard, and external speakers. A document camera can be used to show science-related documents, but it can also be easily repurposed to show larger zoomed-in images of science-related objects, such as rocks and minerals.

Specific Digital Technologies for Science Education

Instructional technologies applied to the teaching of science can be placed in one of four categories based on their purpose: gathering scientific information, data collection and analysis by pupils, creating and using models of scientific phenomena, and communication. Students should gain experience using a variety of technologies in each of those areas. While using probeware for data collection is the default idea for science-specific technology in the classroom, there are many more options. Using online resources—for gathering information, for running simulations, or for communication—is a vast and rich opportunity for students and teachers.

Social Media

Social media can be used to form your own professional learning community (PLC). This group of professionals that you follow through social media can become an excellent source of resources for your classroom. Social media must be used very carefully. Teachers are generally held to a higher code of conduct in their personal lives than other professions, and if too much information is shared, your professional position and reputation could be harmed.

DISCUSSION QUESTIONS

1. What general technologies have been common in the classrooms you have visited?
2. How can science-specific technology applications be used to push the science experience of your students beyond the classroom walls?
3. How can you find good people or organizations to include in your PLC?

PROFESSIONAL PRACTICES ACTIVITIES

1. Find a classroom with a computer, projector, document camera, and interactive whiteboard. Try unhooking all the wires and reconnecting them correctly.

2. At a local school, find out what science-focused instructional technology they have and how it is being used in the classroom. Ask to come observe a day when the students are using it so you can see the excitement technology helps create in students learning science.

3. If you haven't done so already, create a Twitter account and begin to follow some experts in your field.

Connecting Science with Other Subjects

Hill Street Studios/Blend Images/Getty Images

LEARNING GOALS

After reading this chapter, you should understand that . . .

1. Science doesn't happen in isolation but is connected to mathematics when the learning goals from each discipline and the student practice skills from both disciplines are linked.

2. STEM (science, math, engineering and technology) teaching and learning links the knowledge and skills from each area to answer questions and solve problems.

3. Events and issues studied in social studies link to inquiry and problem-based learning in science.

4. Science and English Language Arts are linked with reading and writing goals and student practices.

Integrated learning connects science with other disciplines, right? Try to recall what part of your school day was typically set apart for learning science. All of the science instruction you have experienced has probably occurred during a time that was designated for science. Yet during that science time, you probably did some reading, some math, and maybe looked at the history of the science and social context as well. So even though you were using skills and learning other subjects during science time, chances are that was not often reciprocated! It is time to learn how the walls between these subjects exist only in our minds (and on our schedules!).

Although the curriculum and the school day are often neatly divided into separate subjects, real-world approaches to problems and issues cut across disciplinary lines. Scientists—and our student scientists—for example, use mathematics as a tool to explore, represent, and explain patterns in data from investigations. Mathematical modeling is one way that mathematics is applied in science. Scientists (and student scientists) draw on their language and literacy skills as they read scientific literature, formulate problems, write proposals, plan investigations, record data, and communicate findings and conclusions to others. Furthermore, scientists, student scientists, as well as other citizens enter into discussions and make decisions about societal problems and issues arising from the applications of science and technology. In the real world, then, science, mathematics, reading, writing, social studies, and other disciplines are not isolated from one another, but connected.

Just as scientists use mathematics and language arts as tools, children should have opportunities to apply and enhance their mathematics, reading, and writing skills while investigating the natural world. This heightens the relevance of mathematics and language arts, enhances their usefulness, and promotes greater learning in science. Similarly, in their studies of both science and social studies, children should have the opportunity to examine the cause-and-effect relationships among science, technology, and societal change. Science is often not allotted as many minutes during the school week as other subjects, so whenever connections can be made between subjects to increase the amount of science that is taught, it is a great idea!

Chapter 12 of *A Framework for K–12 Science Education: Practices, Crosscutting Concepts, and Core Ideas* (2012) presented recommendations for the writers of the *Next Generation Science Standards* (NGSS). Recommendation 12 suggests that the NGSS should clearly align with standards in other subject areas, especially mathematics and English/language arts. Such coherence across subject areas is likely to result in increased student learning as students' skills and conceptual understanding are reinforced during the school year. When the NGSS was published in 2013 (NGSS Lead States), the appendixes included one that connects science to the *Common Core State Standards for Mathematics* (CCSSM) and a second appendix connecting the *Common Core State Standards for English Language Arts* & Literacy in History/Social Studies, Science, and Technical Subjects (CCSS).

In the *Next Generation Science Standards* (NGSS), correlations between the performance expectations and the CCSS in English Language Arts and Literacy and Mathematics are specified in the Connection boxes. Some of the connections link the science, which is a very quantitative discipline, with both the content and practices in CCSS mathematics. Literacy skills, for building knowledge and understanding in science, are critical for students' success in science, so the NGSS writing team worked with the CCSS writing team to identify the key literacy connections. This very useful information in the Connection boxes can help you effectively plan and teach lessons and units that effectively integrate science with other subject areas to create interdisciplinary learning experiences.

Integrating Science and Mathematics

Science and mathematics are easily connected. Anyone can quickly see that science as a quantitative discipline applies mathematics skills and practices. Open any mathematics textbook and you will find that many of the word problems and tasks are related to science. Conversely, open any science textbook and you will see examples of how to "do the math" to solve a science question, analyze data, and synthesize results.

A Framework for K–12 Science Education: Practices, Crosscutting Concepts, and Core Ideas (NRC, 2012), which guided the development of the NGSS, reflects the importance of the relationship between science and mathematics in two of its three dimensions. Two Scientific and Engineering Practices show the relationship explicitly: *Analyzing and interpreting data* and *Using mathematics and computational thinking*. The Crosscutting Concepts of *Patterns* and *Scale, proportion, and quantity* are also closely tied to mathematics.

The NRC *Framework* and the *Common Core State Standards for Mathematics* (NGA & CCSSO, 2010) both identify practices for their featured subject area. Though the wording differs, some of the practices are similar for both subjects, as shown in Table 9.1. It is this parallel alignment that allows for natural connections between math and science learning. Within the Practices, *Analyzing and interpreting data* and *Using mathematics and computational thinking* directly utilize mathematical processes and thinking.

The NGSS writing team realized the importance of maintaining coherence between science and mathematics learning as students advance through the grade levels. They collaborated with members of the *Common Core State Standards for Mathematics* writing team to ensure that any mathematics skills or concepts would be taught in math (based on the CCSSM) before students need to apply them in science (Achieve, 2013a).

Being familiar with the *Common Core State Standards for Mathematics* can help you plan effective science instruction. For example, knowing that angle measurement is not developmentally appropriate until fourth grade, as noted in the CCSSM, should lead you to avoid teaching a lesson to your first graders about the tilt of Earth's axis being a cause of seasonal temperature change.

In fact, the development of mathematics concepts, just like science concepts, is often rooted in physical experiences. Children often quantify the world through counting, estimating, and measuring all kinds of

Access the NGSS Appendices at www .nextgenscience.org/get-to-know. To find out more about connections to the CCSSM in the NGSS look at Appendix L.

TABLE 9.1 **Science and Engineering Practices and Mathematics Practices That Are Aligned**

Science and Engineering Practice	Mathematics Practice
Asking questions (for science) and defining problems (for engineering)	Making sense of problems and persevering in solving them
Developing and using models	Modeling with mathematics
Using mathematics and computational thinking	Reasoning abstractly and quantitatively
Engaging in argument from evidence	Constructing viable arguments and critiquing the reasoning of others

Finding Mathematics in the Next Generation Science Standards

Go online to www.nextgenscience.org. From a grade level that you would like to teach, select a "topic page" that interests you. Examine the performance expectations, the foundation boxes, and the connection boxes for evidence of the integration of mathematics and science in the NGSS.

Also, use the links in the NGSS to access related background information from the *Framework* and the *Common Core State Standards*. Appendix L is another section of the NGSS document that summarizes the key math topics relevant to science and the grade level at which they are first expected in the *Common Core State Standards for Mathematics*. Talk about your findings with one or more of your colleagues.

Reflection Questions:

1. What evidence of the integration of mathematics and science do you find?
2. In what ways do the references to mathematics skills and concepts in the different sections of the page seem to be related? How do you know?
3. How do the math and science standards seem to support each other? Use examples to explain your thinking.

real-world variables they encounter in the process of investigating. In school, for example, children may be asked to count the number of seeds found in different fruits or the number of pennies added as cargo to a clay boat. They may estimate weights and volumes in determining whether objects might float or sink. They may also measure the weights of pendulum bobs, lengths of stems of growing plants, or time for an antacid powder or tablet to dissolve in water. Furthermore, they may add weights, subtract the weight of a container from the total weight to find the weight of the contents, multiply lengths and widths to find areas, and divide distances by time to find rates. All of these operations help children begin to quantify objects and events. Complete Exploration 9.1 to find out more about how the mathematical practices are identified in the NGSS documents.

When thinking about elementary and middle school students quantifying the world, consider the task of measurement. Measuring is part of both science and mathematics instruction. As children engage in problem-solving activities in either discipline, they often need skills for measuring and performing operations with length, volume, weight, time, temperature, and other variables. Measuring is founded on the processes of observing and comparing. "Children naturally make comparisons" (National Science Resources Center, 1996, p. 3). To make quantitative comparisons, they stand back to back to see who is taller, line up their feet to see whose are longer, and match their bodies to different-sized clothing to see what will fit.

The logic of something seemingly simple like length measurement is deceptively complex. It encompasses such ideas as the conservation of length, the notion of standard units, unit iteration (counting the number of standard units in a length), and knowledge of how to use standard measuring instruments, such as rulers. According to research by Clements (1999), however, children do not have to master all of these logical complexities to learn to measure the lengths of objects using a ruler, if the teacher provides appropriate scaffolding.

While studying plant growth students often measure and record data about seedlings for analysis later.

Real-world measurements often present a challenge to children. For example, measuring the length of plant roots in germination bags can be difficult because the roots are not straight, but curved and twisted.

A simple ruler cannot be used to directly measure the roots. Children must invent ways to measure them, perhaps by laying a curving string along the roots, then straightening out the string and measuring it with a ruler. What other ways can you think of to solve the problem of measuring curved roots?

The process of measuring length in science contexts provides children an opportunity to rehearse, and consequently enlarge, their measurement knowledge. When using measurement and other mathematics skills in science, children not only practice what they have already encountered in mathematics classes, but also add something new to it. Mathematics schemas are expanded with the new additions from science activities. Children's mathematics skills are then less likely to be bound to specific tasks and are more likely to be transferable and useful in a variety of ways.

The International System of Units (SI) is used to define what we call the **metric system**. Although use of units such as feet and pounds is customary in the United States, the need for SI units has already affected machine tools, packaging, and temperature measurements. Competition with the rest of the world will continue to accelerate the use of SI in business, science, and government.

The metric system is convenient because it is based on the mathematics of place value and uses decimals rather than fractions. Thus, the metric system is often easier to use than U.S. customary units. It is easier for children to add 4.5 cm and 4.2 cm, for example, than to add 1 foot 1-3/4 inches and 2 feet 11-2/3 inches.

American children must continue to learn and be familiar with both metric and customary units, but programs should deemphasize the memorization and use of conversion factors between the two systems. When a student measures something 6.5 cm long, for example, accept that as a description of its length. Do not ask how many inches it is. Students' concepts of a unit of length will develop adequately without knowing the exact equivalent in the U.S. standard unit system.

In science activities, once data has been obtained through measurements, it must be organized and interpreted. Organizing data into diagrams, tables, and graphs is another key step in scientific inquiry. Data tables display numerical data in column form. Graphs provide visual displays of data. Putting data obtained from scientific investigations into tables and graphs better enables students to:

- relate their data to their investigative procedures
- make comparisons among data
- see relationships and patterns
- communicate their data to other people

The types of graphs most often used in scientific applications in elementary and middle schools are bar graphs, histograms, and line graphs. Bar graphs vividly show differences between groups in a set of data. Bar graphs can be used, for example, to show the number of children in a class with each different type of eye or hair color. Comparisons of the number of students in each group are easy to see because of the relative lengths of the bars. Because graphs communicate data in a visual form, they can reveal patterns of information better than data tables. Bar graphs can be constructed in the early grades by cutting strips of graph paper to make measurements and then placing the strips on a piece of paper to represent the length measurement. In this way, students begin to develop visual pictorial representations.

Histograms display the number of data values of a variable that occur within set intervals in a data set. Histograms differ from bar graphs in that the x-axis on a bar graph simply names a category, while the x-axis on a histogram is a number line representing a variable.

Line graphs are more advanced; students from about grade 4 can learn to construct and interpret them. With line graphs, your students can graphically show the relationship between two sets of numerical data that are continuous. A line graph displays visually the changes in a responding or dependent variable in an investigation corresponding to changes in the values of a manipulated or independent variable.

It is scientific convention to plot the manipulated or independent variable on the horizontal x-axis and to plot the responding or dependent variable on the vertical y-axis. The **mnemonic** DRY MIX is helpful for remembering this convention:

The **D**ependent or **R**esponding variable is plotted on the **Y**-axis.

The **M**anipulated or **I**ndependent variable is plotted on the **X**-axis.

Students should understand that in using mathematics in scientific investigations, they will "encounter all the anomalies of authentic problems—inconsistencies, outliers, and errors—which they might not encounter with contrived textbook data" (NRC, 1996, pp. 214, 218). Thus, if certain data points do not fall on a projected trend line, students should consider whether the points might be anomalies or errors. In connecting mathematics and science, it is important that students not only construct tables and graphs but also interpret them. During the analysis process, students will need to look for patterns that result in trends. Is there a general upward trend? Do the points on a line graph increase, then level off, and then gradually decrease? If so what does it mean about the relationship between the variables? Middle school students will also begin to work with lines of best fit where the actual data points are not connected, but a line revealing a pattern or trend is created. Ultimately you will want to help students turn the graphical picture into words by writing a couple of sentences that describe the line and explain the effect that changing the independent variable has on the dependent variable.

At the middle level, when interpreting quantitative data, students also learn the terms *mean, medium, mode,* and *range.* When conducting inquiries, we often ask students to conduct a minimum of three trials. They learn that many measurements contain chance errors that may be unavoidable. Rulers or thermometers may not read the same. So mathematically, finding the mean—the arithmetic average—is a common method to find the central value. The range identifies how spread out the data are. This can be an important analysis tool because if the range in the data is small—for example, with measurements of temperature of 20, 22, and 22—like 2 in the example given, then it shows that the data is less variable. If the data for the temperatures are 14, 22, and 27, then the range is 13 degrees. This group of data is more spread out, which means there is a greater variation. In both of the data sets, the mean is 21 so sometimes looking at the range can be an important mathematical tool to analyze the data. Remember that you can also determine the median, which is the middle value in a set of data ranked from lowest to highest or determining the mode, which is the value that occurs most often and can be used with qualitative data. It is important for students to select the most effective way to compare data as part of the data analysis process.

When appropriate, you may also want to introduce stem-and-leaf plots, which provide a quick way to display 25 or more pieces of data, or box and whisker diagrams, which display data based on the lower extreme, lower quartile, median, upper quartile, and upper extreme. If you need help with these display strategies, talk with a math teacher and discuss when they would be useful for comparing results. Just as with data tables, graphs and stem-and-leaf plots, it is important to help students generate a paragraph summarizing the information in the visual displays. In *Science Experiments by the Hundreds,* 3rd Ed. (Cothron, Giese, & Rezba, 2008), the authors provide examples of investigations that utilize mathematical and computational thinking and require students to analyze and interpret data.

✓ CHECK YOUR UNDERSTANDING 9.1
Click here to gauge your understanding of the concepts in this section.

Science Education as a Component of STEM Education

First, recall that STEM stands for Science, Technology, Engineering, and Mathematics. Second, understand that even though everyone agrees on what STEM stands for, you will find many people and groups use STEM in very different ways. Some people will argue that any project focused on science, technology, engineering, or mathematics is a STEM lesson because it covers "one of the letters." Others will argue that if a project does not incorporate all four aspects, then it is not a STEM lesson. Of course, there are plenty of viewpoints somewhere in between!

The idea of integrating STEM instead of individual science, technology, engineering, or mathematics projects or lessons is increasing. *A Framework for K–12 Science Education: Practices, Crosscutting Concepts, and Core Ideas* (2012) guided the development of the *Next Generation Science Standards* and clearly states that science is no longer to be taught in isolation as single concepts with a laundry list of related vocabulary. The new expectation is for science concepts to be taught as core ideas that are explored through Science and Engineering Practices and connected through explicit relationships to Crosscutting Concepts. Implicit to STEM education is the teaching of integrated bodies of content knowledge and problem-solving processes for learning about them. And while the NGSS (NGSS Lead States, 2013) may not be universally adopted by all states, the recommendations put forth in the *Framework* will significantly impact how science is

 In this video, a hands-on study of robotics illustrates for students **the integration of math and science**. What math/science connections do you observe in this robotics lesson?

taught throughout the nation as textbooks and curriculum designers react to the call for more integrated STEM lessons.

For example, the "E" in STEM, Engineering, is addressed in two of the three dimensions of *A Framework for K–12 Science Education: Practices, Crosscutting Concepts, and Core Ideas*. It is clearly present in the Scientific and Engineering Practices and in the fourth discipline in the Disciplinary Core Ideas.

Two of the eight Practices in the *Framework* differentiate between doing science and doing engineering: *Asking questions (for science) and defining problems (for engineering)*, and *Constructing explanations (for science) and designing solutions (for engineering)*. While science and engineering are distinct disciplines with differing goals, they are synergistic—with advances in science leading to advances in engineering and vice versa. The other six Practices are applicable to the work of both scientists and engineers, illustrating the commonalities between these STEM fields (NRC, 2012).

The inclusion of "Engineering, Technology, and Applications of Science (ETS)" with the three traditional science domains in the *Framework* dimension known as Disciplinary Core Ideas acknowledges their importance to our daily lives and functioning in today's world. In the *Framework*, *engineering* refers to engagement in a systematic design process to solve problems or meet needs that people identify; *technology* refers to human-made objects, systems, or processes developed and used to solve problems and/or meet human needs.

The first core idea in the Engineering, Technology, and Applications of Science discipline is

ETS1: Engineering Design, which focuses on the question: *How do engineers solve problems?* It includes three components:

- ETS1.A—Defining and delimiting an engineering problem, focusing on the questions: *What is a design for?* and *What are the criteria and constraints of a successful solution?*
- ETS1.B—Developing possible solutions, focusing on the question: *What is the process for developing potential design solutions?*
- ETS1.C—Optimizing the design solution, focusing on the question: *How can the various proposed design solutions be compared and improved?*

The second core idea in this discipline is

ETS2: Links among engineering, technology, science, and society, which focuses on the question: *How are engineering, technology, science, and society interconnected?* It includes two components:

- ETS2.A—Interdependence of science, engineering, and technology, focusing on the question: *What are the relationships among science, engineering, and technology?*
- ETS2.B—Influence of engineering, technology, and science on society and on the natural world, focusing on the questions: *How do science, engineering, and the technologies that result from them affect the ways in which people live?* and *How do they affect the natural world?* (NRC, 2012).

Consider a common K–8 science topic, seed germination and growth, and how a science lesson on this topic may have changed over time. In the most traditional sense, and now outdated, your parents may have experienced a lesson about seed germination where they were given a textbook to read about the topic. They were likely asked to then copy key vocabulary words and their definitions. If they were lucky, their textbook may have had some black-and-white pictures of seeds or seedling growth. The result of this lesson was that the goal was met. Students were able to learn the vocabulary terms associated with the topic.

When you were a student, you may have experienced a lesson on seed germination that was somewhat similar. More than likely, however, your textbook contained color pictures and diagrams that were useful in helping you to understand the process. You probably also experienced completing prepared worksheets, corresponding to the textbook reading, instead of copying vocabulary terms from the textbook. There is also a good chance your teacher had seeds for you to look at, and you possibly even planted a seed for the class to observe its growth. Again, the results of this lesson were good: You learned the vocabulary, the diagrams allowed you to visualize the unseen processes, and you were able to connect the unseen processes to the plant growing in your classroom.

A lesson aligned to the *National Science Education Standards* (NRC, 1996) or to NGSS would be more inquiry-based and follow the 5E lesson plan model. To start, the students would be engaged in the topic. Perhaps the teacher would show the whole class an interesting and well-developed plant and ask

Access the NGSS Appendices at www .nextgenscience.org/ get-to-know. To find out more about the ETS DCIs look at Appendix I and Appendix J.

Integration of STEM (especially the T and E) in the
Next Generation Science Standards

EXPLORATION

9.2

Go online to http://www.nextgenscience.org/overview-dci. Examine the performance expectations and the foundation boxes of the NGSS for a grade level of your choosing for evidence of the inclusion of engineering and technology. Talk about your findings with one or more of your colleagues. In particular look for an asterisk in the performance expectations. What new information does it provide?

Reflection Questions:

1. Where in the NGSS did you find connections to engineering, technology, and the applications of science? Why do you think they were placed where they were?
2. Based on your examination of one grade level, do you think that the NGSS suggest that ideas about engineering and technology be taught in isolation or integrated with science ideas? What evidence supports your claim?
3. How do you plan to integrate STEM into your teaching? How will you prepare in order to implement your plan?

students about how the plant got to this stage. This would allow the teacher to introduce and excite the students about the topic of plants and uncover their prior knowledge about seeds and plant germination. Students would then explore the topic. This could be accomplished by giving the students various seeds, the same kinds of soil, and clear plastic sandwich bags. The students could then design experiments to find the optimum conditions for each kind of seed to germinate and then collect data, like measuring the roots. Students would then explain to the class and teacher what they had learned through their experiment. The teacher would take this opportunity to hook vocabulary terms to the students' experiences to reinforce their learning. Students would then extend their knowledge to new situations and cement their new knowledge by applying it to a new situation or scenario. Finally, the students' learning would be evaluated by the teacher to check if they understand the concepts that were intended for the lesson. The results of the evaluation would be used to inform the next day's lesson. The new lesson would be informed by student understanding, and the lesson would likely be a good lesson to teach as the students' experiences with this content would help them anchor new knowledge and new vocabulary terms.

However, a more valuable lesson for students could be experienced. The original seed and germination lesson could be morphed into an integrated STEM lesson. In Exploration 9.2 you learned more about how you can integrate STEM into your teaching. As a STEM lesson it could still follow the 5E instructional *Framework*, but with some changes and additions to "hook" students and determine their prior knowledge. Instead of exploring seed germination in clear plastic bags, the class could incorporate instructional technology and participate in an online learning environment like www.PlantingScience.org. This website would provide some of the materials, both curricular and manipulative, as well as connect students with expert scientists and other classes completing the same challenge. In such an online lesson, some of the materials obviously are not provided, such as soil, growing containers, and supplemental lighting. However, instead of the teacher providing these materials, the students could be asked to design and build, or engineer, a system for growing the plants under specified conditions.

The math, measuring, and graphing, which had perhaps been in the background of the lesson before, would become a more explicit part of the learning process. For example, students might design a specialized measuring tool, a new *technology* to overcome some of the problems they encountered when measuring, or they might design a procedure, another new technology, for data collection that makes the germination or plant growth process easier to manage.

STEM lessons present students with opportunities to integrate skills, practices, and concepts from different disciplines, and they can result in more meaningful learning, aligning with skills required for the twenty-first century. Key to designing successful integrated STEM lessons is to move beyond interesting engineering activities or the use of "cool" technology. Just using a computer or 3-D printer does not make a lesson a STEM lesson. Many teachers have begun to implement robotics lessons since this is an area where we see emerging technologies, and it also motivates students to engage with problem-solving tasks.

Engineering design involves students with solving a problem. How does the teacher engage the students with the engineering design process? Which elements of the ETS DCIs from the progressions matrix in Appendix I are incorporated in this lesson segment? What PEs do you think are being addressed?

For example, there are many lessons available online that ask students to create underwater robots that complete tasks like picking up an object using a mechanical arm, taking a water sample using a syringe, and taking a photo of an underwater object to identify any markings present. In addition to designing and building an underwater remotely operating vehicle, students learn about the science phenomenon of buoyancy, gather and analyze data mathematically, and utilize appropriate technology or build the technology tools needed to complete the tasks. In truly integrated STEM lessons, the students make the connections needed to answer the question or solve the problem.

✔ **CHECK YOUR UNDERSTANDING 9.2**

Click here to gauge your understanding of the concepts in this section.

Integrating Science and Social Studies

▶ Listen to Katy Jo Brown discuss a **yearlong composting study** with her seventh-grade class. What science connections does the compost study allow students to make throughout the year? What social studies connections would this study allow you to address with students?

Social studies cuts across and combines several disciplines. According to the National Council for the Social Studies (1994, 2010):

> Within the school program, social studies [as a discipline] provides coordinated, systematic study drawing on such disciplines as anthropology, archaeology, economics, geography, history, law, philosophy, political science, psychology, religion, and sociology, as well as appropriate content from the humanities, mathematics, and natural sciences (p. 3).

Making connections between science and social studies helps students create a more complete picture of the world. While science emphasizes how the natural world works, social studies focuses on the civic competence needed for active engagement in public life. Addressing ideas in the context of these subject areas simultaneously has two advantages. It helps students understand the impact that scientific discoveries and technological advances have on our culture, economy, and daily life. It also helps them learn how societal needs and political issues affect investment in scientific research and new technologies.

Science, technology, and society (STS) themes are common to social studies and science standards. One of the ten organizing themes of *National Curriculum Standards for Social Studies: A Framework for Teaching, Learning, and Assessment* (NCSS, 2010) is Science, Technology, and Society. This theme focuses on the interrelationships among science, its practical application, technology, social and cultural change, and the ways people interact with the world.

Both science and social studies framework call for students at different grade levels to study common topics, such as the use of natural resources, the history of science and scientists, the effects of humans and physical processes on the environment, and the societal impact of energy usage. In addition, social studies processes shared with science include representation, problem solving, decision making, data collection, data interpretation, and critical thinking.

Examine your state social studies standards and look for the strand for each grade level called Science, Technology, and Society in the Professional Practices Section of the End Matter. Throughout the elementary and middle school grades, students are challenged to understand how science and technology have affected human life past and present. Appropriate to their levels of development, students are expected to:

- describe how science and technology have changed transportation, communication, medicine, agriculture, industry, and recreation
- explain how science and technology have changed the ways people meet their basic needs
- analyze environmental changes brought about by scientific discoveries and technological innovations
- give examples of the contributions of scientists and inventors that have shaped society
- explain how resources, belief systems, economic factors, and political decisions have affected the use of technology from place to place, culture to culture, and society to society
- make predictions about future social, economic, and environmental consequences that may result from future scientific discoveries and technological innovations

Measuring the snowfall.

Wollertz/Shutterstock

TABLE 9.2 Disciplinary Core and Component Ideas from the *Framework* and NGSS Clearly Related to Social Studies Topics

Disciplinary Core Idea
- Component Idea

PS3: Energy
- PS3.D: Energy in Chemical Processes and Everyday Life

PS4: Waves and Their Applications in Technologies for Information Transfer
- PS4.C: Information Technologies and Instrumentation

LS4: Biological Evolution: Unity and Diversity
- LS4.D: Biodiversity and Humans

ESS3: Earth and Human Activity
- ESS3.A: Natural Resources
- ESS3.B: Natural Hazards
- ESS3.C: Human Impacts on Earth Systems
- ESS3.D: Global Climate Change

ETS2: Links Among Engineering, Technology, Science, and Society
- ETS2.B: Influence of Engineering, Technology, and Science on Society and the Natural World

A PDF of *A Framework for K–12 Science Education: Practices, Core Ideas, and Crosscutting Concepts* is available free online from the National Academies Press at www.nap.edu. Type in *Framework for K–12 Science Education* to access the PDF.

Several disciplinary core and component ideas from the third dimension of *A Framework for K–12 Science Education: Practices, Core Ideas, and Crosscutting Concepts* (NRC, 2012) are easily connected to social studies learning goals. These are listed in Table 9.2.

Investigating changes in weather, for the short term (appropriate for elementary), and changes in climate, for the long term (appropriate for middle school), provides an excellent opportunity to merge social studies and science expectations. The following ideas for a weather unit illustrate connections between science and social studies.

Students work in groups to design and construct wind socks to determine what direction the wind is blowing and rain gauges to measure the amount of rainfall in a period of time. They also use thermometers to measure the outside temperature. In using these weather instruments, students have to determine what readings to take and when to take them. You may want your students to understand how they can contribute data to a larger global data set by participating in programs like the Global Learning and Observation to Benefit the Environment (GLOBE) program which is a worldwide, hands-on, international effort to understand the Earth system and our global environment (www.globe.gov). For the social studies connection, link this data collection investigation to everyday issues in the community. Start with asking questions that connect the science data collection to local or regional geography or other social studies topics. What is the impact of changes in the weather and extreme weather events on our community? With more weather events causing damage in a region due to climate change, how can we help our populations be more resilient and know what to do in a crisis (i.e., flood, tornado, thunderstorm, hail, etc.)?

Each day, students take data and record their data in writing on data record sheets or in their science notebooks. Through small-group and class discussion, students reflect on and synthesize their data to describe the local weather. In connecting to social studies, students work in groups to access weather data online and record the weather in different geographic regions. Information available on the Internet includes physical and weather maps of each region and pictures that give identity to each area. A compendium of web resources for weather worldwide can be found on the Franklin Institute website at www.fi.edu. Or the class could communicate through social media with schools across the country or around the world to share student-collected weather data.

In order to apply weather information in decision making, each primary student describes how people in each region across the world dress for their local weather conditions. The students write daily journal entries about the weather, the people, and the unique features of the region they are studying.

As the lesson progresses each day, students develop both science and social studies concepts by exploring how humans collect weather data and how they deal with the physical processes (i.e., winds, warm and cold fronts, precipitation) related to weather and climate. Students also use current events to

EXPLORATION

9.3

Social Studies in *A Framework for K–12 Science Education*

Select one of the component ideas from Table 9.2 that interests you. Read the section of the science framework or the section from the NGSS that describes that component idea in order to find connections with social studies concepts.

Reflect on your reading and discuss your reflections with several of your colleagues.

Reflection Questions:

1. Which component science idea did you select? Why was that component idea of interest to you?
2. What social studies concepts seem easy to connect with the component idea you chose?
3. If you developed a unit that addressed the component science idea you chose and the related social studies concepts, what inquiry questions would you ask? What activities would you have your students do?
4. What are some potential benefits of teaching science and social studies concepts in an integrated unit?

determine how weather affects the way people live. Further, students develop essential computer skills as they become weather watchers.

In concluding the lesson, students answer questions such as: *What weather instruments are used to measure weather conditions? How can weather data best be recorded? How does the weather change? How is weather different in various regions? Why is weather important to us? How does weather affect people in different regions? Why is it helpful to predict the weather?* These questions get to the heart of social studies and science because they lead students to understand the characteristics of weather, the instruments and processes real scientists use to describe and explain weather, the effect weather has on humans, and the many ways humans cope with constantly changing weather phenomena. Select one of the ideas from Table 9.2 and then complete Exploration 9.3.

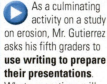 As a culminating activity on a study on erosion, Mr. Gutierrez asks his fifth graders to **use writing to prepare their presentations**. What connections will his students be making between language arts and science? What learning targets did he identify for ELA and for science?

 CHECK YOUR UNDERSTANDING 9.3
Click here to gauge your understanding of the concepts in this section

Integrating Science and English Language Arts

Teachers of all subjects should be engaged in language instruction. As stated in the *Standards for the English Language Arts* (International Reading Association, 1996), "Language is the most powerful, most readily available tool we have for representing the world . . . . Language is not only a means of communication, it is a primary instrument of thought . . . . Encouraging and enabling students to use language effectively is certainly one of society's most important tasks" (p. 12).

Literacy instruction in schools generally includes four areas: reading, writing, speaking, and listening. These critical elements of language learning occur in all curricular areas and should not be separated from substantive content in science, mathematics, social studies, and other subjects. An emphasis on literacy across the curriculum is a natural way for students to learn and use language skills to communicate and reason in specific domains, as well as in their everyday lives.

A Framework for K–12 Science Education: Practices, Crosscutting Concepts, and Core Ideas (NRC, 2012) also strongly supports the ideas of literacy and being scientifically literate.

Being literate in science and engineering requires the ability to read and understand their literatures. Science and engineering are ways of knowing that are represented and communicated by words, diagrams, charts, graphs, images, symbols, and mathematics. Reading, interpreting, and producing text (any form of communication, from printed text to video productions) are fundamental practices of science in particular, and they constitute at least half of engineers' and scientists' total working time. (p. 74)

Finding English Language Arts and Literacy in the
Next Generation Science Standards

Go online to www.nextgenscience.org. From a grade level that you would like to teach, select a "topic page" that interests you. Examine the performance expectations, the foundation boxes, and the connection boxes for evidence that when teaching science, it is important to help students develop specific reading, writing, listening, and speaking skills that make science accessible to them. Also, use the links in the NGSS to access related background information from the *Framework* and the *Common Core State Standards*.

Talk about your findings with one or more of your colleagues.

Reflection Questions:

1. What evidence of the integration of English language arts and science do you find?
2. If you were teaching a unit that addresses the performance expectations on the page you examined, in what ways would your students use literacy skills? What kinds of scaffolding might you need to provide in order for your students to be successful learners?
3. How do the literacy and science expectations seem to support each other? Use examples to explain your thinking.

Select a topic page from the *Next Generation Science Standards* and complete Exploration 9.4. Obtaining, evaluating, and communicating information, the eighth SEP described in Chapter 3 of the *Framework*, is closely tied to elements of literacy. Like the other Science and Engineering Practices from the *Framework*, its component competencies (reading, writing, speaking, and listening in the context of learning science and/or engineering) should be developed over time, beginning in kindergarten. Goals and grade band expectations for the communication Practice are presented on pages 75-77 of the *Framework*.

Access the NGSS Appendices at www .nextgenscience.org/get to know. Select Appendix F and scroll down to page 15 to read a summary of the eighth SEP and examine the related progression matrix.

TABLE 9.3   **Common Core State Standards (CCSS) Reading Standards for Literacy in Science and Technical Subjects for Grades 6–8**

Key Ideas and Details	• Cite specific textual evidence to support analysis of science and technical texts. • Determine the central ideas of conclusions of a text; provide an accurate summary of the text distinct from prior knowledge or opinions. • Follow precisely a multistep procedure when carrying out experiments, taking measurements, or performing technical tasks.
Craft and Structure	• Determine the meaning of symbols, key terms, and other domain-specific words and phrases as they are used in a specific scientific or technical context relevant to grades 6–8 texts and topics. • Analyze the structure an author uses to organize a text, including how the major sections contribute to the whole and to an understanding of the topic. • Analyze the author's purpose in providing an explanation, describing a procedure, or discussing an experiment in a text.
Integration of Knowledge and Ideas	• Integrate quantitative or technical information expressed in words in a text with a version of that information expressed visually (e.g., in a flowchart, diagram, model, graph, or table). • Distinguish among facts, reasoned judgment based on research findings, and speculation in a text. • Compare and contrast the information gained from experiments, simulations, video, or multimedia sources with what is gained from reading a text on the same topic.
Range of Reading and Level of Text Complexity	• By the end of grade 8, read and comprehend science/technical texts in the grades 6–8 text complexity band independently and proficiently.

Source: NGA & CCSSO, 2010, p. 62

Access the NGSS Appendices at www.nextgenscience.org/get-to-know. To find out more about connections to the CCSS in the NGSS look at Appendix M.

The *Common Core State Standards for English Language Arts* & Literacy in History/Social Studies, Science and Technical Subjects (NGA & CCSSO, 2012) (See Table 9.3) recognize that literacy skills, including reading and writing, are essential to science. Specific standards for literacy in science and technical subjects are provided for grades 6 through 12 in a separate section of the CCSS; while for the elementary level, reading and writing in science are integrated into the K–5 standards. Table 9.3 lists the literacy standards included in science and technical subjects for grades 6-8. Use Table 9.2 and complete Exploration 9.5.

EXPLORATION 9.5

Close Reading of the CCSS Reading Standards for Literacy in Science and Technical Subjects for Grades 6–8

Hopefully you read Table 9.3 as you were reading this chapter. If you didn't, please read it to yourself now. Yes, even though it is a table and not formatted as paragraphs of text, it is actually part of the complex text in this book. In this exercise, you will have an opportunity to experience close reading of complex text, something that you might ask your students to do some day.

Close reading is a reading comprehension strategy that involves repeated rereading and thoughtful interaction with a short selection of complex text. Close reading has been described as careful and purposeful rereading (Fisher, 2013). When the strategy is being introduced, the teacher provides text-dependent questions to guide students' interactions with the text. But the goal is for students to do close reading independently and proficiently, when they need to explicitly understand the text, make logical inferences from it, and use evidence in the text to support conclusions that are based on the text (Brown & Kappes, 2012).

With you in the role of a student, try using the close reading strategy! Work with a partner or in a small group. Ask them to select a passage of nonfiction text (two to three paragraphs or a section of text focused on one topic). Listen to the text as your partner reads it aloud or be the reader of the text for the group. This later step highlights the importance of the text in the process. Reread the text again, independently. As you read, circle any terms with which you are not familiar. Look back at the terms you circled. Use context clues to try to understand their intended meaning. Talk about these terms with several of your peers.

Reread the text again, independently. This time examine its structure. Think about how the information is organized in any table or figure. Consider why the author chose this way to present information to readers. Discuss your thinking with at least one other person.

After you reread the text one final time, write a summary that captures the main ideas of this text in your own words. Compare and contrast your summary with several other people.

Reflection Questions:

1. What did you learn about *close reading* by participating in this exploration?
2. During the close-reading process, to what extent were you engaged with the text? Did you actually think about what you were reading? How do you know?
3. In what ways did close reading help you comprehend the text?
4. Do you think this text selection was appropriate for close reading? Why or why not? (Remember to provide evidence to support your claim.)
5. How can you use close reading when students read informational texts or short articles in science? How would you have students provide their evidence supporting a claim?

While teaching science you can engage your students in strategies that will enhance their literacy abilities as they learn science. For example, use instructional strategies that:

- develop, extend, and refine the knowledge base of students

- assist students to organize knowledge into useful schemas or networks

- help students learn vocabulary that is related to topics being studied

- provide students with opportunities to use reading, listening, and viewing behaviors
- supply many opportunities for practice and rehearsal in communicating through writing, speaking, and representing things visually (Ormrod, 2007)

Santa and Alvermann (1991) noted, "Science and reading teachers have very similar goals for their students. Foremost is the pursuit of meaning" (p. vi). In science, students construct meaning from the natural world; in reading, they construct meaning from text. Although investigative processes in science and comprehension processes in reading seem quite different, processing strategies remain at the heart of both disciplines. Both science and reading teachers want their students to be able to describe events, make inferences, interpret information, draw conclusions, and make and test predictions (Padilla, Muth, & Padilla, 1991; Tompkins, 2006; Tovani, 2004).

Contemporary learning theories in both science and reading follow a constructivist view. In the traditional view of reading, meaning resided in the text; the reader's task was to ferret it out. In the constructivist view, the reader creates meaning based on the text and her or his existing knowledge about its content, language, and structure (Tompkins, 2006).

Science text materials, whether in activity guides, laboratory manuals, textbooks, journal articles, or online, are notoriously difficult for students at every level to read. There are a variety of reasons that reading science texts is so challenging.

- They tend to include technical vocabulary, unfamiliar jargon, and lots of big words.
- Even simple words that students may know could have another meaning in science (e.g., volume).
- Their sentence structure is complex, and the passive voice, which may be unfamiliar to students, is used.
- The presented information is often very dense, with so many concepts on a page that it seems overwhelming to the reader.
- Since the precise meaning of each word or clause may be important, they require "close" reading so that information can be extracted accurately.
- They present information through a mix of words, charts, tables, graphs, diagrams, symbols, and equations.
- Visuals may be confusing and difficult to understand.
- Directions are often multistep and difficult (Finley, 1991; NRC, 2012).

A key element in the construction of meaning from text by students is their prior knowledge. This may explain the importance of involving students in exploration with hands-on materials or real-world experiences *before* introducing technical, academic vocabulary or asking them to make sense of science text materials. Students need extensive and repetitive experiences with inquiry-based activities to develop connected, accurate, and useful knowledge. It is this type of knowledge that students must be able to readily access in order to read science books effectively. You may need to scaffold learning to assist students in accessing and using what they already know so that they can better comprehend science text materials.

Finley (1991) and others have suggested various ways that science teachers can help students access and use their existing knowledge. You can help students assess prior knowledge by having them (notice many of these use literacy skills!):

- write initial descriptions and explanations of phenomena
- construct concept maps of what they know
- draw pictures and label diagrams of events, accompanied by written explanations
- present their ideas to the class so that alternative descriptions and explanations might be considered

In addition to helping students acquire and use prior knowledge, teachers can help students approach reading more strategically using both linguistic and nonlinguistic tools (Koba & Mitchell, 2011; Koba & Tweed, 2014). Teachers should assist students in pre-reading, reading, and postreading strategies to help them make sense of what they read (Yopp & Yopp, 2006; Barton & Jordan, 2001).

In beginning a reading assignment in science, students should be clear about what they are expected to learn from the text. A teacher might use a pre-reading strategy like an anticipation guide by having students make predictions about the text content before reading (Padak & Davidson, 1991; Tompkins, 2006). When making predictions about text, children might first examine the illustrations and pictures given in the text. They close the text and make their predictions about words that might appear in it.

For example, in a selection on butterflies, children might infer from a butterfly illustration and their prior knowledge that *caterpillars* would be a word in the text (Yopp & Yopp, 2006). This pre-reading process helps students think about the relationships between the text information and their own prior knowledge. In a case study reported by Padak and Davidson (1991), students who learned to infer text content before reading were able to read for a wider variety of purposes than before. Rather than reading simply to answer the teacher's questions or questions in the passage, they read to learn more about science concepts, to verify predictions that they or others had made, and to connect text presentations to their own prior knowledge. With an anticipation guide, students make their predictions and then using reading strategies they check their predictions and develop comprehension that is revealed by their close reading.

Students often think that they aren't "good" readers. What this really means is that they don't know what to do when they get stuck and the reading doesn't make sense. Students should also be taught to use comprehension-monitoring strategies during reading. Comprehension-monitoring strategies include such tasks as raising questions about the text, clarifying terms, identifying main ideas and supporting statements, and paraphrasing and summarizing text meanings. Using annotation strategies and reading logs are other tools that help. Students can also make and verify inferences and predictions about text meaning. To make an inference we can model a process to have students gather data from the reading, summarize it into statements of evidence, and then make inferences based on the evidence. It is important, especially at the younger grades and with struggling readers, that these strategies are made explicit. They need to be practiced in whole-group settings and then small-group settings before they will become internalized reading strategies. Graphic organizers are tools that can help students at any grade level to development comprehension of informational text materials.

King (1994) has adapted reciprocal reading procedures to science teaching and learning. In King's adaptation, two children work cooperatively in reading a science text, with the children alternating in the roles of dialogue leader and student. King has used prompt cards to successfully teach fourth- and fifth-grade children to deliberately ask themselves and one another questions to access prior science knowledge, comprehend what they have read, and make connections in constructing science explanations.

Discussion of the text after reading is an important way to help students check their comprehension. In discussion, go beyond asking factual questions about what was read. Rather, you should focus on helping students:

- Link text ideas with their prior knowledge and experience
- Make connections between main ideas and supporting details
- Recognize and think about text statements that conflict with their own ideas
- Work to resolve conceptual confusion
- Use concepts presented in the text to explain other real-world phenomena (Roth, 1991)

These pre-reading, reading, and postreading strategies help readers pay attention to how they create meaning based on the text, their own existing content knowledge, and their knowledge about language.

Meaning-making discussions in science can also happen after hands-on activities or other shared learning experiences. Such discourse is sometimes called "science talk," "dialogic discussion," "scientists'

TABLE 9.4   **Recognizing Effective Science Talk**

Science Talk	Not Science Talk
Students explain, clarify, and justify what they have learned.	The teacher is the authority and always controls the discussion.
Generates meaning.	Limits opportunities for sense-making.
Students express and defend their own thinking.	Students guess what their teacher wants them to say.
Teachers do not presume to know the right answers to the questions they ask.	Teachers already know the right answers to the questions they ask and expect students to give them the right answer.
Teacher listens to student responses and waits for other students to respond.	Teacher in the role of evaluator of student responses.

Source: Gagnon & Abell, 2008.

meetings," or "science circles" (Gagnon & Abell, 2008). Table 9.4 presents characteristics of effective science talk—discourse that helps students generate meaning—and characteristics of ineffective discussions in the science classroom.

Science talk allows learners to share their thinking with others and get reactions to it. It offers opportunities for learners to engage in Practice 8 from the *Framework* by listening to others' thinking, sharing their own thinking and receiving feedback about it, evaluating ideas based on evidence, and communicating with other learners (including their teacher). Science talk also provides a time and place for students to practice argumentation (Practice 7 from the *Framework*). Science talk also provides a platform for refining new ideas before writing about them.

The writers of the *Standards for the English Language Arts* (International Reading Association, 1996) assert that "Reading and writing are intertwined . . . . Just as students need an array of strategies to comprehend text written by others, so too do they need to apply an array of strategies as they write" (p. 34).

To build these writing strategies, students need frequent opportunities to write on different topics and for different purposes. Science is a great place to provide students with many opportunities to write.

Writing in science forces students to consider their audience, clarify their questions, organize and present their data more clearly, and form more secure links among data, prior knowledge, and conclusions. Organizing and presenting their findings and conclusions to others helps students make new information their own and connect it to their prior understandings (Worth et al., 2009). Furthermore, the science *Framework* specifically references using writing as a method for analyzing and interpreting data as a Science and Engineering Practice. The NGSS also contain frequent mentions of applying writing skills in the connection to the Common Core sections.

In the science and English language arts skills and practices for students, arguing from evidence is a goal. If this is a new idea for you, then spend some time reviewing articles, links to standards, and examples of lessons that feature this skill. A new resource is available for middle school teachers that provides 20 examples of argument-driven life science inquiries (Enderle et al., 2016) designed to have students gather data, generate arguments, and engage in an argumentation session where they critique claims and evidence. These critical thinking processes help students develop reasoning and ultimately comprehension of important science ideas and phenomena.

Writing might take place in journals or on prepared investigation sheets. Observation journals, or science notebooks, provide an opportunity for students from primary grades through middle school to enhance both their science learning and writing approaches (Santa & Havens, 1991). Science notebooks in particular provide a place for students to keep a record of their science inquiries, their ideas and draft explanations, and any other notes they want to keep track of and refer to later. They even support implementation of the *Next Generation Science Standards* as well as the *Common Core State Standards for ELA* (Campbell & Fulton, 2014). In particular, the authors note that science notebooks help students develop explanations and arguments based on evidence and are a powerful way to help students reveal and develop their thinking about scientific concepts. One organizational scheme that teachers use includes the following:

- Focus Question
- Hypothesis/Prediction
- Planning
- Data/Observations/Diagrams
- Meaning Making Conference
- Claims and Evidence
- Conclusions
- Next Steps/Applications

You will want to ask yourself the following questions before implementing science notebooks. First of all, what should be my goal for using science notebooks? What are the essential components of a science notebook? Are these meant for student learning and will they be assessed formatively? Some research suggests that when science notebooks are nongraded—formatively assessed—and are tools for student use, they can help students develop conceptual understanding. If your students are using notebooks primarily to record inquiry investigations, then they should be able to decide what to record in them, cross out

The NSTA Web Seminar "Connections between the Practices in NGSS, Common Core Math, and Common Core ELA" includes videos demonstrating teacher-guided, productive science talk in classrooms. Strategies and resources to help build teachers' capacity for guiding discussion in the classroom are shared. This resource is archived at www.nsta.org.

information, include drawings or anything else that they decide is important to their learning. They may also use the notebooks to record academic vocabulary and as a place for written feedback and questions for the teacher and then provide space for a reply from the teacher back to the student.

Journal writing in science might also routinely include labeled illustrations as well as narrative descriptions and explanations. Journals may contain observations of a demonstration, personal explanations of a discrepant event, data collected through investigations, reactions to a film or oral presentation, and personal notes from reading an assignment. Journals allow students to write informally and personally explore content.

CHECK YOUR UNDERSTANDING 9.4

Click here to gauge your understanding of the concepts in this section

CHAPTER SUMMARY

Integrating Science and Mathematics

Science and mathematics are two very closely related fields with heavy crossover between them, even when it is unintentional. Students often need to know certain mathematics principles to complete science investigations, and mathematics concepts during mathematics instruction are applied through science-themed problems. Science and mathematics learning by your students can be increased when the connections between the two areas are made explicit. Seemingly mundane tasks such as measurement can be taught in a more robust inquiry-based method when science and mathematics are not viewed as separate topics. Other topics, such as graph construction and interpretation, are so heavily rooted in both content areas that it is very difficult to separate the science and mathematics being taught.

Science Education as a Component of STEM Education

Integrated Science, Technology, Engineering, and Mathematics (STEM) education is becoming an ever-increasing focus in schools and educational policy. Engineering, mathematics, and technology have now become explicit components of the *Next Generation Science Standards* (NGSS). The role of engineering in particular is greatly increased from the previous *National Science Education Standards* (NSES). One way to provide your students with integrated STEM lessons is to start with inquiry-based 5E science lessons and add activities to make clear connections to technology, engineering, and mathematics. Well-conceived and well-executed STEM lessons can serve to increase your students' understanding across many content areas and allow them to easily see real-world connections.

Integrating Science and Social Studies

Science and social studies are connected easily; the fact that one of the ten themes from the National Council for the Social Studies is *Science, Technology, and Society* confirms that connection. Many of the real-world problems facing our planet and population—global climate change and fresh water supplies, for example—are difficult to study without combining science and social studies. Science does not occur in isolation and is heavily influenced by government policy and societal pressures. Studying science topics, such as weather, with a global perspective allows students to learn how factors such as climate have an influence on cultural and societal norms in different parts of the world.

Integrating Science and English Language Arts

Reading and writing skills are vital for student success. Students will find all content areas of school easier with good reading and writing skills. Reading and writing in science requires specialized skills that need to be taught. Students should be taught and practice pre-reading, reading, and postreading strategies to increase their comprehension. Teachers need to check often to see if students are obtaining and understanding the pertinent information from assigned informational texts. New academic vocabulary words are often a significant part of the science curriculum. Inquiry-based lessons give the students concrete examples and experiences on which they can hook these new words. Utilizing science notebooks will help students write about their inquiries and make sense of their learning.

DISCUSSION QUESTIONS

1. Create a graphic organizer that illustrates interconnections between science and mathematics standards at a grade level you would like to teach.

2. In what ways would you expect a truly integrated STEM lesson to be different from a science lesson?

3. How can you incorporate social studies concepts into each of the 5E components of a lesson?

4. How can you teach some of the skills needed to read and comprehend science text during your reading instructional time?

PROFESSIONAL PRACTICES ACTIVITIES

1. How do the curriculum guides in your local schools integrate science and mathematics? Do you consider their approach to be effective? Why or why not? In what ways could the connections be made more effective?

2. Find lesson plans for several STEM lessons online or in instructional units. Evaluate them according to how well they (1) address all of the letters in STEM and (2) are aligned with NGSS or specific dimensions of the *Framework*. Suggest improvements.

3. Contact several local school districts to find out how many minutes are devoted each week to science or social studies. How can you help your students' understandings of both subjects by increasing the connections between them?

4. Identify some children's literature books that have science content or storylines. Is the science accurate? How can you use them in your reading or science instruction?

Making Science Accessible for All Learners

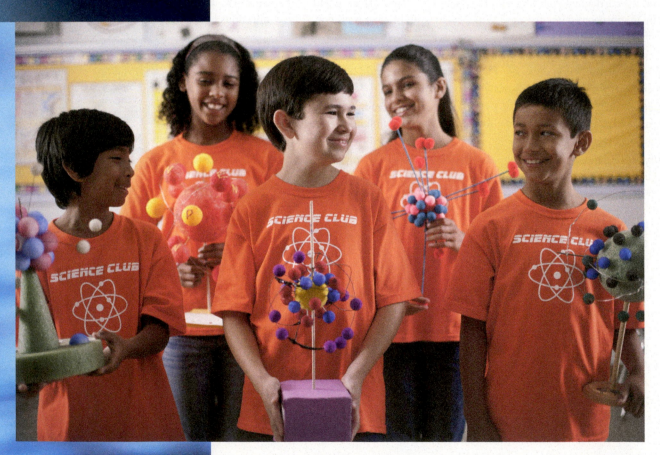

LEARNING GOALS

After reading this chapter, you should know and understand that . . .

1. Equity, diversity, and achievement gaps must be considered when guiding all children to learn science.

2. Teachers of science must utilize the instructional strategies that enable students from linguistically and culturally diverse backgrounds to learn science.

3. The same research-based instructional approaches that are recognized as best practices in any science classroom are effective in an inclusive classroom when appropriate differentiation is used to meet student's individual needs.

4. Providing the least restrictive environment can support the learning of students identified with various disabilities.

5. Students identified as gifted and talented require the use of alternative instructional strategies to maximize their science learning.

Who are the students in an average classroom? Imagine that you are a middle school science teacher. It is likely that you will teach about 100 students each year, four classes of 25 that you meet with each day. If the diversity of your students parallels the diversity of students in the United States during the 2012–2013 school year, then each day, assuming no one is absent, you would work with:

- 49 boys and 51 girls

- 13 students who have been identified with disabilities that make them eligible to receive special education services, and 87 students who have not been identified with disabilities

- 51 students who are white, 16 students who are black, 24 students who are Hispanic, and 9 students who are of other races or ethnicities (Asian, Native Hawaiian or Alaskan, Pacific Islander, American Indian, or two or more races)

- 10 students who have been identified as English language learners (ELL) and are being served in appropriate programs of language assistance, and 90 students who do not qualify for ELL assistance

- 67 students who live in a two-parent household, 24 students who live in a mother-only household, 5 who live in a father-only household, and 4 who have some other family type

- 50 students who are eligible for free or reduced lunch, and 50 students who do not

Which of these statements about diversity surprised you most? How do you think the student diversity in your classes might impact science instruction? What can you do to ensure an equitable science learning environment for your students so that all of them do learn science as described in your state's science standards?

It is quite likely that your elementary or middle school science classroom will contain a diverse group of children. The student population of the United States is diverse in many ways, including gender, race, ethnicity, economic level, location of residence, and family structure. In addition to general education students, you will probably be responsible for teaching students with disabilities, students from different cultural and linguistic backgrounds, and students with special gifts and talents. This chapter focuses on how to effectively engage *all* of your students in science learning by helping you recognize and address their unique needs and capabilities.

Equity, Diversity, and Achievement Gaps in Science Education

The idea that all U.S. citizens should be scientifically literate is not new. The publication, *Science for all Americans* (AAAS, 1990), led to the development of science standards that have continued to change from the *National Science Education Standards* (NSES) (NRC, 1996) to the *Next Generation Science Standards* (NGSS) (NGSS Lead States, 2013).

The *National Science Education Standards* emphasized that science must be for all students: "All students—regardless of race, gender, cultural or ethnic background, disabilities, aspirations, or interest and motivation in science—should have the opportunity to attain high levels of scientific literacy" (NRC, 1996, p. 20). This principle is one of **equity** and **excellence**. It challenged teachers of science to meet the needs of all students, to recognize the diversity of students, and to prepare science experiences to address these differences. The NSES suggested that the goals of science instruction are the same for all learners, stating that: "The understandings and abilities described in the content standards are for all students; they do not represent different expectations for different groups of students" (NRC, 1996, pp. 221–222).

A Framework for K-12 Science Education: Practices, Crosscutting Concepts, and Core Ideas (NRC, 2012), on which the *Next Generation Science Standards* (NGSS) are based, includes an entire chapter about the important topics of equity and diversity: Chapter 11, "Equity and Diversity in Science and Engineering Education." When the NGSS were released, they were accompanied with appendices. Appendix D, "'All Students, All Standards': Making the *Next Generation Science Standards* Accessible to All Students," again emphasized that science learning is for all of our children, not just a select few.

Of course, the issue of equity is not only important in science education. According to the No Child Left Behind Act (NCLB) enacted in 2002, although there may be modifications in materials, instruction, and testing conditions, all students must take the same statewide assessments and be included in statistical analyses. In December 2015, NCLB was replaced by the Every Child Succeeds Act (ESSA). As its name

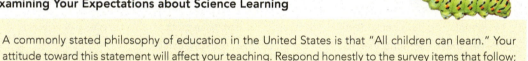

| EXPLORATION 10.1 | Examining Your Expectations about Science Learning |

A commonly stated philosophy of education in the United States is that "All children can learn." Your attitude toward this statement will affect your teaching. Respond honestly to the survey items that follow; don't just give the rating that might be most politically correct. Then reflect on your responses, and if you feel comfortable doing so, discuss your thoughts with your colleagues.

Use this rating scale to indicate your level of agreement with each of the following statements.

5: Strongly Agree   4: Agree   3: Uncertain   2: Disagree   1: Strongly Disagree

1. I think boys are better at science than girls.

2. I think of engineering as a "male profession."

3. I think teaching science to struggling students is a waste of time.

4. I think learning science is less important for students who are experiencing poverty than it is for students who are not.

5. I think students in need of English language acquisition have more difficulty than other students mastering science and engineering concepts.

Reflection Questions:

1. Do your responses indicate by what you do and say that you really believe that all children can learn science? Please explain.

2. In what ways might your attitude about these statements impact your teaching? Why does it matter?

3. Did you find it difficult to respond honestly to this survey? Why or why not?

suggests, ESSA includes provisions that will help to ensure success for *all* students and schools including: advancing equity by upholding critical protections for the United States' disadvantaged and high-needs students and requiring—for the first time—that *all* students in the United States be taught to high academic standards that will prepare them to succeed in college and careers.

A Framework for K–12 Science and Education: Practices, Crosscutting Concepts, and Core Ideas (NRC, 2012) identifies two essential ways of promoting scientific literacy for all students. The first approach is adopting science and engineering standards that reflect high academic goals for all students. The *Next Generation Science Standards* address this. The second approach relates to ensuring that all students have adequate opportunities to learn. Moving toward equity involves providing, for all students, access to quality instructional settings and materials, well-trained and effective teachers, and adequate time devoted to science learning. Exploration 10.1 provides an opportunity for you to examine your own beliefs about science education. Inequities among schools, often related to funding across communities and regions, can result in achievement gaps between different groups of students. Providing inclusive instruction that is motivational for diverse learners is also vital to ensure opportunities to learn. Strategies to address the learning needs of **diverse learners** are presented later in this chapter.

An **achievement gap** exists when there is a **statistically significant difference** between the average scores of different **demographic groups** on an assessment. Achievement gaps are evident based on data from state, national, and international assessments. For example, Table 10.1 presents average **scale scores** for different demographic groups on the 2011 administration of the Eighth Grade National Assessment of Educational Progress (NAEP) for Science. These data have met the test for significance, so they indicate achievement gaps in the areas of race/ethnicity, gender, and family income. Notice the variation of average scores for the various categories of students.

Though achievement gaps on standardized tests in science have been seen with economically disadvantaged, minority, and female students, those gaps should not be attributed to the abilities of these

> Second-grade teacher, Nancy Michael, and eighth-grade teacher, Bernardo de Castro, talk about their diverse classes and their responsibilities and strategies for helping all of their students to learn science. In the classroom footage presented, what evidence do you see that supports the claim that these teachers "walk their talk?"

TABLE 10.1   Data Showing Achievement Gaps

2011—8th Grade Science NAEP Data	
Average scale score = 152	65% of students performed at or above Basic
	32% of students performed at or above Proficient
	2% of students performed at or above Advanced
Race/Ethnicity	**Scale Score**
White	163
Black	129
Hispanic	137
Asian	161
Pacific Islander/Native Hawaiian	139
American Indian/Alaskan Native	141
Two or more races	156
Gender	**Scale Score**
Male	154
Female	149
Income	**Scale Score**
Eligible for Federal Lunch Program	137
Not Eligible for Federal Lunch Program	164

Source: National Center for Education Statistics, 2012.

students. Research shows that when provided with adequate time and support, nearly all students can learn and do science when they make a sustained effort (NRC, 2012).

Although each of these categories of diversity have their own research literature, features of "equitable learning opportunities" for all of them include:

- valuing and respecting the experiences that all students bring from their backgrounds (e.g., homes or communities),
- articulating students' background knowledge (e.g., cultural or linguistic knowledge) with disciplinary knowledge, and:
- offering sufficient school resources to support student learning. (Appendix D in NGSS Lead States, 2013 p.6).

Effective classroom strategies to minimize the achievement gap in each of these categories of diversity are summarized in Table 10.2.

TABLE 10.2 Specific Strategies for Closing Achievement Gaps

Category of Diversity	Effective Classroom Strategies Designed to Close the Achievement Gap
Economically disadvantaged students	• Connecting science education to students' sense of "place" as physical, historical, and sociocultural dimensions • Applying students' knowledge base and cultural practices • Using project-based science learning as a form of connected science
Students from underrepresented racial and ethnic groups	• Culturally relevant pedagogy • Community involvement and social activism • Multiple representation and multimodal experiences • School support systems including role models and mentors of similar racial or ethnic backgrounds.
Female students	• Instructional strategies to increase girls' science achievement and their intentions to continue on in science • Curricula to improve girls' achievement and confidence in science by promoting images of successful females in science • Classrooms' and schools' organizational structure that benefit girls in science (e.g., after school clubs, summer camps, and mentoring programs).

Source: Appendix D in NGSS Lead States, 2013.

Since our nation is so diverse, research into the impact of culture, customs, and environment on learning is important for achieving the goal of equity. By better understanding the reasons for differences in achievement, educators can more effectively design instructional opportunities to minimize those differences.

Low learning expectations for and stereotypical views of certain groups of students have been shown to contribute to inequities in science and engineering learning. Bayer Corporation (2010) conducted a survey of female and minority chemists and chemical engineers in order to better understand the reasons for underrepresentation of these groups in science, technology, engineering, and mathematics (STEM) professions. Respondents gave the U.S. K–12 education system a grade of D for how well it encourages minorities to study STEM subjects and a grade of D+ for its encouragement of girls. Seventy percent of the respondents reported that elementary teachers stimulated and sustained student interest in science more than parents. The survey indicated that regardless of gender, race, or ethnicity, interest in science begins in early childhood with 60 percent of respondents reporting that they were interested in science by age 11. Researchers found the two main reasons for underrepresentation to be lack of quality science and math education programs in poorer school districts (75 percent) and persistent stereotypes that say that STEM isn't for women or minorities.

Suggested ways to close the gender-based achievement gap include:

- Talk with girls as if they are interested in STEM, because many of them are!
- Encourage girls to ask questions about the world, experiment, and problem solve to involve them in Science and Engineering Practices.

- Teach about achievements by females in math and science to counteract the stereotype that males are better than females in these areas.

- Feature female scientists, engineers, and mathematicians as role models to help girls realize that people like them can succeed in STEM professions.

- Teach girls that intellectual skills, including those needed for excelling in STEM, can be developed through effort over time.

- Help girls develop their spatial skills by encouraging them to play with construction toys and 3-D computer games, sketch objects and organisms from different points of view, and use maps and global positioning devices.

- Foster girls' confidence, self-esteem, initiative, and work ethic so that they feel successful and capable in their STEM endeavors (American Association of University Women, 2013; Girl Scout Research Institute, 2012).

Many of these suggestions for helping girls succeed in STEM also apply when working with students who are from other demographic groups that are currently underrepresented in STEM. In Exploration 10.2 you will visit a classroom that actively engages girls in science learning. Since the school-age population of minority and low-income students continues to increase in the United States, the national goal of *science for all* will be challenging to meet until the existing achievement gaps among student demographic groups have been closed (Lee, 2002).

Case Study 5: Girls and the Next Generation Science Standards

EXPLORATION

10.2

Make a virtual visit to a classroom in order to observe the high engagement of girls in a third-grade class learning about life science core ideas through an engineering design approach to problem solving. Access the Case Studies in Appendix D of the NGSS at www.nextgenscience.org/appendix-d-case-studies. Select Case Study 5, and read the vignette "Defining Problems with Multiple Solutions within an Ecosystem." Remember to read the sections of the case study after the vignette to learn how the lessons in the vignette connect to NGSS and *Common Core State Standards* (CCSS) and find out more about research-based instructional strategies that encourage STEM learning by female students.

Reflection Questions:

1. What evidence did you find that the girls in Ms. G's class were actively engaged in learning about ecosystems during this engineering unit?
2. Do you find trying to solve a problem to be more engaging than answering a question? Why or why not? How does this apply to the plan Ms. G developed for the unit?
3. Do you consider this unit to be a good example of a three-dimensional NGSS unit? Provide concrete examples to support your claim.

✔ **CHECK YOUR UNDERSTANDING 10.1**
Click here to gauge your understanding of the concepts in this section.

Helping Students from Linguistically and Culturally Diverse Backgrounds Learn Science

Our nation's motto is *e pluribus unum*, "out of many, one." Nowhere in our society is the rich mosaic of people that embodies the United States better represented than in our schools. Meeting the needs of children from diverse backgrounds in our classrooms has become an important issue in education.

Many students from diverse ethnic backgrounds are in the process of acquiring the U.S. mainstream language, culture, and discourse patterns in schools. For many of these students, a language other than English is spoken at home. Many different terms are used to refer to these students. English Learners or English-learners (ELs) is an inclusive term currently preferred by the U.S. Department of Education's Office of English Language Acquisition (OELA). Other basically synonymous terms include: English-language learners or English Language Learners (ELLs), limited English proficient (LEP) students, and English-as-a-second-language (ESL) students.

Hispanic students make up the large majority of the English Learners in U.S. schools. Statistics change continually, but according to the National Center for Education Statistics, in the 2012–2013 school year, Hispanic students made up 24 percent of the nearly 50 million students enrolled in public elementary and secondary schools. However, only about 5 million of those students qualified as English Learners.

According to the U.S. Census Bureau's 2015 American Community Survey, during the 2013–2014 school year, more than 350 languages were spoken at home by English Learners (ages 5 to 18) around the nation. Of the 5 million ELs counted in that survey, 75.4% spoke Spanish, 2.0% spoke Arabic, 2.0% spoke Chinese, 1.6% spoke Vietnamese, 18.3% percent spoke French/Haitian Creole, and 18.8% spoke other languages (OELA, 2016). Providing equal educational opportunities to students who are not proficient in English is a special challenge, a challenge that grows each school year as the U.S. population becomes more diverse.

Structured inquiry-based science programs, with their emphasis on exploring, investigating, and manipulating concrete materials, and the gradual shift of control from teacher to student, are valuable for students who wrestle with the development of a new language, customs, friendships, and less advantageous community environments. Providing structured inquiry-based activities equalizes the opportunity for success because success is not generally dependent on the students' ability to read a textbook, answer questions from the textbook, or complete worksheets that depend on students' understanding of what they have read. Hands-on structured inquiry-based activities help all students span the gap between their past experiences and the development of language and academic vocabulary within their immediate environment. NGSS-based three-dimensional approaches to science teaching and learning may be even more valuable when working with English Learners, because of the additional focus on discourse and learners' making their thinking visible. The case study in Exploration 10.3 can help you think about strategies that can support students in need of English language acquisition.

Learning language is much more than learning vocabulary. Language learning is a complex process of developing relationships among ideas, terms, and meanings (Lee & Fradd, 1998). A great deal of language can be learned in the context of science and other subjects. Context enables children to build on what they already know to infer the meaning of new words and verbal constructs. When engaged in inquiry, the investigations and activities students experience provide shared context for their learning. Because students have a meaningful, mutual experience to talk about, verbal fluency and literacy naturally grow (Lapp, 2001).

> ▶ All students benefit when teachers activate or **build on students' background knowledge**. Watch this clip and consider: why is this an especially important strategy for working with English language learners?

EXPLORATION
10.3

Case Study 4: English Language Learners and the Next Generation Science Standards

You may have limited experience with classrooms filled with learners whose first language is not English. To introduce you to what that might be like, Access the Case Studies in Appendix D of the NGSS at www.nextgenscience.org/appendix-d-case-studies. Select Case Study 4, then read the vignette, "Developing and Using Models to Represent Earth's Surface Systems," to "see" how a second-grade teacher helps her students overcome language barriers to use models, develop claims, and explain their reasoning using evidence as they study Earth science.

Reflection Questions:

1. What strategies does Ms. H. use to provide English Learners' access to Disciplinary Core Ideas, Practices, and Crosscutting Concepts of science? Please provide evidence of their effectiveness.
2. Create a graphic organizer to summarize the five research-based areas through which teachers can support science and language for students in need of English language acquisition. Include examples of associated strategies from Case Study 4.

As students learn science through inquiry approaches, students have opportunities to develop verbal fluency as they talk about what they are doing, engage in discourse, record their observations, summarize and orally communicate their findings, and create written explanations that draw on their understanding of science concepts. They also read science articles and books, write essays and stories, and do library and Internet research to complement their classroom work (Lapp, 2001).

Language is only one of the internal learning systems students need to learn science and other subjects. Students also need knowledge of facts, concepts, principles, and knowledge of how to apply them in making sense of problem situations (Bransford, Brown, & Cocking, 1999). Inquiry science can help students learn how to construct understanding by teaching them the scientists' approach to answering questions and solving problems—an approach that has proved successful in every culture.

One method of teaching science and English to EL students that became popular in the 1990s is called **sheltered instruction**. This approach is designed to make content in academic subjects comprehensible to ELs while they are developing proficiency in English. With minimum dependency on language, sheltered instruction focuses on concept development and nonlanguage cues and prompts.

Freeman and Freeman (1998) have presented well-thought-out general strategies for using sheltered instruction with English Learners. Lee and Fradd (1998) and Fradd and Lee (1999) have discussed the uses of sheltering within inquiry science lessons. Many of these strategies are also useful for teaching science to all students.

The strategies used for sheltered instruction for students in need of English language acquisition fit easily into the context of the 5E model of instruction, which provides a framework for an inquiry-based lesson. If you are planning to teach a science lesson based on the 5E model using a sheltered approach to a class including English Learners, the following suggestions may be useful.

Preparation. Critical to effective sheltered instruction is the preparation of targeted learning objectives. In addition to science objectives, language objectives should be developed in alignment with state language proficiency benchmarks or language arts standards (Lee & Fradd, 1998).

All 5E Phases. Be careful to integrate listening, speaking, reading, and writing skills into science lessons. ELs are called on to process, manipulate, and display large amounts of new material at a rapid pace in a foreign language (English). Visual aids, adequate time for processing, and opportunities for clarification provide support in this demanding process. Sheltered lessons guide the learning of content information, including inquiry strategies, in ways that ELs can comprehend.

During all phases of a 5E lesson, you should modify your speech and refer to real-world objects and events (or pictures of them) to assist ELs in grasping important science questions, facts, concepts, principles, and procedures. This involves:

- speaking clearly and slowly
- employing pauses, short sentences, simple syntax, and few pronouns and idioms
- using redundancy and discourse markers (OK, like, now, then, finally, you know, etc.), keywords, and outlines
- providing examples and descriptions, *not* definitions
- using visuals, hands-on resources, gestures, and graphic organizers

Successful students develop many skills and strategies that they use when integrating, remembering, and using information. You should explicitly teach learning strategies that enable ELs and other students to develop a toolkit for accomplishing difficult learning tasks. Such strategies might include how to relate new science terms to observed objects, organisms, and events; how to access and use prior knowledge as a context for new learning; how to record new terms and their meanings in science journals; how to utilize "think alouds" while reading and responding to questions, and how to keep initiating questions in mind as inquiry proceeds. Keep in mind that some students will be at the early stages of language development or pre-production and others will be progressing to fluency so consider differentiating the strategies emphasized in order to meet the needs of individual students.

Be sure to provide ample opportunity at each phase of the lesson for students to talk with others in English about their activities and their learning. You should:

- facilitate frequent pair and small-group activities focused on meaningful tasks;
- model and assign tasks requiring turn taking, questioning, supporting/disagreeing, and clarification; and
- model and discuss ways of communicating respect.

This video clip features teachers from different grade levels describing instructional strategies they use to help their English Learners acquire academic language in science. What general themes do you find in the strategies that are suggested?

Engage. Use simple words and simple sentences. Use body language or concrete objects while you explain what you are saying. Avoid idiomatic expressions and rely on non-linguistic representations. Ask clear questions designed to elicit students' current conceptions. Their answers will help you know about previous related experiences your students have had.

Explore. During this phase, students are often involved in small-group activities and are observing and manipulating objects and/or organisms. You should strive to make the goals of the activities clear to all of your students. Cooperative group strategies with assigned tasks can supply structure that can help students stay focused on the investigation. Small-group discussions give students opportunities to Practice taking turns, to ask and answer questions in a reduced risk environment, to respectfully support and/or disagree with peers, and to clarify their thinking. As appropriate for the age level of your students, challenge all class members to keep journals in English.

Explain. You should encourage ELs to contribute to the class discussion about their findings from the explore phase. Summarize what has been presented at frequent intervals. Print the key points on the board, display them with a projector, or refer to a wall chart. As new science terms are introduced in the context of the experiences of the explore phase, post the words on your "word wall," pronounce them clearly, and have your students repeat the pronunciation together.

Elaborate. You should provide opportunities for students to apply their new knowledge to new tasks that involve concepts and skills students have learned. English Learners must have opportunities in the classroom to practice and apply the language skills and content knowledge they have acquired. Trying out new knowledge and practicing new skills in a safe environment, supported by teacher and peer feedback, leads to mastery. Students can reflect on and adjust their performance, initially with assistance and ultimately independently.

Evaluate. Formative and summative assessments of science understandings and English language usage are used. In this way of learning, teaching and assessment are integrated into an ongoing process that provides feedback to students and informs future instruction. For both formative and summative assessment of content learning, consider using a variety of techniques with different levels of language processing requirements to collect assessment data. Such approaches include: individual or small group conferences, personal reflections completed at home, oral retelling, learning logs, and graphic organizers; of course, a scoring guide or rubric for these performance assessments should be aligned with your previously identified science learning objectives.

Sheltered instruction is a generic term; it refers to approaches to instruction designed to make content comprehensible for English Learners. The Sheltered Instruction Observation Protocol (SIOP) Model is currently the only empirically validated model of sheltered instruction. A SIOP classroom is characterized by a consistent, systematic, and concurrent focus on teaching both academic content and **academic language** to ELs. Academic language is considered necessary for success in school. However, much of it is not commonly used in day-to-day conversation. Learn more about academic language in science in Exploration 10.4.

According to the SIOP Model, academic language must be taught to English Learners, and it suggests many instructional techniques to accomplish this goal. The SIOP Model represents an instructional system that has been shown to support content and language development for ELs (Short, Vogt, & Echevarria, 2011). Though a full description of its components and application in the classroom is beyond the scope of this chapter, if you plan to teach science (or other subjects) to English Learners, consider learning more about the SIOP Model of sheltered instruction.

Perhaps the best way to include ELs in your classroom is to view these students as an asset to the learning of all students. ELs can contribute language enrichment for native English-speaking students and abundant occasions for cross-cultural teaching and learning.

Meeting the needs of students from diverse cultural backgrounds has become an important issue in education (Lee, 2002). The National Science Teachers Association recognizes and appreciates the strength and beauty of cultural pluralism. According to NSTA's Position Statement on Multicultural Science Education (2000):

- Children from all cultures should have equitable access to quality science education experiences that enhance success and provide the knowledge and opportunities they need to become successful participants in our democratic society.

- Curricular content should include the contributions of many cultures to our knowledge of science.

Different Types of Terms Found in the Academic Language of Science

Three categories of terms that are found in the academic language of science are

- Terms used across the curricula in many subject areas
- Science content–specific terms
- Polysemous terms (words with multiple meanings in different contexts)

Terms in several grade-band endpoint statements for Disciplinary Core Ideas from *A Framework for K–12 Science Education* (NRC, 2012) have been marked to indicate examples of these three types of terms found in the academic language of science. Read and consider these statements and the markings on their words.

LS1.B—By the end of grade 2. Plants and animals have <u>predictable characteristics</u> at <u>different</u> *stages* of **development**. Plants and animals <u>grow</u> and *change*. Adult plants and animals can have *young*. In many kinds of animals, parents and the **offspring** themselves <u>engage</u> in *behaviors* that help the **offspring** to <u>survive.</u> (p. 146)

PS3.C—By the end of grade 5. When <u>objects</u> **collide**, the <u>contact</u> *forces* <u>transfer</u> **energy** so as to <u>change</u> the objects' **motion**. **Magnets** can <u>exert</u> *forces* on other **magnets** or **magnetizable** <u>materials</u>, *causing* **energy transfer** between them (e.g., <u>leading to changes</u> in **motion**) even when the <u>objects</u> are not *touching*. (p. 127)

Reflection Questions:

1. What marking indicates terms used across the curricula in many subjects? What is your evidence?
2. What marking indicates science content–specific terms? What is your evidence?
3. What marking indicates polysemous terms? What are some nonscience meanings of these words that might already be familiar to students?
4. Which category of terms do you think might be most challenging to teach to ELLs? Why?

- Teachers of science are responsible for exposing all their students to career opportunities in science, technology, and engineering.
- Teachers should know about the learning styles of students from diverse cultures and how their cultures aid or hinder their science learning. The prior cultural experiences of some students may actually interfere with inquiry science. For example, newly arrived students may experience difficulties with scientific inquiry in school because they have not been previously encouraged to ask questions or devise plans for investigation. Students from cultures that respect authority may be more receptive to teachers directing and telling them than to inquiry, exploration, and seeking alternative ways (Lee & Fradd, 1998).

Though students from some cultures may be unfamiliar with inquiry approaches to learning, over time and with explicit instruction and encouragement, they can become proficient in Science and Engineering Practices, including the following: posing questions, devising plans, testing hypotheses, collecting and analyzing data, engaging in science discourse, and constructing theories and explanations (Fradd & Lee, 1999).

When teaching science, your questions can provide necessary scaffolding, advance a meaning-making discussion, and support inquiry investigations; however, you should consider the cultural implications of your questions. Because of students' diverse backgrounds, questions may take on different meanings for different students (Bransford et al., 1999). For example, research indicates that many African American parents engage in different patterns of questioning with their children than do their white counterparts. African American parents are likely to emphasize metaphorical questions ("What is that like?") rather than fact-gathering questions ("What is that?"). Thus, African American students may not understand the purposes of white teachers' inquiry questions.

Some Native American students are averse to responding when called on in class. It may be that they perceive the traditional classroom, where teachers control all activities and interactions, as very different from their community social events, where there are no clear leaders and no clear separation between performers and audience. These students usually perform better one-on-one with the teacher or in cooperative settings with small groups of classmates (Vasquez, 1990). Or it may be that in some Native American communities it is disrespectful to elders for students to ask questions and share their ideas while they are just learning and "know nothing" of the ideas. This makes it difficult for teachers to determine prior knowledge and expect students to engage in open and argumentative discussions.

Also, scientific knowledge frequently does not align with native ways of knowing that have been passed along with their cultural storytelling for generations. For example, they consider rocks and water to have spirits as part of the broader environment and with traditional science learning they are not alive. So as teachers are we asking them to give up their cultural ways of knowing? You must know your students well so that your manner of questioning and presentation does not conflict with their cultural backgrounds. Research indicates that teachers should use praise judiciously when they guide discussions. Praise can provide a signal to students that their contributions to discussion are appropriate. But praise of one student's answer might also tend to stop discussion. Other students may think that the purpose of the inquiry discussion is to find the right answer, not to probe more deeply into nature. Students look to their teacher for guidance and approval. It is also important when providing praise that it is directed toward the work and their response rather than to the student. For example, rather than saying to a student, "you are really smart" you may want to reiterate their idea and ask if any other students shared the same idea and then invite additional contributions from the rest of the students to continue the discussion.

However, it is important to recognize students during individual work and group work for specific work they have done well. Teachers who try to look for good in every student and who inform them specifically and privately about these things are effective. This is part of the formative feedback process. Remember that it is important to let students know what work they are doing well that aligns with the expectations and then guide them with what they should work on next. This doesn't mean giving them the answer but rather making a suggestion or asking a probing question. They also are more likely to enjoy learning because they know what they are supposed to do. It is possible to say something complimentary or neutral to each individual as they come into class or during private discussions. This helps build and maintain positive relationships. As Abraham Maslow indicated in his theory of human needs, we all need to be recognized as valuable persons so our self-concepts continue to grow positively (Maslow, 1987).

 CHECK YOUR UNDERSTANDING 10.2

Click here to gauge your understanding of the concepts in this section.

Teaching Science in an Inclusive Classroom

Your students will have varying intellectual abilities and learning styles, diverse language and cultural backgrounds, and physical, social, and emotional differences. All will enter your classroom having experienced life differently. Thus, their understanding of the world will be different. The varied experiences, background knowledge, and abilities of your students should influence how you plan for and teach science.

"All children are unique. They will achieve understanding in different ways and at different depths as they explore answers to questions about the natural world" (NRC, 1996, p. 20). Though all children are unique, they all benefit when teachers utilize research-based instructional approaches that are recognized as best practices in the science classroom (Spaulding & Flannagan, 2012). These are the methods and strategies you've been reading about in this book.

There are many recommendations that typically appear in articles about successful science teaching in inclusive classes. These include:

- Create a classroom culture that is nurturing and supportive and that fosters mutual respect, self-esteem, self-efficacy, and resilience.

- Understand and address students' needs as learners (learning styles, interests, abilities, IEPs, formative assessment).

- Use multisensory, thematic, and/or cross-disciplinary approaches.

- Encourage collaboration rather than competition.

- Use cooperative learning strategies.

- Provide lessons that are developmentally appropriate and relevant to the learners.

- Employ authentic assessment methods.

- Revisit and apply DCIs, CCCs, and SEPs in multiple contexts over time.

- Have high expectations for all students.

- Encourage students to be responsible for their own learning.

- Actively engage students in inquiry and other constructivist approaches (Alexakos, 2001; Pellino, 2008; Vaughn & Bos, 2012).

The idea of "one size fits all" works about as well in an inclusive classroom as it does in a clothing store—not very well! So rather than expecting all of your students to be comfortable (and successful) following one path to science learning, you should differentiate instruction. Differentiating instruction, like selecting or tailoring clothing, is about meeting the needs of individuals.

To maximize each student's conceptual growth through differentiation, you must consider their ways of learning, their interests, and their responses to instruction, as well as the expected goals and standards that guide the curriculum. Then plan and offer options designed to interest students in learning, help them master content and skills, and show what they know and are able to do.

Differentiated instruction is a model in which teachers plan flexible approaches to instruction in the following areas: content, process, product, affect, and learning environment (Institutes on Academic Diversity, 2009–2012). There are many models for differentiated science instruction currently being used in elementary and middle school settings. Some of them involve **tiers**, levels or groups of students with shared readiness levels, learning styles, or interests.

Adams and Pierce (2003) describe a basic type of differentiation for elementary science classes that they call **tiered learning**. In their example, the entire grade 3 class shares the same content focus, but each teacher-identified student tier follows a slightly different, teacher-prescribed path toward the expected content outcome (see Figure 10.1).

In this example, the students are grouped into three tiers by their readiness to comprehend different books about the reactions of organisms to environmental change. The activity for each tier is designed to be qualitatively different (consisting of varying levels of complexity) from the activities prescribed for other tiers, rather than quantitatively different (expecting different amounts of work).

> ▶ The varied experiences, background knowledge, and abilities of your students should influence **how you plan for and teach science**. What instructional methodologies are recommended for teaching to the varying differences in **inclusive classrooms?**

FIGURE 10.1   Lesson Activity Outline for Lesson Tiered by Content Readiness

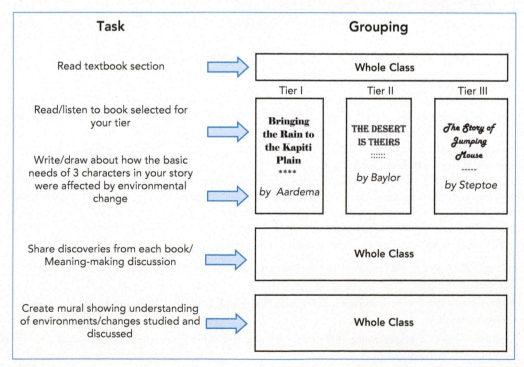

TABLE 10.3 **A Few Examples of Ways to Tier for Differentiated Instruction**

Lesson Tiered By	Lesson Element Differentiated	Example of Activities for Each Tier
Readiness to investigate a science concept (e.g., magnetism)	Hands-on exploration activity	Tier 1—Which of 10 objects are attracted to a magnet? Tier 2—In what ways can the strength of magnetic attraction be measured? (Adams & Pierce, 2003)
Preferred learning style	Vocabulary or concept review	Tier 1—(auditory) Listening stations, oral/aural drill and practice games, songs infused with content (Schoolhouse Rock) Tier 2—(visual) Photographs, drawings, visual models, word cards, flash cards, matching games, graphic organizers Tier 3—(kinesthetic) Three-dimensional models, tracing letters on word cards with fingers, charades, pointing games on poster or body (head, shoulders, knees, and toes actions)
Student interest based on survey data (about how local animals' needs are met)	Field observations and/or library/Internet research project	Students work in groups based on the category of animal they choose to investigate Tier 1—Birds Tier 2—Mammals Tier 3—Insects Tier 4—Reptiles

Table 10.3 shows several other ways to group students into tiers for differentiation. Notice that the number of tiers created may vary; you don't always need three tiers to meet the diverse learning needs of your students.

Please do not confuse the tiered learning approach as described with the multi-tiered **response to intervention** (RTI) process that many schools around the country have adopted to ensure that the educational needs of all learners are met. RTI is based on the use of research-based curricula and evidence-based interventions, and it assumes that all instruction will be presented as it was designed, with fidelity. The three tiers in the RTI process are

- Tier 1—Core Instruction—provided to all learners.

- Tier 2—Supplemental Supports—provided to struggling learners (those not making adequate progress in Tier 1).

- Tier 3—Intensive Interventions—provided to learners with disabilities or significant educational needs (those not making adequate progress in Tier 2) (Hoover, 2011).

However, the RTI process is rarely applied to science learning. This is probably due to the overwhelming emphasis on reading, mathematics, and writing skills measured on high-stakes state tests. What is happening in classroom to meet learning needs is to group students in ways that scaffolds learning based on their individual needs, closes student achievement gaps, and the groups are linked to students grasp of the concepts and phenomena being studied.

Spaulding and Flannagan (2012) developed a framework for effective inclusive science instruction based on the concept of universal design for learning (UDL). Proponents of UDL believe that educational best practices for students with special needs are also effective with general education students, and vice versa. Grounded in a set of research-based educational principles, universal design for learning is intended to give all individuals equal opportunities to learn. UDL curricula typically include:

- Multiple means of representation so that learners can acquire information and content knowledge in a variety of ways.

- Multiple means of expression so that learners may show what they know and are able to do in a variety of ways.

- Multiple means of engagement so that learners are motivated, interested, and challenged in their learning (udlcenter.org).

Among all of the unique students in your class, you may find some that have special learning needs. When considering diverse students, it can be helpful to establish categories. Three accepted categories of diverse learners are students with disabilities, gifted and talented students, and students with linguistically and culturally diverse backgrounds (Mastropieri & Scruggs, 2004).

Project-based learning (PBL) naturally lends itself to differentiated instruction since it is student centered, student driven, and lets teachers meet the needs of students in a variety of ways. PBL can allow for effective differentiation in assessment as well as daily management and instruction. Appropriate differentiation strategies to use during a PBL project include:

- grouping based on academic ability, interest, collaboration skills, or social-emotional traits.

- encouraging students to reflect on their work and set individualized goals for further learning.

- offering mini-lessons, center work, or a variety of resources can empower your students to manage their own learning paths and progress toward the completion of their projects.

- allowing students to show what they know in a variety of ways during both formative and summative assessments.

- providing options in the learning environment by balancing collaboration, independent work, and time for both group and individual instruction because some students learn better on their own, and others learn better in a team (Miller, 2016).

Various forms of differentiation can help you meet the diverse learning needs of the students in your class. You may need to adapt science activities for students who have disabilities, or you may need to work much more closely with them to scaffold learning. Students who are in need of English language acquisition may benefit from special instructional strategies or by working with other students who can help them access material more readily. Gifted and talented students may challenge you to find ways to lead them to ever deeper understanding. Although students in each of these groups may exhibit special learning needs, federal legislation addresses educational modification for only the first category—students with disabilities.

 CHECK YOUR UNDERSTANDING 10.3
Click here to gauge your understanding of the concepts in this section.

Helping Students Identified with Disabilities Learn Science

The Individuals with Disabilities Education Act (IDEA) (1997, amended 2004), which governs the education of students with disabilities, mandates that all students have the right to a full, free public education in the **least restrictive environment**. This means that schools are required to educate students with disabilities with nondisabled students to the maximum extent appropriate for the students with disabilities.

IDEA recognizes about a dozen **disabilities**. The prevalence of each of these disabilities varies greatly (see Figure 10.2). As you can see from the graph, 35 percent of students with disabilities in the 2012–2013 school year were categorized as having specific learning disabilities. To put that into perspective, if you are teaching those 100 students mentioned at the beginning of the chapter that represent the U.S. student population, 13 of your 100 students are eligible for special education services, so it is likely that 4 of your 100 students have specific learning disabilities.

You might wonder how many students are identified as having disabilities and receive most of their education in regular classrooms. Data from the National Center for Education Statistics (nces.ed.gov; 2015) indicate that in the 2012–2013 school year about 13 percent of the public school student population, approximately 6.4 million students, were identified with disabilities and, therefore, required special education services. About 95 percent of school-age children and youth ages 6–21 who were served under IDEA in school year 2011–2012 were enrolled in regular schools. In 2011–2012, 61 percent of students with disabilities spent at least 80 percent of the school day in regular education classrooms. This statistic, noticeably higher than the 31 percent of 1988–1989, illustrates the increase in the prevalence of the Practice of inclusion of students with disabilities in "regular" classrooms over the past two decades.

FIGURE 10.2
Percentage of Disabled
Students by IDEA
Category

Source: Data from the
National Center for
Education Statistics,
nces.ed.gov.

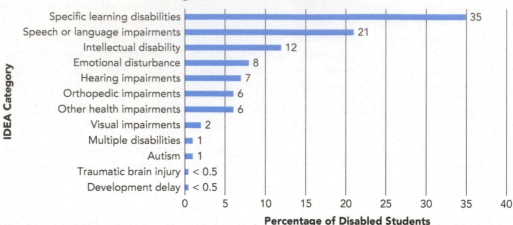

Percentage of Disabled Students by IDEA Category during the 2012-2013 School Year

Students with identified disabilities will enter your classroom with an **individualized education plan** (IEP) in place. An IEP lists specific goals (academic, communication, motor, learning, functional, and socialization) to advance the education of the student with disabilities (nichd.nih.gov). A student's IEP is developed and regularly reviewed by a team that includes parents, general and special education teachers who work with the child, and other school staff. You may be asked to serve on the IEP team of a student identified with disabilities that you teach. Consider IEPs as dynamic, working documents intended to improve student learning, rather than just a set of legalities to be fulfilled. Reviewing a student's IEP goals and objectives is the first step you should take to appropriately plan or modify instructional activities to help that student meet these goals.

For example, one goal in an IEP might read: *Develop communication skills and interactions with peers.* You can help the student to meet this individual learning goal by including him or her in a cooperative learning group during science instruction. Within this group, students may engage in an inquiry activity that requires meaningful student interaction to discover and communicate findings revealed by the data. As part of a cooperative group, the student with a disability is encouraged to communicate about the observed phenomena with his or her peers, and together they can determine how to report their findings.

Instruction for students with disabilities should help them meet the goals on their IEPs while they are learning new concepts and inquiry strategies called for in state and district standards and curriculum frameworks. Research-based instructional strategies that you have learned about for general education students are generally also appropriate when teaching science to students with disabilities. Additional scaffolding or modifications might be necessary to provide the support needed to achieve both science learning goals and the specific goals included in an IEP. Though the IEP goals are unlikely to be specific to science learning, they can and must be addressed during science class.

Appendix D of the *Next Generation Science Standards*, "'All Standards, All Students': Making the *Next Generation Science Standards* Accessible to All Students," points out: "Students with disabilities have their Individualized Education Plans (IEP), specific to the individuals, that mandate the accommodations and modifications that teachers must provide to support student learning in the regular education classroom. By definition, accommodations allow students to overcome or work around their disabilities with the same performance expectations of their peers, whereas modifications generally change the curriculum or performance expectations for a specific student. Two approaches for providing accommodations and modifications are widely used by general education teachers in their classrooms: (1) differentiated instruction and (2) Universal Design for Learning" (Appendix D in NGSS Lead States, 2013, pp. 7–8). You were introduced to those approaches in the previous section of this chapter. Keep in mind that making accommodations is preferable to making modifications, as you try to reach the NGSS goal of "All Standards, All Students." In Exploration 10.5 you will get a glimpse of a science classroom that accommodates students with disabilities.

You may also have some struggling students in your class who are not yet identified as having special learning needs. The response to intervention (RTI) process that was described earlier might reveal that these students are not learning at the same rate as their peers and are in need of differentiated instruction. Perhaps tier 2 interventions are not enough, and tier 3 interventions must be considered. At that point, a struggling student would be referred for evaluation for special education services, and if the student

Appendix D of the Next Generation Science Standards, "'All Standards, All Students': Making the Next Generation Science Standards Accessible to All Students," includes links to case studies. To virtually visit a sixth-grade class that includes several students with disabilities, access the Case Studies in Appendix D of the NGSS at www.nextgenscience.org/appendix-d-case-studies. Select Case Study 3, then read the Vignette titled "Using Models of Space Systems to Describe Patterns." As you read it, imagine that you are a virtual observer in this rural classroom looking for effective strategies the teacher uses to support the students who are disabled in their three-dimensional learning related to the earth-moon-sun relationship. Then, be sure to read the sections of the case study after the vignette to learn how the lessons in the vignette connect to NGSS and CCSS and to delve more deeply into the related research and the context of this vignette.

Reflection Questions:

1. Do you consider this vignette to be a good example of effective three-dimensional teaching and learning? Why or why not?
2. Which of the Universal Design for Learning (UDL) principles did you recognize in Mr. O's classroom: (1) providing multiple means of representation, (2) presenting multiple means of action and expression, and (3) encouraging multiple means of engagement? Identify specific examples.

qualified, an IEP team would develop his or her individualized education plan. Remember that the intent of grouping students is to help them learn and not to track them into a group where they remain. Once students acquire the learning then they may not need the same differentiated instructional approaches. With scaffolding approaches, as teachers we want to slowly withdraw the supports and enable students to be more self-regulated learners.

The following sections offer some concrete ideas for working with students who have varied cognitive differences, students with emotional or behavioral disorders, students with orthopedic disabilities, students who are blind or have low vision, and students who are deaf or hard of hearing.

Science for Students with Specific Learning Disabilities

According to IDEA, the term **specific learning disability** refers to a disorder in one or more of the basic psychological processes involved in understanding or in using spoken or written language. A disorder may manifest itself in imperfect ability to listen, think, speak, read, write, spell, reason, or do mathematical calculations. These disabilities are thought to be caused by differences in brain structure at birth and are often hereditary. Developmental delays related to language, motor skills, or socialization may be associated with the presence of specific learning disabilities (nichd.hih.gov).

Students with learning disabilities (LD) are commonly in the normal range of intelligence. Sometimes, in fact, they are gifted intellectually. However, students with learning disabilities generally achieve below their current grade level, or are several grade levels below where they should be for their age, in one or more basic academic skill areas such as reading, written language, or math.

Students with learning disabilities are a heterogeneous group and can have overlapping problems. This makes it difficult to classify their learning discrepancies and prescribe learning activities and approaches for them. However, research and practical experience support some general strategies to enhance science instruction for students with LD. These include the use of activities-based science, intensive scaffolding, and the teaching of learning strategies—all of which are also recommended for use with students without identified disabilities.

Activities-Based Science. Scruggs and colleagues (1993) report a study of activities-based versus textbook-based instruction in middle school students with learning disabilities. Both approaches were well structured and involved daily review, active engagement by students, formative evaluation of student products, and questioning. In the activities-based lessons, students were challenged to answer questions based on their experience with hands-on materials, while questions in the textbook-based lessons focused on recall of information provided. The science content of both approaches was carefully controlled so that the only difference between the lessons was instructional style. Two science topics were presented—rocks and minerals and electricity and magnetism. Each of the 26 students received both a textbook approach to one subject and an inquiry-oriented approach to the other subject. Testing following each of the instructional modes revealed the activities-based instruction resulted in increased student understanding of the concepts introduced in the units. Students also reported they enjoyed the activities-based lessons more than the textbook-based lessons.

An advantage of inquiry-based science for diverse learners is that it facilitates the efforts of classroom teachers to make appropriate modifications to accommodate different learning needs (Brownell & Thomas, 1998).

Fradd and Lee (1999) have suggested that, rather than debate about whether a textbook or inquiry-based approach is best, it may be worthwhile to consider how to use the two approaches in a complementary way to meet students' needs.

Intensive Scaffolding. One accommodation teachers often make is to provide more scaffolding assistance to certain learners. It can be challenging for some students to generalize from real-world experiences and form new science concepts without very directed scaffolding by the teacher.

Mastropieri and colleagues (1993) investigated these issues. A total of 54 junior high students participated in the study, including 20 general education students, 18 students with learning disabilities, and 16 students with intellectual disabilities. Each student met individually with a researcher and was shown a pendulum and taught how to count the number of complete back-and-forth swings the pendulum made in 10 seconds. Then, the pendulum was set in motion and the student counted the number of swings while the researcher kept the time.

The first pendulum made 10 swings in 10 seconds. The researcher recorded the number of swings on a sticker below the pendulum. Data were collected on three more pendulums. The number of swings each pendulum made in 10 seconds was recorded on a sticker below the appropriate pendulum. Figure 10.3 shows the four pendulums with their stickers (with arrows pointing to them) at the end of the investigation.

FIGURE 10.3
Pendulum Data

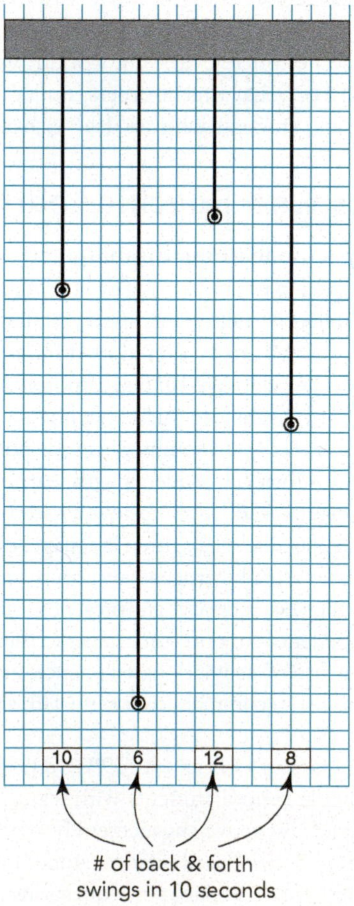

# of back & forth
swings in 10 seconds

Inference is the process of generalizing, or drawing general rules based on a number of specific observations. In a 5E science lesson, students are often asked to generalize during the explain phase from data collected during the explore phase of instruction. The task of students in the pendulum study was to generalize from observations of four instances that the longer a pendulum, the fewer the number of complete back-and-forth swings it makes in 10 seconds.

The researcher's protocol consisted of five prompts to be used in order as needed to help each participant make the correct generalization about pendulum length and rate of swing. The number of prompts needed for a student to be successful on the task was taken as a measure of inductive reasoning (inference)—the lower the number the better.

Prompt 1: "Thinking about these pendulums, can you think of a general rule about pendulums?"

If the student's response was correct, a score of 1 was given.

If the student was not successful, the researcher continued with the next prompt.

Prompt 2: "Compare the number of swings in 10 seconds for the shortest and longest pendulums, and then make a generalization."

If the student responded correctly at this point, a score of 2 was given.

If the student was not successful, the researcher continued with the next prompt.

Prompt 3: "Arrange all of the pendulums in order by length from the shortest to the longest. Compare the number of swings in 10 seconds for each of the pendulums, and then form a generalization."

If the student responded correctly at this point, a score of 3 was given.

If the student was not successful, the researcher continued with the next prompt.

Prompt 4: "Notice that when the pendulums were sequenced in order by length, as the strings got longer, the swinging rate became slower. Try to form a generalization based on this information."

If the student responded correctly at this point, a score of 4 was given.

If the student was not successful, the researcher continued with the next prompt.

Prompt 5: "Isn't it that, as the string gets longer, the number of swings they make get smaller?"

The researcher then demonstrated the rule until the student expressed understanding.

The results indicated that 75 percent of the nondisabled students were successful after the first prompt, and 100 percent were successful by the fourth prompt. For students with LD, 50 percent were successful with the first prompt, while 72 percent were successful after the fourth prompt, and 100 percent were successful by the fifth prompt. For students with mild intellectual disabilities, no students were successful with one prompt, while only 19 percent were successful after four prompts, then finally 100 percent were successful after the fifth prompt.

Students were then asked to apply the rule to a new pendulum problem. The students were shown a new pendulum intermediate in length between the 8-swing pendulum and the 10-swing pendulum and asked how many swings it would make in 10 seconds. On this application problem, 90 percent of the general education students, 50 percent of students with LD, and none of the students with mild intellectual disabilities provided the correct answer.

Mastropieri and colleagues (1993) concluded that general education junior high school students may readily make generalizations from data, with only a moderate amount of scaffolding assistance. Students with learning disabilities may also succeed on an inference task, but may need more assistance.

Teach Learning Strategies. Successful students develop many skills and strategies that they use when integrating, remembering, and using information. However, students with learning disabilities may require explicit instruction in the use of these strategies and/or other continued support.

Dr. Edwin Ellis (2002) advocates "watering up" rather than "watering down" instruction. He has developed a teaching/learning model known as Makes Sense Strategies (MSS). The MSS model is an approach to teaching based on three fundamental instructional principles:

1. Students learn better when they are actively engaged in processing new information in meaningful ways.
2. Increasing the learnability of information or skills is preferable to dumbing it down.
3. Students should not waste time learning trivia.

Approaches to instruction based on these principles can result in more effective learning by students with LD as well as by general education students.

One important learning strategy in the MSS model is **elaboration**. Elaboration of an idea occurs when one transforms an idea without losing the essence of its meaning. Ellis (2002) notes that students with LD often lack the language-based cognitive skills necessary to engage in effective elaboration but can be taught to use elaboration strategies. When teaching students with or without LD to elaborate, teach them how to create a visual image of an idea, how to paraphrase and summarize information about an idea, how to raise a series of questions about the idea, and how to use the idea in drawing inferences and forming predictions. Some students, especially those with LD, may benefit from **procedural facilitators** or **graphic organizers**, charts or sheets that remind them of the steps to follow when they decide to use a particular learning strategy. Figure 10.4 provides an example of a procedural facilitator for elaboration that is designed to support upper elementary students.

Another important learning strategy in the MMS model is **reflection**. According to Ellis (2002), reflection is a powerful tool for developing deep knowledge structures, but promoting it can be considerably more challenging than creating situations that require students to just memorize answers for tests. Important reflective processes for learning and performing include activating background knowledge, anticipating and predicting, establishing goals, relating ideas, and recognizing manifestations of ideas as they appear in other forms and how ideas might be applied in various contexts.

FIGURE 10.4   A Procedural Facilitator for Elaboration

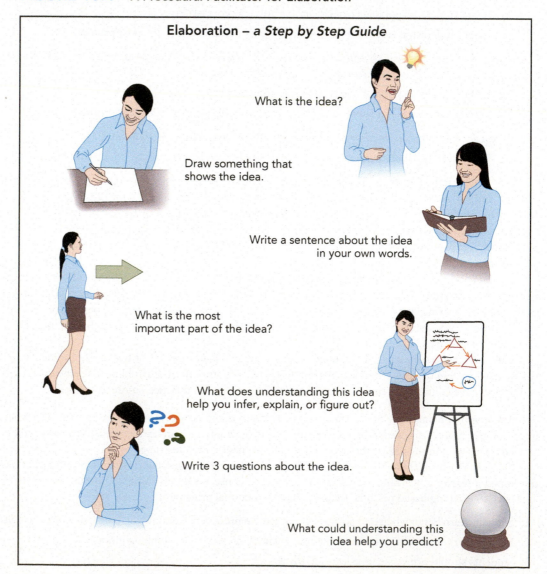

Students with LD may have particular difficulties in collecting, organizing, and using data skills that are critical in science inquiry. Thus, they may benefit from explicit instruction on how to record data and how to construct and interpret charts and graphs.

Cawley and Foley (2002) have emphasized the importance of teaching students with LD the inherent relationships involved in data tables. Help your students learn to recognize relationships by involving them in connecting data to measurement procedures, describing data, filling in blank spaces in data tables, and using data to make predictions of new measurements.

In the pendulum data interpretation study described previously, for example, students with LD benefitted from prompts related to examining the data, arranging it in order to form a concrete graph, and interpreting the graph to form a generalization about pendulum length and time for 10 swings. Overall, the general education students did not need these prompts, presumably because they had already learned how to analyze data. Students with LD should be provided explicit instruction in constructing and working with tables, charts, and graphs.

To teach students with disabilities to use charting and graphing strategies (Mastropieri & Scruggs, 2004), prefamiliarize them with graph paper and various types of charts and graphs, such as bar graphs, histograms, and line graphs. Use concrete examples in your instruction. For example, create a class bar graph based on students' favorite foods, colors, or television shows. Talk with the class about what might be learned from the graph. Is each person's favorite displayed? Is there a "class favorite"? Use pictures of the objects being graphed to help reinforce what the graph represents. Provide a strategy for how to analyze the graph and how to make inferences.

Consider grouping students with and without disabilities together and allow them to record and graph data cooperatively. Peers may be able to assist with some of the more difficult components of the task. As students work together, take time to teach specific cooperative skills, such as taking turns and listening. When teaching cooperative skills, use explicit instruction procedures, such as modeling, pointing out examples and nonexamples, role playing, and providing feedback. In this way, students with and without exceptionalities can learn to actively and successfully be a part of cooperative learning groups.

Many students with LD find it difficult to identify key words and main ideas from text, lectures, or even multimedia presentations. Therefore, they are likely to find taking notes independently quite challenging. Providing a "think sheet" is one way to guide note taking. For example, Figure 10.5 is a "think sheet" designed to be used with a video or multimedia presentation about the water cycle. Rather than taking notes on their own, students fill in the blank spaces about the phases of the water cycle as the information is presented. If a few students still need further support, provide them with think sheets already filled in and ask them to circle the underlined words when they are encountered in the presentation.

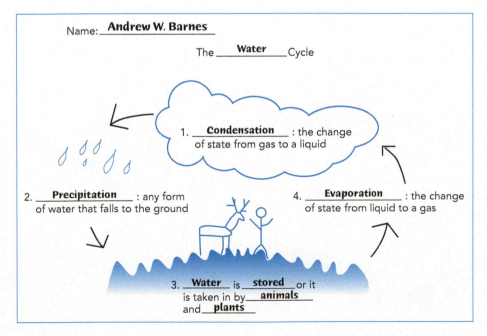

FIGURE 10.5 **Graphic Organizer Modified for a Student with a Disability**

Source: From The Inclusive Classroom: Strategies for Effective Instruction (p. 514), by M. A. Mastropieri and T. E. Scruggs, 2000. Upper Saddle River, NJ: Merrill/ Prentice Hall. Copyright © 2000 by Merrill, an imprint of Prentice-Hall, Inc. Reprinted by permission of Pearson Education, Inc. Upper Saddle River, NJ.

Organization is an area that students with learning disabilities often struggle with. Organizing ideas, facts, and concepts for writing purposes can be especially challenging for them. Many students benefit from visual organizers to organize thoughts and ideas, and visual organizers are particularly helpful to students who have executive function difficulties in order to organize what they know before they put it in writing (Richards, 2008).

Sometimes a little structure for organizing findings can help a lot. If you asked third-grade students to record their findings in their science notebooks as they test items to see which of them are attracted to a magnet and which are not, the student work produced might be quite varied (see Figure 10.6).

Some students, like Aaron and Brianna, used effective recording strategies. Others, like Carlos, recorded findings randomly in their science notebooks, making it hard to draw conclusions from the data. Their notes may be so random that even they can't figure out what they were trying to represent several days later. A few students, like Dan, investigated by touching a magnet to many different objects to see what happened, but wrote no notes about the interaction between the magnet and each item. Notice that Dan just drew an illustration of the title of the investigation in his notebook.

FIGURE 10.6 Organization of Data

Aaron

Which items are attracted to magnets?

Item	Attracted	Not attracted
Eraser		✓
Golf pencil		✓
Post-it™ note		✓
Rubber band		✓
Nail	✓	
Paper clip	✓	
Penny		✓
Aluminum foil		✓
Washer	✓	

Brianna

Which items are attracted to magnets?

Attracted	Not attracted
Nail	Golf pencil
Washer	Rubber band
Paper clip	Eraser
	Aluminum foil
	Post-it™ note
	Penny

Carlos

Which items are attracted to magnets?

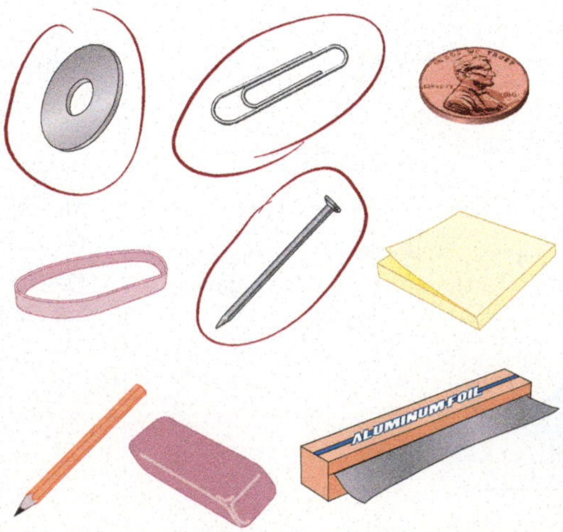

Dan

Which items are attracted to magnets?

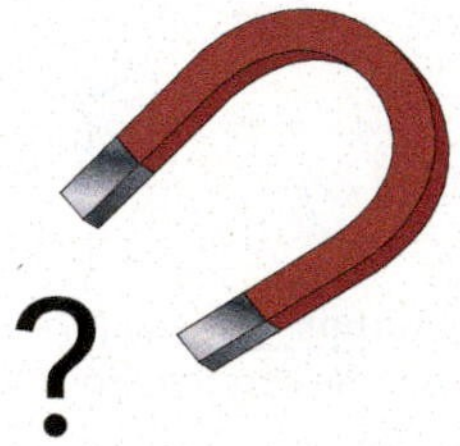

Students who tried with limited success to record might have benefitted by being shown how to use a **t-chart**, a simple frame on which two categories of observations can be organized. In Figure 10.6, Brianna used a t-chart to organize her data.

When introducing this method, you might first provide a sheet with a labeled t-chart on it; when the student is successful when provided this much support, withdraw some of the scaffolding by just offering a blank t-chart that the student would label before completing it. With Practice over time, all you might need to do to support the student is suggest drawing a t-chart in his or her notebook, and the student will be able to take it from there.

The **Venn diagram** is another simple graphic organizer that has been shown to be an effective study tool for students with learning disabilities, especially those with language-processing deficits. It provides a visual frame for comparing and contrasting observations, terms and concepts that can help students to organize their thoughts without having to develop complete sentences (Logsdon, 2016).

Unless students are already familiar with a specific graphic organizer, you will need to teach its purpose and how it is used. A good way to introduce students to Venn diagrams is through a class activity involving things or concepts with which they are already familiar. The lesson plan that follows provides a model of how this might be done.

Lesson Plan

Unit: Technologies used to accomplish different tasks.

Lesson: Writing or recording on paper.

Grade Level: Fourth

Objectives:

- Students will be able to complete a Venn diagram about familiar objects.
- Students understand the implications of the placement of ideas within a Venn diagram and can use that knowledge to interpret a Venn diagram produced by someone else.
- Students will know that a Venn diagram can help them organize information when they want to compare and/or contrast things.

Instruction:

1. Ask the class to suggest some technologies (tools) that help us write on paper.
2. Select one of their suggestions, e.g., a pencil. Ask everyone to take out a pencil and examine it. After about a minute, lead a brainstorming session about pencils; be sure to record all responses on the left side of the board.
3. Select another writing technology that the students suggested, perhaps a crayon. Give students time to examine a crayon, then brainstorm and record (on the right side of the board) students' ideas about crayons.
4. Tell the class that you are going to show them a good way to compare (find ways the two objects are alike) and contrast (find ways the two objects are different).
5. Draw a big oval on the board around the pencil ideas and much of the open space in the center. Draw a second big oval around the crayon ideas and much of the open space in the center. Label the oval on the left "Pencil" and the oval on the right "Crayon."
6. Point out, while tracing around the left oval with your finger, that any ideas in this oval are about pencils; then repeat for the right (crayon) oval.
7. Encourage students to look for ideas that are found in both circles—statements that are the same (e.g., hold in hand when using, cylinder shaped, marks on paper). Provide ample time for them to complete this task. They may work collaboratively if that is convenient.
8. Suggest that if the ideas they found in both brainstormed lists were moved to the part of the diagram where the two ovals overlap they would still apply to each writing object.
9. Demonstrate moving (or rewriting) the idea "hold in hand when using" to the center of the diagram and removing that idea from both brainstormed lists. Point out that this idea is now

inside of both ovals, so it is part of the description of both pencils and crayons. Trace around each oval with your finger to make the point.

10. Continue identifying ideas that are common to the pencil and crayon and moving them to the center of the diagram.

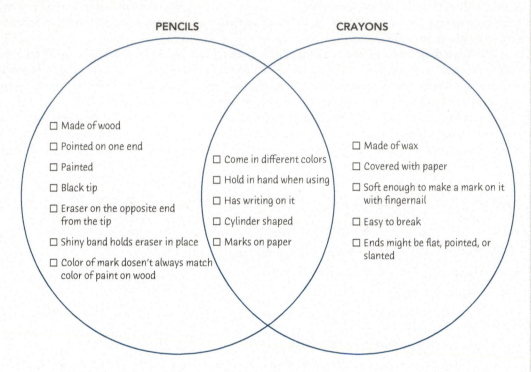

PENCILS   CRAYONS

- ☐ Made of wood
- ☐ Pointed on one end
- ☐ Painted
- ☐ Black tip
- ☐ Eraser on the opposite end from the tip
- ☐ Shiny band holds eraser in place
- ☐ Color of mark dosen't always match color of paint on wood

- ☐ Come in different colors
- ☐ Hold in hand when using
- ☐ Has writing on it
- ☐ Cylinder shaped
- ☐ Marks on paper

- ☐ Made of wax
- ☐ Covered with paper
- ☐ Soft enough to make a mark on it with fingernail
- ☐ Easy to break
- ☐ Ends might be flat, pointed, or slanted

11. When the class agrees that all ideas are correctly placed in the diagram, ask: "How can this diagram help us compare and contrast ideas about pencils and crayons?"

12. Use effective questioning strategies to uncover student thinking about Venn diagrams. Encourage the following ideas to emerge during a meaning-making discussion:

   - The ideas in the center, where the ovals overlap, are ways that pencils and crayons are the same. They apply to both objects.
   - The ideas in the rest of the pencil oval only apply to pencils, and those in the rest of the crayon oval apply only to crayons. So together they can help us see how pencils and crayons are different.
   - Comparing is finding ways that things are alike.
   - Contrasting is finding ways that things are different.

13. Organize the class into small groups. Give each group two related objects to compare and contrast (e.g., technologies used for eating: fork and spoon; technologies used for keeping hands warm in the winter: gloves and mittens; technologies used to contain liquids: bottles and cans; etc.).

14. Tell each group to create a Venn diagram about their objects and be prepared to explain it to the class.

15. During group presentations, use a scoring rubric to evaluate understanding.

Though standards suggest that science learning should be focused on understanding and applying concepts rather than memorizing lists of terms and concepts, there are still times when the skill of memorizing is useful. Students with LD often have difficulty with short-term memory. One of the strategies identified for assisting students with LD is **mnemonics**. In their research, Mastropieri et al. (1993) found the use of mnemonics very effective with students who have LD.

Mnemonic instruction is based on helping learners link new, just taught, information to information they already know. Sometimes the links are fanciful, but researchers have found that mnemonics can help both children and adults commit information to memory, from phone numbers to shopping lists (k8accesscenter.org).

You probably already know a few science-related mnemonics. Do you remember ROY G. BIV? You know, that guy that had something to do with a rainbow. No, that's not the name of the leprechaun standing beside the pot of gold. It is a mnemonic intended to help you remember the order of the colors of the visible spectrum, those colors that make up a rainbow. The letters stand for Red, Orange, Yellow, Green, Blue, Indigo, and Violet. By associating the letters in that funny name with the first letter of the colors, you could list the colors in the proper order just by remembering ROY G. BIV. This is one example of a mnemonic that uses letter strategies; specifically, it employs an acronym, a word with individual letters that represent elements in lists of information (k8accesscenter.org). Never mind that ROY G. BIV is a made-up name. Lots of students have been able to remember it over the years and, therefore, pass the test about the order of the colors in the spectrum.

The other type of letter strategy mnemonic involves **acrostics**, sentences in which the first letter of each word represents information to be remembered. A science example that you may already know is the no-longer-current way to remember the order of the planets in our solar system: *My very educated mother just served us nine pizzas*. Which stood for: Mercury, Venus, Earth, Mars, Jupiter, Saturn, Uranus, Neptune, and Pluto (k8accesscenter.org). But since Pluto was demoted to a dwarf planet in 2007, the sentence should be slightly reworded and made more nutritious. A possible new version is: *My very educated mother just served us nectarines*. As you can probably see, letter strategy mnemonics are good for helping people remember ordered lists of information.

Since mnemonics should be based on correct information, teachers generally present them to the class and demonstrate how to use them as a memory aid. Once students are comfortable using mnemonics and mature enough to create ones that are accurate and appropriate, they can create their own (k8accesscenter.org).

Science for Students with Intellectual Disabilities

On October 5, 2010, President Obama signed Rosa's Law. This legislation changed the official federal language used to refer to "students with mental retardation" to "students with intellectual disabilities" (govtrack.us).

Students with **intellectual disabilities** show greater cognitive discrepancies than students with learning disabilities. To improve the daily functioning (life skills) of these students and to address their IEPs, you might provide learning experiences that promote self-care, home living, community use, communication, self-direction (problem-solving and decision-making skills), and other functional academics as appropriate. Still, unless you emphasize and teach to the science standards that all students are expected to master, they will not be prepared to pass the state science test.

Fortunately, many of the skills found in a functional curriculum integrate well with science objectives, such as daily problem solving and understanding the world around us. When inquiry is focused on authentic, real-life applications, the functional and the academic curricula naturally support each other and are more accessible to all learners. Just think about the science concepts that directly relate to self-care: hand washing as a way to prevent the transmission of germs, why a hair dryer dries hair faster than letting it air dry, wearing layers of clothing to stay warm in cold weather, etc. (Miller, 2012).

Research indicates that students with mild intellectual disabilities learn concepts better when they are guided to construct them through questioning than when the information is presented directly to them. A study of the thinking of fourth-grade students with mild intellectual disabilities during an ecology unit indicated that they *can* actively engage in such processes as observing, describing, comparing, recording, and predicting—with appropriate assistance (Mastropieri, et al, 1993). Yet, remember in the pendulum study discussed previously, students with intellectual disabilities were not successful when inference was required, even when their peers with LD or in general education were.

The research into effective science instruction for students with intellectual disabilities is limited. But emerging research suggests that inquiry-based instructional methods can help students with intellectual disabilities learn both functional and some science content (Miller, 2012).

Science for Students with Emotional Disturbance

According to IDEA, students with **emotional disturbance** exhibit one or more of these characteristics for an extended period of time:

- an inability to learn not due to intellectual, sensory, or health factors
- an inability to exhibit appropriate behavior under ordinary circumstances
- an inability to maintain relationships with peers or teachers
- an inappropriate affect such as depression or anxiety
- an inappropriate manifestation of physical symptoms or fears in response to school or personal difficulties (Code of Federal Regulations, Title 34, §300.8[c][4][i])

Some students with emotional disturbance will act out in class; they will certainly get your attention and that of the other students. Clearly stated classroom and laboratory rules, if fairly and consistently enforced, will go a long way toward maintaining a safe and supportive learning environment for all of your students. But you should ask for advice from special needs teachers and counselors who also work with your students with emotional disturbance. You must be prepared to deal with behaviors that may be exhibited. During an activity, do not put yourself or your class at risk for the sake of inclusion. Students with impulse control or aggression issues, or who exhibit antisocial or obstructional, defiant behaviors, must be carefully monitored during activities utilizing chemicals, open flames, or sharp objects. If you have any concerns, arrange for a co-teacher or a skilled instructional aide to assist in the lab. If any behavioral problems that could impact the safety of you or the class occur, remove the offending student from the lab immediately.

Some problem behaviors, like persistent apathy, may not be disruptive and, therefore, may be easy to overlook. But since apathetic behavior may make it difficult for a child with severe depression to learn effectively, you should help that student make a behavioral change. Realize that some behaviors simply should not be ignored, often for safety reasons, but that getting angry will never solve the problem (Conn, 2001).

Research indicates that punitive discipline rarely corrects the behavior of students with emotional disturbance. Hundreds of research studies reveal that behavioral modification improves not only classroom behaviors but academic performance as well (Ormrod, 2007). Behavior modification is often effective when other techniques are not, because (1) students know exactly what is expected of them; (2) through the gradual process of shaping, students attempt to learn new behaviors only when they are truly ready to acquire them; and (3) students find that learning new behaviors usually leads to success.

Because students with emotional disturbance may be included in your classroom, a few words of wisdom may be helpful. Consider that labels often get in the way of seeing these students as children. Even though they may be impulsive, aggressive, antisocial, disruptive, defiant, or apathetic, you could also identify them as smart, good soccer players, lively, helpful, creative, tenacious, and daring. Picture the student(s) in your class as exhibiting these positive characteristics and choose carefully the words you use to describe them.

Science for Students with Visual Impairments

You may have students with **visual impairments** in your classroom. These are not your students whose vision is corrected by wearing glasses or contacts. Students with *low vision* might need special aids or instruction to read ordinary print. Those who are *functionally blind* typically need to use Braille (a tactile system of communication) for efficient reading and writing. Those who are *totally blind* do not receive meaningful input through the visual sense. These individuals use tactile and auditory means to learn about their environment. *Color blindness* is also a visual impairment that can impact science learning, since color-coded wires or lines on a schematic diagram may be very difficult for a student with color blindness to distinguish.

One of your main tasks, if you teach a student with visual impairments, is to figure out how to adapt classroom materials to make them accessible. Table 10.4 suggests some simple things that you could do on your own to make accommodations for students with low vision. Once you have reviewed Table 10.4, try out Exploration 10.6.

Students with visual impairments often benefit by accessing information about the world through their other senses, especially hearing. No longer do you or another student need to read text aloud to a student with a visual impairment, since audio books, speech synthesizers, screen readers, or talking browsers (assistive technology devices that transform text to speech output) can provide that service.

▶ Fifth-grade teacher Nicole Bay talks about strategies she uses to help students who are sometimes "challenging to teach." As you watch this video of her classroom during some exploration activities, look for times when she uses those strategies.

▶ This video clip shows second-grade students looking for the plant embryos inside soaked lima beans. How did their teacher, Nancy Michael ensure that all of her students could observe and record information about the "baby plants?"

TABLE 10.4 Simple Accommodations for Students with Low Vision

Resource	Ways to Make It More Accessible for Students with Low Vision
Chalkboard, whiteboard, or chart paper	Write bigger, using bold contrasting print. Provide binoculars. Take a photo with an iPad, then stretch out the image with your fingers.
Printed handout	Use enlarge function on copy machine. Use a document camera to project an enlarged image on a screen. Use a large hand lens. Take a photo with an iPad, then stretch out the image with your fingers.
Digitized text	Select highly legible font before printing. Increase font size and line spacing before printing. Use Zoom function on computer. Project computer image on screen.

Helping a Student with Total Blindness Measure Tree Trunks

EXPLORATION

10.6

Design and construct a device that would enable a student with total blindness to measure the circumference of a tree trunk to the nearest centimeter. Test your design by asking blindfolded persons to try it out. Make improvements to the measuring device or the associated instructions for its use based on feedback from the tests.

Reflection Questions:

1. How did you address this problem?
2. In what ways did feedback from blindfolded testers allow you to improve your tree circumference measuring system?
3. What other laboratory tasks might students with total blindness find challenging?
4. What devices or procedures can you suggest that could make hands-on science more accessible to students with blindness?

Talking thermometers, clocks, and timers enable students to be more directly involved in data collection during a laboratory investigation (Watson & Johnson, 2007).

Text that is transformed into Braille is accessible to students who have learned to decode letters composed of patterns of raised dots on a surface through their sense of touch. If a student's IEP calls for them, your special education department should order books in Braille, provide a Braille printer, or purchase a Braille label maker to aid in the identification of chemicals, models, and laboratory equipment. Tactile markings on graduated cylinders, meter sticks, and balances can make measuring accessible to visually impaired students as well (Watson & Johnson, 2007).

If students with visual impairments need assistive technology to turn their ideas into text, they now have several options. There are devices that transform their spoken words into text, or they can use a Braille keyboard to aid their word processing. Technological advances such as these offer students who are blind greater levels of independence as they learn science.

Science for Students with Hearing Impairments

Students who have impaired hearing range in their hearing ability from hard of hearing (use of amplification) to total deafness. Because there are substantial differences between aided and unaided hearing (Turnbull et al., 2004), there is no consensus about how to refer to people with hearing impairments. A people-first approach—persons who are deaf—will be used in this section.

▶ Teachers use a variety of strategies to **make science more accessible for all learners**. Which strategy do some educators think works particularly well for students who are hearing impaired, and why?

One of the major problems for persons who are deaf is language development. Just as incidental learning accounts for the lack of certain kinds of prior knowledge for persons who are blind, persons who are deaf generally struggle with language development. Thus, psychosocial development—an interaction with the world through language—is a key need for students who are deaf or hard of hearing. Sign language, lip reading, and the reading of body and facial movements help these students with communication. However, without intervention, there are increasing gaps in vocabulary, concept formation, and the ability to understand and produce complex sentences for people who are deaf. Without intervention, both language and intellectual development may be affected.

Hands-on activities can help show students differences in the meanings of words. Begin with familiar objects from the students' everyday environment. Stress handling the objects during language/concept development. Introduce other words related to the properties of objects, such as color, size, and texture. This process follows the constructivist learning cycle in which the learner manipulates materials, and then the teacher introduces or "invents" words for the scientific concepts.

A simple first step is to place students in the front of the classroom to improve their opportunity to hear verbally provided instructions and access the teacher if needed. Students that have some hearing may benefit by having **assistive listening systems** in their classrooms. Hearing aids alone may be effective in a quiet environment, but for the student who wears a hearing aid in a typical classroom, the teacher's voice becomes muffled with the background noise, room echo, and distance. Most assistive listening systems use a microphone/transmitter positioned close to the instructor's mouth to transmit the instructor's voice to the receiver worn by the student. Minimizing the background noise in the classroom is a low-tech way to improve the learning environment for students who are hard of hearing.

Your students who are deaf will better understand science videos and TV programming when captioning features are turned on. Computer-aided speech-to-print transcription systems have now been perfected, so lectures can be digitally transcribed (Watson & Johnson, 2007).

Science for Students with Mobility or Motor Impairments

You may have students in your class who use a wheelchair or a walker. The physical layout of your classroom or laboratory is of primary importance to them. Arrange your desks or tables so that every aisle is at least one meter wide. For appropriate wheelchair access, workstations for students with mobility impairments should be at least 91 cm wide and at least 50 cm deep. The height of the table should be adjustable, since the work surface should be no more than 81 cm above the floor, but the space under the tabletop should be at least 73 cm high (Fetters, Pickard, & Pyle, 2003).

Acknowledge the abilities and independence of your student with mobility impairments by always asking if he or she wants help before offering it. Say "Would you like . . . ?" instead of "Here, let me . . ." Never move a student's wheelchair unless the student asks you to do so. Provide appropriate support by having the student work with a lab partner; placing needed lab materials within easy reach; and modifying lab equipment to make it easier to hold by substituting a different size or shape, adding a handle to make it easier to grip, and/or using plastic instead of glass if possible. Allowing extra time is also important (Fetters et al., 2003). Close access to safety equipment such as the eye wash station should be provided.

For field trips and investigations that are conducted outside, special planning is often needed if your class includes a student with a mobility disability. Be sure that the study site is wheelchair or walker accessible and that the bus is equipped. Vignette 10.1 presents a real-world example of this.

Tomasz Markowski/Shutterstock

Vignette 10.1 About Our Seventh-Grade Environmental Field Trip

We have historically done a field trip at the end of the school year at the West Plain Coastal Reserve. It's a fun outdoor field trip with a picnic. Each teacher does an hour-long lesson. The English teacher does nature poetry; someone takes the kids on a hike, and they document it with digital technology; and I take them out into the water to collect invertebrates. This year was a little different, though.

We have a student named Brad, who is in a motorized wheelchair with muscular dystrophy. He has quite a bit of paralysis too. Brad is in seventh grade. He's an amazing kid. He's just one of those sponges who picks up everything I say. Then a little later on, he'll put up a hand and ask an amazingly insightful question about what I said. Like he was really thinking about it. Not just accepting something because I said it. Or he'll relate it to something else—another animal or something. He just really thinks about things, and he wants to be a scientist. He says he wants to be a biologist.

There was no way that he could do the field trip at the West Plain Coastal Reserve. It just wasn't handicap accessible at all. I asked a group of science teachers if anyone else knew another place where we could do a similar field trip. The group suggested the Nature Center in Hammonasset State Park. I called them up, and they had one more opening for the year. They had everything we needed. The nature center itself had bathrooms that were handicapped accessible. They had a beach chair, which is a very cool wheelchair with big wheels that can go out into the sand, onto the shore, and even out into the salt marsh.

We did a program called the three ecosystems tour. Brad met us there. He went in a separate van with one or two friends with him. We used his wheelchair to get to the pavilion area, where we switched him into the beach chair. We did the Sandy Beach first, and the kids had a really good time pushing him in the beach chair on the sandy beach—to the point where I was a little bit worried because they were going fast. He likes to go fast.

We went from the Sandy Beach to the salt marsh to the rocky shore. He was able to go to all three of them—to go right out with the kids. When we were on the rocky shore, he was able to bend over and pick up the crabs and snails with the rest of the kids. He was looking with his friends, but he was able to hold a snail and a crab in his hands. He really enjoyed it.

 CHECK YOUR UNDERSTANDING 10.4
Click here to gauge your understanding of the concepts in this section.

Supporting Science Learning for Students Identified as Gifted and Talented

Students such as Alan, who you will meet in Vignette 10.2, provide a different kind of challenge for teachers. These students have above-average intelligence and possess unusual skills, interests, talents, and attitudes about learning. Words such as *creativity, vitality, potential, motivation,* and *joy* tend to describe their approach to learning, at least in a specific area (Armstrong, 1998). Such students are identified as having special gifts or talents. But keep this in mind: The fact that a student is identified as being gifted and talented does not mean he or she is necessarily excited about learning science! Additionally, most teachers realize that students may be gifted in different ways and may not excel in all content areas.

As a teacher, you will quickly learn that students who are identified as gifted are a very diverse group. Most have general intelligence (scoring well on an IQ test) specific academic ability, creative and productive thinking, leadership ability, and/or abilities in visual and performing arts that stand out from their classmates. Many students who are gifted or talented love to participate in many activities and usually enjoy being challenged with meaningful enrichment activities.

It is important to make gifted and talented (GT) students (sometimes referred to as TAG [talented and gifted] or GATE [Gifted and Talented Education] students) in your classroom feel welcome and accepted.

Vignette 10.2   A Conversation about Relativity with a Gifted and Talented Child

Ten-year-old Alan developed an unlikely interest in Einstein's theory of relativity. Alan's teacher invited a college professor to the classroom to talk about the theory with the boy. The child said to the professor, "I understand that Einstein described the universe in terms of four variables, but I can only think of three of them." As they discussed the problem, the professor told Alan that at age 16, Einstein set this puzzle for himself: *What would happen if I traveled along at the speed of light and held up a mirror to my face?*

What would I see? The professor explained that Einstein needed the three variables of space and an additional variable of time to eventually answer this question at age 26. Somehow, this information helped Alan to bring together a variety of things he had read and thought about. He then took up the explanation, laying out Einstein's problem and solution in such an insightful way that the astounded professor began to understand them more deeply himself.

Previously, these students were accelerated to higher or special pullout classes. Currently, greater emphasis is placed on inclusion, incorporating changes in science content and activities to introduce rigorous levels of abstract and independent thinking and problem-solving skills. Your challenge is to help your gifted and talented students modify, adapt, and learn how to discover new skills and concepts for themselves. An inquiry-based approach is nearly ideal to address that challenge.

Most highly motivated, bright students need little encouragement. For those who do, try these suggestions:

- Provide recognition for their efforts, but be wary of gifted students with know-it-all tendencies. Encourage cooperative efforts.
- Challenge students to come up with questions they think are difficult and then work in small groups with other motivated (GT) students to find answers to the questions.
- Encourage student-initiated projects and alternative activities sometimes in lieu of standard kinds of class activities.
- Introduce elementary and middle grade students to research methods.
- Encourage students to use a variety of media to express themselves in creative ways such as drawing, creative writing, drama, and role playing.
- Help students organize and publish a classroom or school science magazine.

A caution is in order; students who are gifted must also acquire basic knowledge, understandings, and procedures, even as they are given more freedom to move in their own directions. Most of them will soon come to appreciate the depth of knowledge that comes with integrating the three dimensions of NGSS in teaching and learning. However, those too focused on getting perfect scores or competing with others in their class may find this more student-centered approach frustrating, since they have already mastered the skills of succeeding in traditional schooling. A further caution is to remember that your best and brightest student should not be paired with struggling students with the expectation that they are responsible for helping the struggling student learn. This can be problematic as it does not allow the GT student to be challenged and there may be a tendency for the GT student to just "tell" the struggling student the answer so that they do not really learn the concepts.

Your teaching methods can encourage students who are gifted and talented. In our society, students' thinking is often trained to focus on the right answer, which sometimes discourages them from taking risks in academic situations. Many GT students are high achievers; they have come to expect only perfect scores. Students may be confused or feel threatened with failure when they are faced with tasks in which there are either no clear answers or a variety of correct answers. Be sure to use some of these techniques, which generally represent best instructional Practice for all students as you implement NGSS-aligned instructional approaches, to encourage GT students to be less focused on competition and right answers:

1. Use a series of open-ended questions rather than giving information.

2. Use hypothetical, probing questions beginning with "What if . . . ?"

3. Ask students to develop open-ended situations where no one answer is correct.

4. In science tasks involving mathematics, where specific answers are usually required, encourage students to estimate their answers before completing calculations.

5. Instead of information, emphasize concepts, principles, relationships, generalizations, and claims supported by evidence.

6. Provide opportunities and assignments that rely on independent reading and research as appropriate. Ask students to report on their research and investigations; this helps them acquire a sense of sharing knowledge.

7. Provide students with multiple opportunities to learn how to use technology to research information and gather data from a variety of global resources.

8. Challenge students to engage in, and design or originate more open-ended, hands-on inquiry or problem-solving activities.

   • Start by working with the entire class or a group. Later, when routines are established, invite individuals to explore on their own.

   • Keep investigations within the limits of time, ethics, student readiness, and available apparatus. Explore these limitations before suggesting problems.

   • Be alert to the open-endedness of this type of exploration. Expect questions to arise such as, "Suppose we vary the experiment in this way. What will happen?"

   • Do not assume that the gifted student will have a sustained interest in the problem. You must continually check on progress.

Read Exploration 10.7 to find out more about effective strategies to us with gifted and talented students.

Case Study 7: Gifted and Talented Students and the Next Generation Science Standards

EXPLORATION

10.7

Access the Case Studies in Appendix D of the NGSS at www.nextgenscience.org/appendix-d-case-studies. Select Case Study 7, then read the vignette, "Constructing Arguments about the Interaction of Structure and Function in Plants and Animals" to "watch" how Mrs. J. meets the science educational needs of gifted and talented students in her class. Be sure to read the sections of the case study after the vignette to learn how the lessons in the vignette connect to NGSS and CCSS and find out more about research-based instructional strategies that are useful when working with this unique group of learners.

Reflection Questions:

1. How did Mrs. J. apply the following strategies, which are particularly effective for gifted and talented students, in the life science unit described in the vignette? Please provide specific examples in your reflection.
   • Fast pacing
   • Different levels of challenge (including differentiation of content)
   • Opportunities for self-direction
   • Strategic grouping

2. What does "compacting curriculum" mean? Why is it useful in a diverse classroom that includes students who are gifted and talented? In what ways did Mrs. J. use curriculum compacting?

3. Do you think the switch to the NGSS may have some inherent benefits for gifted and talented students who have not yet been officially identified? Why or why not?

Connecting science and mathematics is important for all students, particularly gifted students. Challenge them to go beyond describing what happens and why and explore *how much* or what *quantitative relationships* exist between variables. Ask students to quantify their findings, and encourage them to use graphing when communicating their findings.

Most elementary school teachers have not majored in science and, therefore, find that some of their students know more about certain areas of science than they do. Feeling somewhat incompetent with science content should not stop you from encouraging gifted and talented students to do more advanced work than the rest of the class. Students enjoy seeing their teachers get excited about the results of their work. Facilitate the academic environment of students who are gifted by posing challenging questions and offering constructive feedback. Also, identify community people who are available to work with gifted and talented students in a mentor program. Be sure to provide some guidance to those who are knowledgeable in their fields but do not know how to motivate and teach students.

Remember that for all their knowledge and abilities, gifted students are still elementary or middle school students whose social, emotional, and physical development mirrors the development of their peers. They need your mature adult guidance, professional training, and practical experience. They will seek caring and emotionally stable adults. That's you!

CHECK YOUR UNDERSTANDING 10.5

Click here to gauge your understanding of the concepts in this section.

CHAPTER SUMMARY

Equity, Diversity, and Achievement Gaps in Science Education

The population of the United States is very diverse, and our classrooms and schools reflect this *diversity*. They are filled with a variety of individual learners who each can be described by multiple factors including: race, gender, age, family structure, economic status, culture, ethnicity, language spoken at home, disabilities, aspirations, motivation, and interest in science. According to national science standards, equity is important as we prepare students to live in the twenty-first century; *all* students should have an equal opportunity to attain high levels of scientific literacy as they advance through the grade levels. However, low learning expectations and stereotypical views of some groups of students have been shown to affect science learning as reflected in scores on high-stakes science assessments. This variance in science scores, known as an *achievement gap,* should not be attributed to the abilities of these students. When provided with adequate time and support, nearly all students can learn and do science when they make a sustained effort. Achievement gaps are probably a result of inequities in the system. By better understanding the reasons for observed achievement gaps, teachers of science can design and deliver instruction that brings us closer to the goal of equity in science education.

Helping Students from Linguistically and Culturally Diverse Backgrounds Learn Science

Hands-on science teaching and learning activities have many benefits for students from diverse backgrounds, especially those with limited English proficiency. Sheltered instruction, specifically the SIOP model, offers instructional strategies that support both content and English language learning simultaneously. When teaching, speak clearly and slowly; use pauses, visuals, gestures, a graphic organizer to emphasize important terms, and provide descriptions instead of definitions. Also teach learning strategies such as mnemonics, note-taking skills, etc. Provide ample time for ELs to practice and use their language in small-group and whole-class settings. Learn about the cultural norms of your students and keep their culture in mind when planning and delivering instruction. The population of children from linguistically and culturally diverse backgrounds is growing in the United States, so you are likely to teach these students.

Teaching Science in an Inclusive Classroom

Appropriate science teaching strategies for inclusive classrooms are the same research-based instructional approaches that are recognized as best practices in any science classroom. These approaches include actively engaging all students in scientific inquiry; revisiting and applying DCIs, CCCs, and SEPs in multiple contexts over time; using cooperative learning strategies; and providing relevant, developmentally appropriate, standards-based lessons. It is important to understand the special learning needs of individual students, then address those needs by differentiating instruction. High expectations for all learners and a nurturing and supportive class culture also enhance the science learning in an inclusive classroom.

Helping Students Identified with Disabilities Learn Science

The Individuals with Disabilities Education Act (IDEA) mandates that all students have the right to a full, free public education in the least restrictive environment; yet the identified students often require accommodations based on their disabling conditions. Accommodations are specifically designed to support the learning needs of each identified student by a committee and reported on that student's Individualized Education Plan (IEP). If you teach science to a student with disabilities, you must address both the regular curricular goals and the student's IEP goals. Disabling conditions include those that are cognitive (specific learning disabilities, intellectual disabilities), emotional, and physical (blindness, deafness, mobility issues). Instructional supports vary widely by disabling condition but include providing alternative or multisensory activities, allowing extra time to complete assignments or assessments, teaching study skills, using graphic organizers, applying behavior modification plans, arranging for technologies to aid the senses, and in some cases, an instructional aide.

Supporting Science Learning for Students Identified as Gifted and Talented

Gifted and talented students vary greatly, but in general they are very intelligent, creative, and intensely interested in at least some topics. They do not necessarily love science, but if they do, they are full of questions and often answers as well. Students who have unusual talents or are intellectually gifted can benefit from doing relatively unstructured explorations, engaging in enrichment activities such as studying abstract topics to integrate connections, and observing how math and science are connected. You can maximize their science learning by respecting their abilities, challenging them in areas where growth is needed, and listening and responding to their interests while ensuring that they have a firm foundation of basic concepts and skills.

DISCUSSION QUESTIONS

1. How do you believe issues of diversity and equity relate to achievement gaps between certain groups of students on standardized science assessments?

2. How is it possible to teach science to students who are not fluent in English, when you do not speak their language at all?

3. Why is differentiating instruction so important in inclusive science classrooms, and in what ways can it be done?

4. In what ways is teaching science to students with disabilities more challenging than teaching them other subjects?

5. How do you feel about teaching science to a student who is gifted and talented and especially interested in science? In what ways would you support his or her continued growth?

PROFESSIONAL PRACTICES ACTIVITIES

1. Access state science achievement test results from your state's department of education website. Examine the data to look for evidence of achievement gaps in science scores for several schools or districts in your area. Summarize your findings.

2. Modify a science lesson plan by adding activities designed to help ELs increase their academic vocabulary. If possible, try out the lesson with a class that includes some English Learners.

3. Examine the teacher's guide for a science textbook or a kit-based module to learn what ideas for differentiated instruction are included. Evaluate how well the suggestions in the teacher's guide would help a teacher meet the individual learning needs of students in an inclusive classroom.

4. During your field-based experiences, inconspicuously observe a student with disabilities as he or she participates in a hands-on science activity. Look for accommodations that may be in place, interactions with peers, and student engagement in learning. With your cooperating teacher, discuss specific challenges faced by this learner, the accommodations required by his or her IEP, and the progress this child has already made.

5. Speak with (or follow the blog of) a practicing teacher of science about his or her experiences with gifted and talented students. Determine what he or she found particularly surprising, challenging, or rewarding while working with this special population.

Activities for Teaching Science through Inquiry-Based Instruction

Teaching Inquiry-Based Science Activities

Source: Morgan Lane Photography/Shutterstock

The key to engaging children and young adolescents in inquiry-based learning is the teacher, who plans, guides, scaffolds, questions, informs, explains, and challenges—all in the context of students' experiences with real-world phenomena. Even well-prepared, enthusiastic teachers like you can benefit from a collection of instructional activities to help your students excel in the classroom. A bank of activities provides concrete suggestions for teaching inquiry-based science as well as introducing engineering design to learners in grades K through 8. These activities *do not* comprise a comprehensive science curriculum, but they do represent ideas for three-dimensional instruction designed to help you connect science in the classroom to standards in a practical way. Allowing students to engage in these and similar activities helps them develop a better understanding of science and how the world works while they develop their abilities related to Scientific and Engineering Practices and begin to comprehend the Crosscutting Concepts that connect the sciences and engineering.

There are five sections in the Activities part of this book, this introduction and four more sections that each introduce one of the four major domains: the Physical Sciences, the Life Sciences, the Earth and Space Sciences, and Engineering Design, and present activities related to that domain. As shown in Table 11.1, these domains basically mirror the organization of Disciplinary Core Ideas in *A Framework for K–12 Science Education: Practices, Crosscutting Concepts, and Core Ideas* (NRC, 2012). Sometimes deciding the appropriate domain for an activity was challenging because of the interdisciplinary nature of the learning described. For example, in the sections focused on the sciences you may find some activities that include elements of Engineering Design and/or another scientific domain. Nearly all of the activities found in the Engineering Design section are related to at least one of the traditional science domains.

Many of the included activities have their roots in science topics and process skills traditionally taught in elementary or middle schools, and they align with content standards from the *National Science Education Standards* (NRC, 1996) and state standards based on the NSES. However, these activities have been written with the three dimensions introduced by *A Framework for K-12 Science Education: Practices, Crosscutting Concepts, and Core Ideas* (NRC, 2012) in mind, and are correlated with one or more of the Performance Expectations of the *Next Generation Science Standards* (NGSS Lead States, 2013).

According to the *Framework*, in order to facilitate students' learning, all three dimensions must be woven together in standards, curricula, instruction, and assessments. So the activities in this section are designed to enable learners to explore particular Disciplinary Core Ideas as they engage in certain Scientific and Engineering Practices, while also helping them to make connections to related Crosscutting Concepts.

The activities in this section should be thought of as bare-bones outlines that must be fleshed out through lesson planning and connections to other subjects. Building lesson plans and sequencing activities into instructional units is something that you may do yourself or through collaboration with your grade level team. You should feel free to modify activities to take advantage of instructional technologies and other resources available in your classroom. For example, instead of just asking the suggested question provided in the engage phase of an activity, you might also project a related image from the internet or hang up a colorful poster that focuses on the topic of study. This can be a good way to engage your students with a lesson-level phenomenon that they will try to figure out during the lesson so they can develop an explanation for it.

To assist and guide you in the lesson planning process, the activities follow the same general format. Each activity begins with a descriptive title stated in the form of a question. Just below the title, the intended grade level (for elementary) or grade-level band (for middle school) (according to the NGSS) is presented. Then, the Framework Context Chart suggests how the activity relates to the three dimensions of the *Framework*. The general organization of the Framework Context Chart for each activity is shown in Table 11.2.

Next, one or more NGSS Performance Expectations are identified by their codes (Grade Level or Grade Band-Component Idea Code-Number based on the order it was presented in NGSS) and stated with citations to NGSS. Please note that, used in isolation, the lesson provided is not intended to enable learners to master the NGSS Performance Expectation(s) listed. The given lesson simply helps to build toward deep understanding of that NGSS Performance Expectation.

A *Learning Target* presents the element of the DCI being focused on that is appropriate for learners at the specified grade level or grade band. *Success Criteria* then describe what students should know and be able to do during and following engagement with the activity.

TABLE 11.1   The Three Dimensions of the *Framework*

1. Scientific and Engineering Practices

1. Asking questions (for science) and defining problems (for engineering)
2. Developing and using models
3. Planning and carrying out investigations
4. Analyzing and interpreting data
5. Using mathematics and computational thinking
6. Constructing explanations (for science) and designing solutions (for engineering)
7. Engaging in argument from evidence
8. Obtaining, evaluating, and communicating information

2. Crosscutting Concepts

1. Patterns
2. Cause and effect: Mechanism and explanation
3. Scale, proportion, and quantity
4. Systems and system models
5. Energy and matter: Flows, cycles, and conservation
6. Structure and function
7. Stability and change

3. Disciplinary Core Ideas

Physical Sciences

PS1: Matter and its interactions
PS2: Motion and stability: Forces and interactions
PS3: Energy
PS4: Waves and their applications in technologies for information transfer

Life Sciences

LS1: From molecules to organisms: Structures and processes
LS2: Ecosystems: Interactions, energy, and dynamics
LS3: Heredity: Inheritance and variation of traits
LS4: Biological evolution: Unity and diversity

Earth and Space Sciences

ESS1: Earth's place in the universe
ESS2: Earth's systems
ESS3: Earth and human activity

Engineering, Technology, and Applications of Science

ETS1: Engineering design
ETS2: Links among engineering, technology, science, and society

Source: NRC, 2012, p. 3.

Some activities include a short *Science Background* section intended as a brief review for the lesson planner (you); it is not what the students should know before the lesson or even what they should know after the lesson.

To help you prepare to facilitate an activity with your class, a basic list of *Materials* is given. In some activities, specific numbers or amounts of needed tools, objects, organisms, or supplies is given for each individual, pair, or small group; in other activities, a simple listing is given, leaving it up to you to decide the quantities needed. In activities that have potential safety concerns, relevant *Safety Precautions* are described.

TABLE 11.2   Framework Context Chart

Framework Context	
Scientific and Engineering Practices	**The name of a practice from the *FRAMEWORK* appears here,** followed by a description of the practice as it relates to the activity (with a page reference from the *Framework*).
Crosscutting Concepts	**The name of a Crosscutting Concept from the *FRAMEWORK* appears here,** followed by a description of the Crosscutting Concept as it relates to the activity (with a page reference from the *Framework*).
Disciplinary Core Idea	**Code:** and name of the related DCI from the Framework
Component Idea	**Code:** and name of the component idea from the Framework
Conceptual Understanding	**By the end of grade (___):** Description of progression of learning related to the component idea expected (with a page reference from the Framework)

The body of each activity is organized according to the 5E instructional model, which you learned about in Chapter 5 of this text. This instructional sequence supports effective inquiry teaching and learning. The names of the 5 phases—engage, explore, explain, elaborate, and evaluate—serve as headings for the instructional segments that should be included in an inquiry-based lesson. Suggestions of what you and your students should be doing during each phase of the lesson are described in each activity.

Be sure to look back at the previous chapters of this text, should you need to review information about planning for inquiry-based instruction, grouping students, managing materials, maintaining a safe learning environment, facilitating discourse, asking effective questions, assessing student learning, incorporating technology, integrating other subject areas, meeting the needs of diverse learners, etc.

Additional activities are available in the Pearson Enhanced eText.

It has been left to you to select those activities that best support student learning and lead to mastery of the NGSS or the current science standards of your state. You do not have to be a science specialist to engage your students in these activities, but merely curious and willing to learn along with them. The most important element in these inquiry activities is that students can discover the joy and wonder of science and engineering. And so can you. Have fun!

If you are using the Pearson eText, it is easy to use the Activities Library to search for a specific activity. Click on "Activities Library" in the left navigational bar in your eText to explore activities sorted by Disciplinary Core Ideas, Science and Engineering Practices, and Crosscutting Concepts. Clicking on the "Browse Full Library" option will sort all of the activities by appropriate grade level. You can also do a keyword search using the search box available at the top of the Activities Library page. Each activity is coded by useful criteria, for example, by title, grade level, component idea, or SEP, making it extremely easy to find exactly what you need. All of the activities are downloadable and printable, so you can save what you'll need for use in your classroom.

Physical Sciences

About Physical Sciences

"Physical Sciences" is the first domain included in the Disciplinary Core Ideas, the third dimension of the *Framework*. The Physical Sciences relate to ideas in the traditional fields of chemistry and physics. Physical Science activities are intended to help children develop their understanding of the physical world and how it works. These activities relate to everyday life experiences and help students find answers to fundamental questions about matter and energy, such as: *What is everything made of?* and *Why do things happen?*

TABLE 12.1 Physical Science Core and Component Ideas According to the Framework

Discipline-Related Code	Descriptive Title	Related Question
PS1	**Matter and Its Interactions**	**How can one explain the structure, properties, and interactions of matter?**
PS1.A	Structure and Properties of Matter	How do particles combine to form the variety of substances one observes?
PS1.B	Chemical Reactions	How do substances combine or change (react) to make new substances? How does one characterize and explain these reactions and make predictions about them?
PS1.C	Nuclear Processes	What forces hold nuclei together and mediate nuclear processes?
PS2	**Motion and Stability: Forces and Interactions**	**How can one explain and predict interactions between objects and within systems?**
PS2.A	Forces and Motion	How can one predict an object's continued motion, changes in motion, or stability?
PS2.B	Types of Interactions	What underlying forces explain the variety of interactions observed?
PS2.C	Stability and Instability in Physical Systems	Why are some physical systems more stable than others?
PS3	**Energy**	**How is energy transferred and conserved?**
PS3.A	Definitions of Energy	What is energy?
PS3.B	Conservation of Energy and Energy Transfer	What is meant by conservation of energy? How is energy transferred between objects or systems?
PS3.C	Relationship Between Energy and Forces	How are forces related to energy?
PS3.D	Energy in Chemical Processes and Everyday Life	How do food and fuel provide energy? If energy is conserved, why do people say it is produced or used?
PS4	**Waves and Their Applications in Technologies for Information Transfer**	**How are waves used to transfer energy and information?**
PS4.A	Wave Properties	What are the characteristic properties and behaviors of waves?
PS4.B	Electromagnetic Radiation	What is light? How can one explain the varied effects that involve light? What other forms of electromagnetic radiation are there?
PS4.C	Information Technologies and Instrumentation	How are instruments that transmit and detect waves used to extend human senses?

Source: NRC, 2012.

The activities are organized according to the codes for the core and component ideas for the Physical Science Disciplinary Core Ideas, which are presented in Table 12.1. Physical Science Core Ideas have codes in the format PS#, and are in the rows with the darker background. The Component Ideas have codes in the format PS#.A and are in the rows with the lighter background. Within each cluster of activities for a specific component idea, activities are organized by grade-level bands from low to high. The activities represent only a sampling of instructional plans for lessons; there are some component ideas for which no activities are included.

For a concise description of background information related to Physical Science DCIs and their components, look at Chapter 5 of *A Framework for K–12 Science Education: Practices, Crosscutting Concepts, and Core Ideas* (NRC, 2012), available online from the National Academies Press at www.nap.edu.

There are additional Physical Science activities available to you digitally via the Enhanced Pearson eText. These include:

DCI Component Idea	Title	Grade / Grade-band
PS2.A	What happens to water drops on different surfaces?	Grade 3
PS2.B	How do compass needles interact with current-carrying wires?	Middle School
PS2.B	How can you increase the strength of an electromagnet?	Middle School
PS4.A	How can you make a bottle pipe organ? What affects the pitch of the sound produced by a bottle?	Grade 1
PS4.B	What can we see in the dark?	Grade 1

Activity 1: Which materials do magnets attract?

Grade: 2, Physical Sciences

Framework Context	
Scientific and Engineering Practices	**Planning and Carrying Out Investigations** From the earliest grades, students should have opportunities to carry out careful and systematic investigations, with appropriately supported prior experiences that develop their ability to observe and measure and to record data using appropriate tools and instruments (NRC, 2012, pp. 60–61). **Analyzing and Interpreting Data** At the elementary level, students need support to recognize the need to record observations—whether in drawings, words, or numbers—and to share them with others (NRC, 2012, p. 63).
Crosscutting Concepts	**Patterns** It is important for them (students) to develop ways to recognize, classify, and record patterns in the phenomena they observe (NRC, 2012, p. 86).
Disciplinary Core Idea	**PS1:** Matter and Its Interactions
Component Idea	**PS1.A:** Structure and Properties of Matter
Conceptual Understanding	**By the end of grade 2:** Matter can be described and classified by its observable properties . . . Different properties are suited to different purposes (NRC, 2012, p. 108).

Performance Expectation 2-PS1-1

Plan and conduct an investigation to describe and classify different kinds of materials by their observable properties (NGSS Lead States, 2013, p. 16). www.nextgenscience.org/dci-arrangement/2-ps1-matter-and-its-interactions

Learning Target

A property of objects and materials composed of iron is that they are attracted to magnets.

Success Criteria

The students will:

1. Use a magnet to post a paper in the classroom.
2. Sort objects and materials by whether they are attracted by magnets.
3. Recognize that magnets come in many sizes and shapes.
4. Explain how they can use a magnet to identify most objects and materials that contain iron.

Materials

For each student:

1 refrigerator magnet or magnetic pushpin (available at office supply stores)

For each group:

- Assortment of magnets, including: bar magnets, U-shaped magnets, ring magnets, disc magnets, and other magnets
- Bag of assorted materials that are attracted to magnets (objects containing iron, such as paper clips and most screws and nails) and materials that are not attracted to magnets (such as wood, plastic, and paper objects, and non-iron metallic objects, such as aluminum nails or foil, most soda cans, pennies, and brass fasteners)

Science Background

Iron is the only common kind of metal that magnets attract. Magnets will not stick to such metals as: aluminum, copper, and brass. Magnets stick to steel because steel is mostly iron.

Four hundred years ago, William Gilbert, an English physician, wrote a book titled *On the Loadstone and Magnetic Bodies*. It was the first important work in Physical Science published in England. Gilbert's book provides the first written account of numerous experiments on magnetism, experiments that can be readily carried out in elementary and middle school science today. Gilbert argued for a new method of knowing, dedicating his book to those "ingenuous minds, who not only in books, but in things themselves look for knowledge."

Stainless steel contains iron. However, magnets don't stick to all stainless steel refrigerator doors (as some students may point out). That's because refrigerator doors may be made of ferritic stainless steel, which is magnetic or of austenitic stainless steel that is not magnetic. The difference in the properties of these two kinds of stainless steel is due to their atomic structure and the amount of iron they contain (*Scientific American*, 2006).

Safety Precautions

- Keep electronic media, and credit cards away from magnets, as magnets can destroy information on them. Also, keep magnets away from computer and television screens and antique watches, as magnetism can damage them. Don't use strong magnets like neodymium magnets as they can also disrupt pacemakers and other electronic devices.

- Magnets must be treated with care so as not to destroy their magnetic effects. Magnets can be destroyed by dropping them, exposing them to extreme heat, or storing two magnets of the same type together.

Engage

Ask students to select a finished assignment they are proud of. Give each student a refrigerator magnet or a magnetic pushpin (available at office supply stores). Direct students to post their papers in the classroom using the object you just gave them. Students will try to find surfaces to which the magnet will stick in order to hold up the papers. After all papers are posted, conduct a class discussion about what students noticed and what they wondered as they were completing this task. Student comments could be recorded on a We noticed . . . We wonder Chart.

Explore

Hold up a magnet. Ask: *What kinds of things will stick to the object you were given? How could you find out?* Have the class work in small groups of 3 or 4 students. It would be best if each student in the group had a different type of magnet.

Give each small group of students a bag of materials, some of which are attracted to magnets and some that are not. Instruct students to sort the objects into two piles, according to which objects they predict will stick to the object they were given earlier (a magnet) and which will not. When groups have made their predictions, have them plan an investigation to figure out which objects in the bag stick to the object they were given initially. Remind students to record their predictions and findings in their science notebook in a way that makes sense to them, so they can refer back to their notes later.

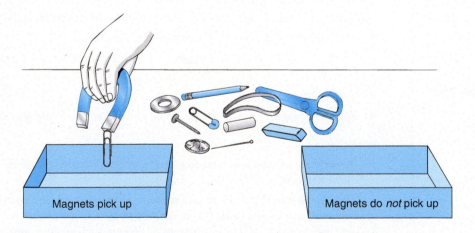

Explain

Ask: *Does anyone know the name of the object they have been using to test the objects in the bag?* (A magnet.) *What have you discovered that magnets do? Are all magnets the same?* (No, they come in different shapes and sizes, but the same things stick to all of them.)

Ask: *How accurate were your predictions? Were you surprised by any objects you tested?* (Students might mention the aluminum nail or the brass fastener.) *Are there any metal objects in the things-that-don't-stick group? What do you think is the difference between the metal objects in the "will stick" and "won't stick" piles?* (Lead the class to the conclusion that some metals are magnetic (attracted to a strong magnet) and others are not.)

Elaborate

Make a chart titled *Objects in the Bag That Contain Iron.* List all of the objects in the bags that are attracted to magnets. Each object listed will include ferrous iron in their composition. (The children don't need to know that!) Post the chart and suggest that the class compare their findings from the explore phase of the lesson with this list. Challenge students to figure out what testing materials with a magnet can tell them about the material's composition.

Evaluate

To check for understanding about which objects are attracted to magnets, ask students to answer the following questions in their science notebook:

1. Where did you post your paper in the classroom? Why did you put it there?
2. Describe and draw a picture of at least 3 magnets. How are they alike? How are they different?
3. What types of things will magnets stick to or will stick to magnets?
4. How could you find other objects in the room that contain iron?
5. How will you know that those objects contain iron?

Activity 2: How can electrical conductors be identified?

Grade: 5, Physical Sciences

Framework Context	
Scientific and Engineering Practices	**Planning and Carrying Out Investigations** Students need opportunities to design investigations so that they can learn the importance of such decisions as what to measure, what to keep constant, and how to select or construct data collection instruments that are appropriate to the needs of an inquiry (NRC, 2012, p. 60). **Analyzing and Interpreting Data** As they engage in scientific inquiry more deeply, they [students] should begin to collect categorical or numerical data for presentation in forms that facilitate interpretation, such as tables and graphs (NRC, 2012, p. 63).
Crosscutting Concepts	**Patterns** It is important for students to develop ways to recognize, classify, and record patterns in the phenomena they observe (NRC, 2012, p. 86).
Disciplinary Core Idea	**PS1:** Matter and Its Interactions
Component Idea	**PS1.A:** Structure and Properties of Matter
Conceptual Understanding	**By the end of grade 5:** Measurements of a variety of properties . . . can be used to identify particular materials (NRC, 2012, p. 108).

Performance Expectation 5-PS1-3

Make observations and measurements to identify materials based on their properties (NGSS Lead States, 2013, p. 43). www.nextgenscience.org/pe/5-ps1-3-matter-and-its-interactions

Learning Target

The electrical conductivity of materials can be observed and measured.

Success Criteria

The students will:

1. Describe the essential properties of an electrical conductor.
2. Explain how to test objects and materials to determine if they are good electrical conductors.
3. Predict whether a given material is an electrical conductor or insulator, based on other observed properties.
4. Design and carry out an investigation to rank the electrical conductivity of at least 5 materials.

Materials

- Batteries (D-cells)
- Bulbs (for battery circuits)
- Wires
- Bulb holders
- Battery holders
- Diverse array of conducting and nonconducting (insulating) materials including paper, cloth, wood, plastics, and metals of different kinds
- Safety goggles
- Light probes and data collection software (optional)

Safety Precautions

Wear safety goggles when handling wires. Their ends are sharp and could damage the eyes. Model appropriate wearing of goggles as a teacher during the engage phase of the lesson.

If, when testing a conductor, the wire, battery, or material being tested gets hot, immediately disconnect the circuit to stop the flow of electricity and prevent accidental burns.

Engage

Display a battery, a bulb, and a wire arranged in a complete circuit so the bulb lights. Then put down the wire. Ask: *If I didn't have a wire, do you think I could complete this circuit with some other object or material so the bulb would light?*

Explore

Make available to each cooperative group a diverse array of conducting and nonconducting (insulating) materials. Provide safety goggles for each students. Instruct students to use the test circuit illustrated to find out which materials could be substituted for the wire and which materials could not.

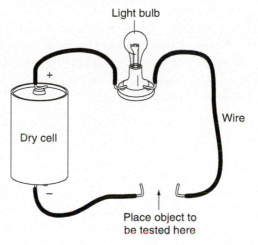

Light bulb

Wire

Dry cell

Place object to be tested here

Students should realize, based on their work with circuits in fourth grade, that they should place the test object (made of metal, cloth, wood, plastic, etc.) between the bare ends of the two pieces of wire as shown. If the bulb lights, then electricity flows easily through that material, so it could be substituted for a wire. If the bulb does not light, then electricity does not flow easily through the material, so it would not be a good substitute for a wire.

Design and use a data table in which to record your findings.

Explain

Ask students to share their findings with the rest of the class. They will probably report that the bulb lit when they tested some of the materials and did not light when they tested other materials. As students describe their findings, summarize the class data on the board using a T-chart with the headings *Bulb Lights* and *Bulb Does Not Light*.

Through discussion, lead children to understand that some materials will conduct electricity. Others will not. Materials that conduct electricity well are called *conductors*. If conductors are substituted for wires, the circuit will be complete and the bulb will light. Materials that do not conduct electricity well are called *insulators* or *nonconductors*. If insulators or nonconductors are substituted for wires, the circuit will not be complete and the bulb will not light.

Ask: *What types of materials are good conductors of electricity?* (Metals.) *How do you know?* (The bulb lights when metals are tested.) *Can you tell which of the metals you tested is the best conductor? How? What types of materials are good insulators of electricity?* (Nonmetals.) *How do you know?* (The bulb does not light when nonmetals are tested.)

Provide an opportunity for students to find and read resources online, in textbooks, and/or in other books that provide additional information about electrical conductors and insulators. Ask them to find statements that support what they discovered during the explore and explain phases of the lesson. Challenge each student to locate at least three "new facts" or "interesting examples" related to electrical insulators and conductors and why they are important in today's world. These should be written on separate index cards for posting on a bulletin board. Later, students can organize these ideas into logical groups and then have a discussion about the ideas presented and how they relate to what they found when testing objects and materials in class.

Elaborate

Challenge students to design and carry out an investigation to place at least 5 materials in order based on electrical conductivity. Most groups will do something related to the brightness of the bulb when the material is placed in the test circuit. If they have access to light probes, they may want to measure the brightness of the bulb. They may want to build multiple testers so they can see all of the bulbs simultaneously and rank order them based on how they look. Through an internet search, they may find other techniques for comparing the brightness of bulbs. Try to accommodate their need for additional materials and equipment.

Evaluate

To assess student understanding about conductors and insulators of electricity, have students respond to the following items:

1. How can you determine if a material is a good conductor or a good insulator of electricity?

2. From the objects/materials you tested, identify at least 3 that were good conductors and at least 3 that were good insulators. What evidence enabled you to classify them?

3. Predict which of these items is a good conductor of electricity. (Display or give each student a new collection of conductors and insulators to consider. Do not give students the testing device. They are only to make predictions.) On what evidence did you base your prediction?

4. Explain the procedure you used to put 5 materials in order according to how well they conduct electricity. Present your results in a data table.

Activity 3: How can their properties help you identify mineral samples?

Grade: 5, Physical Sciences

Framework Context	
Scientific and Engineering Practices	**Planning and Carrying Out Investigations**
	As [elementary students] engage in scientific inquiry more deeply, they should begin to collect categorical or numerical data for presentation in forms that facilitate interpretation, such as tables and graphs. When feasible, computers and other digital tools should be introduced as a means of enabling this practice (NRC, 2012, p. 63).
	Analyzing and Interpreting Data
	At the elementary level, students need support to recognize the need to record observations—whether in drawings, words, or numbers—and to share them with others (NRC, 2011, p. 63).
Crosscutting Concepts	**Patterns**
	It is important for students to develop ways to recognize, classify, and record patterns in the phenomena they observe. For example . . . they can investigate the characteristics that allow classification . . . of materials (e.g., wood, rock, metal, plastic) (NRC, 2012, p. 86).
Disciplinary Core Idea	**PS1:** Matter and Its Interactions
Component Idea	**PS1.A:** Structure and Properties of Matter
Conceptual Understanding	**By the end of grade 5:** Measurements of a variety of properties (e.g., hardness, reflectivity) can be used to identify particular materials (NRC, 2012, p. 108).

Performance Expectation 5-PS1-3

Make observations and measurements to identify materials based on their properties (NGSS Lead States, 2013, p. 43). www.nextgenscience.org/pe/5-ps1-3-matter-and-its-interactions

Learning Target

Minerals can be identified based on their properties.

Success Criteria

The students will:

1. Observe and record the color of various mineral samples.
2. Carry out investigations to identify the observed color, streak color, texture, luster, and transmission of light of various mineral samples.
3. Organize data into a table and analyze similarities and differences among various mineral samples.
4. Use resources to find the names of the minerals they have investigated.
5. Identify three mineral samples they have previously investigated, and recognize a sample that they have not investigated.

Materials

For each group:

- Kits of mineral samples, including such minerals as feldspar, calcite, fluorite, gypsum, graphite, hematite, hornblende, magnetite, mica, and quartz (with identifying numbers 1–12 on the samples [e.g., in each kit the feldspar sample is labeled 1, etc.])
- Index card
- Document camera to project student and group work onto a screen or blank wall
- Copies of Mineral Properties Chart
- Streak plates
- Colored pencils or crayons
- Penlights or flashlights

Engage

Display a set of minerals. If possible, use a document camera to project an image of them onto a screen or a blank wall to enhance viewing by all students. Ask: *What are some ways these minerals are different from each other?* Make a list of the properties suggested for the class to refer to later.

Tell the class: *You will investigate some properties of minerals using a set of samples like these.*

Ask: *How can the way a mineral feels be used to identify the mineral? What are some words that describe the way a mineral feels?* (smooth, rough, rounded edges, and soapy)

Hold a shiny mineral sample in the beam of light coming from an overhead projector or a flashlight; rotate it so it sparkles when viewed by the class. Ask: *What are some words you can use to describe the way light reflects from the surface of this mineral?*

Explore 1: Color

Point out that one of the properties the class mentioned was color. Explain that in this first investigation they will carefully observe each sample and record information about the property of color for each of the minerals in their kit. Distribute kits of minerals and a sheet of paper to each small group of students. On a sheet of paper, each small group should display their data about mineral colors in an organized fashion. Let them know that they will have an opportunity to show their data to the class using the document projector.

Tell the class how much time is available to complete this task. (Ten minutes is probably sufficient.) Circulate through the classroom as students work, encouraging group collaboration.

Explain 1: Color

When time is up, have groups share their mineral sample color data with the class, using the document projector if possible. Encourage the class to discuss the ways each group's data was similar and different and the possible reasons for those findings. (There may be differences in observed color for a given sample number from group to group due to variations among samples of the same mineral.) The organization of the data will probably be different from group to group. Conduct a group discussion about the features of an organized presentation of data. Ask: *Do you think you would organize your data differently if you included other properties in addition to mineral color? If we plan to compare data from each group, would it be helpful to all organize our data on the same table? Why or why not?*

Point out differences in details of the descriptions presented by the groups. Ask: *In what ways might these details be helpful in identifying another sample that was the same mineral as one you have tested? Are there any ways the details might not be helpful?*

Ask: *Does just looking at the color of a mineral give you enough information to identify it?* (Not really.) Explain that while observed color was the first property used to describe the minerals, the observed color of a mineral is not a conclusive clue to its identity, because different samples of the same mineral may have different colors, and different minerals may appear the same color. *Was there more than one black mineral sample in your kit?* (Yes.)

Ask: *Are there other properties of minerals that might help us distinguish one from another?* Suggest that students refer to the list made at the beginning of the lesson, if assistance is needed. Tell the class that, since they will be collecting data about several other properties of minerals, you have prepared a Mineral Properties Table for everyone to use. Distribute the tables to the class and display one using the document camera, if possible. Ask students to describe how to use this table; if they aren't sure, show them how to copy their mineral color data into the column labeled Observed Color. Give students a few minutes to transfer their group data to the Observed Color column of the table, while checking their work for understanding.

Begin a Class Mineral Properties Table representing a summary of the group data. This can be done on a blank Mineral Properties Table sheet under the document camera or as a large version of the chart drawn on the board. The purpose of this class table is to represent all of the groups' data, not just a consensus. Encourage students to suggest how this could be done. For example, if four groups indicated that Sample 8 was brown, one group indicated that Sample 8 was reddish-brown, and one group indicated that Sample 8 was black; on the shared Class Mineral Properties Table the data could be recorded as:

| Brown (4) |
| Reddish-brown (1) |
| Black (1) |

in the cell at the intersection of the Observed Color column and Mineral Sample #-8 row. Students should *not* change the data on their tables to match the class table. The class table simply points out the variety in the observations, if any exists.

Mineral Properties Table						
Mineral Sample #	Observed Color	Streak Color	Texture	Luster	Light Transmission	
1						
2						
3						
4						
5						
6						
7						
8						
9						
10						
11						
12						

Nature of Science

Ask: *Why should we record descriptions of rocks and minerals in a chart?* Explain that building a chart of mineral properties is a way to organize data. Charts of mineral properties help us to summarize observations and identify unknown minerals. Other ways to organize data and information include data tables, graphs, and classification systems. Scientists use all of these ways to display data in order to make it easier to analyze or to make sense of it.

Explore 2: Streak

Tell the class they will now test each mineral by scratching it on a streak plate and then record information about the color of the streak produced by each mineral. Provide each small group with a mineral kit and two streak plates. Demonstrate how one stroke of the mineral across the porcelain plate will usually produce a streak.

Remind students to record their streak color observations in the appropriate row and column of the table for each mineral. Inform the class of how much time they will have to complete this task, and give them that time to work. Monitor their progress and provide scaffolding as needed.

Explain 2: Streak

Ask: *Did the streak test help in any way to tell the black minerals apart?* (The streaks of the black minerals aren't the same, so they help tell the black samples apart.)

Tell the class that the color of the powdered form of a mineral is more consistent than its observable color. Geologists obtain powdered forms of minerals by wiping them across a streak plate. That mineral property, called *streak,* is described in terms of the color of the streak of powdered mineral that is left on the streak plate.

Give groups a chance to share their streak data and represent it appropriately on the Class Mineral Properties Table. Ask: *Was the streak color data more consistent than observed color data, as expected?* Encourage students to discuss why or why not this was the case. Groups may even need to compare streaks for similarity in color to see if they look the same but just were described differently.

Explore 3: Texture

Have students feel each mineral and record their descriptions in the Texture column of their charts. Encourage them to use as much detail as possible in their descriptions. As you monitor their work, suggest that they discuss their ideas as a small group.

Explain 3: Texture

Ask students to describe how they determined the texture of their samples. Discuss whether they found this task easy or difficult and why they felt that way. Give groups a chance to share their texture data and represent it appropriately on the Class Mineral Properties Table.

Explore 4: Luster

Darken the classroom and provide a penlight or flashlight to each group. Suggest that they place the mineral samples on the desktop and then shine the light on each mineral sample and observe how the light reflects from the surface of the mineral. Within groups, encourage students to suggest words that describe how minerals look in the light before entering observations in their Mineral Properties Tables.

If clarification of the kinds of adjectives used to describe luster is needed, find examples in the classroom to illustrate the concept of luster: Compare similar colors of patent leather (shiny) to regular leather (dull, silky), or compare the appearance of various types of white paper (copy paper, glossy paper, tissue, paper towel, etc.). This mini-lesson is intended to let students know that though a sample may still appear brown and round under the light, neither brown nor round are adjectives used to describe a mineral's luster.

Once the class has a better grasp on the type of adjectives that might describe luster, have them describe their samples' luster in their own words in the Luster column of their mineral properties table. Let them know how long they have to complete this task.

Explain 4: Luster

Collect descriptions of luster from the groups and display them on the class chart. There might be a variety of descriptive words suggested. The subtle differences between sparkly and glittery are not important to geologists; simply describing different ways that light reflects from the surface of a sample is their goal.

Tell students that *luster* refers to the way a mineral's surface reflects light. Explain that some minerals have a metal-like luster and are called *metallic.* Other minerals are *nonmetallic.* Some terms you could use to describe the nonmetallic luster of a mineral might be *dull, glassy, waxy, pearly,* and *shiny.* Write the italicized words on the board for future reference. Revisit the students' words and see if any of them are synonyms for the terms geologists typically use to describe luster.

Explore 5: Light Transmission

Challenge students to determine if and how well light passes through their mineral samples. Many will shine a light toward their face and then hold a mineral sample between the light source and their eyes; others will shine a light on a surface, like a desktop or a wall, hold a mineral sample in the beam of light, and look for shadows on the surface. Tell students to make a data table about their discoveries on a sheet of scratch paper. Let the class know at what time you expect them to finish this exploration.

Explain 5: Light Transmission

Ask students to report and discuss their findings. Then introduce or review (if they should have learned this previously) the terms scientists use to describe materials that transmit different amounts of light. Explain and demonstrate with a flashlight and common kitchen materials that materials can be: *transparent,* like clear plastic wrap, letting most of the light pass through them; *translucent,* like waxed paper, letting some of the light pass through them; or *opaque,* like aluminum foil, with no light shining through.

Instruct the class to decide whether each mineral sample was transparent, translucent, or opaque, then have them record the scientific term to describe the light transmission of each sample in the proper column of their Mineral Properties Tables.

Elaborate

Label the heading space of the right column of the Mineral Properties Table "Name of Mineral." Use library and Internet resources to find the names of the mineral samples, and then write mineral names in the proper row of the chart.

Consider creating a narrowed resource, like a webquest or focused mineral identification guide that includes only the 12 minerals in the set being investigated, for students to use if they are overwhelmed by the use of broader resources.

Evaluate

During the explore phases, interact with cooperative groups and look over their Mineral Properties Tables periodically to formatively assess their abilities to observe and describe properties of different minerals. During the elaborate phase, check the accuracy of students' identification of the mineral samples. If some have incorrectly identified minerals, point out the inaccuracies and have them reconsider their research and conclusions.

As a summative assessment, give each student four unlabeled mineral samples and an index card. One sample should be a mineral not included in the set of minerals that were studied earlier; the other three samples should be minerals that are included on the original sets. Note that the four samples are not necessarily the same for each student. Allow each student to use his or her completed Mineral Properties Table to determine the name of three of the minerals and to identify the one that is new.

Have each student:

- write his or her name near one edge of the index card
- fold the card once vertically and once horizontally to form four sections
- tape one mineral sample into each section
- write the names of the three minerals that were part of the original set in the corresponding sections
- write "new" in the section containing the sample that was not part of the original set of minerals

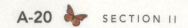

Activity 4: How do the tiny particles that make up pure substances move in different states of matter?

Grades: 6–8, Physical Sciences

Framework Context	
Scientific and Engineering Practices	**Developing and Using Models** More sophisticated types of models should increasingly be used across the grades, both in instruction and curriculum materials, as students progress through their science education. The quality of a student-developed model will be highly dependent on prior knowledge and skill and also on the student's understanding of the system being modeled, so students should be expected to refine their models as their understanding develops. Curricula will need to stress the role of models explicitly . . . so that students come to value this core practice and develop a level of facility in constructing and applying appropriate models (NRC, 2012, p. 59).
Crosscutting Concepts	**Patterns** One major use of pattern recognition is in classification, which depends on careful observation of similarities and differences; objects can be classified into groups on the basis of similarities of visible or microscopic features or on the basis of similarities of function. Such classification is useful in codifying relationships and organizing a multitude of objects or processes into a limited number of groups (NRC, 2012, p. 85). By middle school, students can begin to relate patterns to the nature of microscopic and atomic-level structure . . . (NRC, 2012, p. 86). **Scale, Proportion, and Quantity** From a human perspective, one can separate three major scales at which to study science: (1) macroscopic scales that are directly observable; that is, what one can see, touch, feel, or manipulate; (2) scales that are too small or fast to observe directly; and (3) those that are too large or too slow. Objects at the atomic scale, for example, may be described with simple models, but the size of atoms and the number of atoms in a system involve magnitudes that are difficult to imagine (NRC, 2012, p. 89). **Systems and System Models** An explicit model of a system under study can be a useful tool not only for gaining understanding of the system but also for conveying it to others (NRC, 2012, p. 92). **Structure and Function** For students in the middle grades, the concept of matter having a submicroscopic structure is related to properties of materials; for example, a model based on atoms and/or molecules and their motions may be used to explain the properties of solids, liquids, and gases . . . (NRC, 2012, p. 98).
Disciplinary Core Idea	**PS1:** Matter and Its Interactions
Component Idea	**PS1.A:** Structure and Properties of Matter
Conceptual Understanding	**By the end of grade 8:** Gases and liquids are made of molecules or inert atoms that are moving about relative to each other. In a liquid, the molecules are constantly in contact with each other; in a gas, they are widely spaced except when they happen to collide. In a solid, atoms are closely spaced and vibrate in position but do not change relative locations. Solids may be formed from molecules, or they may be extended structures with repeating subunits (e.g., crystals) (NRC, 2012, pp. 108–109).

Performance Expectation MS-PS1-4

Develop a model that predicts and describes changes in particle motion, temperature, and state of a pure substance when thermal energy is added or removed (NGSS Lead States, 2013, p. 56).

www.nextgenscience.org/pe/ms-ps1-4-matter-and-its-interactions

Learning Target   Particles of a pure substance are arranged and behave (move) differently depending on their state of matter.

Success Criteria   *The students will:*

1. Collect data about the arrangement and behavior of particles in examples of three different states of matter from a simulation (model) that provides molecular-level detail, organize the data, make generalizations from it, and use their data chart as a reference to support their engagement in science discourse.

2. Work collaboratively in a small group to plan, construct, share, explain, and defend their own model to represent their ideas about general differences in the position and motion of the tiny particles (atoms and molecules) in different states of matter.

Materials   *For the class:*

- A clear, tightly sealed, 1-gallon plastic bag filled with air
- A clear, tightly sealed, 1-gallon plastic bag mostly filled with water
- A clear, tightly sealed, 1-gallon plastic bag mostly filled with wooden beads or blocks
- Assorted model-making materials, including: representations of particles (i.e., marbles, coins, beads, beans, cereal) and containers for the models (i.e., plastic or paper plates, petri dishes, vials, small jars, small boxes)

For each small group of students:

- A computer with access to the Internet

For each student:

- A pencil
- A science notebook

Preparation

- Go to the PhET Interactive Simulations home page produced by the University of Colorado Boulder: http://phet.colorado.edu. Look over the website's features, then under the How to Run Simulations tab, select On Line. Under Simulations, select Chemistry, then General Chemistry; scroll down through the alphabetically listed thumbnails until you find States of Matter: Basics, then select it.

- Look over the information on the States of Matter: Basics title page; then under the heading Tips for Teachers, select and read the teacher's guide (pdf). Return to the States of Matter: Basics title page, then select the green Run Now! button. The screen that appears is the workspace for this simulation!

- For this activity, only the first tab (farthest to the left at the top of the screen) should be used.

- To save class time, before your students arrive, check the computers the students will use to be sure that an up-to-date version of Java is installed; then follow the instructions you used above to try out the simulation so that it will run smoothly when the class is ready to gather data from this animated model.

Engage   Invite three students to the front of the room, give each of them one of the tightly sealed plastic bags, and ask them to hold up their bags so all can see them. Ask the class: *What do the contents of these bags exemplify?* Hopefully, some students will recognize that each bag contains a different state of matter. Ask the class to suggest the term that scientists use for the state of matter that mostly fills each bag; each suggestion should be directed to one of the bag holders. The bag holder being addressed then writes the term as a heading on the board near where he or she is standing. If several terms are suggested for the same bag holder, for example, water and liquid, he or she should write them on the board. After the brainstorming is done, let the class have a brief discussion to reach consensus about the proper words to use to identify the states of matter. Have the three bag holders indicate that these are the terms that scientists use for states of matter by circling that term. If other terms are examples of matter in that state, they should be labeled as examples. If some terms simply don't belong, just erase them quietly.

Ask: *What was it about the contents of each bag that convinced you, just by looking, that it was an example of that state of matter?* Holding up the bag with the beads or blocks, ask: *What was it about the contents of this bag that made you think it holds solids?* Holding up the bag of air, ask: *What was it about the contents of this bag that convinced you to say it is filled with a gas?* Holding up the bag that is mostly filled with water, ask: *Why did you decide that this bag contains a liquid?*

Explore

Tell the class: *Today you will use a computer simulation in a small group to explore the behavior of particles that are too tiny to be observed directly in four different pure substances in each of the three states of matter. Please create a table in your science notebook to organize the data you collect. You only need to use the controls in the gray area on the right side of the computer screen to get the needed information to complete the chart. Look carefully for everything that changes as you make different selections for the atoms and molecules and the state they are in.*

After you observe arrangements and motions and other information, record your findings in the proper cells of your chart using words and/or pictures. Once you have information for each state of each substance in the simulation, then look over your data and write a generalization about the behavior of particles when matter is in that particular state. You may speak quietly in your small group to refine your ideas and thinking before you write about it.

(Consider providing templates similar to the one that follows for any students who still need scaffolding in order to effectively record data in a usable manner.)

Name of Substance	State of Matter		
	Solid	Liquid	Gas
Neon			
Argon			
Oxygen			
Water			

Explain

Invite students to bring their data to a meaning-making discussion. Ask students to talk about their generalizations and the evidence that supports their thinking. Encourage students to follow appropriate norms for scientific discussion and argumentation.

Consider the students' ideas and the information about the grade band endpoint that appears in the *Frameworks* context box that appears at the beginning of the lesson. Assist your students in reaching consensus for the generalization statements for each state of matter.

Encourage students to discuss the reasons that computer simulation provides a useful model for considering the arrangement and motion of the tiny particles that make up a substance. Talk about how the models used in the simulation help us understand at least certain parts of what is really happening, but certain parts of the model might not really apply to reality, i.e., the colors of the atoms in the animations.

Elaborate

Challenge the students to work in small groups to create models that illustrate their three generalization statements. They may use the materials available to the class to make physical models, act out the motions of the particles using classmates in a role play, or create a drawing (a two-dimensional model) to make a model that effectively describes their generalizations.

Each group will be asked to present their model and explain why they consider it to be an effective model for communicating the ideas they were trying to get across to their classmates.

Evaluate

You could informally assess students' achievement of Success Criterion 1 by monitoring group work, looking over the data charts they created based on information provided by the computer simulation during the explore phase of the lesson, and noticing how effectively learners use their recorded data to support science talk during the explain phase of the lesson.

In order to assess Success Criterion 2, work with your class to develop an analytic rubric that identifies three or four criteria that should be considered when assessing the models and accompanying presentations developed in the elaborate phase of the lesson. For each criterion, describe the level of work expected for each component for four levels of achievement: Expert, Proficient, Emergent, Novice. Provide the rubric to groups to guide their preparation of their presentations, and specify the amount of time they have to share and explain their models. Be sure that each group has a copy of the rubric to refer to in order to guide their work in planning, completing, practicing, and delivering their information.

Provide students with sticky notes, and following each group presentation, have students each write a brief, positive message to that group about their model and/or presentation. Remind students to focus on the work, not the people involved. With practice, middle schoolers can learn to provide positive feedback to their peers.

After all groups have presented, if time allows, provide time for more science talk about the models that were produced and in what ways they were effective.

Activity 5: How does heating or cooling affect air in a container?

Grade: 2, Physical Sciences

Framework Context	
Scientific and Engineering Practices	**Constructing Explanations** Early in their science education, students need opportunities to engage in constructing and critiquing explanations. They should be encouraged to develop explanations of what they observe when conducting their own investigations and to evaluate their own and others' explanations for consistency with the evidence (NRC, 2012, p. 69).
Crosscutting Concepts	**Cause and Effect: Mechanism and Explanation** In the earliest grades, as students begin to look for and analyze patterns . . . in their observations of the world . . . and also begin to consider what might be causing these patterns and relationships and design tests that gather more evidence to support or refute their ideas (NRC, 2012, p. 88).
Disciplinary Core Idea	**PS1:** Matter and Its Interactions
Component Idea	**PS1.B: Chemical Reactions** [though this activity simply lays the groundwork for the study of this broad topic.]
Conceptual Understanding	**By the end of grade 2:** Heating or cooling a substance may cause changes that can be observed (NRC, 2012, p. 110).

Performance Expectation 2-PS1-4
Construct an argument with evidence that some changes caused by heating or cooling can be reversed and some cannot (NGSS Lead States, 2012, p. 16). www.nextgenscience.org/pe/2-ps1-4-matter-and-its-interactions

Learning Target
Heating or cooling air may cause an effect that can be observed.

Success Criteria
The students will:

1. Develop generalizations about how warming or cooling affects air.
2. Predict the ways an inflated balloon will change if it is cooled in a freezer for an hour, and explain their reasoning.

Materials

For each student:

- Safety goggles (to protect eyes from splashes or popped bubbles)

For each small group:

- Liquid soap solution about 2 cm deep in a pie pan (without holes) or plastic dish
- Ice water in a deep container
- Test tube, medicine vial, and/or a small juice can
- Paper towels (for cleanup and hand drying)
- Cafeteria tray or basin (to contain spills)

For the class:

- Balloon
- Empty 2-liter soda bottle

- Basin of hot water
- Basin of cold water (use ice water with the ice removed for best results)
- Liquid soap solution supply (4 liters of water, 170 ml dishwashing soap, 40 ml glycerin [available in pharmacies or from chemical supply companies])
- Large empty can, with the top removed

Safety Precautions   When working with materials that could splash, both teachers and students should wear safety goggles.

Engage

Place the basins of hot and cold water on a demonstration table. Don't let the students know what is in the basins. Partially inflate the balloon and stretch the open end over the open mouth of the 2-liter bottle. Hold up the balloon/bottle system for the class to see. With a flourish, as if presenting a magic trick, lower the bottle into the tub of cold water. Ask the amazed children to talk about what they observe. Then, lower the bottle into the tub of hot water. Encourage the children to discuss their new observations.

Ask: *What do you think made the balloon on the bottle change? Was it really magic? What do you think is inside of the bottle and balloon system?* (Air.) *What do you think is in each basin?*

Do not indicate whether the students' ideas are correct or incorrect; they will make some discoveries on their own during the explore phase of the lesson.

Explore

Squirt some liquid soap into a large container of water with a wide opening at the top. Stir the water. Dip the open end of a test tube, medicine vial, or small juice can into the soapy water so that a soap film forms across the end of the container. Challenge students to get the soap film to expand. One way to get the soap film to expand is for students to wrap their hands around the container (without squeezing) so that their hands cover as much of the container as possible.

Ask: *What do you observe?*

Get a soap bubble on a small container, such as a test tube or medicine vial. Put the container in the container of ice water. Ask: *What happens to the soap bubble?*

Explain

Ask: *Were you able to change the shape of the soap film? How? Why did the soap bubble expand when you held the container in your hands? Why did the soap bubble go down into the container when you placed the container in ice?*

Through their explorations, the students should note that when they hold the container in their hands, the air in the container is heated and the soap film expands, becomes dome-shaped, and eventually pops. When they place the container in the ice water, the bubble film bends into the container, because the air in the container contracted when it became cold, and it took up less space, pulling the bubble film into the container until it breaks.

Through discussion of their observations and explanations of why the changes occurred, lead students to understand this principle about heat and air pressure:

Air expands (takes up a greater volume) when it is heated. Thus, air in a closed container exerts more pressure on its container when it is heated. Air contracts (takes up a smaller volume) when it is cooled. Thus, air in a closed container exerts less pressure on its container when it is cooled.

Elaborate

Obtain a large can, such as a vegetable can from the school cafeteria. Dip the open end of the can into soap solution in order to form a soap film over the open end of the large can. Let several students wrap their hands around it to see if they can get the soap film to expand. Ask children to describe what they see and to explain why it happens.

Evaluate

To assess if students can apply the principles they have been investigating to a new situation, have them answer the following questions:

1. You blow up a red balloon so that it is 40 cm around its widest part. Then you put the balloon into the freezer for an hour. What do you predict will be true about the balloon immediately after it is taken out of the freezer compared to before it was placed in the freezer?

2. For each pair of answers below, circle the answer you predict to be true.

The balloon will be blue.	The balloon will be red.
The air in the balloon will be colder.	The air in the balloon will be warmer.
The balloon will be larger.	The balloon will be smaller.
The balloon's circumference will be less than 40 cm.	The balloon's circumference will be more than 40 cm.
The air in the balloon is exerting more pressure on the balloon.	The air in the balloon is exerting less pressure on the balloon.

3. Then write an explanation of why you expect the changes you have circled.

Activity 6: What are the distinguishing properties of common white powders?

Grade: 5, Physical Sciences

Framework Context	
Scientific and Engineering Practices	**Planning and Carrying Out Investigations** At all levels, they [students] should engage in investigations that range from those structured by the teacher—in order to expose an issue or question that they would be unlikely to explore on their own (e.g., measuring specific properties of materials)—to those that emerge from students' own questions (NRC, 2012, p. 61).
Crosscutting Concepts	**Patterns** It is important for students to develop ways to recognize, classify, and record patterns in the phenomena they observe. For example . . . they can investigate the characteristics that allow classification . . . of materials (e.g., wood, rock, metal, plastic) (NRC, 2012, p. 86).
Disciplinary Core Idea	**PS1:** Matter and Its Interactions
Component Idea	**PS1.A:** Structure and Properties of Matter
Conceptual Understanding	**By the end of grade 5:** Measurements of a variety of properties . . . can be used to identify particular materials (NRC, 2012, p.108).
Component Idea	**PS1.B:** Chemical Reactions
Conceptual Understanding	**By the end of grade 5:** When two or more different substances are mixed, a new substance with different properties may be formed; such occurrences depend on the substances and the temperature (NRC, 2012, p. 110).

Performance Expectations 5-PS1-3

Make observations and measurements to identify materials based on their properties (NGSS Lead States, 2013, p. 43). www.nextgenscience.org/pe/5-ps1-3-matter-and-its-interactions

5-PS1-4

Conduct an investigation to determine whether the mixing of two or more substances results in new substances (NGSS Lead States, 2013, p. 43). www.nextgenscience.org/pe/5-ps1-4-matter-and-its -interactions

Learning Target

Common white powders can be identified based on their properties and reactions in chemical tests.

Success Criteria

The students will:

1. Use simple tools and instruments that extend the senses to gather data.
2. Carry out chemical indicator tests to determine how different powders react with water, iodine, and vinegar.
3. Accurately record and analyze data.
4. Use data to draw conclusions.

Materials

For each pair or small group of students:

- Small quantities of salt, granulated sugar, baking soda, cornstarch, and flour
- Dropper
- Plastic spoon
- Resealable bag (large enough to hold recording chart)
- Hand lenses (magnifiers)

- Toothpicks
- Safety goggles
- Small labeled containers of water, vinegar, and iodine
- Copies of recording chart
- Black marker

Safety Precautions

- Students and any adults in the room should wear safety goggles for these investigations with powders.
- Students must not taste any of the powders or liquids.
- Students should wash their hands after they test each powder.
- Dispose of extra dry powders in the trash; do not put powders in the sink as they may clog drains.

Engage

Ask: *How are sugar and salt different? How are they alike? If you have several white powders, how can you tell them apart?* Encourage all students to share their ideas.

Tell the students they will be observing some powders with a magnifier and doing chemical tests, acting like scientists (e.g., forensic chemists) to see what happens when different indicators (water, vinegar, and iodine) are added to different powders.

Explore

Distribute a data table sheet, a plastic bag, and a black marker to each pair or small group of students. Instruct them to use the black marker to color in the blank cells on the row labeled *Visual*; then place that data table sheet into the plastic bag and seal it for use as a *lab tray*. Each test, described by the row and column headings, will take place in a specific cell on the lab tray. Explain that they will be doing one test (one row on the lab tray) at a time. Demonstrate how they should conduct tests directly on the lab tray; placing a small amount (about 1/4 tsp) of powder in the column headed with the powder's name.

Tell students to use the other data table to record their findings through writing and/or drawing. Explain that for each test, they should record their observations in the cell that corresponds to the cell on the lab tray. They should check the row and column headings on the record sheet to confirm that they are recording the data in the right place. The data table provides a record of observations and experiments that they can refer to later.

Briefly go over the tests that they will be conducting before distributing the rest of the materials. To prevent spills and/or random mixing, you may limit the liquids that they have to what they need to do the tests on each row separately. Model the wearing of safety goggles during the tests involving liquids to set a good example for the class.

Visual observation. Place a small spoonful of each powder in the proper cell of the visual test row. Use a hand lens to visually observe each powder. Describe and draw the appearance of the magnified powder in the appropriate cell of the data table.

Water tests. Place a small spoonful of each powder in the water test row on the lab tray (plastic bag with record sheet inside). Add several drops of water and mix with a toothpick to see what happens. Observations should be recorded in the data tables.

Iodine tests. Place a small spoonful of each powder in the iodine test row of the lab tray. Add a drop or two of iodine to each powder and write down the results in their data tables. Caution the students to be careful. Iodine must not be tasted and can stain hands and clothing.

Vinegar tests. Place a small spoonful of each powder in the vinegar test row of the lab tray. Add a drop or two of vinegar to each powder and write down the results in their data tables.

Explain

Compare. Discuss the properties of the four powders that have been revealed through the different chemical tests. Help students to compare the results of their tests with the master chart of properties of white powders shown in the diagram. If necessary, ask students to repeat tests to see what happens.

Properties of White Powders				
Observations	Powder 1 Granulated Sugar	Powder 2 Table Salt	Powder 3 Baking Soda	Powder 4 Cornstarch
Visual (Magnifying Glass)	White crystals	White box-shaped crystals	Fine white powder	Fine yellowish-white powder
Water Test	Dissolves in water	Dissolves in water	Turns water milky	Makes water cloudy
Iodine Test	Turns yellow with iodine	No reaction with iodine	Turns yellow-orange with iodine	Turns red, then black with iodine
Vinegar Test	Dissolves in vinegar	No reaction with vinegar	Fizzes with vinegar	Gets thick, then hard with vinegar

Elaborate

Ask: *If you had a mixture of powders, how could you find out what is in the mixture?*

Give each pair or small group of students small samples of a mixture of two white powders, flour and one of the original white powders. Be sure to keep track of which mixture each group gets. Do not tell the students what each mixture contains.

Ask: *What powders are these?* Challenge children to determine if each powder is one they have encountered previously, and if so, which one. (Children would not have studied the properties of flour.) Ask: *What is the evidence for your conclusions?*

Clean Up. Students should throw away plastic bags and toothpicks, return powders and test supplies to teacher-designated spot, and clean and dry anything dirty, including their hands. Caution students not to put any of the powders in the sink since they can clog drains.

Evaluate

Let students present and discuss their procedures and their conclusions. Ask students to explain the basis for their conclusions. Use the following checklist as an assessment tool to monitor the quality of the presentations:

- Explained their procedure clearly
- Conducted tests with the mixture in the same way as with single powders previously
- Referred to data table of properties of single powders
- Used that data as evidence of conclusion
- Stated conclusion clearly
- Recognized that the other powder in the mixture must be a powder not yet studied
- Correctly identified the powder that they had previously studied that was in their mixture

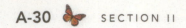

Activity 7: How do salt crystals form?

Grades: 6–8, Physical Sciences

Framework Context	
Scientific and Engineering Practices	**Asking Questions and Defining Problems** Students at any grade level should be able to ask questions of each other about the texts they read, the features of the phenomena they observe, and the conclusions they draw from their models or scientific investigations (NRC, 2012, p. 56). **Planning and Carrying Out Investigations** At all levels, they should engage in investigations that range from those structured by the teacher—in order to expose an issue or question that they would be unlikely to explore on their own (e.g., measuring specific properties of materials)—to those that emerge from students' own questions (NRC, 2012, p. 61). **Obtaining, Evaluating, and Communicating Information** Students should be able to interpret meaning from text, to produce text in which written language and diagrams are used to express scientific ideas, and to engage in extended discussion about those ideas (NRC, 2012, p. 76).
Crosscutting Concepts	**Structure and Function** By the middle grades, students begin to visualize, model, and apply their understanding of structure and function to more complex or less easily observable systems and processes (e.g., the structure of water and salt molecules and solubility, Earth's plate tectonics). For students in the middle grades, the concept of matter having a submicroscopic structure is related to properties of materials; for example, a model based on atoms and/or molecules and their motions may be used to explain the properties of solids, liquids, and gases or the evaporation and condensation of water (NRC, 2012, pp. 97–98).
Disciplinary Core Idea	**PS1:** Matter and Its Interactions
Component Idea	**PS1.B:** Structure and Properties of Matter
Conceptual Understanding	**By the end of grade 8:** Solids may be formed from molecules, or they may be extended structures with repeating subunits (e.g., crystals) (NRC, 2012, p. 109).

Performance Expectation MS-PS1-1   Develop models to describe the atomic composition of simple molecules and extended structures (NGSS Lead States, 2013, p. 56). www.nextgenscience.org/pe/ms-ps1-1-matter-and-its-interactions

Learning Target   Solids, such as sodium chloride, may be extended structures with repeating subunits (crystals).

Success Criteria   *The students will:*

1. Conduct an investigation in order to observe the formation of salt crystals from a saltwater solution.

2. Develop questions related to the formation of salt crystals and find answers to those questions through research and/or investigations.

3. Communicate information to answer questions related to the formation of salt crystals.

Materials
- Salt
- Tablespoons
- Jar lids or petri dish bases

- Small paper cups (3 oz.)
- Magnifying lenses
- Water
- String
- Digital microscope (optional)
- Sentence strips
- Markers
- Masking tape
- Safety goggles
- Access to library and Internet resources

Engage

Guide students to examine a grain of table salt through a magnifying lens. If a digital microscope is available, use it to show the class salt grains under higher magnification by displaying the image on a TV or computer monitor or projecting it onto a screen. Ask: *What do you see? What does a salt grain look like? What are crystals? How are crystals formed?*

Explore

Guide students to conduct these activities within their cooperative groups and to record the answers to the following questions in their science notebooks:

1. Obtain a tablespoon of salt, a jar lid, a small glass of water, and a piece of string about 30 cm long. Mix the salt into the glass of water. Stir the water well. Let the solution stand for a few minutes until it becomes clear.

   Ask: *What happens to the salt?*

2. Very gently pour some of the salt solution into the jar lid. Put a piece of string in the solution, letting one end hang out, as in diagram (a). Let the solution stand for several days where the lid will not be disturbed.

   Ask: *What do you predict will happen to the salt solution?*

3. After several days have passed, use your magnifying lens to look at the materials in the lid. Lift the string out of the jar lid. Examine the string with your magnifying lens. Describe what you see with the hand lens. See diagram.

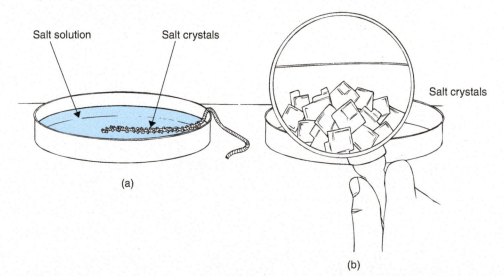

Explain

Bring students together for a whole-class discussion about their findings. Have each group describe and show their results to the class. Ask: *How are the materials in the lid different from your original salt solution? Why do you now have a solid when you started out with a liquid? What name could you give to the formations in the lid?*

   Tell the class: **Crystals** *are nonliving substances found in nature that are formed in various geometrical shapes. These are crystals of* **halite,** *the mineral we use for table salt.*

Ask students to share and defend their ideas about the crystal formation they observed. Points that should emerge from the discussion include: Salt was dissolved in the water in the lid; when the salt water stood for several days, the water evaporated, leaving behind crystals of salt.

Elaborate

Challenge each student in the class to brainstorm at least three questions they have about table salt, halite, or the process of evaporative crystal formation. Each question should be written legibly in marker on a separate sentence strip.

Tape the questions to the classroom wall or the board; then, with help from the class, move identical or similar questions together into clusters. (You may quietly remove any off-topic or inappropriate questions at this time.) Ask the class how these questions could be answered. Lead the students into a discussion about the difference between questions that require scientific investigations to answer and those that could be answered through library or Internet research.

With the students working in pairs, let them select a question from the board to investigate further. Provide access to pertinent library and Internet resources. A browser search for "formation of halite" returned many useful sites.

Each student pair should prepare a short paper and/or presentation describing their findings about the question they selected. Collaboratively developing a rubric for the product of this research will ensure that students understand your expectations, and you will be aware of their concerns. One criterion you might want to include is that they relate their findings to the explore phase of this activity.

Evaluate

Allow time for all students to share the product of their research—what they learned that helped to answer their selected question and how they found those answers. Use the rubric to guide scoring.

Activity 8: How do you balance an equal-arm balance?

Grade: 3, Physical Sciences

Framework Context	
Scientific and Engineering Practices	**Using Mathematics and Computational Thinking** Increasing students' familiarity with the role of mathematics in science is central to developing a deeper understanding of how science works. A significant advance comes when relationships are expressed using equalities first in words and then in algebraic symbols—for example, shifting from distance traveled equals velocity multiplied by time elapsed to $s = vt$. Students should have opportunities to explore how such symbolic representations can be used to represent data, to predict outcomes, and eventually to derive further relationships using mathematics (NRC, 2012, p. 66). **Constructing Explanations and Designing Solutions** The goal for students is to construct logically coherent explanations of phenomena that incorporate their current understanding of science, or a model that represents it, and are consistent with the available evidence (NRC, 2012, p. 52).
Crosscutting Concepts	**Systems and System Models** Students' thinking about systems in terms of component parts and their interactions, as well as in terms of inputs, outputs, and processes, gives students a way to organize their knowledge of a system, to generate questions that can lead to enhanced understanding, to test aspects of their model of the system, and, eventually, to refine their model (NRC, 2012, p. 93). Students' models should incorporate a range of mathematical relationships among variables (at a level appropriate for grade-level mathematics) and some analysis of the patterns of those relationships (NRC, 2012, p. 94).
Disciplinary Core Idea **Component Idea** **Conceptual Understanding**	**PS2:** Motion and Stability: Forces and Interactions **PS2.A:** Forces and Motion **By the end of grade 3:** An object at rest typically has multiple forces acting on it, but they add to give zero net force on the object. Forces that do not sum to zero can cause changes in the object's speed or direction of motion (Boundary: Qualitative and conceptual, but not quantitative addition of forces are used at this level) (NRC, 2012, p. 115).

Performance Expectation 3-PS2-1

Plan and conduct an investigation to provide evidence of the effects of balanced and unbalanced forces on the motion of an object (NGSS Lead States, 2013, p. 25). www.nextgenscience.org/pe/3-ps2-1 -motion-and-stability-forces-and-interactions

Learning Target

The number and position of weights on an equal-arm balance determine whether it will balance.

Success Criteria

The students will:

1. Use these qualitative rules to predict and explain balance on an equal-arm balance:

   Symmetry rule. Equal weights at equal distances will balance [see diagram (a)].

   Relational rule. Heavier weights close in can balance lighter weights farther out [see diagram (b) and diagram (c)].

2. Demonstrate and explain that balance occurs when the product of weights and distances on one side of the pivot equals the product of weights and distances on the other side of the pivot.

Science Background

An equal-arm balance is a system consisting of a crossbar pivoted in the center and weights that can be placed at different positions on each side of the bar, as is shown in the diagram. The amount of each weight and its distance from the central pivot point are the relevant factors in determining balance.

Materials   Equal-arm balance with hanging weights (masses) for each pair or small group of students (Plastic equal-arm balances are often referred to as *math balances*).

Engage   Ask: *What affects the balance of an equal-arm balance scale? How can you predict accurately whether a balance will be level?*

Explore   Distribute balances to your students. Give the children the following balance problems, one at a time. Allow ample time for students to work on each problem and discuss their findings before giving the next one. Be noncommittal about patterns they may discover.

1. Place two weights at the second peg from the center on the left side of the balance. Leaving the left side always the same, find at least three different ways to balance the crossbar by adding weights to a peg on the other side. (You can use as many weights as necessary, but be sure to add weights to only one peg at a time on the right side, not to two or three pegs.) Use drawings, words, or data columns to show what you did. Tell your teacher what you did to balance the crossbar.

2. Start with two weights on the left side at the third peg from the center. Find at least four ways to balance the crossbar. (Remember, you can use as many weights as necessary, but be sure to add weights to only one peg on the right side, not to two or three pegs.) Write down what you did and show your work to your teacher.

3. Start with four weights at the third peg on the left side. How many ways can you find to balance the crossbar? (Remember to add weights from only one peg at a time on the other side.)

4. Set up your own combinations of weights and distances on one side of the balance and use your developing knowledge to predict what might be done to the other side to produce balance.

Explain   Ask: *What did you do to balance the crossbar? Can you find patterns in the different ways you found to balance the crossbar? How can you test to determine if the pattern you found is a general one, applying in all cases?*

Through discussion, lead your students to understand the following balance patterns or rules:

Symmetry rule. Equal weights at equal distances will balance [see diagram (a)]

Relational rule. Heavier weights close in can balance lighter weights farther out [see diagram (b) and diagram (c)]

Both of these rules are qualitative or nonnumerical rules. They are understood by most upper elementary children, but they may not be stated explicitly.

Elaborate   Depending on math competency and grade level, some students *may* be ready to use formal mathematics to coordinate weights and distances. Differentiate instruction for students who do not yet have the mathematical skills required for this stage of the lesson.

Challenge students to work with their data from step *b* to find a mathematical rule for the balance, a rule involving doing something with the actual numbers.

The mathematical rule for the balance is:

$$(W_L) \times (D_L) = (W_R) \times (D_R)$$

where W = weights, D = distances, L = left side, and R = right side of the balance. Thus, the product of the weight and distance on one side is equal to the product of weight and distance on the other side.

Lead students to try this rule for themselves, using the data from different trials. If the crossbar is balanced, the products of the weights and distances on the left side will always equal the products on the right side for each of these three cases.

Interestingly, this rule applies even if weights are placed on more than one peg on each side. Then, the sum of the weights multiplied by their distances on one side must equal the sum of the weights multiplied by their distances on the other side.

Evaluate

Use these or similar multiple-choice items to assess the students' understanding of the principles related to equal-arm balances.

For all students:

1. If one blue weight is near the pivot on the left side of the balance and one blue weight is near the end of the beam on the right side of the balance:

   A. The beam will be level (balanced).

   B. The right side of the beam will be lower than the left side of the beam.

   C. The left side of the beam will be lower than the right side of the beam.

2. If three blue weights are at the end of the left side of the beam and two blue weights are at the end of the right side of the beam:

   A. The beam will be level (balanced).

   B. The right side of the beam will be lower than the left side of the beam.

   C. The left side of the beam will be lower than the right side of the beam.

3. Which of the following is *not* a true statement about the balance?

   A. Equal weights at equal distances will balance.

   B. Equal weights at different distances will not balance.

   C. A heavier weight far out can balance a lighter weight close in.

   D. A lighter weight far out can balance a heavier weight close in.

   E. Different weights at equal distances will not balance.

Only for students who investigated the balance quantitatively:

4. On the right side of the balance beam there is a 10-gram weight on the second peg from the pivot point. Where should you put a 5-gram weight to make the beam balance?

   A. On the second peg from the pivot point on the left side of the balance beam

   B. On the fourth peg from the pivot point on the left side of the balance beam

   C. On the fifth peg from the pivot point on the left side of the balance beam

   D. On the 10th peg from the pivot point on the left side of the balance beam

5. The right side of the balance beam has a 5-gram weight on the 10th peg from the pivot. The left side of the balance beam has a 10-gram weight on the sixth peg from the pivot. Which statement best describes the position of the balance beam?

   A. It is level.

   B. The right side is up.

   C. The left side is up.

Answer Key: (1. B; 2. C; 3. D; 4. B; 5. B)

Activity 9: Can magnets interact with objects through different materials?

Grade: 3, Physical Sciences

Framework Context	
Scientific and Engineering Practices	**Asking Questions** Students should ask questions of each other about the features of the phenomena they observe and the conclusions they draw from scientific investigations (NRC, 2012, p. 56). **Planning and Carrying Out Investigations** At all levels, students should have opportunities to plan and carry out investigations . . . that emerge from students' own questions (NRC, 2012, p. 61). **Constructing Explanations** Scientific explanations link scientific theory with specific observations; i.e., they may describe the mechanisms that support cause and effect inferences about them (NRC, 2012, p. 67). Students should be encouraged to develop explanations of what they observe when conducting their own investigations and to evaluate their own and others' explanations for consistency with the evidence (NRC, 2012, p. 69).
Crosscutting Concepts	**Cause and Effect:** Mechanism and Explanation Argumentation starting from students' own explanations of cause and effect can help them appreciate standard scientific theories that explain the causal mechanisms in the systems under study. Strategies for this type of instruction include asking students to argue from evidence when attributing an observed phenomenon to a specific cause (NRC, 2012, p. 89).
Disciplinary Core Idea	**PS2:** Motion and Stability: Forces and Interactions
Component Idea	**PS2.B:** Types of Interactions
Conceptual Understanding	**By the end of grade 3:** Magnetic . . . forces between a pair of objects do not require that the objects be in contact—for example, magnets push or pull at a distance. The sizes of the forces . . . depend on the properties of the objects and their distances apart and, for forces between two magnets, on their orientation relative to each other (NRC, 2012, p. 117).
Disciplinary Core Idea	**PS3:** Energy
Component Idea	**PS3.C:** Relationship Between Energy and Forces
Conceptual Understanding	**By the end of grade 3:** Magnets can exert forces on other magnets or on magnetizable materials, causing energy transfer between them (e.g., leading to changes in motion) even when the objects are not touching (NRC, 2012, p. 127).

Performance Expectation 3-PS2-3

Ask questions to determine cause-and-effect relationships of electric or magnetic interactions between two objects not in contact with each other (NGSS Lead States, 2013, p. 25). www.nextgenscience.org/pe/3-ps2-3-motion-and-stability-forces-and-interactions

Learning Target

Magnetic forces act through most materials, although the magnetic interaction decreases with the thickness of the materials.

Success Criteria

1. Recognize that magnetism acts through most materials.
2. Investigate how the strength of the magnetic interaction varies with distance.

Materials

- Magnets (a variety of kinds, if possible)
- Paper clips

- Variety of materials—paper, cardboard, plastic, glass, aluminum foil, steel, wood, clipboard, etc.
- Books

Engage

Ask: *Will magnets work through paper and other materials? How do you know? How could you find out?*

Explore

Ask students to investigate if a magnet will attract a paper clip through different materials. Remind them to record their procedures and findings in their science notebooks so they can refer to their notes later. If possible, be sure that each member of a group is using a different type of magnet.

Students should try a variety of materials with various thicknesses if possible. If students don't think of trying multiple layers of materials on their own, you might say: *I see the magnet worked through one sheet of paper. Does it work through two sheets? . . . three sheets?*

Explain

Ask: *What did you find out about magnetic forces acting through various materials?* Facilitate a class discussion about their observations. Encourage students to provide evidence for their claims.

Ask: *Why do you think we got such a variety of results?* (We didn't all have the same magnets. Different magnets were different strengths. The thicknesses of the materials we tested were different.)

The discussion should lead to the idea that the strength of the magnetic interaction decreases with the thickness of the material or maybe just with the distance between the magnet and the paper clip. Lots of new questions related to this topic will probably emerge.

Elaborate

Challenge students to investigate one of the questions that they still have about magnets acting through materials, such as:

- *How many pages of a book can magnets act through?*
- *Does the material matter or is it just the thickness of the material (or the space between the magnet and the paperclip)?*
- *Which magnet acts through the greatest thickness?*

In their science notebooks, students should record the question they are investigating and a description of the procedures they used. Suggest that they develop a chart on which to record their data, and, if appropriate, they might even graph their data to make it easier to analyze. Finally, each group should present a summary of their investigation and their finding to the class.

Evaluate

Develop rubrics to guide evaluation of (1) written work in their science notebooks and (2) the group presentations. Sharing the rubrics with the students before they start their investigation can give them a clear idea of your expectations.

Activity 10: What happens when two ring magnets interact?

Grade: 3, Physical Sciences

Framework Context	
Scientific and Engineering Practices	**Asking Questions** Students should ask questions of each other about the features of the phenomena they observe and the conclusions they draw from scientific investigations (NRC, 2012, p. 56). **Planning and Carrying Out Investigations** At all levels, students should have opportunities to plan and carry out investigations . . . that emerge from student's own questions (NRC, 2012, p. 61). **Constructing Explanations** Scientific explanations link scientific theory with specific observations; i.e., they may describe the mechanisms that support cause and effect inferences about them (NRC, 2012, p. 67). Students should be encouraged to develop explanations of what they observe when conducting their own investigations and to evaluate their own and others' explanations for consistency with the evidence (NRC, 2012, p. 69).
Crosscutting Concepts	**Cause and Effect:** Mechanism and Explanation By the upper elementary grades, students should have developed the habit of routinely asking about cause-and-effect relationships in the systems they are studying, particularly when something occurs that is, for them, unexpected. The question "What conditions were critical for that (attraction or repulsion between ends of bar magnets) to happen?" relates to cause and effect (NRC, 2012, p. 89).
Disciplinary Core Idea **Component Idea** **Conceptual Understanding**	**PS2:** Motion and Stability: Forces and Interactions **PS2.B:** Types of Interactions **By the end of grade 5:** Magnetic . . . forces between a pair of objects do not require that the objects be in contact—for example, magnets push or pull at a distance. The sizes of the forces . . . depend on the properties of the objects and their distances apart and, for forces between two magnets, on their orientation relative to each other (NRC, 2012, p. 117).

Performance Expectation 3-PS2-3
Ask questions to determine cause-and-effect relationships of electric or magnetic interactions between two objects not in contact with each other. *Clarification Statement:* . . . examples of a magnetic force could include the force between two permanent magnets . . . (NGSS Lead States, 2013, p. 25). www.nextgenscience.org/pe/3-ps2-3-motion-and-stability-forces-and-interactions

Learning Target
The interactions between two permanent ring magnets depend on their orientation and their distance apart.

Success Criteria
The students will:

1. Correctly use the terms *force, attract,* and *repel* to describe the interactions between magnets.
2. Realize that magnets can exert forces at a distance, that is, without touching the object being pushed (repelled) or pulled (attracted).
3. Develop questions about magnetic interactions based on their exploration, design and conduct investigations to answer their questions, and discuss their findings with the class.

Materials
For each group of students:

- Three or four ring magnets
- A pencil

Engage
Ask: *How do two ring magnets interact with each other?*

Explore
Give each pair or small group of students three or four ring-shaped magnets. Ask the students to find out what happens when magnets interact. Suggest that they record their observations and new questions on an I notice, I wonder chart.

Allow time for exploration. If necessary, challenge students to try:

- using one magnet to move another magnet without the two magnets touching; and

- placing several ring magnets over a pencil in different ways to see what happens.

Explain
Ask: *What did you do to test how the magnets interact? What did you find out about how the two magnets interact?* Building on the children's activities, use discussion and expository teaching to help them understand the terms *attract, repel,* and *force* in the context of magnetic interactions.

- When two magnets or a magnet and an object pull or stick together, we say they attract.
- When two magnets push apart, we say they repel.
- A force is a push or a pull. We can see some forces, such as when you push someone in a swing. Some forces, such as magnetic forces, are invisible and act without direct contact between objects.
- Magnets can attract or repel each other. When two magnets come together, there is a force of attraction. When two magnets push apart, there is a force of repulsion.

Ask: *What did you wonder about as you explored?* Collect the questions by writing them on the board or on chart paper.

Elaborate
Tell students: *In your group, select one of the questions you still wonder about. Design an investigation that will help you answer that question. Carry out your investigation. Then, prepare a poster showing what you found out.*

Evaluate
Give each group a copy of the rubric so they have a clear idea of the expectations for their poster:

Rubric

Exemplary: Poster —

- Includes all components of Proficient
- Is very neat, easy to read, and well organized

Proficient: *Poster includes —*

- Clear statement of the question being investigated
- Clear statement of your procedure
- Clear statement of what you found out
- Correct use of the terms *attract, repel,* and *force*

Developing: *Poster includes —*

- At least two of the components of Proficient

Needs Improvement: *Poster includes —*

- Fewer than two of the components of Proficient

Activity 11: How do the ends of bar magnets interact with each other?

Grade: 3, Physical Sciences

Framework Context	
Scientific and Engineering Practices	**Constructing Explanations** Scientific explanations link scientific theory with specific observations; i.e., they may describe the mechanisms that support cause and effect inferences about them (NRC, 2012, p. 67). Students should be encouraged to develop explanations of what they observe when conducting their own investigations and to evaluate their own and others' explanations for consistency with the evidence (NRC, 2012, p. 69). **Engaging in Argument from Evidence** Students can begin by constructing an argument for their own interpretation of the phenomena they observe. They need instructional support to go beyond simply making claims—that is, to include reasons or references to evidence and to begin to distinguish evidence from opinion (NRC, 2012, p. 73).
Crosscutting Concepts	**Cause and Effect: Mechanism and Explanation** By the upper elementary grades, students should have developed the habit of routinely asking about cause-and-effect relationships in the systems they are studying, particularly when something occurs that is, for them, unexpected. The question "What conditions were critical for that (attraction or repulsion between ends of bar magnets) to happen?" relates to cause and effect (NRC, 2012, p. 89).
Disciplinary Core Idea **Component Idea** **Conceptual Understanding**	**PS2:** Motion and Stability: Forces and Interactions **PS2.B:** Types of interactions **By the end of grade 5:** Magnetic . . . forces between a pair of objects do not require that the objects be in contact—for example, magnets push or pull at a distance. The sizes of the forces . . . depend on the properties of the objects and their distances apart and, for forces between two magnets, on their orientation relative to each other (NRC, 2012, p. 117).

Performance Expectation 3-PS2-3

Ask questions to determine cause-and-effect relationships of electric or magnetic interactions between two objects not in contact with each other. *Clarification Statement:* . . . examples of a magnetic force could include the force between two permanent magnets . . . (NGSS Lead States, 2013, p. 25). www.nextgenscience.org/pe/3-ps2-3-motion-and-stability-forces-and-interactions

Learning Target

Like poles of bar magnets repel and unlike poles of bar magnets attract.

Success Criteria

The students will:

1. Correctly use the terms *force*, *attract*, and *repel* to describe the interactions between the ends of two magnets.
2. Develop a way to determine like poles of unmarked magnets.
3. Identify evidence that supports the claim that like poles of magnets repel and unlike poles attract.

Materials

- Bar magnets (3 for each small group)
- Masking tape
- Red and blue crayons
- Ring magnets
- Horseshoe magnets

Preparation   Place masking tape over the ends of the bar magnets so the N-pole and S-pole designations are obscured.

Engage   Ask: *How do bar magnets interact with each other? How could we find out?*

Explore   Provide each group with three identical bar magnets with taped ends. Challenge the students to find a way to determine which ends of the magnets are the same or alike. Give the class plenty of time to explore. Encourage students to discuss their reasoning within their groups and support their claims about which ends are the same with evidence.

Explain   Ask: *What did you find out?* The students should arrive at the idea that if the ends of two magnets are the same, then they interact in the same way with the end of the third magnet. For example, if the ends of two magnets both attract the same end of a third magnet, the ends of the first two magnets must be the same or alike. Tell children to use red and blue crayons to designate the like ends of the three magnets.

Say to the class: *Now that you know which ends of the magnets are alike and which are unlike, can you "find a pattern that describes" or "make a claim about" how like and unlike ends of magnets interact?*

Through exploration, discussion, and productive questioning, encourage students to provide evidence to support the following claim:

- When two magnets are brought together, like ends repel (push one another apart), while unlike ends attract (pull one another together).

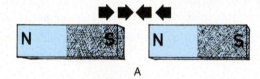

Elaborate   Ask the students to determine if this claim holds with other types of magnets, such as ring-shaped or horseshoe magnets. Provide appropriate magnets and adequate time for student groups to design and carry out their investigations and discuss their findings with the class.

Evaluate   To check for student understanding about the interaction of the ends of magnets, have them answer the following items:

Fill in the blanks, so that the following sentences are true.

1. When like ends of magnets are brought close together, they _____.

2. When unlike ends of magnets are brought close together, they _____.

Activity 12: What evidence reveals the presence of magnetic fields?

Grades: 6–8, Physical Sciences

Framework Context	
Scientific and Engineering Practices	**Asking Questions and Defining Problems** Students at any grade level should be able to ask questions of each other about the texts they read, the features of the phenomena they observe, and the conclusions they draw from their models or scientific investigations (NRC, 2012, p. 56).
Crosscutting Concepts	**Patterns** . . . it is important for [students] to develop ways to recognize, classify, and record patterns in the phenomena they observe (NRC, 2012, p. 86).
Disciplinary Core Idea **Component Idea** **Conceptual Understanding**	**PS2:** Motion and Stability: Forces and Interactions **PS2.B:** Types of Interactions **By the end of grade 8:** Forces that act at a distance (. . . magnetic) can be explained by force fields that extend through space and can be mapped by their effect on a test object (. . . a magnet . . .) (NRC, 2012, p. 118).

Performance Expectation MS-PS2-5

Conduct an investigation and evaluate the experimental design to provide evidence that fields exist between objects exerting forces on each other even though the objects are not in contact (NGSS Lead States, 2013, p. 59). www.nextgenscience.org/pe/ms-ps2-5-motion-and-stability-forces-and-interactions

Learning Target

Iron filings can make magnetic fields visible.

Success Criteria

The students will:

1. Demonstrate procedures for mapping magnetic fields.
2. Describe variations in the strength of a magnetic field.
3. Use the concept of magnetic force fields to explain how magnetic forces act at a distance.

Materials

- Magnets (bar, and other types)
- Iron filings
- Food storage bags
- Digital camera (optional)
- Magnetic compasses

Preparation

Sprinkle iron filings into a large, transparent, food storage bag so that a thin layer covers about three-fourths of the area of one side of each bag. Prepare a bag for each cooperative group of students.

Engage

Ask: *How do you think magnets will interact with the material in this storage bag?*

Explore

Ask students, working in small groups, to explore what happens when a magnet touches or is brought near a bag containing iron filings. Give students these instructions:

- Spread an iron filings bag out flat on your desk. Do not open the bag. Tap the bag lightly so that the iron filings are evenly distributed. Slide a bar magnet under the bag. Tap the bag again so that the iron filings move about. (See the diagram.)

- Draw a diagram and/or capture a digital image to show what happened to the iron filings in the bag. Complete an I notice, I wonder chart about your explorations with a single bar magnet.
- Explore what happens to the iron filings in the bag when two bar magnets are placed end to end a few centimeters apart so that the magnets attract under the iron filings bag. Draw a diagram and/or capture a digital image showing the reaction of the iron filings. Complete an I notice, I wonder chart about your explorations with this arrangement of two bar magnets.
- Explore what happens to the iron filings in the bag when two bar magnets are placed end to end a few centimeters apart so that the magnets repel under the iron filings bag. Draw a diagram and/or capture a digital image showing the reaction of the iron filings. Complete an I notice, I wonder chart about your explorations with this arrangement of two bar magnets.
- If time allows, investigate one or more of the *I wonder Questions* your group developed using the materials available.

Explain

Encourage groups to share their findings and to look for and discuss similarities and differences in the patterns formed by the iron filings when a magnet or multiple magnets were under the bag. Facilitate discussion about what might have caused the patterns that were formed. Introduce the concept of a magnetic force field if it doesn't emerge from the conversation. Explain that the particles of iron become tiny magnets when they are in a magnetic field so they move (align) according to the magnetic lines of force in the field.

Ask: *What did you observe about the magnetic field around a single bar magnet? What did you observe about the magnetic field for attracting bar magnets? What did you observe about the magnetic field for repelling bar magnets? Do you think that parts of the magnetic field are stronger than other parts? What evidence supports your claim?*

Explain that all magnets have two regions where the magnetic interaction with other magnets or magnetic materials is strongest. If any groups investigated magnets that were not bar magnets, ask them to share their diagrams/images of the iron filings, so that this claim can be evaluated. These regions, where the magnetic field is strongest, are called *poles*. Point out that the concentration of iron filings is greatest at the poles of the magnets.

Take time to let groups share questions that emerged and that they investigated; encourage them to make meaning of their observations in the context of previous observations.

Elaborate

Replicate the positions of the magnet(s) and the bag of iron filings on the table from the explore phase of the lesson. This time, slowly move the compass slightly above the bag as you watch what happens to the compass needle when the compass is moved through different parts of the magnet's field. Develop an effective way to record your findings so you can share them later. Create an *I notice, I wonder chart* based on the discussion in your small group.

Refer to print and online resources to find answers to some of your *I wonder Questions*.

Evaluate

Ask each student group to create a Frequently Asked Questions (FAQ) list, with answers, about magnetic fields. You can decide the level of guidance to provide, i.e., specific questions that must be included, the number of questions to be included on the list, whether the answers to the questions should be based on findings from the activity, references, or both.

A related middle school activity may be accessed via the Enhanced Pearson eText. It is titled:
"How do compass needles interact with current-carrying wires?" and addresses the DCI Component Idea PS2.B.

Activity 13: What is an electromagnet, and how can you make one?

Grades: 6–8, Physical Sciences

Framework Context	
Scientific and Engineering Practices	**Obtaining, Evaluating, and Communicating Information** Students should write accounts of their work, using journals to record observations, thoughts, ideas, and models. They should be encouraged to create diagrams and to represent data and observations with plots and tables, as well as with written text, in these journals (NRC, 2012, p. 77).
Crosscutting Concepts	**Systems and System Models** Students should also be asked to create plans—for example, to draw or write a set of instructions for building something—that another child can follow (NRC, 2012, p. 93).
Disciplinary Core Idea	**PS2:** Motion and Stability: Forces and Interactions
Component Idea	**PS2.B:** Types of Interactions
Conceptual Understanding	**By the end of grade 8:** Electric and magnetic (electromagnetic) forces can be attractive or repulsive, and their sizes depend on the magnitudes of the charges, currents, or magnetic strengths involved and on the distances between the interacting objects (NRC, 2012, p. 117).
Disciplinary Core Idea	**PS3:** Energy
Component Idea	**PS3.C:** Relationship Between Energy and Forces
Conceptual Understanding	**By the end of grade 8:** . . . two magnetic and electrically charged objects interacting at a distance exert forces on each other that can transfer energy between the interacting objects (NRC, 2012, p. 127).

Performance Expectation MS-PS2-3

Ask questions about data to determine the factors that affect the strength of electric and magnetic forces. *Clarification Statement:* Examples of devices that use electric and magnetic forces could include electromagnets . . . (NGSS Lead States, 2013, p. 59). www.nextgenscience.org/pe/ms-ps2-3-motion-and-stability-forces-and-interactions

Learning Target

Electromagnets produce magnetic effects.

Success Criteria

The students will:

1. Construct an electromagnet based on observation of another electromagnet.
2. Write and draw diagrams to instruct others how to construct an electromagnet.
3. Demonstrate and describe the effect of an electromagnet on various iron-containing objects when circuit is complete and incomplete.

Materials

For each pair of students:

- D-cell
- Two 50-cm lengths of insulated (enameled) copper wire
- Iron filings in a sealed plastic bag
- 10 small paper clips
- Pair of wire strippers /cutters

For the class:

- Document camera, visual presenter, or video camera (optional)
- Projection screen or blank wall (optional)
- Extra D-cells
- Safety goggles for each student and the teacher

Engage

Show students examples of electromagnets used in industry. You might find the following YouTube videos to be useful: https://www.youtube.com/watch?v=BQA5VDXE7ts. https://www.youtube.com/watch?v=DB9F3pUlrxI.

Ask students: What seems to be happening in these videos? (Device picking up metal objects.) What forces do you think are involved? (magnetism, gravity) Could permanent magnets do this? (no) Why or why not? (Their magnetism can't be turned off, the materials it picked up wouldn't drop off.)

Since this is the engage phase of the lesson, remember you are not looking for "correct" answers, simply current thinking of the students. Ask: *How can we make an electromagnet?*

Safety Precautions

Do not let the wire and terminal remain in contact for more than a few seconds because

- intense heat builds up, and you could get a burn through the insulation; and
- the electrical energy in the battery will be used up quickly.

Wear safety goggles when working with wires. Their ends are pointy and are therefore a safety hazard for your eyes and the eyes of others.

Explore

1. Challenge students to build an electromagnet like the one shown. Be sure to explain the Safety Precautions to the class. Distribute materials to pairs of students.

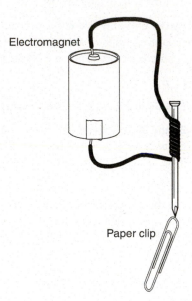

Electromagnet

Paper clip

2. Ask each student to create step-by-step instructions using words and drawings describing how to build an electromagnet. Once instructions are completed, tell students to exchange instructions with another student pair and then try to follow the written instructions to construct another electromagnet. Collaborate with the other pair of students to improve clarity of instructions.

3. Suggest that students find out what happens when they bring the nail close to the baggie with the iron filings or the pile of paper clips when the wires are connected to the D-cell and when they are not. Record observations in science notebook through words and drawings.

Explain

Ask: *What happens to the iron filings and the paper clip when the circuit is completed (or when the wire is touched to the battery)? What happens to the iron filings and the paper clip when the circuit is broken (or when the wire is removed from the battery)? What is the evidence that the nail became a magnet temporarily?*

Facilitate the discussion so that the class realizes that when a loop of wire is placed around an iron object and current runs through the wire, the system becomes an electromagnet. The electromagnetic effect is suddenly reduced when current no longer runs through the wire.

Elaborate

Extend the learning through another activity: "How Can You Increase the Strength of an Electromagnet?" This activity is available in a digital format if you are using the e-book version of this text.

Evaluate

Informally assess the students' conversation and actions as they build their electromagnets in small groups and listen carefully to the responses during discourse in the explain phase.

A related middle school activity may be accessed via the Enhanced Pearson eText. It is titled: "How can you increase the strength of an electromagnet?" and addresses the DCI Component Idea PS2.B

Activity 14: What factors affect the rate of swing of a pendulum?

Grade: 3, Physical Sciences

Framework Context	
Scientific and Engineering Practices	**Planning and Carrying Out Investigations** In the elementary years, students' experiences should be structured to help them learn to define the features to be investigated, such as patterns that suggest causal relationships (e.g., What features of a ramp affect the speed of a given ball as it leaves the ramp?). The plan of the investigation, what trials to make, and how to record information about them, then needs to be refined iteratively as students recognize from their experiences the limitations of their original plan. These investigations can be enriched and extended by linking them to engineering design projects—for example, how can students apply what they have learned? (NRC, 2012, p. 60)
Crosscutting Concepts	**Cause and Effect: Mechanism and Prediction** By the upper elementary grades, students should have developed the habit of routinely asking about cause-and-effect relationships in the systems they are studying, particularly when something occurs that is, for them, unexpected. The questions "How did that happen?" or "Why did that happen?" should move toward "What mechanisms caused that to happen?" and "What conditions were critical for that to happen?" (NRC, 2012, p. 89).
Disciplinary Core Idea **Component Idea** **Conceptual Understanding**	**PS2:** Motion and Stability: Forces and Interactions **PS2.C:** Stability and Instability in Physical Systems **By the end of grade 3:** A system can change as it . . . shifts back and forth (e.g., a swinging pendulum) . . . Examining how the forces on and within the system change as it moves can help to explain the system's patterns of change (NRC, 2012, p. 119).

Performance Expectation 3-PS2-2

Make observations and/or measurements of an object's motion to provide evidence that a pattern can be used to predict future motion (NGSS Lead States, 2013, p. 25). www.nextgenscience.org/pe/3-ps2-2-motion-and-stability-forces-and-interactions

Learning Target

The length of a pendulum determines both its period and its frequency. Its pattern of motion is predictable.

Success Criteria

The students will:

1. Demonstrate procedures for measuring the rate of a pendulum's swing.
2. Design controlled experiments to test hypotheses about factors that might affect the rate of a pendulum's swing.
3. Record, analyze, and draw accurate conclusions from data.

Science Background

A pendulum is a system involving something hanging from a fixed point, which when pulled back and released swings back and forth. A tire hanging on a rope from a strong tree branch is an example of a pendulum you might find in a backyard. The weight at the bottom of a pendulum is called a **bob**. The force of gravity and the inertia of the bob due to its motion keep it swinging back and forth until all of its energy is lost to friction at the pivot point.

In 1602, Galileo Galilei noticed the regular motion of pendulums by observing swinging lanterns in a chapel. He realized that this regular motion would be useful for measuring time. The length of time it takes a pendulum bob to make one complete swing (from its release until it swings down and away then back to near the release point) is known as the *period* of the pendulum. The number of complete swings the pendulum bob makes in a certain length of time is known as the pendulum's *frequency*.

Students typically identify three variable factors that might affect the rate of swing or frequency of a pendulum: the weight of the pendulum bob, the angle at which it is released, and the length of the pendulum string. Determining which factors are indeed relevant requires that students conduct controlled investigations in which one factor at a time is varied and its effect on the rate of swing of the pendulum is determined, while the other two variables are controlled or left unchanged.

Surprisingly, only the length affects the rate of swing. Varying the weight of the pendulum bob or the angle at which the pendulum is released has no effect on its rate of swing.

Materials

- Stopwatch or watch with a second hand for each group; or clock with a second hand for the whole class
- Paper clips
- Pennies
- Ball of string
- Craft sticks with notched ends or pencils (to support the pendulums)
- Masking tape (to tape the pendulum support to a desk)

Preparation

For the demonstration that initiates the engage phase, tie a paper clip to one end of a long piece of string and insert one or more pennies into the paper clip. Suspend the pendulum from a craft stick by sliding the other end of the string into the notch of a tongue depressor as shown on the left side of the drawing. Students can adjust the length of string as needed by sliding it along the notch of the tongue depressor. Or tie the other end of the string around a pencil as shown on the right side of the drawing. Attach the craft stick or pencil so that the pendulum can swing freely and all students can observe its motion.

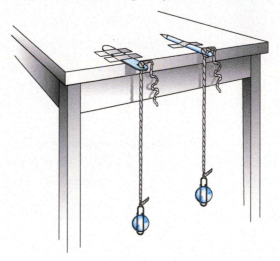

Engage

Show students the pendulum you prepared. Tell them that this system is known as a pendulum. Demonstrate what happens when you pull back the bob and release it. Ask: *Do all pendulums swing at the same rate, or do some swing slower or faster? How can you measure how fast a pendulum swings?*

Explore

Provide each cooperative group with the materials to make a pendulum similar to the one you demonstrated. Lead the students to count the number of swings of their pendulum in 15 seconds. Explain that this is called the rate of swing (or frequency) of the pendulum. Define a swing as one complete back-and-forth cycle.

Ask: *How can you get a pendulum to swing faster or slower (more or fewer swings in 15 seconds)?* Challenge the students to identify the things about their pendulum that they could possibly change.

After some discussion, ask students to focus on these three separate, measurable *variables* that might make a pendulum swing faster or slower:

1. Length of the pendulum
2. Weight or number of pennies that make up the pendulum bob
3. Angle at which the pendulum is released

Then tell them to design and conduct controlled experiments to answer the questions they have asked. If you think your class would benefit from having a template on which to record data, distribute copies of this chart.

Pendulum Data Table					
Does length affect the rate of swing of a pendulum?		Does weight affect the rate of swing of a pendulum?		Does the release angle affect the rate of swing of a pendulum?	
What variable did you manipulate?		What variable did you manipulate?		What variable did you manipulate?	
What variables did you control?		What variables did you control?		What variables did you control?	
What responding variable did you measure?		What responding variable did you measure?		What responding variable did you measure?	
Length of Pendulum	Rate (number of swings in 15 seconds)	Weight of Pendulum (number of pennies)	Rate (number of swings in 15 seconds)	Angle of Pendulum Release	Rate (number of swings in 15 seconds)
20 cm		1		small	
40 cm		2		medium	
60 cm		3		large	
What can you conclude about length and rate of swing?		What can you conclude about weight and rate of swing?		What can you conclude about the angle of release and rate of swing?	

This data table is not only a place for students to record measurements so they can remember them but also a "think sheet" that facilitates the planning and conducting of investigations, guides the students in recognizing relationships, and assists them in drawing conclusions.

Monitor students' experiments and provide assistance with the procedures, logic, and data interpretation for controlled experiments. Ask the students to record what they do and what they find out.

When students have had ample time to explore, help the class to standardize the way they measure weight, length, angle, and rate (number of back-and-forth swings in 15 seconds). At this time you should be ready to introduce the use of a data table like the one illustrated to help students organize their investigations, keep track of their data, and interpret their data to form conclusions.

Explain

Encourage students to share their findings as you facilitate a discussion about the factors that affect the rate of a pendulum.

If students have changed more than one variable at a time (for example, changing length and weight together), discuss with them the importance of experimental design. Ask: *Why must you change only one variable at a time when investigating? Why must other variables be kept constant?* (So you can be sure which of the variables really made a difference.)

Elaborate

Challenge students to notice pendulums in the world around them or find examples of pendulums in books or magazines or on the Internet. Grandfather clocks, swings, and trapezes are all forms of pendulums.

Evaluate

Assessment task for cooperative learning groups:

- Instruct students to create a pendulum that swings from one extreme to the other in one second (7.5 complete back-and-forth swings in 15 seconds). They should record the steps they followed to achieve their goal.

- Use the following rubric to assess levels of group performance in solving the task.

Exemplary:

- Includes all of the bullets from the Proficient Level.
- The pendulum's rate is exactly 7.5 complete back-and-forth swings in 15 seconds.

Proficient:

- The steps they followed were clearly described.
- They only varied the length of the string, since they knew that the mass of the bob and the angle of release do not affect the rate of the pendulum's swing.
- They referred to their data table from previous trials to estimate a reasonable string length to try.
- The pendulum's rate is between 7 and 8 complete back-and-forth swings in 15 seconds.

Developing:

- One or two of the bullets from the Proficient Level were not observed.

Little Understanding:

- No more than two of the bullets from the Proficient Level were observed.

Assessment task for individuals:

- Ask students to explain in writing: *How would you adjust a grandfather clock that was running too fast? too slow?* (Students should realize that the pendulum must be lengthened for the clock to slow down and shortened for the clock to run faster.)

Activity 15: What energy changes occur in a swinging pendulum system?

Grades: 6–8, Physical Sciences

Framework Context	
Scientific and Engineering Practices	**Developing and Using Models**
	Use [provided] computer simulations . . . as a tool for understanding and investigating aspects of a system, particularly those not readily visible to the naked eye (NRC, 2012, p. 58).
	Planning and Carrying Out Investigations
	. . . students also should have opportunities not only to identify questions to be researched but also to decide what data are to be gathered, what variables should be controlled, what tools or instruments are needed to gather and record data in an appropriate format, and eventually to consider how to incorporate measurement error in analyzing data (NRC, 2012, p. 61).
Crosscutting Concepts	**Systems and System Models**
	. . . it is often useful to conceptually isolate a single system for study. To do this, scientists and engineers imagine an artificial boundary between the system in question and everything else. They then examine the system in detail while treating the effects of things outside the boundary as either forces acting on the system or flows of matter and energy across it . . . (NRC, 2012, p. 92).
	As students progress, their models should move beyond simple renderings or maps and begin to incorporate and make explicit the invisible features of a system, such as interactions, energy flows, or matter transfers (NRC, 2012, p. 94).
Disciplinary Core Idea	**PS3:** Energy
Component Idea	**PS3.A:** Definitions of Energy
Conceptual Understanding	**By the end of grade 8:** Motion energy is properly called kinetic energy . . . A system of objects may also contain stored (potential) energy, depending on their relative positions. For example, energy is stored—in gravitational interaction with Earth—when an object is raised, and energy is released when the object falls or is lowered (NRC, 2012, p. 123).
Component Idea	**PS3.B:** Conservation of Energy and Energy Transfer
Conceptual Understanding	**By the end of grade 8:** When the motion energy of an object changes, there is inevitably some other change in energy at the same time (NRC, 2012, p. 125).
Component Idea	**PS3.C:** Relationship between Energy and Forces
Conceptual Understanding	**By the end of grade 8:** . . . when energy is transferred to an Earth-object system as an object is raised, the gravitational field energy of the system increases. This energy is released as the object falls; the mechanism of this release is the gravitational force (NRC, 2012, p. 127).

Performance Expectations MS-PS3-2

Develop a model to describe that when the arrangement of objects interacting at a distance changes, different amounts of potential energy are stored in the system. Clarification Statement: Emphasis is on relative amounts of potential energy, not on calculations of potential energy . . . Examples of models could include representations, diagrams, pictures, and written descriptions of systems (NGSS Lead States, 2013, p. 61). www.nextgenscience.org/pe/ms-ps3-2-energy

MS-PS3-5

Construct, use, and present arguments to support the claim that when the kinetic energy of an object changes, energy is transferred to or from the object (NGSS Lead States, 2013, p. 61). www.nextgenscience.org/pe/ms-ps3-5-energy

Learning Target As a pendulum swings, energy transfers between potential and kinetic energy.

Success Criteria *The students will:*

1. Describe through words and/or pictures the continual transfer of energy between kinetic and potential that occurs in a swinging, frictionless pendulum system in the context of the position and motion of that pendulum's bob.

2. Use their knowledge of the conservation of mechanical energy in an ideal (frictionless) pendulum system to determine the potential energy (PE) and kinetic energy (KE) of the system when the bob is at a different location, when they are given the PE of the system when the bob is initially released.

3. Write or select a question related to the level of friction acting on a pendulum system, design and conduct an experiment to answer that question, then present their investigation and findings to the class.

4. Describe at least three ways that the level of friction acting on the pendulum system affects its motion.

Materials *For the whole class:*

- A demonstration pendulum suspended from the ceiling (length of pendulum = 1.5 m, mass of pendulum bob = 0.5 kg)
- A T-chart graphic organizer for an *I notice, I wonder Chart,* drawn or projected on the board or chart paper

For each small group or pair of students:

- Computer with access to the Internet
- Exploration Guide

For each student:

- Pencil
- Science notebook

Preparation

- Go to the *PhET – Interactive Simulations Homepage* produced by the University of Colorado Boulder: **http://phet.colorado.edu**. Look over the website's features, then under the *How to Run Simulations* tab, select *On Line.* Then under *Simulations* select *Physics;* scroll down through the alphabetically listed thumbnails until you find *Pendulum Lab,* then select it.

- Look over the information on the Pendulum Lab title page, then under the heading *Tips for Teachers* select and read the *teacher's guide* (pdf). Return to the Pendulum Lab title page, then select the green *Run Now! Button.* The screen that appears is the workspace for this simulation!

- To save class time, before your students arrive open the simulation found at http://phet.colorado.edu from PhET Interactive Simulations, University of Colorado, on all of the computers they will use.

Engage Start the demonstration pendulum swinging by pulling the bob (the mass at the end of the string) away from its resting position, then releasing it. Have the class watch this moving system for about 30 seconds. Ask: *What do you think this system is called?* (Depending on their previous experience, some students may recognize that it is a *pendulum.*) Either confirm that it is called a pendulum or introduce the term *pendulum* for this type of swinging system. Ask: *How would you describe the parts of this pendulum?* (Students will probably say it has a long string, attached to the ceiling, and a heavy object [mass or weight] on the other end.) Tell them that the heavy object is called a *bob.*

Instruct the class to observe the swinging pendulum again, this time watching the motion of the bob. Start the pendulum swinging again as you did before and let the class watch how the bob moves for about 30 seconds. Then have them create an *I notice, I wonder chart* about the motion of the bob in their science notebooks. After several minutes, ask students to share their ideas with the class; write those ideas on the class *I notice, I wonder chart* for further reference.

Explore

Tell the class that they will have an opportunity to learn more about pendulums by using a computer simulation. Working in pairs or small groups (depending on the number of computers available), they will use the simulation to provide information to complete the Exploration Guide (which is included after the lesson description). Remind the class to (1) talk with their partner or the rest of the group about what they observe and the relationships they discover, and (2) write about their findings in their science notebook since they may refer to their notes during later discussions.

Explain

Bring the class together in a discussion circle and facilitate a class discussion about what they learned from their exploration of simulated pendulums. If the discussion lags, refer to the suggested questions that are included in the Exploration Guide in to order to guide exploration. For your information, expected answers are shown in an answer key right after the Exploration Guide, but the purpose of the exploration phase is not to find all of the correct answers immediately. The exploration phase is intended to provide shared experiences for the students so that they can make claims backed up by evidence and argue scientifically with their peers in order to develop a deeper understanding of the concepts.

When the students start talking about KE and PE, take time to tell them that KE stands for *kinetic energy* and that PE stands for *potential energy*. Rather than just telling them that kinetic energy is energy of motion, help them recognize the relationship they have noticed between the speed (velocity) of the bob and the height of the KE bar. Then let them know that in physics, kinetic energy is the proper term for motion energy. Likewise, rather than simply announcing that the gravitational potential energy in this system is a type of stored energy due to its position relative to Earth, ask them to describe the position of the bob when the PE is highest and when the PE is zero. Then tell them that when we pull the bob to start the pendulum swinging that we are adding energy to the system and that energy is released when the bob moves down to its lowest possible position because of gravity.

Ask the class if they noticed any major differences between the simulated pendulum and the demonstration pendulum. (Answers may vary, but hopefully someone will suggest that the demonstration pendulum eventually slows down and stops while the pendulum in the simulation keeps going, and going.) Tell them that by setting the friction slider at none, we created an ideal simulated pendulum, one that does continue to swing forever. Explain that this never happens in the real world because there is always at least a little friction between the bob and the air it moves through and between the string and where it is tied on its support.

Elaborate

Have the students return to their computers. They will now have the opportunity to investigate the effect of different amounts of friction on the pendulum's motion. Give them five to ten minutes to explore the function of the *friction slider* and try out the *photogate timer* and/or the *other tools,* which they may use this time. Challenge the students to develop an investigable question related to this topic, then design and carry out a simulated experiment that will answer their question. If you think your students need some scaffolding to be successful in this task, consider providing a list of investigable questions from which they may choose. Some possible questions include:

- What is the effect of different levels of friction on the length of time a pendulum will continue to swing?
- In what ways does the level of friction affect the energy in the pendulum system?
- What is the relationship between different levels of friction and the amount of thermal energy produced?
- What is the effect of different levels of friction on the angle of the pendulum's swing over time?
- What is the effect of different levels of friction on the period of the pendulum over time?
- Does the thermal energy rise at a constant rate? If not, how does its rate of increase vary?

Evaluate

Work with your class to develop an analytic rubric that identifies three or four criteria that should be considered when assessing group presentations of their research from the elaborate phase of the lesson. For each criterion, describe the level of work expected for each component for four levels of achievement: Expert, Proficient, Emergent, Novice. Provide the rubric to groups to guide their preparation of their presentations, and specify the amount of time they have to share their investigation question, procedure, results, and conclusions.

Encourage students to take notes about the findings of other groups in the science notebooks. After all groups have presented, if time allows, provide time for more science talk about the experimental designs used and the conclusions drawn.

Administer the following quiz to the class. Students should work and respond individually.

1. Use words and/or pictures to describe how the position and motion of the bob of an ideal (frictionless) pendulum relates to the varying amount of kinetic and potential energy in the swinging system.

2. Use the information presented in this diagram of an ideal (frictionless) pendulum to correctly fill in the blanks below. The pendulum bob was released from point a.

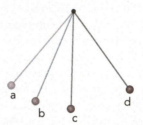

At **a** KE = _____ Joules

PE = 10 Joules

At **b** KE = 5 Joules

PE = _____ Joules

At **c** KE = _____ Joules

PE = 0 Joules

At **d** KE = _____ Joules

PE = _____ Joules

3. Describe at least three ways that the level of friction acting on the pendulum system affects its motion.

Exploration Guide for the *Pendulum Lab**

*Computer program from PhET Interactive Simulations, University of Colorado, http://phet.colorado.edu.

In the green box:

- Use the sliders to make your simulated pendulum similar to our demonstration pendulum.

$$\text{Length} = 1.5 \text{ m} \quad \text{Mass} = 0.5 \text{ kg}$$

- Leave *Show 2nd pendulum* unchecked.
- Leave the *friction slider* at the far left of the scale, so the friction in the simulated system is none.
- Start with *real time* selected.
- Stay on *Earth*.
- Leave *velocity, acceleration, photo-gate timer,* and *other tools* unchecked.
- Show *energy of 1*.

1. Start the pendulum swinging by left-clicking and dragging its bob to the release position you want to try, then lift your finger off the left-click button.

2. Try out different release points, watch the pendulum move, and see what happens on the Energy bar graph. Talk with your partner or group about what you notice and wonder. Keep records of your findings in your science notebook. After a little while, try out the play/pause button, change the speed so you can see the motion better, and see what happens when you check **velocity**.

Some questions that might guide your exploration include:

(Remember to make notes in your science notebook.)

1. At what point(s) in the swing is the bob stationary (not moving)?

2. At what point(s) in the swing is the bob moving the fastest?

3. What seems to determine the total energy in the system?

4. What is the relationship among KE, PE, and Total?

5. When is the KE the highest?

6. When is the PE the highest?

7. What happened when you checked *velocity?* How did that help you answer some other questions? Which one(s)?

8. How does the speed (velocity) of the bob relate to the KE in the system? . . . the PE?

9. How does the position of the bob relate to the KE in the system? . . . the PE?

10. In what ways is the simulated pendulum like the demonstration pendulum, and how is it different?

Answer Key for the Exploration Guide for the Pendulum Lab

Use to help you guide the meaning-making discussion during the explain phase.

1. When it is at the top of each side of the swing.

2. When it is directly under the pivot point where it is suspended from the ceiling; at the lowest point it can be.

3. The height at which the bob was released.

4. In this system, with no friction, the total energy = KE + PE. The energy cycles between being all KE and no PE to being no KE and all PE.

5. The KE is highest when the pendulum bob is moving the fastest, as it passes through the lowest point in the system.

6. The PE is highest when the pendulum bob is the greatest distance above the earth, at the top of each swing.

7. When *velocity* is checked, a green arrow extends out of the bob showing the speed and direction of movement (the velocity) of the bob. Because the size of the green arrow varies with the speed that the bob is moving, it can help us decide when the bob is stopped and when it is moving fastest. So it can help us answer questions 1 and 2.

8. As the speed (velocity) of the bob increases, the KE of the system increases and the PE of the system decreases.

9. As the position of the bob moves from the bottom to the top of the system, the PE of the system increases and the KE of the system decreases.

10. The simulated pendulum was designed to be the same length and have a bob of the same mass as the demonstration pendulum. In both, the bob could be pulled back to different angles before it was released. The simulated pendulum system had no friction, which never happens in the real world.

Activity 16: What makes things get hotter?

Grade: 4, Physical Sciences

Framework Context	
Scientific and Engineering Practices	**Constructing Explanations** Students need opportunities to engage in constructing and critiquing explanations. They should be encouraged to develop explanations of what they observe when conducting their own investigations and to evaluate their own and others' explanations for consistency with the evidence (NRC, 2012, p. 69). By the middle grades, students recognize that many of the explanations of science rely on models or representations of entities that are too small to see . . . (NRC, 2012, p. 70).
Crosscutting Concepts	**Cause and Effect:** Mechanism and Explanation By the upper elementary grades, students should have developed the habit of routinely asking about cause-and-effect relationships in the systems they are studying, particularly when something occurs that is, for them, unexpected. The questions "How did that happen?" or "Why did that happen?" should move toward "What mechanisms caused that to happen?" and "What conditions were critical for that to happen?" (NRC, 2012, p. 89).
Disciplinary Core Idea **Component Idea** **Conceptual Understanding**	**PS3:** Energy **PS3.B:** Conservation of Energy and Energy Transfer **By the end of grade 4:** Energy is present whenever there are moving objects, sound, light, or heat. When objects collide, energy can be transferred from one object to another, thereby changing their motion. In such collisions, some energy is typically also transferred to the surrounding air; as a result, the air gets heated and sound is produced (NRC, 2012, p. 125).

Performance Expectation 4-PS3-3

Ask questions and predict outcomes about the changes in energy that occur when objects collide (NGSS Lead States, 2013, p. 35). www.nextgenscience.org/pe/4-ps3-3-energy

Learning Target

The kinetic energy of moving particles can be transformed into heat energy.

Success Criteria

The students will:

1. Explain their ideas about why motion makes things get hotter.

Science Background

Moving things have energy known as kinetic energy or mechanical energy. Bending, rubbing, stretching, and shaking things cause them or the particles that they are made of to move, thus giving them kinetic energy. Energy can change from one form to another. Heat is also a form of energy. In this investigation, students experience multiple examples of motion causing heating (kinetic energy transforming into heat energy), which causes the temperature to increase.

Materials

For each pair or small group of students:

- Brass brad
- Wool cloth
- Piece of metal
- Pencil with eraser
- Notebook paper
- Baby food jar with screw top or small plastic food storage container with secure lid
- Sand

- Small thick towel
- Thermometer or temperature probes with CBL software on computers

For the class:

- 1 piece of wire coat hanger or heavy gauge craft wire (~25 cm long)

Engage

Hold up the piece of wire coat hanger. Ask the class: *If you touched this, how do you think it would feel?* If its temperature is not mentioned, lead them to also consider that property. Let several students feel the wire before you start and report their observations, especially about temperature, to the class. Bend a 6-inch piece of wire hanger back and forth ten times as shown. Let the students quickly touch the wire at the point where you bent it.

Ask: *How does the wire feel now?* (The wire got hotter.) *What do you think will happen if I bend the wire more times, for example, 20, 25, 30, 35 times?* (Each time the wire gets hotter.)

Safety Precautions

Try out this activity first to find out how many bends will make the wire too hot for students to safely touch.

Explore

In cooperative groups, have students explore actions that cause materials to heat up. For example, rub your hands together very fast and hard, or rub a brass brad on a piece of wool, metal on paper, or a pencil eraser on paper and quickly touch it to the tip of your nose.

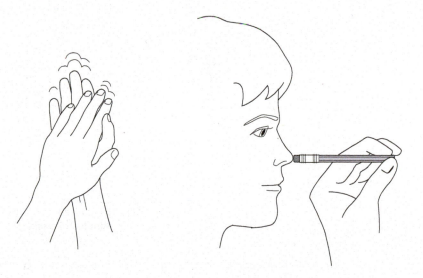

Have groups each complete an *I notice, I wonder chart* about their observations and the questions they generate.

If temperature probes and CBL software are available for student use, students could use this technology to make their observations quantitative rather than just qualitative.

Explain

Ask: *What did you observe in each case? How was heat produced in these activities?* Guide students to understand that bending things and rubbing things produces heat. Encourage the class to discuss other examples of motion producing heat that they have experienced.

Elaborate

Hold up a baby food jar three-fourths full of sand. Ask: *What do you think will happen to the sand in a baby food jar if you shake it many times?* Hint: *Think back to the previous activity.*

For each cooperative group, fill a baby food jar three-fourths full of sand, screw on the jar top, and then wrap it with a thick towel. Each person should take a turn doing the following things:

1. Measure the initial temperature of the sand, then shake the sand vigorously for five minutes.

2. Measure the temperature of the sand.

3. Write your findings on a record sheet like the one shown.

Person	Minutes of Shaking	Temperature in °C
1	5	
2	10	
3	15	
4	20	
5	25	

4. Pass the jar to the next person.

5. When everyone has had a turn, compare the temperature of the sand from the first to the last reading.

6. How were they different? (The temperature was higher after each shaking.)

7. Set up axes on a grid as shown; then graph the data from the record sheets.

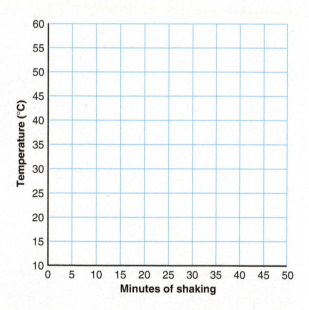

8. Analyze the graph, look for patterns of change, and discuss your thinking.

Ask: *What did you observe? What do your data indicate? What do you think was the source of the heat energy in the sand?*

Evaluate

Ask students to express their explanation of why and/or how motion causes heating in writing and through labeled drawings. Then allow them to explain their ideas to each other. If you want this evaluation to be summative, create a rubric to guide scoring.

Activity 17: How can you construct a circuit in which a bulb lights?

Grade: 4, Physical Sciences

Framework Context	
Scientific and Engineering Practices	**Obtaining, Evaluating, and Communicating Information** Students should be asked to engage in the communication of science, especially regarding the investigations they are conducting and the observations they are making. Careful description of observations and clear statement of ideas, with the ability to both refine a statement in response to questions and to ask questions of others to achieve clarification of what is being said (NRC, 2012, p. 76).
Crosscutting Concepts	**Systems and System Models** Students should describe objects [circuits] . . . in terms of their parts and the roles those parts play in the functioning of the object, . . . and they should note relationships between the parts (NRC, 2012, p. 93).
Disciplinary Core Idea **Component Idea** **Conceptual Understanding**	**PS3:** Energy **PS3.B:** Conservation of Energy and Energy Transfer **By the end of grade 3:** Energy can also be transferred from place to place by electric currents, which can then be used locally to produce motion, sound, heat, or light (NRC, 2012, p. 125).

Performance Expectation 4-PS3-4

Apply scientific ideas to design, test, and refine a device that converts energy from one form to another (NGSS Lead States, 2013, p. 35). www.nextgenscience.org/pe/4-ps3-4-energy

Learning Target

Current electricity carries energy as it flows through a closed circuit. That energy can be converted into light and heat as it moves through the bulb.

Success Criteria

The students will:

1. Demonstrate and explain through words and drawings how to make a bulb light in various ways, given one or two batteries and one or two wires.
2. State a rule that summarizes the arrangement of and connections between components of a simple complete circuit.
3. Be able to identify circuit drawings that represent complete circuits (i.e., the bulb will light if the illustrated circuit is actually constructed) and those that do not (i.e., the bulb will not light if the illustrated circuit is actually constructed).

Science Background

Current electricity refers to a movement of electrical charge along a conducting path. In this activity, electrical energy produced by a D-cell (commonly called a battery) is converted to heat and light in a light bulb. In this system, for electrical energy to be transferred to the bulb, there must be a complete conducting path—a *complete circuit*—from one end of the battery along the conducting material (typically wires) through the filament of the light bulb along more conducting material to the other end of the battery.

Materials

For each student, at least:

- One flashlight bulb
- One battery (1.5-volt D-cell)
- One 15–25 cm wire (with insulation removed from ends)
- Safety goggles

(Students initially need their own materials but will later combine materials with those of one or more other students.)

Safety Precautions   Discussing safe habits to use with electricity is a must.

- Caution children not to experiment with anything but 1.5-volt flashlight batteries (D-cells) and flashlight bulbs. There is no danger of electrical shock from these batteries.
- Children should wear safety goggles to protect their eyes from the sharp ends of the copper wires used in the activities.
- Tell children that if their wire gets hot, they should do something different with the connections of the wire(s).
- Children should never experiment with the electricity from wall sockets or from car batteries.
- Do not use electrical appliances near water; for example, do not use a hair dryer near a water-filled sink.
- When you pull an electrical cord out of a wall socket, grasp it by the plug and pull firmly.

Engage   Tell a story about some hikers who lost their flashlight in a dark cave. One hiker had an extra battery, another had an extra bulb, and a third had a wire. *Can you help them light the bulb so they can get out of the cave?*

Explore   Give each child a small flashlight bulb, a length of wire, and a 1.5-volt D-cell. (*Note:* A 1.5-volt D-cell is commonly referred to as a battery, although batteries actually have multiple cells.) Ask: *Can you make the bulb light?* Let the children work to light the bulb. Some children may take 20 minutes or longer to light the bulb. Resist the temptation to step in and "teach" them how to light the bulb. Encourage them to keep trying on their own. As they succeed, the children develop confidence in their own abilities to learn about electrical circuits.

As each child lights the bulb, ask: *Can you find another way to light the bulb?* Students may experiment by placing the bulb on its side or on the other end of the battery. If two or more children want to cooperate at this point, let them. More hands may be helpful. Be accepting and reinforcing of the children's efforts.

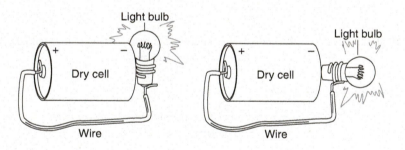

Ask children, individually, to draw pictures of what they did to light the bulb with one battery and one wire. Look at the children's drawings carefully to see if they have observed that the electrical path (circuit) is a continuous or complete one.

Explain   Ask the children to explain their drawings to you and to one another. Look at the drawings carefully to see if the wires touch the bulb on the bottom and the side.

Ask: *What two places must you touch a bulb for it to light? Where must the battery be touched?*

Referring to actual circuits and drawings, children should state, explain, and write the complete circuit rule:

For a bulb to light,

- the bulb must be touched on the side and the bottom;
- the battery must be touched on both ends; and
- there must be a continuous path through the battery, bulb, and wires.

Elaborate

Give each pair of children a second wire. Ask: *Can you make the bulb light using two wires?* Children may simply twist the two wires together and make one wire of them. If so, ask: *Can you use two wires to light the bulb without the bulb touching the battery?* Also ask them to draw a picture of what they did to light the bulb using two wires, with the bulb not touching the battery.

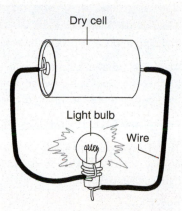

Dry cell

Light bulb

Wire

Evaluate

As a self-evaluation of their understanding of how to light a bulb with just one battery and one wire, ask each child to do Prediction Sheet 1. For each frame, the students should ask themselves: *Will the bulb light?* and then write *Yes* or *No* in the frame to record their prediction. After making predictions for all the frames, students should test their predictions by setting up a circuit like the one shown to try it and see. When all the children have completed the prediction sheet and checked it, go back over it with them. Ask: *Will this one light? Why won't it light? What could you do to get it to light?*

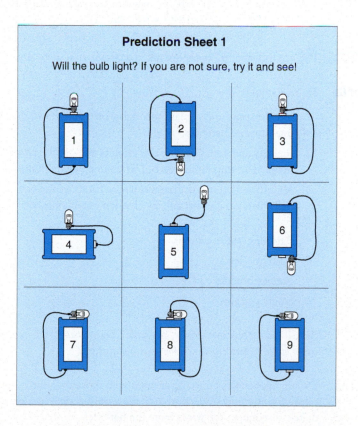

Prediction Sheet 1

Will the bulb light? If you are not sure, try it and see!

Activity 18: What happens when there is more than one bulb or battery in a circuit?

Grade: 4, Physical Sciences

Framework Context	
Scientific and Engineering Practices	**Planning and Carrying Out Investigations** At all levels, they should engage in investigations that range from those structured by the teacher—in order to expose an issue or question that they would be unlikely to explore on their own to those that emerge from students' own questions (NRC, 2012, p. 61).
Crosscutting Concepts	**Energy and Matter: Flows, Cycles, and Conservation** The ability to examine, characterize, and model the transfers and cycles of matter and energy is a tool that students can use across virtually all areas of science and engineering (NRC, 2012, p. 95).
Disciplinary Core Idea	**PS3:** Energy
Component Idea	**PS3.B:** Conservation of Energy and Energy Transfer
Conceptual Understanding	**By the end of grade 4:** Energy can also be transferred from place to place by electric currents, which can then be used locally to produce motion, sound, heat, or light (NRC, 2012, p. 125).

Performance Expectation 4-PS3-4

Apply scientific ideas to design, test, and refine a device that converts energy from one form to another (NGSS Lead States, 2013, p. 35). www.nextgenscience.org/pe/4-ps3-4-energy

Learning Target

The arrangement of components in a circuit affects the energy conversion by the components.

Success Criteria

The students will:

1. Demonstrate and explain through words and drawings different ways to light multiple bulbs with one or more batteries.
2. Identify and construct parallel circuits and use the complete circuit rule to explain why the other bulbs in a series circuit go out when one bulb is removed from its holder.
3. Identify and construct parallel circuits and use the complete circuit rule to explain why the other bulbs in a parallel circuit stay lit when one bulb is removed from its holder.

Materials

- Batteries, bulbs, wires
- Bulb holders
- Battery holders
- Safety goggles

Engage

Ask: *What happens when you try two bulbs? Try two batteries. Can you use three batteries and two bulbs? Does the orientation of the batteries matter? How could you find out?*

Safety Precautions

Do not allow children to experiment with more than three batteries. More batteries can result in burned-out bulbs. Remind students that if the wires become hot, the bulbs will not light, and they should immediately disconnect the wires from the batteries.

Children should wear safety goggles to protect their eyes from the sharp ends of the copper wires used in the activities.

Explore

Let children explore and discover. As they try different arrangements, have them complete an *I notice, I wonder chart* to record their observations and questions.

As the children try different arrangements, the need for "bulb holders" and "battery holders" arises. Give the children bulb holders and battery holders and demonstrate how to use them.

Children may discover that when batteries are placed end-to-end (in series), a positive terminal of one battery must be connected to the negative terminal of an adjacent battery.

Explain

Encourage children to share and discuss the information on their *I notice, I wonder charts* with the class. If conversation lags, ask: *Who tried one battery and three bulbs? What did you notice? Did this make you wonder anything? What? Did everyone that tried this notice the same thing?*

Ask: *Can you trace the complete circuit path for each circuit you have built?* Help children see that the bulb holder is constructed so that one part of it is connected to the metal side of a bulb and another part is connected to the bottom base of the bulb. The terminals of the bulb holder are then connected to the battery. The bulb holder is doing the same thing the children were doing with their hands when they made the bulb light. The bulb holders provide a complete circuit path for the electricity.

Display the diagram of a series circuit.

Bulb and bulb holder

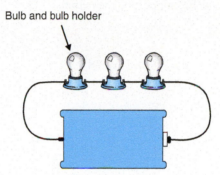

Tell the students that electricians, scientists, and engineers call this circuit a *series circuit* because the bulbs are lined up in a series and electricity flows from bulb to bulb.

Ask students to identify series circuits that they have built (either the actual circuits or diagrams of them) and provide evidence that supports their claim that each is a *series circuit*.

Display the diagram of a parallel circuit.

Bulb and bulb holder

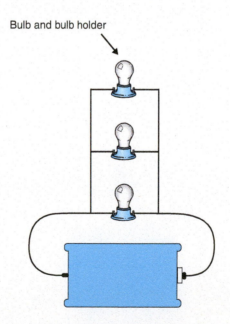

Tell students that this circuit is called a parallel circuit because there are parallel paths through the bulbs for the electricity. Each bulb is part of an independent circuit with the battery.

Ask students to identify parallel circuits that they have built (either the actual circuits or diagrams of them) and provide evidence that supports their claim that each is a parallel circuit.

Develop class definitions for series circuits, parallel circuits, and those circuits that are neither series or parallel.

Elaborate

Have student groups construct series and parallel circuits like those in the diagrams. Ask: *What will happen to the other bulbs in the circuit if one of the bulbs is removed from its holder? Try it and see.* (In a series circuit, the other bulbs will go out; in a parallel circuit, the other bulbs will remain lit.)

Evaluate

Have students:

1. Use a graphic organizer to summarize their findings about the similarities and differences between series and parallel circuits.

2. Make a claim about the type of circuit that would be best for a string of holiday lights and give evidence supporting their claim.

Activity 19: What affects the final temperature of a water mixture?

Grades: 6–8, Physical Sciences

Framework Context	
Scientific and Engineering Practices	**Planning and Carrying Out Investigations** Students need opportunities to design investigations so that they can learn the importance of such decisions as what to measure, what to keep constant, and how to select or construct data collection instruments that are appropriate to the needs of an inquiry (NRC, 2012, p. 60).
Crosscutting Concepts	**Patterns** Noticing patterns is often a first step to organizing and asking scientific questions about why and how the patterns occur (NRC, 2012, p. 85). **Scale, Proportion, and Quantity** As students deepen their understanding of algebraic thinking, they should be able to apply it to examine their scientific data to predict the effect of a change in one variable on another (NRC, 2012, p. 91).
Disciplinary Core Idea	**PS3:** Energy
Component Idea	**PS3.A:** Definitions of Energy
Conceptual Understanding	By the end of grade 8: Temperature is not a measure of energy; the relationship between the temperature and the total energy of a system depends on the types, states, and amounts of matter present (NRC, 2012, p. 123).
Component Idea	**PS3.B:** Conservation of Energy and Energy Transfer
Conceptual Understanding	**By the end of grade 8:** The amount of energy transfer needed to change the temperature of a matter sample by a given amount depends on the nature of the matter, the size of the sample, and the environment (NRC, 2012, p. 126).

Performance Expectation MS-PS3-4

Plan an investigation to determine the relationships among the energy transferred, the type of matter, the mass, and the change in the average kinetic energy of the particles as measured by the temperature of the sample (NGSS Lead States, 2013, p. 61). www.nextgenscience.org/pe/ms-ps3-4-energy

Learning Target

When samples of water at two different temperatures are mixed together, the resulting temperature depends on the starting temperature of each sample, the mass of each sample, the temperature of the surrounding environment, and time.

Success Criteria

The students will:

1. Design and conduct investigations to determine the final temperature of water mixtures.
2. Recognize that when mixing samples of water together, the final temperature of the mixture depends on the initial temperatures of the samples, the volume of the samples, and the amount of heat lost to the environment.

Materials

- Styrofoam cups (minimum capacity = 250 ml)
- Supply of hot water
- Supply of cold water
- Graduated cylinders
- Thermometers or temperature probes with appropriate software
- Stirring spoons

- Safety goggles
- Paper towels

Engage

Ask: *What happens to the temperature of bath water when you add hot water to cold water? Does the amount of hot water and cold water matter? How could you predict the new temperature when hot and cold water are mixed?*

Safety Precautions

Wear safety goggles because of splashing danger.

Wipe up any spills immediately to minimize risk of slipping on wet surfaces.

Explore

Tell students to plan an investigation to determine the final temperature when hot and cold water are mixed. Students could plan and conduct the following activity in cooperative groups:

1. Pour the following volumes of water at the indicated temperatures into separate Styrofoam cups:
   - 100 ml of hot water
   - 100 ml of cold water
   - 50 ml of hot water
   - 50 ml of cold water
   - 150 ml of hot water
   - 150 ml of cold water

2. Measure and record the temperature of the 100-ml samples of water in a copy of the prepared data table (see illustration). If possible, make all temperature measurements in degrees Celsius.

3. In a third cup, carefully mix and stir the two 100-ml samples of water.

4. Measure and record the final temperature.

5. Repeat steps 2, 3, and 4 for the following mixtures:
   - 150 ml of hot water and 50 ml of cold water
   - 150 ml of cold water and 50 ml of warm water

   Instruct cooperative group recorders to record their data on the class master data table.

Temperature of Water Mixtures			
	Amount of Water in Each Container	**Initial Temperature of Water**	**Final Temperature of Mixture**
Mixture 1	100 ml		
	100 ml		
Mixture 2	150 ml		
	50 ml		
Mixture 3	50 ml		
	150 ml		
Mystery Mixture			Predicted _____
			Measured _____

Explain

Ask: *What patterns do you see in the class data? In what ways do these patterns help you predict the final temperature of the mixtures?* Lead students to notice that if the volumes of two samples of water are the same, the final

temperature will be halfway between the two initial temperatures. If the volumes of the two samples are different, the final temperature will be nearer the initial temperature of the larger sample.

Ask: *Was there a pattern of change in the data over time? What do you think may have caused this pattern of change?* If they notice that the temperatures of the samples get closer to room temperature over time, a reasonable explanation of the cause of this change is: (1) if the original sample was colder than room temperature, heat from the environment would have warmed it up over time; and (2) if the original sample was warmer than room temperature, heat from the warmer water was lost to the environment over time.

Elaborate

Tell students you are going to give them a new water-mixing problem, but they will need to predict the final temperature before they mix the water samples and take data.

Prepare a large container of cold water at near freezing temperature (but with no ice). Prepare another large container of water at room temperature. Give materials managers a cup of cold water and a cup of room temperature water.

Instruct groups they are going to mix 175 ml of cold water with 50 ml of warm water. Ask groups to make a prediction of the final temperature and then to conduct the investigation. Predictions do not need to be exact. For example, a group may just predict that the final temperature will be halfway between the temperatures of the two samples or very near the temperature of the larger sample.

Instruct recorders to record the predicted and final temperatures of their mixtures on a class chart. Invite students to present and discuss their predictions, the basis of the predictions, and the final temperatures obtained.

Explain that the final temperature of a mixture depends on both the initial temperatures and volumes of the samples. When a large volume of water is mixed with a smaller volume of water, the final temperature will be nearer the initial temperature of the large volume. There are actually mathematical ratios here that can be dealt with at upper grades.

Ask: *What have you done in this investigation that is like what scientists do?* Lead students to understand that they have formulated a problem, planned and conducted an investigation, used a thermometer and graduated cylinder to collect data, recorded data in a table, interpreted the data and formed an explanation for experimental results, and tested the explanations through a prediction. These are some of the things scientists do.

Evaluate

Use the following item to check student understanding of the principle presented in this lesson:

1. The water that comes from your cold faucet is 10°C. The water that comes from your hot faucet is 72°C. If you mix equal parts of water from each faucet in the bathtub, what will be the initial temperature of your bath water? How do you know? (41°—Since I put in equal amounts of the two temperatures of water, the resulting temperature is halfway between the two temperatures.)

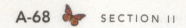

Activity 20: How does the length of a vibrating stick affect the sound produced?

Grade: 1, Physical Sciences

Framework Context	
Scientific and Engineering Practices	**Planning and Carrying Out Investigations** In the elementary years, students' experiences should be structured to help them learn to define the features to be investigated, such as patterns that suggest causal relationships (NRC, 2012, p. 60).
Crosscutting Concepts	**Cause and Effect: Mechanism and Explanation** In the earliest grades, as students begin to look for and analyze patterns . . . in their observations of the world . . . they can also begin to consider what might be causing these patterns and relationships and design tests that gather more evidence to support or refute their ideas (NRC, 2012, p. 88).
Disciplinary Core Idea	**PS4:** Waves and Their Applications in Technologies for Information Transfer
Component Idea	**PS4.A:** Wave Properties
Conceptual Understanding	**By the end of grade 1:** . . . vibrating matter can make sound (NRC, 2012, p. 131).

Performance Expectation 1-PS4-1

Plan and conduct investigations to provide evidence that vibrating materials can make sound and that sound can make materials vibrate (NGSS Lead States, 2013, p. 10). www.nextgenscience.org/pe/1-ps4 -1-waves-and-their-applications-technologies-information-transfer

Learning Target

Sound is produced by vibrating objects. The pitch of a sound produced by a vibrating object depends on the frequency of vibration. The length of the vibrating object affects the frequency of vibration.

Success Criteria

The students will:

1. Recognize the rapid back-and-forth motion of objects as *vibration* and compare rates of vibration.
2. Recognize that pitch is a way of describing how high or low a sound is and compare sounds of various pitches.
3. Demonstrate, describe, and explain how the pitch of a sound may be varied.

Materials

For each student:

- Craft stick (15 cm long)

Engage

Ask: *How can you use a craft stick to create sounds?*

Explore

Instruct students to hold a 15-cm craft stick firmly against a desk with one hand. With the other hand, they should pluck the overhanging part of the stick, causing it to vibrate. Remind the students to observe carefully while carrying out this procedure.

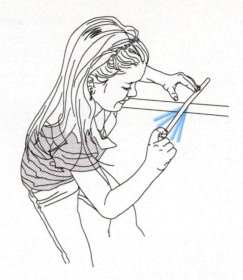

Explain

Ask: *What did you hear?* (A sound.) *What did you see?* (Part of the craft stick was moving up and down.) *What did you feel?* (Possibly, the end of the craft stick moving up and down.) *What is meant by vibration?* (A rapid back-and-forth motion.) *Which part of the craft stick vibrates and produces sound? Were all the sounds produced by the craft sticks the same?* (No, not exactly.) *How were they different?* (They were different notes, some high, some lower. Some children may mention the term *pitch* to describe this difference.)

Ask: *What is meant by the pitch of a sound? How can you change the pitch of a vibrating craft stick?*

Elaborate

Challenge students to produce a high-pitched sound by vibrating the stick and to produce a low-pitched sound by vibrating the stick. Then have them try to make pitches that fall in between. Remind students to observe carefully and to pay attention to what they are changing about the craft stick. Then let them discuss their findings.

Ask: *What did you do to change the pitch of the vibrating craft stick?* (Change the amount of the craft stick hanging over the edge of the desk.) *How did you make your lowest pitch?* (Hold the craft stick so that most of it hangs over the edge of the desk.) *How did you make your highest pitch?* (Hold the craft stick so that only a little of it hangs over the edge of the desk.) *Does the craft stick vibrate faster or slower when more of it hangs over the edge of a desk?* (It vibrates slower when more of it hangs over the edge of the desk.) *How is the speed of vibration related to the pitch of the sound produced?* (The faster the vibration, the higher the pitch of the sound produced.) Consider asking students to demonstrate their ideas with the craft sticks to support the answers to these questions.

Evaluate

To check for understanding of the relationship among length of vibrating object, speed of vibration, and pitch of the sound produced, have the students respond to the following assessment items:

1. Complete the following table to describe the relationships among variables in this investigation. The words to choose from are: Fast, High, Long, Low, Short, Slow.

Length of craft stick hanging over the edge of the table	Speed of vibration	Pitch of the sound produced

Rulers hanging over edge of table.

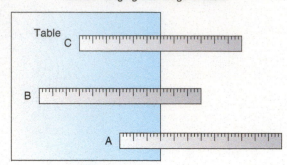

2. Which of the rulers shown in the drawing would produce the lowest pitched sound when plucked? (A.) What evidence supports your claim?

3. Which of the rulers shown in the drawing would vibrate the fastest when plucked? (B.) What evidence supports your claim?

Activity 21: How is sound produced by a banjo?

Grade: 1, Physical Sciences

Framework Context	
Scientific and Engineering Practices	**Planning and Carrying Out Investigations** In the elementary years, students' experiences should be structured to help them learn to define the features to be investigated, such as patterns that suggest causal relationships (NRC, 2012, p. 60).
Crosscutting Concepts	**Cause and Effect: Mechanism and Explanation** In the earliest grades, as students begin to look for and analyze patterns . . . in their observations of the world . . . they can also begin to consider what might be causing these patterns and relationships and design tests that gather more evidence to support or refute their ideas (NRC, 2012, p. 88).
Disciplinary Core Idea	**PS4:** Waves and Their Applications in Technologies for Information Transfer
Component Idea	**PS4.A:** Wave Properties
Conceptual Understanding	**By the end of grade 2:** . . . vibrating matter can make sound (NRC, 2012, p. 131).

Performance Expectation 1-PS4-1

Plan and conduct investigations to provide evidence that vibrating materials can make sound and that sound can make materials vibrate (NGSS Lead States, 2013, p. 10). www.nextgenscience.org/pe/1-ps4-1-waves-and-their-applications-technologies-information-transfer

Learning Target

The pitch of a vibrating stretched rubber band depends on the length of the rubber band that is vibrating.

Success Criteria

The students will:

1. Demonstrate, describe, and explain the generation of sound by various vibrating sources.
2. Define pitch as how high or low a sound is.
3. Demonstrate, describe, and explain how the pitch of a sound may be varied.

Materials

- Rubber bands of varying lengths and thicknesses
- Small, open boxes or plastic cups
- Stringed instrument (optional)

Engage

Ask: *What vibrates to produce sound in a stringed musical instrument, such as a banjo?*

Explore

Suggest that students make model banjos by stretching rubber bands of varying lengths and thicknesses over a small box or plastic cup. Encourage students to pluck the rubber bands to produce sounds. Remind them to observe carefully with both their eyes and ears and to record their observations in their science notebooks using words and drawings.

Explain

Assemble the class into a discussion circle. Encourage students to refer to their science notebooks as they have a science talk about their initial experiences with the rubber band banjos.

Ask: *What part of a rubber band banjo vibrates to produce sound? What is your evidence?*
Ask: *What do you think might affect the pitch of the sound from a banjo?*

Instruct students to investigate how the pitch of a sound is varied on a rubber band banjo by varying the tension and thickness of the rubber bands. Ask: *What variables can you change to vary the pitch of a rubber band banjo?* (Length, thickness, and tension of the rubber bands.) *How do you vary the loudness of the banjo?*

Elaborate

Ask: *How can you vary the pitch of the sound produced by a stringed musical instrument, such as a guitar or ukulele?* Allow students to observe how strings of differing thickness and different lengths produce different pitches in guitars, ukuleles, or other stringed instruments. Demonstrate how the tension of a string can be varied to produce high- and low-pitched sounds with a guitar or other stringed instrument.

Evaluate

Challenge students to create a stringed instrument on which they can play a scale of eight ascending notes (eight notes in a row, each with a higher pitch). Each student will explain his or her stringed instrument to the class and then play a scale. Give the following rubric to the students to aid in their preparation, then use it to evaluate their instruments and presentations. Total possible score is 35. If you want an approximate grade on a 100-point scale, just multiply the score from the rubric by 3. A student who was judged Exemplary in all categories would have a grade of 105. A student who was judged Proficient in all categories would have a grade of 84. A student who was judged Developing in all categories would have a grade of 42.

Criteria	Exemplary (5 Points)	Proficient (4 Points)	Developing (2 Points)
Appearance	Very attractive; shows much effort and care in construction	Looks OK; some effort and care in construction is evident	Sloppy; shows little effort; careless construction
Sturdiness	Very sturdy; looks like it will withstand repeated use	Somewhat sturdy; didn't fall apart before or during performance, but looks like it might	Not sturdy; falls apart before or during performance
Safety	Completely safe, all potential safety issues addressed	Seems safe, if instrument is used properly	Obvious that someone could be harmed during the use of this instrument
Explanation	Tells (in an interesting, organized manner) their name, name of their instrument, what is vibrating, and how different pitches are produced	Presents most information described in Exemplary; but presentation not very enthusiastic or interesting; or presentation is unorganized	Not informative, not interesting, unprepared, or silly
Speaking Skills	Presenter speaks clearly and at a proper volume for audience to hear; uses good eye contact; and holds instrument so it is visible to all	One of the desired elements from Exemplary not achieved	Two or more of the desired elements from Exemplary not achieved
Playing of Scale	All 8 notes of scale are played in order from low pitch to high pitch and are all "in key"	8 different pitches are played, they are in order from low pitch to high pitch, but they are not "in key"	Instrument produces fewer than 8 pitches or scale not played in order
Volume of Instrument	All notes produced can be easily heard throughout the classroom	Most notes produced can be heard in the classroom	Can't hear many notes, too quiet

A related Grade 1 activity may be accessed via the Enhanced Pearson eText. It is titled: "How can you make a bottle pipe organ?" and addresses the DCI Component Idea PS4.A.

Activity 22: How do transparent, translucent, and opaque materials differ?

Grade: 1, Physical Sciences

Framework Context	
Scientific and Engineering Practices	**Developing and Using Models** Young students should be encouraged to devise pictorial and simple graphical representations of the findings of their investigations and to use these models in developing their explanations of what occurred (NRC, 2012, p. 58). **Engaging in Argument from Evidence** Young students can begin by constructing an argument for their own interpretation of the phenomena they observe and of any data they collect. They need instructional support to go beyond simply making claims—that is, to include reasons or references to evidence and to begin to distinguish evidence from opinion (NRC, 2012, p. 73).
Crosscutting Concepts	**Patterns** It is important for [students] to develop ways to recognize, classify, and record patterns in the phenomena they observe (NRC, 2012, p. 86). **Cause and Effect: Mechanism and Explanation** . . . events that occur together with regularity are clues that scientists can use to start exploring causal, or cause-and-effect, relationships, which pervade all the disciplines of science and at all scales.
Disciplinary Core Idea **Component Idea** **Conceptual Understanding**	**PS4:** Waves and Their Applications in Technologies for Information Transfer **PS4.B:** Electromagnetic Radiation **By the end of grade 1:** Some materials allow light to pass through them, others allow only some light through, and others block all the light and create a dark shadow on any surface beyond them (i.e., on the other side from the light source), where the light cannot reach (NRC, 2012, p. 134).

Performance Expectation 1-PS4-3

Plan and conduct investigations to determine the effect of placing objects made with different materials in the path of a beam of light. *Clarification Statement:* Examples of materials could include those that are transparent (such as clear plastic), translucent (such as wax paper), opaque (such as cardboard) (NGSS Lead States, 2013, p. 10). www.nextgenscience.org/pe/1-ps4-3-waves-and-their-applications-technologies-information-transfer

Learning Target

Light passes easily through transparent materials; they do not cast shadows when illuminated. Some light passes through translucent materials; they cast dim shadows when illuminated. No light passes through opaque materials; they cast dark shadows when illuminated.

Success Criteria

The students will:

1. Identify materials that are transparent, translucent, and opaque.
2. Describe what they see through each of these materials when placed over an object or held between them and a light.
3. Compare and contrast the appearance of shadows cast by transparent, translucent, and opaque objects.

Materials

For each student group:

- Transparent materials (clear plastic wrap, clear glass)
- Translucent materials (wax paper, cloudy plastic, tissue paper)

- Opaque materials (cardboard, aluminum foil, wood)
- White paper

Engage

Allow students to examine a small object placed underneath a sheet of wax paper or a piece of cloudy plastic. Ask: *What do you see? Why is the object not easily seen?*

Explore

Give each group of students some samples of transparent, translucent, and opaque materials. Ask the students to place one kind of material at a time over a printed page. For each material, have students sort material into these three categories: (1) can see through it easily; (2) can see through it but not very clearly; (3) cannot see through it. Encourage students to record which materials are in which category in their science notebooks. Provide graphic organizers as supportive scaffolding for students who would benefit from that assistance.

Provide white paper for students to use as mats on their desk or table. Close the window shades so that the main light source in the room is the overhead lights. Suggest that they hold each object or material a little (about 5 cm) above the white paper mat and observe any shadows that appear. Encourage students to record their shadow observations in their science notebooks as well.

Explain

Ask: *Through which of the materials could you see the print on the page easily? Through which of the materials could you tell there was print on the page, but it could not be seen clearly? Through which of the materials was it impossible to see the print on the page?* List the student responses in three columns on the board. Introduce the terms *transparent, translucent,* and *opaque* by adding them as headings to the three-column chart on the board. Guide students to understand that light is transmitted through transparent media, such as air, water, and glass, so the print was clearly visible. Translucent materials transmit some light, so the print was not so clear. Opaque materials do not transmit any of the light energy striking them, so the print was not possible to see.

Then ask the class to relate their shadow observations to the chart and explain how the appearance of the shadows can serve as evidence of what happens to the light with the different materials.

Elaborate

Using the same materials as before, let the students look through them at the lights on the ceiling of the classroom. Ask: *In terms of how much light comes through, what is the difference between the transparent, translucent, and opaque materials?*

Challenge children to draw pictures (models) that show their current understanding of the interaction of light with the three different types of materials. Encourage them to use their models to explain their reasoning to others in their small group and/or to the whole class.

Evaluate

To check student understanding about this concept, ask students to write, draw, or talk about three different things they could do to identify whether an object or material is transparent, translucent, or opaque.

Activity 23: How can shadows be changed?

Grade: 1, Physical Sciences

Framework Context	
Scientific and Engineering Practices	**Constructing Explanations** [Students] should be encouraged to develop explanations of what they observe when conducting their own investigations and to evaluate their own and others' explanations for consistency with the evidence (NRC, 2012, p. 69).
Crosscutting Concepts	**Patterns** It is important for [students] to develop ways to recognize, classify, and record patterns in the phenomena they observe (NRC, 2012, p. 86).
Disciplinary Core Idea **Component Idea** **Conceptual Understanding**	**PS4:** Waves and Their Applications in Technologies for Information Transfer **PS4.B:** Electromagnetic Radiation **By the end of grade 1:** Some materials allow light to pass through them, others allow only some light through, and others block all the light and create a dark shadow on any surface beyond them (i.e., on the other side from the light source), where the light cannot reach (NRC, 2012, p. 134–135).

Performance Expectation 1-PS4-3

Plan and conduct investigations to determine the effect of placing objects made with different materials in the path of a beam of light. *Clarification Statement:* Examples of materials could include those that are transparent (such as clear plastic), translucent (such as wax paper), opaque (such as cardboard) (NGSS Lead States, 2013, p. 10). www.nextgenscience.org/pe/1-ps4-3-waves-and-their-applications-technologies-information-transfer

Learning Target

The shape, length, and direction of a shadow depends on the position of the light and the object casting the shadow.

Success Criteria

The students will:

1. Describe in what ways the shadow of the same object can change when the light source creating the shadow moves.
2. Compare and contrast the shapes and sizes of shadows.
3. Relate the relative position of the light source to the length and direction of the shadow produced.

Materials

For each student team:

- Flashlight
- Two large sheets of white paper
- Scissors
- Plastic funnel
- Pencil or crayon
- Wooden block

Engage

Ask: *Are shadows of the same object always the same size and shape?* Encourage students to share their ideas.

Explore

Working with a partner, students should put a funnel on a large sheet of white paper. Suggest that they use the flashlight to make a shadow of the funnel on the paper. Encourage them to try shining the flashlight from different positions. Ask: *How does the shadow change?*

Suggest that students do the following to record the size and shape of two shadows. One student should shine the flashlight on the funnel while the other one traces and cuts the shadow shape out with the scissors, in this sequence:

1. First, while holding the flashlight low and to the side, trace and cut out the shadow of the funnel. Label it "low."

2. Next, switch roles with your partner. Put a new piece of white paper under the funnel, hold the flashlight high, and then trace and cut out the shadow of the funnel. Label it "high."

3. Compare the size and shape of the two cutout shadows.

Explain

Ask: *Are both of your shadow shapes the same?* (No.) *How are they different?* (They are different sizes and shapes.) *Which one is longer?* (The one labeled "low" is longer.) *Which one is shorter?* (The one labeled "high" is shorter.) *What caused the difference in shapes?* (The position of the light source.) Try to lead the students to the conclusion that the position of the light source affects the shadow's size and shape. When the light source is low, shining on the object from the side, the shadow is long, and when the light source is high, shining down on the object from above, the shadow is short.

Elaborate

Ask: *What happens to the shadow if you move the light source in an arc from one side of the object, over it, and to the other side of the object?* This simulates the apparent motion of the sun in the sky and provides background experience for future activities.

Evaluate

To see if students understand the relationship between the position of a light source and the length and direction of the shadow of a wooden block on a table, have students match the following statements:

Position of Light Source	Length and Direction of Shadow
1. Light is directly above the block.	A. Very long shadow to the left of the block
2. Light is on the table on the right side of the block.	B. Very long shadow to the right of the block
3. Light is above the table to the right side of the block.	C. Medium-long shadow to the right of the block
4. Light is on the table on the left side of the block.	D. No shadow or very short shadow all around the block
5. Light is above the table to the left side of the block.	E. Medium-long shadow to the left of the block

Activity 24: How does light reflect from a mirror?

Grade: 1, Physical Sciences

Framework Context	
Scientific and Engineering Practices	**Analyzing and Interpreting Data** At the elementary level, students need support to recognize the need to record observations—whether in drawings, words, or numbers—and to share them with others (NRC, 2012, p. 63). **Using Mathematics and Computational Thinking** As soon as students learn to count, they can begin using numbers to find or describe patterns in nature (NRC, 2012, p. 66).
Crosscutting Concepts	**Patterns** It is important for [students] to develop ways to recognize, classify, and record patterns in the phenomena they observe (NRC, 2012, p. 86).
Disciplinary Core Idea **Component Idea** **Conceptual Understanding**	**PS4:** Waves and Their Applications in Technologies for Information Transfer **PS4.B:** Electromagnetic Radiation **By the end of grade 1:** Mirrors and prisms can be used to redirect a light beam. (Boundary: The idea that light travels from place to place is developed through experiences with light sources, mirrors, and shadows, but no attempt is made to discuss the speed of light.) (NRC, 2012, p. 135).

Performance Expectation 1-PS4-3

Plan and conduct investigations to determine the effect of placing objects made with different materials in the path of a beam of light. *Clarification Statement:* Examples of materials could include those that are reflective (such as a mirror) (NGSS Lead States, 2013, p. 10). www.nextgenscience.org/pe/1-ps4-3-waves -and-their-applications-technologies-information-transfer

Learning Target

The location of the light source in relation to a shiny reflective surface determines the direction the light will reflect off of that surface.

Success Criteria

The students will:

1. Describe the reflection of light off shiny reflecting surfaces.

Materials

For each cooperative group:

- Light-ray source (flashlight, cardboard, scissors or knife, transparent tape)
- Mirror
- Rubber band
- Wood block
- Pencils or markers
- White poster board or large sheet of white paper

Preparation

Create a light-ray source by making a stiff cardboard shield about the diameter of a flashlight, cutting a slit in the shield, and attaching the shield over the lens of a strong flashlight with transparent tape. A light ray is formed when light from the flashlight passes through the slit.

Engage

Ask: When you look in a mirror, do you always see yourself?
 Hold a mirror facing the class. Adjust it so everyone might see themselves or another student's face. *Ask: Do you see yourself in the mirror?* (Only students directly in front of the mirror should say yes.) Ask a student who is looking into the mirror at an angle: *What or who do you see in the mirror?* (Someone or something on the other side of the classroom.) After some discussion, ask: *What is the pattern of who sees what in the mirror?*

Explore

In each cooperative group, lay the light-ray source on a white poster board so you can see the light ray on the poster board. Attach a small plane mirror to a block of wood with a rubber band. Put the mirror in the path of light. Tell children to mark a spot on the poster board and to orient the mirror so that the reflected ray hits the spot. Instruct the students to initially use trial and error to align the mirror so that the reflected light ray hits the desired spot. Gradually, the students should make and test predictions of how the mirror should be aligned to direct the reflected light ray to the spot. Suggest that they use drawings or trace the paths of the light on the poster board as a way to record their observations.

Explain

Ask: How does light reflect from a mirror? What pattern did you detect about how light reflects? How did you know how to align a mirror to make a reflected light ray hit a desired spot? Lead students to understand that the angle formed between a reflected light ray and a mirror is the same as the angle between the incoming light ray and the mirror.

Elaborate

Have students explore the rays and mirror positions again to check if the statement that "the angle between the reflected light ray and a mirror is the same as the angle between the incoming light ray and the mirror" is indeed true. Suggest that they place the edge of an index card against the reflective surface of the mirror. Then shine a light ray toward the mirror. Draw lines on the index card showing the incoming and reflected rays. By folding the index card at the point the light ray hit the mirror, students can check if the lines drawn on the card touch when folded. This would confirm that the angles with the edge were the same. If students know how to use a protractor, they can use it to compare the angles the rays made with the edge of the index card.

Evaluate

To assess student understanding of the way a light beam would reflect from a plane mirror, have students respond to this item:

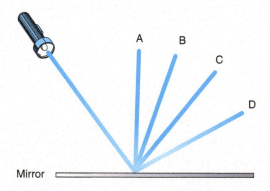

1. In this illustration, which line represents the reflected ray? How do you know?

Activity 25: What happens when light passes from one transparent material to another?

Grades: 6-8, Physical Sciences

Framework Context	
Scientific and Engineering Practices	**Constructing Explanations** [Students] should be encouraged to develop explanations of what they observe when conducting their own investigations and to evaluate their own and others' explanations for consistency with the evidence (NRC, 2012, p. 69).
Crosscutting Concepts	**Systems and System Models** As students progress, their models should move beyond simple renderings or maps and begin to incorporate and make explicit the invisible features of a system, such as interactions, energy flows, or matter transfers (NRC, 2012, p. 94).
Disciplinary Core Idea **Component Idea** **Conceptual Understanding**	**PS4:** Waves and Their Applications in Technologies for Information Transfer **PS4.B:** Electromagnetic Radiation **By the end of grade 5:** The path that light travels can be traced as straight lines, except at surfaces between different transparent materials (e.g., air and water, air and glass) where the light path bends (NRC, 2012, p. 135).

Performance Expectation MS-PS4-2

Develop and use a model to describe that waves are reflected, absorbed, or transmitted through various materials. *Clarification Statement:* Emphasis is on both light and mechanical waves. Examples of models could include drawings, simulations, and written descriptions (NGSS Lead States, 2013, p. 63). www.nextgenscience.org/pe/ms-ps4-2-waves-and-their-applications-technologies-information-transfer

Learning Target

Light bends (refracts) when it passes through a boundary between two different transparent materials at an angle not equal to 90 degrees.

Success Criteria

The students will:

1. Describe the path of a light ray as it passes between air and water or other transparent material.
2. Operationally define refraction as the bending of light as it passes at an angle not equal to 90 degrees into or out of a transparent object.
3. Use the concept of refraction to explain several optical phenomena.

Materials

For the teacher:

- Transparent drinking glass, partially full of water
- Pencil

For each group:

- Coin
- Paper cup or opaque plastic cup
- Small piece of clay or sticky tack
- Pitcher or beaker (from which to pour water)
- Flashlight
- Black rubber or plastic comb
- Two transparent, cylindrical containers (jars) of different diameters
- White paper

Engage

Insert a pencil into the transparent glass partially filled with water so that half of the pencil is in water and half of it out of water. With this system placed in a location where the entire class can see it, ask: *What do you see? Why do you think the pencil seems distorted?*

Use this discrepant event activity to assess students' prior knowledge. In the activities that follow in the explore and explain phases of inquiry, you can build on student ideas, developing concepts and principles to construct an explanation of the broken or bent pencil phenomenon.

Explore

Give each small group a coin, a cup, clay or sticky tack, and a container of water from which it is easy to pour. Ask the students to follow these instructions:

As a group:

- anchor the coin to the center of the bottom of the inside of the cup with a little piece of clay or sticky tack.

Taking turns, let each member of your group:

- Look down into the open top of the cup in order to see the coin in the bottom of the cup from above. (a)
- Move back gradually so the coin is just out of sight, hidden by the opaque side of the cup. (b)
- Remain in that position, observing what's happening in the cup, while another student slowly pours water into the cup.

Suggest that students quietly write or draw about what they saw happening in their science notebooks, while keeping their observations to themselves until everyone in the group has had a chance to observe the phenomenon. Then encourage the group to discuss these questions: *What did you see happening?* (The coin slowly appeared to float into view as the water level rose.) *Why do you think this happened?* Remind students to use evidence to support their claims. Challenge groups to create an illustration (model) to communicate their explanation to the rest of the class.

Explain

In a large group, invite each small group to describe and discuss their observations and explanatory models with the class. Some of the ideas listed below may emerge through discussion, and/or you may want to use this illustration and the following points to provide an explanation of the floating coin phenomenon.

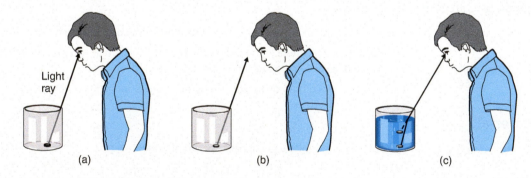

Light ray

(a)   (b)   (c)

- Light ordinarily travels in straight lines. (a), (b)
- In refraction, light rays bend as they go from one medium, such as water, to another medium, such as air. (c)
- Light refracts or bends outward when it goes from water into air. (c)
- As the light rays reflected from the coin emerge from the water, they bend outward and follow a new path that carries them to your eyes. (c)
- The illusion created is that the light rays followed a straight-line path and came directly from a coin floating high in the water. (c)

Explain that light rays are bent when they pass into and out of a clear material, such as water, plastic, or glass. The bending of light rays is called *refraction*.

Display the pencil in a glass of water that you used during the engage phase of the lesson.

Ask: *Now, why do you think the pencil appeared distorted in the glass of water?* Facilitate student discourse about possible explanations for the phenomenon, again reminding students to provide evidence that supports their claims. Lead the students to understand that the water bent or refracted the light rays coming from the pencil, causing it to appear distorted (broken or bent).

Elaborate

Provide each group with a flashlight, a comb, and two cylindrical jars of different diameters. Show them how to form rays of light by laying the flashlight on a white poster board and shining the flashlight through the teeth of the comb.

Instruct students to follow these directions:

1. Fill a jar almost full of water, place it in the path of the rays, and observe what happens.

2. Repeat the procedure with the other jar.

3. Record your observations. Include any differences you observed.

Ask: *What did you observe? In what ways did the patterns of light differ between the two jars? Which jar, the larger or smaller diameter one, bent the light rays more and caused them to converge nearer to the jar? What evidence do you have that supports your claim?* Lead students to recognize that the smaller jar, which had the greater curvature of its surface, caused more bending of the light rays.

Evaluate

Ask students to:

1. Define refraction in their own words.

2. Describe, using words and drawings, what happens to a light ray as it passes through the surface of a transparent object or material at various angles.

3. Provide an example of an optical phenomenon that is caused by refraction. Create a model that explains what happens to the light in this system.

Activity 26: How can a pinhole viewer provide evidence about how light travels?

Grades: 6–8, Physical Sciences

Framework Context	
Scientific and Engineering Practices	**Planning and Carrying Out Investigations** At all levels, students should engage in investigations that range from those structured by the teacher—in order to expose an issue or question that they would be unlikely to explore on their own to those that emerge from students' own questions (NRC, 2012, p. 61). **Analyzing and Interpreting Data** Once collected, data must be presented in a form that can reveal any patterns and relationships and that allows results to be communicated to others . . . .Such analysis can bring out the meaning of data and their relevance so that they may be used as evidence (NRC, 2012, p. 61). **Constructing Explanations** Students need opportunities to engage in constructing and critiquing explanations. They should be encouraged to develop explanations of what they observe when conducting their own investigations and to evaluate their own and others' explanations for consistency with the evidence (NRC, 2012, p. 69).
Crosscutting Concepts	**Cause and Effect** Students should have developed the habit of routinely asking about cause-and-effect relationships in the systems they are studying, particularly when something occurs that is, for them, unexpected. Argumentation starting from students' own explanations of cause and effect can help them appreciate standard scientific theories that explain the causal mechanisms in the systems under study (NRC, 2012, p. 89).
Disciplinary Core Idea	**PS4:** Waves and Their Applications in Technologies for Information Transfer
Component Idea	**PS4.B:** Electromagnetic Radiation
Conceptual Understanding	**By the end of grade 8:** The path that light travels can be traced as straight lines . . . (NRC, 2012, p. 135).

Performance Expectation MS-PS4-2

Develop and use a model to describe that waves are reflected, absorbed, or transmitted through various materials. *Clarification Statement:* Emphasis is on both light and mechanical waves. Examples of models could include drawings, simulations, and written descriptions (NGSS Lead States, 2013, p. 63). www .nextgenscience.org/pe/ms-ps4-2-waves-and-their-applications-technologies-information-transfer

Learning Target

Within a uniform transparent material, light travels in a straight line. The images produced by a pinhole viewer provide evidence for this claim.

Success Criteria

The students will:

1. Construct a pinhole viewer and compare the appearance of the object being viewed and the image that is produced.
2. Explain why the appearance of the image on the wax paper in the pinhole viewer provides evidence that light travels in a straight line.
3. Investigate how the size and number of holes letting light into a pinhole viewer affects the image produced on its wax paper screen, and develop and defend their explanations of the cause-and-effect relationships related to the observed phenomena.
4. Predict the appearance of the image on the wax paper screen of a pinhole viewer when they know the appearance of what is being viewed.

Materials

For each student:

- 2 plastic cups, opaque (16 oz) or two cardboard tubes
- 2 rubber bands
- Scissors
- Copy of each Recording Sheet: *(masters follow)*
    - Difference in Image
    - Difference in Number and Arrangement of Holes
    - Difference in Size of Hole

For each cooperative group:

- Aluminum foil
- Wax paper
- Masking tape
- Pushpin
- Paper clip, large
- Nail
- Pencil

For whole class:

- Overhead projector
- 1 sheet of construction paper *(with a large arrow-shaped hole cut out of the middle of it)*
- Screen or blank wall

DIFFERENCE IN IMAGE

Appearance of Arrow on Screen	Appearance of Arrow on Wax Paper in Pinhole Viewer
↑	
→	
←	
↓	

Describe how the image on the wax paper compares with the image on the screen.

What does the pinhole viewer seem to do to the image?

DIFFERENCE IN NUMBER AND ARRANGEMENT OF HOLES

Number of Holes	Appearance of Holes in Aluminum Foil	Prediction of Image on Wax Paper	Actual Image on Wax Paper
1			
2			
3			
4			

Describe how the number of holes in the aluminum foil affects the image produced.

Describe how the arrangement of holes in the aluminum foil affects the image produced.

Watch this lesson unfold in Don Boushee's fifth-grade classroom. Consider why the lesson segments are presented in the order they are.

DIFFERENCE IN SIZE OF HOLE

Hole Size	Prediction of Image on Wax Paper	Actual Image on Wax Paper
• Pin Hole		
● Paperclip Hole		
● Nail Hole		
● Pencil Hole		

Describe how the size of the hole affects the image produced.

Engage

Ask: *What kind of path do you think light follows as it moves? What have you seen that provides evidence for your claim?* Students are helping to identify possible lesson-level phenomena.

Explore

Have students follow these directions to construct their pinhole viewers. It may be helpful to demonstrate pinhole viewer construction for the class.

1. Cut the bases off of both plastic cups.
2. Cut a circle of wax paper and a circle of aluminum foil about 3 cm larger than the mouth of the cup.
3. Place the circle of wax paper on the mouth of one of the cups. Use a rubber band and some tape to hold the wax paper in place.
4. Hold the other cup so that the mouths of the two cups are together with the wax paper in between. Tape the cups together.
5. Place the circle of aluminum foil over one of the open ends of one of the cups. Secure it in place with a rubber band and tape.
6. Use the pushpin to poke a small hole in the center of the aluminum foil.

Place the construction paper with the arrow-shaped hole on the overhead projector so that a large, bright arrow pointing upward appears on the screen or wall.

Encourage the students to hold their pinhole viewers with the aluminum foil end toward the bright arrow and look into the open end. Ask: *What do you see on the wax paper screen in your pinhole viewer? How does it compare to the bright arrow on the wall?* Tell students to record their observations on the first row of the chart on the *Difference in Image* sheet by drawing what they see on the wax paper in the pinhole viewer.

Shift the orientation of the construction paper so the bright arrow on the screen or wall appears to point toward the right. Have students look into their pinhole viewers and record the appearance of this arrow on the wax paper in the viewer. Reorient the construction paper two more times, first projecting a left-pointing arrow, then a downward-pointing arrow.

Have the students answer the questions at the bottom of the *Difference in Image* sheet: *Describe how the image on the wax paper compares with the image on the screen. What does the pinhole viewer seem to do to the image?*

Explain

Encourage students to share and discuss their observations and the answers to their questions. The consensus should be that the arrow on the wax paper in the pinhole viewer is smaller, not as bright, and the other way around, flipped, or backwards compared to the arrow on the wall.

Introduce the term *inverted* meaning "reversed in position."

Ask: *How does the image on the screen provide more evidence that light travels in straight lines?* Draw this figure below on the board. Ask: *Where does the ray of light from the top point of the arrow land on the wax paper after it goes through the pinhole?* (On the bottom.) *Where does the ray of light from the base of the arrow land on the wax paper, after it goes through the pinhole?* (On the top.) Lead students to the conclusion that if the light travels in straight lines through the pinhole, then the image on the wax paper is inverted compared to the bright arrow on the wall. Remind students that there are rays coming from all lit parts of the arrow, not just the ends, and as they pass through the pinhole, the inverted image forms on the wax paper.

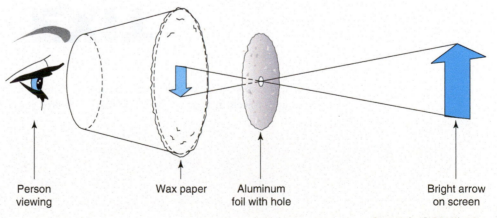

Person viewing   Wax paper   Aluminum foil with hole   Bright arrow on screen

Elaborate

Ask: *What would happen to the image on the wax paper in the pinhole viewer if the number or arrangement of the holes in the aluminum foil was changed?* Point out that the record sheet titled *Difference in Number and Arrangement of Holes* includes a chart on which they can record the appearance of the holes in the foil, their predictions of the image on wax paper, and their observations of the image on wax paper. Mention that the last three rows are left open for them to decide the number and arrangement of the holes. Tell the class that the bright arrow on the wall will stay in the pointing-upward position for all of their observations. Suggest that cooperation and sharing of pinhole viewers can reduce the replacement of aluminum foil, then allow them to investigate.

For an additional surprise, if students don't try rotating their pinhole viewers as they are observing with multiple holes, suggest that they try that.

Have students summarize their findings by responding to the two items at the bottom of the record sheet: *Describe how the number of holes in the aluminum foil affects the image produced. Describe how the arrangement of holes in the aluminum foil affects the image produced.*

Encourage groups to share their observations and summaries with the class. Ask: *Explain why you saw what you did on the wax paper during this investigation.*

Ask: *What would happen to the image on the wax paper in the pinhole viewer if the size of the hole in the aluminum foil was changed?* Point out that the record sheet titled *Difference in Size of Hole* includes a chart on which they can record the size of the hole in the foil, their predictions of the image on wax paper, and their observations of the image on wax paper. Mention that the last two rows are left open for them to try other sizes of holes. Provide groups with additional aluminum foil and suggest that one person make the hole shown on the first row, another make the hole for the second row, etc. Tell the class that the bright arrow on the wall will stay in the pointing-upward position for all of their observations; then encourage them to investigate.

Have students summarize their findings by responding to the item at the bottom of the record sheet: *Describe how the size of the hole affects the image produced.*

Encourage groups to share their observations and summary with the class. Ask: *Explain why you saw what you did on the wax paper during this investigation.*

Evaluate

Ask students to respond to these items in their science notebooks:

1. You use your pinhole viewer to look at a brightly lit EXIT sign. What will the image on the wax paper in the pinhole viewer look like?

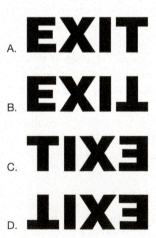

2. Explain why the appearance of the image on the wax paper in the pinhole viewer provides evidence that light travels in a straight line. You may use words and/or drawings.

Activity 27: What is white light?

Grades: 6–8, Physical Sciences

Framework Context	
Scientific and Engineering Practices	**Developing and Using Models** Students should be asked to use diagrams, maps, and other abstract models as tools that enable them to elaborate on their own ideas or findings and present them to others (NRC, 2012, p. 58). **Engaging in Argument from Evidence** Learning to argue scientifically offers students not only an opportunity to use their scientific knowledge in justifying an explanation and in identifying the weaknesses in others' arguments but also to build their own knowledge and understanding (NRC, 2012, p. 73).
Crosscutting Concepts	**Systems and System Models** Teaching students to explicitly craft and present their models in diagrams, words, and, eventually, in mathematical relationships serves three purposes. It supports them in clarifying their ideas and explanations and in considering any inherent contradictions; it allows other students the opportunity to critique and suggest revisions for the model; and it offers the teacher insights into those aspects of each student's understanding that are well founded and those that could benefit from further instructional attention (NRC, 2012, p. 94).
Disciplinary Core Idea	**PS4:** Waves and Their Applications in Technologies for Information Transfer
Component Idea	**PS4.B:** Electromagnetic Radiation
Conceptual Understanding	**By the end of grade 8:** A wave model of light is useful for explaining brightness, color, and the frequency-dependent bending of light at a surface between media (prisms). However, because light can travel through space, it cannot be a matter wave, like sound or water waves (NRC, 2012, p. 135).

Performance Expectation MS-PS4-2

Develop and use a model to describe that waves are reflected, absorbed, or transmitted through various materials. *Clarification Statement:* Emphasis is on both light and mechanical waves. Examples of models could include drawings, simulations, and written descriptions (NGSS Lead States, 2013, p. 63). www.nextgenscience.org/pe/ms-ps4-2-waves-and-their-applications-technologies-information-transfer

Learning Target

White light is composed of many colors (wavelengths) of light. Several phenomena provide evidence for this claim.

Success Criteria

The students will:

1. Recognize that white light is composed of many colors of light.
2. Identify and describe several phenomena that provide evidence that support the claim that white light is made of many colors.

Materials

- Prism
- Sheet of heavy, white cardboard
- Scissors
- Felt markers or crayons
- String
- Flashlights
- Colored filters (red, green, blue) for flashlights (these can be cut from colored clear plastic report covers)

Engage

Obtain a prism. Place the prism in the path of a strong beam of light as indicated in the diagram.
Ask: What do you see? What happened to the white light when it passed through the glass prism? What colors do you see?

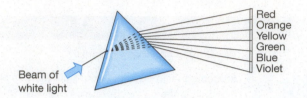

Explore

This part of the activity can be done in small groups or as a whole group investigation.

Put a different colored filter on each of three flashlights. Darken the room for the best effect. Shine each of the flashlights on three different places on a white sheet of paper. Draw and color (or label) a picture to show how the paper looks.

Shine two of the flashlights so their beams overlap on the paper. Draw and color (or label) a picture to show how the paper looks.

Repeat this step with all possible pairs of colors (red-blue; blue-green; green-red).

Shine all three flashlights so their beams all overlap on the paper. Draw and color (or label) a picture to show how the paper looks.

Explain

Ask: *What did the prism do to the light?* (It separated white light into different colors.) *What does that tell you about the composition of white light?* (It is made up of different colors of light.) *What evidence supports your claim?*

Ask: *What happened when you mixed colored light beams from flashlights?* (A different color appeared.) Have students share what color was produced by each pair of overlapped colored light beams and what colors were produced when all three colored light beams were overlapped. Creating Venn diagrams based on student observations on the board might be helpful during this discussion. The class should agree that when these three colors of light were mixed, white light was produced. Ask: *Does this evidence also support the claim that white light is a combination of different colors of light? Why or why not?*

Elaborate

Introduce another way of mixing colors of light. Challenge students to construct spinning color wheels by following these directions:

1. Cut out a circle about 10 cm in diameter from stiff cardboard.

2. Divide the circle into three pie-shaped sections.

3. Use red, green, and blue markers or crayons to color each section a different color.

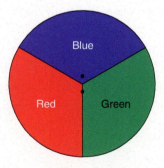

4. Punch two small holes about a centimeter apart in the center of the cardboard circle.

5. Pass a string about 60 cm long through the two holes; tie the free ends of the string forming a loop.

6. Hold the loop by the ends and turn the cardboard color wheel many times, twisting the string as you go.

7. Pull the two ends of the string suddenly and watch the color wheel spin. What do you see? What colors do you observe as the color wheel is spinning?

Encourage students to share their observations with the class. Expected comments include: *The wedges of color seem to disappear. The whole wheel looks white when it spins.* Ask: *What did the color wheel do to the light?* (It combined different colors to form a white color.) Ask: *Why do you think this happened?* Lead students to the idea that red, green, and blue light were reflecting from the wheel, and when it was spinning fast, our eyes couldn't see the sections separately so the reflected light mixed together so it looked white.

To further extend the lesson, let different groups color their color wheel sections differently. Have groups compare what they see with different color wheels.

Invite student groups to report on their procedures and findings related to their color wheels.

Evaluate

To assess student understanding about the composition of white light, have the class respond to the following questions in their science notebook:

1. What evidence have you seen that white light is made up of many colors? Draw models that illustrate your thinking and help you explain your ideas to others. Use the following rubric to evaluate student responses to the question.

Exemplary:

- Clearly explains all three examples presented in the lesson.
- White light separated into colors by a prism.
- Colored beams mix to create white light.
- Spinning color wheel.

Proficient:

- Clearly explains two of the examples presented in the lesson.

Developing:

- Clearly explains only one of the examples presented in the lesson.

Lacks Understanding:

- None of the examples presented in the lesson are suggested as evidence.

Activity 28: What are digital images made of, and how are they produced, transmitted, and displayed?

Grade: 4, Physical Sciences

Framework Context	
Scientific and Engineering Practices	**Developing and Using Models** Conceptual models . . . are . . . explicit representations that are in some ways analogous to the phenomena they represent. Conceptual models allow scientists . . . to better visualize and understand a phenomenon under investigation . . . (NRC, 2012, p. 56). The quality of a student-developed model will be highly dependent on prior knowledge and skill and also on the student's understanding of the system being modeled, so students should be expected to refine their models as their understanding develops (NRC, 2012, p. 59). **Engaging in Argument from Evidence** . . . students should argue for the explanations they construct, defend their interpretations of the associated data, and advocate for the designs they propose. Meanwhile, they should learn how to evaluate critically the scientific arguments of others and present counterarguments. Learning to argue scientifically offers students not only an opportunity to use their scientific knowledge in justifying an explanation and in identifying the weaknesses in others' arguments but also to build their own knowledge and understanding (NRC, 2012, p. 73).
Crosscutting Concepts	**Scale, Proportion, and Quantity** As students deepen their understanding of algebraic thinking, they should be able to apply it to examine their scientific data to predict the effect of a change in one variable on another, for example . . . (NRC, 2012, p. 91).
Disciplinary Core Idea **Component Idea** **Conceptual Understanding**	**PS4:** Waves and Their Applications in Technologies for Information Transfer **PS4.C:** Informational Technologies and Instrumentation **By the end of grade 4:** Digitized information (e.g., the pixels of a picture) can be stored for future recovery or transmitted over long distances without significant degradation (NRC, 2012, p. 137).

Performance Expectation 4-PS4-3

Generate and compare multiple solutions that use patterns to transfer information. *Clarification Statement:* Examples of solutions could include drums sending coded information through sound waves. Using a grid of 1's and 0's representing black and white to send information about a picture, and using Morse code to send text (NGSS Lead States, 2013, p. 37). www.nextgenscience.org/pe/4-ps4-3-waves-and-their-applications-technologies-information-transfer

Learning Target

Digital pictures are composed of pixels. A string of binary digits, 1's and 0's, specify which pixels are black and which are white to generate a black-and-white image.

Success Criteria

The students will:

1. Collaboratively construct and use evidence to defend models that represent their understanding of processes involved in creating, storing, transmitting, and displaying digital images.

2. Make claims about relationships between various quantities and dimensions related to digital imagery, and support their claims with evidence, while critically listening to the claims of others and defending their claims through appropriate scientific discourse.

Materials

- Computer connected to a digital projector (lesson was developed using a computer running Microsoft Windows 7, but could be adapted for other platforms)
- Projection screen, whiteboard, or blank wall

- Student computers with access to Paint in the Accessories menu (1 for each pair or small group of students) (lesson was developed using computers running Microsoft Windows XP, but could be adapted for other platforms)
- "Exploring Pixels" Sheets (a master for preparing these is included at the end of the lesson)
- Black markers
- 8 cm × 8 cm blank sheets of white paper (for their initial drawing)
- Transparent grids of different sized squares (masters for preparing these are included at the end of the lesson)
- Adding machine tape
- Pencils
- Small sticky notes
- Graph paper (1 cm × 1 cm grid)

Engage

From the *Start* menu of your computer, select *Pictures*. Double click an image from one of the files stored there. Maximize the window that opens by clicking the *maximize icon* at the top right corner of the window. Project the image on a screen, whiteboard, or plain wall in the classroom.

Direct the class's attention to the image; then ask: *What is that?* (Students will probably name or describe the image.) *Is it a real _____? (Fill in the blank with whatever the image shows.)* (Students will probably decide that it is just a picture or image of the real thing.) *How can this image from a different place and a different time be here in our classroom? How do you think the process works?* Encourage the students to talk with a partner or in a small group about their responses to these questions for about two minutes. Invite groups to briefly share their thinking with the rest of the class.

Ask: *What do you think this picture is made up of?* (Some students might describe various objects shown on the screen, but that is not really what was being asked.) *Do you think we could tell what the picture is made up of if we looked at it more closely? How could we do that?* (Students might suggest moving closer to the screen, using a hand lens or a microscope, or using the computer to zoom in on it.) Select the magnifier below the image and slowly move the slider up. Ask: *What does the image appear to be made of?* (Lots of little squares.) Each of these is known as a *pixel,* which is short for *picture element.*

Explore

Let students work in pairs or small groups to find out more about pixels in digital images. The lesson was designed to use the *Paint* program located in the *Accessories* folder of a computer running *Microsoft Windows XP.* The *Exploring Pixels* sheet, included at the end of the lesson, will help get students started and guide their exploration. Monitor their work and remind them to follow the guidelines and stay focused on the questions on the sheet.

Explain

Bring the class together in a discussion circle to share the discoveries they made during the explore phase of the lesson. Encourage students to support their claims with evidence, perhaps using images they saved during their exploration or by demonstrating their ideas for the rest of the class. If necessary, guide the discussion so that the following concepts emerge:

- Digital images are composed of pixels.
- When an image is magnified, the number of pixels stays the same, but each one becomes larger.
- The size of an image is determined by its length and width in pixels and the magnification selected.
- An image produced at a low magnification will appear pixelated when viewed at higher magnifications; the higher the magnification, the more pixelated it appears.

Everything that a computer does is based on zeros and ones. The basic unit of information in computers and telecommunications is known as a *bit,* which is short for *binary digit.* A bit can have only two values: numerically either 0 or 1.

In math you may have studied about different number systems. The binary number system, also known as *Base 2,* has only 2 digits: 0 and 1. Its name makes sense because the prefix *bi* means two. The decimal system, also known as *Base 10,* which is commonly used by humans in daily life, has 10 digits: 0, 1, 2, 3, 4, 5, 6, 7, 8, and 9. Its name also makes sense because the prefix *deci* means ten.

Ask: *If you followed the guidelines for Exploring Pixels, what colors were the pixels in your image?* (Black or white.) This type of image is called a *bitonal image,* meaning that it is made up of only two colors of picture elements.

Ask: *How could a digital image like those you made during the explore phase of the lesson be translated into a series of bits (zeros and ones) so it could be stored in a computer's memory or on a memory card and transmitted through wires or wirelessly to other devices?* If students need a hint, suggest that each pixel could be represented by one bit of information: white = 0 and black = 1. Show an example of a tiny image like this:

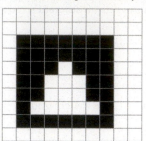

If a scanner read each row of the image from left to right starting at the top, the binary code for this image would be:

000000000000000000000011111110001111111000111011100011000110001100011000100000100011111110000000000000

Ask: *How many bits should be in this code? How do you know?*

Tell the class that this series of numbers could be stored in a memory device or transmitted bit by bit to another device. Ask: *How could this sequence of numbers be turned back into a digital image?*

Elaborate

Challenge groups of students to model the process of scanning a simple black-and-white drawing, transmitting the code to a computer, and displaying the image on a monitor. Encourage them to think of the steps involved; then model each step in order to illustrate the whole process.

This outline of the steps should assist you in providing scaffolding assistance as needed. But only give assistance after students have first grappled with the challenge.

Step	Suggested Materials/Actions
Draw simple picture	Black marker, blank 8 cm×8 cm white paper
Scan the picture (Replicate picture with pixels)	Select a transparent grid to lay over drawing, indicate value of each pixel, either 0/1 or white/black
Write sequence of code	Turn the values of the pixels into a list of numbers
Transmit code to computer across the room one number at a time	Voice, visual signals (hand signs), audible tones, sticky notes, etc.
Store code in computer's memory	Adding machine tape
Transmit code to the video processor	Voice, visual signals (hand signs), audible tones, sticky notes, etc.
Display the image on monitor	Graph paper

Show students the available tools: a black marker, an 8 cm by 8 cm blank sheet of white paper (for their initial drawing), transparent grids of different sized squares (black line masters are included at the end of this activity), adding machine tape, graph paper (1 cm square grid), sticky notes. Groups may use additional tools if they want to.

Explain that their model may be a poster, a skit, or some other product that demonstrates their knowledge of the processes involved with making, storing, and displaying digital images.

Evaluate

During the explore phase of the lesson, informal evaluation of students' abilities to investigate relationships among variables related to digital imagery would be appropriate, even though that practice is not overly emphasized in this activity. Observation of the small group work could reveal students' level of competency in planning and carrying out investigations and making sense of the data collected.

Give each group an opportunity to share their model of the digital imaging process. With the help of the class, you might create an analytic rubric for scoring the products. Consider including criteria such as: order of steps in the process; data in proper form for that step; effectiveness of analogies between model and reality; and strength of argument supporting their proposed model.

Encourage students to consider the alternative ways other groups developed their models and identify the elements of the model they found most meaningful or effective. These ideas could be shared orally or in writing as complimentary notes to specific teams.

"Exploring Pixels" Sheet

GUIDELINES

Tabs you might use:

    File—to save an image you create or to open a new file

    View—only *Tool Bar* should be checked

- Use *Zoom* to:
  - Be sure that *Show Grid* is checked.
  - Select *Custom . . .* to monitor and change percent image is enlarged.

Image—*Draw Opaque* should be checked

- Select *Attributes* to find information about the digital image
- Select *Clear Image* if you want to start a new drawing
- Be sure that *Pixels* is selected in the *Units* box and that *Colors* is selected in the *Colors* box

Tools you might use:

    Magnifier—another way to zoom or change the percent the image is enlarged

    Pencil—to draw a thin line

    Paint Brush—to draw lines of different thicknesses

Things to try: *Be sure to record your findings!*

    Draw something on the screen.

    Change the magnification to see what happens.

    Change the width and length in pixels to see what happens.

    Save the image.

    Compare images you have saved—Do you have notes about the length, width, magnification, etc.?

Questions to answer: *Remember to have some supporting evidence!*

1. When an image is magnified—
   - What happens to the number of pixels?
   - What happens to the size of each pixel in the image?
2. What factors affect the size of an image?
3. What happens to an image drawn at a low magnification as the magnification increases? *(Hint: Set the magnification to 1X or 100%. Set the Width to 150 pixels and the Height to 100 pixels. Draw something on the screen. Increase the magnification gradually.)*
4. What happens to an image drawn at high magnification as the magnification decreases?
5. What are all of your digital images made up of?

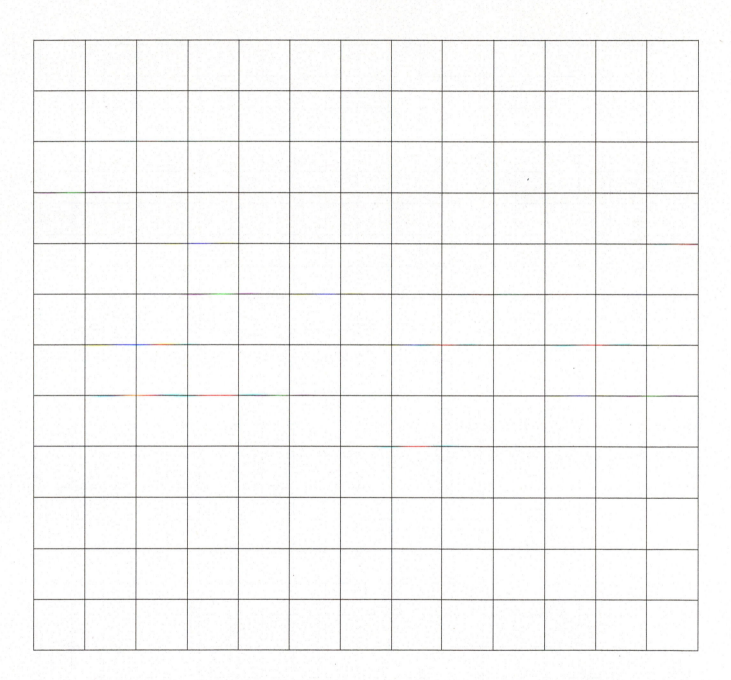

Copy this sheet onto transparencies for use during the elaborate phase of the lesson.

Grid with Large Squares

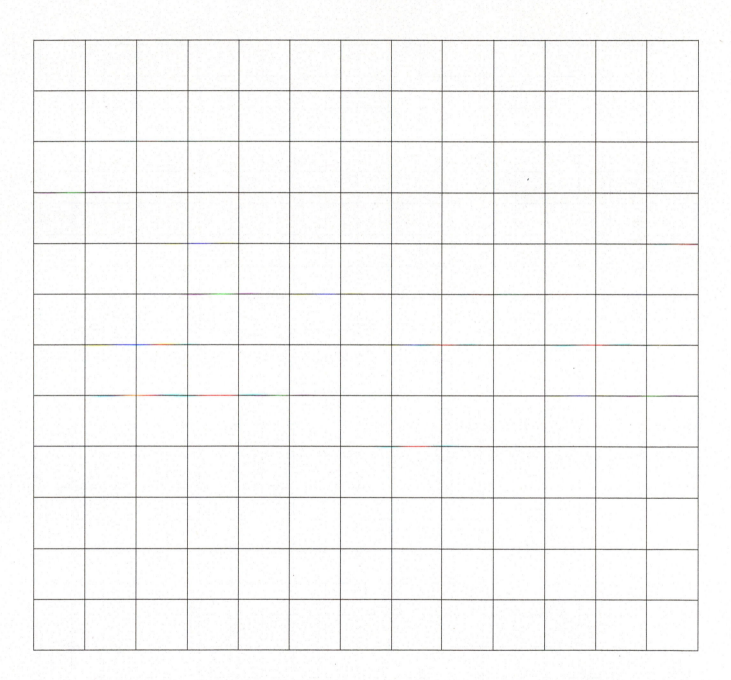

Copy this sheet onto transparencies for use during the elaborate phase of the lesson.

Grid with Medium Squares

Copy this sheet onto transparencies for use during the elaborate phase of the lesson.

Grid with Small Squares

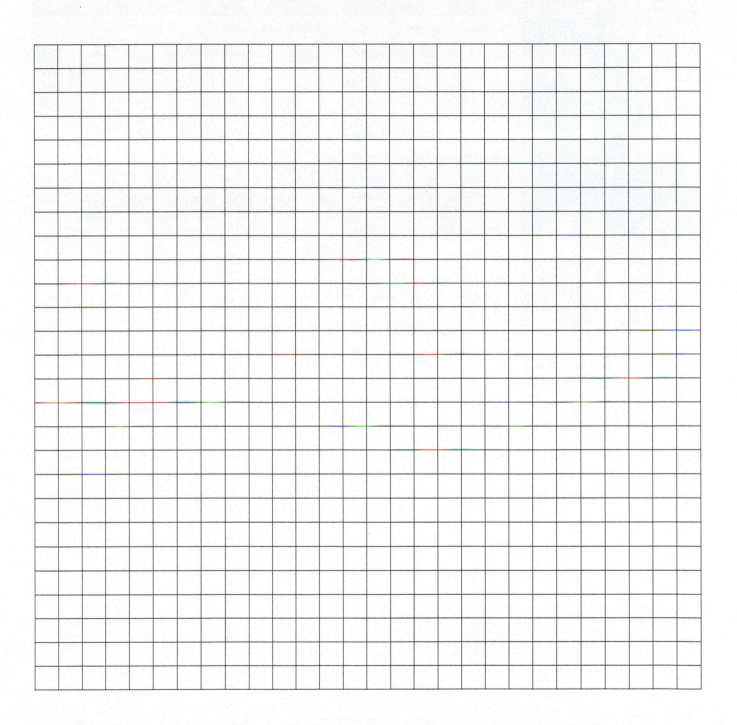

Activity 29: Why are most modern communication technologies digital?

Grades: 6–8, Physical Sciences

Framework Context	
Scientific and Engineering Practices	**Obtaining, Evaluating, and Communicating Information** Students need sustained practice and support to develop the ability to extract the meaning of scientific text from books, media reports, and other forms of scientific communication because the form of this text is initially unfamiliar— expository rather than narrative, often linguistically dense, and reliant on precise logical flows. Students should be able to interpret meaning from text, to produce text in which written language and diagrams are used to express scientific ideas, and to engage in extended discussion about those ideas (NRC, 2012, p. 76). **Engaging in Argument from Evidence** As they grow in their ability to construct scientific arguments, students can draw on a wider range of reasons or evidence, so that their arguments become more sophisticated. In addition, they should be expected to discern what aspects of the evidence are potentially significant for supporting or refuting a particular argument (NRC, 2012, p. 73).
Crosscutting Concepts	**Structure and Function** As students develop their understanding of the relationships between structure and function, they should begin to apply this knowledge when investigating phenomena that are unfamiliar to them. They recognize that often the first step in deciphering how a system works is to examine in detail what it is made of and the shapes of its parts (NRC, 2012, p. 98).
Disciplinary Core Idea **Component Idea** **Conceptual Understanding**	**PS4:** Waves and Their Applications in Technologies for Information Transfer **PS4.C:** Informational Technologies and Instrumentation **By the end of grade 8:** Many modern communication devices use digitized signals (sent as wave pulses) as a more reliable way to encode and transmit information (NRC, 2012 p. 137).

Performance Expectation MS-PS4-3

Integrate qualitative scientific and technical information to support the claim that digitized signals are a more reliable way to encode and transmit information than analog signals. *Clarification Statement:* Emphasis is on basic understanding that waves can be used for communication purposes. Examples could include using fiber-optic cable to transmit light pulses, radio wave pulses in Wi-Fi devices, and conversion of stored binary patterns to make sound or text on a computer screen (NGSS Lead States, 2013, p. 63). www.nextgenscience.org/pe/ms-ps4-3-waves-and-their-applications-technologies-information-transfer

Learning Target

Digitized signals (sent as wave pulses) are a reliable way to encode and transmit information.

Success Criteria

The students will:

1. Collaborate to locate, read, evaluate, and summarize information found on the Internet that relates to the digital revolution and digital communication devices.

2. Closely read a one-page article about the differences between analog and digital signals and then create a T-chart contrasting the two signals.

3. Use only the information from their T-chart to inform their writing of a paragraph that identifies which signal (analog or digital) they think is better and presents evidence to support their claim.

Materials

- Computers with Internet access, at least one for each pair of students
- Sentence strips (each with one of the questions from the engage phase of the lesson, and some extras for new questions that emerge during discussion and research)
- Sticky notes (assorted sizes)

- Pens and pencils
- Chart paper
- Markers
- Copies of a one-page article titled "Difference Between Analog and Digital Signals," available at www.thedifferencebetween.net
- Highlighters
- Blank paper
- Writing paper or access to a word processor

Engage

Say the following to the class; after each question pause for students' ideas to be shared through discussion and discourse. This entire lesson segment should take between 10 and 15 minutes.

*You may have heard of **the digital revolution**.*

1. *How would you define it?*
2. *What do you think it has to do with modern communication devices and systems?*
3. *Why do you think the digital revolution occurred or is occurring?*
4. *What kinds of devices are now available in digital versions? (Be specific.)*
5. *What is so special about digital communication devices and systems? How could we find out the answers to these questions?*

As you ask each numbered question, post the corresponding sentence strip above a sheet of chart paper already posted around the classroom. If additional questions come up, write them on a sentence strip and post them over a sheet of chart paper, too.

Explore

Tell the class that they will have an opportunity to access the Internet and to collaborate in order to find, read, analyze, and summarize information about the digital revolution. Let them know that they will share a computer with a partner (either assign their partner or allow them to select someone to work with for this project). Each pair of students should use one or more web browsers to search for websites that might have information that would help them answer any or all of the posted questions. *As you and your partner find information that relates to a particular question, summarize important ideas from that site on a sticky note, list the URL so you can find the site again if you need to refer to it later, and write your names on the back of the sticky. As notes are completed, stick them to the chart paper under the question they address.*

It will be easy to tell from your seats how many responses each question's chart has. Rather than continuing to search for information about a question that already has lots of input, adjust your Internet search to focus on one of the questions that only has a few notes on it.

As students are working, you should be available to provide assistance and redirection if necessary. Remind them to use the reading and summarization skills that they have learned and used in other subjects. This first step might take between 20 and 30 minutes.

When you think enough information has been collected and posted, divide the class into small groups based on the number of questions posted along with a fair number of sticky notes; each small group will now work on one question poster. Choose a group-forming strategy you believe would work best for your class, and be sure each group has a chart to work with. Their first task is to read all of the sticky notes and place them in clusters of similar ideas on their chart paper. Next they should develop titles for each cluster of notes they formed and summarize main points within each cluster. If someone remembers an idea from their earlier research that they didn't write down but would like to add now, they or another team member may go back online to find, read, summarize the site, and add that extra sticky. This second step should take between five and ten minutes.

Next, each team's job is to make a poster featuring some kind of visual organizer that presents information that helps to answer the question that their group arranged in clusters. They should be able to complete that task in 10 to 15 minutes.

Finally, let the class know that each group will have two minutes to present their poster to the class and to explain why they chose to use the visual organizer that they selected. Allow them five minutes to plan and practice their presentation.

Explain

In some logical order, invite the groups to present their posters to the class. Let the students know that there will be a little time for questions and additional scientific discourse after all the groups present. Tape all of the posters to the wall for future reference.

Elaborate

Ask: *In your Internet research, what did you learn about the differences between digital and analog signals?* Distribute a copy of the article "Difference Between Analog and Digital Signals" to each student. Remind the class of the close-reading strategies that they have been practicing in their classes. After reading the article together orally, tell students to reread it to themselves, while highlighting words that are unfamiliar. Make dictionaries available as a reference.

Each student is expected to independently complete a T-chart that illustrates the ways these two signals differ. With input from your class, develop a rubric to guide their work and to establish criteria and levels for assessment of the T-charts.

Evaluate

Encourage students to use the rubric described previously to self-assess and make revisions to the T-chart they created before turning it in for scoring by you.

When the T-charts are returned, have a class discussion about any lingering misconceptions that seemed to be held by many of your students; use appropriate review/reteach strategies to address those ideas. Then ask the students to write a paragraph that identifies which signal they consider to be "better" and support their claim with evidence. When scoring the paragraph, focus on how well their evidence supported their claim.

Life Sciences

Source: Demerzel21/Fotolia

"Life Sciences" is the second domain included in the Disciplinary Core Ideas, the third dimension of the *Framework*. Specific fields of science that are typically considered to be Life Sciences include: biology, botany, zoology, environmental science, ecology, genetics, medical sciences, and biophysics, just to name a few. Like the other disciplinary areas, Life Science has no distinct boundaries; since the laws of physics and chemistry apply and our Earth is the one place in the universe where we know there is life, the lines between the science disciplines are often blurred.

The inquiry-based activities included in this section are designed to help students learn Life Science core ideas through the use of Science and Engineering Practices. They are not designed to be a curriculum or a complete lesson and are merely examples of lesson activities that are aligned to the three dimensions found in the NGSS standards.

At first glance, you might wonder about the organization of the Life Science activities. Instead of being arranged traditionally, by topic with all of the plant activities together and all the animal activities together, they are arranged in order by the Disciplinary Core Idea code on which they focus and then sequenced by grade level. In other words, the activities at the beginning of the Life Science section relate to structure and function (LS1.A), and K–2 activities focusing on structure and function precede grade 3–5 activities about the same component idea.

As shown in the following table, in *A Framework for K–12 Science Education: Practices, Crosscutting Concepts, and Core Ideas* (NRC, 2012), this disciplinary area includes four core ideas: LS1: From Molecules to Organisms: Structures and Processes; LS2: Ecosystems: Interactions, Energy, and Dynamics; LS3: Heredity: Inheritance and Variation of Traits; and, LS4: Biological Evolution: Unity and Diversity.

Life Science Core and Component Ideas

Discipline-Related Code	Descriptive Title	Related Question
LS1	**From Molecules to Organisms: Structures and Processes**	**How do organisms live, grow, respond to their environment, and reproduce?**
LS1.A	Structure and Function	*How do the structures of organisms enable life's functions?*
LS1.B	Growth and Development of Organisms	*How do organisms grow and develop?*
LS1.C	Organization for Matter and Energy Flow in Organisms	*How do organisms obtain and use the matter and energy they need to live and grow?*
LS1.D	Information Processing	*How do organisms detect, process, and use information about the environment?*
LS2	**Ecosystems: Interactions, Energy, and Dynamics**	**How and why do organisms interact with their environment, and what are the effects of these interactions?**
LS2.A	Interdependent Relationships in Ecosystems	*How do organisms interact with the living and nonliving environments to obtain matter and energy?*
LS2.B	Cycles of Matter and Energy Transfer in Ecosystems	*How do matter and energy move through an ecosystem?*
LS2.C	Ecosystem Dynamics, Functioning, and Resilience	*What happens to ecosystems when the environment changes?*
LS2.D	Social Interactions and Group Behavior	*How do organisms interact in groups so as to benefit individuals?*
LS3	**Heredity: Inheritance and Variation of Traits**	**How are characteristics of one generation passed to the next? How can individuals of the same species and even siblings have different characteristics?**
LS3.A	Inheritance of Traits	*How are the characteristics of one generation related to the previous generation?*
LS3.B	Variation of Traits	*Why do individuals of the same species vary in how they look, function, and behave?*

Discipline-Related Code	Descriptive Title	Related Question
LS4	**Biological Evolution: Unity and Diversity**	**How can there be so many similarities among organisms yet so many different kinds of plants, animals, and microorganisms? How does biodiversity affect humans?**
LS4.A	Evidence of Common Ancestry and Diversity	*What evidence shows that different species are related?*
LS4.B	Natural Selection	*How does genetic variation among organisms affect survival and reproduction?*
LS4.C	Adaptation	*How does the environment influence populations of organisms over multiple generations?*
LS4.D	Biodiversity and Humans	*What is biodiversity, how do humans affect it, and how does it affect humans?*

(NRC, 2012, p. 142)

For a concise description of background information related to the Life Sciences core and component ideas, look at Chapter 6 of *A Framework for K–12 Science Education: Practices, Crosscutting Concepts, and Core Ideas* (NRC, 2012), available online from the National Academies Press at www.nap.edu.

There are additional Life Science activities available to you digitally via the Enhanced Pearson eText. These include:

DCI Component Idea	Title	Grade / Grade-band
LS1.A	What structures (parts) help a tree survive?	Grade 1
LS2.A	How are seeds inside a pod (fruit) alike and different?	Grade 1
LS1.D	How do plants respond to light?	Grade 1

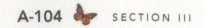

Activity 30: What are seeds and where are they found?

Grade: 1, Life Sciences

Framework Context	
Scientific and Engineering Practices	**Constructing Explanations and Designing Solutions** Early in their science education, students need opportunities to engage in constructing and critiquing explanations. They should be encouraged to develop explanations of what they observe when conducting their own investigations and to evaluate their own and others' explanations for consistency with the evidence (NRC, 2012, p. 69). **Obtaining, Evaluating, and Communicating Information** Students should be able to interpret meaning from text, to produce text in which written language and diagrams are used to express scientific ideas, and to engage in extended discussion about those ideas. From the very start of their science education, students should be asked to engage in the communication of science, especially regarding the investigations they are conducting and the observations they are making (NRC, 2012, p. 76).
Crosscutting Concepts	**Structure and Function** Exploration of the relationship between structure and function can begin in the early grades through investigations of accessible and visible systems in the natural and human-built world (NRC, 2012, p. 97). **Patterns** Patterns in the natural world can be observed, used to describe phenomena, and used as evidence (NRC, 2012, p. 233).
Disciplinary Core Idea	**LS1:** From Molecules to Organisms: Structures and Processes
Component Idea	**LS1.A:** Structure and Function
Conceptual Understanding	**By the end of grade 2:** Plants . . . have different parts (roots, stems, leaves, flowers, fruits) that help them survive, grow, and produce more plants (NRC, 2012, p. 144).

Performance Expectation 1-LS1-1

Use materials to design a solution to a human problem by mimicking how plants . . . use their external parts to help them survive, grow and meet their needs (NGSS Lead States, 2013, p. 12).
www.nextgenscience.org/pe/1-ls1-1-molecules-organisms-structures-and-processes

Learning Target

Seeds, found in fruits, are a plant part from which new plants can grow.

Success Criteria

The students will:

1. Record observations of seeds in a variety of fruits.

2. Develop an explanation for seeds being contained in fruits.

3. Make conceptual connections between observations of seeds in fruit in the "real world" and text describing the same organizational structure.

4. Communicate their current understanding about where seeds are found in words and drawings.

Materials

- Paper plates
- Hand lenses
- Assortment of seeds (they may be from seed packets that are past their expiration date)
- Assortment of other small, non-seed objects such as: gravel, candy sprinkles, chocolate chips, beads, etc.

- Plastic knives
- Variety of fresh fruits (Children might be encouraged to bring a fruit from home. Tomatoes, apples, corn on the cob, blueberries, cherries, cantaloupes, bean and pea pods, strawberries, peaches, and bell peppers are interesting fruits for children to observe.)
- Paper towels
- Safety goggles
- Science notebooks
- The book: *A Fruit Is a Suitcase for Seeds* by Jean Richards or a similar children's text about seeds found in fruit

Engage

Give each pair or small group of students, hand lenses and an assortment of approximately ten seeds and about five non-seed objects on a paper plate. Allow students several minutes to observe and talk about their materials. Then ask the class: *What is on your group's plate? Are all of the objects seeds? How do you know? How are seeds different from the non-seeds? Where do seeds come from?*

The purpose of this phase of the lesson is to uncover students' current thinking, not to present facts or decide who is correct.

Explore

Display the fruit you have collected. Ask: *Are there seeds in each of these fruits? How many seeds are in each of the fruits? How can we find out?*

Distribute paper plates, plastic knives, and several fruits to each group. Tell children to use their plastic knives to cut their fruits open. They should find and observe the seeds in each one. Remind students to keep notes about their discoveries in their science notebooks using words and drawings.

Suggest that groups discuss why seeds would be produced inside fruits. Ask: *What might the fruit do for the seeds?*

Explain

Ask questions about their exploration, such as: *Did you find seeds in your fruit? How many seeds did you find? What are the characteristics of the seeds? How are they alike? How are they different?*

Through questioning and discussion, lead the students to the ideas that fruits are produced by plants, fruits are considered a plant part, and seeds are found in fruit. Also have students share their ideas about why seeds are found in fruits. Lead them to consider the idea that the fruit protects the seeds.

Elaborate

Share a book about seeds and fruit with the class. *A Fruit Is a Suitcase for Seeds* by Jean Richards is an example of children's literature focused specifically on the content of this lesson. During reading, encourage students to talk about connections they see between information in the text and their discoveries during the explore and explain phases of the lesson.

Evaluate

There are multiple opportunities to formatively assess students' use of science Practices throughout the lesson. Be sure to monitor student work and interactions as they explore fruit and participate in class discussions.

As a summative assessment, you might check for understanding about where seeds are found. Have students produce an additional page for the book presented during the elaborate phase of the lesson based on one or more of the fruits examined in class. The student-produced pages should include drawings and a sentence or two about the fruit they choose to focus on. Also, challenge your students to produce a second additional book page explaining why seeds are contained in fruits.

Activity 31: How do plants get the water they need to function and to grow?

Grade: 5, Life Sciences

Framework Context	
Scientific and Engineering Practices	**Constructing Explanations and Designing Solutions** They should be encouraged to develop explanations of what they observe when conducting their own investigations and to evaluate their own and others' explanations for consistency with the evidence (NRC, 2012, p. 69). **Engaging in Argument from Evidence** They [students] should learn how to evaluate critically the scientific arguments of others and present counterarguments. In addition, they should be expected to discern what aspects of the evidence are potentially significant for supporting or refuting a particular argument (NRC, 2012, p. 73).
Crosscutting Concepts	**Energy and Matter** Students should be asked to recognize the conservation of matter and the flow of matter into, out of, and within systems under study (NRC, 2012, p. 96).
Disciplinary Core Idea	**LS1:** From Molecules to Organisms: Structures and Processes
Component Idea	**LS1.C:** Organization for Matter and Energy Flow in Organizations
Conceptual Understanding	**By the end of grade 5:** Plants acquire their material for growth chiefly from air and water and process matter they have formed to maintain their internal conditions (NRC, 2012, p. 148).

Performance Expectation 5-LS1-1

Support an argument that plants get the materials they need for growth chiefly from air and water (emphasis is on the idea that plant matter comes mostly from air and water not from soil) (NGSS Lead States, 2013, p. 47). www.nextgenscience.org/pe/5-ls1-1-molecules-organisms-structures-and-processes

Learning Target

Plants can transport water using vessels in their roots, stems, and leaves.

Success Criteria

Students will be able to:

1. Carry out investigations about how water is transported through the stem of a plant.
2. Recognize that one of the functions of plant stems is to transport water up through a plant.
3. Develop visual models of processes they think cause water to rise in stems of plants, and use them to explain their thinking to others.
4. Use evidence to support an argument about the mechanical processes involved in water rising up through plant stems.

Materials

- White carnations
- Geranium or celery stem
- Red and blue food coloring
- Drinking glass or clear plastic cup
- Paper towel
- Access to the Internet

Preparation

Place the stem of a white carnation in a cup containing water with blue food coloring. Leave the carnation in the water until blue color can be observed in the flower and stem.

Engage

Ask: *What color are carnations naturally? How does water get from the roots of a plant to the leaves? How do you think a florist produces blue carnations? If you wanted to change a white carnation into a multicolored carnation, what would you do? How could you find out if your idea was correct?*

Explore

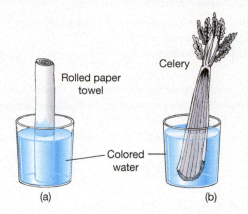

Rolled paper towel

Celery

Colored water

(a)   (b)   (c)

Organize students into small groups. Have each group fill a cup with water, tint it with food coloring, and add a rolled paper towel, as in diagram (a).

To encourage science talk, ask: *What do you see happening to the paper towel? Why do you think this happens?* Encourage students to create visual models to illustrate their explanations.

In the next activity, students will investigate the question: *How could this work in plants?* Tell students to put some water in the drinking glass and add the food coloring. Cut a small slice off the bottom of the celery stem. Observe the cut end with a magnifying glass and draw a picture of what you observe. Set the stem into the glass of colored water as in diagram (b). Allow it to sit in a sunny area for two hours. At the end of this period, cut open the stem with with a cross-cut and then with a lengthwise cut. See diagram (c). Encourage students to discuss the results and to create visual diagrams to illustrate their observations and then create explanations of what happened.

Explain

Ask: *What has happened to the celery stem? What parts of the stem appear to contain the colored water? How do you know? Make a claim and cite your evidence. What can you conclude about one of the functions of a stem?* Encourage classroom discourse that results from asking these questions.

Introduce *xylem,* the structures within the stem that carry water upward in plants. Appropriate descriptions may be found in your science textbook, in a library resource, or online. Note that there are two ideas in the literature about the process for the upward motion of water through plant stems. Some sources cite capillary action as the process cause, while others credit transpiration as the major cause. Be prepared to help students understand these ideas.

Elaborate

You could use one or more of the following questions as a starter for an elaboration activity depending on your instructional goals and the interests or skills of your students. You might differentiate by assigning specific prompts to selected students, or you might use the motivation of personal choice by allowing students to select the prompt they want to work on for this phase of the lesson.

Prompts:

1. What do you think might happen if you put half of a split stem in one color of water and the other half in another color of water? Try it and see.

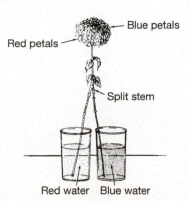

Blue petals

Red petals

Split stem

Red water   Blue water

Product for evaluation: Prepare a report or a poster that describes your procedure, documents your results, and presents a claim about the outcome that is supported by evidence.

2. What do you think might happen to the upward movement of water in a stem when the plant is in the dark or out of sunlight? How could you find out?

Product for evaluation: Design and conduct an experiment to check your prediction. Write a lab report about your investigation.

3. What causes water to rise to the top of a plant through its stem? Conduct research on the Internet to find out. Use your favorite web browser to search for: *capillary action in plants*. What happens if the stem is partially severed?

Product for evaluation: Produce a chart describing various theories about the mechanism that causes water to rise through a plant's stem, then write a persuasive paper making an evidence-based argument to support the hypothesis you claim to be correct.

Evaluate

Use the following multiple-choice item to check student understanding about the concept developed by this activity (the expected answer is C).

The carnation and celery activities demonstrate that stems:

A. Hold the entire plant in place
B. Get water from the soil
C. Transport water to the upper parts of a plant
D. Determine the color of the flower

Rubrics for the products should be developed collaboratively with you and the class. A thorough understanding of the expected products generally leads to better work. All products should be shared with the rest of the class so students have an opportunity to communicate effectively and defend their thinking.

Activity 32: How do we inhale and exhale and why is this process important?

Grades: 6–8, Life Sciences

Framework Context	
Scientific and Engineering Practices	**Developing and Using Models** Conceptual models . . . are . . . explicit representations that are in some ways analogous to the phenomena they represent. Conceptual models allow scientists . . . to better visualize and understand a phenomenon under investigation . . . . Although they do not correspond exactly to the more complicated entity being modeled, they do bring certain features into focus while minimizing or obscuring others. Because all models contain approximations and assumptions that limit the range of validity of their application and the precision of their predictive power, it is important to recognize their limitations (NRC, 2012, p. 56). **Engaging in Argument from Evidence** Use an oral and written argument supported by evidence to support or refute an explanation or a model for a phenomenon (NGSS Lead States, 2013, p. 69).
Crosscutting Concepts	**Structure and Function** Students can also examine more complex structures, such as subsystems of the human body, and consider the relationship of the shapes of the parts to their functions. By the middle grades, students begin to visualize, model, and apply their understanding of structure and function to more complex or less easily observable systems and processes (NRC, 2012, p. 97). **Systems and System Models** Systems may interact with other systems; they may have sub-systems and be a part of larger complex systems (NGSS Lead States, 2013, p. 68). Students should be able to discuss the interactions within a system and realize the importance of the physical, chemical, and biological interactions and their relative importance (NRC, 2012, p. 94).
Disciplinary Core Idea	**LS1:** From Molecules to Organisms: Structures and Processes
Component Idea	**LS1.A:** Structure and Function
Conceptual Understanding	**By the end of grade 8:** In multicellular organisms, the body is a system of multiple interacting subsystems. These subsystems are groups of cells that work together to form tissues or organs that are specialized for particular body functions (NRC, 2012, p. 144).

Performance Expectation: MS-LS1-3
Use argument supported by evidence for how the body is a system of interacting sub-systems composed of groups of cells (Assessment is limited to the circulatory, excretory, digestive, respiratory, muscular, and nervous systems.) (NGSS Lead States, 2013, p. 67). www.nextgenscience.org/pe/ms-ls1-3-molecules -organisms-structures-and-processes

Learning Target:
Breathing processes allow organisms to intake needed oxygen and remove waste gases (carbon dioxide).

Success Criteria: *The students will:*

1. Construct and observe a model of the lungs that demonstrates the mechanism behind breathing.
2. Evaluate the accuracies and inaccuracies of the breathing lung model.
3. Explain how the structure of the lung/diaphragm system relates to how it functions to provide an exchange of gases needed for organisms to live.
4. Construct an argument based on evidence to explain how the respiratory subsystem works to maintain oxygen within living organisms and remove carbon dioxide.

Preparation
You may wish to punch a hole in the plastic cups before class begins. Heat the tip of an ice pick or large ten-penny nail, in a gas flame on a stove or in the flame of a Bunsen burner. Remember that you need to

have a wooden handle or wrap the end with tape to keep you from burning your hand. The heated tip of the ice pick will pierce the bottom of the plastic cups easily. Wiggle the hot ice pick to create a hole in the cups that has the same diameter as the straws do. If you have a cork borer, it will work well. Wear appropriate safety goggles and gloves while working with open flames and hot materials.

Materials

For each student:

- Index card
- Pencil
- Sheet of white construction paper
  Crayons or markers

For each small group:

- Clear plastic cup with a hole in its base the same diameter as the straw
- Drinking straw
- Small plastic bag
- Small balloon
- Rubber band
- Scissors
- Silicone sealant or modeling clay

Engage

Instruct the students to take a deep breath: Breathe in . . . Hold it . . . Breathe out. Have them focus on how their body moves as they continue deep breathing. Ask: *How do your lungs work to inhale and exhale gases? How do your lungs work with the skeletal and muscular systems?* Ask students to make a drawing (a two-dimensional model) on an index card showing how they think breathing works.

Construct

Guide student groups to build a model of part of the respiratory system. Tell them to follow these steps:

1. Obtain a plastic drinking straw, a small plastic bag, two rubber bands, a clear plastic cup with a hole already punched in the bottom, a small balloon, and scissors.

2. Cut the straw in half.

3. Stretch and blow up the balloon a few times.

4. Using a tightly wound rubber band, attach the balloon to the straw. Be sure the balloon does not come off when you blow into the straw and that the rubber band does not crush the straw.

5. Push the free end of the straw though the cup's hole and pull until the balloon is in the middle of the cup. Seal the area around the hole with silicone sealant or modeling clay.

6. Place the open end of the cup into the small plastic bag and fold the bag around the cup, securing it tightly with the other rubber band. The plastic bag should be loose, not stretched taut, across the cup's opening.

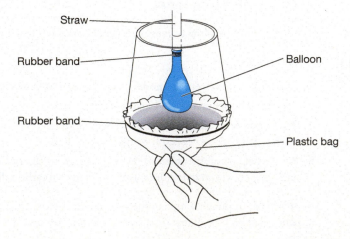

Straw — Rubber band — Balloon — Rubber band — Plastic bag

Explore

Ask the class: *What do you think might happen to the balloon if you pull down on the plastic bag at the bottom of the cup?* Tell them to try it so they can find out. Remind them to record their observations of the system. Then ask: *What do you think might happen if you pushed up on the plastic bag?* Try it to find out and record your observations.

Explain

Assemble the students as a whole group and ask: *What changes did you observe in the system? Why do you think these changes happened? Where in your body do you have something that works like this?*

Referring to a model or illustration of the chest cavity, such as the one shown below, guide students to identify the parts of the body and describe how they function. Ask: *In what ways is this physical model like the lungs? In what ways is the model an accurate representation for this part of the respiratory system? In what ways is the model inaccurate or incomplete?*

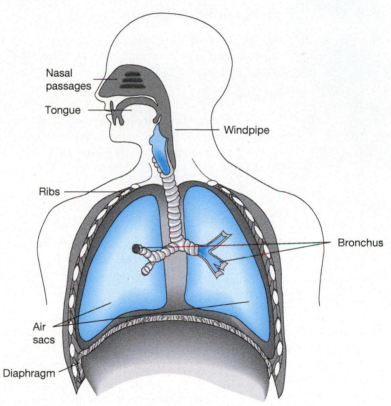

Nasal passages

Tongue

Windpipe

Ribs

Bronchus

Air sacs

Diaphragm

Respiratory system

Elaborate

To reinforce the information about "How Breathing Works," show a short video clip of the same name that is available online from ed.ted.com. As you view the video, do the activities it suggests, note any important concepts that are developed, and record any new questions you have.

Facilitate a discussion about the video after viewing it. Ask students to mention any ideas presented in the video that gave them ideas about how the breathing model could be improved.

Evaluate

Ask students to make a new drawing (a two-dimensional model) on construction paper showing their current thinking about how your lungs work to inhale and exhale gases. Challenge them to express all that they know about how breathing works on this poster.

In addition, ask students to make a T-chart listing accuracies of the breathing model in the left column and inaccuracies of the breathing model in the right column. Then make a list of suggestions about ways the model could be improved.

Have students write a brief paper explaining in their own words how the structures involved in the mechanism of breathing relate to the structure of the respiratory system.

Activity 33: What role do seeds play in a plant life cycle?

Grade: 3, Life Sciences

Framework Context	
Scientific and Engineering Practices	**Planning and Carrying Out Investigations** From the earliest grades, students should have opportunities to carry out careful and systematic investigations, with appropriately supported prior experiences that develop their ability to observe and measure and to record data using appropriate tools and instruments (NRC, 2012, pp. 60–61). **Developing and Using Models** Young students should be encouraged to devise pictorial and simple graphical representations of the findings of their investigations and to use these models in developing their explanations of what occurred (NRC, 2012, p. 58).
Crosscutting Concepts	**Patterns** Elementary students can observe and record patterns in the similarities and differences between plants and their offspring. In the upper elementary grades, students should also begin to analyze patterns in rates of change—for example, the growth rates of plants under different conditions (NRC, 2012, p. 86).
Disciplinary Core Idea **Component Idea** **Conceptual Understanding**	**LS1:** From Molecules to Organisms: Structures and Processes **LS1.B:** Growth and Development of Organisms **By the end of grade 3:** Reproduction is essential to the continued existence of every kind of organisms. Plants and animals have unique and diverse life cycles that include being born (sprouting in plants), growing, developing into adult, reproducing, and eventually dying (NRC, 2012, p. 146).

Performance Expectation 3-LS1-1
Develop models to describe that organisms have unique and diverse life cycles but all have in common birth, growth, reproduction, and death (NGSS Lead States, 2013, p. 27). www.nextgenscience.org/dci-arrangement/3-ls1-molecules-organisms-structures-and-processes

Learning Target
"Birth" in flowering plants starts with the sprouting (germination) of seeds, which begins the growth process.

Success Criteria
Students will be able to:

1. Define *germination* in their own words.
2. Observe and describe with drawings and words the sequence of events in the germination of a seed.
3. Plan and conduct inquiry to determine the conditions needed for plant germination.
4. Develop an explanatory model that shows and explains the plant-sprouting process that is the start of a plant life cycle.
5. Determine what conditions are needed for seeds to germinate or sprout.

Materials
- A quart-size plastic storage bag for each child for each condition tested
- Paper towels
- Stapler

- Lima bean seeds
- Ruler

Engage

Ask: *What are some things we do with seeds?* When students suggest that we plant them, ask: *What happens to seeds when they are planted?* Explain that if we plant the seeds in the soil, we cannot see what happens to them underground. Tell them we will place the seeds in a plastic bag and observe what happens for a few days. Ask: *What conditions are needed for sprouting to occur?*

Explore

Give each child a quart-size plastic storage bag. Show students how to line the inside of the bag with a paper towel. Place eight or nine staples along the bottom portion of the bag about 4 to 5 cm from the bottom. Place five lima bean seeds above the staples inside the bag, as in the illustration. Gently pour water into the bag, being careful not to dislodge the seeds (the water should bulge slightly at the bottom of the bag to about a finger's thickness). There should be enough water to keep the seeds moist, but the seeds should not rest in water. Some of the seeds will germinate within 24–48 hours. Others may take longer. To vary the conditions, set up some bags without water, and place some bags in a light place and others in a dark place.

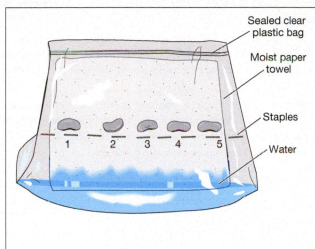

Sealed clear plastic bag

Moist paper towel

Staples

Water

- Line a quart-size sealable, transparent storage bag with a moist paper towel.
- Place nine staples across the bag about 4 to 5 cm from the bottom, as shown in the diagram.
- Position five seeds to be germinated above the staples.
- The seeds may be presoaked for about 24 hours.
- Gently pour water from a small container into the bag, being careful not to dislodge the seeds (the water should bulge slightly at the bottom of the bag to about a finger's thickness).

The water will soak the paper towel and keep the seeds moist. The staples keep the seeds from lying in the water at the bottom of the bag. The transparent bag allows the seeds and roots to be observed.

Children should observe their germinating seeds and developing plants regularly for two weeks or more, recording daily in their investigation journals or on a prepared chart any changes in color, length, shape, texture, special features, and so on. To make the growth sequence clear, ask students to make drawings of changes they observe for one of their germinated bean seeds.

This investigation is a good one to promote careful measurement. Tell students to use a ruler to measure the length of the stem and root each day and to record the measurements in a chart. You can also cut out strips of 1-cm-square graph paper and measure each day. The strips can then be used to make a graphical model. The chart should show length in centimeters for each day observed. The measurement data, when displayed in a graph, provides a picture of growth.

If this is their first experience measuring lengths in an investigation, rather than measuring with a ruler, students can cut a green strip of paper to the length of the stem and a brown strip of paper to the length of the root. If the strips of paper are attached to a time line, such as a calendar, with the green strip above the line and the brown strip below, a visual display of growth over two or three weeks can be seen. At grade three, this investigation provides daily practice with metric measurements. Students should also have ample opportunities to make and test their predictions relevant to the conditions needed for seed germination.

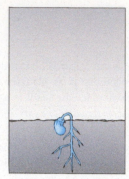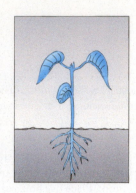

Explain

From their observational data, you want children to discover the sequence of growth changes for the beans from day to day—to learn that the root appears first and grows downward, that the stem is connected to the root and grows upward carrying the cotyledon with it, and that leaves grow on the stems.

In addition to observing the sequence of growth, students should also learn to recognize the seed coat, cotyledons, and embryo part of seeds, and the root, stems, and leaves of the developing plants. Provide the names of these seed and plant parts.

Elaborate

Have students add labels for seed and plant parts to the sequential drawings they have recorded. They should also recognize that parts of the plant are growing and parts of the seed are reducing in size.

Evaluate

A good opportunity for peer assessment is available at the end of the elaborate phase. Students can exchange their recorded data with a peer and check for such things as correct placement of labels; neat, detailed drawings; and meaningful comments. A class discussion to select the criteria to assess creates focus for the analysis of each other's work. Students could write comments about their partner's work or just talk to their partner about his or her work.

To evaluate student awareness of the changes that occur during the germination and plant growth process, have them write a description of how their seed changed into a seedling over time.

Activity 34: What are the stages in an insect life cycle?

Grade: 3, Life Sciences

Framework Context	
Scientific and Engineering Practices	**Planning and Carrying Out Investigations** From the earliest grades, students should have opportunities to carry out careful and systematic investigations, with appropriately supported prior experiences that develop their ability to observe and measure and to record data using appropriate tools and instruments (NRC, 2012, pp. 60–61). **Developing and Using Models** Young students should be encouraged to devise pictorial and simple graphical representations of the findings of their investigations and to use these models in developing their explanations of what occurred (NRC, 2012, p. 58).
Crosscutting Concepts	**Stability and Change** A system can be stable on a small time scale, but on a larger time scale it may be seen to be changing. For example, when looking at a living organism over the course of an hour or a day, it may maintain stability; over longer periods, the organism grows, ages, and eventually dies (NRC, 2000, p. 99). **Patterns** Elementary students can observe and record patterns in the similarities and differences between plants and their offspring. In the upper elementary grades, students should also begin to analyze patterns in rates of change—for example, the growth rates of animals under different conditions (NRC, 2012, p. 86).
Disciplinary Core Idea	**LS1:** From Molecules to Organisms: Structures and Processes
Component Idea	**LS1.B:** Growth and Development of Organisms
Conceptual Understanding	**By the end of grade 3:** Reproduction is essential to the continued existence of every kind of organism. Plants and animals have unique and diverse life cycles that include being born, growing, developing into adults, reproducing, and eventually dying (NRC, 2012, p. 146).

Performance Expectation 3-LS1-1

Develop models to describe that organisms have unique and diverse life cycles but all have in common birth, growth, reproduction, and death (NGSS Lead States, 2013, p. 27). www.nextgenscience.org/dci-arrangement/3-ls1-molecules-organisms-structures-and-processes

Learning Target

Insects like beetles have a larval stage in their life cycle called mealworms that grow and develop based on the conditions.

Success Criteria

The students will:

1. Observe and document the metamorphosis of a mealworm over an extended period of time.
2. Compare and contrast various life cycles.
3. Gather, summarize, and present information about another insect's life cycle.
4. Develop an explanatory model that shows and explains the metamorphosis process that is part of an insect life cycle.
5. Determine what conditions are needed for larvae to grow and develop.

Materials

- Jars with covers (clear plastic, if possible) or baby food jars with holes cut in the lids
- Mealworms (from pet shop or science supply company) or flour that has larvae in it

- Dry branmeal (or dry oatmeal)
- Metric rulers
- Hand lenses
- Spoons
- Pictures or drawings of mealworms at different times during their life cycle (these can be made during the explore phase of the lesson)
- Tape or glue
- Document camera (optional)
- Projection screen (optional)
- Digital microscopes or cameras (optional)

Engage

Ask: *What are the stages people go through as they grow and change? What are the stages in some other animals' life cycles?*

Display a picture of a mealworm or use a document camera to project the image of a real mealworm onto the screen or board. Ask: *How could we find out what stages this animal goes through?*

Explore

Students should work in small groups, but each student will have their own mealworms in a container. Tell the class to make "homes" for their mealworms by spooning dry bran meal or dry oatmeal to a depth of 2 to 3 cm in a clear plastic cup. The cup should have a tight-fitting lid that has several small air holes punched in it. Gently place two mealworms into the cup.

Have the students observe their mealworms, briefly. Then ask the class to suggest ways that the mealworms might change over time. (They are likely to suggest: color, length, shape, etc.). Ask the class to suggest how they could record those changes in an organized way. You can have them measure length and mass to determine if they are growing bigger. Depending on their experience with previous data collection, you might want to provide a template for daily observations, you could have them make mini-books from folded paper with a page for each date observations were made, or you could let students devise their own record-keeping strategies.

Have students observe their mealworms daily (or at least several times a week) and record any changes in appearance or behavior. Careful sketching of the mealworms is encouraged, but photos of the mealworms could be made as well if appropriate technology is available. Observations should continue for three to four weeks in order to observe most of the phases (stages) of their life cycle. Many mealworms transition to the next stage when additional moisture is available so a small piece of apple introduced into the container may be necessary to trigger the change.

Explain

Using their charts or logs as a reference, students should discuss how the mealworms have changed over time. Ask: *What happened to the mealworms? Did they all change in the same way? Did they all change at the same time? How do you know? Which stage do you think is the adult? Why do you think so?*

Introduce the term metamorphosis for this type of change during an organism's life cycle. Using pictures of mealworms at different stages of growth, discuss how these living things grow. Point out that when people grow, they change but not in such extreme ways as a metamorphosing insect. Human children, teenagers, and adults look a lot like each other, while mealworm larvae, pupae, and adults don't look much alike at all. Help the students make a table comparing the stages of mealworms' lives with humans' lives, like the one shown:

Stages	
Humans	**Mealworms**
Child	Larva
Teenager	Pupa
Adult	Adult

In addition, guide students to make a diagram, similar to the one shown, and include photos or drawings to visualize the stages of mealworm metamorphosis.

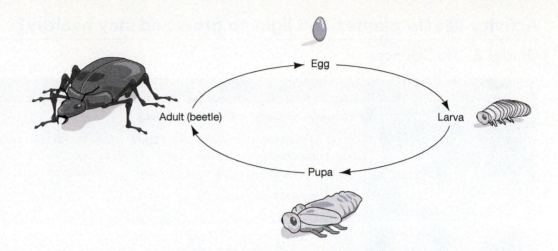

Elaborate

Have students use print and online resources to learn about the life cycles of mealworms and other insects. Students should report back to their class about their findings. Ask: *Are all insect life cycles just like the mealworm's life cycle? If not, how are they different?*

Evaluate

The products created during the lesson (the observation chart or booklet during the explore phase and the research reports on the life cycles of other insects) could be assessed. A rubric or checklist indicating your expectations for these products would guide student work and your scoring of it.

To assess student knowledge about the series of changes that occur during mealworm metamorphosis, prepare cards with drawings or photographs of mealworms during their life cycle. (You could take these pictures with a digital microscope or camera during the explore phase of the investigation.) Give each student a set of the cards. Have them put them in order to represent the mealworm's life cycle. Ask them to label the stages of the mealworm life cycle using terms they learned during this lesson. Finally, ask them to complete their visual model and explain why they arranged the cards the way they did.

Activity 35: Do plants need light to grow and stay healthy?

Grade: 2, Life Sciences

Framework Context	
Scientific and Engineering Practices	**Planning and Carrying Out Investigations** Students need opportunities to design investigations so that they can learn the importance of such decisions as what to measure, what to keep constant, and how to select or construct data collection instruments that are appropriate to the needs of an inquiry (NRC, 2012, p. 60). **Analyzing and Interpreting Data** At the elementary level, students need support to recognize the need to record observations—whether in drawings, words, or numbers—and to share them with others. As they engage in scientific inquiry more deeply, they should begin to collect categorical or numerical data for presentation in forms that facilitate interpretation, such as tables and graphs (NRC, 2012, p. 63). Students should use observations (firsthand or from media) to describe patterns in the natural world in order to answer scientific questions (NGSS Lead States, 2013, p. 6).
Crosscutting Concepts	**Cause and Effect** Students should begin to look for and analyze patterns—whether in their observations of the world or in the relationships between different quantities in data (e.g., the sizes of plants over time)—they can also begin to consider what might be causing these patterns and relationships and design tests that gather more evidence to support or refute their ideas (NRC, 2012, pp. 88–89). Patterns in the natural and human designed world can be observed and used as evidence (NGSS Lead States, 2013, p. 18).
Disciplinary Core Idea	**LS1:** Structure and Function
Component Idea	**LS1.C:** Organization for Matter and Energy Flow in Organisms
Conceptual Understanding	**By the end of grade 2:** Plants need . . . light to live and grow (NRC, 2012, p. 147).
Disciplinary Core Idea	**LS2:** Ecosystems: Interactions, Energy, and Dynamics
Component Idea	**LS2.A:** Interdependent Relationships in Ecosystems
Conceptual Understanding	**By the end of grade 2:** Plants depend on . . . light to grow . . . . Different plants survive better in different settings because they have varied needs for . . . sunlight (NRC, 2013, p. 151).

Performance Expectations 2-LS2-1   Plan and conduct an investigation to determine if plants need sunlight and water to grow (students should test one variable at a time) (NGSS Lead States, 2013, p. 18). www.nextgenscience.org/pe/2-ls2-1 -ecosystems-interactions-energy-and-dynamics

Learning Target   Plants depend on light to grow.

Success Criteria   *Students will:*

1. Collaboratively design and conduct an investigation about whether plants need light to grow and stay healthy.
2. Collect observational data over an extended time period.
3. Analyze small-group and whole-class data.
4. Use data-based evidence to support their claims.

Materials

For each small group:

- Two similar healthy plants growing in separate similar pots with plant labels indicating the light conditions they need in the garden (full sun, part sun/part shade, shady). Each group should have a pair of a type of plant that is different from other small groups.
- Graduated cylinder or measuring cup
- Crayons
- Permanent marker
- Water
- Digital camera or other device for taking pictures of the plants (optional)

For each student:

- Science notebook or chart on which to record data

Engage

Arrange your class into small groups. Provide each group with two similar healthy plants growing in separate similar pots. Ask: *Do your small group's two plants appear to be the same? In what ways? What are some things you could count or measure about your plants that would let your group compare them? Do you think your two plants will look like each other three weeks from now? Why? What might their appearance in three weeks depend on?*

Explore 1

Have groups use a permanent marker to label one of their pots A and the other one B. Give student groups time to observe and compare their two plants and record their findings in their science notebooks. Suggest that they use a three-column chart to organize their data, if you believe that scaffolding would be helpful. The chart might look like this:

	Plant A	Plant B
Number of leaves		
Color of leaves		
Height of plant		
Appearance of leaves		
Other observations group thinks of (add extra rows if needed)		

If they don't think of measuring their plants, show some measuring tools they may use such as tape measures or rulers. As you circulate, monitor students' notebook entries and provide scaffolding through questioning as needed.

Then ask groups to look for evidence in their data that supports the claim: "Our group's two plants are basically alike." Suggest that they talk with their group about the evidence they find.

Explain 1

Bring class together to talk about their findings and their evidence lists. It is likely that students might have difficulty accepting that their two plants are similar if one plant is several centimeters taller than the other or if one plant has several more leaves than the other.

Explore 2

Ask: *Do you think plants need light in order to grow and stay healthy? How could your group use your two plants to find out?*

Assuming the class has mastered the basics of designing a fair test, allow ample time for groups to design investigations to find out. Inform the class that they may observe and record data about their plants for three weeks. Have each group write down their planned procedure in words and drawings. Then tell the groups to review at least one other group's work and add comments using sticky notes. One comment, marked with a plus sign (+) should be about something that they think is especially well done, while the second comment note, marked with a question mark (?), should be about something that they question (i.e., think it would be better done differently or think was omitted).

If the class is just learning to design fair tests, involve the whole class in collaborative planning of the investigation through strategic questioning and discourse. Remind them that only one factor that might affect the plants should be changed at a time. If necessary, lead students to suggest that one plant should be put in a dark place, and the other plant should be put in a place where it gets sunlight or artificial light. Record major steps of the procedure on chart paper for the students to refer to as they work.

Explain 2

Bring the class together and have the groups share their suggested procedures. Ask: *Is there anything else that should be kept the same to make this experiment a fair test?* If students don't suggest that they each be watered the same amount, lead them to that idea.

Have students record their first observation of the plants in their investigation journals or on charts that you provide. If digital cameras, or other technologies that can capture images, are available for students to use, encourage groups to take pictures of both of their plants as another means of monitoring change over time.

Let students know that they will observe the plants twice each week for the next three weeks. Each time they will draw and write about how the plants look and photograph them if possible.

Explain 3

After each weekly observation, ask: *What do you see? Do your group's two plants still look basically alike? If not, why not? How did you determine the growth and/or the health of your two plants? Why do you think this happened?*

Finally, after the last observation, ask: *Do you think plants need light to grow and stay healthy? What evidence do you have that supports your claim? Did all groups have similar findings?*

It is likely that the class will agree that plants need light to grow and stay healthy. This concept lays the groundwork for studies about photosynthesis in later grades.

Elaborate

Ask: *Did some of the groups' plants seem to survive longer in the dark than others? Which ones? How do you know? What is the evidence for your claim? How could we visually compare the conditions of the plants?* They may suggest a graph something like this:

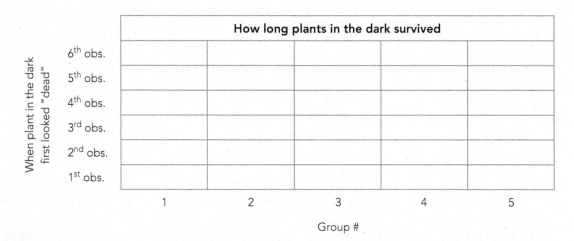

Discuss several alternative ways to visually display the class findings. Discuss which best shows how long the plants in the dark survived.

Tell the groups to look at the plant identification tags in their pots. Ask: *Is there anything on the plant tag that has something to do with how much light that type of plant needed?* Students will probably notice the symbol or words that indicate whether the plant should be planted in a sunny, shady, or partly shady part of the garden. Add this information to the graph under each group number. Then ask them to look for patterns in the graph; specifically, *Did the plants with a "shady" tag survive longer than the others? Did the plants with a "full sun" tag appear dead first?* Involve the class in science talk about why patterns found make sense or don't make sense.

Evaluation

There are multiple opportunities for formative and informal assessment during this lesson: Listen for students' ideas during small-group and whole-class discussion, monitor students' work in science notebooks, and observe group interactions to assess cooperation, collaboration, and respect for others' ideas.

As a summative assessment at the end of the lesson, you might ask students to answer the questions in writing or orally during a one-on-one conversation with you:

1. Do plants need light to grow and stay alive?

2. What evidence from your investigation supports your claim?

3. What else did you learn from this investigation?

Activity 36: Is the air we breathe in the same as the air we breathe out?

Grades: 6–8, Life Sciences

Framework Context	
Scientific and Engineering Practices	**Planning and Carrying Out Investigations** As they become more sophisticated, students also should have opportunities not only to identify questions to be researched but also to decide what data are to be gathered, what variables should be controlled, what tools or instruments are needed to gather and record data in an appropriate format, and eventually to consider how to incorporate measurement error in analyzing data (NRC, 2011, p. 61). **Constructing Explanations and Designing Solutions** As students' knowledge develops, they can begin to identify and isolate variables and incorporate the resulting observations into their explanations of phenomena. Using their measurements of how one factor does or does not affect another, they can develop causal accounts to explain what they observe (NRC, 2012, pp. 69–70).
Crosscutting Concepts	**Energy and Matter: Flows, Cycles, and Conservation** By middle school, a more precise idea of energy—for example, the understanding that food or fuel undergoes a chemical reaction with oxygen that releases stored energy—can emerge. The common misconceptions can be addressed with targeted instructional interventions (including student-led investigations), and appropriate terminology can be used in discussing energy across the disciplines (NRC, 2012, p. 96).
Disciplinary Core Idea **Component Idea** **Conceptual Understanding**	**LS1:** From Molecules to Organisms: Structures and Processes **LS1.C:** Organization for Matter and Energy Flow in Organisms **By the end of grade 8:** Within individual organisms, food moves through a series of chemical reactions in which it is broken down and rearranged to form new molecules, to support growth, or to release energy. In most animals and plants, oxygen reacts with carbon-containing molecules (sugars) to provide energy and produce carbon dioxide (NRC, 2012, p. 148).

Performance Expectation MS-LS1-5

Construct a scientific explanation based on evidence for the cycling of matter and flow of energy into and out of organisms (NGSS Lead States, 2013, p. 225). www.nextgenscience.org/pe/ms-ls1-5-molecules-organisms-structures-and-processes

Learning Target

Through the process of cellular respiration, food (sugar) in the presence of oxygen, is broken down and usable energy is provided to the organisms and carbon dioxide is released as a waste product.

Success Criteria

The students will:

1. Design and conduct an investigation to determine if the concentration of carbon dioxide is the same in inhaled and exhaled air.

2. Construct an explanation based on scientific evidence for why exhaled air contains a greater concentration of carbon dioxide that inhaled air contains.

3. Design and conduct an investigation related to activities that may affect the concentration of carbon dioxide in exhaled air.

4. Develop a claim based on evidence for why the concentration of carbon dioxide changes with each inhalation and exhalation.

Materials

- Balloons (all the same size and shape, 12" works fine)
- Balloon pumps, handheld

- Drinking straws
- Rubber bands
- Scissors
- Duct tape
- Limewater (saturated solution of calcium hydroxide in water)
  - Gallon of distilled water
  - Calcium hydroxide (aka: slaked lime, hydrated lime, and pickling lime)
  - Teaspoon
  - Filter paper
  - Funnel
- Stopwatch or timer accurate to 0.1 second
- Transparent beakers (250 ml) or 8-oz or 9-oz plastic cups
- Metric tape measures
- Safety goggles
- Science notebooks
- Dry ice (optional)
- Funnel with ~2 cm-wide stem (optional)
- Tablespoon (optional)

Preparation

CO$_2$ Balloons

If you have dry ice, prepare several CO$_2$ balloons, as follows. Put the nozzle of a balloon over the stem of the funnel. Pour one or two tablespoons of dry ice powder or chunks into the funnel and into the balloon. Wrap a rubber band firmly around the nozzle of the balloon. The balloon will slowly inflate as the dry ice changes from solid to gaseous CO$_2$.

Limewater

Wear safety goggles while preparing this solution. If limewater splashes onto skin, immediately rinse the affected area with tap water. Limewater is a strong base.

Put 1 teaspoon of calcium hydroxide in a clean glass or plastic one-gallon max jar or jug. Fill container with distilled or tap water. Put the lid or cap on the container and shake vigorously for several minutes. Then let the solution stand for one day. A little sediment will be at the bottom of the container (it is supposed to be there as the solution is saturated). Carefully pour the clear solution from the top of the jar through a filter in a funnel into other glass or plastic containers for storage. Filter it a second time to remove even more of the undissolved sediment. Be sure to label storage containers—**Limewater.** For safety protocols, use your favorite Internet browser to access MSDS sheets for calcium hydroxide and limewater solution; print them for your records.

Engage

Ask the class to sit quietly and focus on their breathing. After about a minute, ask: *Do you think that what you breathe in (inhale) is the same as what you breathe out (exhale)?* Discussion may include mention of volume, temperature, composition, and moisture of the air. Focus on what they think about the composition of the gases in the air. Ask: *Do you think that inhaled and exhaled air contains the same mixture of gases? What gases do you think would have different concentrations? Why? How could we find out?*

On the board, write: *Is the concentration of carbon dioxide the same in inhaled and exhaled air?*

Explore

Tell the class that limewater is an indicator for carbon dioxide. If you made CO$_2$ balloons, do the following demonstration (Everyone in the classroom, including you, must wear safety goggles as limewater is an eye irritant. If limewater splashes onto skin, immediately rinse the affected area with tap water. Limewater is a strong base.)

- Pour about 100 ml of limewater into a clean beaker or cup.
- To avoid releasing much gas from the balloon, pinch the nozzle closed between the rubber band and the body of the balloon. Have someone loosen the rubber band on the nozzle. Insert one end

of a drinking straw into the nozzle of the balloon and then close the nozzle around the straw with the rubber band and/or a piece of duct tape. Keep pinching the nozzle during all of this; you don't want to release the carbon dioxide from the balloon yet!

- Tell the class to watch carefully for a change in the limewater.
- Submerge the other end of the straw into the limewater in the cup.
- Release your pinch on the nozzle.
- CO_2 from the balloon will flow into the limewater causing bubbles.
- The limewater will change from clear to cloudy. This indicates the presence of a high concentration of CO_2 in the gas that is bubbling into the limewater. Chemically when carbon dioxide is bubbled through limewater, calcium carbonate ($CaCO_3$) is formed. Since calcium carbonate is less soluble than calcium hydroxide, it precipitates out as a white suspended solid that makes the liquid look cloudy.

While pointing at the question written on the board at the end of the engage phase of the lesson, ask the class: *How does having an indicator for carbon dioxide help us answer our question?*

Challenge small groups of students to write procedures for an investigation that will answer the question that is posted on the board. Display the materials that are available for the students to use in their investigations, including balloons, balloon pumps, drinking straws, rubber bands, duct tape, scissors, limewater, stopwatch or timer, beakers or cups, metric tape measures, and safety goggles. Tell the class that all proposed procedures must be turned in to you and approved before anyone receives materials to complete the lab activity. As groups work on their procedures, circulate through the room providing scaffolding through appropriate questioning.

Once all procedures have been approved, review safety rules (goggles, skin contact, spill cleanup), then permit students to get their materials and conduct their investigations. Remind them to record their findings in their science notebooks.

Explain

Bring the class together to share each group's procedure and results. Some questions you might ask to facilitate the discussion include: *What happens when air that would have been inhaled is bubbled through limewater? What happens when air that was exhaled was bubbled through limewater? Why does the limewater stay clear? Why does the limewater turn cloudy? What was your independent or manipulated variable? What was your dependent or responding variable? How did you ensure that your experiment was controlled? Based on our class findings, is there more carbon dioxide in the air you breathe in (inhale) or in the air you breathe out (exhale)? What is your evidence?*

Students may realize that air contains some CO_2 and wonder why that is not detected by the limewater test. Explain that concentration of carbon dioxide in air (inhaled air) is too low to be detected by this procedure.

Have students read a section in their text or listen to a mini-lecture about where the carbon dioxide in the exhaled air came from. Basically, during cellular respiration oxygen reacts with carbon-containing molecules (sugars), releasing energy and producing carbon dioxide.

Elaborate

Ask the students to brainstorm questions they have about activities that might change the concentration of carbon dioxide in their exhaled breath. They may wonder if CO_2 levels rise after strenuous exercise or if holding one's breath affects the concentration of CO_2.

Let groups of students write investigations that would help them answer a question of their choice. Once their procedures have been approved, allow them time to conduct their investigation.

Tell them that they must complete a lab report about their investigation and present it to the rest of the class.

Evaluate

Observation of students as they plan and carry out investigations in the explore and elaborate phases of the lesson allows for formative assessment that will inform your teaching.

Ask students to write an evidence-based paragraph explaining why exhaled air contains a higher concentration of carbon dioxide than inhaled air.

The reports and presentations created during the elaborate phase of the lesson can also serve as a summative assessment. Use a standard lab report rubric or construct one especially for this investigation.

Activity 37: How do sensory receptors respond to stimuli?

Grades: 6–8, Life Sciences

Framework Context	
Scientific and Engineering Practices	**Obtaining, Evaluating, and Communicating Information** Students need sustained practice and support to develop the ability to extract the meaning of scientific text from books, media reports, and other forms of scientific communication because the form of this text is initially unfamiliar—expository rather than narrative, often linguistically dense, and reliant on precise logical flows. Students should be able to interpret meaning from text, to produce text in which written language and diagrams are used to express scientific ideas, and to engage in extended discussion about those ideas (NRC, 2012, p. 76).
Crosscutting Concepts	**Cause and Effect** Students should learn to argue from evidence when attributing an observed phenomenon to a specific cause (NRC, 2012, p. 89).
Disciplinary Core Idea **Component Idea** **Conceptual Understanding**	**LS1:** From Molecules to Organisms: Structures and Processes **LS1.D:** Information Processing **By the end of grade 8:** Each sense receptor responds to different inputs (electromagnetic, mechanical, chemical), transmitting them as signals that travel along nerve cells to the brain (NRC, 2012, p. 149).

Performance Expectation MS-LS1-8

Gather and synthesize information that sensory receptors respond to stimuli by sending messages to the brain for immediate behavior or storage as memories (NGSS Lead States, 2013, p. 223). www .nextgenscience.org/pe/ms-ls1-8-molecules-organisms-structures-and-processes

Learning Target

Each sense receptor responds to different inputs and transmits them as signals that travel along nerve cells to the brain where they are processed as behaviors or memories.

Success Criteria

The students will:

1. Gather, synthesize, and communicate information about types of stimuli that cause sensory receptors to respond.

2. Classify human senses and those unique to other animals according to the type(s) of sense receptors involved.

3. Make claims based on evidence about the cause-and-effect relationship that occurs in the brain's information processing.

Materials

- Science notebooks
- 5 sentence strips, each labeled with one of the types of sensory receptors
  - mechanoreceptors
  - chemoreceptors
  - electromagnetic receptors
  - thermoreceptors
  - nociceptors
- Computers or mobile devices with access to the Internet (at least one for each small group of students)
- Decks of Amazing Animal Senses Cards from the Neuroscience for Kids website, http://faculty. washington.edu (one set for each small group); print the pages on cardstock, and then cut into cards

Engage

Ask students to work individually during this phase of the lesson. Tell the students that they will have five minutes to write down a list of as many things as they can think of that they can sense about the world around them from their seats. Promise (and follow through with) a prize for the longest lists, if you think that would be motivational. Beside each thing they sense, they must identify the sense they used. For example, a student's list might start like this:

Thing Sensed	Sense Used
Bell ringing	hearing
Tight shoe	touch
Yellow pencil	sight
Cold air	touch

As students are listing, walk around the room carrying something with a strong odor, making small sounds and touching students' arms with a pencil or brushing a sheet of paper over the tiny hairs on students' arms without actually coming in contact with their skin.

When time is up, have students tally the number of things sensed with each sense, then do a class tally to determine which sense you seem to pay most attention to as a class.

Explore

Arrange the class into small groups. Each small group should have one or more computers or mobile devices to access the Internet. Tell the class that human sensory receptors are classified into five categories. Display the five sentence strips in Set A. Assign or let each group choose one of the sentence strips to research. Send everyone to the Boundless website, www.boundless.com, to begin their research. Tell them to search for *Categorizing Sensory Receptors* in the site. If necessary, help groups identify the section of the article that relates to their sentence strip. Then challenge the group to make a visual presentation on a piece of chart paper that illustrates important ideas about the type of sensory receptor on their sentence strip. Provide more specific guidance for your class if you think it would be helpful. For example, you could provide a list of information that should be on the poster, such as:

- The term on the sentence strip
- Definition of the term in writing and presented visually (through drawings or symbols)
- Examples of this type of sensory receptor in humans

Let the class know how much time they have to complete their posters and that they will need to explain their work to the rest of the class. If groups finish before time is up or all other groups are finished, encourage them to browse the Internet to find additional information about their topic.

Explain

Have all groups present their posters to the class. Encourage the students in the audience to ask questions of the presenting group and to take notes in their science notebooks. If there are major gaps or inaccuracies in the information presented on the posters, revisit the text as a whole class and add the ideas to an extra poster below the initial group poster.

Elaborate

Point out to the class that so far we've focused on human sensory receptors but that other fascinating sensory receptors are found throughout the animal kingdom. For this activity you may want students to work in their old small groups or to form new ones. Give each small group a deck of Amazing Animal Senses Cards.

Challenge each group to create a graphic organizer for the cards on a sheet of chart paper. The goal is for the entire deck to be arranged in logical groups and/or sequences; both tape and markers may also be used in this project. All posters will be posted on the walls in the classroom for future use, and groups will be asked to explain them to the rest of the class.

Evaluate

The group posters and the associated presentations can be assessed. As a summative assessment, let students use their notes and the posters in the room to complete this table by putting Xs in cells to indicate that the row label and the column label match.

Activity 38: How do disruptions to an ecosystem affect its populations?

Grades: 6–8, Life Sciences

Framework Context	
Scientific and Engineering Practices	**Planning and Carrying Out Investigations** As they become more sophisticated, students also should have opportunities not only to identify questions to be researched but also to decide what data are to be gathered, what variables should be controlled, what tools or instruments are needed to gather and record data in an appropriate format . . . (NRC, 2012, p. 61). **Analyzing and Interpreting Data** In middle school, students should have opportunities to learn standard techniques for displaying, analyzing, and interpreting data; such techniques include different types of graphs . . . (NRC, 2012, p. 63).
Crosscutting Concepts	**Systems and System Models** An explicit model of a system under study can be a useful tool not only for gaining understanding of the system but also for conveying it to others. Models of a system can range in complexity from lists and simple sketches to detailed computer simulations or functioning prototypes (NRC, 2012, p. 92). **Stability and Change** . . . students should come to recognize that both the regularities of a pattern over time and its variability are issues for which explanations can be sought. Examining these questions in different contexts . . . broadens students' understanding that stability and change are related and that a good model for a system must be able to offer explanations for both (NRC, 2012, p. 101).
Disciplinary Core Idea	**LS2:** Ecosystems: Interactions, Energy, and Dynamics
Component Idea	**LS2.A:** Interdependent Relationships in Ecosystems
Conceptual Understanding	**By the end of grade 8:** Organisms and populations of organisms are dependent on their environmental interactions both with other living things and with nonliving factors. Growth of organisms and population increases are limited by access to resources. In any ecosystem, organisms and populations with similar requirements for food, water, oxygen, or other resources may compete with each other for limited resources, access to which consequently constrains their growth and reproduction. Similarly, predatory interactions may reduce the number of organisms or eliminate whole populations of organisms (NRC, 2012, p. 152).
Component Idea	**LS2.C:** Ecosystem Dynamics, Functioning, and Resilience
Conceptual Understanding	**By the end of grade 8:** Ecosystems are dynamic in nature; their characteristics can vary over time. Disruptions to any physical or biological component of an ecosystem can lead to shifts in all of its populations (NRC, 2012, p. 155).

Performance Expectations MS-LS2-1	Analyze and interpret data to provide evidence for the effects of resource availability on organisms and populations or organisms in an ecosystem (NGSS Lead States, 2013, p. 225). www.nextgenscience.org/pe/ms-ls2-1-ecosystems-interactions-energy-and-dynamics
MS-LS2-4	Construct an argument supported by empirical evidence that changes to physical or biological components of an ecosystem affect populations (NGSS Lead States, 2013, p. 225). www.nextgenscience.org/pe/ms-ls2-4-ecosystems-interactions-energy-and-dynamics
Learning Target	Ecosystems are dynamic in nature and change based on changes to both biotic and abiotic factors.

Success Criteria *The students will:*

1. Use a computer simulation to explore the dynamic nature of ecosystems.

2. Use evidence from computer simulations to explain how populations of organisms depend on their environmental interactions with both biotic and abiotic factors in the ecosystem to maintain stability.

3. Design simulated experiments to address questions about environmental interactions.

4. Analyze and interpret evidence provided by the simulations to infer the changes that would result based on changes within the ecosystem populations and physical conditions.

Materials

- Science notebooks
- Computers (at least one for each pair of students)
  - Download and launch the activity *Experiment with Ecosystems* found on the Concord Consortium's website at www.concord.org.
- LCD projector for whole-class display of computer screen (optional)
- Screen or blank wall (optional)

Engage

Ask the class: *Do you think ecosystems stay the same or change over time? Explain your thinking. If you think ecosystems change over time, what do you think might change? What are some things that might cause these changes?*

Explore 1

Explain to the class that they will use a computer simulation that will let them change factors in a virtual ecosystem and model the changes over a much shorter time period than would happen in the real world. If you have an LCD projector, display the simulation *Experiment with Ecosystems* for the whole class to see while presenting basic instructions:

- Collaboration and thinking as a team will lead to success.
- Ask for help if necessary.
- Read carefully, since the simulation provides background information and has hyperlinks if you need to check the definition of any words appearing in blue (page 1).
- Use the arrows near the compass at the bottom of the screen to navigate through the pages (page 1).
- Answer questions (page 2). (Tell the class whether to answer on the computer or in their science notebooks.)
- Follow the instructions that are given for the *Missing Grass Experiment* (page 4).
- Use control buttons to explore the simulation's functions and figure out the challenge (page 4).
- Continue as the program instructs until page 5 is finished.

If no LCD projector is available, consider listing the basic instructions on the board and quickly explaining them to the class.

Have the class work in pairs. Each pair should have a computer on which *Experiment with Ecosystems* is loaded. Allow adequate time for students to try out their ideas in the simulated environment.

Explain 1

Bring the class together to talk about their findings in a meaning-making discussion. If you are able to project the program on a screen or blank wall, do so as you get input from the students about questions they answered, how they solved the challenges, what conclusions they can make, etc.

Lead the class to understand that any disruption to one component of an ecosystem can lead to changes in other components. Ask the class: *What was the disruption you caused in your virtual ecosystem?* (All the grass died.) *What are some possible causes of this in the real world?* (Drought, disease, pests.) *What did you hypothesize would happen to the ecosystem?* (Answers will vary.) *What changes did your disruption cause?* (The rabbits died, then the hawks left.) *How did the graph show this?* (Population lines dropped to zero.) *Explain why you think the disruption in the grass population caused these changes in the rabbit and hawk populations.*

Explore 2

Tell students to continue with page 6 of the simulation. Follow basic instructions as before to complete the *Fox Experiment*. Stop when you finish with page 8.

Explain 2

Bring the class back together to talk about their findings in the *Fox Experiment*. Again, if you are able to project the program on a screen or blank wall, do so as you get input from the students about questions they answered, how they solved the challenges, what conclusions they can make, etc.

What was the disruption to the virtual ecosystem this time? (The introduction of foxes.) *What did you hypothesize would happen because of the introduction of the foxes?* (Answers will vary.) *What changes in other components of the ecosystem seemed to occur because of the introduction of the foxes? How did the graph lines show that? How do you know that these changes were caused by the introduction of the foxes? Did everyone get the same result? If you ran the simulation several times, did you always get the same results? What happened to the graph lines this time? Was your hypothesis confirmed?* (Answers will vary.) *Is there one right answer? How could you use statistics to determine a reasonable answer?*

Elaborate

Ask students to come up with other questions about the virtual ecosystem that they would like to investigate. Return to page 9 of the simulation. Design and carry out an investigation to answer your selected question. Run the simulation several times to be sure that the results are stable.

Evaluate

Write a lab report about the simulation you conducted during the elaborate phase. Be sure to include:

1. The question being investigated
2. Your hypothesis about what you expect to happen
3. The procedure you used (what settings you selected before or during the investigation)
4. How many times you repeated the simulation
5. A picture of the graph and the ecosystem representation
6. A written description of the results
7. Your evidence-based explanation of why your results occurred
8. Any other comments you would like to add
9. Any additional questions you would like to investigate

Activity 39: How do the social interactions and group behavior of ants and honeybees help to maintain their colonies?

Grade: 3, Life Sciences

Framework Context	
Scientific and Engineering Practices	**Obtaining, Evaluating, and Communicating Information** Students need sustained practice and support to develop the ability to extract the meaning of scientific text from books, media reports, and other forms of scientific communication because the form of this text is initially unfamiliar—expository rather than narrative, often linguistically dense, and reliant on precise logical flows. Students should be able to interpret meaning from text, to produce text in which written language and diagrams are used to express scientific ideas, and to engage in extended discussion about those ideas (NRC, 2012, p. 76). **Engaging in Argument from Evidence** Students can construct scientific arguments where they draw on a wide range of reasons or evidence, so that their arguments become more sophisticated. In addition they should be able to discern what aspects of evidence are potentially significant for supporting or refuting a particular argument (NRC, 2012, p. 73).
Crosscutting Concepts	**Cause and Effect** Students should begin to look for and analyze patterns—whether in their observations of the world or in the relationships between different quantities in data (e.g., the sizes of plants over time)—they can also begin to consider what might be causing these patterns and relationships and design tests that gather more evidence to support or refute their ideas (NRC, 2012, pp. 88–89). Patterns in the natural and human designed world can be observed and used as evidence (NGSS Lead States, 2013, p. 18).
Disciplinary Core Idea **Component Idea** **Conceptual Understanding**	**LS2:** Ecosystems: Interactions, Energy, and Dynamics **LS2.D:** Social Interactions and Group Behavior **By the end of grade 2:** Groups can be collections of equal individuals, hierarchies with dominant members, small families, groups of single or mixed gender, or groups composed of individuals similar in age. Some groups are stable over long periods of time; others are fluid, with members moving in and out. Some groups assign specialized tasks to each member; in others, all members perform the same or a similar range of functions (NRC, 2012, p. 156).

Performance Expectation 3-LS2-1 Construct an argument that some animals form groups that help members survive (NGSS Lead States, 2013, p. 28). www.nextgenscience.org/dci-arrangement/3-ls2-ecosystems-interactions-energy-and-dynamics

Learning Target Being part of a group helps animals obtain food, defend themselves, and cope with changes. Groups may serve different functions and vary dramatically in size.

Success Criteria *The students will:*

1. Gather and synthesize information about social structures and assigned tasks found in colonies of some insects.
2. Work collaboratively to present factual information about either ants or honeybees to their peers through a creative performance.
3. Prepare and engage in arguments from evidence and be prepared to critique the arguments of peers.

Materials
- Articles describing the social structure of an ant colony and a honeybee colony. (Make enough copies of each for half of the class.)

- Articles with pertinent information on these topics can be accessed at http://animal.discovery.com.
- Select *Wild Animals* from the menu bar, then select *Insects & Arachnids,* then scroll down a little and select the box labeled *Insects.*
- In the *search window* at the top right corner of the screen, enter *ant colony,* click on the *Read Article* box beside the article "Ant" (http://animal.discovery.com). The part of the article that is focused on the social structure of an ant colony begins with the heading "The Ant Colony" and ends right before the heading "Kinds of Ants."
- In the *search window* at the top right corner of the screen, enter *social bees,* click on the *Read Article* box beside the article "Bee" (http://animal.discovery.com). The part of the article that is focused on the social structure of a bee colony begins with the heading "Social Bees" and ends right before the heading "Beekeeping."

- Science notebooks
- Chart paper
- Markers
- Variety of materials for costumes, props, etc., for presentations during the evaluate phase of the lesson
- Video camera for recording final student presentations (optional)
- Tripod (optional)

Engage

Ask: *What do you know about the social interactions of ants in an anthill or honeybees in a hive? Do they all pitch in and help out as needed to keep the colony functioning, or do individual members of the colony have assigned tasks? How do you know?*

Explore

Organize the class into an even number of small groups. Give students in half of the small groups the article titled "Ant Colony" and the students in the other small groups the article titled "Social Bees."

Instruct students to closely read their articles and take notes about the roles that different castes of social insects take on. Suggest that they use lists and graphic organizers when appropriate. Encourage them to discuss the information as they read, since talking about text helps students to make sense of it. If you think that providing a template for note-taking would be useful scaffolding for students in your class, develop and distribute them to the students.

Explain

Bring the students together in a discussion circle to talk about their findings. Encourage groups who read about ants to verify and improve each other's findings and groups who read about bees to verify and improve each other's findings. Then suggest that opposite groups make connections with their work to compare and contrast the social interactions of the two different types of insect colonies. Recommend that students create graphic organizers to effectively summarize the important information that is shared.

Elaborate

Students should return to their original small groups. Challenge each group to produce a creative but factual presentation about the social structure of the insect colony they read about and summarized. They might role-play, do a puppet show, a broadcast interview, etc. Provide ample time for groups to work, but announce a firm deadline at the time you make the assignment.

Collaborate with your class to develop criteria and levels of achievement for a rubric for scoring the presentations. Student involvement with the creation of the rubric helps to ensure that they will know what is expected and self-assess their presentation during rehearsals.

Evaluate

On the day of presentations, arrange to use the stage at your school, or organize your classroom so that each presenting group has sufficient space for their production. Make a video recording of the presentations so that you can review group work at a later time for scoring and thoroughly take in their performance. When you have the next open house, consider showing the student presentations on a video monitor in your room. Parents always like to see their children in action!

Activity 40: In what ways do young animals resemble their parents?

Grade: 1, Life Sciences

Framework Context	
Scientific and Engineering Practices	**Planning and Carrying Out Investigations** From the earliest grades, students should have opportunities to carry out careful and systematic investigations, with appropriately supported prior experiences that develop their ability to observe and measure and to record data using appropriate tools and instruments (NRC, 2012, pp. 60–61). **Analyzing and Interpreting Data** At the elementary level, students need support to recognize the need to record observations—whether in drawings, words, or numbers—and to share them with others (NRC, 2012, p. 63). **Constructing Explanations and Designing Solutions** Students should develop explanations of what they observe when conducting their own investigations and to evaluate their own and others' explanations for consistency with the evidence (NRC, 2012, p. 69).
Crosscutting Concepts	**Patterns** Elementary students can observe and record patterns in the similarities and differences between parents and their offspring. Students should also begin to analyze patterns of change (NRC, 2012, p. 86).
Disciplinary Core Idea	**LS3:** Heredity: Inheritance and Variation of Traits
Component Idea	**LS3.C:** Inheritance of Traits
Conceptual Understanding	**By the end of grade 1:** Young animals are very much, but not exactly, like their parents and also resemble other animals of the same kind (NRC, 2012, p. 158).

Performance Expectation 1-LS3-1

Make observations to construct an evidence-based account that young animals are like, but not exactly like, their parents (NGSS Lead States, 2013, p. 13). www.nextgenscience.org/dci-arrangement/1-ls3-heredity-inheritance-and-variation-traits

Learning Target

Offspring are like their parents, but not exactly.

Success Criteria

The students will:

1. Talk with a partner about similarities and differences between adult animals and their offspring.
2. Know that an animal's young or a person's child or children are known as offspring.
3. Make observations to use when constructing an evidence-based account that young animals are very much, but not exactly, like their parents.
4. Follow the patterned text of a children's book to create additional pages with accurate information about an animal and its offspring.

Materials

- Family picture showing multiple generations. (Find one online by using your favorite web browser to search for *multigenerational family pictures* or bring yours from home.)
- Pictures of different species of animals, each showing adult(s) with offspring. (Use your favorite web browser to search for *pictures of animals and their offspring.*) You will need at least one picture for each pair of students in your class.
- Set of 4 sentence strips (pink, yellow, green, blue) for each pair of students

- Crayons or markers
- Tape
- A copy of the book, *Is Your Mama a Llama?* by Deborah Guarino

Engage

Show the class the multigenerational family picture. Ask: *What is this a picture of? What do you notice about the people in this picture? Do you think that some of the people in this picture are related? What family members do you think it shows? Why do you think that? What evidence do you have to support your claim?*

Explore

Have students work in pairs. Give each pair of students one picture of an adult animal with its offspring or a picture of an animal family. Tell the students that the pictures you have given them show one (or more) young animal with one (or both) parents. Encourage each pair of students to talk with each other about their picture.

The following questions could be spoken and/or written on the board (depending on the age and reading abilities of your students) to guide their discussion.

1. In what ways does the young animal look like its parent(s)?
2. In what ways does the young animal look different from its parent(s)?
3. Is it easy to tell that the young animal is the same type of animal as its parent(s)? Why or why not?
4. What kinds of animals are shown in your picture? (It's OK if you don't know or aren't sure.)

If your class is able to write words, give each pair of students a set of sentence strips and a crayon or marker. Refer back to the previous questions:

- Post a green sentence strip beside question 1. Tell the class to use their green sentence strip to list ways the young animal(s) is (are) like the adult(s) in their picture. Provide additional green sentence strips if they need them.
- Post a pink sentence strip beside question 2. Tell the class to use their pink sentence strip to list ways the young animal(s) is (are) different from the adult(s) in their picture. Provide additional pink sentence strips if they need them.
- Post a blue sentence strip beside question 3. Tell the class to write their answer to question 3 on their blue sentence strip.
- Post a yellow sentence strip beside question 4. Tell the class to identify the animals shown on their picture on the yellow sentence strip. Assure them that it is OK if they aren't sure of what their animals are called.

If your class is not able to write yet, you will gather this information from your students orally during the next phase of the lesson.

Explain

Have the whole class come together for a meaning-making discussion about animals and their young. Students should sit beside their partners in a large circle and bring along their animal family picture and sentence strips (if they made them).

Tell the class that they have been looking at pictures of adult animals and their offspring. Be sure students understand that the term **offspring** refers to an animal's young or a person's child or children. Ask pairs of students to hold up their pictures and to point to the animal that is the offspring of the parent or parents in their picture. Take a little time to have students explain their choices.

Create a chart summarizing the work of all of the pairs of students. If students have made sentence strips, they can tape them to the chart; if not, you can write student ideas on the chart.

Picture of animals	>>>
Name of animals in picture (yellow strips)	>>>
Ways young are like parent(s) (green strips)	>>>

Picture of animals	>>>
Ways young are different from parent(s) (pink strips)	>>>
Easy to tell that parents and offspring are same type of animal? Why? (blue strips)	>>>

Encourage students to talk about how characteristics shared by adult and young animals help them move, eat, etc. Guide children in the process of looking for patterns of data on the class chart. Draw conclusions based on the data; e.g., the young are more like their parents than different from them.

Elaborate

Read the book *Is Your Mama a Llama?* by Deborah Guarino with your class. Discuss how the information in the book relates to the information you learned from your pictures. Also talk about the pattern of the text.

Challenge pairs of students to create additional pages for the book based on the picture they had or another picture that is not already included in the book.

Evaluate

Student work can be formatively assessed during the explore and explain phases of the lesson, based on the sentence strips produced or the oral explanations given. The additional book pages developed during the elaborate phase can be evaluated both on the accuracy of science content and on language arts skills such as rhyming and following patterns in text.

Activity 41: How can mutations result in variation of traits?

Grades: 6–8, Life Sciences

Framework Context	
Scientific and Engineering Practices	**Planning and Carrying Out Investigations** As they become more sophisticated, students also should have opportunities not only to identify questions to be researched but also to decide what data are to be gathered, what variables should be controlled, what tools or instruments are needed to gather and record data in an appropriate format . . . (NRC, 2012, p. 61). **Developing and Using Models** Use (provided) computer simulations or simulations developed with simple simulation tools as a tool for understanding and investigating aspects of a system, particularly those not readily visible to the naked eye (NRC, 2012, p. 58).
Crosscutting Concepts	**Cause and Effect** Cause and effect relationships may be used to predict phenomena in natural systems. . . . argumentation starting from students' own explanations of cause and effect can help them appreciate standard scientific theories that explain the causal mechanisms in the systems under study (NRC, 2012, p. 89).
Disciplinary Core Idea	**LS3:** Heredity: Inheritance and Variation of Traits
Component Idea	**LS3.B:** Variation of Traits
Conceptual Understanding	**By the end of grade 8:** In addition to variations that arise from sexual reproduction, genetic information can be altered because of mutations. Though rare, mutations may result in changes to the structure and function of proteins. Some changes are beneficial, others harmful, and some neutral to the organism (NRC, 2012, p. 16).

Performance Expectation MS-LS3-2

Develop and use a model to describe why asexual reproduction results in offspring with identical genetic information and sexual reproduction results in offspring with genetic variation (NGSS Lead States, 2013, p. 73). www.nextgenscience.org/pe/ms-ls3-2-heredity-inheritance-and-variation-traits

Learning Target

Variations can arise from sexual reproduction or through mutations and change the appearance of an organism.

Success Criteria

The students will:

1. Use a computer simulation to investigate patterns of inheritance of traits in fruit flies.
2. Analyze phenotypes of parents and varieties of offspring to determine the genotypes of the organisms.
3. Use evidence from a computer simulation to support a claim about whether a mutation is harmful, helpful, or neutral.
4. Create a visual organizer to summarize the harmful, helpful, and neutral aspects of the mutation known as sickle cell disease.
5. Generate an explanatory model that shows the cause-and-effect relationship of gene transmission from parents to offspring and the resulting genetic variation.

Materials

- Science notebooks
- Computer with access to the Internet (at least one for each pair of student)
- Websites accessed:

- http://star.mit.edu
- www.pbs.org
- LCD projector for whole-class display of computer screen
- Screen or blank wall
- Copies of (one for each pair of students):
  - Backgrounder article related to "A Mutation Story" video segment
  - *StarGenetics Tutorial 1,* Sections 1–3 only (from the StarGenetics home page, select *Sample Exercises* from the menu on the left side of the screen; then select the link to *Tutorial 1*)
  - *Fruit Fly Exercise 1—Level 1* (from the StarGenetics home page, select *Sample Exercises* from the menu on the left side of the screen; then select the link to *Fruit Fly Exercise 1—Level 1*)

Engage

Ask the class: *When you hear the word mutation what do you think of? Do you think that all mutations are harmful to the organism? Why or why not?*

Explore

Pairs of students working at computers should access http://star.mit.edu; select the *StarGenetics* tool, then select *Video Tutorial* from the menu on the left side of the screen. The tutorial will introduce them to the basic operation of the simulation they will use to model inheritance of traits in fruit flies.

Distribute a copy of *StarGenetics Tutorial 1* to each pair of students. Instruct the class to select *Home* from the menu on the left side of the screen, then press the *Start* button to run the application. Instruct them to follow the instructions that appear on the screen until they see the simulation workspace. Give them ample time to work through the tutorial. Use a computer attached to an LCD projector if any part of the process needs to be demonstrated for the class.

Distribute a copy of *Fruit Fly Exercise —Level 1* to each pair of students. Encourage them to use this exercise to guide their exploration of the simulation, but also allow them to use the simulator to investigate other fruit fly crosses. As the class works through this exercise, circulate and monitor their progress. If some students need assistance, either provide guidance (not answers) yourself or ask other students to help them.

Explain

Bring the class together to talk about their findings in a meaning-making discussion. If you are able to project the simulation on a screen or blank wall, do so as you get input from the students about questions they answered, how they used the simulation, what fruit fly crosses (matings) provided the information they were looking for, what conclusions they can make, etc.

Ask the class whether they think the mutation carried by the fly named "grounded" represents a positive, negative, or neutral mutation. Remind students to support their claims with evidence from the simulations that they have run.

Elaborate

Tell the class that sometimes it is difficult to determine whether a mutation is harmful or helpful to an organism. Show the video segment titled "A Mutation Story" that you can find on the Public Broadcasting System's website www.pbs.org.

Provide a copy of the backgrounder for "A Mutation Story" that accompanies the video on the website for each student to read closely. Encourage students to use the "reading in the content area" strategies that have been introduced in science and language arts to help them identify words that are new to them and main ideas of the article.

Evaluate

As a summative evaluation for this lesson, have individual students create a visual organizer, for example, a Venn diagram or T-chart, illustrating reasons that sickle cell disease is a genetic disease caused by a mutation that may be considered harmful, helpful, or neutral under different conditions.

Activity 42: How can fossils help us learn about life and environments long ago?

Grade: 3, Life Sciences

Framework Context	
Scientific and Engineering Practices	**Analyzing and Interpreting Data** Students should be able to collect categorical or numerical data for presentation in forms that facilitate interpretation, such as tables and graphs. When feasible, computers and other digital tools should be introduced to enable this Practice (NRC, 2013, p. 63).
Crosscutting Concepts	**Patterns** One major use of pattern recognition is in classification, which depends on careful observation of similarities and differences; objects can be classified into groups on the basis of similarities of visible or microscopic features or on the basis of similarities of function. Such classification is useful in codifying relationships (NRC, 2012, p. 85). **Scale, Proportion, and Quantity** Students can express quantities of time. They can also use estimation to help them develop a sense of time scales relevant to various objects, systems, and processes (NRC, 2012, p. 91).
Disciplinary Core Idea **Component Idea** **Conceptual Understanding**	**LS4:** Biological Evolution: Unity and Diversity **LS4.A:** Evidence of Common Ancestry and Diversity **By the end of grade 3:** Fossils provide evidence about the types of organisms (both visible and microscopic) that lived long ago and also about the nature of their environments. Fossils can be compared with one another and to living organisms according to their similarities and differences (NRC, 2012, p. 162).

Performance Expectations 3-LS4-1

Analyze and interpret data from fossils to provide evidence of organisms and environments in which they lived long ago (NGSS Lead States, 2013, p. 30). www.nextgenscience.org/pe/3-ls4-1-biological-evolution -unity-and-diversity

Learning Target

Fossils provide evidence about organisms that lived long ago and the environments in which they lived.

Success Criteria

The students will:

1. Observe images of fossils and infer the type of organism or organism part from which it was formed.

2. Look at artist's conceptions of the appearance of the organism or organism part from which a fossil was formed and determine key characteristics.

3. Compare images of fossils with one another and with living organisms.

4. Contrast images of fossils with images of currently living organisms.

5. Explain how a fossil provides evidence of something that was alive long ago.

6. Explain how a fossil provides evidence of ancient environments.

Materials

- Computers with Internet access (at least one for each small group of students) with the website *Fossils for Kids* bookmarked: (www.fossilsforkids.com)

- Science notebooks

- LCD projector and screen or blank wall (optional)

Engage

Write the word *fossils* on the board. Tell the class to start thinking about what they know about fossils. Distribute three sticky notes to each student. Ask students to write three things they know about fossils. Tell them to write only one idea on each sticky note.

Walk around the room and collect the sticky notes as students finish. Quickly sort through the notes and organize them into like topics on the board. If some statements are incorrect or off-topic, simply don't post them at this time. Briefly point out ideas that relate to the upcoming lesson.

Explore

Organize the class into small groups or pairs. Each should have access to a computer with access to the Internet. Have students bring up the *Fossils for Kids* website at www.fossilsforkids.com, click to enter, click on the image for the *Now and Then* page. Display the same page with the LCD projector if you want to demonstrate the procedures for this part of the lesson.

Tell the students to make a table with three columns and six rows on the next blank page in their science notebook. Then instruct them to read the paragraph at the top of the page. Before they click on any of the images, challenge students to write, in the corresponding cell in the table, their thoughts about what organism or organism part the fossil shown came from. Tell them you are not worried if they are correct but want them to be sure to try. Let them know that they may discuss their thinking quietly with others in their small group if they would like.

Next, have the students look more closely at each image by clicking on the picture, then scroll down to see an artist's idea of what the entire organism looked like millions of years ago. If there are captions below the pictures, be sure to read them. Invite them to follow any hyperlinks on these pages as well for further information. Suggest that they add a few notes to the table in their science notebook for future reference. They may use the backwards arrow at the top left of the screen to go back and select another fossil image to examine closely.

Explain

Bring the students together in a discussion circle to talk about their findings. Encourage students to talk to each other about what they learned or still wonder about rather than simply answering any questions you pose.

Ask the class to describe similarities among the organisms and organism parts that were included on this webpage. Hopefully, someone will mention that the hard things became fossils and soft things did not. Talk about where they think the different fossils were found and what evidence they have to support their thinking (perhaps they read it in the captions). Talk about whether they think the environment in which the organism was fossilized long ago was the same or different from the recent environment where the fossil was discovered.

If students did click on the hyperlinks, they would have seen the table titled *The Sands of Time* that provides information about the age of various fossils. Briefly show the class the chart and briefly describe it.

Mention that scientists who study fossils are known as paleontologists. Point out that they often compare fossils to one another and with recent organisms to find similarities and differences. Such studies enable them to learn about how organisms may have changed over time.

Elaborate

Have the students work again in their small groups. Have them find a set of fossil images to compare and contrast. There are several places on the *Fossils for Kids* website for students to look: the *Shark Teeth* page, the *Shark Tooth Hill Virtual Museum* page, and the *Invertebrate* page. Or they could use their favorite web browser to find other images. Also suggest that they find images of related recent organisms to compare with fossils.

Evaluate

Have students explain in writing how fossils provide evidence about the types of organisms that lived long ago and the environments found on Earth long ago.

Activity 43: How does the environment influence populations of organisms over multiple generations?

Grades: 6–8, Life Sciences

Framework Context	
Scientific and Engineering Practices	**Using Mathematics and Computational Thinking** Students should be able to express relationships using equalities first in words and then in algebraic symbols. Students should be able to able to represent data, to predict outcomes and to determine relationships using mathematics. Students should gain experience using computers to record measurements taken with probes or instruments to take multiple measurements. Students should also use computer programs to transform their data into tabular and/or graphical forms and use the representations to aid in identifying patterns (NRC, 2012, p. 58). **Obtaining, Evaluating, and Communicating Information** Students need sustained practice and support to develop the ability to extract the meaning of scientific text from books, media reports, and other forms of scientific communication because the form of this text is initially unfamiliar—expository rather than narrative, often linguistically dense, and reliant on precise logical flows. Students should be able to interpret meaning from text, to produce text in which written language and diagrams are used to express scientific ideas, and to engage in extended discussion about those ideas (NRC, 2012, p. 76). **Constructing Explanations and Designing Solutions** Construct an explanation that includes qualitative or quantitative relationships between variables that describe phenomena (NRC, 2012, p. 70).
Crosscutting Concepts	**Cause and Effect** Phenomena may have more than one cause, and some cause and effect relationships in systems can only be described using probability (NGSS Lead States, 2013, p. 74). **Systems and System Models** An explicit model of a system under study can be a useful tool not only for gaining understanding of the system but also for conveying it to others. Models of a system can range in complexity from lists and simple sketches to detailed computer simulations or functioning prototypes (NRC, 2012, p. 92).
Disciplinary Core Idea	**LS4:** Biological Evolution: Unity and Diversity
Component Idea	**LS4.B:** Natural Selection
Conceptual Understanding	**By the end of grade 8:** Genetic variations among individuals in a population give some individuals an advantage in surviving and reproducing in their environment. This is known as natural selection. It leads to the predominance of certain traits in a population and the suppression of others (NRC, 2012, p. 165).
Component Idea	**LS4.C:** Adaptation
Conceptual Understanding	**By the end of grade 8:** Adaptation by natural selection acting over generations is one important process by which species change over time in response to changes in environmental conditions. Traits that support successful survival and reproduction in the new environment become more common; those that do not become less common. Thus, the distribution of traits in a population changes. In separated populations with different conditions, the changes can be large enough that the populations, provided they remain separated (a process called reproductive isolation), evolve to become separate species (NRC, 2012, p. 166).

Performance Expectations
MS-LS4-4

Construct an explanation based on evidence that describes how genetic variations of traits in a population increase some individuals' probability of surviving and reproducing in a specific environment. www .nextgenscience.org/pe/ms-ls4-4-biological-evolution-unity-and-diversity

MS-LS4-6

Use mathematical representations to support explanations of how natural selection may lead to increases and decreases of specific traits in populations over time (NGSS Lead States, 2013, p. 74). www .nextgenscience.org/pe/ms-ls4-6-biological-evolution-unity-and-diversity

Learning Targets

1. Natural selection leads to the predominance of certain traits in a population.

2. Adaptation by natural selection is the mechanism by which species change over time in response to changes in environmental conditions.

3. Traits that support survival become more common and those that do not become less common.

Success Criteria

The students will:

1. Use a simulation to explore how the rate of environmental change affects evolutionary changes in organisms.

2. Gather and synthesize information about real-world examples of adaptation by natural selection acting over generations.

3. Write a report that relates the findings about adaptation by natural selection acting over generations from a simulation and research about the topic.

4. Use mathematical representations to support explanations of natural selection that lead to increases and decreases in specific traits in populations over time.

Materials

- Science notebooks
- Computers or mobile devices (at least one for each small group of students)
  - Download and launch the activity *Changes in the Environment* found on the Concord Consortium's website at www.concord.org
  - Internet access
- LCD projector for whole-class display of computer screen (optional)
- Screen or blank wall (optional)

Engage

Ask the class: *How would you define natural selection? What does it mean for a species to adapt? What does it mean for a species to go extinct?*

Explore

Explain to the class that because they will be examining changes that take very long to happen, they will use a computer simulation that will model the changes over a much shorter time period. If you have an LCD projector, display the simulation *Changes in the Environment* for the whole class to see while presenting basic instructions:

- Read carefully, since the simulation provides background information and has hyperlinks if you need to check the definition of any words appearing in blue (page 1).
- Use the arrows near the compass at the bottom of the screen to navigate through the pages (page 1).
- Follow the instructions that are given (page 2).
- Use control buttons to explore the simulation's functions and figure out the challenge (page 2).
- Answer questions (page 3). (Tell the class whether to answer on the computer or in their science notebooks.)
- Continue as the program instructs until page 12 is finished.
- Collaboration and thinking as a team will lead to success.
- Ask for help if necessary.

If no LCD projector is available, consider listing the basic instructions on the board and quickly explaining them to the class.

Have the class work in pairs. Each pair should have a computer on which *Changes in the Environment* is loaded. Allow adequate time for students to try out their ideas in the simulated environment.

Explain

Bring the class together to talk about their findings in a meaning-making discussion. If you are able to project the program on a screen or blank wall, do so as you get input from the students about questions they answered, how they solved the challenges, what conclusions they can make, etc.

Lead the class to understand that the mountain-building process illustrated in this simulation takes millions of years although they spent less than an hour watching the simulation. Ask the class: *When you quickly raised the height of the mountains, what happened to the plant populations?* The plants on both sides of the mountain range withered and died. The plants could not survive long enough in the new environments to produce seeds, so that species of plants ceased to exist in that area. Then ask: *When you gradually raised the height of the mountains, what happened to the plant population?* There was time for several generations of plants to grow and reproduce. There was more variation in the plants on each side of the mountain range. So as the mountains continued to grow, making the environment change, a few plants on each side of the mountain range produced seeds because they were sufficiently adapted to the new environmental conditions while those that were not sufficiently adapted to the new conditions withered and died.

This gradual change in the surviving species as the environment changes has been called *natural selection* or *survival of the fittest.* The evolutionary process has also been called *adaptive radiation,* in which a species diversifies over many generations due to genetic variation and some adaptations happen to be better able to survive and reproduce in specific environmental niches or conditions.

Elaborate

Tell the class that they simulated adaptive radiation but that they should also understand that this evolutionary process occurs in the real world. Assign some Internet research to help your class make these connections. A PBS series, *Evolution,* at www.pbs.org/wgbh/evolution, presents a rich online collection of articles and other features that serve as appropriate complex text for middle school students to use to pursue this topic. Among these resources is a library article with multiple hyperlinks titled "Adaptive Radiation: Darwin's Finches," a film clip named "Hummingbird Species in the Transitional Zones," and an interactive presentation called "An Origin of Species" with an associated "Species Gallery." This website also contains several options for teacher professional development about evolutionary biology, in case you need to review any concepts before teaching them.

Depending on the technical reading skills of your class, either select one article for all students to read or one presentation to view, identify main ideas in, and discuss with the class; or have groups of students read or view different features, then share summaries of them with the rest of the class. Be sure to encourage science talk about the information presented.

Evaluate

Have students write a report about *adaptation by natural selection acting over generations.* Suggest that they support their claims with evidence from both the plant simulation and readings about finches.

Activity 44: How many different kinds of living things are in the habitats around our school?

Grade: 3, Life Sciences

Framework Context	
Scientific and Engineering Practices	**Planning and Carrying Out Investigations** Students need opportunities to design investigations so that they can learn the importance of such decisions as what to measure, what to keep constant, and how to select or construct data collection instruments that are appropriate to the needs of an inquiry. They also need experiences that help them recognize that the laboratory is not the sole domain for legitimate scientific inquiry and that, for many scientists (e.g., earth scientists, ethologists, ecologists), the "laboratory" is the natural world where experiments are conducted and data are collected in the field . . . . From the earliest grades, students should have opportunities to carry out careful and systematic investigations, with appropriately supported prior experiences that develop their ability to observe and measure and to record data using appropriate tools and instruments (NRC, 2012, pp. 60–61). **Analyzing and Interpreting Data** At the elementary level, students need support to recognize the need to record observations—whether in drawings, words, or numbers—and to share them with others (NRC, 2012, p. 63). **Obtaining, Evaluating, and Communicating** From the very start of their science education, students should be asked to engage in the communication of science, especially regarding the investigations they are conducting and the observations they are making. Careful description of observations and clear statement of ideas, with the ability to both refine a statement in response to questions and to ask questions of others to achieve clarification of what is being said begin at the earliest grades (NRC, 2012, p. 76).
Crosscutting Concepts	**Systems and System Models** Starting in the earliest grades, students should be asked to express their thinking with drawings or diagrams and with written or oral descriptions. They should describe objects or organisms in terms of their parts and the roles those parts play in the functioning of the object or organism, and they should note relationships between the parts (NRC, 2012, p. 93).
Disciplinary Core Idea	**LS4:** Biological Evolution: Unity and Diversity
Component Idea	**LS4.D:** Biodiversity and Humans
Conceptual Understanding	**By the end of grade 3:** Populations live in a variety of habitats, and change in those habitats affects the organisms living there (NRC, 2012, p. 167).

Performance Expectation 3-LS4-4 Make a claim about the merit of a solution to a problem caused when the environment changes and the types of organisms that live there also change (NGSS Lead States, 2013, p. 30). www.nextgenscience.org/pe/3-ls4-4-biological-evolution-unity-and-diversity

Learning Target Environmental changes to an environment may result in changes to the populations that live there.

Success Criteria *The students will:*

1. Investigate the diversity of organisms on a small plot of land.
2. Refine research procedures based on ideas of their peers and initial investigational experiences.

3. Collaborate to collect, organize, and share data with their class.

4. Explain the value of biodiversity in ecosystems.

Materials

- Meter sticks or metric tapes
- Garden stakes or paint stirrers
- Caution tape or ribbon
- Science notebooks
- Hand lenses
- Field guides for your area for plants, insects, etc.
- Computers with access to Internet (optional)
- Digital cameras, portable digital microscopes, handheld devices with cameras, etc. (optional)
- Document camera and screen or blank wall (optional)

Engage

Ask the class: *How many different kinds of plants and animals do you think we could find around our school? Do you think we would find the same kinds of living things in different parts of the school grounds? How could we find out?*

Explore

Review behavior guidelines and safety rules for investigations in the field. Remind students not to touch any of the organisms in their study plot.

Take the class outside to explore the schoolyard for different microhabitats; e.g., a flower bed, a shady area under a tree, a sunny spot on the lawn, etc. For this investigation, students should work in groups of three or four. Assign groups or allow them to select an area to study. Give each group a meter stick or tape measure, four garden stakes or paint stirrers, and ribbon or caution tape to mark off a square study plot, 2 meters on each side, in one of the microhabitats identified.

Let the students know that each group should study their plot to determine the variety of living things it has. Give the students about ten minutes to talk with the others in their small group about how they plan to observe, classify, count, and record the living things they find in their study plot. Then tell them to try out their observation and data collection plan in their plot for about 15 minutes.

Explain

Have the whole class come together for a meaning-making discussion about their study plot, the organisms they observed, and how they recorded their data. If a document camera is available, let students use it to show the class their notes in their science notebooks. Focus the science talk on strategies used to organize and report the data. Some groups may have made a map indicating where in their plot each organism was found. Some may have made a list of the organisms they observed by name or by simple drawings in the order they observed them. Others may have created categories such as plants and animals, or green things, crawling things, and flying things. Talk about the advantages of each method. Emphasize that scientists share ideas and that using someone else's approach is appropriate if you give credit to the people you learned it from.

Introduce the print and online field guides that are available for reference, and discuss with the class whether it would be better to use them in the field or to refer to them when reviewing their notes back in the classroom.

Remind the class that their goal is to find out how many different organisms are in each study plot, not the total count of organisms. Explain that different groups used different investigational methods during their exploration and that it would be fairer if all groups used similar methods. Explain that they're going to make another set of investigations, but this time using more similar methods.

Ask the class if they had enough time to find and record information about all of the different types of organisms in their study plot. Also check to see if they need additional tools for their observations, such as hand lenses, rulers, digital cameras, etc.

Elaborate

Plan another visit to the study plots in the field. Go over the strategies that the whole class will try to use this time. Set a reasonable length of time to make observations based on recommendations made during the explore phase of the lesson. You may decide to have groups continue to study the same plot or to ask them to switch to one they did not observe during the explore phase of the lesson.

Tell each group that they are expected to present a report about the variety of organisms in their plot. Let them know that they will have time to complete their organization and display of data after they come back into the classroom and that they may use the document camera to share their records with the class.

Evaluate

Informal formative assessment should occur throughout the lesson, during fieldwork and science talks. By watching and listening to students, you will learn a lot about their understanding of biodiversity in their plot.

The final presentations of each group may be summatively assessed. Consider developing a simple rubric for scoring the group presentations; a rubric would also help groups self-evaluate their recording and presentation methods as they prepare and practice before speaking to the class.

Hold one more general discussion after the group presentations. Ask: *Were the same organisms found in each of the study plots? Did they all have the same variety of plants and animals? Which plot seemed to have the most different organisms? . . . the least? Why do you think this was the case? Which is better (for the health and survival of the plot), having a plot with lots of different organisms or having a plot with just a few organisms? What if a disease made one of the organisms in the plot die off? Which plot would be most severely affected? Does what we learned by studying the plots apply to the whole world? Why or why not?*

Earth and Space Sciences

Source: Minerva Studio/Shutterstock

"Earth and Space Sciences" (ESS) is the third domain included in the Disciplinary Core Ideas, the third dimension of the *Framework*. ESS is quite interdisciplinary, including the study of physics, chemistry, and life science concepts. For example, the study of the properties of rocks and minerals that make up Earth's crust have traditionally been studied in an earth science unit, but according to the Disciplinary Core Ideas introduced by the *Framework* and embedded in the *Next Generation Science Standards,* those Disciplinary Core Ideas are located in the discipline of physical sciences. The activities in this section are organized in the same way. If you are looking for an activity about the properties of minerals, please look in the physical science activities section.

Earth is our home planet. Its place in space, its interacting systems, and humanity's impact on it are of prime importance. Specific fields of science that are typically considered to be an Earth/space science include: astronomy, astrophysics, cosmology, planetary science, lunar science, geology, geomorphology, volcanology, seismology, paleontology, oceanography, meteorology, etc.

As shown in the following table, in *A Framework for K–12 Science Education: Practices, Crosscutting Concepts, and Core Ideas* (NRC, 2012) this disciplinary area includes three core ideas; ESS1: Earth's Place in the Universe, ESS2: Earth's Systems, and ESS3: Earth and Human Activity.

Earth and Space Sciences Core and Component Ideas

Discipline-Related Code	Descriptive Title	Related Question
ESS1	**Earth's Place in the Universe**	**What is the universe, and what is Earth's place in it?**
ESS1.A	The Universe and Its Stars	*What is the universe, and what goes on in stars?*
ESS1.B	Earth and the Solar System	*What are the predictable patterns caused by Earth's movement in the solar system?*
ESS1.C	The History of Planet Earth	*How do people reconstruct and date events in Earth's planetary history?*
ESS2	**Earth's Systems**	**How and why is Earth constantly changing?**
ESS2.A	Earth Materials and Systems	*How do arth's major systems interact?*
ESS2.B	Plate Tectonics and Large-Scale System Interactions	*Why do the continents move, and what causes earthquakes and volcanoes?*
ESS2.C	The Roles of Water in Earth's Surface Processes	*How do the properties and movements of water shape Earth's surface and affect its systems?*
ESS2.D	Weather and Climate	*What regulates weather and climate?*
ESS2.E	Biogeology	*How do living organisms alter Earth's processes and structures?*
ESS3	**Earth and Human Activity**	**How do Earth's surface processes and human activities affect each other?**
ESS3.A	Natural Resources	*How do humans depend on Earth's resources?*
ESS3.B	Natural Hazards	*How do natural hazards affect individuals and societies?*
ESS3.C	Human Impacts on Earth Systems	*How do humans change the planet?*
ESS3.D	Global Climate Change	*How do people model and predict the effects of human activities on Earth's climate?*

Source: NRC, 2012, p. 171.

For a concise description of background information related to Earth and Space Science DCIs and their components, look at Chapter 7 of *A Framework for K–12 Science Education: Practices, Crosscutting Concepts, and Core Ideas* (NRC, 2012), available online from the National Academies Press at www.nap.edu.

There are additional Earth and space science activities available to you digitally via the Enhanced Pearson eText. These include:

DCI Component Idea	Title	Grade/Grade-band
ESS1.B	How can shadows tell you when it is local noon?	Grade 5
ESS1.B	What causes the phases of the moon to change during a lunar month?	Middle School
ESS1.B	How do the planets in our solar system compare in size?	Middle School
ESS2.C	What part of Earth's water is in the oceans?	Grade 5
ESS3.D	What are greenhouse gasses and how do they contribute to global warming?	Middle School

Activity 45: How does the position of the sun in the sky change throughout the day?

Grade: 1, Earth and Space Sciences

Framework Context	
Scientific and Engineering Practices	**Planning and Carrying Out Investigations** At all levels, [students] should engage in investigations that range from those structured by the teacher—in order to expose an issue or question that they would be unlikely to explore on their own—to those that emerge from students' own questions (NRC, 2012, p. 61). **Engaging in Argument from Evidence** Young students can begin by constructing an argument for their own interpretation of the phenomena they observe and of any data they collect. They need instructional support to go beyond simply making claims—that is, to include reasons or references to evidence and to begin to distinguish evidence from opinion (NRC, 2012, p. 73).
Crosscutting Concepts	**Patterns** It is important for them [students] to develop ways to recognize, classify, and record patterns in the phenomena they observe (NRC, 2012, p. 86).
Disciplinary Core Idea	**ESS1:** Earth's Place in the Universe
Component Idea	**ESS1.A:** The Universe and Its Stars
Conceptual Understanding	**By the end of grade 2:** Patterns of the motion of the sun, moon, and stars in the sky can be observed, described, and predicted (NCR, 2012, p. 174).
Component Idea	**ESS1.B:** The History of Planet Earth
Conceptual Understanding	**By the end of grade 2:** Some events on Earth occur in cycles, like day and night . . . (NRC, 2012, p. 178).

Performance Expectation 1-ESS1-1

Use observations of the sun, moon, and stars to describe patterns that can be predicted. Clarification Statement: Examples of patterns could include that the Sun and Moon appear to rise in one part of the sky, move across the sky, and set . . . (NGSS Lead States, 2013, p. 14). www.nextgenscience.org/pe/1-ess1 -1-earths-place-universe

Learning Target

Each day the sun follows a similar pattern as it appears to move across the sky.

Success Criteria

The students will:

1 Observe, record, and look for patterns in the apparent daily motion of the sun across the sky.

Materials

- Science notebooks or copies of sheets showing a panoramic view of landmarks on the horizon from a selected observation point near your school
- Pencils and/or crayons

Engage

Say to the class: *I'd like you to vote with your bodies. Don't move until you hear the options. If you think that the sun changes positions in the sky during the day, move to the front of the room.* (Post a sentence strip that says: "The sun changes positions in the sky during the day." in the front of the room.) *If you think that the sun stays in one position in the sky during the day, move to the back of the room.* (Post a sentence strip that says: "The sun stays in one position in the sky during the day." in the back of the room.) *Now, move—vote with your bodies.*

Once the students have moved to their selected part of the classroom, point out how many students support each claim. Then ask students to discuss with others in their group the reasons they agree with the statement they selected. After a few minutes, ask each group to share with the whole class some of the reasons they talked about. Make a chart listing the evidence each group presents under the claim (sentence strip) they support.

Ask the class: *How could we gather more evidence about this?* Make a list of the suggestions offered.

Safety Precaution

Do not allow students to look directly at the sun. Suggest that students simply refer to surrounding objects to define a general position for the sun (e.g., "The sun is above the maple tree," or, "The sun is almost overhead"). Shading their eyes with their hand or another opaque object is another possible strategy.

Explore

Considering the students' suggestions for gathering more evidence about the motion of the sun in the sky during the day, provide opportunities for the class to observe and record the position of the sun in the sky throughout the day for several days.

Early in the morning on a sunny day, take the class outside to a good spot to see the sun in the context of the surroundings. Students should record their observations in a science journal by drawing a representation of the sun in the sky in relation to landmarks (trees, buildings, flagpoles, etc.) to help them show the sun's position at the time of each observation. Remind students to record the date and time of their observation. If you believe some or all of your students would benefit from some scaffolding, create a sketch or photo of a panorama of the horizon showing the landmarks from the observation spot so that students only need to draw in the position of the sun on a sheet printed with a copy of your sketch.

Throughout the day, about once each hour if possible, return to the same spot outside with the class to mark the sun's current position.

Explain

After making the final afternoon observation, ask: *What did you find out about the position of the sun in the sky during the day?* Encourage students to use their drawings to describe the changes in the sun's position. Lead students to understand that it started out low over there in the morning, moved higher in the sky around noon, then kept moving that way in the afternoon. Introduce the cardinal directions if you think your students would benefit from that level of detail.

Encourage students to talk about what will happen when the sun continues to move along its apparent path. They might bring up sunset, when the sun goes below the horizon, and mention that then it gets dark and becomes night. Ask: *When do you think the sun will be visible again, and where will it be on our pictures?* Discuss the difference between day and night.

Elaborate

Ask: *Do you think the sun's position will change the same way tomorrow? . . . next week? . . . next month? How could we find out?* Assist the students in continuing their investigation of sun positions throughout the school year and help them look for patterns in their findings. Identified patterns might include the cycle of day and night, changes in the length of day and night throughout the seasons, etc.

Evaluate

To check student understanding about how the sun's position changes throughout the day, after several days of observing have them fill in the blanks in the following story.

Early in the morning the sun is low in the _____.

During the morning the _____ rises higher in the sky.

At noon the sun is almost _____.

In the evening the sun is low in the _____.

This is a pattern because _____.

Activity 46: How can we describe the positions of objects in the sky?

Grades: 6–8, Earth and Space Sciences

Framework Context	
Scientific and Engineering Practices	**Planning and Carrying Out Investigations** Students need opportunities to design investigations so that they can learn the importance of such decisions as what to measure, what to keep constant, and how to select or construct data collection instruments that are appropriate to the needs of an inquiry (NRC, 2012, p. 60).
Crosscutting Concepts	**Patterns** It is important for students to develop ways to recognize, classify, and record patterns in the phenomena they observe (NRC, 2012, p. 86).
Disciplinary Core Idea	**ESS1:** Earth's Place in the Universe
Component Idea	**ESS1.A:** The Universe and Its Stars
Conceptual Understanding	**By the end of grade 8:** Patterns of the apparent motion of . . . the moon . . . in the sky can be observed, described, [and] predicted . . . (NRC, 2012, p. 174).

Performance Expectation MS-ESS1-1

Develop and use a model of the Earth-sun-moon system to describe the cyclic patterns of lunar phases, eclipses of the sun and moon, and seasons (NGSS Lead States, 2013, p. 78). www.nextgenscience.org/pe/ms-ess1-1-earths-place-universe

Learning Target

Compass directions and angles can be used to describe the position of objects in the sky including the moon.

Success Criteria

The students will:

1. Use compass directions and angles to describe the position of objects in the sky.
2. Observe and describe the position of the moon in the sky.

Materials

- Cardinal direction signs
- Ten index cards each labeled with a large number from 1 to 10
- Masking tape or sticky tack
- Adding machine tape
- "Handy Angle Measurements" sheet

Preparation

Post cardinal directions—north, south, east, and west—on the classroom walls. Post the 10 index cards at various locations on the walls and ceiling of the classroom. Put a strip of adding machine tape all the way around the room at the students' seated eye level. This represents the horizon.

Engage

Ask: *How could you explain to someone where to look for a particular object in the sky? What kinds of measurements and units might be helpful?* Ask several students to describe the location of something in the classroom. Discuss alternative approaches.

Explore

Point out the cardinal directions signs posted in the room. Distribute copies of the "Handy Angle Measurements" sheet shown on the next page. Demonstrate how to extend your arm, and discuss the angles represented by the different parts of the hand. Mention that the adding machine tape around the room represents the horizon, the starting point for their angle measurements. Ask the students to try to measure the angle from the horizon line to the point straight overhead using an outstretched arm and clenched fist. It should take approximately nine fists, since the angle from the horizon to the point overhead (zenith) is 90 degrees and each fist represents about 10 degrees.

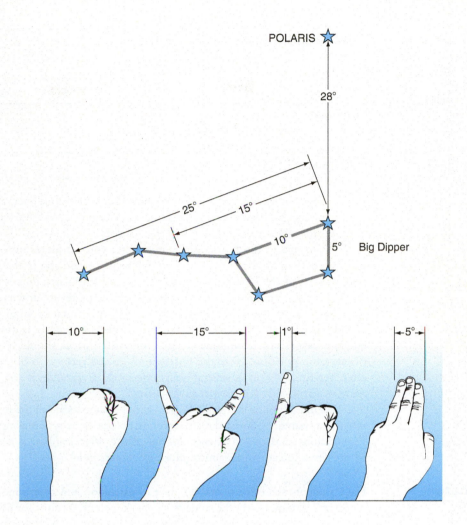

Have students number from 1 to 10 on a sheet of paper. Ask them to use cardinal directions and angle measurements to describe the position of each index card number posted in the room, from their seat.

Note: Because the cards are relatively close to the observers, the observing position will affect the results. Do not expect students in different parts of the room to have the same direction and angle measurement for each card.

Explain

Ask: *How were you able to describe the positions of the index cards?* (By finding the direction to look and measuring how high above the horizon with my outstretched hand.) *Could you use this same technique to describe the position of objects in the sky? What would you need to know to be successful?* (Cardinal directions.)

Safety Precautions

Caution students to never look directly at the sun. The sun is very bright. Looking at it could cause blindness. Only use the technique introduced in this activity to describe the location of the moon, stars, and planets.

Elaborate

Apply this measuring technique to describing the position of the moon in the sky. Find out how the moon moves across the sky during the night. Determine the cardinal directions around your observation point. A compass, street map, or locating Polaris (the North Star) should help.

Record your observations in a data table like the one shown.

Time of Observation	Direction	Angle above the Horizon
7:30 p.m.		

Time of Observation	Direction	Angle above the Horizon
8:00 p.m.		
8:30 p.m.		
9:00 p.m.		
9:30 p.m.		
10:00 p.m.		

Observe and record the position of the moon at half-hour intervals. Describe how the moon moves during the night. Develop an investigation to determine how the position of the moon at a given hour changes from night to night. Ask: *What did you find?*

If you live in the Northern Hemisphere, you can determine your latitude by measuring the position of Polaris above the horizon. Polaris is the end star in the handle of the Little Dipper. The pointer stars of the Big Dipper are helpful in finding Polaris. Polaris is *not* the brightest star in the sky. To find it, face the northern horizon. Look for the patterns shown in the Handy Angle Measurement diagram. The orientation of the Big Dipper will vary, but its pointer stars always point toward Polaris. Decide which star is Polaris. Determine how many degrees it is above the horizon using the Handy Angle Measurement technique. That number of degrees should be the same as the latitude of your observation position. Note the position of Polaris relative to objects on the ground (trees, houses, etc.). Try finding Polaris several hours later. Ask: *Is it still in the same angle above the horizon? Is it still in the same place relative to the objects on the ground?*

You might notice that while Polaris is in the same location, the nearby star patterns have seemed to move in a counterclockwise direction around Polaris. Activity 5, Making a Star Clock, in the GEMS (Great Explorations in Math and Science) Module *Earth, Moon, and Stars,* is a good activity related to the motion of the circumpolar constellations (those around the pole).[1]

Evaluate

Have students share the results of their investigation and determine the approximate location for the moon at 7:00 p.m. Direct the students to check their predictions for homework and summarize how they calculate and determine positions of the moon at night. In the morning, students should share their ideas with classmates.

---

[1]For many good astronomy activities, see GEMS (Great Explorations in Math and Science), 1986. *Earth, Moon, and Stars,* by Cary I. Sneider. Lawrence Hall of Science, Berkeley, CA.

Activity 47: How do shadows caused by the sun change during the day?

Grade: 5, Earth and Space Sciences

Framework Context	
Scientific and Engineering Practices	**Analyzing and Interpreting Data** At the elementary level, students need support to recognize the need to record observations—whether in drawings, words, or numbers—and to share them with others. As they engage in scientific inquiry more deeply, they should begin to collect categorical or numerical data for presentation in forms that facilitate interpretation, such as tables and graphs (NRC, 2012, p. 63). **Constructing Explanations** [Students] should be encouraged to develop explanations of what they observe when conducting their own investigations and to evaluate their own and others' explanations for consistency with the evidence (NRC, 2012, p. 69).
Crosscutting Concepts	**Patterns** It is important for them [students] to develop ways to recognize, classify, and record patterns in the phenomena they observe (NRC, 2012, p. 86).
Disciplinary Core Idea **Component Idea** **Conceptual Understanding**	**ESS1:** Earth's Place in the Universe **ESS1.B:** Earth and the Solar System **By the end of grade 5:** . . . the rotation of Earth about an axis between its North and South poles, cause observable patterns. These include . . . daily . . . changes in the length and direction of shadows . . . (NRC, 2012, p. 176).

Performance Expectation 5-ESS1-2

Represent data in graphical displays to reveal patterns of daily changes in length and direction of shadows, day and night, and the seasonal appearance of some stars in the night sky. (NGSS Lead States, 2013, p. 49). www.nextgenscience.org/pe/5-ess1-2-earths-place-universe

Learning Target

The position of the sun in the sky determines the length and direction of the shadows produced.

Success Criteria

The students will:

1. Observe how the length and direction of shadows change during the day.
2. Relate the position of the sun in the sky to the length and direction of the shadows it produces.

Materials

- Flagpole or fence post
- Sidewalk chalk
- Paint stirrers (to use as stakes in the lawn)
- Sticky notes or index cards and masking tape
- Metric tapes
- Protractors
- Science notebooks

Engage

Ask: *Do you think that shadows outdoors change during the day? How might we find out?*

Safety Precaution

Caution students to never look directly at the sun. The sun is very bright. Staring at it could cause blindness. Students should simply refer to surrounding objects to define a general position for the sun (e.g., "The sun is above the maple tree," or, "The sun is almost overhead"). Shading their eyes with their hand or another opaque object is another possible strategy to avoid looking directly at the sun.

Explore

On a sunny day, take the class outside to the flagpole or a fence post early in the morning.

Ask: *Does the flagpole or fence post have a shadow? How could we mark the position of this shadow?*

Show the students the sidewalk chalk and paint stirrers if they need a hint. Have the students identify the "end" of the shadow, that is, the part cast by the top of the flagpole or the fence post. If the end of the shadow falls on concrete, sidewalk chalk can be used to mark its position. If the end of the shadow falls on grass, a paint stirrer can be used as a stake to mark its position. Record the time of the observation either in chalk on the concrete or with pencil on the paint stirrer. Throughout the day, about once each hour if possible, return to the flagpole or fence post with the class to mark the shadow's current position.

Explain

After making the final afternoon observation, ask: *What did you find out about how the shadow changed during the day?* (It started out long on that side, then got shorter, then got longer on the other side.) *Why do you think the shadow changed in this way?* (Because the sun seemed to move across the sky.) *How did the position of the sun change during our observations today?* (Indicating directions, lead students to understand that it started out low over there in the morning, moved higher in the sky around noon, then kept moving that way in the afternoon.) Develop the concept that the sun appeared to move from east to west in the sky during the day and that caused the size, shape, and direction of the shadow to change over time.

Elaborate

Ask: *Do you think the flagpole or fence post shadow will change the same way tomorrow? Next week? Next month? How could we find out?* Assist the students in continuing their investigation of shadow positions throughout the school year and help them look for patterns in their findings.

Suggest that the students use appropriate tools to quantify the data they collect. Metric measuring tapes and protractors could be used to facilitate measurement of shadow length and direction.

Evaluate

To check student understanding about how shadows change throughout the day, have them fill in the blanks in the following story.

Early in the morning the sun is low in the _____.

When I am outside early on a sunny morning my shadow is _____ and points toward the _____.

During the morning the _____ rises higher in the sky.

My shadow gets _____.

My shadow is _____ at noon when the sun is almost _____.

During the afternoon my shadow becomes _____.

In the evening the sun is low in the _____.

My shadow is _____ and points toward the _____.

A related Grade 5 activity may be accessed via the Enhanced Pearson eText. It is titled: "**How can shadows tell you when it is local noon?**" and addresses the DCI Component Idea ESS1.B.

Activity 48: How does the appearance of the moon's shape change over time?

Grades: 6–8, Earth and Space Sciences

Framework Context	
Scientific and Engineering Practices	**Planning and Carrying Out Investigations** At all levels, they [students] should engage in investigations that range from those structured by the teacher—in order to expose an issue or question that they would be unlikely to explore on their own—to those that emerge from students' own questions (NRC, 2012, p. 61).
Crosscutting Concepts	**Patterns** It is important for students to develop ways to recognize, classify, and record patterns in the phenomena they observe (NRC, 2012, p. 86).
Disciplinary Core Idea **Component Idea** **Conceptual Understanding**	**ESS1:** Earth's Place in the Universe **ESS1.B:** Earth and the Solar System **By the end of grade 8:** The orbits of Earth around the sun and of the moon around Earth, together with the rotation of Earth about an axis between its North and South poles, cause observable patterns. These include day and night; . . . phases of the moon; and different positions of the . . . moon . . . at different times of the day, month . . . (NRC, 2012, p. 176).

Performance Expectation MS-ESS1-1

Develop and use a model of the Earth-sun-moon system to describe the cyclic patterns of lunar phases, eclipses of the sun and moon, and seasons. (NGSS Lead States, 2013, p. 78). www.nextgenscience.org/pe/ms-ess1-1-earths-place-universe

Learning Target

The appearance of the moon in Earth's sky changes from night to night. This cyclic pattern is observable and can be predicted.

Success Criteria

The students will:

1. Observe the moon at the same time each night for a week and record the moon's shape each night.
2. Make predictions about the moon's apparent shape for the next few days.
3. Put pictures of different moon phases in order according to how the moon's appearance changes throughout a month.

Materials

- Black construction paper
- Soft white chalk
- Copies of the Phases of the Moon as Seen from the Earth, cut apart into a set of eight cards
- Tape
- Blank paper

Engage

Distribute materials to the students. Give them five minutes to draw the shape of the moon. Post the pictures for all to see. Ask: *Are all the drawings the same shape?* (No.) Sort them so that similar shapes are grouped together. Ask representatives from each group to tell why they drew the moon the way they did. Ask: *Can everyone's drawing be correct even if they are different shapes?* (Yes.) *How can this be?* (The moon doesn't always appear the same shape.) *How could we find out how the appearance of the moon's shape changes over time?* (Hopefully, someone will suggest observing and recording the moon's appearance in the sky for a week or so.)

Explore

Have the students take home a large sheet of black construction paper and some white chalk and then observe the moon daily for a week. They should divide their paper into eight equal rectangles as shown.

Moon Calendar by Suzy	11/5	11/6	11/7
11/8	11/9	11/10	11/11

▶ Visit a fifth-grade classroom to see an alternative method of organizing and analyzing observations of the moon over time. Which approach do you prefer? Why?

Students can use the first rectangle for the title and their name and the remaining seven spaces for their daily observations. It is best to begin this assignment several days after the new moon when fair weather is expected—the waxing crescent moon should be visible in the western sky shortly after sunset. Assuming it is clear, the moon should be visible in the evening sky for the next week. If there is an overcast night, students should indicate on their chart that the sky was cloudy.

Explain

At the end of the observation period, students should bring their moon calendars to class to share and compare. Ask: *How did the moon's shape seem to change during the week?* Have them see if everyone's observations supported the same conclusions. Ask: *Did more of the moon appear to be illuminated each night?* Tell the students that the apparent shape of the moon is known as its *phase*. Use a chart like this to introduce the names of the phases. Challenge the students to identify which phases they observed.

New moon	Waxing crescent	First quarter	Waxing gibous
Full moon	Waning gibous	Last quarter	Waning crescent

Phases of the Moon as Seen From the Earth

Elaborate

Ask students to predict what the moon will look like for the next few days and then make observations to check their predictions.

To continue the investigation as a class project, each night have three students draw the shape of the moon on an index card. Have the three students compare their drawings and arrive at one drawing that represents their observations. Post the drawing on the appropriate month/date cell on a bulletin board calendar. As a pattern develops, have the class predict the next day's moon phase.

Evaluate

Provide students with sets of pictures or diagrams showing various phases of the moon. Challenge them to tape the pictures to a sheet of paper to illustrate their understanding of how the phases of the moon change during a month. Ask them to write a brief paragraph that tells the story of how the apparent shape of the moon visible from Earth changes over time.

Now that your students know how the apparent shape of the moon changes over time when viewed from Earth, they may be interested in what causes the phases of the moon. A related Grade 5 activity may be accessed via the Enhanced Pearson eText. It is titled: "What causes the phases of the moon to change during a lunar month?" and addresses the DCI Component Ideas ESS1.B.

Activity 49: How spread out are the planets in our solar system?

Grades: 6–8, Earth and Space Sciences

Framework Context	
Scientific and Engineering Practices	**Developing and Using Models** Conceptual models . . . are . . . explicit representations that are in some ways analogous to the phenomena they represent. Conceptual models allow scientists . . . to better visualize and understand a phenomenon under investigation . . . (NRC, 2012, p. 56). **Obtaining, Evaluating, and Communicating Information** Obtaining, Evaluating, and Communicating Information Students need sustained practice and support to develop the ability to extract the meaning of scientific text from books, media reports, and other forms of scientific communication because the form of this text is initially unfamiliar—expository rather than narrative, often linguistically dense, and reliant on precise logical flows. Students should be able to interpret meaning from text, to produce text in which written language and diagrams are used to express scientific ideas, and to engage in extended discussion about those ideas (NRC, 2012, p. 76).
Crosscutting Concepts	**Scale, Proportion, and Quantity** Understanding scale requires some insight into measurement . . . in order to identify something as bigger or smaller than something else—and how much bigger or smaller—a student must appreciate the units used to measure it and develop a feel for quantity (NRC, 2012, p. 90).
Disciplinary Core Idea	**ESS1:** Earth's Place in the Universe
Component Idea	**ESS1.B:** Earth and the Solar System
Conceptual Understanding	**By the end of grade 8:** The solar system consists of the sun and a collection of objects, including planets, their moons, and asteroids that are held in orbit around the sun by its gravitational pull on them (NRC, 2012, p. 176).

Performance Expectations

MS-ESS1-2   Develop and use a model to describe the role of gravity in the motions within galaxies and the solar system. *Clarification Statement*: . . . Examples of models can be physical (such as the analogy of distance along a football field . . .) or conceptual (such as mathematical proportions relative to the size of familiar objects such as students' school or state) (NGSS Lead States, 2013, p. 78). www.nextgenscience.org/pe/ms-ess1-2-earths-place-universe

MS-ESS1-3   Analyze and interpret data to determine scale properties of objects in the solar system. *Clarification Statement:* Emphasis is on the analysis of data from Earth-based instruments, space-based telescopes, and spacecraft to determine similarities and difference among solar system objects. Examples of scale properties include the sizes of an object's layers (such as crust and atmosphere), surface features (such as volcanoes), and orbital radius. Examples of data include statistical information, drawings and photographs, and models (NGSS Lead States, 2013, p. 78). www.nextgenscience.org/pe/ms-ess1-3-earths-place-universe

Learning Target   The planets in the solar system are at different distances from the sun as they orbit around it.

Success Criteria   *The students will:*

1. Demonstrate and describe a scale model of our solar system.
2. Name the planets in order of distance from the sun.

3. Conduct research about the planets in the solar system and their orbital paths in order to refine the model presented in class.

Materials

- Ten sentence strips, each labeled with one of the solar system bodies (Sun, Mercury, Venus, Earth, Mars, Jupiter, Saturn, Uranus, Neptune, and Pluto)
- Science notebooks
- Pencils

Engage

Ask students to draw a picture showing what they know about the orbits of the planets around the sun in our solar system. To assess students' prior knowledge, ask: *How many planets did you include? Could you name the planets? Do you think you placed the planets in the right order from the sun? Are the orbits of the planets all the same distance apart? What is a scale model? Was your drawing a scale model? Why or why not?*

Explain

Select ten students to represent the major bodies in the solar system. Give each of them a labeled sentence strip to hold.

Select a starting place at one edge of the playground or at the end of a very long hall. Instruct the sign-holding students to follow these instructions for constructing the model solar system.

1. The "sun" stands at one end of the area.
2. Mercury takes four small steps from the sun.
3. Venus takes three small steps outward from Mercury.
4. Earth takes two small steps beyond Venus.
5. Mars takes five small steps beyond Earth.
6. Jupiter takes 34 small steps beyond Mars.
7. Saturn takes 40 small steps beyond Jupiter.
8. Uranus takes 90 small steps beyond Saturn.
9. Neptune takes 100 small steps beyond Uranus.
10. Pluto takes 88 small steps beyond Neptune.

Tell the class that the positions of the students with the signs represent the average distance between the major bodies in the solar system. With the holders remaining in their places and holding up their signs, all the students should observe the spacing and think about these questions: *Which planets' orbits are closest together? Which ones are really spread out? Are the planets' orbits spaced at equal distances from the sun?*

Explain

Upon returning to the classroom, discuss the students' responses to the questions. Important ideas to emerge from the discussion include the following:

- The first four planets—Mercury, Venus, Earth, and Mars—do not have much distance between their orbits. These planets are known as the *inner planets*.
- The rest of the planets—Jupiter, Saturn, Uranus, and Neptune—have rather large distances between their orbits. These planets are known as the *outer planets*.
- Pluto, once considered a planet, was reclassified as a dwarf planet in 2006. Pluto's average distance from the sun is represented in the model we created on the playground.

Explain that the major bodies in the solar system are not usually lined up as in our model. The model does not show the actual positions of the major bodies in the solar system, just the relative spacing of their orbits.

Elaborate

Students can research information regarding the major bodies in the solar system in order to understand more accurate models and representations of the solar system. They should develop an alternative model that uses scale to illustrate their relative distances from the sun.

Evaluate

To assess student knowledge of the relative positions of the planets in our solar system, have students respond to the following items.

1. List the planets in order by their distance from the sun.

2. Which of the following statements best describes the location of the planets in our solar system?

   A. The planets are all lined up in a straight line.

   B. The planets' orbits are equal distances apart.

   C. The inner planets' orbits are closer together than the orbits of the outer planets.

   D. The planets are all the same distance from the sun.

Another activity about the scale of objects in the solar system, titled: "How do the planets in our solar system compare in size?" may be accessed via the Enhanced Pearson eText. It addresses DCI Component Idea ESS1.B

Activity 50: What is core sampling, and how can we use it to infer patterns in rock layers in the Earth's crust?

Grade: 4, Earth and Space Sciences

Framework Context	
Scientific and Engineering Practices	**Developing and Using Models** Students should be asked to use diagrams, maps, and other abstract models as tools that enable them to elaborate on their own ideas or findings and present them to others (NRC, 2012, p. 58). **Planning and Carrying Out Investigations** At all levels, they should engage in investigations that range from those structured by the teacher—in order to expose an issue or question that they would be unlikely to explore on their own (e.g., measuring specific properties of materials)—to those that emerge from students' own questions (NRC, 2012, p. 61). **Constructing Explanations and Designing Solutions** Asking students to demonstrate their own understanding of the implications of a scientific idea by developing their own explanations of phenomena, whether based on observations they have made or models they have developed, engages them in an essential part of the process by which conceptual change can occur (NRC, 2012, p. 68).
Crosscutting Concepts	**Patterns** It is important for students to develop ways to recognize, classify, and record patterns in the phenomena they observe. For example . . . they can investigate the characteristics that allow classification . . . of materials (e.g., wood, rock, metal, plastic) (NRC, 2012, p. 86). **Cause and Effect: Mechanism and Explanation** By the upper elementary grades, students should have developed the habit of routinely asking about cause-and-effect relationships in the systems they are studying, particularly when something occurs that is, for them, unexpected. The questions "How did that happen?" or "Why did that happen?" should move toward "What mechanisms caused that to happen?" (NRC, 2012, p. 89).
Disciplinary Core Idea	**ESS1:** Earth's Place in the Universe
Component Idea	**ESS1.C:** The History of Planet Earth
Conceptual Understanding	**By the end of grade 5:** Local, regional, and global patterns of rock formations reveal changes over time due to Earth forces, such as earthquakes (NRC, 2012, p. 178).

Performance Expectation 4-ESS1-1

Identify evidence from patterns in rock formations and fossils in rock layers to support an explanation for changes in a landscape over time (NGSS Lead States, 2013, p. 39). www.nextgenscience.org/pe/4-ess1-1-earths-place-universe

Learning Target

Data about rock layers in Earth's crust can be obtained by examining core samples.

Success Criteria

The students will:

1. Model a procedure used by scientists to investigate rock layers in the Earth's crust.
2. Draw two-dimensional models that illustrate their understanding of the internal structure (layers) of their model based on core samples collected from it.
3. Compare and contrast actual cross-sections of the model with the drawings based on the core samples.

Materials

For each group:

- A layered cupcake
- Clear plastic straws
- Plastic knives

Preparation

In this activity, straws will be used to take core samples of layered cupcakes. Layered cupcakes may be made by the teacher or a parent volunteer as follows:

1. Use either different flavors or white batter mixed with food coloring.
2. Put batter in four layers in foil or paper cups.
3. Bake the cupcakes. Add frosting if desired.

Engage

Show students a cupcake. Ask: *What do you think is inside the cupcake? How could we find out without eating it or cutting into it? How can scientists learn what's underground?*

Explore

Provide groups of students with one cupcake on a paper plate, five clear plastic straws cut into thirds, a plastic knife, drawing paper, and markers. Do *not* remove the foil or paper cup from the cupcake.

Instruct students to draw what they think the inside of the cupcake looks like. Show and tell students how to take side "core samples," as in diagram (a):

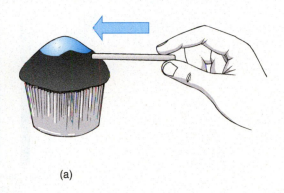

(a)

1. Carefully insert a straw into the side of the cupcake, rotate slightly, remove, and place sample on paper plate.
2. Repeat with another straw.

Instruct students to take two side core samples of their cupcake. Ask: *Can you determine what the entire cupcake looks like with these two core samples? If not, what must you do?*

Instruct students to take three samples by inserting the straw straight down into the cupcake, as shown in diagram (b):

(b)

Compare these samples with those taken from the side, as in diagram (c):

Core samples of
cupcake

(c)

Ask: *How are they different? Based on your core samples, what do you infer is inside the cupcake?*
Instruct students to make drawings of what they now think the inside of the cupcake looks like.

Explain

Post the student drawings. Ask: *On what data did you base your drawing? How sure are you of the accuracy of your drawing? Why?*

Provide students this background information:

Geologists study Earth and use many devices to discover what is under the surface. Core sampling is done by putting hollow drilling tubes into the ground and extracting a sample of what the tubes went through.

Ask: *How does your straw sampling of the cupcake compare and contrast with core sampling done by geologists?*

Elaborate

Ask: *How could you find out what the inside of your cupcake looks like?* Tell students to use the plastic knives to cut down and separate the cupcakes into halves. Have them draw what the inside of the cupcake actually looks like. Ask: *How do your direct observations compare with your inferences and your drawings? Can geologists check the inferences they make from their core samples, the way you checked the inside of your cupcake? Why or why not?*

Evaluate

To assess student understanding about the use of data from core sampling, show students pictures of cores from a different cupcake. Challenge them to draw what the inside of the cupcake looks like when sliced vertically through the center and horizontally through the center, based on the data. Then ask them to explain why they drew the inside of this cupcake the way they did.

Activity 51: How does the geologic time scale display scientists' understanding of the history of Earth?

Grades: 6–8, Earth and Space Sciences

Framework Context	
Scientific and Engineering Practices	**Developing and Using Models** Students should be asked to use diagrams, maps, and other abstract models as tools that enable them to elaborate on their own ideas or findings and present them to others (NRC, 2012, p. 58). The quality of a student-developed model will be highly dependent on prior knowledge and skill and also on the student's understanding of the system being modeled, so students should be expected to refine their models as their understanding develops (NRC, 2012, p. 59). **Using Mathematics and Computational Thinking** Increasing students' familiarity with the role of mathematics in science is central to developing a deeper understanding of how science works. Students should have opportunities to explore how such symbolic representations can be used to represent data, to predict outcomes, and eventually to derive further relationships using mathematics (NRC, 2012, p. 66). **Obtaining, Evaluating, and Communicating Information** Students need sustained practice and support to develop the ability to extract the meaning of scientific text from books, media reports, and other forms of scientific communication because the form of this text is initially unfamiliar—expository rather than narrative, often linguistically dense, and reliant on precise logical flows. Students should be able to interpret meaning from text, to produce text in which written language and diagrams are used to express scientific ideas, and to engage in extended discussion about those ideas (NRC, 2012, p. 76).
Crosscutting Concepts	**Scale, Proportion, and Quantity** Understanding scale requires some insight into measurement . . . in order to identify something as bigger or smaller than something else—and how much bigger or smaller—a student must appreciate the units used to measure it and develop a feel for quantity (NRC, 2012, p. 90).
Disciplinary Core Idea	**ESS1:** Earth's Place in the Universe
Component Idea	**ESS1.C:** The History of Planet Earth
Conceptual Understanding	**By the end of grade 8:** The geologic time scale interpreted from rock strata provides a way to organize Earth's history (NRC, 2012, p. 178).

Performance Expectation MS-ESS1-4

Construct a scientific explanation based on evidence from rock strata for how the geologic time scale is used to organize Earth's 4.6-billion-year-old history (NGSS Lead States, 2013, p. 78). www.nextgenscience.org/pe/ms-ess1-4-earths-place-universe

Learning Target

Earth's history can be described by a geologic time scale. Evidence for the construction of the geologic time scale, which presents only relative (not absolute) dates is found in rock strata and the fossil record.

Success Criteria

The students will:

1. Develop and use a model of the geologic time scale of Earth.

2. Describe the sequence major geologic events that have occurred throughout the history of Earth.

Materials

For the teacher:

- A sign representing each Time Period on the Geologic Time Scale (Today, Quaternary period, Tertiary Period, Cretaceous Period, Jurassic Period, Triassic Period, Permian Period, Pennsylvanian Period, Mississippian Period, Devonian Period, Silurian Period, Ordovician Period, and Cambrian Period). Label each sign with the name and age in years as shown on the table below.
- A different colored sign representing each Era on the Geologic Time Scale (Cenozoic, Mesozoic, Paleozoic, Precambrian).

For each group:

- A roll of adding machine tape

Engage

Earth was formed approximately 4.6 billion years ago. Many geologic events have taken place during that time. Ask students to contribute ideas to a KWL chart that shows what they currently *know* about the Geologic Time Scale or the history of Earth in the K section of the chart. In the W section of the chart, students should contribute their ideas about what they *want to know* about the history of Earth.

Explore

Select 13 students to represent the major Time Periods that represent the Geologic Time Scale. Give each of them a labeled sentence strip to hold. Select four students to hold signs representing the Eras in the Geologic Time Scale.

    Select a starting place at one edge of the playground or a football field. Instruct the sign-holding students to follow these instructions for constructing the model geologic time scale. One meter = 100,000,000 years! Begin with Today and measure off the distance for each time period and era.

Era	Time Period	Age (years)	Distance in meters (1 m = 100 mya)	Distance in cm
Cenozoic	Today Quaternary period Tertiary period	0.00 1,600,000 66,000,000	0.0 .016 meters .66 meters	
Mesozoic	Cretaceous period Jurassic period Triassic period	144,000,000 208,000,000 245,000,000	1.44 meters 2.08 meters 2.45 meters	
Paleozoic	Permian period Pennsylvanian period Mississippian period Devonian period Silurian period Ordovician period Cambrian period	286,000,000 320,000,000 360,000,000 408,000,000 438,000,000 505,000,000 570,000,000	2.86 meters 3.20 meters 3.60 meters 4.08 meters 4.38 meters 5.05 meters 5.70 meters	
Precambrian		4,500,000,000	45 meters	

    Tell the class that the positions of the students with the signs represent the time span between each major geologic period. With the holders remaining in their places and holding up their signs, all the students should observe the spacing and think about these questions: *Which eras are closest together? Which ones are really spread out? What does this tell you about the history of Earth?*

Explain

Upon returning to the classroom, discuss the students' responses to the questions.

Allow students to learn more about specific geologic events through library and Internet research. Students can research various life forms and geologic processes for each Era and Time Period. Have students add to the KWL chart what they have *learned* about geologic time.

This might be an appropriate time for a review about ratios and proportions. *What is the scale of this model?* (1 m on this model = approximately 100,000,000 years.)

Ask: *How do scientists know that various organisms lived on Earth during these time periods?* (The fossil record provides clues to organisms that lived in different environments.)

Elaborate

Have students use a roll of adding machine tape to create a visual representation of the geologic time scale. Hint: Use a scale of 1 cm = 1 million years. Students should calculate the correct scale labeling each Era and Time Period. Have students draw pictures of geologic events and life forms on the adding machine tape.

Evaluate

Have student teams present their geologic time scale models to the class. Evaluate student understanding by creating a rubric with the class based on essential elements required for the model. For example, assessment of the model could include accurate scaling and inclusion of living organisms, as well as major geologic events, for each era.

Encourage students to discuss what the class should include in the L section, what they have *learned*. Assess student understanding through the evaluation of the KWL chart that students created throughout the lesson.

Activity 52: How can living things produce forces that can change Earth's surface?

Grade: 4, Earth and Space Sciences

Framework Context	
Scientific and Engineering Practices	**Constructing Explanations** [Students] should be encouraged to develop explanations of what they observe when conducting their own investigations and to evaluate their own and others' explanations for consistency with the evidence (NRC, 2012, p. 69).
Crosscutting Concepts	**Cause and Effect: Mechanism and Explanation** By the upper elementary grades, students should have developed the habit of routinely asking about cause-and-effect relationships in the systems they are studying, particularly when something occurs that is, for them, unexpected. The questions "How did that happen?" or "Why did that happen?" should move toward "What mechanisms caused that to happen?" and "What conditions were critical for that to happen?" (NRC, 2012, p. 89).
Disciplinary Core Idea	**ESS2:** Earth's Systems
Component Idea	**ESS2.A:** Earth Materials and Systems
Conceptual Understanding	**By the end of grade 5:** Water, ice, wind, living organisms, and gravity break rocks, soils, and sediments into smaller particles and move them around (NRC, 2012, p. 181).
Component Idea	**ESS2.E:** Biogeology
Conceptual Understanding	**By the end of grade 5:** Living things affect the physical characteristics of their regions (e.g., plants' roots hold soil in place, beaver shelters and human-built dams alter the flow of water, plants' respiration affects the air). Many types of rocks and minerals are formed from the remains of organisms or are altered by their activities (NRC, 2012, p. 190).

Performance Expectation 4-ESS2-1

Make observations and/or measurements to provide evidence of the effects of weathering or the rate of erosion by water, ice, wind, or vegetation (NGSS Lead States, 2013, p. 40). www.nextgenscience.org/pe /4-ess2-1-earths-systems

Learning Target

Growing plants exert forces on earth materials in which they grow. The presence of vegetation can affect Earth's surface over time.

Success Criteria

The students will:

1. Explain how rocks on Earth's surface can be changed by vegetation.
2. Describe how water and living organisms break rocks and soil into smaller particles.

Materials

For the teacher:

- A large rock
- Chart paper
- Two plastic vials or medicine bottles with snap lids
- Dry bean seeds
- Water

Engage

Display a large rock. Ask: *How could this rock be broken?* List students' suggestions on chart paper for use later in the lesson.

Explore

Fill both of the vials or medicine bottles with as many dry beans as will fit. Add as much water as you can to one vial of beans. Snap the lids on both vials.

Ask: *What do you think might happen to the two vials?*

Observe both vials the next day.

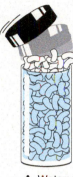

A Water   **B** No water

Explain

Bring the class together for discussion. Ask: *What do you observe? Why do you think it happened?* Lead students to understand that in the container with water, the beans expanded and lifted the lid off. In the vial without water, there was no observable change.

Refer back to the chart developed during the engage phase of the lesson. Lead students to realize that all ideas on the list are related to force. Remind students that force is needed to make something move. Ask: *Was there force involved when the lid came off one of our containers? How do you know?*

Ask: *How could the force of germinating seeds and growing plants produce changes in Earth's surface?* Help students infer that swelling and growing plants change the land by breaking up rocks and soil just as the swelling beans lifted the vial's lid off.

Elaborate

Ask students to find places on the school grounds or on concrete walks where plants grow through and crack rocks.

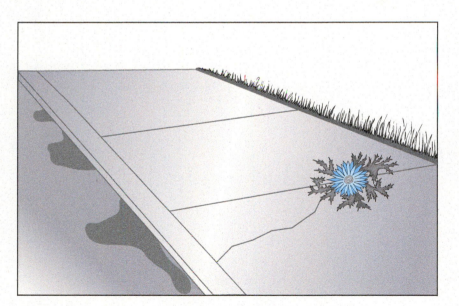

Evaluate

Have students draw and write in their science notebooks about their observations during the explore and elaborate phases of the lesson. By looking over this work, you can formatively assess their observation and recording skills.

To assess their understanding of the concept that growing plants can affect Earth's surface, display the rock used during the engage phase of the lesson; then ask children to respond to the following questions:

1. Could a plant break this rock?
2. Why or why not?
3. What evidence supports your answer?

Activity 53: Which parts of Earth experience the most earthquakes?

Grade: 4, Earth and Space Sciences

Framework Context	
Scientific and Engineering Practices	**Planning and Carrying Out Investigations**
	At all levels, they should engage in investigations that range from those structured by the teacher—in order to expose an issue or question that they would be unlikely to explore on their own—to those that emerge from students' own questions (NRC, 2012, p. 61).
	Constructing Explanations
	[Students] should be encouraged to develop explanations of what they observe when conducting their own investigations and to evaluate their own and others' explanations for consistency with the evidence (NRC, 2012, p. 69).
	Obtaining, Evaluating, and Communicating Information
	Students need sustained practice and support to develop the ability to extract the meaning of scientific text from books, media reports, and other forms of scientific communication because the form of this text is initially unfamiliar—expository rather than narrative, often linguistically dense, and reliant on precise logical flows. Students should be able to interpret meaning from text, to produce text in which written language and diagrams are used to express scientific ideas, and to engage in extended discussion about those ideas (NRC, 2012, p. 76).
Crosscutting Concepts	**Patterns**
	It is important for students to develop ways to recognize, classify, and record patterns in the phenomena they observe (NRC, 2012, p. 86).
Disciplinary Core Idea	**ESS2:** Earth's System
Component Idea	**ESS2.B:** Plate Tectonics and Large-Scale System Interactions
Conceptual Understanding	**By the end of grade 5:** The locations of mountain ranges, . . . earthquakes, and volcanoes occur in patterns. Most earthquakes and volcanoes occur in bands that are often along the boundaries between continents and oceans (NRC, 2012, p. 183).

Performance Expectation 4-ESS2-2

Analyze and interpret data from maps to describe patterns of Earth's features (NGSS Lead States, 2013, p. 40). www.nextgenscience.org/pe/4-ess2-2-earths-systems

Learning Target

Most earthquakes occur in bands that are along the boundaries between continents and oceans.

Success Criteria

The students will:

1. Use the Internet to collect scientific monitoring data about recent earthquake activity.
2. Plot earthquake data on a world map.
3. Look for patterns in the geographic distribution of earthquakes on Earth.
4. Write a paragraph about the distribution of earthquakes on Earth during the last week.

Materials

For the teacher:

- World map
- Map pins, sticky dots, or erasable markers

For each group:

- Copy of a world map
- Internet access

Engage

Display a world map in the classroom. Ask: *Where do earthquakes occur on Earth?* List student ideas on the board, or use sticky notes to identify locations on the map.

Explore

Have teams of students plot the location of earthquakes on a world map. Use the Internet and the United States Geologic Survey (USGS) website to locate the earthquakes that have happened in the last seven days (earthquake.usgs.gov). There will be many earthquakes, so have each team of students choose 20 to plot on their maps, or to avoid having groups collect data on the same events, assign a date for each group to monitor.

Explain

Ask: *Where are some places that earthquakes have occurred on Earth in the past seven days?*

Add these places to the class map or board from the beginning of the class. Show students the current Earthquake Map from the USGS site.

Ask: *If we look at all of the earthquakes that have happened in the past seven days, what patterns do you notice about the location of earthquakes?*

Guide students to see the pattern that earthquakes happen along certain boundaries between oceans and continents.

Ask: *What do you think happens to the land during an earthquake? How does it change?* Students should indicate that you might feel movement and see buildings or structures break. Explain that scientists use this data to learn more about earthquakes and how to keep people safe.

Elaborate

Guide students to related readings in texts or online that provide further information about how scientists monitor earthquake activity using seismographs.

Evaluate

To assess student understanding of earthquake patterns, have students write at least a paragraph to summarize their understanding in their science notebook. Remind students that any claims they make about the distribution of earthquakes should be supported by the data they collected and/or other research they have done.

Activity 54: How have Earth's plates moved over time?

Grades: 6–8, Earth and Space Sciences

Framework Context		
Scientific and Engineering Practices	**Developing and Using Models** Students should be asked to use diagrams, maps, and other abstract models as tools that enable them to elaborate on their own ideas or findings and present them to others (NRC, 2012, p. 58). **Constructing Explanations** [Students] should be encouraged to develop explanations of what they observe when conducting their own investigations and to evaluate their own and others' explanations for consistency with the evidence (NRC, 2012, p. 69). **Obtaining, Evaluating, and Communicating Information** Students need sustained practice and support to develop the ability to extract the meaning of scientific text from books, media reports, and other forms of scientific communication because the form of this text is initially unfamiliar—expository rather than narrative, often linguistically dense, and reliant on precise logical flows. Students should be able to interpret meaning from text, to produce text in which written language and diagrams are used to express scientific ideas, and to engage in extended discussion about those ideas (NRC, 2012, p. 76).	
Crosscutting Concepts	**Cause and Effect: Mechanism and Explanation** Argumentation starting from students' own explanations of cause and effect can help them appreciate standard scientific theories that explain the causal mechanisms in the systems under study. Strategies for this type of instruction include asking students to argue from evidence when attributing an observed phenomenon to a specific cause (NRC, 2011, p. 89). **Energy and Matter: Flows, Cycles, and Conservation** The ability to examine, characterize, and model the transfers and cycles of matter and energy is a tool that students can use across virtually all areas of science and engineering (NRC, 2012, p. 95).	
Disciplinary Core Idea **Component Idea** **Conceptual Understanding**	**ESS2:** Earth's Systems **ESS2.B:** Plate Tectonics and Large-Scale System Interactions **By the end of grade 8:** Plate tectonics . . . explains the past and current movements of the rocks at Earth's surface and provides a *Framework* for understanding its geological history (NRC, 2012, p. 183).	

Performance Expectation MS-ESS2-3   Analyze and interpret data on the distribution of fossils and rocks, continental shapes, and seafloor structures to provide evidence of the past plate motions (NGSS Lead States, 2013, p. 80). www.nextgenscience.org/pe/ms-ess2-3-earths-systems

Learning Target   There are multiple lines of observable evidence that support the theory of plate tectonics.

Success Criteria   *The students will:*

1. Investigate the movements of plates and plate boundaries on Earth.
2. Describe how plate movements change the land.

Science Background   The Earth is made up of lithospheric plates that move the Earth's crust. Plate boundaries are areas of Earth where plates meet, usually between continental and oceanic plates. Plates move in different ways. Convergent boundaries are where plates move toward each other and result in the formation of mountains, volcanoes, and trenches. Divergent boundaries are areas where plates move away from each other and result in midocean ridges and valleys. Transform boundaries are areas where plates slip past each other. All movements of the plates result in earthquake activity.

Materials

For each group:

- Cardboard
- 2 sponges
- Cornstarch
- Aluminum foil
- Water
- Chart paper
- Safety goggles

Engage

Ask: *What do you already know about Earth's plates? In what ways do you think the Earth's plates might move?* Create a class chart that shows student ideas related to the movement of the Earth's plates.

Safety Precautions

Wear safety goggles while working with the cornstarch/water mixture to protect eyes from splashes.

Explore

Have students create a model of plate boundary movements by using a cornstarch/water mixture (mixed to the consistency of thick, slow-running lava), and cardboard and sponges to represent the plates. Guide each team of students to conduct this investigation:

1. Lay a piece of aluminum foil on the table to use for easy cleanup.
2. Cut two pieces of cardboard the same size as the sponges and label them "ocean plates."
3. Use two sponges and label them "continental plates."
4. Pour a small amount of cornstarch/water mixture onto the aluminum foil. Do not make the cornstarch mixture too thick or it will not flow.
5. Take one continental plate (sponge) and one oceanic plate (cardboard) and lay them on the mixture. Model convergent plate movement by pushing them together. Create a data chart to record observations. A sample observation chart is shown here:

Plate Boundaries	Movement	Observations
Continental/Oceanic	Convergent	
Continental/Continental	Convergent	
Oceanic/Oceanic	Divergent	
Continental/Oceanic	Transform	

6. Model convergent plate movement by pushing a continental and continental plate together.
7. Model divergent plate movement by pushing an oceanic and oceanic plate together.
8. Model transform plate movement by pushing a continental and oceanic plate against each other.

Explain

Students should use their data to explain how plates move and what happens to the land above plate movements. Student explanations should include the movement of the plates and use appropriate vocabulary that explains the movements. Teacher clarification may be needed to help students make connections between the plate movement and landforms found on Earth. For example, convergent plates create mountain ranges, and divergent boundaries create valleys.

Elaborate

Using books or Internet resources, students should examine maps and diagrams of plate boundary movement. Have students find real locations on Earth that are examples of convergent plate movement, divergent plate movement, and transform plate movement. Students should add the information collected through research to their data chart from the explore phase.

Evaluate

To assess student understanding of plate movements, use the data chart and observations from the investigation in the explore phase. Students should be able to write a summary of plate movement and describe different locations on Earth as evidence of their understanding. An exemplary example would also include explanations of how plate movements affect Earth's surface and change the land.

Activity 55: What part of Earth's surface is covered by oceans?

Grade: 5, Earth and Space Sciences

Framework Context	
Scientific and Engineering Practices	**Developing and Using Models** Students should be asked to use diagrams, maps, and other abstract models as tools that enable them to elaborate on their own ideas or findings and present them to others (NRC, 2012, p. 58). **Using Mathematics and Computational Thinking** Increasing students' familiarity with the role of mathematics in science is central to developing a deeper understanding of how science works. Students should have opportunities to explore how such symbolic representations can be used to represent data, to predict outcomes, and eventually to derive further relationships using mathematics (NRC, 2012, p. 66).
Crosscutting Concepts	**Scale, Proportion, and Quantity** Understanding scale requires some insight into measurement . . . in order to identify something as bigger or smaller than something else—and how much bigger or smaller—a student must appreciate the units used to measure it and develop a feel for quantity (NRC, 2012, p. 90).
Disciplinary Core Idea	**ESS2:** Earth's Systems
Component Idea	**ESS2.C:** The Roles of Water in Earth's Surface Processes
Conceptual Understanding	**By the end of grade 5:** Nearly all of Earth's available water is in the ocean (NRC, 2012, p. 185).

Performance Expectation 5-ESS2-2
Describe and graph the amounts and percentages of water and fresh water in various reservoirs to provide evidence about the distribution of water on Earth (NGSS Lead States, 2013, p. 50). www.nextgenscience.org/pe/5-ess2-2-earths-systems

Learning Targets
Approximately 70 percent of Earth's surface is covered by ocean. Mathematical sampling techniques can be used to gather data.

Success Criteria
The students will:

1. Use a sampling method to estimate the percentage of Earth's surface covered by oceans.
2. Compare the findings from the sampling method with information about the percentage of Earth's surface covered by ocean found in library and Internet references.

Materials
For each group:

- Inflatable globe (preferably showing natural land features rather than political boundaries)

Engage
Hold up the inflatable globe. Ask: *What is this globe a model of?* (Earth.) *How is it like the real Earth and how is it different? What is shown on the globe's surface?* (Land and oceans.) *About how much of the Earth is covered by oceans? How could we use the globe to find out?*

Explore
Tell the class we need to collect data by using a sampling method. Help the students follow these steps:

1. Show the class a two-column table with the headings "Ocean" and "Land."
2. Select a student to be the record keeper.
3. Instruct one student to toss the inflatable globe to another student.

4. The person who catches the globe will look to see if his or her right thumb is on an ocean or land part of the globe's surface and report this information to the record keeper.

5. The record keeper will make a tally mark in the appropriate column on the table.

6. Then the inflatable globe should be tossed to another student and the process repeated.

7. Continue for a total of 100 tosses.

Explain

Ask: *How many times out of 100 tosses was the catcher's right thumb on an ocean area?* (Approximately 70 times.) *How many times out of 100 tosses was the catcher's right thumb on a land area?* (Approximately 30 times.)

Ask: *Why do you think the catcher's right thumb was on an ocean area more often than on a land area?* (Because more of the surface of the inflatable globe is ocean area so there is more chance of the catcher's right thumb being on an ocean.) Discuss the term *percent* with the class. *What percent of the times was the catcher's thumb on an ocean area?* (The answer should be close to 70 percent.) *What percent of the times was the catcher's thumb on a land area?* (Answer should be close to 30 percent.)

Elaborate

Challenge the class to use their textbooks or other references to find out what they say about the percent of Earth's surface that is covered by oceans. (70 percent.) Encourage the class to discuss how well and why the sampling technique they used worked to estimate the relative area of land and ocean on Earth's surface.

Evaluate

Have each student write a short paper about this activity. Papers should include:

1. A description of the sampling procedure used.

2. An explanation of why the sampling procedure is expected to produce a reasonable estimate of the percent of the surface of Earth covered by oceans.

3. A claim about the percent of the surface area of Earth that is covered by oceans based on the survey procedure.

4. A claim about the percent of the surface area of Earth that is covered by oceans based on evidence found in library and/or Internet resources.

5. A comparison of the two claims and an explanation of their similarities or differences.

A related Grade 5 activity may be accessed via the Enhanced Pearson eText. It is titled: "What part of Earth's water is in the oceans?" and addresses the DCI Component Idea ESS2.C.

Activity 56: What is condensation? How does it occur?

Grades: 6–8, Earth and Space Sciences

Framework Context	
Scientific and Engineering Practices	**Constructing Explanations** [Students] should be encouraged to develop explanations of what they observe when conducting their own investigations and to evaluate their own and others' explanations for consistency with the evidence (NRC, 2012, p. 69). **Obtaining, Evaluating, and Communicating Information** Students need sustained practice and support to develop the ability to extract the meaning of scientific text from books, media reports, and other forms of scientific communication because the form of this text is initially unfamiliar—expository rather than narrative, often linguistically dense, and reliant on precise logical flows. Students should be able to interpret meaning from text, to produce text in which written language and diagrams are used to express scientific ideas, and to engage in extended discussion about those ideas (NRC, 2012, p. 76).
Crosscutting Concepts	**Cause and Effect: Mechanism and Explanation** By the upper elementary grades, students should have developed the habit of routinely asking about cause-and-effect relationships in the systems they are studying, particularly when something occurs that is, for them, unexpected. The questions "How did that happen?" or "Why did that happen?" should move toward "What mechanisms caused that to happen?" (NRC, 2012, p. 89).
Disciplinary Core Idea **Component Idea** **Conceptual Understanding**	**ESS2:** Earth's Systems **ESS2.C:** The Roles of Water in Earth's Surface Processes **By the end of grade 8:** Water continually cycles among land, ocean, and atmosphere via transpiration, evaporation, condensation and crystallization, and precipitation as well as downhill flows on land (NRC, 2012, p. 185).

Performance Expectation MS-ESS2-4

Develop a model to describe the cycling of water through Earth's systems driven by energy from the sun and the force of gravity (NGSS Lead States, 2013, p. 80). www.nextgenscience.org/pe/ms-ess2-4-earths -systems

Learning Target

Condensation is the process by which a gas, when sufficiently cooled, changes state to become a liquid.

Success Criteria

The students will:

1. Define condensation and list common, real-world examples of this process.
2. Explain condensation and describe the conditions for condensation to occur.

Materials

For the teacher:

- A cold can of soda

For each group:

- Clean, empty vegetable or fruit cans
- Water
- Ice

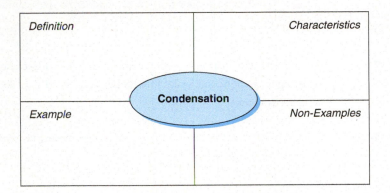

Engage

Hold up a cold soda can. Drops of water will probably appear on the outside surface of the can. Ask: *What do you see on the outside of this soda can? Where do you think these droplets came from?*

Explore

Provide each group two identical, empty vegetable cans. Give students these instructions:

1. Add the same amount of water to each can so that they are about three-fourths full.
2. Place ice in one of the cans so that the water is almost to the top of the can.
3. Stir the water in each can.
4. Observe the outside of each can.

Explain

Ask: *What happened to the outside of each can as you stirred the water?* (Moisture collected on the outside of the container with ice water.) *What conditions were necessary for the water to appear on the outside of the can?* (The can had to be cool.) *Where did the water come from?*

If students suggest that cold water soaked through the can, ask: *How could we test this hypothesis?*

Hint: You might put food dye in the water and then observe to see if any of the food coloring actually soaked through the can.

Ask: *People often say that a glass of ice water is sweating; why is this explanation incorrect?*

Provide this explanation of condensation:

When water evaporates, it goes into the air as water vapor. If moist air comes into contact with a surface that is cool enough, then water vapor condenses (changes from a gas to a liquid) from the air and collects on the cool surface.

Elaborate

Ask: *What is the source of the warm, moist air in each of these examples of condensation? What is the surface on which water condenses in each case?* Allow students to use library and Internet resources to confirm their answers.

- Formation of clouds. (Warm, moist air in the atmosphere rises and cools. As the water vapor cools, it condenses on dust particles.)
- Dew. (Warm, moist air is cooled as it mixes with cooler air near the surface of Earth. As the water vapor cools, it condenses on the grass and other surfaces.)
- Vapor trails. (Warm, moist air from the exhaust of a jet mixes with cooler air high in the atmosphere. As the water vapor cools, it condenses on dust particles in the atmosphere.)
- Moisture on bathroom mirrors after a hot shower. (Warm, moist air produced during the hot shower condenses on the cooler bathroom mirror.)

Evaluate

To check student understanding about the concept of condensation, ask students to use the Frayer model, a graphic organizer that helps students develop their vocabularies.

Definition	Characteristics
Condensation	
Example	Non-Examples

Activity 57: What are stalactites and stalagmites, and how are they formed?

Grades: 6–8, Earth and Space Sciences

Framework Context	
Scientific and Engineering Practices	**Planning and Carrying Out Investigations** At all levels, [students] should engage in investigations that range from those structured by the teacher—in order to expose an issue or question that they would be unlikely to explore on their own (e.g., measuring specific properties of materials)—to those that emerge from students' own questions (NRC, 2012, p. 61). **Constructing Explanations** [Students] should be encouraged to develop explanations of what they observe when conducting their own investigations and to evaluate their own and others' explanations for consistency with the evidence (NRC, 2012, p. 69). **Obtaining, Evaluating, and Communicating Information** Students need sustained practice and support to develop the ability to extract the meaning of scientific text from books, media reports, and other forms of scientific communication because the form of this text is initially unfamiliar—expository rather than narrative, often linguistically dense, and reliant on precise logical flows. Students should be able to interpret meaning from text, to produce text in which written language and diagrams are used to express scientific ideas, and to engage in extended discussion about those ideas (NRC, 2012, p. 76).
Crosscutting Concepts	**Cause and Effect: Mechanism and Explanation** By the upper elementary grades, students should have developed the habit of routinely asking about cause-and-effect relationships in the systems they are studying, particularly when something occurs that is, for them, unexpected. The questions "How did that happen?" or "Why did that happen?" should move toward "What mechanisms caused that to happen?" (NRC, 2012, p. 89).
Disciplinary Core Idea	**ESS2:** Earth's Systems
Component Idea	**ESS2.C:** The Roles of Water in Earth's Surface Processes
Conceptual Understanding	**By the end of grade 8:** Water's movements—both on the land and underground—cause weathering and erosion, which change the land's surface features and create underground formations (NRC, 2012, p. 185).

Performance Expectation MS-ESS2-2

Construct an explanation based on evidence for how geoscience processes have changed Earth's surface at varying time and spatial scales (NGSS Lead States, 2013, p. 80). www.nextgenscience.org/pe/ms-ess2-2-earths-systems

Learning Target

Movement of water underground can cause weathering erosion that creates underground formations in certain types of rocks.

Success Criteria

The students will:

1. Investigate how stalactites and stalagmites are formed.
2. Explain how water plays a role in the formation of underground formations.

Materials

For each group:

- Paper towel
- Epsom salt
- Spoon
- 30 cm (1 ft) of thick string
- Large tin can
- Two small jars or clear plastic cups
- Two heavy washers

Helen Bass

Engage

Display a picture of the inside of a cavern showing stalactites and stalagmites. Ask: *Where do you think this picture was taken? How do you think rock formations like these formed?*

Safety Precautions

Wear safety goggles when working with Epsom salt and Epsom salt solutions.

Explore

Allow students to carry out this investigation in cooperative groups:

1. Fill the large tin can about three-quarters full of water. Add Epsom salt one spoonful at a time, stirring vigorously after each addition, until no more will dissolve.
   Note: Epsom salt crystals will fall to the bottom of the can when no more will dissolve.
2. Fill the two small jars or plastic cups with the Epsom salt solution and place the containers 5 cm (2 in.) apart on the paper towel. Tie a heavy washer to each end of the string. Place one washer in each of the small jars or paper cups.

Note: Arrange the string in the cups so that you have at least 5 cm between the string and the paper towel.

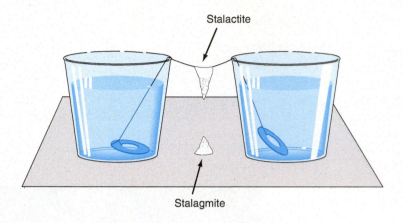

Stalactite

Stalagmite

3. Observe the jars or cups, the paper towel, the string, and the washer daily. Record the observations on a record sheet or in your science journals.

Explain

Bring the whole class together to discuss the results of the investigation. Ask: *What did you observe? What is the substance deposited on the string and on the paper towel? How did they get there? What is your evidence?*

Help students learn the difference between stalactites and stalagmites. Point out that the deposits that hang down are called **stalactites** (*c* for ceiling), while those that point up are called **stalagmites** (*g* for ground).

Ask: *Is the crystal formed on the string like a stalactite or a stalagmite? Why do you think so? Is the crystal formed on the paper towel like a stalactite or a stalagmite? Why do you think so?*

Nature of Science

Children sometimes fail to understand the link between causes and effects because they think of an investigation in terms of its component parts rather than its interactions. Scientists use the notion of *system* to help them think in terms of components and interactions. Explain that a system is a collection of components that interact to perform some function. Examples of systems are a school system and the city water system.

Thinking of an investigation as a **system** made up of parts that interact with one another can help to broaden children's thinking. Ask: *What are the components of our investigation system?* (Containers, Epsom salt, water, string, washers, paper towels.) *How does each component interact with other components? What is your evidence?*

By observing small systems, we can draw inferences about what happens in larger systems of the world. Ask: *How is what we observed like what might happen in a cavern in the Earth?*

Elaborate

Encourage students to learn more about rock features in caverns and caves through library and internet research. Each research group could prepare an educational brochure or commercial encouraging travel to a specific underground attraction. Through their research they will probably find that other underground features exist, including columns and helectites.

Evaluate

Before research begins, have the class help you develop a rubric describing the criteria and expectations for the brochures and commercials. These rubrics will guide student work and serve as a scoring guide when you assess their final products.

Activity 58: How does temperature vary from place to place and over time?

Grade: 3, Earth and Space Sciences

Framework Context	
Scientific and Engineering Practices	**Planning and Carrying Out Investigations** At all levels, they should engage in investigations that range from those structured by the teacher—in order to expose an issue or question that they would be unlikely to explore on their own (e.g., measuring specific properties of materials)—to those that emerge from students' own questions (NRC, 2012, p. 61). **Analyzing and Interpreting Data** As [elementary students] engage in scientific inquiry more deeply, they should begin to collect categorical or numerical data for presentation in forms that facilitate interpretation, such as tables and graphs. When feasible, computers and other digital tools should be introduced as a means of enabling this Practice (NRC, 2012, p. 63). **Constructing Explanations** [Students] should be encouraged to develop explanations of what they observe when conducting their own investigations and to evaluate their own and others' explanations for consistency with the evidence (NRC, 2012, p. 69).
Crosscutting Concepts	**Cause and Effect: Mechanism and Explanation** In the earliest grades, as students begin to look for and analyze patterns . . . in their observations of the world . . . and also begin to consider what might be causing these patterns and relationships and design tests that gather more evidence to support or refute their ideas (NRC, 2012, p. 88).
Disciplinary Core Idea **Component Idea** **Conceptual Understanding**	**ESS2:** Earth's Systems **ESS2.D:** Weather and Climate **By the end of grade 5:** Weather is the minute-by-minute to day-by-day variation of the atmosphere's condition on a local scale. Scientists record the patterns of the weather across different times and areas so they can make predictions about what kind of weather might happen next (NRC, 2012, p. 188).

Performance Expectation 3-ESS2-1

Represent data in tables and graphical displays to describe typical weather conditions expected during a particular season (NGSS Lead States, 2013, p. 80). www.nextgenscience.org/pe/3-ess2-1-earths-systems

Learning Target

Air temperature can be measured, and it varies over time and from place to place. Patterns of temperature over time enable scientists to make predictions about the weather.

Success Criteria

The students will:

1. Investigate temperatures in various locations and explain how temperatures vary from place to place and over time.
2. Describe patterns and trends in local weather conditions.

Materials

For each group:

- Thermometers, spirit-filled, digital, or portable temperature probes
- Science notebooks

Engage

Ask: *How does the temperature vary from place to place? Is the temperature the same inside and outside the classroom? Is the temperature the same everywhere on the school grounds? Is the temperature the same in the shade and the sun? How could we find out?*

Explore

Guide students to measure and compare the temperature at various locations: near the floor and near the ceiling of the classroom, inside and outside the classroom, in the sun and in the shade, and at different places on the school grounds. Remind them of the importance of recording their findings in an organized manner so that they can make sense of it later.

Explain

Have students share their findings with the class. Ask them to suggest ways that we can display class data so it will be meaningful. They might suggest using maps, charts or tables, and/or graphs. Discuss the differences in the temperatures at different locations and the possible reasons for these differences.

Elaborate

Ask: *Is the temperature the same throughout the day?* Give student groups time to design an investigation to answer that question. Allow students to measure the outside temperature every hour. Have each group make a presentation to the class, describing its investigation procedure and discussing the temperature differences observed.

Evaluate

To assess student understanding about the reasons for different temperatures at different places and at different times during the day, ask students to respond to the following multiple choice questions and give reasons for their answers:

1. Where would you expect it to be cooler on a sunny day?

   A. in the shade

   B. in the sun

   Write a few paragraphs to support your selected answer with evidence and/or logical reasoning.

2. On a sunny day, when would you expect the outside temperature to be highest?

   A. early in the morning

   B. midmorning

   C. noon

   D. late afternoon

   E. just before sunset

   Write a few paragraphs to support your selected answer with evidence and/or logical reasoning.

Activity 59: How do organisms use and/or change the land, water, or air around them?

Grade: K, Earth and Space Sciences

Framework Context	
Scientific and Engineering Practices	**Analyzing and Interpreting Data** At the elementary level, students need support to recognize the need to record observations—whether in drawings, words, or numbers—and to share them with others (NRC, 2012, p. 63).
Crosscutting Concepts	**Cause and Effect: Mechanism and Explanation** In the earliest grades, as students begin to look for and analyze patterns . . . in their observations of the world . . . and also begin to consider what might be causing these patterns and relationships and design tests that gather more evidence to support or refute their ideas (NRC, 2012, p. 88).
Disciplinary Core Idea	**ESS2:** Earth's Systems
Component Idea	**ESS2.E:** Biogeology
Conceptual Understanding	**By the end of grade 2:** Plants and animals (including humans) depend on the land, water, and air to live and grow. They in turn can change their environment (NRC, 2012, p. 190).

Performance Expectation K-ESS2-2

Construct an argument supported by evidence for how plants and animals (including humans) can change the environment to meet their needs (NGSS Lead States, 2013, p. 7). www.nextgenscience.org/pe/k-ess2-2-earths-systems

Learning Target

Plants and animals depend on their environment to live and alter their environment as they live there.

Success Criteria

The students will:

1. Describe ways a variety of organisms depend on the land, water, and air in their environment to survive.
2. Describe various ways that organisms change the environment in which they live.

Materials

- Chart paper
- Science notebooks
- Pencils
- Simple digital cameras or iPads
- Pictures of organisms and their environments
- Selected library or Internet resources that focus on how organisms depend on Earth's resources and/or how they change their environment by living where they do

Engage

Ask: *What are some ways that people depend on the land, air, and water in order to live? What are some ways that people change the environment by living where they do?* Record students' ideas on a chart or other type of graphic organizer for use later in the lesson.

Explore

Take students outside to the schoolyard or another natural, non-paved area near your school to observe local organisms in their natural environment.

    Safety notice: Be sure to set boundaries to limit how far students may go when exploring. Be sure that they are dressed appropriately for field exploration (hat, sunscreen, insect repellent, closed-toed shoes, long pants, jacket if it is cold out, etc.). Avoid areas that contain poison ivy or that are likely to be homes for venomous snakes or stinging insects. Arrange to have many adult helpers to assist you in supervising and the students in collecting information.

Assign students to work with a partner or in a small group. Students should take along their science notebooks and a pencil. If possible, let each group take out a simple digital camera or an iPad. Tell students to take pictures or make drawings of plants and animals they observe. They should also try to capture images that provide evidence that a plant or animal is using the environment in order to meet its basic needs. For example, students may observe a bird's nest as evidence that a bird uses grass and mud to create its shelter. Also encourage students to look for evidence of plants or animals changing their environment, such as ants or other insects moving natural items from the environment.

Explain

When you and the class return to the classroom, let student groups prepare to share images, drawings, and/or notes they made in the field. Encourage science talk among the whole class; and depending on the grade level of the students, either have them write ideas on charts, graphic organizers, or sentence strips, or have adult helpers scribe for them.

Summarize the discussion by pointing out clear examples of the land, air, and/or water meeting an organism's needs or an organism changing the environment in some way.

Elaborate

Make available a variety of media such as books and Internet resources to have students identify more examples of plants and/or animals for which the environment helps meet their needs and/or the organism changes the environment. Assist each child, or pair of children, in selecting an organism they would like to learn more about, and help them find appropriate informational resources.

Have students research the organisms they chose and then create a grade-level appropriate project or performance (poster, labeled picture or photograph, role play, brochure, etc.) or presentation that shows how their organism relies on the land, air, and water in its habitat and/or alters the area it occupies.

Evaluate

Working with your students, create a rubric for assessing their projects or presentations. Some suggested criteria to consider when assessing student work might include:

- The name of the organism is given
- Pictures, drawings, and verbal or written descriptions communicate how the land, air, or water are utilized to meet its needs
- Pictures, drawings, and verbal or written descriptions communicate how the organism impacts the land, air, or water in its environment.

Activity 60: How do people use natural resources?

Grade: K, Earth and Space Sciences

Framework Context	
Scientific and Engineering Practices	**Engaging in Argument from Evidence** They [young children] need instructional support to go beyond simply making claims—that is, to include reasons or references to evidence and to begin to distinguish evidence from opinion (NRC, 2012, p. 73). **Obtaining, Evaluating, and Communicating Information** Students should be able . . . to produce text in which written language and diagrams are used to express scientific ideas, and to engage in extended discussion about those ideas. From the very start of their science education, students should be asked to engage in the communication of science (NRC, 2012, p. 76).
Crosscutting Concepts	**Systems and System Models** Starting in the earliest grades, students should be asked to express their thinking with drawings or diagrams and with written or oral descriptions. Such experiences help them . . . realize the importance of representing one's ideas so that others can understand and use them (NRC, 2012, p. 93).
Disciplinary Core Idea	**ESS3:** Earth and Human Activity
Component Idea	**ESS3.A:** Natural Resources
Conceptual Understanding	**By the end of grade 2:** Humans use natural resources for everything they do: for example, they use soil and water to grow food, wood to burn to provide heat or to build shelters, and materials such as iron or copper extracted from the Earth to make cooking pans (NRC, 2012, p. 192).

Performance Expectation K-ESS3-1

Use a model to represent the relationship between the needs of different plants and animals (including humans) and the places they live (NGSS Lead States, 2013, p. 8). www.nextgenscience.org/pe/k-ess3-1-earth-and-human-activity

Learning Target

Humans use natural resources for everything they do.

Success Criteria

The students will:

1. Collaborate to develop the concept of natural resources.
2. Consider things in the classroom that people use and describe how they are used, what they are made of, and/or where they came from.
3. Provide evidence that supports the claim that humans use natural resources for everything they do.
4. Communicate ideas about natural resources in writing and orally with others in their class.

Materials

- Sentence strips with the following terms boldly written on them: Natural Resources, Not Natural Resources, Can't Decide, water, air, soil, rocks, minerals, rain, food, trees, paper, pencils, plants, animals, minerals, energy, fossil fuels, sunlight, wood, houses, cars, books
- Blank sentence strips
- Tape
- Markers or chalk
- Chart paper

Engage

Bring the class to the rug and direct their attention to the stack of sentence strips you are holding. On the board or wall where all can see, post the first three strips as the headings of three columns. Tell the class: I'll hold up a sentence strip for everyone to see. Each of you should decide in which column the word on that sentence strip should be placed. I'll call on someone to tell me where to post the sentence strip and tell us why it should be placed in that column. If you disagree with the placement, don't say anything yet. This is like brainstorming; we will politely accept all ideas right now. Then I'll hold up another word on a sentence strip, and so forth, until they are all posted.

When all word strips have been posted in one of the three columns, involve the class in discourse about their placement. Encourage students to suggest moving any strips they want as long as they express a good reason to do so. Limit this discussion to about five minutes.

Then ask: *Based on these examples we have organized and discussed, how would you define* **natural resources** *in your own words?* Record students' preliminary definitions on the board for future reference.

Explore

Organize the class into small groups and give each some blank sentence strips and crayons or markers. Model the activity for the class:

- Fold a blank sentence strip into thirds. (The sections do not need to be exactly the same size.)
- Identify something in the classroom that you use.
- In the center section of the sentence strip, write the name of and/or draw a picture of the selected thing.
- In the left section of the sentence strip, write a description or draw a picture of how the selected thing is used.
- In the right section of the sentence strip, list what the selected thing is made of or what it comes from.

Your sentence strip might look something like this:

To write with.	Pencil	Wood, metal, rubber, paint, graphite

Instruct students to work collaboratively in their small group to complete as many sentence strips as possible in the time allowed (about 15 minutes).

Explain

Have the groups bring their sentence strips to a whole-class discussion. Encourage students to share and compare ideas generated during the explore phase of the lesson. Ask: *Which of the things identified in the classroom and shown in the center section of a sentence strip are used by people to stay alive? Explain your thinking. Does that lead anyone to think of additional sentence strips to make? What are they?* (Air might be suggested; we need air to breathe in order to stay alive.)

Continue the discourse by asking: *Would you say that everything people use is made of or comes from natural resources? Why or why not? What evidence on the sentence strips supports your claim? Are all the things listed in the right section of the sentence strips natural resources? Should they be? If there are things listed that are not natural resources, what are they made of or where did they come from?*

Have the class look at the chart they constructed during the engage part of the lesson. Ask: *Do you see any changes we should make in the placement of things on this chart? What are they? Why should they be moved?* Make changes in the chart if the class agrees on those changes. The column labeled Natural Resources should now be reasonably accurate.

Elaborate

Re-form small groups. Ask each small group to select one of the natural resources that is listed on the class chart. Encourage each group to select a different natural resource for the focus of their writing. Distribute a sheet of chart paper and crayons or markers to each small group. Challenge groups to make a poster that presents evidence that supports their claim that their selected natural resource is important to their group.

Share your expectations for the posters. Criteria might include:

- The claim is clearly written as a heading.
- The selected natural resource is highlighted in some consistent way.
- At least four reasons that the claim is true are given.

- The reasons are accurate, based on facts.
- All statements relate to the group's selected natural resource.

For a group that selects air, the poster might look like this:

> **Air** is an important natural resource to our group because:
>
> – We breathe **air**. We need to breathe to stay alive.
> – We eat vegetables that come from plants. Plants need **air** to stay alive and grow.
> – We eat meat. Meat comes from animals like cows and pigs. Animals breathe **air** in order to stay alive and grow.
> – We can cook our food over a fire. Fires need **air** in order to burn.
>
> So our group needs **air**!

Allow the class to work collaboratively within their groups for about 15 minutes to complete their posters.

Evaluate

Allow each small group five minutes to present, explain, and defend their poster to the class. Use the criteria presented in the elaborate section of the lesson to guide scoring.

Activity 61: Where are mineral resources and fossil fuels found on our planet and why?

Grades: 6–8, Earth and Space Sciences

Framework Context	
Scientific and Engineering Practices	**Obtaining, Evaluating, and Communicating Information** Students should be able to interpret meaning from text, to produce text in which written language and diagrams are used to express scientific ideas, and to engage in extended discussion about those ideas (NRC, 2012, p. 76). Students should write accounts of their work, using journals to record observations, thoughts, ideas, and models. They should be encouraged to create diagrams and to represent data and observations with plots and tables, as well as with written text, in these journals. . . . Furthermore, students should have opportunities to engage in discussion about observations and explanations and to make oral presentations of their results and conclusions as well as to engage in appropriate discourse with other students by asking questions and discussing issues raised in such presentations (NRC, 2012, p. 77).
Crosscutting Concepts	**Cause and Effect: Mechanism and Explanation** Argumentation starting from students' own explanations of cause and effect can help them appreciate standard scientific theories that explain the causal mechanisms in the systems under study. Strategies for this type of instruction include asking students to argue from evidence when attributing an observed phenomenon to a specific cause (NRC, 2012, p. 89).
Disciplinary Core Idea **Component Idea** **Conceptual Understanding**	**ESS3:** Earth and Human Activity **ESS3.A:** Natural Resources **By the end of grade 8:** Minerals, fresh water, and biosphere resources are limited, and many are not renewable or replaceable over human lifetimes. These resources are distributed unevenly around the planet as a result of past geological processes (NRC, 2012, p. 192).

Performance Expectation MS-ESS3-1
Construct a scientific explanation based on evidence for how the uneven distributions of Earth's mineral, energy, and groundwater resources are the result of past and current geoscience processes (NGSS Lead States, 2013, p. 83). www.nextgenscience.org/pe/ms-ess3-1-earth-and-human-activity

Learning Target
Minerals and energy resources are distributed unevenly in Earth's crust because of past and current geoscience processes.

Success Criteria
The students will:

1. Use maps to determine patterns of distribution of minerals and energy resources in Earth's crust.
2. Acquire and discuss information about the formation of fossil fuel deposits that are being extracted today.
3. Locate, read, analyze, summarize, present, and discuss information about mineral resources found in Earth's crust.

Materials
- Computers or other digital devices with access to the Internet
- Physical/political map of the United States displayed for the class
- Copies of a simple outline map of the United States that shows state boundaries, such as a free map available online. (http://www.waterproofpaper.com/printable-maps/united-states-maps/printable-map-of-the-united-states-labeled.pdf)

- Science notebooks
- Small sticky notes

Engage

Ask the class: *Where on Earth are minerals found? How do prospectors know where to find mineral deposits? What are fossil fuels? How do oil and gas exploration companies know where to start drilling? How do miners know where to dig?*

Explore

Let students work in pairs at a computer with access to the internet. Have them use a web browser to locate maps that show geographic information about energy and mineral deposits in the United States. Some suggested sites include: MAPS ETC (http://etc.usf.edu/maps/galleries/us/minerals/index.php); USGS – Minerals Information (http://minerals.usgs.gov/minerals/pubs/mapdata/); AGI: American Geosciences Institute (http://www.americangeosciences.org/critical-issues/search-maps-visualizations). Challenge the class to to find and use maps to explore the distribution of minerals and energy resources across the United States. You may want to assign one fossil fuel and one mineral resource to each student pair in order to focus their investigation. (More than one pair may focus on the same fossil fuel.) Distribute copies of the U.S. outline maps for recording observations. Encourage that additional notes be made in science notebooks.

Use the following prompts and questions to guide their exploration:

1. According to the map, our mineral resource is found in sufficient quantities to extract in the following states of the United States:_____.

2. According to the map, our fossil fuel resource is found in the following states:_____.

3. The map symbols show areas where the resources are concentrated enough to make extraction of the mineral or fossil fuel economically viable. What distribution patterns seem to emerge?

4. Do either of the resources you are investigating seem to be associated with the distribution of other resources shown on the *United States Energy & Minerals map*? If so, in what ways?

5. Does the distribution of the resources you are investigating seem to be associated with any of the features on the physical/political map? If so, in what ways?

Explain

Bring the class together to share and discuss their findings. Students might want to use sticky notes or other strategies to show the distribution of the resources they studied on the physical/political map. Remind students to support the claims they make about the distribution of resources with evidence. Point out that traces of resources are widespread on Earth's surface, but that the symbols on the maps show the locations of deposits that are concentrated enough to make extraction of the identified resources economically beneficial.

Provide background information about the formation of fossil fuel resources. You might show a video, suggest a section to read from a textbook, or refer them to *The Energy Story* at www.energyquest.ca.gov to read segments of Chapter 8: "Fossil Fuels—Coal, Oil, and Natural Gas."

Involve the class in a meaning-making discussion about what the surface of the Earth was like while fossil fuels being extracted now were being formed.

Elaborate

Let each pair of students use the Internet to find information about the formation of deposits of the mineral they investigated during the explain phase. Have them create a five-slide PowerPoint presentation summarizing their findings and relating the distribution of their mineral resource on Earth to the conditions experienced as the mineral was forming. Involve the class in the development of a rubric to guide scoring of the presentations. Criteria might include:

- Appropriate title slide
- Factual information
- Description of conditions during mineral deposit formation
- Connection between distribution patterns and geological conditions during formation
- Supports claims with evidence
- Proper spelling and grammar

- References correctly cited
- Both partners actively involved in oral presentation

Evaluate   Monitor student work during the explore phase of the lesson and encourage ongoing self-assessment. Make note of student involvement in science talk during the explain phase.

Give each student pair an opportunity to present their PowerPoint summary of findings from the elaborate phase of the lesson. Provide feedback based on the rubric.

Activity 62: What types of severe weather happen in our area?

Grade: K, Earth and Space Sciences

Framework Context	
Scientific and Engineering Practices	**Analyzing and Interpreting Data** At the elementary level, students need support to recognize the need to record observations—whether in drawings, words, or numbers—and to share them with others (NRC, 2012, p. 63).
Crosscutting Concepts	**Patterns** It is important for them [students] to develop ways to recognize, classify, and record patterns in the phenomena they observe (NRC, 2012, p. 86).
Disciplinary Core Idea **Component Idea** **Conceptual Understanding**	**ESS3:** Earth and Human Activity **ESS3.B:** Natural Hazards **By the end of grade 2:** Some kinds of severe weather are more likely than others in a given region. Weather scientists forecast severe weather so that communities can prepare for and respond to these events (NRC, 2012, p. 193).

Performance Understanding K-ESS3-2

Ask questions to obtain information about the purpose of weather forecasting to prepare for, and respond to, severe weather (NGSS Lead States, 2013, p. 8). www.nextgenscience.org/pe/k-ess3-2-earth-and -human-activity

Learning Target

Different areas are more likely to experience different severe weather events than others. Predictions of severe weather events can help people prepare for them in order to stay safe.

Success Criteria

The students will:

1. Record information about a severe weather event they have experienced and discuss that information with their peers.
2. Monitor and record severe weather events forecast for their area and at least one other geographic area.
3. Explain the importance of accurate forecasts about predicted severe weather events.

Materials

- Drawing paper
- Crayons
- Computer with access to the Internet or a severe weather app for your computer, phone, or tablet
- Newspaper article or recorded broadcast about a recent severe weather event
- Science notebooks

Engage

Remind your students about a severe weather event that recently affected your area. Challenge each child to draw a picture of what that weather event was like and to use words or sentences to describe the event, too. Provide drawing paper and crayons, and set a time limit of about ten minutes to complete this task.

Explore

Organize the class into small discussion groups of about four students each. Within their small groups, encourage students to talk about their drawings. Some questions to guide discussion include: *What do you remember most about this weather event? Were you frightened during this weather event? Why or why not? Did you expect this weather event to happen or did it surprise you? If you expected it, what caused you to expect it?*

Read a newspaper story or play a recorded broadcast about the recent local severe weather event to the class. When students return to their small groups, challenge each student to tell the others in their group one thing they learned about the weather event from the story or broadcast.

Explain

Ask each small group to share with the class one or two important ideas that they talked about during their discussion. Remind the class that you chose this weather event to think and talk about because it was considered a "severe" weather event. That means it was expected to or actually did cause damage, loss of human life, or disrupt normal activities in a major way. Ask: *What do you think it was about the weather event that we have been discussing that made it "severe"? Why do you think it is important for weather forecasters to alert people to possible severe weather conditions?*

Show the class the website or the severe weather application they will monitor throughout the year. Explain that we will keep track of severe weather in our area as well as severe weather in one or two other places (these additional places should be far away from your community). With the help of the class, create a table or calendar on which to record severe weather conditions in the locations your class is monitoring. Demonstrate the use of the chart for the first week or so, then assign students to be in charge of this data collection and recording.

Elaborate

Every month, have the class look at the severe weather data they have been collecting. Look at the records of severe weather in your community first. Ask questions such as: *What kinds of severe weather did we record? For how many days was each kind of severe weather recorded? For how many days was no severe weather recorded for our location?* Have students repeat with data from the other location(s) that your class is monitoring.

Encourage discussion about the data: Ask: *Do our different locations seem to have the same kinds of severe weather? How do you know? Which locations seem to have the most of each type of severe weather? Why do you think this is?*

Evaluate

After ongoing investigation and discussion related to severe weather, ask students to answer the following questions (orally or in writing, depending on language skills of the students):

- What do you think the difference is between weather and severe weather?
- Which types of severe weather should we be most concerned about in our community? How do you know?
- Why is it important for weather forecasters to predict severe weather?

Activity 63: How can maps of the distribution of natural hazards help scientists predict future occurrences?

Grades: 6–8, Earth and Space Sciences

Framework Context	
Scientific and Engineering Practices	**Planning and Carrying Out Investigations** At all levels, they should engage in investigations that range from those structured by the teacher—in order to expose an issue or question that they would be unlikely to explore on their own—to those that emerge from students' own questions (NRC, 2012, p. 61). **Constructing Explanations** [Students] should be encouraged to develop explanations of what they observe when conducting their own investigations and to evaluate their own and others' explanations for consistency with the evidence (NRC, 2012, p. 69). **Obtaining, Evaluating, and Communicating Information** Students need sustained practice and support to develop the ability to extract the meaning of scientific text from books, media reports, and other forms of scientific communication because the form of this text is initially unfamiliar—expository rather than narrative, often linguistically dense, and reliant on precise logical flows. Students should be able to interpret meaning from text, to produce text in which written language and diagrams are used to express scientific ideas, and to engage in extended discussion about those ideas (NRC, 2012, p. 76).
Crosscutting Concepts	**Patterns** Noticing patterns is often a first step to organizing and asking scientific questions about why and how the patterns occur (NRC, 2012, p. 85). **Cause and Effect: Mechanism and Explanation** Argumentation starting from students' own explanations of cause and effect can help them appreciate standard scientific theories that explain the causal mechanisms in the systems under study. Strategies for this type of instruction include asking students to argue from evidence when attributing an observed phenomenon to a specific cause (NRC, 2012, p. 89).
Disciplinary Core Idea **Component Idea** **Conceptual Understanding**	**ESS3:** Earth and Human Activity **ESS3.B:** Natural Hazards **By the end of grade 8:** Mapping the history of natural hazards in a region combined with an understanding of related geologic (and meteorological) forces can help forecast the locations and likelihoods of future events (NRC, 2012, p. 194).

Performance Expectation MS-ESS3-3

Analyze and interpret data on natural hazards to forecast future catastrophic events and inform the development of technologies to mitigate their effects (NGSS Lead States, 2013, p. 83). www.nextgenscience.org/pe/ms-ess3-3-earth-and-human-activity

Learning Target

Patterns of past occurrences of natural hazards make it possible to predict areas where future natural hazards may occur. Some natural hazards can be more accurately predicted than others.

Success Criteria

The students will:

1. Examine maps displaying the geographical locations of occurrences of natural hazards.
2. Explain patterns that exist related to natural hazards.
3. Explain why some natural hazards are more accurately predictable than others.

Materials

For each group:

- Access to the internet and library resources
- Maps showing the geographic distribution of various categories of severe weather (use a web browser to search for: frequency of thunderstorms, distribution of blizzards, etc.) and other natural disasters
- Computer with projection capabilities

Engage

Ask: *What are examples of natural hazards?* (Student responses may include: earthquakes, volcanoes, and various types of severe weather.)

Explore

Organize your class into small groups. Each will select or be assigned a natural hazard to research. Challenge groups to find maps that show the geographical distribution of the natural hazard they are monitoring. Have each group write a description of where their natural hazard is most likely to occur based on the information presented on maps they found through an Internet search.

Explain

Student groups should share the information they learned and data they collected about natural hazards and their locations. After all groups have presented, ask: *What patterns do you notice regarding the location of different natural hazards?*

Elaborate

Student groups should continue researching their selected natural disaster, now focusing on the geological or meteorological factors that contribute to their distribution on Earth. In addition, they should investigate how accurately scientists can predict occurrences of the natural disaster their group is studying and the reasons for this level of predictability.

Challenge each group to prepare a five-minute presentation summarizing the research methods they used, the conclusions they developed, and additional questions they have. Work collaboratively with the class to develop a rubric to guide their work and your scoring of their final product.

Evaluate

Formatively assess students' collaborative and research skills throughout the lesson, offering appropriate scaffolding as needed. The group presentation completed during the elaborate phase of the lesson will be scored based on the rubric developed jointly by you and the class and will serve as the summative assessment for this lesson.

Activity 64: What is in our trash? How could we reduce the waste we create?

Grade: K, Earth and Space Sciences

Framework Context	
Scientific and Engineering Practices	**Planning and Carrying Out Investigations** At all levels, they should engage in investigations that range from those structured by the teacher—in order to expose an issue or question that they would be unlikely to explore on their own—to those that emerge from students' own questions (NRC, 2012, p. 61). **Analyzing and Interpreting Data** At the elementary level, students need support to recognize the need to record observations—whether in drawings, words, or numbers—and to share them with others (NRC, 2012, p. 63).
Crosscutting Concepts	**Patterns** Once they are students, it is important for them to develop ways to recognize, classify, and record patterns in the phenomena they observe (NRC, 2012, p. 86). **Cause and Effect: Mechanism and Explanation** In the earliest grades, as students begin to look for and analyze patterns . . . in their observations of the world . . . and also begin to consider what might be causing these patterns and relationships and design tests that gather more evidence to support or refute their ideas (NRC, 2012, p. 88).
Disciplinary Core Idea **Component Idea** **Conceptual Understanding**	**ESS3:** Earth and Human Activity **ESS3.C:** Human Impacts on Earth Systems **By the end of grade 2:** Things that people do to live comfortably can affect the world around them. But they can make choices that reduce their impacts on the land, water, air, and other living things (NRC, 2012, p. 195).

Performance Understanding K-ESS3-3

Communicate solutions that will reduce the impact of humans on the land, water, air, and/or other living things in the local environment (NGSS Lead States, 2013, p. 8). www.nextgenscience.org/pe/k-ess3 -3-earth-and-human-activity

Learning Target

Humans produce trash, but there are ways that they can decrease the amount of trash they produce. Limiting the amount of trash produced is good for the environment.

Success Criteria

The students will:

1. Investigate the composition of their classroom trash.
2. Record, analyze, and draw conclusions from data.
3. Design strategies to decrease the amount of classroom trash produced.
4. Implement selected strategies and monitor the impact on trash production.
5. Discuss positive and negative impacts of trash reduction strategies on the classroom and the world.

Materials

- Protective gloves
- Trash bags, various sizes
- Trash cans
- Wastebaskets
- Recycling bins

- Balances or scales with masses if necessary
- Measuring tapes, meter sticks, and/or rulers
- Science notebooks
- Graph paper
- Markers
- Chart paper, white board, black board, interactive whiteboard

Preparation

Without the knowledge of the children, for each day during the week before beginning the lesson, collect and save all the trash in the room in plastic bags. If you want your class to just compare all the trash thrown away or left behind each day, after school put trash from all classroom receptacles, the floor, etc., together in a plastic bag labeled with the date and day of the week. If you want your class to compare where the trash was left in the room, bag the trash from the different classroom collection places, i.e., trash can, recycling bin, floor, in separate bags each day. Keep all of the bags for each day together for later use, out of student sight if possible.

Engage

Ask: *How much stuff do you think we throw away in our classroom each day? How could we find out? What ways could we measure the stuff that is thrown away? Which measuring method(s) do you think would be best? Why?*

Explore

Organize the class into small groups. There should be one small group for each day of trash you have saved. Provide each student with a pair of protective gloves. Show them the tools they may use to analyze and quantify the trash from the day they receive. Distribute the collected trash bags, one group receiving last Monday's trash, another group receiving last Tuesday's trash, etc.

Tell the students to examine the trash from their day. Suggest that they might classify their trash, measure it, make charts and graphs, and write words and sentences in their science notebooks. Allow each group to pursue their own questions for investigation. Only provide suggestions, or better yet—guiding questions, when they are stuck.

Tell the class to create a report about their trash to share with the rest of the class. Distribute chart paper and markers to each group. Let the groups know how much time they have to complete their reports and alert the class often to how much time they have left to work.

Explain

Ask each group to describe their investigation and share the data they collected. Involve the class in science talk about the various approaches groups used. Encourage students to advocate for their methods if they still believe they are appropriate. Discuss similarities and differences in the amount and types of trash thrown away each day. Encourage groups to share other features of the trash they analyzed that interested them. Perhaps they noticed there was a lot of blank space on the papers they found. They might mention that the unused portions could be used before the whole thing was discarded. Perhaps they noticed that trash was not always put in the proper container; i.e., paper was in the trash can instead of in the recycling bin.

Present a short video or read text from a book that helps students understand that resources are used to provide the things we use every day. The more we use, sometimes wastefully, the more resources are depleted. Data about how many sheets of paper come from a tree, etc., can help students see the bigger picture when it comes to not being wasteful.

Elaborate

Back in their small groups, ask students to suggest one or two changes they could make personally or as a class that should result in less classroom trash being produced. Share ideas with the whole class, then reach consensus on one approach to try and implement it in the classroom for the next week, collecting trash daily for analysis the following week. Do a group write of the procedure to be followed in this investigation.

Share the new data, and compare the data from before and after the new approaches were implemented. This is a good point in the lesson to use math skills such as addition and subtraction. Draw conclusions about the effectiveness of the new approaches. What were the benefits of our trash reduction strategies? Were there any drawbacks in implementing our trash reduction strategies? Explain.

Evaluate

There are numerous opportunities for assessment during this lesson. During the explore phase, look for cooperative and collaborative group work, productive science talk, and effective use of science notebooks for data collection and analysis as well as jotting down things they notice and wonder. The group presentations that occur during the explain phase could be scored with a checklist or a rubric. During the elaborate phase, science talk, notebooking, and engagement in making sense of the data also could be evaluated.

For a summative writing task to encourage reflection on the activity and synthesis of the ideas developed, ask: *What are some ways we are wasteful in our daily lives? What changes can we make to solve that problem? Provide evidence to support your claims.*

Activity 65: What are some effects of water pollution?

Grade: 5, Earth and Space Sciences

Framework Context	
Scientific and Engineering Practices	**Planning and Carrying Out Investigations** At all levels, [students] should engage in investigations that range from those structured by the teacher—in order to expose an issue or question that they would be unlikely to explore on their own (e.g., measuring specific properties of materials)—to those that emerge from students' own questions (NRC, 2012, p. 61). **Constructing Explanations** [Students] should be encouraged to develop explanations of what they observe when conducting their own investigations and to evaluate their own and others' explanations for consistency with the evidence (NRC, 2012, p. 69).
Crosscutting Concepts	**Cause and Effect: Mechanism and Explanation** Argumentation starting from students' own explanations of cause and effect can help them appreciate standard scientific theories that explain the causal mechanisms in the systems under study. Strategies for this type of instruction include asking students to argue from evidence when attributing an observed phenomenon to a specific cause (NRC, 2012, p. 89).
Disciplinary Core Idea **Component Idea** **Conceptual Understanding**	**ESS3:** Earth and Human Activity **ESS3.C:** Human Impacts on Earth Systems **By the end of grade 5:** Human activities in agriculture, industry, and everyday life have had major effects on the land, vegetation, streams, ocean, air and even outer space (NRC, 2012, p. 196).

Performance Expectation 5-ESS3-1

Obtain and combine information about ways individual communities use science ideas to protect the Earth's resources and environment (NGSS Lead States, 2013, p. 51). www.nextgenscience.org/pe/5-ess3-1-earth-and-human-activity

Learning Target

Water pollution can affect land, vegetation, streams, and the ocean. Individuals can help reduce water pollution.

Success Criteria

The students will:

1. Investigate the effects of several types of water pollution on the growth of aquatic algae.
2. Communicate information about the impact of human activities on our environment.

Materials

For each student:

- Safety goggles

For each group:

- Four quart-sized or 2-liter clear containers (plastic soda bottles, food jars with covers, etc.)
- Tap water aged for three to four days
- Soil and/or gravel from an aquarium or pond
- Water with algae and other aquatic microorganisms from a freshwater aquarium or a pond
- Measuring cups and spoons
- Plant fertilizer

- Hand lenses for each group
- Optical or digital microscopes (optional)
- Liquid laundry detergent (not green)
- Motor oil
- Vinegar

Preparation

Two weeks in advance of conducting this activity, four jars should be set up by you and designated student helpers for each cooperative group of students:

1. Fill four containers one-third full with aged tap water, add 4 cm of pond soil or aquarium gravel, and then fill the rest of the jar with pond water and algae.
2. Add 1 teaspoon of plant fertilizer to each jar, stir well, and loosely screw on the jar covers.
3. Put the jars near the window in indirect light or under a strong artificial light.
4. Label the jars A, B, C, and D.

Engage

Ask: *What things do people do, sometimes unknowingly, that result in water pollution? How can water pollution affect water environments in ways that are detrimental to the organisms that live in or depend on the water?*

Explore

Guide students to conduct this investigation:

1. Provide each group of students the four jars that were set up two weeks earlier. The jars contain pond water, algae, pond soil or aquarium gravel, and fertilizer.
2. Instruct the groups to observe and describe on their record sheets how each jar looks. Make sure students use hand lenses.
3. Students should add 2 tablespoons of detergent to jar A, enough motor oil to cover the surface of jar B, and 1/4 to 1/2 cup (250 ml) of vinegar to jar C. Jar D will not have any additive. See the diagram.

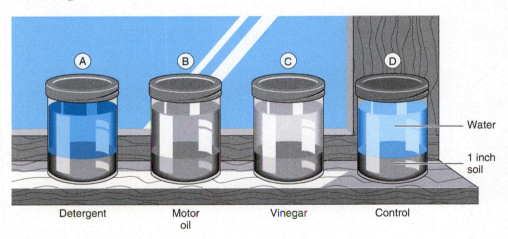

4. Students should loosely cover the jars and return them to the light as before.
5. Ask: *What do you think might happen in each of the jars?*
6. Provide time for students to observe and record their observations two to three times a week. After four weeks, groups should summarize their observations.

Explain

Ask: *What changes did each jar go through? Why do you think jars A, B, and C went through such changes?*

Elaborate

Guide students to related readings in texts or online that provide further information about the effects of these pollutants on water and on organisms exposed to the polluted water.

Ask:

1. How could you apply these findings?
2. How might you set up activities to try to reverse the effects of the pollutants used in jars A, B, and C?
3. Where in everyday life do we see the effects of water pollution like that in jars A, B, and C?
4. How could these effects be prevented?

Evaluate

Assess student understanding of the effects of water pollution through the evaluation of student responses in the explore and elaborate sections of the lesson. Student understandings and explanations should include the effects of pollution on organisms and plant life. Students can create brochures or public service announcements describing what they learned and include suggestions regarding how to prevent water pollution in their area.

Activity 66: What will happen if Earth's mean temperature continues to rise?

Grades: 6–8, Earth and Space Sciences

Framework Context	
Scientific and Engineering Practices	**Analyzing and Interpreting Data** Students need opportunities to analyze large data sets and identify correlations. Increasingly, such data sets—involving temperature, pollution levels, and other scientific measurements—are available on the Internet. . . . Such data sets extend the range of students' experiences and help to illuminate this important Practice of analyzing and interpreting data (NRC, 2012, p. 62). **Obtaining, Evaluating, and Communicating Information** Beginning in upper elementary and middle school, the ability to interpret written materials becomes more important. Early work on reading science texts should also include explicit instruction and practice in interpreting tables, diagrams, and charts and coordinating information conveyed by them with information in written text (NRC, 2012, p. 76).
Crosscutting Concepts	**Cause and Effect: Mechanism and Explanation** Argumentation starting from students' own explanations of cause and effect can help them appreciate standard scientific theories that explain the causal mechanisms in the systems under study. Strategies for this type of instruction include asking students to argue from evidence when attributing an observed phenomenon to a specific cause (NRC, 2011, p. 89).
Disciplinary Core Idea **Component Idea** **Conceptual Understanding**	**ESS3:** Earth and Human Activity **ESS3.D:** Global Climate Change **By the end of grade 8:** If Earth's global mean temperature continues to rise, the lives of humans and other organisms will be affected in many different ways (NRC, 2012, p. 198).

Performance Expectation MS-ESS3-5

Ask questions to clarify evidence of the factors that have caused the rise in global temperatures over the past century (NGSS Lead States, 2013, p. 83). www.nextgenscience.org/pe/ms-ess3-5-earth-and-human-activity

Learning Target

Trends in Earth's global mean temperature provide evidence of global climate change. Continued global warming will adversely affect life on Earth as we know it.

Success Criteria

The students will:

1. Examine historical trends in Earth's global mean temperature to the present.
2. Closely read a scientific article dealing with expected consequences of continued global warming and summarize the information presented.
3. Create a poster summarizing at least five expected consequences of continued global warming on Earth and providing evidence to support any claims that are made.

Materials

For each student:

- Science notebooks

For each small group of students:

- Access to the internet
- A web browser
- Ability to print or capture graphs and/or tables from identified websites

- A short, scientific article about an expected consequence of Earth's continued warming. (Select readings appropriate for your students from a series called "Temperature Rising," published periodically in the Environmental Section of the *New York Times* beginning in 2010 or simply search for "effects of global warming" with your web browser.)

Engage

Ask: *Do you think global warming is real? Why or why not? How could we find out?*

After a few minutes, tell the class that you aren't interested in whether human activity causes global warming. You are just interested in whether the Earth's global mean temperature has been rising.

Have students write their ideas in their science journals. Ask students to share their ideas with one or two other students. Invite students to share their thinking with the class and remind them to use evidence to explain any claims they make.

Explore

Challenge small groups of students to search the Internet to find data and graphs about Earth's global mean temperature over time from two or more websites. Copy or print the information you find and note the URL so you can locate the source again if needed.

Compare the information you collect. Discuss similarities and differences in the data and/or graphs, general trends in the shape of the graphs, and how the graphs were constructed. Also consider whether the source (sponsor of the website) would be considered trustworthy in the scientific community and why or why not. Make notes about your findings in your science notebook or in a computer document.

Explain

Bring the class together to discuss the various representations of the global mean temperature of Earth over time that were found. Encourage representatives from various groups to contribute to the discussion. Talk about the reliability of the sources, any major differences that appeared, and try to reach consensus about the general conclusions that can be drawn from the graphs.

Give students time to write again about the question asked in the engage phase of the lesson; this time considering the data collected, compared, and discussed during the explore phase. Assure students that scientists often modify and revise their thoughts as they gather additional information.

Have students share their findings from the experiment and explain how the results relate to temperature changes on the Earth. Have students make predictions about the potential impact of global warming on living things.

Working in pairs, small groups, or as a class, students should brainstorm a list of their ideas related to these questions. Explain to the students that not everyone agrees about global warming and climate change.

Elaborate

Tell the class that most scientists expect that the global mean temperature of Earth will continue to rise unless drastic changes are soon made in the use of our planet's resources. Have the class brainstorm a list of possible consequences resulting from continued global warming. Write all suggestions on the board for future reference.

Assign each small group a scientific article related to the projected effects of global warming to closely read and discuss for the purpose of uncovering its main ideas.

Each group will make a brief presentation to the class summarizing the projected effect of continued global warming presented in the scientific article they read. As students listen to other groups' presentations, they should make notes about the information presented, since they will need to use that information as they complete the evaluation phase of this activity.

Evaluate

Each student is expected to create a poster or wall chart that addresses the question: What will happen if Earth's temperature continues to rise? Work with the class to identify expected criteria and levels defining success, before they start on their projects. For example:

Criteria	Exemplary	Proficient	Developing
Number of Expected Consequences Adequately Described	More than 4	4	3 or fewer
Claims and Evidence	Supporting evidence from multiple sources is presented for most claims	Supporting evidence from at least one source is presented for all claims	Some claims are not supported by supporting evidence
Visual Presentation	Consistent design elements are apparent, and appropriate graphic organizers are incorporated	Information is clearly organized and easy to understand	Information is not well organized, and/or poster or chart is hard to make sense of

You will be able to use this collaboratively developed rubric to guide summative scoring for this project.

A related middle school activity may be accessed via the Enhanced Pearson eText. It is titled: "What are greenhouse gases, and how do they contribute to global warming?" and addresses the DCI Component Idea ESS3.D.

section

V

Engineering, Technology, and Applications of Science

Source: Mesut Dogan/Shutterstock

Engineering, Technology, and Applications of Science is the fourth domain included in the Disciplinary Core Ideas, the third dimension of the *Framework*. Instead of focusing on another natural science discipline, this final disciplinary area emphasizes the importance of understanding the human-built world. The fields of science and engineering rely on each other and develop synergistically. Scientists rely on tools, objects, systems, and procedures developed by engineers to further their studies, while engineers use scientific concepts to invent and improve the technologies they produce.

As shown in the following table, in *A Framework for K–12 Science Education: Practices, Crosscutting Concepts, and Core Ideas* (NRC, 2012) this disciplinary area includes two core ideas, ETS1: Engineering Design and ETS2: Links among Engineering, Technology, Science, and Society.

Engineering, Technology, and Applications of Science Core and Component Ideas

Discipline-Related Code	Descriptive Title	Related Question
ETS1	**Engineering Design**	**How do engineers solve problems?**
ETS1.A	Defining and Delimiting an Engineering Problem	*What is design for?* *What are the criteria and constraints of a successful solution?*
ETS1.B	Developing Possible Solutions	*What is the process for developing potential design solutions?*
ETS1.C	Optimizing the Design Solution	*How can the various proposed design solutions be compared and improved?*
ETS2	**Links Among Engineering, Technology, Science, and Society**	**How are engineering, technology, science, and society interconnected?**
ETS2.A	Interdependence of Science, Engineering, and Technology	*What are the relationships among science, engineering, and technology?*
ETS2.B	Influence of Engineering, Technology, and Science on Society and the Natural World	*How do science, engineering, and the technologies that result from them affect the ways in which people live? How do they affect the natural world?*

Source: NRC, 2012, p. 203.

There is an additional engineering design activity available to you digitally via the Enhanced Pearson eText. It is:

DCI Component Ideas	Title	Grade / Grade-band
ETS1.B, ETS1.C, PS2.A	Which guardrail design works best?	Middle School

During the development of the *Next Generation Science Standards,* there was significant public comment and ongoing discussion within the writing team about the best way to include these ideas in the architecture of the NGSS. When the standards were released in April 2013, the first core idea in Engineering, Technology, and Applications of Science, ETS1: Engineering Design, remained in the Disciplinary Core Ideas (DCI) section of the foundation boxes, while the second core idea in this disciplinary area, ETS2: Links among Engineering, Technology, Science, and Society, appears in the Crosscutting Concepts (CC) section of the foundation boxes.

For this reason, all of the activities found in this section focus on learning about the application of engineering design to the problems in our world. Many of the activities included in the first three core disciplinary areas, the Physical, Life, and Earth/Space Sciences, could be modified slightly, perhaps by adding an engineering design component in the 5E phases of the lesson if appropriate, to encompass the fourth disciplinary area as well.

For a concise description of background information related to Engineering, Technology, and Applications of Science core and component ideas look at Chapter 8 of *A Framework for K–12 Science Education: Practices, Crosscutting Concepts, and Core Ideas* (NRC, 2012), available online from the National Academies Press at www.nap.edu.

Activity 67: How can we protect our eyes from the sun?

Grades: K–2, Engineering, Technology, and Applications of Science

Framework Context	
Scientific and Engineering Practices	**Asking Questions and Refining Problems** Student should ask questions to define the problem to be solved and to elicit ideas that lead to the constraints and specifications for its solution (NRC, 2012, p. 56).
Crosscutting Concepts	**Structure and Function** Exploration of the relationship between structure and function can begin in the early grades through investigations of accessible and visible systems in the natural and human-built world (NRC, 2012, p. 97).
Disciplinary Core Idea **Component Idea** **Conceptual Understanding**	**ETS1: Engineering Design** **ETS1.A: Defining and Delimiting an Engineering Problem** **By the end of grade 2:** A situation that people want to change . . . can be approached as a problem to be solved through engineering. Such problems may have many acceptable solutions. Asking questions, making observations, and gathering information are helpful in thinking about problems. Before beginning to design a solution, it is important to clearly understand the problem (NRC, 2012, p. 205).

Performance Expectations K-2-ETS1-1

Ask questions, make observations, and gather information about a situation people want to change to define a simple problem that can be solved through the development of a new or improved object or tool (NGSS Lead States, 2013, p. 23). www.nextgenscience.org/pe/k-2-ets1-1-engineering-design

1-PS4-3

Plan and conduct investigations to determine the effect of placing objects made with different materials in the path of a beam of light. (NGSS Lead States, 2013, p. 11). www.nextgenscience.org/pe/k-2-ets1-1-engineering-design

Learning Target

Before beginning to design a solution, it is important to clearly understand the problem.

Success Criteria

The students will:

1. Identify the sun shining in through the windows as a situation they want to change that could be approached as an engineering problem.

2. Explain why it is important to thoroughly understand the problem before beginning to design a solution for it.

3. Do things—such as ask questions, make observations, and gather information—to help them think more effectively about the problem.

4. Recognize that there may be many acceptable solutions to the identified problem.

Materials

- Classroom with sunny window
- Masking tape
- Chart paper
- Markers
- Aluminum foil

Engage

On a sunny day, point out that the sun is shining on some parts of the room. Ask: *Is the sunlight bothering anyone?* Ask: *How can we protect our eyes from the sun?*

Explore

Several times during the day, call attention to the parts of the room in sunlight, and discuss if the sunlight bothers anyone. Encourage students to ask questions about and make observations of the sunlight coming into the room through the windows and to keep track of how it changes during the day. Encourage them to think about the effects of the sunlight on their classroom and their classmates. Suggest that they consider science concepts that relate to this phenomenon: i.e., the sun produces light, windows are transparent, shades block the light (are opaque), the sun seems to move across the sky during the day. Remind them to record their ideas using pictures and writing in their science notebooks so that they can refer to them later.

Explain

Facilitate a discussion about what the class noticed when watching the patterns of sunlight change during the day; record words and phrases on a flip chart as appropriate. Ask: *What problems did the sun cause? What did we try to learn about the problem before trying to solve it? What else should we know about the problem before trying to solve it? How could we find out those things? Why is it important to understand the problem before trying to solve it?*

Make a brainstormed list about possible things we could do to help solve the problem(s). Point out that there is often more than one way to solve a problem.

The brainstormed list is likely to include things they could do (procedures) to solve the problem, such as close a window shade or move a desk, and things they could make (objects or systems) to solve the problem, such as a freestanding sun screen. Help the students categorize the various types of technologies on their list.

Elaborate

With the students working together in small groups, ask each group to design a solution to the identified problem, and record their plan on a sheet of chart paper. They may select one of the approaches already suggested, combine several of the ideas, or come up with a new idea. When they have your permission, each group should implement its design and determine how effectively it solved the problem.

Evaluate

Each group should present its design to the class, make a claim about the effectiveness of the design, and offer evidence supporting their claim. Informally evaluate the students' use of scientific argumentation, monitor their discussion for objective comments rather than personal attacks, and notice their realization that there are often multiple ways to solve a problem.

Activity 68: How can we use technology to keep our plants watered?

Grades: K–2, Engineering, Technology, and Applications of Science

Framework Context	
Scientific and Engineering Practices	**Asking Questions (for Science) and Defining Problems (for Engineering)** Students at any grade level should be able to ask questions of each other about the texts they read, the features of the phenomena they observe, and the conclusions they draw from their models or scientific investigations. For engineering, they should ask questions to define the problem to be solved and to elicit ideas that lead to the constraints and specifications for its solution (NRC, 2012, p. 56). **Developing and Using Models** Young students should be encouraged to devise pictoral and simple graphical representations of the findings of their investigations and to use these models in developing their explanations of what occurred (NRC, 2012, p. 58). **Analyzing and Interpreting Data** Students need support to recognize the need to record observations—whether in drawings, words, or numbers—and to share them with others. As they engage in scientific inquiry more deeply, they should begin to collect categorical or numerical data for presentation in forms that facilitate interpretation, such as tables and graphs (NRC, 2012, p. 63).
Crosscutting Concepts	**Structure and Function** Exploration of the relationship between structure and function can begin in the early grades through investigations of accessible and visible systems in the natural and human-built world (NRC, 2012, p. 97).
Disciplinary Core Idea	**ETS1:** Engineering Design
Component Idea	**ETS1.A:** Defining and Delimiting an Engineering Problem
Conceptual Understanding	**By the end of grade 2:** A situation that people want to change or create can be approached as a problem to be solved through engineering. Such problems may have many acceptable solutions. Asking questions, making observations, and gathering information are helpful in thinking about problems. Before beginning to design a solution, it is important to clearly understand the problem (NRC, 2012, p. 205).
Component Idea	**ETS1. B:** Developing Possible Solutions
Conceptual Understanding	**By the end of grade 2:** Designs can be conveyed through sketches, drawings, or physical models. These representations are useful in communicating ideas for a problem's solutions to other people (NRC, 2012, p. 207).
Component Idea	**ETS1.C:** Optimizing the Design Solution
Conceptual Understanding	**By the end of grade 2:** Because there is always more than one possible solution to a problem, it is useful to compare designs, test them, and discuss their strengths and weaknesses (NRC, 2012, p. 209).

Performance Expectations K-2-ETS1-1

Ask questions, make observations, and gather information about a situation people want to change to define a simple problem that can be solved through the development of a new or improved object or tool (NGSS Lead States, 2013, p. 23). www.nextgenscience.org/pe/k-2-ets1-1-engineering-design

K-2-ETS1-2   Develop a simple sketch, drawing, or physical model to illustrate how the shape of an object helps it function as needed to solve a given problem (NGSS Lead States, 2013, p. 23). www.nextgenscience.org/pe/k-2-ets1-2-engineering-design

K-2-ETS1-3   Analyze data from tests of two objects designed to solve the same problem to compare the strengths and weaknesses of how each performs (NGSS Lead States, 2013, p. 23). www.nextgenscience.org/pe/k-2-ets1-3-engineering-design

K-LS1-1   Use observations to describe patterns of what plants and animals (including humans) need to survive (NGSS Lead States, 2013, p. 7) www.nextgenscience.org/pe/k-ls1-1-molecules-organisms-structures-and-processes

Learning Targets

1. A problem can be solved using an engineering design process.
2. Representations are useful in communicating ideas for a problem's solutions to other people.
3. It is useful to compare and test designs.

Success Criteria

The students will:

1. Define an engineering problem related to watering their plants during school breaks.
2. Collect data about the watering needs of their plants to inform the design process.
3. Make sketches or drawings to visualize the elements of proposed design solutions.
4. Communicate proposed design solutions to others.
5. Compare designs and discuss their strengths and weaknesses.
6. Reach consensus on solution(s) to try out, implement those solutions, and evaluate their success as solutions to the problem.

Materials

- Plants in pots (preferably young but established plants grown and tended by the class as a whole rather than individual pots considered the "property" of each child)
- Water
- Variety of containers, trays, tubes
- Paper
- Crayons
- Pencils
- Science notebooks

Engage

Tell the class that you were thinking about the upcoming school vacation (winter break, spring break, summer) and that you are worried about keeping the plants in the room watered. Since no one will be at school to water the plants (which hopefully is the students' job), ask if they think we could design a solution to this problem.

Explore 1

Remind the class that to be able to solve a problem, we really need to understand what the problem is. Have them brainstorm some of the things we already know about the problem. The resulting list might include: the length of time we will be gone, that our plants need water to stay alive, that some plants need more water than others, that we usually water the plants with a watering can or a pitcher, that water can flow through tubes, that water drips.

Then have them brainstorm about things that we should find out before starting our design solution. They might suggest: how much water each pot needs, how long it takes for the soil to dry out, whether too much water can harm a plant, how long plants can survive in a pot between waterings.

Have small groups of students (or the whole class with your guidance) plan and conduct investigations that will result in the data needed to inform their designs. Note: It is important to have lots of plants in lots of pots since some may not survive the investigation. Provide adequate scaffolding during the investigation to ensure that data is recorded in an organized way; you might provide a data table or work with the students to develop one. There will be many opportunities for learning through mini-lessons that address specific needs the students encounter during this phase of the lesson.

Explain 1

Let students present the findings of their investigations. Discuss the conclusions that can be drawn and how their discoveries are important as they design a solution to the plant-watering problem.

Explore 2

Have the students talk in pairs or small groups about possible solutions to the problem. Challenge them to draw or sketch the idea their pair or group thinks is best. They may ask what they will be able to use to solve the problem (they are asking about the constraints). Tell them they may use anything they can think of in this plan and then later you will decide as a class which might be possible. Let them know how long they have to work on their drawings and that they will explain their design solution to the rest of the class.

Explain 2

Each group will present their idea and respond to questions that other students have about their work. Help them compare and contrast the ideas using a chart or some other type of graphic organizer. Suggest that they look for strengths and weaknesses in each proposed design. Encourage scientific argumentation when students question whether specific approaches will work; suggest that they go back to the data to look for evidence that supports any claims that are made.

Discuss which designs (either original or modified) are actually feasible based on the availability of resources. Help the class to reach consensus on several designs that they will actually try out.

Elaborate

Trying out designs should happen well before the school break. Provide needed materials for students to build prototypes of the design solutions selected to be tested. Careful observation of the plants, moisture in the soil, etc., should allow students to make adjustments in their plans as they see the need to do so. They should be watching for things that could be improved and make those improvements to see if they really matter. Good records of procedures, modifications, and observations are vital when trying to design a solution to an engineering problem.

After ample opportunities to test and refine the prototypes, have students compare and contrast the solutions to decide which of the solutions would work and which would work best.

Evaluate

This activity is a long-term performance task, and the children are just beginning to learn about the engineering design process. Evaluation should be formative throughout the activity. Classroom and small-group discourse, data collection and reflections in notebooks, and careful observation of students as they work provide assessment data to consider. Look for growth in willingness to propose suggestions, ask questions, and challenge each other's thinking.

Activity 69: How can you improve your telephone?

Grades: K–2, Engineering, Technology, and Applications of Science

Framework Context	
Scientific and Engineering Practices	**Developing and Using Models** Young students should be encouraged to devise pictorial and simple graphical representations of the findings of their investigations and to use these models in developing their explanations of what occurred (NRC, 2012, p. 58). **Analyzing and Interpreting Data** Students need support to recognize the need to record observations—whether in drawings, words, or numbers—and to share them with others. As they engage in scientific inquiry more deeply, they should begin to collect categorical or numerical data for presentation in forms that facilitate interpretation, such as tables and graphs (NRC, 2012, p. 63).
Crosscutting Concepts	**Structure and Function** Exploration of the relationship between structure and function can begin in the early grades through investigations of accessible and visible systems in the natural and human-built world (NRC, 2012, p. 97).
Disciplinary Core Idea **Component Idea** **Conceptual Understanding** **Component Idea** **Conceptual Understanding**	**ETS1:** Engineering Design **ETS1.B:** Developing Possible Solutions **By the end of grade 2:** Designs can be conveyed through sketches, drawings, or physical models. These representations are useful in communicating ideas for a problem's solutions to other people (NRC, 2012, p. 207). **ETS1.C:** Optimizing the Design Solution **By the end of grade 2:** Because there is always more than one possible solution to a problem, it is useful to compare designs, test them, and discuss their strengths and weaknesses (NRC, 2012, p. 209).

Performance Expectations K-2-ETS1-2

Develop a simple sketch, drawing, or physical model to illustrate how the shape of an object helps it function as needed to solve a given problem (NGSS Lead States, 2013, p. 23). www.nextgenscience.org/pe/k-2-ets1-2-engineering-design

K-2-ETS1-3

Analyze data from tests of two objects designed to solve the same problem to compare the strengths and weaknesses of how each performs (NGSS Lead States, 2013, p. 23). www.nextgenscience.org/pe/3-5-ets1-3-engineering-design

1-PS4-1

Plan and conduct investigations to provide evidence that vibrating materials can make sound and that sound can make materials vibrate (NGSS Lead States, 2013, p. 11). www.nextgenscience.org/pe/1-ps4-1-waves-and-their-applications-technologies-information-transfer

Learning Targets

1. A problem can be solved through engineering.
2. Representations are useful in communicating ideas for a problem's solutions to other people.

Success Criteria

Students will:

1. Construct homemade telephones.
2. Explain the operation of a homemade telephone using the concepts of vibrating source, conducting material, and receiver.

3. Design and carry out investigations to determine the best type of materials for a homemade telephone.

4. Demonstrate abilities of technological design.

Materials

- 7-meter lengths of string, wire, or nylon fishing line, etc.
- Cups of various kinds (Styrofoam, waxed cardboard, plastic, large, small) with a small hole in the base made in advance with a nail or a drill.
- Paper clips, toothpicks

Engage

Ask: *What do telephones let you do? How can you design a "telephone" that will enable you to communicate across some distance? What parts will your homemade telephone system need? How will you know if your homemade telephone system works? How will your telephone be better than existing telephones?*

Explore

Challenge pairs of students to use materials provided to design and construct a homemade "telephone." Instruct them to try out their homemade telephones with their partners.

Explain

Ask: *What is the original source of sound for your telephones? What is set in vibration in the mouthpiece of the telephone? What is the conductor of sound? How is the sound detected at the other end of the telephone? What would your phone need to be able to do to improve on its existing functions?*

A homemade telephone is a human-constructed product that connects well to scientific principles. Many concepts introduced in the activities on sound are used in this activity. The voice of one partner sets particles of air in vibration. The cup/mouthpiece of the string telephone is then set in vibration. The sound energy produced by the vibrating cup is conducted along the string to the other cup. Thus, the second cup is set in vibration. This vibrating cup sets the air in vibration, producing sound. The sound is then carried to the ear. Designing, constructing, and evaluating homemade telephones provides a good introduction to the technological design cycle.

Elaborate

Challenge students to improve the quality of their homemade telephones by investigating the effects of different string or wire media, different types of cups, and different ways to hold the string or wire against the bottom of the cups. Tell students to come up with standard ways to test their telephones so they can decide which parts are most effective. If you have a microphone probe to use with CBL software, this would be a great time to introduce that technology.

Evaluate

Ask each pair of students to create a labeled drawing and brief explanation of the homemade telephone they constructed that they think worked best. Distribute the following checklist to guide their work, and then use it to evaluate their products.

Checklist: The first three items on the checklist are to help you label your work and the other items are part of your explanation.

- ☐ Fit on one page.
- ☐ Include first and last name of both partners.
- ☐ Include a neat sketch of your homemade telephone in use.
- ☐ Label the following parts of your homemade telephone on the sketch: vibrating source, conducting material, and receiver.
- ☐ Indicate the length of the conducting material (in centimeters).
- ☐ Identify the materials used to make each part of your homemade phone.
- ☐ Include a description of how your phone works.
- ☐ Include an explanation of why this phone was the best one you designed.

Activity 70: How could you do product testing to determine which snow shovel is best?

Grades: 3–5, Engineering, Technology, and Applications of Science

Framework **Context**	
Scientific and Engineering Practices	**Asking Questions and Defining Problems** Define a simple design problem that can be solved through the development of an object, tool, process, or system and includes several criteria for success and constraints on materials, time, or cost (NRC, 2012, p. 56). **Planning and Carrying Out Investigations** Plan and conduct an investigation collaboratively to produce data to serve as the basis for evidence, using fair tests in which variables are controlled and the number of trials is considered. Students also recognize the limitations of their original plans (NRC, 2012, p. 60). **Constructing Explanations and Designing Solutions** Generate and compare multiple solutions to a problem based on how well they meet the criteria and constraints of the design problem. Students can begin to identify and isolate variables and incorporate the resulting observations into their explanations. Using their measurements of how one factor does or does not affect another, they can develop causal accounts to explain what they observe . . . They should be encouraged to revisit their initial ideas and produce more complete explanations that account for more of their observations (NRC, 2012, pp. 69–70).
Crosscutting Concepts	**Influence of Engineering, Technology and Science on Society and the Natural World** People's needs and wants change over time, as do their demands for new and improved technologies. Engineers improve existing technologies or develop new ones to increase their benefits, decrease known risks, and meet societal demands (NGSS Lead States, 2013, p. 53).
Disciplinary Core Idea	**ETS1:** Engineering Design
Component Idea	**ETS1.A:** Defining and Delimiting an Engineering Problem
Conceptual Understanding	**By the end of grade 5:** The success of a designed solution is determined by considering the desired features of a solution (criteria). Different proposals for solutions can be compared on the basis of how well each one meets the specified criteria for success . . . (NRC, 2012, p. 205).
Component Idea	**ETS1.B:** Developing Possible Solutions
Conceptual Understanding	**By the end of grade 5:** Research on a problem should be carried out—for example, through Internet searches, market research, or field observations—before beginning to design a solution (NRC, 2012, p. 207).
Component Idea	**ETS1.C:** Optimizing the Design Solution
Conceptual Understanding	**By the end of grade 5:** Different solutions need to be tested in order to determine which of them best solves the problem, given the criteria and the constraints (NRC, 2012, p. 209).

Performance Expectations 3-5-ETS1-1	Define a simple design problem reflecting a need or a want that includes specified criteria for success and constraints on materials, time, or cost. www.nextgenscience.org/pe/3-5-ets1-1-engineering -design
3-5-ETS1-2	Generate and compare multiple possible solutions to a problem based on how well each is likely to meet the criteria and constraints of the problem. www.nextgenscience.org/pe/3-5-ets1-2-engineering -design

3-5-ETS1-3 Plan and carry out fair tests in which variables are controlled and failure points are considered to identify aspects of a model or prototype that can be improved (NGSS Lead States, 2013, p. 53). www .nextgenscience.org/pe/3-5-ets1-3-engineering-design

Learning Targets

1. Possible solutions to a problem can be limited by available materials and resources.
2. Research on a problem should be carried out before beginning to design a solution.
3. Different solutions need to be tested in order to determine which of them best solves the problem.

Success Criteria

The students will:

1. Analyze existing snow shovels pictured on websites or in catalogs.
2. Describe the relationship between form and function in a prototype (model) snow shovel they design and construct.
3. Evaluate and compare models of snow shovels based on criteria they develop and tests they conduct.

Materials

- Computers with Internet access and a web browser
- Printer
- Hardware store catalog pages displaying various types of snow shovels
- Markers
- Chart paper
- Scissors
- Tape or glue stick
- Collection of various types of shovels (optional)
- Variety of materials from which to construct prototype shovels for testing
- Sand, snow, or other granular material for testing

Engage

Share this scenario with your class:

On a cold winter morning you learned that school was cancelled for the day. During the night there was a snowstorm in your area. The meteorologist on the local morning news reported that between 10 and 12 inches of fluffy snow covers your city. Your job is to clear the snow from the sidewalks by your home by lunchtime.

Then ask: *What are some ways you could solve this problem?* When shoveling the snow is suggested, ask: *What tool would you use to do that?* (A shovel.)

Explore

Tell the class that they will work in small groups to investigate the design of snow shovels. They will have access to pictures of many types of snow shovels, either online or in a hardware catalog. Challenge them to collaborate within their group to do the following:

1. Select six to eight snow shovels to compare and contrast. On a piece of chart paper, create a chart or other graphic organizer to show your ideas about how they are similar and different. Be sure to consider the shape (form) of the shovel and its parts in relationship to how it works to solve the problem it was designed to address (function).
2. Write your group's expectations for an effective snow shovel (i.e., what you should be able to do with it). Use a separate yellow sticky note for each expectation suggested by your group.

Explain

Post the groups' graphic organizers on the wall for all to see. Invite each group to present their work and explain what it shows. Encourage discourse about the ideas shared. Emphasize the relationships between form and function that were identified by the students or encourage them to find those relationships now.

Title a sheet of chart paper "Expectations for an effective snow shovel." Collect one sticky note at a time from each group; have them explain the expectation statement on that note. Each group's addition should be different from those already posted. Keep adding notes until all ideas have been displayed and discussed.

Tell the class that engineers refer to expectations like these as *criteria*. If all important criteria are met, the designed solution for a problem should be successful. Ask: *Are there other criteria we should add to this chart? Are there any criteria that we should remove?* Add and/or remove sticky notes as needed.

Elaborate

Challenge small groups of students to make models of at least two of the snow shovels that they have pictures of. Have them work as groups to determine ways to test their models. Remind them to record the testing protocols they develop.

Within their groups, have students decide whether the class criteria developed for actual shovels earlier would be reasonable for the models they will test. They may modify the performance expectations for their models if they think it is necessary.

After testing the models, each group should identify the model shovels that successfully met the criteria. Suggestions for improvement should be made for any model shovels that did not meet all criteria.

Evaluate

Formatively assess students during all phases of the lesson and as the objectives are addressed. As a summative assessment, ask individual students to write a brief report about their groups' models, testing procedures, criteria, and results. Suggest that within their reports they compare the performance of at least two models they tested and describe the importance of identifying criteria and testing models in the engineering design process.

Activity 71: How can you make the best boat using a variety of materials?

Grades: 3–5, Engineering, Technology, and Applications of Science

Framework Context	
Scientific and Engineering Practices	**Asking Questions and Defining Problems** Define a simple design problem that can be solved through the development of an object, tool, process, or system and includes several criteria for success and constraints on materials, time, or cost (NRC, 2012, p. 56). **Planning and Carrying Out Investigations** Plan and conduct an investigation collaboratively to produce data to serve as the basis for evidence, using fair tests in which variables are controlled and the number of trials is considered. Students also recognize the limitations of their original plans (NRC, 2012, p. 60). **Constructing Explanations and Designing Solutions** Generate and compare multiple solutions to a problem based on how well they meet the criteria and constraints of the design problem. Students can begin to identify and isolate variables and incorporate the resulting observations into their explanations. Using their measurements of how one factor does or does not affect another, they can develop causal accounts to explain what they observe . . . They should be encouraged to revisit their initial ideas and produce more complete explanations that account for more of their observations (NRC, 2012, pp. 69–70).
Crosscutting Concepts	**Influence of Engineering, Technology and Science on Society and the Natural World** People's needs and wants change over time, as do their demands for new and improved technologies. Engineers improve existing technologies or develop new ones to increase their benefits, decrease known risks, and meet societal demands (NGSS Lead States, 2013, p. 53).
Disciplinary Core Idea	**ETS1:** Engineering Design
Component Idea	**ETS1.A:** Defining and Delimiting an Engineering Problem
Conceptual Understanding	**By the end of grade 5:** Possible solutions to a problem are limited by available materials and resources (constraints). The success of a designed solution is determined by considering the desired features of a solution (criteria). Different proposals for solutions can be compared on the basis of how well each one meets the specified criteria for success or how well each takes the constraints into account (NRC, 2012, p. 205).
Component Idea	**ETS1.B:** Developing Possible Solutions
Conceptual Understanding	**By the end of grade 5:** Tests are often designed to identify failure points or difficulties, which suggest the elements of the design that need to be improved (NRC, 2012, p. 207).
Component Idea	**ETS1.C:** Optimizing the Design Solution
Conceptual Understanding	**By the end of grade 5:** Different solutions need to be tested in order to determine which of them best solves the problem, given the criteria and the constraints (NRC, 2012, p. 209).

Performance Expectations 3-5-ETS1-1

Define a simple design problem reflecting a need or a want that includes specified criteria for success and constraints on materials, time, or cost. www.nextgenscience.org/pe/3-5-ets1-1-engineering-design

3-5-ETS1-2

Generate and compare multiple possible solutions to a problem based on how well each is likely to meet the criteria and constraints of the problem. www.nextgenscience.org/pe/3-5-ets1-2-engineering-design

3-5-ETS1-3

Plan and carry out fair tests in which variables are controlled and failure points are considered to identify aspects of a model or prototype that can be improved (NGSS Lead States, 2013, p. 53). www.nextgenscience.org/pe/3-5-ets1-3-engineering-design

Learning Targets

1. Possible solutions to a problem can be limited by available materials and resources.
2. Research on a problem should be carried out before beginning to design a solution.
3. Different solutions need to be tested in order to determine which of them best solves the problem.

Success Criteria

The students will:

1. Describe the importance of having clear criteria for an engineering design project.
2. Describe the effect of various constraints on an engineering design project.
3. Distinguish between constraints and criteria.
4. Test and improve possible solutions to the problem.
5. Compare possible solutions to a problem based on how well each meets criteria and/or takes constraints into account.

Materials

- Index cards (4″ × 6″)
- Copy paper rectangles (4″ × 6″)
- Aluminum foil rectangles (4″ × 6″)
- Basin of water
- Pennies
- Stopwatch or clock with second hand
- Metric ruler

Engage

Ask: *What is a boat? What are the essential characteristics of boats? What must a boat do to be useful? What are boats made of? Are all boats made of the same materials? Is one design better than another based on the material that it is made from?*

Explore

Let each student select one rectangle to use as the only building material for a model boat. Allow only 2 minutes for boat construction. Boats may not be tested during the construction period. Collect all boats, then announce the criteria for successful boats:

- Float for at least 5 minutes
- Hold a cargo of 20 pennies
- Be at least 12 cm long and 6 cm wide

Determine which boats meet the criteria for a successful boat.

Explain

Bring the class together for a whole-group discussion. Ask: *Why do you think so few boats were successful? Do you think we would have had more successful boats if we all knew the criteria for success ahead of time? What were the criteria? If the criteria were different, do you think your boat would be successful?*

Besides criteria, engineering design projects often have constraints. What were the constraints you had during the explore phase of the lesson? (One type of building material, only a 4″ × 6″ rectangle to use, limited time to construct, no testing during construction.)

Elaborate

Your group may now define its own criteria for success and set its own constraints. Find out if each of the three construction materials can be used to build a successful boat. Different construction materials might be prone to different design flaws. As a group, make some prototype boats from each of the available construction materials and test them. If they are not successful, try to make improvements.

Evaluate

Write a report about your boat investigations from the elaborate phase of the lesson. This checklist should guide your writing:

- What criteria are you using to judge success?
- What constraints have you established?
- Which materials were successful for boat construction?
- What design flaws emerged during your investigations?
- How did you address the design flaws that emerged?
- Based on your criteria and constraints, which of your boats do you think is best, and why?

Activity 72: Which structures are most likely to withstand an earthquake?

Grades: 3–5, Engineering, Technology, and Applications of Science

Framework Context	
Scientific and Engineering Practices	**Asking Questions and Defining Problems** Define a simple design problem that can be solved through the development of an object, tool, process, or system and includes several criteria for success and constraints on materials, time, or cost (NRC, 2012, p. 56). **Planning and Carrying Out Investigations** Plan and conduct an investigation collaboratively to produce data to serve as the basis for evidence, using fair tests in which variables are controlled and the number of trials is considered. Students also recognize the limitations of their original plans (NRC, 2012, p. 60). **Constructing Explanations and Designing Solutions** Generate and compare multiple solutions to a problem based on how well they meet the criteria and constraints of the design problem. Students can begin to identify and isolate variables and incorporate the resulting observations into their explanations. Using their measurements of how one factor does or does not affect another, they can develop causal accounts to explain what they observe . . . They should be encouraged to revisit their initial ideas and produce more complete explanations that account for more of their observations (NRC, 2012, pp. 69–70).
Crosscutting Concepts	**Influence of Engineering, Technology and Science on Society and the Natural World** People's needs and wants change over time, as do their demands for new and improved technologies. Engineers improve existing technologies or develop new ones to increase their benefits, decrease known risks, and meet societal demands (NGSS Lead States, 2013, p. 53).
Disciplinary Core Idea	**ETS1:** Engineering Design
Component Idea	**ETS1.A:** Defining and Delimiting an Engineering Problem
Conceptual Understanding	**By the end of grade 5:** Possible solutions to a problem are limited by available materials and resources (constraints). The success of a designed solution is determined by considering the desired features of a solution (criteria). Different proposals for solutions can be compared on the basis of how well each one meets the specified criteria for success or how well each takes the constraints into account (NRC, 2012, p. 205).
Component Idea	**ETS1.B:** Developing Possible Solutions
Conceptual Understanding	**By the end of grade 5:** An often productive way to generate ideas is for people to work together to brainstorm, test, and refine possible solutions. . . . Tests are often designed to identify failure points or difficulties, which suggest the elements of the design that need to be improved. At whatever stage, communicating with peers about proposed solutions is an important part of the design process, and shared ideas can lead to improved designs (NRC, 2012, p. 207).
Component Idea	**ETS1.C:** Optimizing the Design Solution
Conceptual Understanding	**By the end of grade 5:** Different solutions need to be tested in order to determine which of them best solves the problem, given the criteria and the constraints (NRC, 2012, p. 209).
Component Idea	**ESS3:** Earth and Human Activity
Conceptual Understanding	**ESS3.B:** Natural Hazards
	By the end of grade 5: A variety of hazards result from natural processes (e.g., earthquakes, tsunamis, volcanic eruptions, severe weather, floods, coastal erosion). Humans cannot eliminate natural hazards but can take steps to reduce their impacts (NRC, 2012, p. 193).

Performance Expectations
3-5-ETS1-1

Define a simple design problem reflecting a need or a want that includes specified criteria for success and constraints on materials, time, or cost. www.nextgenscience.org/pe/3-5-ets1-1-engineering-design

3-5-ETS1-2

Generate and compare multiple possible solutions to a problem based on how well each is likely to meet the criteria and constraints of the problem. www.nextgenscience.org/pe/3-5-ets1-2-engineering-design

3-5-ETS1-3

Plan and carry out fair tests in which variables are controlled and failure points are considered to identify aspects of a model or prototype that can be improved (NGSS Lead States, 2013, p. 53). www.nextgenscience.org/pe/3-5-ets1-3-engineering-design

4-ESS3-2

Generate and compare multiple solutions to reduce the impacts of natural Earth processes on humans (NGSS Lead States, 2013, p. 36) www.nextgenscience.org/pe/4-ess3-2-earth-and-human-activity

Learning Targets

1. Possible solutions to a problem can be limited by available materials and resources.

2. Research on a problem should be carried out before beginning to design a solution.

3. Different solutions need to be tested in order to determine which of them best solves the problem.

4. Humans cannot eliminate natural hazards but can take steps to minimize the impacts.

Success Criteria

The students will:

1. Use prototype models to investigate the effect of earthquakes on simple and more complex structures.
2. Identify evidence that supports or refutes the claim that the simulated earthquakes in the model were consistent.
3. Use the engineering design process to solve a problem.
4. Prepare a report documenting their engineering design project.

Materials

For each small group of 4 students:

- 2 cafeteria serving trays (18″ × 14″)
- 4 ping pong balls
- 3 large rubber bands (that each stretch to at least 20″)
- 3 empty matchboxes (approximately 12 cm × 7 cm × 3 cm)
- 20 index cards (3″ × 5″)
- Scissors
- Rulers

Engage

Show the class still photos or video clips of destruction of buildings during earthquakes. Ask: *Based on these images, what is a major problem faced by people living in earthquake-prone areas?* (Earthquakes cause their buildings to collapse.) What are some ways that engineering might help solve this problem?

Explore

Tell the class they will have a chance to use models to explore the effect of earthquakes on different building designs.

First, they need something to simulate a small-scale earthquake. This device, called a **shake table,** should create a similar shaking motion that is about the same strength each time it is used.

After constructing their shake table, each small group should follow this procedure to simulate an earthquake: While one student holds the bottom tray in place, another student pulls the top tray gently, then releases it.

Introduce the three empty matchboxes as buildings for their model. Suggest that they conduct fair tests to determine the safest way to build (orient) buildings so that they are most likely to survive the shaking of an earthquake without falling over. If necessary, remind them to record their procedures and results and to repeat the investigation multiple times.

Encourage each group to collect evidence that supports the claim that the simulated earthquake's strength and motion is similar each time they follow the procedure.

Explain

Involve the class in a discussion, asking questions such as: *What was the purpose of the shake table in your model? What problem was it designed to solve?*

Remind the class that in engineering:

- The term ***constraint*** refers to the available materials and resources that limit possible solutions to a problem. Then ask: *What were the constraints that limited the design of the shake table?*
- The term ***criteria*** refers to the desired features of a successful designed solution. Then ask: *What were the criteria for a successful shake table? Do you think the simulated earthquakes your group produced were about the same each time? What evidence supports your claim? Why does it matter?*

Have groups share their findings with the class and discuss general conclusions that can be drawn from their observations of the matchbox buildings during the simulated earthquakes. Ideas about what makes the best building might emerge. Ask: *What criteria might a construction engineer or architect use when designing a building?* (Size, cost of materials, occupancy limits, cost of the land, cost of construction, safety.)

Encourage discussion about the ways that the model used in the explore phase of the lesson was like a real earthquake with real buildings and how it was different.

Elaborate

Have students work with a partner to design, construct, test, and improve an earthquake-safe home for model people that are 6 cm tall. They want a two-story house with ceilings at least 10 cm high. The only available building material is index cards, only 20 of them. They want to move in within 20 minutes and expect their home to remain standing in good condition after three simulated earthquakes.

Evaluate

Have students document the engineering design process for this model house. Reports should answer the following questions:

1. What is the engineering problem you were trying to solve?
2. What criteria defined a successful designed solution?
3. What constraints limited your options?
4. How did you develop possible design solutions?
5. Which design solutions did you test and/or compare? (You could use drawings or sketches to document this.)
6. How were your tests conducted? Why did you choose this procedure?
7. What improvements did you make? What prompted you to make those improvements?
8. What are the strengths and weaknesses of your final design?

Activity 73: How can you design a healthy aquarium environment?

Grades: 3–5, Engineering, Technology, and Applications of Science

Framework Context	
Scientific and Engineering Practices	**Planning and Carrying Out Investigations**
	Plan and conduct an investigation collaboratively to produce data to serve as the basis for evidence, using fair tests in which variables are controlled and the number of trials is considered. Students also recognize the limitations of their original plans (NRC, 2012, p. 60).
	Constructing Explanations and Designing Solutions
	Generate and compare multiple solutions to a problem based on how well they meet the criteria and constraints of the design problem. Students can begin to identify and isolate variables and incorporate the resulting observations into their explanations. Using their measurements of how one factor does or does not affect another, they can develop causal accounts to explain what they observe . . . They should be encouraged to revisit their initial ideas and produce more complete explanations that account for more of their observations (NRC, 2012, pp. 69–70).
Crosscutting Concepts	**Influence of Engineering, Technology and Science on Society and the Natural World**
	People's needs and wants change over time, as do their demands for new and improved technologies. Engineers improve existing technologies or develop new ones to increase their benefits, decrease known risks, and meet societal demands (NGSS Lead States, 2013, p. 53).
Disciplinary Core Idea	**ETS1:** Engineering Design
Component Idea	**ETS1.B:** Developing Possible Solutions
Conceptual Understanding	**By the end of grade 5:** Research on a problem should be carried out—for example, through Internet searches . . . or field observations—before beginning to design a solution. An often productive way to generate ideas is for people to work together to brainstorm, test, and refine possible solutions. . . . At whatever stage, communicating with peers about proposed solutions is an important part of the design process, and shared ideas can lead to improved designs (NRC, 2012, p. 207).
	LS2: Ecosystems: Interactions, Energy, and Dynamics
Disciplinary Core Idea	**LS2.C:** Ecosystem Dynamics, Functioning, and Resilience
Component Idea	
Conceptual Understanding	**By the end of grade 5:** When the environment changes in ways that affect a place's physical characteristics, temperature, or availability of resources, some organisms survive and reproduce, others move to new locations, yet others move into the transformed environment, and some die (NRC, 2012, p. 155).

Performance Expectations 3-5-ETS1-1	Define a simple design problem reflecting a need or a want that includes specified criteria for success and constraints on materials, time, or cost. www.nextgenscience.org/pe/3-5-ets1-1-engineering-design
3-5-ETS1-2	Generate and compare multiple possible solutions to a problem based on how well each is likely to meet the criteria and constraints of the problem. www.nextgenscience.org/pe/3-5-ets1-2-engineering-design
3-5-ETS1-3	Plan and carry out fair tests in which variables are controlled and failure points are considered to identify aspects of a model or prototype that can be improved (NGSS Lead States, 2013, p. 53). www.nextgenscience.org/pe/3-5-ets1-3-engineering-design
3-LS4-4	Make a claim about the merit of a solution to a problem caused when the environment changes and the types of plants and animals that live there may change (NGSS Lead States, 2013, p. 27). www.nextgenscience.org/pe/3-ls4-4-biological-evolution-unity-and-diversity

Learning Targets

1. Possible solutions to a problem can be limited by available materials and resources.
2. Research on a problem should be carried out before beginning to design a solution.
3. Different solutions need to be tested in order to determine which of them best solves the problem.
4. When the physical environment of an environment changes, some organisms survive and some die.

Success Criteria

1. Conduct research about appropriate criteria and constraints for classroom aquaria.
2. Identify and describe the parts of an aquarium habitat, and describe how the parts of this system interact.
3. Design and construct an aquarium habitat.

Materials

- Clear plastic basins (6 liter), fish bowls, small aquaria, etc.
- Variety of aquatic plants (approximately 10 cm in height)
- Guppies, goldfish, or other fish
- Water
- Fish food
- Snails
- Other supplies as needed by the class

Engage

Ask: *What is an aquarium? What lives in an aquarium? What are some of the things fish, plants, and other organisms need in order to survive in an aquarium? How must an aquarium be constructed and maintained to support living things? How could you find out?*

Explore

Suggest that the class brainstorm a list of the parts or components that should be included in an aquarium system. Ideas that emerge might include topics such as:

- the container (size, shape, material)
- material on the bottom of the aquarium system (composition, grain size, depth, color, preparation)
- water (amount, preparation, fresh or salt)
- plants (size, types, number)
- fish (size, types, number)
- snails (size, types, number)
- temperature/light (placement)
- food
- air
- maintenance issues

This list might provide structure for developing strategies for researching and organizing information gathered. Small groups of students might be in charge of gathering information on particular factors/topics to then share with the class. Be sure that more than one small group is researching each topic to ensure rich discussion during the next phase of the lesson.

Provide access to Internet resources and related books. Ask the librarian at your school to assist in finding appropriate resources and in guiding student research. Discuss procedures for evaluating sources and describe expectations for sharing information with the class during the explain phase of the lesson.

Science Background

Basic information about setting up an aquarium is provided for your use. It is *not* intended to be shared directly with the students but may give you needed background to guide and scaffold their research.

Container. Obtain a 4- to 6-liter (1 to 1.5 gallons), rectangular, clear plastic container with strong walls. The container should have a large surface area to allow gas exchange with the atmosphere but should not be too shallow. Wash the container well with water, but not soap.

Sand. Obtain a supply of coarse white sand. Rinse the sand in a bucket to remove debris. Add white sand to a depth of about 4 cm to the bottom of the aquarium container.

Water. Age tap water in an open container for 24 to 48 hours to allow chlorine in the water to escape. You may choose to use bottled spring water (but not distilled water). Gently pour the water into the container, perhaps over clean paper to prevent disturbing the sand.

Plants. Obtain water plants from a pond or purchase them from a science supply company or a local pet shop. Root about two sprigs of waterweed (elodea) and two sprigs of eelgrass in the sand. Add some duckweed as a floating plant. Overplanting is better for your aquarium than underplanting. Allow 1 to 2 weeks for the plants to become acclimated to the water before adding animals.

Fish. Purchase small fish from a pet store or obtain some free from an aquarium hobbyist. Obtain male and female guppies or goldfish. Place the plastic bag containing the fish in your aquarium water for a few hours for the water temperatures in the bag and the aquarium to become equal. Use a dip net to add three to four fish to the aquarium. A rule of thumb is not to have more than 1 cm of fish (excluding tail) per liter of water. Dispose of the plastic container and water the fish came in.

Snails. Add several small pond snails to your aquarium.

Care. Add a plastic lid to your aquarium. Lift the corners of the lid to allow exchange of gases between the water and the atmosphere. Thus, you will not need a pump for aeration. Keep a supply of aged tap water available to replace evaporated water as necessary, keeping the water in the aquarium at a predetermined level.

Temperature. Place your aquarium in the room so that it can get light, but not direct sunlight. Too much light will promote the growth of algae (which can, if you desire, be observed and studied by students). The aquarium should be maintained at room temperature ($70°$ to $78°$F or $21°$ to $25°$C). A gooseneck lamp with a 60- to 75-watt bulb can be used to warm the water if necessary. Adjust the lamp so the bulb is a few centimeters above the water, until the temperature is maintained at the desired level. Check with your principal about school regulations concerning leaving the lamp on over the weekend.

Food. Feed the fish a small amount (a pinch) of commercial fish food every other day (or as instructed on the package). Do not overfeed. Uneaten food will decay, polluting the water. Fish can go as long as 2 weeks without food. Fish may supplement their diet by eating from the water plants. Snails do not require any special food. They eat water plants or the debris that collects on the bottom of the aquarium.

Explain

Tell the class that each group in turn will have an opportunity to contribute information about setting up an aquarium until all ideas have been shared. Take time for needed scientific argumentation if conflicting information emerges.

Discuss why it was important to conduct research about aquaria and how to build and maintain them before getting too deep into the design process.

Food jar
aquarium

Soda bottle
aquarium

Elaborate

Have each small group draw a plan of their proposed aquarium habitat, based on the class's research findings. Then let them construct a prototype and monitor the system over time. Each group should develop a plan for observing and recording information about their aquarium for several months. Let them determine the data they will collect based on their interests and questions they might have. (How often will I need to add water? Will the fish reproduce? Will the fish grow bigger?)

Evaluate

Informally assess students' research and scientific argumentation skills as they work collaboratively on this project. Encourage students to discuss the relationship between their plans and their prototypes.

Activity 74: How can you keep your soup hot?

Grades: 6–8, Engineering, Technology, and Applications of Science

Framework Context	
Scientific and Engineering Practices	**Asking Questions and Defining Problems** Define a design problem that can be solved through the development of an object, tool, process, or system and includes multiple criteria and constraints, including scientific knowledge that may limit possible solutions (NGSS Lead States, 2013, p. 86). **Developing and Using Models** Develop a model to generate data to test ideas about designed systems, including those representing inputs and outputs (NGSS Lead States, 2013, p. 86). **Analyzing and Interpreting Data** Analyze and interpret data to determine similarities and differences in findings (NGSS Lead States, 2013, p. 86). **Engaging in Argument from Evidence** Evaluate competing design solutions based on jointly developed and agreed-upon design criteria (NGSS Lead States, 2013, p. 87).
Crosscutting Concepts	**Influence of Science, Engineering, and Technology on Society and the Natural World** All human activity draws on natural resources and has both short- and long-term consequences, positive as well as negative, for the health of people and the natural environment. The uses of technologies and limitations on their use are driven by individual or societal needs, desires, and values; by the findings of scientific research; and by differences in such factors as climate, natural resources, and economic conditions (NGSS Lead States, 2013, p. 86).
Disciplinary Core Idea **Component Idea** **Conceptual Understanding** **Component Idea** **Conceptual Understanding** **Component Idea** **Conceptual Understanding**	**ETS1: Engineering Design** **ETS1.A:** Defining and Delimiting an Engineering Problem **By the end of grade 8:** The more precisely a design task's criteria and constraints can be defined, the more likely it is that the designed solution will be successful. Specification of constraints includes consideration of scientific principles and other relevant knowledge that is likely to limit possible solutions (NRC, 2012, p. 205). **ETS1.B:** Developing Possible Solutions **By the end of grade 8:** A solution needs to be tested, and then modified on the basis of the test results in order to improve it. There are systematic processes for evaluating solutions with respect to how well they meet criteria and constraints of a problem (NRC, 2012, p. 208). **PS3.B:** Conservation of Energy and Energy Transfer **By the end of grade 8:** Energy is transferred out of hotter regions or objects and into colder ones by the processes of conduction, convection, and radiation (NRC, 2012, p. 126).

Performance Expectations MS-ETS1-1

Define the criteria and constraints of a design problem with sufficient precision to ensure a successful solution, taking into account relevant scientific principles and potential impacts on people and the natural environment that may limit possible solutions. www.nextgenscience.org/pe/3-5-ets1-1-engineering-design

MS-ETS1-4

Develop a model to generate data for iterative testing and modification of a proposed object, tool, or process such that an optimal design can be achieved (NGSS Lead States, 2013, p. 86). www.nextgenscience.org/dci-arrangement/ms-ets1-engineering-design

MS-PS3-3   Apply scientific principles to design, construct, and test a device that either minimizes or maximizes thermal energy transfer (NGSS Lead States, 2013, p. 58). www.nextgenscience.org/pe/ms-ps3-3-energy

Learning Targets

1. The more precisely a design task's constraints can be defined, the more successful the design solution will be.

2. A solution needs to be tested and then modified on the basis of the test results in order to improve it.

3. Heat moves from regions that are hotter to regions that are colder by the process of conduction.

Success Criteria

The students will:

1. Describe the importance of having clear criteria and constraints for an engineering design project.
2. Investigate factors that may affect how quickly hot water cools in a container.
3. Identify criteria and constraints for a container intended to keep hot soup hot.
4. Test and improve possible solutions to the problem.
5. Make a labeled sketch or drawing that illustrates the flow of energy in the designed system.

Materials

- Hot plate and tea kettle (only handled by teacher for safety reasons)
- Thermometers or temperature probes, interfaces, and computer or other device running appropriate MBL software
- Water
- Variety of containers, cups, and bowls (different sizes, shapes, materials, etc.)
- Variety of materials to use as insulators (Styrofoam, cotton, bubble wrap, cloth, tissue paper, etc.)
- Tape (transparent or masking)
- Other household materials requested by students as available

Engage

Say to the class: *Have you ever arrived at the dinner table a little late only to find your soup is too cold? Sure, you could put it back in the microwave and zap it for a minute to solve that problem, but is there a way to prevent the problem in the first place? What are some of the factors that might affect your soup cooling off?*

Students might suggest: how long it was sitting there, the shape of the bowl it was in, the material of the bowl it was in, the amount of soup in the bowl, the temperature of the soup when it was poured into the bowl, the surface area of the soup exposed to the air, etc.

Explore

Organize the students into small groups for this investigation. Let each group select one of the suggested factors to investigate. Encourage at least one group to investigate each suggested factor, or, if necessary, assign one of the factors to at least one group.

Have groups design a controlled experiment in which the factor they are studying is the independent variable and the temperature of the soup (hot water) is the dependent variable. Instruct them to keep other variables constant. They should compare at least four different levels of the independent variable (i.e., four different bowl shapes, four different bowl materials, four different amounts of hot water, etc.).

If they are using a thermometer to monitor temperature change, they will need to determine at what interval to monitor the temperature, create a data table for their observations, and construct a line graph to visually illustrate the change in temperature over time. If they are using a temperature probe, they will be able to watch as the line graph of the temperature change is displayed on the computer monitor or other display screen.

Explain

Each group will report the findings from their investigation, share their graph with the whole class, and recommend how best to keep the "soup" hot when only altering the factor they studied, their independent variable.

Encourage the class to discuss the data presented and ask each other for clarification of their procedures and findings. Discuss the scientific principle involved in this investigation: that energy moves from hotter regions to cooler regions. Look for evidence in the data that supports that claim. Talk about why the rate of change of the temperature differs in different investigations.

Tell the class that soon each group will use the information they have gathered as a class during the engage phase of the lesson to help them design a container for the soup that will be better. Ask the class if they have been provided with enough information for them to design something they think will be successful. Ask them what would be helpful to know.

Hopefully criteria and constraints will be suggested. Then, as a class, establish criteria and constraints that will guide the elaborate phase of the lesson.

Elaborate

Challenge each group to design a soup container that meets the stated criteria and takes into consideration the identified constraints. Provide ample time so that they can test and improve their design several times.

Evaluate

Ask students to write a report about their new design developed during the elaborate phase of the lesson. Provide this checklist to guide their writing:

- What criteria are you using to judge success?
- What constraints limit your design?
- How does energy move through your designed system? (This can be illustrated using arrows on a labeled drawing of your design.)
- Why did you design the new container the way you did? (Consider individual factors.)
- Did it work as well as you expected it would? Why do you think this was the case?

Activity 75: How can you design a "better" roller coaster?

Grades: 6–8, Engineering, Technology, and Applications of Science

Framework Context	
Scientific and Engineering Practices	**Asking Questions and Defining Problems** Define a design problem that can be solved through the development of an object, tool, process, or system and includes multiple criteria and constraints, including scientific knowledge that may limit possible solutions (NGSS Lead States, 2013, p. 86). **Developing and Using Models** Develop a model to generate data to test ideas about designed systems, including those representing inputs and outputs (NGSS Lead States, 2013, p. 86). **Analyzing and Interpreting Data** Analyze and interpret data to determine similarities and differences in findings (NGSS Lead States, 2013, p. 86). **Engaging in Argument from Evidence** Evaluate competing design solutions based on jointly developed and agreed-upon design criteria (NGSS Lead States, 2013, p. 87).
Crosscutting Concepts	**Influence of Science, Engineering, and Technology on Society and the Natural World** All human activity draws on natural resources and has both short- and long-term consequences, positive as well as negative, for the health of people and the natural environment. The uses of technologies and limitations on their use are driven by individual or societal needs, desires, and values; by the findings of scientific research; and by differences in such factors as climate, natural resources, and economic conditions (NGSS Lead States, 2013, p. 86).
Disciplinary Core Idea	**ETS1:** Engineering Design
Component Idea	**ETS1.A:** Defining and Delimiting an Engineering Problem
Conceptual Understanding	**By the end of grade 8:** The more precisely a design task's criteria and constraints can be defined, the more likely it is that the designed solution will be successful. Specification of constraints includes consideration of scientific principles and other relevant knowledge that are likely to limit possible solutions (NRC, 2012, p. 205).
Component Idea	**ETS1.B:** Developing Possible Solutions
Conceptual Understanding	**By the end of grade 8:** Research on a problem should be carried out—for example, through Internet searches, market research, or field observations—before beginning to design a solution. . . . Tests are often designed to identify failure points or difficulties, which suggest the elements of the design that need to be improved. At whatever stage, communicating with peers about proposed solutions is an important part of the design process, and shared ideas can lead to improved designs. There are many types of models, ranging from simple physical models to computer models. They can be used to investigate how a design might work, communicate the design to others, and compare different designs (NRC, 2012, p. 207).

Performance Expectations MS-ETS1-1

Define the criteria and constraints of a design problem with sufficient precision to ensure a successful solution, taking into account relevant scientific principles and potential impacts on people and the natural environment that may limit possible solutions. www.nextgenscience.org/pe/3-5-ets1-1-engineering-design

MS-ETS1-3   Analyze data from tests to determine similarities and differences among several design solutions to identify the best characteristics of each that can be combined into a new solution to better meet the criteria for success. www.nextgenscience.org/pe/3-5-ets1-3-engineering-design

MS-ETS1-4   Develop a model to generate data for iterative testing and modification of a proposed object, tool, or process such that an optimal design can be achieved (NGSS Lead States, 2013, p. 86). www.nextgenscience .org/dci-arrangement/ms-ets1-engineering-design

Learning Targets

1. The more precisely a design task's constraints can be defined, the more successful the design solution will be.

2. A solution needs to be tested and then modified on the basis of the test results in order to improve it.

3. A solution needs to be determined based on how well it meets the criteria and constraints of a problem.

Success Criteria

The students will:

1. Describe the importance of having clear criteria for an engineering design project.
2. Use various types of models to represent and test roller coaster designs.
3. Evaluate the pros and cons of the various types of models they used.
4. Test and improve possible design solutions.
5. Maintain good records of their investigations.

Materials

- White construction paper
- Pencils
- Computers connected to the Internet, with bookmarked roller coaster design simulations that you have selected prior to the lesson. (There are many available; just search for "Design a Roller Coaster Interactive" using your favorite web browser.)
- Engineering log (or science notebook)
- Foam pipe insulation
- Marbles
- Masking tape
- Metric tape measures

Engage

Distribute sheets of white construction paper and pencils to the students. Tell the class: *An amusement park company has decided to build a new entertainment attraction in your area. Since they know that many of their customers will be middle school students, they are holding a contest for best roller coaster design. You'll have five minutes to draw a sketch of your proposed roller coaster on your sheet of paper. They have asked that you draw the elements (hills, valleys, and loops) of your coaster in order from left to right across your page, even though the start and end of the coaster will connect when it is actually built.*

If questions related to criteria or constraints are asked during the drawing time, *do not* provide answers; simply say that you do not know. Only clarify questions about how to draw the picture, with the start of the coaster at the left side of the paper and the end of the coaster at the right side of the paper. Collect the papers after five minutes of drawing time, then post them on a bulletin board for use later in the lesson.

Explore

Provide students with access to several computer simulations that allow them to design and test roller coasters. They may work individually, in pairs, or in small groups depending on the availability of computers. Challenge them to design several coasters using at least two of the available programs. Tell students to sketch each design they test, describe the outcome of the ride, and identify the program they were using. They should keep these records in their engineering logs or science notebooks.

Explain

Ask students to bring their notes from the explore phase to a discussion circle. Facilitate discourse among the students about their experiences with the simulations. Some questions that might generate discussion are:

- What were some differences between successful roller coasters and those that were unsuccessful?
- How were the simulations you tried alike and different? Which simulation did you prefer? Why? What did you learn about roller coaster design from the computer simulations?
- Where is the coaster car when it is moving very slowly? Where is the coaster car when it is moving very fast? What do these observations have to do with potential and kinetic energy?
- In a successful roller coaster, which hill is highest? Why?

Tell the class that you have heard back from the amusement park company about the design contest. Unfortunately, many of the designs were disqualified, either because the coaster would not travel successfully to the end of the track, would cost too much to build, or had some inherent safety issues. The company still is interested in our help with this project and has asked us to submit new designs and prototypes based on revised criteria and constraints.

Elaborate

Tell students they may now design a physical model of a successful roller coaster. Show the class the foam pipe insulation, marbles, and tape, and identify how many/much of each of these resources they may use. Decide as a whole class what criteria will describe a successful model roller coaster; list those criteria on the board for further reference. Also list the constraints that limit the design, such as the resources available to each group.

Before student groups may get the materials to construct their model roller coaster, they must make a labeled drawing of their proposed design and show it to you. Check the drawing to be sure the constraints have been considered, i.e., that they are using the allowed resources in their design.

Allow time for students to build their model roller coaster, test it, and make improvements if necessary. Then let each group demonstrate their coaster for the rest of the class and explain why it worked successfully.

Evaluate

Students' work should be assessed informally throughout the lesson by listening to their science talk within their small groups and during whole-class discourse.

Using their engineering logs or science notebooks, have students review their notes from this activity and then respond to the following prompts in writing as a reflection on this engineering design project:

1. Why is it important to have clear criteria when designing a solution for an engineering problem?
2. You used various types of models during this investigation. Make a chart listing the types of models used and showing the benefits and drawbacks of each type of model.
3. Write three keys to designing a successful coaster.

Details of Some Important Science Process Skills

Science process skills were introduced in Chapter 2 of *Teaching Science Through Inquiry-Based Instruction*. Appendix A provides more in depth information and context about the science process skills typically associated with science teaching and learning in elementary and middle schools. These include: observing, measuring, inferring, classifying, questioning, communicating, analyzing and interpreting data, predicting, hypothesizing, and experimenting. Relationships between science process skills and the Science and Engineering Practices in NGSS are also discussed in Appendix A.

Observing

Observation is the process of gathering information about the world around us. When you observe, you make use of at least one of your senses. Often several senses are used simultaneously. You might use aids to your senses, such as a hand lens, a microscope, or a microphone with an amplifier and a speaker to better study details while viewing or listening to a phenomenon. Effective observation includes noticing relevant details of the thing or event being observed and its surroundings. Exploration A.1 provides an opportunity for you to make some observations and reflect on many aspects of that science process skill.

Observations are either qualitative or quantitative. A **qualitative observation** describes the qualities or properties of the object, organism, or event that is observed. A qualitative description

> ▶ To see an example of a fourth-grade teacher and his students engaged in observation, watch this video clip and notice how the teacher introduces the process skill of observation to the students. Think about how you would do this with students and what you want to remember about how it worked. Are these students making qualitative or quantitative observations? What questions does the teacher ask to guide the students' observations?

Observing Fruit

EXPLORATION

A.1

Get a piece of fruit. It can be an apple, a blueberry, a cherry, a grape, or even a bell pepper! (Yes! Scientifically, bell peppers are fruits because they contain seeds. The part of the plant that forms to protect the developing seeds is called the fruit. The nonscientific term *vegetable* refers to any fleshy part of the plant that we eat.) Using safe procedures and tools, open your fruit and make observations.
Spend a few minutes observing your piece of fruit. Record your observations.

Reflection Questions:

1. Which senses did you use? Did you use all appropriate senses? How did you determine which senses were appropriate for this task?
2. How did the tools improve your senses? What other tools do you wish you had?
3. Did you make qualitative observations? What characteristics of your fruit did you describe?
4. Did you make quantitative observations? For example, did you count anything about your fruit or *measure* its size in standard or nonstandard units?
5. What changes did you make to your fruit? For example, did you crush it? Cut it? Other actions? What additional observations did that enable you to make?
6. Did you ask *questions* about your fruit that might be investigated through further observations or tests? For example, did you wonder about what happens to the fruit when you cook it? When you keep it for several weeks? Are the seeds edible?
7. How did you *communicate* your observations? Did you make a written list or perhaps a chart or table that might facilitate *comparisons*? Did you include drawings?
8. Are your *recorded* observations detailed enough that someone else reading them could *identify* your fruit if it was mixed with other fruits of the same kind?

Notice the other process skills in italics that are often associated with observing.

of a leaf might be: "It is green, oval shaped, and waxy with a serrated edge." **Quantitative observations** involve numbers, and are based on counting or measurement. They quantify things about the object, organism, or event being observed. A quantitative description of the same leaf might be: "It is 5 cm long with one central vein and 35 points on its serrated edge."

Children use their senses to explore their world from the day they are born—actually earlier. If you visit the infants' section at a toy store, you will find a variety of playthings designed to enable babies to make sounds to hear, feel textures, and look at contrasting colors. In preschool and kindergarten, young learners associate parts of their bodies with their five senses. Their teacher might encourage this with the following statements and questions:

"What do you notice about this?" a kindergarten teacher asks her class as she points to a rock on the table. "Yes, it is a rock. But can you tell me more about it? What color is it? What part of your body tells you that? What else can you learn about it by looking at it?" Then she asks the children, "How could you learn about the rock if your eyes are closed? Which part of your body would you use? What could you find out about it by using that sense?"

Young children tend to observe globally, so they frequently miss potentially relevant details. They often see what they expect to see, and they may focus more on differences than similarities. As they develop skills in observing, children learn to observe for detail, to see what is actually there, and to pay attention to both similarities and differences (Harlen & Jelly, 1990). Other indicators of observation skills, along with classroom examples related to the study of properties of Earth materials, are presented in Table A.1.

Learning to be a good observer is a lifelong task. Observing, like other process skills, is learned more effectively when practiced in the context of lessons designed to teach science concepts, than when taught in isolation. Although Exploration A.1 was intended to introduce you to the science process skill of observing, by observing a piece of fruit you were also gathering information related to LS1.A, the first component idea (Structure and Function) of the first life science disciplinary core idea (From Molecules to

TABLE A.1 Observation Skill Indicators and Example Question-Driven Activities

Indicators of Observation (Listed in order from least to most sophisticated)	Actions and Questions (Related to the study of properties of Earth materials)
Point out obvious ways that two objects look the same and ways that they look different (similarities and differences).	Provide two rock samples, granite and sandstone, ask: How are these two objects alike? How are they different?
Use multiple senses when exploring objects or materials.	Provide a cup of soil, ask: How does this material look? What color is it? Are all of its parts the same color? The same size? How does it feel? Describe its texture and weight. How does it smell? Describe its odor. Does it smell like something else you've experienced before? What? How does it sound when it is poured? (Note: Questions about the sense of taste were not included due to safety issues.)
Identify similarities (characteristics or properties) between objects, even if differences are more obvious.	Provide a spoonful of sand and a sample of obsidian, ask: How are these things alike? What are some other ways that they are the same?
Make enough observations to answer the question or test the hypothesis being investigated.	To answer the investigable question: "Do all rocks sink in water?" provide a varied assortment of rock samples including pumice. Ask: How many rocks will you need to test to answer this question? To test the hypothesis that beans grow faster in potting soil than in sand, provide containers, potting soil, sand, and bean seeds. Ask: How many seeds should you plant in each material? Why? How often should you look at your beans? Why? For how many days should you observe your bean plants? Why?
Use appropriate tools to extend your students' senses.	Provide a fine-grained rock sample such as basalt and a hand lens and/or binocular or digital microscope. Ask: Describe the appearance of the rock's surface. What can you notice now that was not visible with just your eyes?

Indicators of Observation (Listed in order from least to most sophisticated)	Actions and Questions (Related to the study of properties of Earth materials)
Distinguish from your many observations those that best help answer your question and justify your choices.	A rock was found in the school yard. Students collected data about its location, surface features and colors, texture, and general size. Ask: Which observations about the rock will help you determine whether it is igneous or sedimentary? Why?
Ensure that the results obtained are as accurate and precise as they can reasonably be and repeat observations where necessary.	Students are using stream tables to learn about the deposition of sediments. Ask: How will you ensure that your observations are accurate? Will watching the formation of one model river be enough to answer your questions? How can you be confident in your conclusions?

Source: Harlen, 2006.

Organisms: Structures and Processes) (NRC, 2012). In a primary classroom you might encourage children to focus on the external features of this plant part. In an upper elementary classroom, you might suggest that students also look at internal structures of the fruit. These more detailed observations may lead to inferences about the function of the fruit.

Some other ways to help your students become better observers include:

- Providing interesting things to observe.

- Allowing plenty of time for observation.

- Letting students just explore before giving them a task.

- Introducing a similar object to enable comparison, after initial observation. This encourages more detailed examination of the original object.

- Introducing appropriate tools to enable more detailed observation when students are ready to move on.

- Encouraging students to take things apart so they can better observe their parts and how they work.

- Persuading students to talk informally about their observations, since hearing the point of view of others can lead to more careful observing (Harlen, 2006).

Observing may be the most basic science process skill. It is a core skill in most elementary and middle school investigations and is embedded in the practice of most professional scientists. But observation rarely occurs in isolation. Observing is interrelated with other science process skills. It often leads to communicating: recording through writing, drawing, or making charts; and/or discussion among learners. Observing something surprising or interesting frequently generates questions, and then more observations are needed to answer them. Focus on science phenomena and help students generate questions. Then make observations of the properties and characteristics of things to provide the basis for comparing, contrasting, and classifying them. When observations are considered with prior knowledge, inferences can be made. And observations become quantitative observations when measurement is used. Ultimately, the observations will be needed to generate evidence that can be used to answer questions.

Observing is a skill often directly involved in these NGSS Science and Engineering Practices (NGSS Lead States, 2013):

- *Asking questions and defining problems*

- *Developing and using models*

- *Planning and carrying out investigations*

- *Obtaining, evaluating, and communicating information*

Measuring

It is often important in science to quantify observations by measuring. For example, knowing the length of the roots and stems of developing plants and how these variables change from day to day can be important for understanding plant growth (DCI: LS1.B). Accurate measurements not only enhance descriptions, but they can also improve the quality of predictions and explanations of natural phenomena. Measuring makes it possible to compare objects that are far apart, that is, separated in space rather than placed side by side. Exploration A.2 focuses on how important the science process skill of measuring is in our daily lives.

Measuring is based on the processes of observing and comparing that children do naturally (NSRC, 1996). They stand back to back to see who is taller, line up their feet to see whose are longer, or use handy objects like pencils or plastic spoons as nonstandard units to measure length. However, these nonstandard units have a main disadvantage. Because spoons and pencils, as well as children's arm spans and bodies, vary in length, it is difficult to use them to consistently compare objects that cannot be held side by side. Standard units of measure solve this problem.

You may be wondering, "Isn't measurement a topic children learn about in math class?" Certainly it is! In the CCSSM you can examine the Measurement & Data domain to learn what measurement concepts and skills students are expected to master as they progress through the grades.

Even so, according to the National Science Education Standards (NRC, 1996), science lessons at different grade levels can help students learn different aspects of the measuring process. CCSSM encourage increased rigor in conceptual understanding and procedural fluency by expecting students to apply mathematical knowledge in real-world contexts. Science experiences offer many opportunities for such applications.

Correlations between DCIs and CCSSM are included in Appendix L of the Next Generation Science Standards. This tool helps to explain the information about science and math connections presented in the connection box for each NGSS performance expectation. For each grade level, related mathematics content standards are organized by Disciplinary Core Ideas addressed at that grade.

The Next Generation Science Standards were developed with the Common Core State Standards for Mathematics (CCSSM) in mind. Care was taken to assure that measuring concepts and skills needed for students to successfully complete grade-level NGSS Performance Expectations should have been addressed already according to the CCSSM.

Table A.2 summarizes key measurement concepts relevant to science learning and the grade at which they are first expected in CCSSM. Please realize that you may build foundations for concepts by involving your class informally with concepts at earlier grade levels than indicated in Table A.2. For example, even though the concept of volume is not expected to be mastered until fifth grade, in first grade students might compare volumes of different boxes by packing them full of cubic units, then counting the little cubes. Though third graders don't often think of volume as a three-dimensional quantity, they can learn to read the volume of a liquid in a graduated cylinder since they should be able to read a value based on the height of the liquid from the one-dimensional scale displayed as milliliters on the side of the cylinder.

▶ Watch some students using graduated cylinders in an investigation about sound. How is the teacher supporting their measurement skills? What other process skills are addressed in this video clip?

EXPLORATION A.2

Measurement in Your Daily Life

While the TV or radio is tuned to a local news program, walk around your home. Look and listen for measurement tools, references to measurements, and/or units of measure.

Record your findings and ideas on a table like the one that follows. For example, I have an alarm clock in my bedroom. So, I started filling in my table with information about that measuring tool:

Room	Measuring Tool	What It Measures	Units	Use/Importance
Bedroom	Alarm Clock	Time	Hours, minutes, seconds	Wake me up, keep track of the time

Reflection Questions

1. What did you learn from this exploration?
2. What surprised you?
3. How would you summarize your use of measurement tools at home?

TABLE A.2 Key Measurement Concepts for Science Learning

Measurement concepts relevant to science learning	Grade first expected
Describe measurable attributes of objects. (length, weight, etc.) Compare objects based on the same measureable attribute (e.g., longer, tallest, heavier, etc.)	K
Seriation–ordering a set of objects by length Measure lengths indirectly and by iterating length units	1
Standard units of length (e.g., inch, centimeter, etc.) Combine and compare lengths using addition	2
Area Perimeter Problem solving involving measuring and estimating intervals of time, liquid volumes, and masses of objects	3
Converting from a larger unit to a smaller unit in the same system Angles	4
Converting units within a given measurement system Volume	5
Converting units across measurement systems (e.g., inches to cm)	6
Measure attributes derived from two different attributes such as speed (derived by dividing distance by time) or density (derived by dividing mass by volume) Circumference and area of circles	7
Volumes of cones, cylinders, and spheres	8

Source: Based on the Common Core State Standards Writing Team, 2012.

In elementary and middle school science, children should have many opportunities to practice using and reading metric rulers, meter sticks, thermometers, balances, spring scales, timers of various kinds, graduated cylinders, measuring cups, and other measuring instruments. Students must learn both how to use the tools and be able to select the appropriate tool for the situation. Middle school students apply their measurement knowledge and skills in new ways as they investigate quantities that require derived units, such as density, speed, velocity, and acceleration. Algebraic and geometric concepts developed primarily in math classes enable seventh and eighth graders to use angular measurements, work with proportion and scale, and relate units of distance, area, and volume. More sophisticated measuring tools—such as triple-beam balances; temperature, light, and dissolved oxygen probes; pH paper; and GPS devices—may be available to use in laboratory and field experiences. The importance of repeated measurements and issues of experimental error are also considered in middle school science.

Acting as engineers, students might design a device or procedure for measuring an attribute of interest, such as color—through an analysis of pixel values on a digital image. For her eighth-grade Invention Convention project, a girl from Connecticut patented a device to determine if ice on a pond was thick enough to walk on safely! Made of a PVC pipe and a remote-controlled electric motor, the invention indirectly measures ice thickness. When walking on ice is unsafe, activating the motor causes the pipe to rise, alerting the observer of the danger. This happens because the friction between the thin layer of ice and the pipe is too weak to prevent the motor from raising the pipe. As the ice thickens, the friction between the ice layer and the pipe increases, finally keeping the pipe from rising when it is safe to walk on the pond (Musante, 2012).

Measuring is associated with several other science process skills. It enables quantitative observation and more specific communication about data. It provides numerical data for interpretation and analysis and to inform prediction.

Like observing, measuring is a science process skill often directly involved in these NGSS Science and Engineering Practices:

- *Asking questions and defining problems*
- *Developing and using models*
- *Planning and carrying out investigations*
- *Obtaining, evaluating, and communicating information*
- *Analyzing and interpreting data*
- *Using mathematics and computational thinking*

Inferring

An **inference** is an interpretation of observations based on prior knowledge and experiences. You could also think of an inference as a reasonable conclusion or opinion based on known facts or evidence. When inferring, you use experiences and knowledge to fill in gaps about observed events and information. For example, when a skunk sprays, you can observe that it smells bad. But to say that a skunk sprays to protect itself is an inference, a possible explanation based on previous experiences and your observational evidence. Complete Exploration A.3 to gain familiarity with the science process skill of inferring.

In the early 1990s, astronomers announced the discovery of planets orbiting distant stars. These planets were not directly observed, even with telescopes. Some of these exoplanets were discovered when astronomers observed that the brightness of certain stars varied according to a pattern. Based on those observations they inferred that planets orbiting around those stars periodically block the stars' light as seen from Earth.

Inferring doesn't just occur in scientific contexts. When a young woman receives a small box from her boyfriend as a gift, she might infer that inside it is a special piece of jewelry. When you hear sirens, you might infer that an emergency vehicle is nearby, even if you don't see it or know its exact location.

Inferring is an important cognitive skill in both science and in reading. In inquiry science, through firsthand experiences, inferring merges new information gathered through direct observation with the learner's prior knowledge. In reading, inferring is a valued, high-level interpretive skill. New information comes from text resources instead of the senses. In both subjects, the goal is to use evidence to support claims (Douglas et al., 2006).

EXPLORATION

A.3

What Is Inferring?

Four children tilt, rattle, and smell a small box to discover the object inside. As they explore:

Andy says, "It makes a sound like something inside is sliding when the box is tilted long ways."
Bonnie says, "It makes a sound like something inside is rolling when the box is tilted sideways."
Charlie says, "It smells like peppermint."
Doreen says, "I think there's a round piece of candy in the box."

Reflection Questions

1. Which of the students is making an inference instead of an observation about the contents of the box? Why did you select that answer?
2. What is the shape of the object in the box? How do you know?
3. Was your answer to Question 2 an observation or an inference? Why?
4. How would you define inferring?

FIGURE A.1 Where does the moisture on the outside of a glass of ice water come from? What is your evidence?

Inferring can lead to developing understanding of science concepts, such as condensation, which is related to DCI: PS1.A. Moisture sometimes appears on the outside of a glass full of ice water, as is illustrated in Figure A.1. Some people might say, "The glass is sweating." Is this statement an observation or an inference? It is, of course, an inference. Did the moisture on the glass come from inside the glass to the outside (sweating) or from outside the glass (perhaps from water vapor in the air condensing)? What investigations might be carried out to help students decide between the two inferences about the source of the water on the outside of the glass?

One way to gather evidence about where the moisture on the outside of the glass of ice water came from is to put red food coloring in the water. Then when moisture forms, check it carefully for any hint of red. The observation that the moisture contains no sign of red supports the inference that it likely came from the air surrounding the glass, rather than from the water in the glass.

Scientific inferences are based on observations and prior knowledge. Children often experience difficulties in distinguishing between their observations and their inferences (NRC, 2007). Encourage your students to explicitly state the observations and prior knowledge on which their inferences are based. When they claim that a statement is an observation, you might ask, "What sense did you use in making that observation?" When they draw inferences, you might ask: "What is your evidence?" and "Why do you think so?" Helping children distinguish between observations (evidence of the senses) and inferences (conclusions based on evidence) is important to their understanding of science.

Inferring is most obvious in the following Science and Engineering Practices:

- *Asking question and defining problems*
- *Developing and using models*
- *Constructing explanations and designing solutions*
- *Engaging in argument from evidence*

Classifying

When **classifying**, you organize objects according to their common properties (characteristics, attributes, or features). Classification can result in the formation of groups of objects or putting things in order. Classifying things requires not only that you observe properties but also that you look for relationships among the properties. This enhances your understanding of the structure and function of the things. Also, placing an object or organism within a group means you already know something about it, if you are familiar with the characteristics of the group. Additionally, grouping things with other things gives you an added way to search for information about them by direct observation, in the library, or online (National Aquarium in Baltimore, 1997).

Sometimes things are classified on the basis of single properties that are directly observed by the senses. Classification depends on students' abilities to make comparisons using their senses. For older students, they also become proficient at contrasting as a skill that supports their ability to classify. For example, using your sense of sight, you can sort autumn leaves by their color or sort rocks by their size into the categories of boulders, pebbles, and gravel. Which senses let you sort the coins by different properties in Exploration A.4?

EXPLORATION A.4

Classifying Coins

Find 10 coins. It doesn't matter what their denomination is or how many of each you have. Drop them on the table. Do not turn any of the coins over during this activity, just slide them into groups.

- Sequence your coins in order based on one property. Record your sequence and identify the property on which it was based.
- Sort your coins into groups. Record the categories you used.
- Make a list of all the ways you can separate the coins into just two distinct groups.

Reflection Questions

1. Were all of the ways you organized coins, examples of classification? Why or why not?
2. What strategies did you use to sequence the coins? Why did you select that approach?
3. What strategies did you use to sort the coins? Why did you select that approach?
4. How is sequencing different than grouping or sorting?
5. How many different ways can the coins be separated into just two distinct groups?

Classification can be based on recognition of certain features. For example: the side of a coin can be classified as heads or tails based on the imprint that shows; monarch butterflies can be classified as male or female based on the color patterns on their wings. Some organisms and materials can be classified according to how they behave. Animals that are active during the day are known as diurnal, while those that are active at night are classified as nocturnal. Materials are classified as solids, liquids, or gasses based on how they fill a container.

Some things are classified based on the results of a test. For example, children can learn more about magnetism by sorting objects into piles based on whether or not they are attracted to magnets. They can learn more about the properties of density and buoyancy by sorting objects based on whether or not they float when placed in water. Liquids can be classified as acids or bases based on the color change of litmus paper, or they can be arranged in order by acidity based on the color change of pH paper.

Sequencing, or serial ordering, is a simple form of classifying that involves placing objects in order by a given property. Students can line up by height or by age. Coins can be put in order by their diameter, thickness, mass, value, date minted, etc. Toy cars can be ordered by how quickly they crossed the finish line after rolling down a ramp. Photographs taken at different stages during the growth of a plant can be sequenced or put in order by date.

Classification systems clarify relationships between and among individual or groups of things. The same set of objects may be sorted in multiple ways; which method is best depends on what property is deemed most important to consider (Settlage & Southerland, 2012). If you were investigating birds' diets, which of these characteristics would you select to group a variety of birds: feather color, length of wings, shape of beak, size of eyes? Because birds use their beaks to eat, beak shape seems to be a relevant characteristic to use.

Special ways of classifying often introduced in elementary science are binary and multistage classification. In a **binary classification system**, a set of objects is divided into two groups on the basis of whether each object has a particular property. For example, you could classify a set of buttons into two groups based on the number of holes they have. One group might consist of all the buttons that have four holes; the other group would be made up of all buttons that do not have four holes.

In a **multistage classification system**, the objects in the original set are sorted again and again so that a hierarchy of sets and subsets is formed. For example, the four-hole buttons in our example of binary classification might be further classified as being round or not round. Four-hole round buttons might then be classified as being plastic or not plastic. Figure A.2 shows an example of a multistage classification of button properties.

Buttons were used in the previous examples of classification systems because of their simplicity. They don't have much to do with any science concepts, but they are familiar objects that are easy to describe. Buttons are also a technology—an object, system, or process designed to solve a problem. So their use in introducing classification is easily justifiable in a STEM lesson.

Focusing on similar properties in classifying can lead to understandings about the most significant properties of objects and their functions. For example, a focus on the four-hole property of buttons might lead to a question about why some buttons have four holes and others do not. What is the function of the holes? Do buttons without holes have some characteristics that substitute for the holes (such as another

FIGURE A.2   **A Multistage Classification of Button Properties**

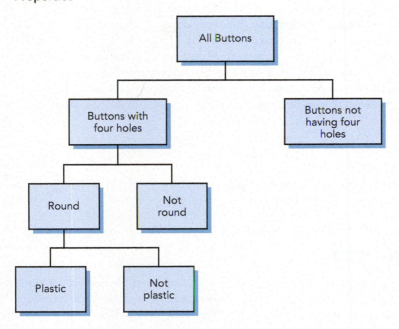

means to attach them to garments)? Think about what science ideas your students might discover through classifying shells, minerals, rocks, seeds, plants, insects, even circuits or writing tools.

Dichotomous keys, used to identify objects or organisms, are based on multistage classification systems. The word *dichotomous* means divided into two parts. In a dichotomous key, a series of steps, each with two choices, leads the user to the name of an item. Figure A.3 shows a group of leaves and a dichotomous key to identify them. It is important to note that keys are created by people and only help us to identify a specific group of objects or organisms for which they were created. In that respect they are changeable and they won't work for other objects.

The process of classifying seems to come naturally to some young children. Without being explicitly taught to do so, some toddlers organize blocks by color or shape as part of their play. It seems that they want to create some kind of order in their world. Students are expected to understand and use more complex skills of classification as they progress through the grade levels.

FIGURE A.3   **Leaves to Identify Using a Dichotomous Key**

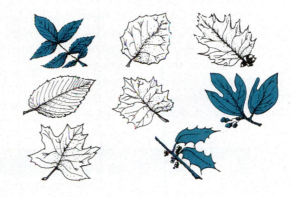

1. Is it a compound leaf?	Yes—It is Ash. No—Go to question 2.
2. Is the leaf lobed?	Yes—It is Sassafras. No—Go to question 3.
3. Is its base symmetrical?	Yes—Go to question 4. No—It is Elm.
4. Is its leaf margin spined?	Yes—It is Holly. No—It is Aspen.

Patterns, one of the crosscutting concepts in the *Framework*, is related to the process skill of classification. The *Framework* states, "Observed patterns of forms and events guide organization and classification, and they prompt questions about relationships and the factors that influence them" (NRC, 2012, p. 84).

Classification relies on observation. The properties of objects, organisms, and events must be observed before they can be compared or contrasted. Things can be classified based on their measurements. Observed similarities and differences form the basis for classification—both sorting and sequencing. Questions often arise after classifying things. Shared properties within groups can lead to inferences about all members of that group. Again, the interrelationship of process skills is apparent. You are most likely to use the science process skill, classifying, while engaging in the following Science and Engineering Practices:

- *Asking questions and defining problems*
- *Analyzing and interpreting data*
- *Using mathematics and computational thinking*
- *Constructing explanations and designing solutions*

Questioning

Questioning is a very important science process skill; one that is obviously a component of the Science and Engineering Practice, *Asking Questions (for science) and Defining Problems (for engineering)*. "Science begins with a question about a phenomenon, such as 'Why is the sky blue?' or 'What causes cancer?' and seeks to develop hypotheses that can provide explanatory answers to such questions. A basic practice of the scientist is formulating empirically answerable **questions** about phenomena, establishing what is already known, and determining what questions have yet to be satisfactorily answered" (NRC, 2012, p. 50).

Many science questions arise from phenomena that have been observed in the world around us.

Vignette A.1　Wondering about Cats

During their study of pets, Ms. Scruggs arranged to have a cat, trained as a companion animal, visit her third-grade class. As the children observed and discussed the cat, Ms. Scruggs suggested making a class "We Notice/We Wonder" chart on the board. She had used this strategy with these students before. She labeled the left column of this two-column chart "We Notice . . . " In this column, she wrote students' observations and discoveries as they interacted with the cat. She labeled the right column "We Wonder . . . " In this column, she recorded questions that students mentioned as they observed the cat. After a few minutes, the chart looked like this:

Ms. Scruggs congratulated the class for wondering about some very interesting things and then asked, "How could we answer the questions we wonder about?"

Through discussion the class decided that:

- Questions 1, 4, and 6 might be answered through library or internet research.
- We need to talk to the owner of the cat's parents to answer question 2.

We Notice . . .	We Wonder . . .
The cat's fur is black and white.	1. Are most cats black and white?
	2. Were this cat's parents black and white?
	3. What fraction of this cat's fur is each color?
The pupils of the cat's eyes change shape as the brightness of the room changes.	4. Why do the cat's eyes look different than human eyes? Why do they change based on the brightness of the light?
The cat purrs when I pet him.	5. Does petting make the cat happy or angry?
	6. How does the cat make that noise?

(continued)

- For question 3, we could take pictures of the cat, then put a grid over the pictures and count how many squares there are of each color to estimate what fraction of his fur is black and what fraction is white.
- For question 5, we would have to know how a cat looks and behaves when it is happy and when it is angry and then watch the cat when we pet it.

Mrs. Scruggs then pointed to a previously introduced term on the word wall—*investigable question*—and asked the class, "Are any of the questions we are wondering about *investigable*?"

A student raised her hand, "Yes! Questions 3 and 5 are investigable because we could figure out an answer on our own and give reasons why our answer makes sense."

Another student offered, "All of the rest of the questions are *noninvestigable*; we couldn't really answer them by ourselves in the classroom without asking for or looking up information."

Vignette A.1 illustrates how observation of even everyday events can lead to questions, some of which can be answered by applying science process skills. But it is not just students who come up with questions this way. In 2010, four engineers published a scientific paper describing their answer to the age-old question, "How do cats drink?" During breakfast one morning, one of the researchers noticed his cat lapping, which led to questions for investigation and a multiyear project (Wade, 2010).

Children wonder about many things, and they can ask many questions. But which questions can be investigated through their own activities? Generally, *why* questions are noninvestigable. Vignette A.2 focuses on a class trying to develop investigable questions about how the Amazon River changes its course over time.

Vignette A.2   The Twisting River

While Mr. Moss, a sixth-grade teacher, was developing a unit about landforms, he located a satellite image that shows part of the Amazon Rain Forest.

He thought this phenomenon would engage his students in figuring out more about a middle school DCI element, ESS2.C.5 - *Water's movements—both on the land and underground—cause weathering and erosion, which change the land's surface features and create underground formations.* Its content is graphically illustrated in Figure A.4.

FIGURE A.4

Mr. Moss projected the image on the whiteboard so the whole class could see it. He asked his class: "What do you think this is?", then allowed several minutes for the students to talk about their ideas with their tablemates.

Ideas that were generated included: "We think it's a map with a squiggly line drawn on it in chalk"; "It must be a map because it has a distance scale in the corner"; "We think it's a picture of part of Earth's surface taken from space"; "Well, if it is a satellite image it must show someplace with lots of vegetation; see how green it is"; "Look, there are some labels on the picture"; "I think the term oxbow lake has something to do with rivers"; and "Isn't *Rio* the Spanish word for river? Maybe that white squiggle is what a river in a Spanish-speaking country looks like from space."

"What great ideas," said Mr. Moss, "you are looking at an image of part of the Amazon Rain Forrest and that white feature is the Amazon River."

Erin asked, "Why is the river such a weird shape?"

Mr. Moss replied, "That's a good question, but how will we figure out the explanation?"

Jorge jumped into the conversation, "Oh yeah, remember last week when Mr. Moss said *why* questions are usually hard to answer through direct investigation. We should try to come up with some questions that are more investigable."

(continued)

The class generated the following related questions that led to investigations which should help them figure out an explanation for the twisty river phenomenon and better understand the targeted disciplinary core idea element:

- How does running water affect soil?
- What erosion patterns are caused by running water?
- What factors affect the rate of erosion?

- What determines the direction that water flows?
- What factors affect the shape of a river?
- Which sediments are moved furthest by moving water?
- What other rivers look like this from space?
- How could we make a model that demonstrates how rivers become so twisty?

▶ Watch a fifth grade class use pinhole viewers to investigate how light travels.

With your help, children can learn to improve their questioning skills. As you emphasize the importance of questions for investigation, ask the students how they could investigate the questions they ask. Also guide them to reformulate some of the questions they ask, and provide them many good models of scientific questions.

For example, a science textbook might state that "Light travels in straight lines." Students might wonder, *Why does light travel in straight lines*? It would be difficult, if not impossible, for children to answer this *why question* from their own investigations. You can help them develop a related question that can be investigated, by asking "How could you investigate how light travels?" You could focus the discussion even further by asking, "What evidence would support the claim that light travels in straight lines?" Students could construct pinhole viewers, then investigate this question: "What happens to the image of an arrow when seen in a pinhole viewer?" Writing this focus question in their science notebooks or journals helps the students to clarify their purposes and keep those purposes in mind as they continue to investigate. The observation that the image on the screen of a pinhole viewer is inverted leads to the inference that light travels in straight lines. Ray diagrams can help students visualize how light travels through the pinhole. Both the observation of the inverted image and the diagram that models the phenomenon support the claim that light travels in straight lines.

▶ At the onset of a classroom inquiry on earthworms, fourth-grade teacher Glen McKnight asks students to generate questions they hope to answer during their study of earthworms. Make a list of the questions students ask. Why did McKnight reformulate the question on earthworms' hearts?

Asking questions related to the world around us and recognizing that different questions are answered in different ways are important skills for *doing science*. Questions that lead to inquiry-based investigations might develop from everyday experiences, other hands-on activities, the results of another investigation, information from books or electronic sources, teacher demonstrations, or even lectures if they relate to students' experience and interest (NRC, 1996).

Good questions for initiating inquiry:

- lead to interesting new knowledge about the world.
- lead to a deeper understanding of the nature of science and scientific understanding.
- require students to gather observable evidence and use it with developing knowledge to generate answers.
- require a variety of science processes to answer them.
- may require students to
    - observe, compare, and classify objects and organisms.
    - infer and predict.
    - identify and measure variables.
    - plan and conduct controlled experiments.

Questioning is a science process skill also recognized as a key part of the first NGSS Science and Engineering Practice: *Asking questions and defining problems* (NGSS Lead States, 2013). Questioning is a skill that often applied in the other seven SEPs as well. Think about the questions students might ask when:

- *Developing and using models*
- *Planning and carrying out investigations*
- *Analyzing and interpreting data*
- *Using mathematics and computational thinking*

- *Constructing explanations and designing solutions*
- *Engaging in argument from evidence*
- *Obtaining, evaluating, and communicating information.*

Communicating

Communicating is a science process skill that is clearly evident in the Science and Engineering Practice: *Obtaining, evaluating and communicating information.* **Communicating** collectively refers to the recording, organizing, and reporting of observations, measurements, experiments, findings, and conclusions. The skill of communicating is considered necessary for students to complete the process of conceptual change. This idea is explored more deeply in Chapter 4: Learning Science with Understanding. According to the *Benchmarks for Science Literacy,* "An important part of students' explorations is telling others what they see, what they think, and what it makes them wonder about. Children should have lots of time to talk about what they observe and to compare their observations with others" (American Association for the Advancement of Science, 1993, p. 10). In addition to oral discourse (on-topic speaking and listening for the purpose of creating understanding), communications might take the form of drawings, written reports, journal entries, data tables, graphs, emails, blogs, websites, digital presentations, videos, and podcasts. Children might even use music, art, and role playing to communicate their understanding. Do you want to talk about the need for communication to help students complete the process of conceptual change? It is also what scientists do. There is a chance to reinforce that idea across these process skills.

When students inquire, their questions, investigations, observations, and explanations or conclusions might be communicated through a science journal or notebook. The written records should be developed as the investigation unfolds, with questions, data, and conclusions recorded.

The OWL chart is a tool for student recording and reflection. OWL stands for I Observe, I Wonder, and I Learn. It is another useful organizer, similar to the *We notice . . . , We wonder . . . chart* you read about previously. Figure A.5 shows you both organizers side by side.

The We Notice/We Wonder chart, introduced earlier, is a useful organizer for some science recording. Look back at it to examine its structure. Notice that the left column of this two-column chart is labeled "We Notice . . . " In this column, students write their observations and discoveries as they explore objects, organisms, and events. Notice that the right column is labeled "We Wonder . . . " In this column, students write questions that come to mind as they are exploring. These questions can lead to further inquiry investigations. Individual students might create I Notice/I Wonder charts when not working in groups.

Scientists keep accurate records of data collected, so they are prepared to recall data taken, make comparisons of the data, draw inferences, make predictions, and analyze their data to generate explanations. For similar reasons, students should also keep accurate records.

During an inquiry-based activity, you should provide time for students to record their findings. Recording data will be a natural part of the work of some students; other students will need encouragement to stop and record their findings. Initially allow the students to use their own methods of recording data. Many will use sentences in making records. If so, encourage them to also use labeled drawings and lists (Fulton & Campbell, 2014).

> ▶ Watch some fourth graders creating I notice . . . /I wonder . . . charts in their science notebooks as they investigate melting ice cubes in stream tables. How does this approach help to engage the students in their learning?

FIGURE A.5 OWL Chart and We Notice/We Wonder Student Reflection Tools

OWL Chart			We Notice.../We Wonder...Chart	
I Observe	I Wonder	I Learn	We Notice	We Wonder

After discussions with the class about which of their observations are likely to be useful in answering the focus question and which are likely to be less useful, you might prepare a data sheet for students to fill in. Over time, with practice and appropriate scaffolding, students will be able to develop their own data tables.

When developing explanations, students should use writing and drawing to connect their observations with new conceptions and explanations that are developed through discussion or introduced by the teacher. Through writing, students make their thinking visible, both to themselves and to teachers (Fulton & Campbell, 2014). Writing helps students to reflect on their data, offer their own interpretations, and better understand the new conceptions and explanation given by teachers. Further, writing gives teachers an important performance product to use in formative assessment.

Some ways that you might help your students develop communication, reporting, argumentation, and reflection skills as they are learning science (Harlen, 2006) include:

- Organize your class so that students can work and discuss in small groups.

- Make science talk and meaning-making discussion, along with data collection and informal recording (perhaps in science notebooks), part of the planned structure of science investigations.

- Allow time for records to be made and used in reporting and reflecting.

- Introduce a variety of techniques for recording and communicating results, such as charts, tables, graphs, labeled diagrams, and other graphic organizers.

- Discuss the appropriateness of ways of organizing and presenting information for particular purposes and audiences. Help students be clear about whether they are communicating to share data and evidence, or present reasoning and explanations.

In science activities, once data have been obtained, they must be organized and interpreted. Data tables and graphs are common means of displaying data. Data tables typically display data in columns and rows. This organization can help you identify patterns within qualitative data. In Chapter 2, Table 2.8 shows an example of a data table used in an investigation of white powders. Data tables are also used to organize quantitative data. However, putting measurement data into graphs better enables students to discover relationships and patterns that help them make sense of the data. Graphs also facilitate the construction of inferences based on data.

The types of graphs most often used in scientific applications in elementary and middle schools are bar graphs, histograms, and line graphs. As a teacher, it is important that you know their characteristics, their similarities and differences, and when each of them is appropriate to use when graphing data. Graphs and tables are ways of displaying data, organizing it visually to make it easier to analyze and interpret.

Bar graphs display the number of things in various, discrete categories. The relative lengths of the bars make it easy to compare the numbers in each category.

For example, during their study of types of animals, a kindergarten class constructed a bar graph about their pets (see Figure A.6). Notice that the types of pets the children have are listed along the bottom line. The order of the pet type categories doesn't matter, so they could be arranged alphabetically, by size, or just randomly from left to right. Each category is discrete, separate from the next. For example, an included pet might be a turtle or a hamster, but there are no hamster-turtles. The number scale on the

FIGURE A.6   Bar Graph of Pets

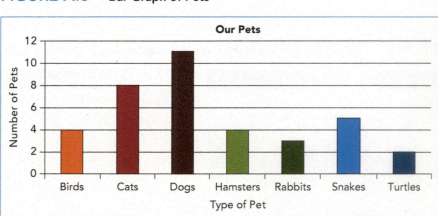

left side of the graph simplifies finding out how many of each kind of animal the class has. From this bar graph, it is easy to see the types of pets the children in this class have. This graph also shows that if everyone brought their pets to school, there would be eight cats in the classroom, there would be more pet dogs than pet cats, and there would be twice as many birds as turtles.

Bar graphs are normally constructed on grid paper. The categories on bar graphs are usually listed along the bottom line, known as the *horizontal axis* or *x-axis*. Because the categories are *discrete* (not sequential or dependent on each other), their order along the axis doesn't matter. The line on the left, known as the *vertical axis* or the *y-axis,* is a number line that starts at zero at the *origin* (where the x-axis and y-axis intersect), with numbers on the horizontal grid lines, increasing as the axis extends upwards. The intervals between the numbers should represent equal values, but counting by any convenient number is fine as long as the scale is consistent. A title and clearly labeled axes are important parts of a bar graph.

Simple bar graphing is typically introduced in kindergarten, with the teacher constructing a class graph based on data from the children. In first grade, students become more involved with whole-class graphing and begin to construct bar graphs on their own, with teacher assistance. Bar graphs are not just associated with the primary grades, however. Their appropriate use depends on the variables being graphed. For example, a seventh-grade class that has been surveying the woods beside their school might construct a bar graph to illustrate the number of various species of trees found in the study area. The graph shows a concise picture of the biodiversity in their woods, which could support students' understanding of LS4.D (Core Concept—Biological evolution: Unity and diversity; Component Idea—Biodiversity and humans).

Histograms display the *number of times* a *number event* occurs in a large set. They are used to represent the frequency of occurrence of quantified data. Vignette A.3 presents an example of the use of a histogram by a class that grew tomatoes.

Vignette A.3   Tomato Data

Some sixth graders were harvesting tomatoes from their school garden. They noticed a great variety in the size of tomatoes when they ripened (first turned bright red on the plant). The students considered measuring the diameter or the circumference of each ripe tomato, but realized their irregular shapes might complicate that approach. They had just learned about *mass* as a measure of the amount of matter, so they decided to measure the mass of each tomato they picked. As soon as each tomato was red enough to be judged ripe by the harvesters, they used a balance to measure the mass of each tomato to the nearest gram, recorded their data in a table, then constructed the histogram (shown in Figure A.7) summarizing the frequency of different masses of the tomatoes harvested.

FIGURE A.7   Histogram of Ripe Tomato Masses

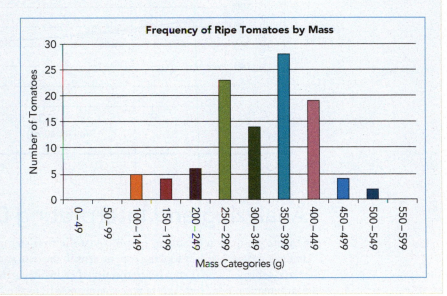

Histograms differ from bar graphs in that the *x*-axis on a bar graph simply names a category, while the *x*-axis on a histogram is a number line representing a continuous variable. Histograms are similar to simple bar graphs except that each bar represents a range of values rather than just a single category.

A familiar example of data that might be displayed in a histogram is how many students made each grade on a test. All possible scores are arranged in a number line on the *x*-axis; the width of the bars is based on the scores that yield each letter grade; the *frequencies,* or number of occurrences, of grades are arranged in a number line on the *y*-axis. Once the data is plotted, you can quickly see the distribution of letter grades in the class.

Line graphs are more advanced; they are typically introduced in fourth or fifth grade. With line graphs, your students can graphically show numerical data about variables that are continuous. A line graph displays visually the changes in a **responding** or **dependent variable** in an investigation corresponding to changes in the values of a **manipulated** or **independent variable**.

As an example, consider Vignette A.4 that describes an investigation about the rate of cooling of a sample of hot water contained in an uncovered Styrofoam cup.

Vignette A.4　Water Temperature Data

Students wanted to find out how the temperature of the water varies with time. The students began with a cup of hot water. They measured the initial temperature of the water and then measured the temperature every five minutes as the water cooled. Figure A.8 shows the line graph constructed from their data.

By analyzing the graph, the class concluded that the temperature decreased in a regular (predictable) way with time. Then the teacher demonstrated how they could use the graph to predict the temperature of the water at different times.

FIGURE A.8　**Graph of how the temperature of water changes with time as the water cools.** The small squares represent the water temperature each time it was measured, then a best-fit curve was drawn to show the cooling trend over time.

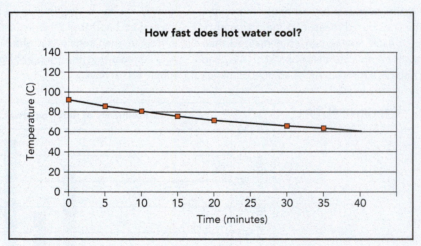

Analyzing and Interpreting Data

Organizing data in a table or graph is just the first step in making sense of the data. The next step, analyzing data, involves looking for patterns in the data such as similarities, disparities trends, and other relationships. The last step is interpreting data, which is thinking about what the patterns might mean. Mathematical concepts and practices appropriate to the learners' grade level are often applied when analyzing data, especially statistical approaches. Starting in the lower grades, students look for values in the data that are the highest or lowest (at the extremes) and identify relationships between data points, such as greater than, less than, and equal. In upper elementary grades, students learn to describe a set of data by determining the range, the mode, and the median. Students in middle school learn to calculate the mean, determine quartiles, identify outliers, and find a line or curve of best fit and describe correlations (TeacherVision, 2015).

Look back at the graphs presented earlier and consider how they might be analyzed. Remember, data can be looked at in many ways; scientists and students typically apply multiple approaches to data analysis.

After the data is analyzed, it must be interpreted. Connections must be made between what the data shows and what is known about the science behind the phenomenon being studied.

Analyzing and interpreting data is a science process skill that is also one of the NGSS Science and Engineering Practices (NGSS Lead States, 2013): *Analyzing and interpreting data.*

Predicting

It is often important in science to predict future occurrences. A **prediction** is a forecast of a future outcome based on initial observations, knowledge of patterns and relationships in data. Predictions look forward to what might happen. Inferences, in contrast, look backward; as explained earlier, inferences are types of explanations of what has already happened.

Predictions are greatly enhanced when measurement data is organized into graphs to illustrate a trend. For example, look again at the graph in Figure A.8. Even though the students did not plot the temperature of the water after 25 minutes or after 40 minutes, they could use the best fit line from the first trial to predict the water temperature at those times if they repeat the investigation. They could simply draw vertical lines up from the 25- and 40-minute marks on the x-axis until they each intersect the *line-of-best-fit* drawn based on the existing data. Then they could draw horizontal lines left to the y-axis to find their intersections on the temperature scale. A reasonable prediction for the temperature after 25 minutes is about 104°F, while a reasonable prediction for the temperature after 40 minutes is about 90°F. Some estimation from the graph is necessary in both cases. The first prediction in this example is called an **interpolation** because it is between (*inter-*) available data points; the second prediction is called an **extrapolation** because it is outside (*extra-*) the collected data points.

Figure A.9 presents a sample test item involving predicting. The item is from the National Assessment of Educational Progress (NAEP) for grade 4, but it is like those that might appear on statewide tests. It might help you appreciate how helpful line graphs can be when making predictions.

To answer the question in Figure A.9, students would first determine the trend of the data from the data table, that the air temperature increases about 1° or 2°C every hour. From this pattern, they could then predict that the temperature at 12:00 noon would be closest to 25°C, which is answer choice C.

FIGURE A.9   A Sample Test Item for Assessing Skills in Predicting
Sample Test Item. It is a cloudless, sunny day. A student measures the temperature of the air outside every hour. She collects the following data.

Time	Air Temperature
8:00 a.m.	18°C
9:00 a.m.	19°C
10:00 a.m.	21°C
11:00 a.m.	23°C

What will the air temperature outside most likely be at noon?

A.   18°C

B.   21°C

C.   25°C

D.   32°C

Source: National Assessment of Educational Progress (NAEP) released test item, grade 4, 2005.

Or they could construct a line graph of the data, then use the procedure for extrapolating described in the water cooling example.

Like other science process skills, students' prediction skills develop over the years through multiple experiences and practice. The following list, based on Harlen's work (2006), describes some indicators of developing predicting skills:

- Young children try to make predictions based on preconceived ideas. For example, if they think that plants continue to grow bigger over time, they may predict that a tomato plant will eventually become the size of a tree if they wait long enough.

- As their understanding of prediction improves, children begin to realize that a prediction is not just a guess. A child might say, "I don't know what is going to happen to that crystal if it gets wet. I've never seen one like that before! I would just be guessing."

- With more experience children tend to use evidence from previous experiences to make more meaningful predictions. A child who remembers seeing a rainbow after a rainstorm may tell an adult, "We need to get ready to watch for the rainbow" the next time the weather is rainy.

- Reasonable predictions begin to emerge when students understand a science concept well enough to have formed a hypothesis about the idea. A child who understands that if something is made of metal it is a good conductor of electricity will be able to make valid predictions about which objects can be used to complete an open circuit and cause the bulb to light.

- Development of prediction skills improve as students recognize patterns in their observations and base predictions on those patterns. A student involved in a moon phase project who notices the crescent moon in the evening sky appearing to grow a little more illuminated (more of the moon is visible) each night could accurately draw how the moon will look on the next few nights.

- Further development is obvious when that student can also explain the reasoning behind her drawings. "I could predict the moon's appearance in the future because I've been watching it, and two nights ago it was skinny like this [pointing to a thin crescent drawing], and last night it was fatter like this [pointing to a drawing of a more robust crescent]. So, I just extended that pattern in my drawings and made my predicted moons a little fatter each night."

- Their ability to use relevant science concepts to justify a prediction is an indication that children possess fairly sophisticated prediction skills. "Because plants do photosynthesis and use energy from the sun to grow, I predict that the plants on the windowsill will grow bigger and better than those in the windowless, dark storage closet."

Work through Exploration A.5 to practice distinguishing predictions from other types of science-related statements.

EXPLORATION

A.5

Identifying Predictions

Which of the statements listed below are probably predictions?
- That black bear sighted in the town square today weighs at least a ton.
- Based on my gas gauge reading, I don't need to stop for gasoline before I go home tonight.
- Since he is walking, that toddler probably is at least one-year-old.
- The meteorologist forecasts a foot of snow in this region for next Tuesday.
- The population of this city will double in ten years.
- I hope it rains tomorrow, so I don't need to water the grass.

Reflection Questions

1. Why did you select the statements you did?
2. What is your operational definition of a prediction?

Predicting is another cognitive skill that is used in both science and literacy instruction. Prediction builds commitment to learning, since it gives both scientists and readers a stake in the results. It gives students a purpose to either continue investigating or reading to find out if their prediction turns out to be correct (Douglas et al., 2006).

Like other science process skills, predicting is closely linked with others. Scientists typically base their predictions on their hypotheses. Then they conduct experiments to see if their predictions are accurate. If they are, the hypothesis is "supported" and may be verified in future investigations. If the predictions are not accurate, the hypothesis is "not supported" by the results of the experiment.

Predicting is a science process skill often directly involved in these NGSS Science and Engineering Practices (NGSS Lead States, 2013): *Developing and using models* and *Planning and carrying out investigations*.

Hypothesizing

The process of formulating and testing hypotheses is one of the core activities of scientific investigations. A **hypothesis** is a prediction based on observations suggesting a possible answer to a scientific question that can be studied through investigation. "The term 'hypothesis' is used by scientists for an idea that may contribute important explanations to the development of a scientific theory. Scientists use and test hypotheses in the development and refinement of models and scenarios that collectively serve as tools in the development of a theory" (Michaels, Shouse, & Schweingruber, 2008, p. 5). In K–8 science classrooms, all investigations should start with a scientific question, but do not always need a hypothesis. Hypotheses really don't apply to engineering design activities.

Hypotheses are often stated in an *if . . . then* form. For example,

If more magnets are added to the magnets stack, *then* more washers will stick to the stack.

If more weights are added to the bottom of the string, *then* the pendulum will make more cycles in 15 seconds.

Hypotheses guide scientists in choosing what data to collect, what available data to pay attention to, what additional data to seek, and possible ways to interpret the data in an investigation. To be useful, a hypothesis should suggest what observational evidence would support it and what evidence would refute it.

To test a hypothesis, students will typically need to conduct a controlled experiment. For example, suppose children wonder how the temperature of water affects the time for an effervescent tablet to dissolve in it. They hypothesize, "If the water is warmer, a tablet will dissolve in it more quickly." To test this hypothesis, the children conduct an investigation in which the temperature of the water is systematically varied. They decide to use water temperatures of 40°F, 60°F, and 80°F. Then, they measure the time for the tablet to completely dissolve for each temperature. All other variables, such as the type of container, the volume of water, and the size and type of tablet, remain fixed. Then they analyze the data to see whether or not the hypothesis is supported.

Formal hypothesizing is often introduced in middle school science classrooms. But the ideas that lead to this skill begin at earlier grades, when students begin to try to explain something in terms of other factors that affect it. A child's statement, "If the sun has already set, then night has started," is an example of this kind of thinking. Children go through stages of explaining things by referring to related experiences or naming (or blaming) specific ideas without really understanding them (e.g., "Gravity made me fall down!"). Sometimes children suggest a possible cause for something that could not be easily tested or verified (e.g., "My goldfish died because it didn't like the other fish in the bowl"). As their hypothesizing skills develop, students come to realize that more than one explanation fits the evidence. A boy who has been gaining weight might explain the cause of this problem in any or all of these ways: "I eat too much." "I don't eat the right foods." "I don't get enough exercise." Or "My parents are overweight, too." Eventually, with enough practice and appropriate teacher support, students start developing testable hypotheses that explain why things that they observe happen (e.g., "That swing goes faster because its chains are shorter. If I make the chains on both swings the same length, they will both move back and forth at the same rate"). Hopefully, these students will come to realize, like practicing scientists, that explanations are tentative and that they might be found inadequate and in need of change when scientists collect new evidence in the future.

Before you watch the video, think about what you understand about providing controlled experiments for students. How do the students know that it is a fair test? Seventh-grade students have been asked to design an experiment to determine what affects the frequency of a simple pendulum. Why can't students figure out if the length, weight, or angle affects the pendulum's frequency? How do the teacher's questions assist student thinking?

Hypothesizing is a science process skill typically involved in these NGSS Science and Engineering Practices (NGSS Lead States, 2013):

- *Developing and using models*
- *Planning and carrying out investigations*
- *Constructing explanations and designing solutions*

Experimenting

An experiment is more than a hands-on science activity. When experimenting, scientists or students control circumstances deliberately and precisely to obtain evidence to test hypotheses and arrive at explanations. By varying just one condition in the experiment, scientists and students can hope to identify its effects on what happens, uncomplicated by changes in other conditions (American Association for the Advancement of Science, 1990). Elementary school students seem to understand controlled experiments better when they think of them as **fair tests**.

Controlled experiments involve (1) deliberately changing one variable at a time, (2) observing the effect on another variable, while (3) holding all other variables constant. A controlled investigation might be used to answer questions such as these:

- What factors affect the rate of swing of a pendulum?
- How does adding compost to potting soil affect plant growth?
- Which brand of paper towel is the best buy, considering such factors as absorbency, wet strength, quality, and cost per sheet?

Working with variables is a particularly important part of experimenting. A **variable** is a property of objects or events that can change, has variations, or has differing amounts. The changing height and weight of a growing child, the time a candle can burn under a glass jar, and the amount of rainfall in a day are all examples of variables. The different colors of children's shoes is also an example of a variable.

Three types of variables are important in scientific investigations:

- An **independent variable** (also called a **manipulated variable**) is a variable that the experimenter deliberately changes or manipulates in an investigation.
- A **dependent variable** (also called a **responding variable**) is a variable that changes in an investigation in response to changes in the independent variable. You could say that the dependent variable "depends" on the independent variable.
- **Controlled variables** are variables that are deliberately kept constant or unchanged in an investigation in order not to confound the results—that is, so the investigation is a fair test.

Vignette A.5 illustrates experimenting and the three types of variables.

Table A.3 gives the meaning and examples of each of the three types of variables in the sunlight absorption experiment.

TABLE A.3   Definitions and Examples of Types of Variables

Variable Type	Definition	Example
Independent or Manipulated	Variable that is deliberately changed	Color of paper wrapped around the cans in color and sunlight absorption investigation
Dependent or Responding	Variable that responds to manipulated changes	Change in temperature of the water in each can
Controlled variable	Variable that remains unchanged in an experiment	Type of container; amount of water in each can; time each can was left in sunlight

Most of the other science process skills are embedded in experimentation. How many can you find in Vignette A.5?

When students are experimenting, all of the NGSS Science and Engineering Practices (NGSS Lead States, 2013) are likely to be involved, with the possible exception of *Developing and using models*.

Vignette A.5   Sunlight Absorption Experiment

The students in a fifth-grade class wondered why NASA chose white as the color for astronauts' space suits. Several students thought the reason might relate to the sunlight absorbed by the space suit. Challenged by the teacher, the students reformulated their question to: "Do different-colored materials absorb sunlight differently?" The teacher then guided the students as they designed and carried out a controlled experiment to help answer their question.

Working in cooperative groups, each team took two identical, empty vegetable cans and wrapped one with black construction paper and the other with white construction paper, filled the cans with equal amounts of water, and placed them side by side in sunlight for a period of time. What were the manipulated, responding, and controlled variables in the sunlight absorption investigation? The manipulated variable in the investigation was the color (light or dark) of the can; the color of the can was the variable that the investigators deliberately changed. The responding variable was the change in temperature of the water in the cans; the change in temperature was the outcome variable the investigators measured for each trial. To make the temperature test a fair one, in each investigation trial the teams would have to control such variables as the size of the cans and materials they were made from, the amount of water in each can, and the time the cans were left in sunlight.

Noting that the water in the dark can got warmer in the investigation of each team, the children, with the teacher's scaffolding assistance, concluded that it had absorbed more sunlight which was transformed to heat energy. In answer to their original question, the color of a material does make a difference in the absorption of sunlight. Generalizing from their observations, the children stated this principle: *Darker colored materials absorb more heat from sunlight than lighter colored materials*.

Returning to their initial question, the fifth graders reasoned that NASA chose white for astronauts' suits because white suits reflect sunlight and do not absorb extra heat like the darker-colored suits. Follow-up reading activities and direct instruction from the teacher confirmed this inference.

References

Chapter 1

Achieve. (April 2013 a.). Appendix H—Understanding the Scientific Enterprise: The Nature of Science in the Next Generation Science Standards. Retrieved from http://www.nextgenscience.org/sites/ngss/files/Appendix%20H%20-%20The%20Nature%20of%20Science%20in%20the%20Next%20Generation%20Science%20Standards%204.9.13.pdf.

Achieve. (April 2013 b.). Appendix L---Connections to the Common Core State Standards for Mathematics. Retrieved from http://nextgenscience.org/sites/default/files/Appendix-L_CCSS%20Math%20Connections%2006_03_13.pdf

Achieve. (April 2013 c.). Appendix M---Connections to the Common Core State Standards for Literacy in Science and Technical Subjects. Retrieved from http://www.nextgenscience.org/sites/default/files/Appendix%20M%20Connections%20to%20the%20CCSS%20for%20Literacy_061213.pdf

Achieve. (April 2013 d.). Appendix F—Science and Technology Practices in the NGSS. Retrieved from http://www.nextgenscience.org/sites/ngss/files/Appendix%20F%20%20Science%20and%20Engineering%20Practices%20in%20the%20NGSS%20_0.pdf.

Achieve. (April 2013 e.). Appendix E---Progressions Within the Next Generation Science Standards. Retrieved from http://www.nextgenscience.org/sites/default/files/Appendix%20M%20Connections%20to%20the%20CCSS%20for%20Literacy_061213.pdf

Achieve. (April 2013 f.). Appendix G—Crosscutting Concepts in the Next Generation Science Standards. Retrieved from http://www.nextgenscience.org/sites/ngss/files/Appendix%20F%20%20Science%20and%20Engineering%20Practices%20in%20the%20NGSS%20_0.pdf.

Achieve. (April 2013 g.). Appendix I—Engineering Design in the NGSS. Retrieved from http://www.nextgenscience.org/sites/ngss/files/Appendix%20I%20%20Engineering%20Design%20in%20NGSS%20-%20FINAL_V2_1.pdf.

Achieve. (April 2013 e.). Appendix A—Conceptual Shifts in the Next Generation Science Standards. Retrieved from http://www.nextgenscience.org/sites/ngss/files/Appendix%20A%20%20 4.11.13%20Conceptual%20Shifts%20in%20the%20Next%20Generation%20Science%20Standards.pdf.

Achieve. (April 2013 f.). How to Read the *Next Generation Science Standards (NGSS)*. Retrieved from http://nextgenscience.org/sites/ngss/files/How%20to%20Read%20NGSS%20-%20Final%204-19-13.pdf.

Achieve. (April 2013 h.). Appendix J---Science, Technology, Society and the Environment. Retrieved from http://www.nextgenscience.org/sites/default/files/APPENDIX%20J%204.15.13%20for%20Final%20Release.pdf

American Association for the Advancement of Science. (1990). *Science for all Americans. Online.* Chapter 1: The Nature of Science. Retrieved from http://www.project2061.org/publications/sfaa/online/chap1.htm.

American Association for the Advancement of Science. (1993). *Project 2061: Benchmarks for science literacy.* New York: Oxford University Press.

American Association for the Advancement of Science. (2001). *Atlas of science literacy,* Volume 1. Co-published by AAAS Project 2061 and the National Science Teachers Association.

American Association for the Advancement of Science. (2007). *Atlas of science literacy,* Volume 2. Co-published by AAAS Project 2061 and the National Science Teachers Association.

Champagne, A. L. & Kouba, V. L. (2000). Writing to inquire: Written products as performance measures. In J.J. Mintzes, J.H. Wandersee, & J. D. Novak (Eds.), *Assessing science understanding: A human constructivist view* (pp. 223–248). New York: Academic Press.

Fordham Institute. (2012). The state of state standards 2012. Retrieved from www.edexcellence.net/publications/the-state-of-state-science-standards-html.

Johnson, M. (2011). NASA's Kepler mission confirms its first planet in habitable zone of sun-like star. *NASA: Kepler—A Search for Habitable Planets.* Retrieved from http://www.nasa.gov/mission_pages/kepler/news/kepscicon-briefing.html.

Judson, H. F. (1980). *The search for solutions.* New York: Holt, Rinehart & Winston.

Langdon, D., McKittrick, G., Beede, D., Khan, B., and Doms, M. (2011). STEM: Good jobs now and for the future, ESA Issue Brief #03-11, Economics and Statistics Administration, Department of Commerce. www.esa.doc.gov/sites/default/files/reports/documents/stemfinalyjuly14_1.pdf

Mestre, J. P. and Cocking, R. R. (2002). Applying the science of learning to the education of prospective science teachers. In Bybee, R. W. (Ed.), in *Learning science and the science of learning.* Arlington, VA: NSTA Press.

Michaels, S., Shouse, A. W., Schweingruber, H. A., & National Research Council (U.S.). (2008). *Ready, set, science!: Putting research to work in K-8 science classrooms.* Washington, DC: National Academies Press.

National Academies of Science. (2006). *Rising above the gathering storm.* Washington, DC: National Academies Press.

National Assessment Governing Board. (2010). *Science framework for the 2011 National Assessment of Educational Progress.* Washington, DC: National Assessment Governing Board.

National Assessment Governing Board. (2014). *Science framework for the 2015 National Assessment of Educational Progress.* Washington, DC: National Assessment Governing Board.

National Center for Improving Science Education. (1989). *Getting started in science: A blueprint for elementary school science education.* Washington, DC: The Network, Inc.

National Research Council (NRC). (1996). *National science education standards.* Washington, DC: National Academies Press.

National Research Council (NRC). (2000). *Inquiry and the national science education standards: A guide for teaching and learning.* Washington, DC: National Academies Press.

National Research Council (NRC). (2007). *Taking science to school: Learning and teaching science in grades K–8.* Washington, DC: National Academies Press.

National Research Council. (2012). *A framework for K–12 science education: Practices, crosscutting concepts, and core ideas.* Committee on a Conceptual Framework for New K–12 Science Education Standards. Board on Science Education, Division of Behavioral and Social Sciences and Education. Washington, DC: The National Academies Press.

National Science Teachers Association (NSTA). (2000). NSTA position statement: The nature of science. Retrieved from http://www.nsta.org/about/positions/natureofscience.aspx

National Science Teachers Association (NSTA). (2002). NSTA position statement: Elementary school science. Retrieved from www.nsta.org/about/positions/elementary.aspx.

National Science Teachers Association (NSTA). (2003). NSTA position statement: Science education for middle level students. Retrieved from www.nsta.org/about/positions/middlelevel.aspx.

NGSS Lead States. (2013). *Next generation science standards: For states, by state*s. Washington, DC: National Academies Press.

OECD (2012). *Education at a Glance 2012: OECD Indicators,* OECD Publishing. http://dx.doi.org/10.1787/eag-2012-en.

Ramirez, A. (2016). "A Case for Curiosity." Edutopia. Retrieved from www.edutopia.org/blog/a-case-for-curiosity-ainissa-ramirez.

Technical Research Centre of Finland (VTT) (2012, February 27). 60-year-old definition of surface tension on solids revised. *ScienceDaily*. Retrieved July 26, 2012, from http://www.sciencedaily.com/releases/2012/02/120227111200.htm.

U.S. Government. (2015). Every Student Succeeds Act. www.help.senate.gov/imo/media/The_Every_Child_Achieves_Act_of_2015--summary.pdf.

"What is science?" Understanding Science. (2012). University of California Museum of Paleontology. Retrieved from http://undsci.berkeley.edu/article/0_0_0/whatisscience_03.

Zembal-Saul, C., McNeill, K. L., & Hershberger, K. (2013). *What's your evidence?: Engaging K-5 students in constructing explanations in science.* Boston: Pearson.

National Research Council (NRC). (2000). *How people learn: Brain, mind, experience, and school.* Expanded Edition. Washington, DC: National Academies Press.

National Research Council (NRC). (2005). *America's lab report: Investigations in high school science.* Washington, DC: National Academies Press.

National Research Council (NRC). (2005). *How students learn: Science in the classroom.* Washington, DC: National Academies Press.

National Research Council (NRC). (2007). *Ready, set, science!: Putting research to work in K–8 science classrooms.* Washington, DC: National Academies Press.

National Research Council (NRC). (2009). *Learning science in informal environments: People, places, and pursuits.* Washington, DC: National Academies Press.

National Research Council. (2012). *A framework for K–12 science education: Practices, crosscutting concepts, and core ideas.* Committee on a Conceptual Framework for New K–12 Science Education Standards. Board on Science Education, Division of Behavioral and Social Sciences and Education. Washington, DC: National Academies Press.

National Research Council (NRC). (2012). *Education for life and work: Developing transferable knowledge and skills in the 21st Century.* Washington, DC: National Academies Press.

Chapter 2

Achieve. (April 2013 a.). Appendix H—Understanding the Scientific Enterprise: The Nature of Science in the Next Generation Science Standards. Retrieved from http://www.nextgenscience.org/sites/ngss/files/Appendix%20H%20-%20The%20Nature%20of%20Science%20in%20the%20Next%20Generation%20Science%20Standards%204.9.13.pdf.

Achieve. (April 2013 d.). Appendix F—Science and Technology Practices in the NGSS. Retrieved from http://www.nextgenscience.org/sites/ngss/files/Appendix%20F%20%20Science%20and%20Engineering%20Practices%20in%20the%20NGSS%20_0.pdf.

Achieve. (April 2013 e.). Appendix E---Progressions Within the Next Generation Science Standards. Retrieved from http://www.nextgenscience.org/sites/default/files/Appendix%20M%20Connections%20to%20the%20CCSS%20for%20Literacy_061213.pdf

Achieve. (April 2013 g.). Appendix I—Engineering Design in the NGSS. Retrieved from http://www.nextgenscience.org/sites/ngss/files/Appendix%20I%20%20Engineering%20Design%20in%20NGSS%20-%20FINAL_V2_1.pdf.

Achieve. (April 2013 h.). Appendix J—Science, Technology, Society and the Environment. Retrieved from http://www.nextgenscience.org/sites/default/files/APPENDIX%20J%204.15.13%20for%20Final%20Release.pdf.

American Association for the Advancement of Science. (1990). *Science for all Americans. Online.* Chapter 1: The Nature of Science. Retrieved from www.project2061.org/publications/sfaa/online/chap1.htm.

American Association for the Advancement of Science. (1993). *Project 2061: Benchmarks for science literacy.* New York: Oxford University Press.

Anderson, L. W. & Krathwohl, D. R. (Eds.). (2001). *A taxonomy for learning, teaching, and assessing: A revision of Bloom's taxonomy of educational objectives.* New York: Longman.

Full Option Science System (FOSS). (2000). *Overview: Physics of sound.* Nashua, NH: Delta Education.

Heritage, M. (2010). *Formative assessment: Making it happen in the classroom.* Thousand Oaks, CA: Corwin Press.

Michaels, S., Shouse, A. W., & Schweingruber, H. A., and National Research Council (U.S.). (2008). *Ready, set, science! Putting research to work in K–8 science classrooms.* Board on Science Education, Center for Education, Division of Behavioral and Social Sciences and Education. Washington, DC: National Academies Press.

National Research Council. (1996). *National science education standards.* Washington, DC: National Academies Press.

National Research Council. (2012). *A framework for K–12 science education: Practices, crosscutting concepts, and core ideas.* Committee on a Conceptual Framework for New K–12 Science Education Standards. Board on Science Education, Division of Behavioral and Social Sciences and Education. Washington, DC: National Academies Press.

National Science Board. (2004). Science and Engineering Indicators 2004. National Science Foundation, Division of Science Resources Statistics. Arlington, VA. (NSB 04-01). Retrieved from www.nsf.gov/statistics/seind04/c1/c1s3.htm.

National Science Teachers Association (NSTA). (2003). NSTA position statement: Scientific inquiry. Retrieved from www.nsta.org/about/positions/inquiry.aspx.

NGSS Lead States. (2013). *Next generation science standards: For states, by state*s. Washington, DC: National Academies Press.

Roth, K. J., Druker, S. L., Garnier, H. E., Lemmens, M., Chen, C., Kawanaka, T., Rasmussen, D., Trubacova, S., Okamoto, Y., Gonzales, P., Stigler, J., & Gallimore, R. (2006). *Highlights from the TIMSS 1999 Video Study of eighth-grade science teaching* (NCES

2006-17). U.S. Department of Education, National Center for Education Statistics. Washington, DC: U.S. Government Printing Office.

Tweed, A. (2009). *Designing effective science instruction: What works in science classrooms.* Alexandria, VA: NSTA Press.

Chapter 3

American Association for the Advancement of Science. (1993). *Project 2061: Benchmarks for science literacy.* New York: Oxford University Press.

American Association for the Advancement of Science. (2001). *Atlas of science literacy.* Co-published by AAAS Project 2061 and the National Science Teachers Association.

Baron, E. B. (1992). Discipline strategies for teachers. Fastback, 344. Bloomington, IN: Phi Delta Kappa Educational Foundation.

Barton, M. L., & Jordan, D. (2001). *Teaching reading in science: A supplement to teaching reading in the content areas* (2nd ed.). Alexandria, VA: ASCD.

Dean, C., Hubbell, E., Pitler, H., & Stone, B. (2012). *Classroom instruction that works: Research-based strategies for increasing student achievement.* (2nd ed.). Alexandria, VA: Association for Supervision and Curriculum Development.

Gerlovich, J. A. (1996). Developments in laboratory safety. In J. Rhoton and P. Bowers (Eds.). *Issues in science education.* Arlington, VA: National Science Teachers Association.

Jones, F. (2000). *Tools for teaching.* Santa Cruz, CA: Fredric H. Jones & Associates.

Kagan, S. (1994). *Cooperative learning.* San Clemente, CA: Kagan Publishing.

Lowery, L. (1998). How new science curriculums reflect brain research. *Educational Leadership.* 56(3), 26-30.

Marzano, R. J. & Marzano, J. S. (2003). The key to classroom management. *Educational Leadership, 61*(1), 6-13.

Marzano, R., & Pickering, D. (1997). *Dimensions of learning trainer's manual,* 2nd Edition. Alexandria, VA: Association for Supervision and Curriculum Development.

Marzano, R., Pickering, D., & Pollock, J. (2003). *Classroom management that works: Research-based strategies for every teacher.* Alexandria, VA: Association for Supervision and Curriculum Development.

National Research Council. (1996). *National science education standards.* Washington, DC: National Academies Press.

National Research Council. (2000). *How people learn: Brain, mind, experience, and school: Expanded Edition.* Washington, DC: The National Academies Press,

National Research Council. (2005) *How students learn: Science in the classroom.* Washington, DC: The National Academies Press.

National Research Council. (2007). *Taking science to school: Learning and teaching science in grades K–8.* Committee on Science Learning, Kindergarten through Eighth Grade. Richard A. Duschl, Heidi A. Schweingruber, and Andrew W. Shouse (Eds.). Board on Science Education, Center for Education. Division of Behavioral and Social Sciences and Education. Washington, DC: The National Academies Press.

National Research Council. (2012). *A framework for K–12 science education: Practices, crosscutting concepts, and core ideas.* Committee on a Conceptual Framework for New K–12 Science Education Standards. Board on Science Education, Division of Behavioral and Social Sciences and Education. Washington, DC: The National Academies Press.

National Science Teachers Association (NSTA). (2008). NSTA position statement: Responsible use of live animals and dissection in the science classroom. Retrieved from http://www.nsta.org/about/positions/animals.aspx

Rosenthal, R. (1998). Covert communication in classrooms, clinics, and courtrooms. *Eye on Psi Chi 3*(1): 18–22.

Weiss, I., Pasley, J., Smith, S., Banilower, E., & Heck, D. (2003). *Looking inside the classroom: A study of K–12 mathematics and science education in the United States.* Chapel Hill, NC: Horizon Research.

Wiggins, G. P. & McTighe, J. (2005). *Understanding by design* (Expanded second edition.). Alexandria, VA: Association for Supervision and Curriculum Development.

Wong, H., & Wong, R. (2009). *The first days of school: How to be an effective teacher* (2nd ed.). Mountain View, CA: Harry K. Wong Publications.

Chapter 4

Anderson, C. W. (1987). Strategic teaching in science. In B. F. Jones et al. (Eds.), *Strategic teaching and learning: Cognitive instruction in the content areas.* Alexandria, VA: Association for Supervision and Curriculum Development.

Banilower, E., Cohen, K., Pasley, J., & Weiss, I. (2010). *Effective science instruction: What does research tell us?* (2nd ed.). Portsmouth, NH: RMC Research Corporation, Center on Instruction.

Bransford, J. D., Brown, A. L., & Cocking, R. R. (Eds.). (1999). *How people learn: Brain, mind, experience, and school.* Washington, DC: National Academies Press. (Also available at www.nap.edu.)

Brown, A. L., & Campione, J. C. (1998). Designing a community of young learners: Theoretical and practical lessons. In N. L. Lambert & B. L. McCombs (Eds.), *How students learn: Reforming schools through learner-centered education.* Washington, DC: American Psychological Association.

Chi, M. T. H. (2005). Commonsense conceptions of emergent processes: Why some misconceptions are robust. *Journal of the Learning Sciences, 14*(2), 161–199.

Clement, J., Brown, D., & Zietsman, A. (1989). Not all preconceptions are misconceptions: Finding anchoring conceptions for grounding instruction on students' intuitions. *International Journal of Science Education, 11,* 554–565.

Confrey, J. (1990). What constructivism implies for teaching. In R. B. Davis, C. A. Maher, & N. Noddings (Eds.), *Constructivist views on the teaching and learning of mathematics. Journal for Research in Mathematics Education monograph, 4,* 107–122.

Hogan, K. & Pressley, M. (1997). Scaffolding scientific competencies within classroom communities of inquiry. In K. Hogan & M. Pressley (Eds.), *Scaffolding student learning: Instructional approaches and issues.* Cambridge, MA: Brookline Books.

Jirout, J., & Klahr, D. (2011). Children's scientific curiosity: In search of an operational definition of an elusive concept. Working paper. TED Research Group, Carnegie Mellon University.

Konicek-Moran, R., & Keeley, P. (2015). *Teaching for conceptual understanding in science.* Arlington, VA: NSTA Press.

Loucks-Horsley, S., Hewson, P., Love, N., & Stiles, K. (1998). *Designing professional development for teachers of science and mathematics.* Thousand Oaks, CA: Corwin Press.

Lowery, L. (1998). How new science curriculums reflect brain research. *Educational Leadership* (November 26–30).

National Research Council. (1996). *National science education standards.* Washington, DC: National Academies Press.

National Research Council. (2007). *Taking science to school: Learning and teaching science in grades K–8.* Committee on Science Learning, Kindergarten through Eighth Grade. Richard A. Duschl, Heidi A. Schweingruber, and Andrew W. Shouse (Eds.). Board on Science Education, Center for Education. Division of Behavioral and Social Sciences and Education. Washington, DC: National Academies Press.

National Research Council. (2012). *A framework for K–12 science education: Practices, crosscutting concepts, and core ideas*. Committee on a Conceptual Framework for New K–12 Science Education Standards. Board on Science Education, Division of Behavioral and Social Sciences and Education.

National Science Teachers Association. (2014). *Crosscutting concepts*. NGSS@NSTA Hub. Accessed May 12, 2016 from http://ngss .nsta.org/CrosscuttingConceptsFull.aspx.

Ormrod, J. (2004). *Human learning*. Upper Saddle River, NJ: Merrill/ Prentice Hall.

Posner, G. J., Strike, K. A., Hewson, P. W., & Gertzog, W. A. (1982). Accommodation of a scientific conception: Toward a theory of conceptual change. *Science Education, 66,* 211–227.

Roth, K. (1991). Reading science texts for conceptual change. In C. M. Santa & D. V. Alverson (Eds.), *Science learning: Processes and applications*. Newark, DE: International Reading Association.

Stepans, J. (2003). Targeting students' science misconceptions: Physical science concepts using the conceptual change model. Tampa, FL: Showboard.

Strike, K. A., & Posner, G. J. (1985). A conceptual change view of learning and understanding. In L. H. T. West & A. L. Pines (Eds.), *Cognitive structure and conceptual change* (pp. 189–210). Orlando: Academic Press.

Trowbridge, L., & Bybee, R. (1996). *Teaching secondary school science* (6th ed.). Upper Saddle River, NJ: Merrill/Prentice Hall.

Vygotsky, L. S. (1962). *Thought and language*. Cambridge, MA: MIT Press.

Chapter 5

The Access Center. (n.d.). *Using mnemonic instruction to facilitate access to the general education curriculum*. Retrieved August 22, 2012 from www.k8accesscenter.org/training_resources/ Mnemonics.asp.

Banchi, H. & Bell, R. (2008). The many levels of inquiry. *Science and Children, 46*(2), 26–29.

Banilower, E., Cohen, K., Pasley, J., & Weiss, I. (2010). *Effective science instruction: What does research tell us?* (2nd ed.). Portsmouth, NH: RMC Research Corporation, Center on Instruction.

Bell, P., & Shouse, A. (2015). Practice Brief 4: Are there multiple instructional models that fit with the science and engineering practices in NGSS? (Short answer: Yes.). STEM teaching tools. http://stemteachingtools.org/brief/4dcfdfs.

Bell, R. L., Smetana, L., & Binns, I. (2005). Simplifying inquiry instruction: Assessing the inquiry level of classroom activities. *The Science Teacher, 72*(7), 30–33.

Bransford, J. D., Brown, A. L., & Cocking, R. R. (Eds.). (1999). *How people learn: Brain, mind, experience, and school*. Washington, DC: National Academies Press. (Also available at www.nap.edu.)

Brown, A. L., & Campione, J. (1994). Guided discovery in a community of learners. In K. McGilly (Ed.), *Classroom lessons: Integrating cognitive theory and classroom practice*. Cambridge, MA: MIT Press.

Bybee, R. W. (2000). Teaching science as inquiry. In J. Minstrell & E. van Zee (Eds.), *Inquiring into inquiry learning and teaching in science*. Washington, DC: American Association for the Advancement of Science.

Bybee, R. W. (2013). *Translating the NGSS for classroom instruction*. Arlington, VA: NSTA Press.

Bybee, R. W. (2014). The BSCS 5E instructional model: Personal reflections and contemporary implications. *Science and Children 53*(8): 10–13.

Bybee, R. W. (2015). *The BSCS 5E instructional model: Creating teachable moments*. Arlington, VA: NSTA Press.

Bybee, R. W., Taylor, J. A., Gardner, A., Van Scotter, P., Carlson Powell, J., Westbrook, A., & Landes, N. (2006). The BSCS 5E Instructional Model: Origins, Effectiveness, and Applications: A Report Prepared for the Office of Science Education National Institutes of Health. Retrieved from http://science.education. nih.gov/houseofreps.nsf/b82d55fa138783c2852572c9004f5566 /$FILE/Appendix%20D.pdf.

Eisenkraft, A. (2003). Expanding the 5E model: A proposed 5E model emphasizes "transfer of learning" and the importance of eliciting prior understanding. *The Science Teacher, 70*(6), 57–59.

Haury, D. L. (1993). Teaching science through inquiry. *ERIC CSMEE Digest* (March), 359(48).

Keeley, P., Eberle, F., & Farrin, L. (2005). Formative assessment probes: Uncovering students' ideas in science. *Science Scope, 28*(4), 18–21.

Kirschner, P., Sweller, J., & Clark, R. (2006). Why minimal guidance during instruction does not work: An analysis of the failure of constructivist, discovery, problem-based, experiential, and inquiry-based teaching. *Educational Psychologist, 41*(2), 75–86. Lawrence Erlbaum Associated, Inc.

Klahr, D. & Nigam, M. (October, 2004). The equivalence of learning paths in early science instruction: Effects of direct instruction and discovery learning. *Psychological Science*. vol. 15. no. 10. pp. 661-667.

Kratochvil, D. W. & Crawford, J. J. (1971). *Science Curriculum Improvement Study*. Palo Alto, CA: American Institutes for Research in the Behavioral Sciences. Retrieved from www.eric .ed.gov/PC.

Michaels, S., Shouse, A. W., & Schweingruber, H. A. (2008). *Ready, set, science! Putting research to work in K–8 science classrooms*. Board on Science Education, Center for Education, Division of Behavioral and Social Sciences and Education. Washington, DC: National Academies Press.

National Research Council. (1996). *National science education standards*. Washington, DC: National Academies Press.

National Research Council. (2000). *Inquiry and the national science education standards: A guide for teaching and learning*. Washington, DC: National Academies Press.

National Research Council. (2001). *Classroom assessment and the national science education standards*. Washington, DC: National Academies Press.

National Research Council. (2007). *Taking science to school: Learning and teaching science in grades K–8*. Committee on Science Learning, Kindergarten through Eighth Grade. Richard A. Duschl, Heidi A. Schweingruber, and Andrew W. Shouse (Eds.). Board on Science Education, Center for Education. Division of Behavioral and Social Sciences and Education. Washington, DC: National Academies Press.

National Research Council. (2012). *A framework for K–12 science education: Practices, crosscutting concepts, and core ideas*. Committee on a Conceptual Framework for New K–12 Science Education Standards. Board on Science Education, Division of Behavioral and Social Sciences and Education. Washington, DC: National Academies Press.

Rowe, M. B. (1973). *Teaching science as continuous inquiry*. New York: McGraw-Hill.

Trowbridge, L., & Bybee, R. (1996). *Teaching secondary school science* (6th ed.). Upper Saddle River, NJ: Merrill/Prentice Hall.

Vasquez, J. A. (2008). *Tools and traits for highly effective science teaching, K–8.* Portsmouth, NH: Heinemann.

Chapter 6

American Association for the Advancement of Science. (1993). *Project 2061: Benchmarks for science literacy.* New York: Oxford University Press.

Blosser, P. E. (1991). How to ask the right questions. Arlington, VA: NSTA. Also available at www.nsta.org/pdfs/201108BookBeatH owToAskTheRightQuestions.pdf.

Bransford, J. D., Brown, A. L., & Cocking, R. R. (Eds.). (1999). *How people learn: Brain, mind, experience, and school.* Washington, DC: National Academies Press. (Also available at www.nap.edu.)

Carin, A. A. & Sund, R. B. (1978). *Creative questioning and sensitive listening techniques: A self-guided approach.* Upper Saddle River, NJ: Merrill/Prentice Hall.

Douglas, R., Klentschy, M. P., & Worth, K. (2006). *Linking science & literacy in the K–8 classroom.* Arlington, VA: NSTA Press.

Elstgeest, J. (2001). The right question at the right time. In *Primary science: Taking the plunge* (2nd ed) Wynne Harlen (Ed.). (pp. 25–34). Portsmouth, NH: Heinemann.

Furtak, E. M. & Ruiz-Primo, M. A. (2005). Questioning cycle: Making students' thinking explicit during scientific inquiry. *Science Scope, 28*(4), 22–25.

Martens, M. L. (1999). Productive questions: Tools for supporting constructivist learning. *Science and Children, 36*(8), 24–53.

McTighe, J., & Wiggins, G. (2013). *Essential questions: Opening doors to student understanding.* Alexandria, VA: ASCD.

Michaels, S., O'Connor, M. C., Hall, M. W., & Resnick, L. B. (2010). Accountable talk sourcebook: For classroom conversation that works (Version 3.1) University of Pittsburgh.

Michaels, S., Shouse, A. W., & Schweingruber, H. A. (2008). *Ready, set, science! Putting research to work in K–8 science classrooms.* Board on Science Education, Center for Education, Division of Behavioral and Social Sciences and Education. Washington, DC: National Academies Press.

National Research Council. (1996). *National science education standards.* Washington, DC: National Academies Press.

National Research Council. (2007). *Taking science to school: Learning and teaching science in grades K–8.* Committee on Science Learning, Kindergarten through Eighth Grade. Richard A. Duschl, Heidi A. Schweingruber, and Andrew W. Shouse (Eds.). Board on Science Education, Center for Education. Division of Behavioral and Social Sciences and Education. Washington, DC: The National Academies Press.

National Research Council. (2012). *A framework for K–12 science education: Practices, crosscutting concepts, and core ideas.* Committee on a Conceptual Framework for New K–12 Science Education Standards. Board on Science Education, Division of Behavioral and Social Sciences and Education. Washington, DC: The National Academies Press.

Olson, J. K. (2008). The crucial role of the teacher: Choosing questions and timing to improve your effect on students' learning. *Science and Children, 46*(2), 45–49.

Ormrod, J. (2004). *Human learning.* Upper Saddle River, NJ: Merrill/ Prentice Hall.

Rowe, M. B. (1973). *Teaching science as continuous inquiry.* New York: McGraw-Hill.

Rowe, M. B. (1987). Wait-time: Slowing down may be a way of speeding up. *American Educator, 11*(1), 38–47.

Texas A&M Center for Mathematics and Science Education. (2005). Effective research-based science instruction. Austin, TX: Texas Education Agency. Retrieved from http://72.14.209.104/search?q=cache:q4rfHv7MDMYJ: www3.science.tamu.edu/cmse/tsi/.

Texas A&M Center for Mathematics and Science Education. (2006). Texas science initiative meta-analysis of national research regarding science teaching: Executive summary. Austin, TX: Texas Education Agency. Retrieved from http://72.14.209.104/ search?q=cache:AWfRsosvXPIJ:www3.science.tamu.edu/cmse/ tsi/ExecutiveSum.

Tienken, C. H., Goldberg, S., & DiRocco, D. (2009). Questioning the questions. *Kappa Delta Pi Record* (pp. 39–43). Retrieved from www.kdp.org/publications/pdf/record/fall09/RF09_Tienken .pdf.

Tilson, J. L. (2007). Discourse circles. Retrieved from http:// scienceandliteracy.org/sites/scienceandliteracy.org/files/biblio/ tilson_discoursecirclesconnect_pdf_47687.pdf.

Weiss, I. R., & Pasley, J. D. (2004). What is high-quality instruction? *Educational Leadership, 45*, 24–29.

Wheatley, M. J. (2007). *Finding our way: Leadership for uncertain times.* San Francisco: Berrett-Koehler.

Winokur, J., Worth, K., & Heller-Winokur, M. (2009). Connecting science and literacy through talk. *Science and Children, 47*(3), 46–49.

Worth, K., Winokur, J., Crissman, S., Heller-Winokur, M., & Davis, M. (2009a). *The essentials of science and literacy: A guide for teachers.* Portsmouth, NH: Heinemann.

Worth, K., Winokur, J., Crissman, S., Heller-Winokur, M., & Davis, M. (2009b). *Science and literacy: A natural fit.* Portsmouth, NH: Heinemann.

Chapter 7

Achieve. (April 2013). How to Read the Next Generation Science Standards (NGSS). Retrieved from http://nextgenscience.org/ sites/ngss/files/How%20to%20Read%20NGSS%20-%20 Final%204-19-13.pdf.

Black, P., & Wiliam, D. (1998a). Assessment and classroom learning. *Assessment in Education, 5,* 7-74.

Black, P., & Wiliam, D. (1998b). Inside the black box: Raising standards through classroom assessment. *Phi Delta Kappan, 80*(2), 139-144, 146-148.

Colburn, A. (2009). The prepared practitioner: An assessment primer. *The Science Teacher, 76*(4), 10.

Duke Academic Resource Center. (n.d.) What is the difference between assessment and evaluation? Retrieved June 16, 2012 from http://web.duke.edu/arc/documents/The%20 difference%20between%20assessment%20and%20evaluation .pdf.

Edmondson, K. M. (1999). Assessing science understanding through concept maps. In J. J. Mintzes, J. H. Wandersee, & J. D. Novak (Eds.). Assessing science understanding: A human constructivist view (pp. 223–248). New York: Academic Press.

Heritage, M. (2007). Formative assessment: What do teachers need to know and do? *Phi Delta Kappan, 89*(2), 140-145.

Jarolimek, J., & Foster, C. D., Sr. (1997). *Teaching and learning in the elementary school* (6th ed.). Upper Saddle River, NJ: Merrill/ Prentice Hall.

Keeley, P., Eberle, F., & Farrin, L. (2005). Formative assessment probes: Uncovering students' ideas in science: 25 Formative assessment probes. Arlington, VA: NSTA Press.

Keeley, P. (2011). Formative assessment probes: With a purpose. *Science and Children, 48*(9).

Keeley, P. (2012). Formative assessment probes: The daytime moon. *Science and Children, 49*(5), 28–30.

Kentucky Department of Education. (n.d.). Designing a performance assessment. Frankfort, KY: Author.

Kizlik, B. (2012). Measurement, assessment, and evaluation in education. Retrieved from www.adprima.com/measurement.htm.

Kohn, A. (2015). Who's Asking?. *Educational Leadership, 73*(1), 16-22.

Long, K. (2011). Formative Assessment in the FOSS Program. FOSS Newsletter #37. (Spring 2011). Retrieved from http://lhsfoss.org/newsletters/last/FOSS37.formative.html.

National Center for Education Statistics (2011). The Nation's Report Card: Science 2009(NCES 2011–451). Institute of Education Sciences, U.S. Department of Education, Washington, D.C.

National Center for Education Statistics. (2012). NAEP Questions Tool. Retrieved from http://nces.ed.gov/nationsreportcard/itmrlsx.

National Research Council. (1996). *National science education standards.* Washington, DC: National Academies Press.

National Research Council. (2000). *Inquiry and the national science education standards: A guide for teaching and learning.* Washington, DC: National Academies Press.

National Research Council. (2001). *Classroom assessment and the national science education standards.* Washington, DC: National Academies Press.

National Research Council. (2007). Taking science to school: Learning and teaching science in grades K–8. Committee on Science Learning, Kindergarten through Eighth Grade. Richard A. Duschl, Heidi A. Schweingruber, and Andrew W. Shouse (Eds.). Board on Science Education, Center for Education. Division of Behavioral and Social Sciences and Education. Washington, DC: National Academies Press.

NGSS Lead States. (2013). *Next generation science standards: For states, by states.* Washington, DC: National Academies Press.

Novak, J. (1995). Concept mapping: A strategy for organizing knowledge. In S. Glynn & R. Duit (Eds.), *Learning science in the schools: Research reforming practice.* Mahwah, NJ: Erlbaum.

Rosenshine, B. (1997). Advances in research on instruction. In J. Lloyd, E. Kameanui, & D. Chard (Eds.), *Issues in educating students with disabilities* (pp. 197–221). Mahwah, NJ: Erlbaum.

Shepard, L., Hammerness, K., Darling-Hammond, L., & Rust, F. (2005). Assessment. In L. Darling-Hammond & J. Bransford (Eds.), *Preparing teachers for a changing world: What teachers should learn and be able to do* (pp. 275–326). San Francisco, CA: Jossey-Bass.

Shepardson, D. P. & Britsch, S. J. (2001). Tools for assessing and teaching science in elementary and middle schools. In D. P. Shepardson (Ed.), *Assessment in science: A guide to professional development and classroom practice* (pp. 119–147). Boston: Kluwer.

Smouse, C. (2010, June 18). Interesting article about assessment and evaluation. Rea, J. B. (June 2010) You say ee-ther and I say eye-ther: Clarifying assessment and evaluation. ASTD (American Society of Training and Development). Links newsletter. Retrieved from http://deinfocus.blogspot.mx/2010/06/interesting-article-about-assessment.html#!/2010/06/interesting-article-about-assessment.html.

Sterling, D. R. (2005). Assessing understanding. *Science Scope, 28*(4), 33–37.

Chapter 8

Bell, R. L., & Trundle, K. C. (2008). The use of computer simulation to promote scientific conceptions of moon phases. *Journal of Research in Science Teaching. 45*(3), 346–372.

EQuIP Rubric for Lessons & Units: Science. (2016). Retrieved from http://www.nextgenscience.org/resources/equip-rubric-lessons-units-science

Henderson, J. R. (2016). "T is for thinking: The ICYouSee guide to critical thinking." www.icyousee.org.

Metcalf, S. J., & Tinker, R. F. (2004). Probeware and handhelds in elementary and middle school science. *Journal of Science Education and Technology, 13*(1), 43-49.

National Research Council. (1996). *National science education standards.* Washington, DC: National Academies Press.

National Research Council. (2012). *A framework for K–12 science education: Practices, crosscutting concepts, and core ideas.* Committee on a Conceptual Framework for New K–12 Science Education Standards. Board on Science Education, Division of Behavioral and Social Sciences and Education. Washington, DC: National Academies Press.

Park, J. C., & Slykhuis, D. A. (2006). Guest editorial: Technology proficiencies in science teacher education. *Contemporary Issues in Technology and Teacher Education, 6*(2), 218–229.

Reiser, B. J. (2013, September). *What professional development strategies are needed for successful implementation of the Next Generation Science Standards?* White paper presented to the Invitational Research Symposium on Science Assessment. K–12 Center at ETS. Retrieved from www.ride.ri.gov/Portals/0/Uploads/Documents/Instruction-and-Assessment-World-Class-Standards/Science/NGSS/Reiser_What_PD_Strategies_are_Needed_for_NGSS.pdf

Chapter 9

Achieve. (January, 2013a). Appendix K–Connections to the Common Core State Standards for Mathematics in NGSS Public Release II. Retrieved from www.nextgenscience.org/sites/ngss/files/Appendix%20K%20%E2%80%93%20Connections%20to%20the%20Common%20Core%20State%20Standards%20for%20Mathematics%20-%20FINAL.pdf.

Achieve. (April 2013b). Appendix I—Engineering Design in the NGSS. Retrieved from www.nextgenscience.org/sites/ngss/files/Appendix%20I%20%20Engineering%20Design%20in%20NGSS%20-%20FINAL_V2_1.pdf.

Barton, M. L., & Jordan, D. L. (2001). *Teaching reading in science.* Arlington, VA: Association for Supervision and Curriculum Development.

Brown, S., & Kappes, L. (2012). Implementing the Common Core State Standards: A primer on "close reading of text." Washington, DC: Aspen Institute. Accessed from www.aspeninstitute.org/sites/default/files/content/docs/pubs/CR.Primer.print.pdf.

Campbell, B. & Fulton, L. (2014). *Science notebooks: Writing about inquiry* (2nd ed.). Portsmouth, NH: Heinemann.

Clements, D. (1999). Teaching length measurement: Research challenges. *School Science and Mathematics, 99*(1), 5–11.

Cothron, J., Giese, R., & Rezba, R. (2004). *Science experiments by the hundreds* (2nd ed.). Dubuque, IA: Kendall-Hunt.

Enderle, P. J., Bickel, R., Gleim, L. K., Granger, E., Grooms, J., Hester, M., Murphy, A., Sampson, V., & Southerland, S. A. (2016). *Argument-driven inquiry for life science: Lab investigations for grades 6-8.* Arlington, VA: NSTA Press.

Finley, F. N. (1991). Why children have trouble learning from science texts. In C. M. Santa & D. E. Alvermann (Eds.), *Science learning: Processes and applications*. Newark, DE: International Reading Association.

Fisher, D. (2013). Close Reading and the CCSS, Part 1. McGraw-Hill Education. www.mhecommoncoretoolbo.com/close-reading-and-the-ccss-part-1.html.

Gagnon, M. J. & Abell, S. K. (2008). Making time for science talk. In Readings in science methods, K–8: An NSTA press journals collection, E. Brunsell (Ed.). 183–185. Arlington, VA: NSTA Press.

International Reading Association. (1996). Standards for the English language arts (a project of the International Reading Association and the National Council of Teachers of English). Newark, DE: Author.

King, A. (1994). Guiding knowledge construction in the classroom: Effects of teaching children how to question and how to explain. *American Educational Research Journal, 31*(2), 338–368.

Koba, S. & Mitchell, C. T. (2011). *Hard-to-teach science concepts: A framework to support learners, grades 3-5*. Arlington, VA: NSTA Press.

Koba, S. & Tweed, A. (2014). *Hard-to-teach biology concepts: Designing instruction aligned to the NGSS*. Arlington, VA: NSTA Press.

National Council for the Social Studies. (1994). Expectations of excellence: Curriculum standards for the social studies. Washington, DC: Author.

National Council for the Social Studies. (2010). *National curriculum standards for social studies: A framework for teaching, learning, and assessment*. Silver Spring, MD: Author.

National Governors Association Center for Best Practices & Council of Chief State School Officers. (2010). Common Core State Standards for Mathematics Washington, DC: Authors.

National Research Council. (1996). *National science education standards*. Washington, DC: National Academies Press.

National Research Council. (2012). *A framework for K–12 science education: Practices, crosscutting concepts, and core ideas*. Committee on a Conceptual Framework for New K–12 Science Education Standards. Board on Science Education, Division of Behavioral and Social Sciences and Education. Washington, DC: National Academies Press.

National Science Resources Center. (1996). *Science and technology for children: Comparing and measuring*. Burlington, NC: Carolina Biological Supply.

Ormrod, J. (2007). *Human learning* (5th ed.). Upper Saddle River, NJ: Merrill/Prentice Hall.

Padak, N. D. & Davidson, J. L. (1991). Instructional activities for comprehending science text. In C. M. Santa & D. E. Alvermann (Eds.). *Science learning: Processes and applications*. Newark, DE: International Reading Association.

Padilla, M. J., Muth, K. D., & Padilla, R. K. (1991). Science and reading: Many process skills in common. In C. M. Santa & D. V. Alvermann (Eds.), *Science learning: Processes and applications*. Newark, DE: International Reading Association.

Roth, K. (1991). Reading science texts for conceptual change. In C. M. Santa & D. V. Alverson (Eds.), *Science learning: Processes and applications*. Newark, DE: International Reading Association.

Santa, C. M. & Alvermann, D. E. (Eds.). (1991). *Science learning: Processes and applications*. Newark, DE: International Reading Association.

Santa, C. M. & Havens, L. T. (1991). Learning through writing. In C. M. Santa & D. E. Alvermann (Eds.). *Science learning: Processes and applications*. Newark, DE: International Reading Association.

Tompkins, G. E. (2006). *Literacy for the 21st century* (4th ed.). Upper Saddle River, NJ: Pearson/Merrill.

Tovani, C. (2004). *Do I really have to teach reading? Content comprehension, grades 6-12*. Portland, ME: Stenhouse Publishers.

Worth, K., Winokur, J., Crissman, S., Heller-Winokur, M., & Davis, M. (2009). *Science and literacy: A natural fit*. Portsmouth, NH: Heinemann.

Yopp, H. K. & Yopp, R. H. (2006). Primary students and informational texts. *Science and Children, 44*(3), 22–25.

Chapter 10

Adams, C. M., & Pierce, R. L. (2003). Teaching by tiering. *Science and Children, 41*(3): 30–34.

Alexakos, K. (2001, March). Inclusive classrooms, a multicultural look at the national science education standards. *The Science Teacher, 68*(3): 40–43.

American Association for the Advancement of Science. (1990). *Science for all Americans. Online*. Chapter 1: The Nature of Science. Retrieved from www.project2061.org/publications/sfaa/online/chap1.htm.

American Association of University Women. (2013, August). Fast Facts: Science, Technology, Engineering, and Mathematics (STEM). Retrieved from www.aauw.org/files/2013/09/quick-facts-on-STEM.pdf.

Armstrong, T. (1998). *Awakening genius in the classroom*. Alexandria, VA: Association for Supervision and Curriculum Development.

Bayer. (2010, March 22). U.S. Women and Minority Scientists Discouraged from Pursuing STEM Careers, National Survey Shows. Bayer: Science for a better life. Retrieved from www.bayerus.com/News%5CNewsDetail.aspx?ID=862593F0-F489-B4D0-283DB12C656EA899.

Bransford, J. D., Brown, A. L., & Cocking, R. R. (Eds.). (1999). *How people learn: Brain, mind, experience, and school*. Washington, DC: National Academies Press. (Also available at www.nap.edu.)

Brownell, M. T., & Thomas, C. W. (1998). An interview with Margo Mastropieri: Quality science instruction for students with disabilities. *Intervention in School and Clinic, 32*, 118–122.

Cawley, J. F., & Foley, T. E. (2002). Connecting math and science for all students. *Teaching Exceptional Children, 34*(4), 14–19.

Civic Impulse. (2016). S. 2781 — 111th Congress: Rosa's Law. Retrieved from www.govtrack.us/congress/bills/111/s2781.

Code of Federal Regulations, Title 34, §300.8(c)(4)(ii) Individuals with disabilities act. Retrieved from http://ecfr.gpoaccess.gov/cgi/t/text/text-idx?c=ecfr&rgn=div8&view=text&node=34:2.1.1.1.1.1.36.7&idno=34.

Conn, K. (2001). Supporting special students: Including special needs students in the science classroom. *The Science Teacher, 68*(3), 32–35.

Ellis, E. S. (2002). Watering up the curriculum for adolescents with learning disabilities, Part II: Goals for the affective dimension. *LD Online*. Retrieved from www.ldonline.org/articles/5742.

Every Student Succeeds Act (ESSA). (n.d.). Retrieved March 3, 2016, from www.ed.gov/essa.

Fetters, M., Pickard, D. M., & Pyle, E. (2003, February). Making science accessible: Strategies to meet the needs of a diverse student population. *Science Scope. 26*(5): 26–29.

Fradd, S. H. & Lee, O. (1999). Teachers' roles in promoting science inquiry with students from diverse language backgrounds. *Educational Researcher, 28*(6), 14–20.

Freeman, D. & Freeman, Y. (1998). *Sheltered English instruction* (ERIC Digest).

Girl Scout Research Institute. (2012). Generation STEM: What girls say about science, technology, engineering, and math. Retrieved from www.girlscouts.org/content/dam/girlscouts-gsusa/forms-and-documents/about-girl-scouts/research/generation_stem_full_report.pdf.

Hoover, J. J. (2011). *Response to intervention models: Curricular implications and interventions.* Upper Saddle River, NJ: Prentice Hall.

Institutes on Academic Diversity. (2009-2012). Differentiation central. Retrieved from www.diffcentral.com/index.html.

Lapp, D. (2001). Bridging the gap. *Science Link* (Newsletter of the National Science Resources Center), *12*(1), 2.

Lee, O. (2002). Promoting scientific inquiry with elementary students from diverse cultures and languages. In W. C. Secada (Ed.), *Review of research in education* (Vol. 26, pp. 23–69). Washington, DC: American Educational Research Association.

Lee, O., & Fradd, S. H. (1998). Science for all, including students from non-English-language backgrounds. *Educational Researcher, 27*(4), 12–19.

Logsdon, A. (2016). Using graphic organizers as study guides. www.verywell.com/using-graphic-organizers-as-study-guides-2162650.

Maslow, A. H. (1987). *Motivation and personality* (3rd ed.). New York: Harper and Row.

Mastropieri, M. A., & Scruggs, T. E. (2004). *The inclusive classroom: Strategies for effective instruction.* Upper Saddle River, NJ: Merrill/Prentice Hall.

Mastropieri, M. A., Scruggs, T. E., & Butcher, K. (1993). How effective is inquiry learning for students with mild disabilities? *The Journal of Special Education, 31*(2), 199–211.

Miller, A. (2016). *6 Strategies for Differentiated Instruction in Project-Based Learning.* Retrieved from www.edutopia.org/blog/differentiated-instruction-strategies-pbl-andrew-miller?page=9.

Miller, B. (2012). Ensuring meaningful access to the science curriculum for students with significant cognitive disabilities. *Teaching Exceptional Children* (July 2012). Retrieved from www.highbeam.com/doc/1P3-2708950191.html.

National Center for Education Statistics. (2012). NAEP Questions Tool. Retrieved March 1, 2016 from http://nces.ed.gov/nationsreportcard/itmrlsx.

National Center for Education Statistics. The Condition of Education - Participation in Education - Elementary/Secondary Enrollment - Children and Youth with Disabilities - Indicator May (2015). (n.d.). Retrieved from http://nces.ed.gov/programs/coe/indicator_cgg.asp.

National Center on Universal Design for Learning. (n.d.). The Three Principles. Retrieved April 22, 2016, from www.udlcenter.org/aboutudl/whatisudl/3principles

National Research Council. (1996). *National science education standards.* Washington, DC: National Academies Press.

National Research Council. (2012). *A framework for K–12 science education: Practices, crosscutting concepts, and core ideas.* Committee on a Conceptual Framework for New K–12 Science Education Standards. Board on Science Education, Division of Behavioral and Social Sciences and Education. Washington, DC: National Academies Press.

National Science Teachers Association (NSTA). (2000). NSTA position statement: Multicultural science education. Retrieved fromwww.nsta.org/about/positions/multicultural.aspx.

NGSS Lead States. (2013). *Next generation sciences standards: For states, by state*s. Washington, DC: National Academies Press.

No Child Left Behind. (2002). Retrieved March 1, 2016, from www2.ed.gov/nclb/landing.jhtml.

Office of English Language Acquisition (OLEA). (2014). Fast Facts —Languages Spoken by English Learners. Retrieved from www.ncela.us/files/fast_facts/OELA_Fast_Facts_All_Languages_Update_508_11_5._15.pdf

Ormrod, J. (2007). *Human learning,* (5th ed.). Upper Saddle River, NJ: Merrill/Prentice Hall.

Pellino, K. M. (2008). The effects of poverty on teaching and learning. Retrieved from URLwww.teach-nology.com/tutorials/teaching/poverty/print.htm.

Public Law 108-446. (2004). *IDEA 2004.* Retrieved from www.ldonline.org/features/idea2004#law.

Richards, R. G. (2008). The writing road: Reinvigorate your students' enthusiasm for writing. *LD online.* Retrieved from www.ldonline.org/article/5608?theme=print.

Scruggs, T. E., Mastropieri, M. A., Bakken, J. P., & Brigham, F. J. (1993). Reading versus doing: The relative effects of textbook-based and inquiry-oriented approaches to science learning in special education classrooms. *Journal of Special Education, 27*(1), 1–15.

Short, D. J., Vogt, M. E., & Echevarria, J. (2011). *The SIOP model for teaching science to English learners.* Boston, MA: Pearson. Retrieved from http://siop.pearson.com/about-siop/index.html

Spaulding, L. S., & Flannagan, J. S. (2012). DIS_2ECT: A framework for effective inclusive science instruction. *Teaching Exceptional Children, 44*(6): 6–14.

The Access Center. (n.d.). *Using mnemonic instruction to facilitate access to the general education curriculum.* Retrieved August 22, 2012 from http://www.k8accesscenter.org/training_resources/Mnemonics.asp.

Turnbull, A., Turnbull, R., Shank, M., & Smith, S. J. (2004). *Exceptional lives: Special education in today's schools* (4th ed.). Upper Saddle River, NJ: Merrill/PrenticeHall.

U.S. Department of Education. (2004). *Building the legacy: IDEA 2004.* Retrieved from: http://idea.ed.gov/explore/view/p/%2Croot%2Cstatute%2CI%2CA%2C602%2C30%2C.

Vasquez, J. A. (1990). Teaching to the distinctive traits of minority students. *The Clearing House, 63,* 299–304.

Vaughn, S., & Bos, C. S. (2012). *Strategies for teaching students with learning and behavior problems* (8th ed.). Upper Saddle River, NJ: Prentice Hall.

Watson, S. & Johnson, L. (2007, March). Assistive technology in the inclusive science classroom. *The Science Teacher, 74*(3): 34–38.

Appendix A

American Association for the Advancement of Science. (1990). *Science for all Americans.* Online. Chapter 1: The Nature of Science. Retrieved from http://www.project2061.org/publications/sfaa/online/chap1.htm.

American Association for the Advancement of Science. (1993). *Project 2061: Benchmarks for science literacy.* New York: Oxford University Press.

The Common Core State Standards Writing Team. (2012). *Progressions for the Common Core State Standards in Mathematics (draft).* Retrieved from https://commoncoretools.files.wordpress.com/2012/07/ccss_progression_gm_k5_2012_07_21.pdf.

Douglas, R., Klentschy, M. P., & Worth, K. (2006). *Linking science & literacy in the K–8 classroom.* Arlington, VA: NSTA Press.

Fulton, L., & Campbell, B. (2014). *Science notebooks: Writing about inquiry* (2nd ed.). Portsmouth, NH: Heinemann.

Harlen, W. (2006). *Teaching, learning and assessing science 5–12* (4th ed.). London: Sage Publications.

Harlen, W. & Jelly, S. (1990). *Developing science in the primary classroom.* Portsmouth, NH: Heinemann.

Michaels, S., Shouse, A. W., & Schweingruber, H. A. (2008). *Ready, set, science! Putting research to work in K–8 science classrooms.* Board on Science Education, Center for Education, Division of Behavioral and Social Sciences and Education. Washington, DC: National AcademiesPress.

Musante, F. (2012). *Newtown student receives patent for ice safety measurement process.* Retrieved from http://patch.com/connecticut/newtown/newtown-student-receives-patent-for-ice-safety-measura955c678ae from the Newtown Patch.

National Aquarium in Baltimore. (1997). *Living in water: An aquatic science curriculum.* Dubuque, IA: Kendall/Hunt.

National Research Council. (1996). *National science education standards.* Washington, DC: National Academies Press.

National Research Council. (2007). *Taking science to school: Learning and teaching science in grades K–8.* Committee on Science Learning, Kindergarten through Eighth Grade. Richard A. Duschl, Heidi A. Schweingruber, and Andrew W. Shouse (Eds.). Board on Science Education, Center for Education. Division of Behavioral and Social Sciences and Education. Washington, DC: National Academies Press.

National Research Council. (2012). *A framework for K–12 science education: Practices, crosscutting concepts, and core ideas.* Committee on a Conceptual Framework for New K–12 Science Education Standards. Board on Science Education, Division of Behavioral and Social Sciences and Education. Washington, DC: National Academies Press.

National Science Resources Center. (1996). *Science and technology for children: Comparing and measuring.* Burlington, NC: Carolina Biological Supply.

NGSS Lead States. (2013). *Next generation science standards: For states, by states.* Washington, DC: National Academies Press.

Settlage, J., & Southerland, S. A. (2012). *Teaching science to every child: Using culture as a starting point* (2nd ed.). New York: Routledge.

TeacherVision, 2015. *Analyzing data.* Retrieved from www.teachervision.com/skill-builder/graphs-and-charts/48946.html.

Wade, N. (2010). For cats, a big gulp with a touch of the tongue. *The New York Times (online).* Retrieved from www.nytimes.com/2010/11/12/science/12cats html#.

5E instructional model a series of instructional phases (engage, explore, explain, elaborate, evaluate) designed to result in students learning science with understanding.

academic language vocabulary needed for success in school; includes three types of terms: those used in multiple subject areas, science content–specific terms, and polysemous terms (words with multiple meanings in different contexts).

accept one way a teacher might respond to student answers; involves acknowledging, reinforcing, or repeating a student's answer.

accountable talk discourse that promotes learning and sharpens student thinking by reinforcing their ability to use knowledge appropriately.

achievement gap when there is a statistically significant difference between the average scores of different demographic groups on an assessment.

acrostics sentences in which the first letter of each word represents information to be remembered; a type of letter strategy mnemonic.

affective related to attitudes and emotions.

analytic analyzed by components; multiple performance criteria and levels of achievement in each criterion are part of an analytic rubric.

asking questions a science process skill; the first task in inquiry; part of the first Scientific and Engineering Practice in the *Framework*.

assessment a process of gathering information about student learning for decision making.

assistive listening system electronic components that help people with hearing loss hear better in group situations.

bar graph a visual representation of data; displaying the number of items in various discrete categories by the relative length of the bars.

binary classification system a method of sorting or organizing in which a set of things is divided into two groups based on a particular property.

classifying sorting things into groups based on the properties or characteristics of those things.

closed question a question that has only one right answer and can often be answered with a single word; it calls for factual knowledge and convergent thinking.

cognitive related to thinking, knowing, or understanding.

communicating a science process skill; also an inquiry task; sharing information.

community of learners classroom in which students engage in reflection, discussion, and inquiry with each other and their teacher, who is also a learner.

component ideas subordinate ideas that relate to (support) Disciplinary Core Ideas in the *Framework*; include sets of grade band "endpoints."

concept map a visual representation of a concept and its connections to subconcepts.

confirmation activities laboratory exercises designed to verify a concept that has already been taught through text or lecture.

confirmatory assessment a quiz, test, or performance task administered a long time after the concept or skill was taught; designed to measure what learners retain from their earlier studies; perhaps administered at the end of a course or grade level.

connection boxes part of the layout of *Next Generation Science Standards* located at the end of each standard; shows connections between *Next Generation Science Standards* and *Common Core State Standards for Language Arts and Mathematics*.

constructed-response item a question on an assessment that requires students to express answers in their own words and/or drawings; i.e., a short-answer or essay item.

constructivism a learning theory that posits that learners construct new knowledge.

controlled experiment an investigation in which one variable is deliberately changed at a time, the effect on another variable is observed, and all other variables are held constant; at elementary grade levels this might be described as a fair test.

controlled variable a factor in an experiment that is kept the same to ensure that it is a fair test.

convergent coming together; a convergent question leads toward one correct answer.

cooperative groups small groups of students working cooperatively on an educational task; a classroom arrangement that is supportive of social-constructivist teaching and learning.

cooperative learning an educational approach that supports a positive, student-centered classroom culture in which students work together in groups to achieve a common learning outcome while individual accountability for learning is maintained.

Crosscutting Concepts one of the three dimensions of the *Next Generation Sciences Standards*; abbreviated as CCCs; singular is Crosscutting Concept (CCC); there are seven CCCs in the NGSS.

demographic group a segment of the population; could be based on age, gender, race, ethnicity, income, etc.

dependent variable a factor in an experiment that depends on the manipulation of the independent variable; sometimes called a responding variable.

diagnostic assessment a test, quiz, or other assessment method administered before teaching a lesson or unit to gather data about learners' prior knowledge, interests, abilities, or preferences; sometimes called *preassessment* or *pretesting*.

dichotomous key a tool for identifying objects or organisms based on multistage classification systems; it uses a series of steps, each with two choices, to lead the user to the name of an item.

differentiated instruction a flexible approach to instruction based on student's learning needs and interests.

differentiation a variety of instructional strategies and lesson adaptations used by educators to instruct a diverse group of students in a learning environment; often used in heterogeneously grouped classrooms.

directed inquiry a laboratory exercise in which the teacher specifies the question or problem, and the procedures to be used by students; also known as structured inquiry; sometimes called a cookbook lab.

disabilities conditions recognized by the Individuals with Disabilities Education Act (IDEA) that may interfere with learning; students with disabilites are often described as learners with special needs.

Disciplinary Core Ideas one of the three dimensions of the *Next Generation Science Standards*; abbreviated as DCIs; singular form is Disciplinary Core Idea (DCI).

discourse expressing one's own questions, observations, concepts, ideas, and thinking, while listening to and reflecting on the ideas of others.

discrepant event a scientific phenomenon that has a surprising or unusual outcome for students to consider.

diverse learners a varied population of students that teachers are expected to teach; differences are demographic, intellectual, experiential, physical, cultural and linguistic; in learning styles, motivation, etc.

EL stands for English Learner, the current term for referring to students who are in need of English language acquisition to be successful learners in their classes. The plural form of EL is ELs.

ELL stands for English language learners, a term that was used in the past to refer to ELs including students for which English was not their first language or the language spoken in their home. The plural form of ELL is ELLs.

elaboration a learning strategy that is an important part of the Makes Sense Strategies (MSS); occurs when one transforms an idea without losing the essence of its meaning; involves recognizing the idea, showing the idea through a drawing, writing a sentence about the idea in your own words, identifying the most important part of the idea, becoming aware of what the idea helps you infer, explain, or figure out; writing three questions about the idea, and stating what knowing the idea could help you predict.

emotional disturbance a category of disability listed in the Individuals with Disabilities Education Act (IDEA); a student with emotional disturbance may consistently act out in class, be unable to exhibit appropriate behavior, be unable to maintain relationships with teachers or other students, or seem depressed or anxious or fearful.

equitable equal, fair; when referring to questions, those that are inclusive, potentiality answerable by all students regardless of background or experience.

equity same learning opportunities for all students.

essential questions questions that relate to an idea that is foundational in science and revisited multiple times in a K-12 learning sequence; they address puzzling ideas that signal the need for inquiry to answer them.

evaluation using assessment data in judging student performance and making decisions about learning and instruction.

excellence very high quality.

extend one way a teacher might respond to student answers; involves adding something new to a student's answer.

extrapolation a prediction about values of data beyond the observed data set.

fair test an elementary school–level description of a controlled experiment.

formal assessment planned efforts to gather data about student learning; typically scheduled and systematically recorded; typically summative and scored or graded.

formative assessment a practice quiz or performance task administered during instruction to inform teachers of what students know, understand, and can do; enables teachers to plan ongoing instruction; typically not graded and focuses on student feedback.

formative assessment probes tools for uncovering student ideas (conceptions and misconceptions); generally used during the engage phase of a lesson.

foundation boxes part of the layout of the *Next Generation Science Standards* located between the performance expectations and the connection boxes; include statements from the three dimensions of the *Framework* related to the performance expectation.

Framework in this book, this term refers to *A Framework for K–12 Science Education: Practices, Crosscutting Concepts, and Core Ideas* (NRC, 2012); the document that provided the basis of the *Next Generation Science Standards* (NGSS).

full inquiry a lesson that includes all of the five essential features of classroom inquiry.

grade band "endpoints" statements from the *Framework* that describe what students should understand about a component idea at the end of grades 2, 5, 8, and 12.

graphic organizers visual displays that show relationships among terms, facts, concepts, or ideas; there are many forms: chart, concept map, Venn diagram, storyboard, flow chart, etc.

guided inquiry a laboratory exercise in which the teacher specifies the question or problem but students plan procedures and determine how to gather and analyze results.

habits of mind attitudes and ways of thinking scientists are expected to exhibit; i.e., curiosity, critical and analytic thinking, desire for knowledge, reliance on evidence, willingness to modify explanations when they are not supported by evidence, honesty, cooperation in investigating questions, and solving problems.

histogram a visual representation of data; a type of graph that shows the frequency of occurrence of quantified data in specified intervals.

holistic taken as a whole; when using a holistic rubric, teachers consider the student product created as a whole, they compare the student work with several descriptors, and they determine at which level the student is performing; the score range is typically between 0 and 4.

hypothesis a statement about a possible answer to a question that could be answered by investigating; a prediction about the expected outcome of an experiment.

I-Checks formative assessments embedded in FOSS 3 modules after each investigation; short for "I check my own understanding."

independent variable a factor in an experiment that is changed on purpose by the experimenter; sometimes called a manipulated variable.

individualized education plan an official document listing specific academic, communication, motor, learning, functional, and socialization goals to advance the education of a student with disabilities, developed and reviewed regularly by a team including parents, teachers, and other school staff; sometimes refered to as an IEP.

inequitable unequal, unfair; when referring to questions, those that are not accessible by all students due to lack of comparable background experience.

inference an interpretation of observations based on what was observed and prior knowledge.

informal assessment gathering data about student learning "on the fly," not scheduled or standardized or systematically recorded; may include using asking questions, listening to student discussion, looking over student work, checklists; they are typically formative, not graded.

inquiry the method of teaching and learning science emphasized in the *National Science Education Standards*; a term that was often misused, resulting in the introduction of Scientific and Engineering Practices in the *Next Generation Science Standards*.

inquiry-based a constructivist approach to science teaching and learning advocated by the *National Science Education Standards*.

instructional model sequence of teaching and learning designed to accomplish a learning goal.

intellectual disabilities cognitive discrepancies that are more severe than learning disabilities; students with intellectual disabilities used to be known as students with mental retardation.

interpolation a prediction about values of data expected between two observed data points.

knowing mental process generally relating to facts and things that can be directly observed.

large-scale assessments tests or performance tasks administered across a district, state, nation, or internationally that are designed to make decisions about high-stakes issues such as modifying science programs.

LD learning disabilities.

learner response devices "clickers" or mobile electronic devices that enable students to respond to questions for display or discussion.

learning goals broad science concepts and practices that guide a unit of study; in the planning process, they should be identified before selecting instructional strategies.

learning progressions research-based pathways or sequences that suggest how the understanding of ideas develops as learners progress through school; a guiding principle of *A Framework for K–12 Science Education* upon which the *Next Generation Science Standards* were based.

learning targets short term, student-friendly learning expectations; they guide the selection of instructional activities and teaching strategies.

least restrictive environment the educational setting appropriate for students with disabilities; as much like a regular class setting with nondisabled students as possible considering educational needs and safety.

levels of inquiry a continuum of lessons that differ based on the amount of learner self-direction and teacher direction involved; from very student directed to very teacher directed the sequence is open inquiry, guided inquiry, directed inquiry, and confirmation lab.

line graph a visual representation of data that is appropriate for showing numerical data about continuous (not discrete) variables.

manipulated variable the factor in an experiment that is changed on purpose by the experimenter to answer a question or test a hypothesis; sometimes called the independent variable.

measuring quantifying variables using appropriate instruments and units (standard or nonstandard).

metacognition thinking about one's own thinking.

metric system the common name of the measurement system that uses the following basic units: meter for length or distance, gram for mass, second for time, liter for capacity; officially known as the International System of Units (SI).

mnemonic a memory device, i.e., an acrostic or the use of pegwords.

multistage classification system a method of sorting or organizing things so that objects in the set are sorted into groups, then each group is sorted into subgroups, etc.

nature of science, the characteristics of science, i.e.: testable, replicable, reliable, tentative, collaborative, and evidence based.

NGSS *Next Generation Science Standards,* standards based on the *Framework,* released in April 2013.

NSES *National Science Education Standards,* released in 1996.

observation the action of gathering information about one's surroundings by using appropriate senses.

open inquiry a science lesson or unit that involves all of the essential features of classroom inquiry and is very student directed.

open-ended question a question that has many acceptable answers so it typically invites many students to answer; it encourages divergent thinking, reflection, and helps to build toward understanding.

partial inquiry a lesson that includes at least one, but not all five of the essential features of classroom inquiry.

performance assessment a task that requires students to demonstrate their understanding of a concept and/or abilities to perform a skill.

performance expectations what a student is expected to know and be able to do on an assessment; or statements in the *Next Generation Science Standards* that integrate the three dimensions of the *Framework* into an assessment target.

person-centered when describing a question, one focused on learners' ideas and thinking; usually includes the word *you* or *your* in its construction; ask for personal ideas without suggesting that there is one right or best answer.

phenomena objects or events used to anchor NGSS units or lessons by engaging students in figuring out explanations about interesting real-world core ideas; they must be academically productive, but don't need to be phenomenal; phenomenon is the singular form of phenomena.

physical environment the surroundings in a classroom, non-human aspects of a classroom that affect learning, including: arrangement of desks, posted resources, accessible equipment and materials, lighting, temperture, etc.

practice to do something repeatedly in the same way to improve a performance.

prediction a forecast of a future outcome based on knowledge of patterns and relationships in data.

probe one way a teacher might respond to student answers; asking the student a question based on their answer, they might ask for elaboration, clarification, justification, or verification.

procedural facilitators scaffolds used to assist students with learning disabilities in meaningfully accessing the general curriculum, i.e., checklists, structures to help self-monitoring, examples for imitation, visual representation to make cognitive processes visible.

productive questions teachers' questions that promote learners' activity and reasoning.

qualitative observation a description of qualities or properties of the thing(s) observed.

quantitative observation a description of the thing(s) observed that involves numbers, based on counting or measurement.

question what is asked; or in science, a possible starting point for inquiry.

response to intervention Known as the RTI process; based on the use of research-based curricula and evidence-based interventions; its three tiers are: Tier 1 – Core Instruction, Tier 2 – Supplemental Supports, and Tier 3 – Intensive Interventions.

reflection   a powerful strategy for developing deep knowledge; introspective thinking, deep consideration.

rehearsal   to do a series of similar, but not identical, tasks to reinforce learning and make it more generalizable.

reliable   in educational assessment, a test is reliable if it is likely that a given student would make a similar score if repeatedly given the same test several times under the same conditions (i.e., with no additional learning).

responding variable   the factor in an experiment that responds or changes due to manipulation of the independent variable, also called a dependent variable.

rubric   a scoring guide that helps to make scoring of essays and/or performance tasks more objective; they may be holistic or analytic.

science   a way to study and answer questions about the natural world through collection and analysis of observation-based evidence.

science education   teaching and facilitating learning about science facts, concepts, and inquiry skills; includes aspects of curriculum, instruction, and assessment.

Scientific and Engineering Practices   one of the three dimensions introduced by the *Framework;* referred to as Science and Engineering Practices in the NGSS; also referred to as: Practices, or Science and Engineering Practices; abbreviated as SEPs; the singular is Scientific and Engineering Practice (SEP); there are eight Practices in the NGSS.

scientific literacy   ability to think scientifically and to understand the scientific point of view; a goal for all citizens in the *National Science Education Standards* of 1996.

selected-response item   a question on an assessment that involves identifying the correct answer from a list of possible answers, i.e., multiple-choice, true-false, or matching items; also known as a forced-choice item.

sequencing   putting things in order by the value of a specific property; serial ordering, a type of classification.

sheltered instruction   a method of teaching science and English to English Learners that focuses on concept development and nonlanguage cues and prompts.

social constructivism   a learning theory that posits that learners construct new knowledge more effectively when they talk and work with others, including teachers.

specific learning disability   a disorder in one or more of the basic psychological processes involved in understanding or in using spoken or written language.

statistically signficant difference   when the results of an assessment or experiment are not likely to be due to chance alone.

STEM   an acronym for Science, Technology, Engineering, and Mathematics.

structured inquiry   a laboratory exercise in which the teacher specifies the question or problem, and the procedures to be used by students; also known as directed inquiry; sometimes called a cookbook lab.

student-initiated inquiry   a lesson or lab activity in which learners develop the question to be investigated; also known as open inquiry.

subject-centered   when describing learning, an environment where students generate questions which guide the instructional process.

summative assessment   a quiz, test, or performance task administered soon after the completion of a lesson or a unit to evaluate what has been learned and to assign grades.

t-chart   a graphic organizer composed of two columns, each with a heading; useful for organizing two categories of observations.

three dimensions   organizing structure of *A Framework for K–12 Science Education* upon which the *Next Generation Science Standards* were based. The three dimensions are Scientific and Engineering Practices, Crosscutting Concepts, and Disciplinary Core Ideas.

tiered learning   a basic type of differentiation of instruction; whole class shares the same content focus, but teacher designs different learning paths and qualitatively different objectives for student groups formed based on their readiness to comprehend various texts and activities.

tiers   levels or groups of students formed on the basis of readiness levels, learning styles, or interests.

traditional assessment items   test questions that are in a customary form, i.e., multiple-choice, true-false, matching, short-answer, or essays.

understanding   mental processing generally relating to comprehension.

valid   in educational assessment, a test is valid if the test measures what it is purported to measure; the items on a valid test must be aligned with the content and skills that were taught.

variable   a property of objects or events that can change, has variations, or has differing amounts.

Venn diagram   a graphic organizer composed of circles; provides a visual frame for comparing and contrasting terms and concepts.

visual impairments   a category of disability listed in the Individuals with Disabilities Education Act (IDEA); students whose visual challenges cannot be corrected by wearing glasses or contacts are described as having visual impairments.

wait time 1   the pause that follows a question by the teacher.

wait time 2   the pause that follows a burst of responses from students before the teacher responds or asks another question.

wait times   intervals between a teacher asking a question and calling on a student to answer it; wait times longer than three seconds are recommended to encourage a variety of positive student behaviors.

zone of proximal development   a term used by Vygotsky to refer to the gap between what learners can do on their own and what they can do with assistance.

Index